Rover 214 & 414 Owners Workshop Manual

Mark Coombs

Models covered
Rover 214 and 414 models fitted with eight- or sixteen-valve 1397 cc 'K-series' engine

Covers major mechanical features of Cabriolet
Does not cover Diesel engine models

(1689 - 3W1)

ABCDE
FGHIJ
K

Haynes Publishing
Sparkford Nr Yeovil
Somerset BA22 7JJ England

Haynes Publications, Inc
861 Lawrence Drive
Newbury Park
California 91320 USA

Restoring and Preserving our Motoring Heritage

Few people can have had the luck to realise their dreams to quite the same extent and in such a remarkable fashion as John Haynes, Founder and Chairman of the Haynes Publishing Group.

Since 1965 his unique approach to workshop manual publishing has proved so successful that millions of Haynes Manuals are now sold every year throughout the world, covering literally thousands of different makes and models of cars, vans and motorcycles.

A continuing passion for cars and motoring led to the founding in 1985 of a Charitable Trust dedicated to the restoration and preservation of our motoring heritage. To inaugurate the new Museum, John Haynes donated virtually his entire private collection of 52 cars.

Now with an unrivalled international collection of over 210 veteran, vintage and classic cars and motorcycles, the Haynes Motor Museum in Somerset is well on the way to becoming one of the most interesting Motor Museums in the world.

A 70 seat video cinema, a cafe and an extensive motoring bookshop, together with a specially constructed one kilometre motor circuit, make a visit to the Haynes Motor Museum a truly unforgettable experience.

Every vehicle in the museum is preserved in as near as possible mint condition and each car is run every six months on the motor circuit.

Enjoy the picnic area set amongst the rolling Somerset hills. Peer through the William Morris workshop windows at cars being restored, and browse through the extensive displays of fascinating motoring memorabilia.

From the 1903 Oldsmobile through such classics as an MG Midget to the mighty 'E' Type Jaguar, Lamborghini, Ferrari Berlinetta Boxer, and Graham Hill's Lola Cosworth, there is something for everyone, young and old alike, at this Somerset Museum.

Haynes Motor Museum

Situated mid-way between London and Penzance, the Haynes Motor Museum is located just off the A303 at Sparkford, Somerset (home of the Haynes Manual) and is open to the public 7 days a week all year round, except Christmas Day and Boxing Day.

Acknowledgements
Thanks are due to Champion Spark Plug who supplied the illustrations showing spark plug conditions, to Holt Lloyd Limited who supplied the illustrations showing bodywork repair, and to Duckhams Oils who provided lubrication data. Thanks are also due to Sykes-Pickavant Limited, who provided some of the workshop tools, and to all those people at Sparkford who helped in the production of this Manual.

A book in the **Haynes Owners Workshop Manual Series**

Printed by J. H. Haynes & Co. Ltd., Sparkford, Nr Yeovil, Somerset BA22 7JJ, England

ISBN 1 85010 689 4

British Library Cataloguing in Publication Data
A catalogue record for this book is available from the British Library

We take great pride in the accuracy of information given in this Manual, but vehicle manufacturers make alterations and design changes during the production run of a particular vehicle of which they do not inform us. No liability can be accepted by the authors or publishers for loss, damage or injury caused by any errors in, or omissions from, the information given.

Contents

Spark plug condition and bodywork repair colour pages between pages 32 and 33

Rover 214 Si

Rover 414 SLi

About this manual

Its aim

The aim of this Manual is to help you get the best value from your vehicle. It can do so in several ways. It can help you decide what work must be done (even should you choose to get it done by a garage), provide information on routine maintenance and servicing, and give a logical course of action and diagnosis when random faults occur. However, it is hoped that you will use the Manual by tackling the work yourself. On simpler jobs it may even be quicker than booking the car into a garage and going there twice, to leave and collect it. Perhaps most important, a lot of money can be saved by avoiding the costs a garage must charge to cover its labour and overheads.

The Manual has drawings and descriptions to show the function of the various components so that their layout can be understood. Then the tasks are described and photographed in a clear step-by-step sequence.

Its arrangement

The Manual is divided into Chapters, each covering a logical sub-division of the vehicle. The Chapters are each divided into Sections, numbered with single figures, eg 5; and the Sections into paragraphs (or sub-sections), with decimal numbers following on from the Section they are in, eg 5.1, 5.2, 5.3 etc.

It is freely illustrated, especially in those parts where there is a detailed sequence of operations to be carried out. There are two forms of illustration: figures and photographs. The figures are numbered in sequence with decimal numbers, according to their position in the Chapter – eg Fig. 6.4 is the fourth drawing/illustration in Chapter 6. Photographs carry the same number (either individually or in related groups) as the Section or sub-section to which they relate.

There is an alphabetical index at the back of the Manual as well as a contents list at the front. Each Chapter is also preceded by its own individual contents list.

References to the 'left' or 'right' of the vehicle are in the sense of a person in the driver's seat, facing forward.

Unless otherwise stated, nuts and bolts are removed by turning anti-clockwise, and tightened by turning clockwise.

Vehicle manufacturers continually make changes to specifications and recommendations, and these, when notified, are incorporated into our Manuals at the earliest opportunity.

We take great pride in the accuracy of information given in this Manual, but vehicle manufacturers make alterations and design changes during the production run of a particular vehicle of which they do not inform us. No liability can be accepted by the authors or publishers for loss, damage or injury caused by any errors in, or omissions from, the information given.

Project vehicles

The main project vehicle used in the preparation of this Manual, and appearing in many of the photographic sequences was a 1990 414 SLi. Additional work was carried out and photographed on a 1990 214 Si.

Introduction to the Rover 214 & 414

The Rover 214 Hatchback and 414 Saloon models covered in this Manual are a much-developed version of the original 213 and 216 models Rover first launched in 1984. The 214 five-door model was the first to be introduced in October 1989, and was closely followed by the 414 model which was introduced in March 1990. The 214 model range was further updated in September 1990 when a three-door variant was introduced.

All models are fitted with the new 1.4 litre 'K' series engine. The 214 S model (first introduced in September 1990) has an eight-valve single overhead camshaft version of the engine which is fed by a SU KIF carburettor, whereas all other 214 and 414 models are equipped with a sixteen-valve double overhead camshaft version of the engine which is controlled by a Rover/Motorola Modular Engine Management System single-point fuel-injection (MEMS-SPi). Both versions of the engine are able to accept a full range of emission control systems, up to and including a three-way regulated catalytic converter, and designed to require the minimum of servicing.

The five-speed transmission, which is a joint development by Rover and Peugeot engineers, is of Peugeot design and produced by Rover; it is fitted to the left-hand end of the engine. The complete engine/transmission assembly is mounted transversely across the front of the car and drives the front wheels through unequal-length driveshafts.

The front suspension incorporates MacPherson struts and the rear is of the double wishbone type.

Braking is by discs at the front and drums at the rear, with a dual-circuit hydraulic system. On all models in the range, an Anti-lock Braking System (ABS) was offered as an optional extra. If ABS is fitted braking is by discs both at the front and rear.

General dimensions and weights

Dimensions

Overall length:	
214 models	4220 mm
414 models	4370 mm
Overall width (including mirrors)	1940 mm
Overall height (at kerb weight)	1400 mm
Wheelbase	2550 mm
Turning circle	10 200 mm

Weights

Kerb weight – car unladen, less options, but with full fuel tank, coolant and all fluids, tools and spare wheel:

214 S – three-door	995 kg
214 Si – three-door	1020 kg
214 S – five-door	1025 kg
214 Si – five-door	1030 kg
214 SLi – five-door	1050 kg
214 GSi – five-door	1065 kg
414 Si – four-door	1020 kg
414 SLi – four-door	1040 kg

Note: *Add 5 kg if a catalytic converter is fitted*

Maximum gross vehicle weight	1580 kg
Maximum roof rack load	65 kg
Maximum towing weight – with braked trailer:	
214 S models	900 kg
All other models	1000 kg
Towing hitch downward load	50 kg

Jacking, towing and wheel changing

Note: *On models fitted with side skirt/sill extension trim panels, the access panel must first be removed from the trim panel to gain access to jacking points 2, 3, 4 and 5 (see accompanying illustration).*

To change a wheel, have the car parked on firm, level ground, apply the handbrake firmly and select first or reverse gear. Remove the spare wheel, tools and jack from the luggage compartment.

Remove the roadwheel trim (where fitted) and slacken the roadwheel nuts through half to one turn each, working in a diagonal sequence. Using chalk or similar, mark the relationship of the roadwheel to the hub.

Place chocks at the front and rear of the roadwheel diagonally opposite the one to be changed, then locate the jack head in the jacking point nearest to the wheel to be changed. Ensure that the jack base is located on firm ground and jack up the car.

When the wheel is clear of the ground remove the nuts and lift off the wheel. Check that the threads and the wheel-to-hub mating surfaces are clean and undamaged. The threads may be cleaned with a brass wire brush if rusty. Apply a thin smear of anti-seize compound (Holts Copaslip) to the threads (and also to the roadwheel-to-hub mating surfaces) to prevent the formation of corrosion, and clean the inside of the roadwheel to be fitted.

On refitting, align the marks made on removal (if the same roadwheel is being fitted) and moderately tighten the nuts. Lower the

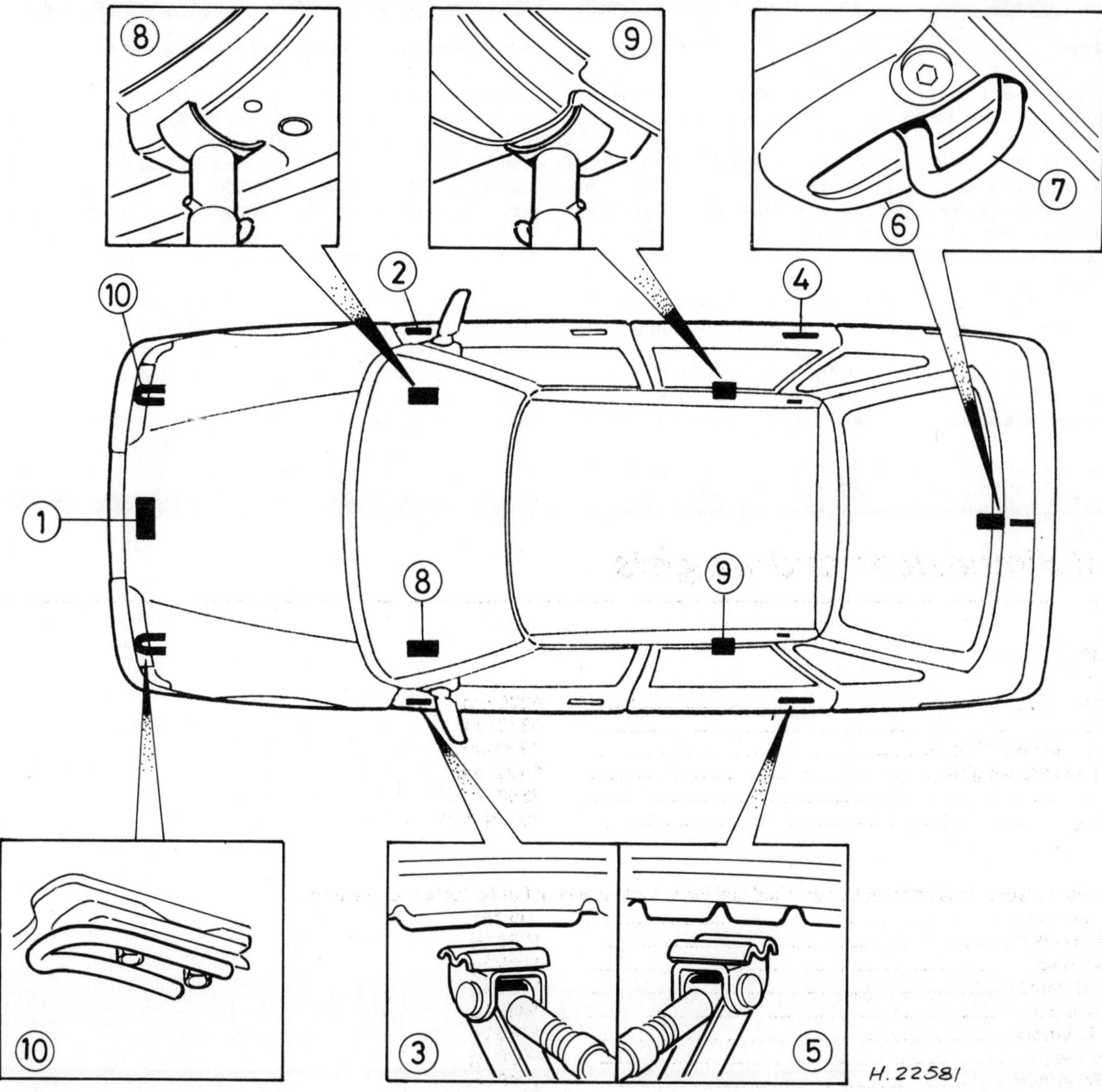

Jacking towing and supporting points

1 Front central jack location pad
2 Right-hand sill front jacking/support point
3 Left-hand sill front jacking/support point
4 Right-hand sill rear jacking/support point
5 Left-hand sill rear jacking/support point
6 Rear reinforced jack location pad
7 Rear towing eye
8 Front underbody longitudinal support points
9 Rear underbody longitudinal support points
10 Front towing eyes

Front towing eye

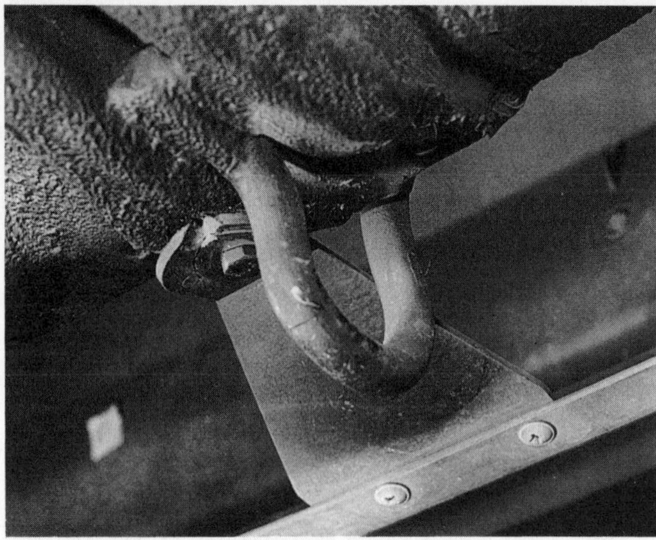

Rear towing eye – for towing light vehicles only

car and then tighten securely the nuts, working in progressive stages and in a diagonal sequence, to the specified torque wrench setting if possible.

Refit the roadwheel trim (where applicable) and check the tyre pressure. With the spare wheel in position, remove the chocks and stow the jack and tools. If a new roadwheel has been fitted, have it balanced as soon as possible. If the roadwheel nuts were tightened using the car's wheelbrace, check as soon as possible that they are tightened to the specified torque wrench setting.

When jacking up the car to carry out repair or maintenance tasks position the jack as follows; see the accompanying illustration for details:

If the front of the car is to be raised, firmly apply the handbrake and place the jack head under point 1. Jack the car up and position the axle stands either on the sills at points 2 and 3, or the underbody longitudinal supports at points 8.

To raise the rear of the car, chock the front wheels and place the jack head under point 6, the reinforced location pad immediately in front of the rear towing eye. The axle stands should be placed either on the sills at points 4 and 5 or the underbody longitudinal supports at points 9.

To raise the side of the car, place the jack head under the sill at point 2 or 3 (as applicable) at the front, then jack up the car and position an axle stand under the longitudinal support at point 8. Remove the jack and position it under point 4 or 5 (as applicable) then jack up the rear of the car and position an axle stand under the longitudinal support at point 9.

Never work under, around or near a raised car unless it is adequately supported in at least two places with axle stands or suitable sturdy blocks.

The car may be towed for breakdown recovery purposes, but only using the towing eyes positioned at the front and rear of the vehicle (photos). These eyes are intended only for towing other vehicles (or being towed by them) and must not be used for lifting the car either directly or indirectly.

Note: *On no account should the car be towed with the front wheels on the ground if the transmission is faulty or the transmission oil level is low. If the car is being towed with the wheels on the ground, it must not be towed at speeds in excess of 30 mph (50 kmh) or for a distance in excess of 30 miles (50 km).*

Buying spare parts and vehicle identification numbers

Buying spare parts

Spare parts are available from many sources; for example, Rover garages, other garages and accessory shops, and motor factors. Our advice regarding spare part sources is as follows.

Officially appointed Rover garages – This is the best source for parts which are peculiar to your car, and are not generally available (eg complete cylinder heads, internal gearbox components, badges, interior trim etc). It is also the only place at which you should buy parts if the vehicle is still under warranty. To be sure of obtaining the correct parts, it will be necessary to give the storeman your car's vehicle identification number, and if possible, take the old parts along for positive identification. Many parts are available under a factory exchange scheme – any parts returned should always be clean. It obviously makes good sense to go straight to the specialists on your car for this type of part, as they are best equipped to supply you.

Other garages and accessory shops – These are often very good places to buy materials and components needed for the maintenance of your car (eg oil filters, spark plugs, bulbs, drivebelts, oils and greases, touch-up paint, filler paste, etc.). They also sell general accessories, usually have convenient opening hours, charge lower prices and can often be found not far from home.

Motor factors – Good factors will stock all the more important components which wear out comparatively quickly (eg exhaust systems, brake pads, seals and hydraulic parts, clutch components, bearing shells, pistons, valves, etc.). Motor factors will often provide new or reconditioned components on a part exchange basis – this can save a considerable amount of money.

Vehicle identification numbers

Modifications are a continuing and unpublicised process in vehicle manufacture, quite apart from major model changes. Spare parts manuals and lists are compiled upon a numerical basis, the individual vehicle identification numbers being essential to correct identification of the component concerned.

When ordering spare parts, always give as much information as possible. Quote the car model, year of manufacture, body and engine numbers as appropriate.

The *vehicle identification plate* is situated at the bottom of the passenger side door pillar (photo). It gives the VIN (vehicle identification number), vehicle weight information and paint and trim colour codes.

The *vehicle identification number* is given on the vehicle identification plate and is repeated, stamped onto the centre of the engine compartment bulkhead (photo).

The *body number* is stamped into a plate fixed to the left-hand side of the spare wheel well, in the luggage compartment.

The *engine number* is stamped into a raised pad on the front left-hand end of the cylinder block/crankcase, next to the transmission (photo).

The *transmission number* is marked on a label stuck on the top of the transmission, near the clutch cable abutment.

The *carburettor number* (where applicable) is stamped into a metal identification tag attached to one of the carburettor suction chamber screws.

Vehicle identification plate on passenger door pillar

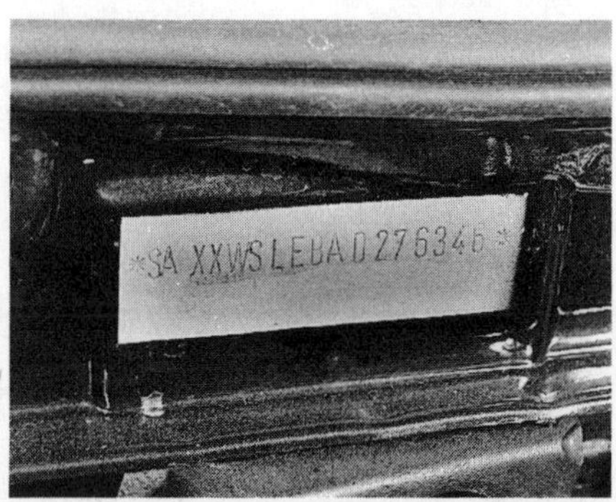

Vehicle identification number on engine compartment bulkhead

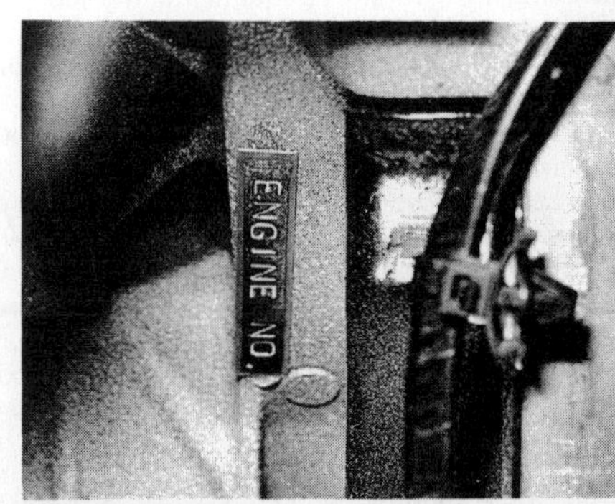

Engine number on front of cylinder block/crankcase

Safety first!

However enthusiastic you may be about getting on with the job in hand, do take the time to ensure that your safety is not put at risk. A moment's lack of attention can result in an accident, as can failure to observe certain elementary precautions. There will always be new ways of having accidents, and the following points do not pretend to be a comprehensive list of all dangers; they are intended rather to make you aware of the risks and to encourage a safety-conscious approach to all work you carry out on your vehicle.

Essential DOs and DON'Ts

DON'T rely on a single jack when working underneath the vehicle. Always use reliable additional means of support, such as axle stands, securely placed under a structural part of the vehicle that you know will not give way.
DON'T attempt to loosen or tighten high-torque nuts (eg wheel hub nuts) while the vehicle is on a jack; it may be pulled off.
DON'T start the engine without first ascertaining that the transmission is in neutral (or 'Park' where applicable) and the handbrake applied.
DON'T suddenly remove the filler cap from a hot cooling system - cover it with a cloth and release the pressure gradually first, or you may get scalded by escaping coolant.
DON'T attempt to drain oil, automatic transmission fluid, or coolant until you are sure it has cooled sufficiently to avoid scalding you.
DON'T grasp any part of the engine, exhaust or catalytic converter without first ascertaining that it is sufficiently cool to avoid burning you.
DON'T allow brake fluid or antifreeze to contact vehicle paintwork.
DON'T syphon toxic liquids such as fuel, brake fluid or antifreeze by mouth, or allow them to remain on your skin.
DON'T inhale dust - it may be injurious to health (see *Asbestos* below).
DON'T allow any spilt oil or grease to remain on the floor - wipe it up straight away, before someone slips on it.
DON'T use ill-fitting spanners or other tools which may slip and cause injury.
DON'T attempt to lift a heavy component which may be beyond your capability - get assistance.
DON'T rush to finish a job, or take unverified short cuts.
DON'T allow children or animals in or around an unattended vehicle.
DON'T park vehicles with catalytic converters over combustible materials such as dry grass, oily rags, etc if the engine has recently been run. As catalytic converters reach extremely high temperatures, any such materials in close proximity may ignite.
DON'T run vehicles equipped with catalytic converters without the exhaust system heat shields fitted.
DO wear eye protection when using power tools such as an electric drill, sander, bench grinder, etc., and when working under the vehicle.
DO use a barrier cream on your hands prior to undertaking dirty jobs - it will protect your skin from infection as well as making the dirt easier to remove afterwards; but make sure your hands aren't left slippery. Note that long term contact with used engine oil can be a health hazard.
DO keep loose clothing (cuffs, tie, etc.) and long hair well out of the way of moving mechanical parts.
DO remove rings, wristwatch, etc., before working on the vehicle - especially the electrical system.
DO ensure that any lifting tackle or jacking equipment used has a safe working load rating adequate for the job, and is used precisely as recommended by the manufacturer.
DO keep your work area tidy - it is only too easy to fall over articles left lying around.
DO get someone to check periodically that all is well when working alone on the vehicle.
DO carry out work in a logical sequence and check that everything is correctly assembled and tightened afterwards.
DO remember that your vehicle's safety affects that of yourself and others. If in doubt on any point, get specialist advice.
IF, in spite of following these precautions, you are unfortunate enough to injure yourself, seek medical attention as soon as possible.

Asbestos

Certain friction, insulating, sealing, and other products - such as brake linings, brake bands, clutch linings, gaskets, etc. - contain asbestos. *Extreme care must be taken to avoid inhalation of dust from such products since it is hazardous to health.* If in doubt, assume that they *do* contain asbestos.

Fire

Remember at all times that petrol is highly flammable. Never smoke, or have any kind of naked flame around, when working on the vehicle. But the risk does not end there - a spark caused by an electrical short-circuit, by two metal surfaces contacting each other, by careless use of tools, or even by static electricity built up in your body under certain conditions, can ignite petrol vapour, which in a confined space is highly explosive.

Whenever possible disconnect the battery earth terminal before working on any part of the fuel or electrical system, and never risk spilling fuel on to a hot engine or exhaust. Catalytic converters run at extremely high temperatures, and consequently can be an additional fire hazard. Observe the precautions outlined elsewhere in this Section.

It is recommended that a fire extinguisher of a type suitable for fuel and electrical fires is kept handy in the garage or workplace at all times. Never try to extinguish a fuel or electrical fire with water.

Note: *Any reference to a 'torch' appearing in this Manual should always be taken to mean a hand-held battery-operated electric lamp or flashlight. It does NOT mean a welding/gas torch or blowlamp.*

Fumes

Certain fumes are highly toxic and can quickly cause unconsciousness and even death if inhaled to any extent, especially if inhalation takes place through a lighted cigarette or pipe. Petrol vapour comes into this category, as do the vapours from certain solvents such as trichloroethylene. Any draining or pouring of such volatile fluids should be done in a well ventilated area.

When using cleaning fluids and solvents, read the instructions carefully. Never use materials from unmarked containers - they may give off poisonous vapours.

Never run the engine of a motor vehicle in an enclosed space such as a garage. Exhaust fumes contain carbon monoxide which is extremely poisonous; if you need to run the engine, always do so in the open air or at least have the rear of the vehicle outside the workplace. Although vehicles fitted with catalytic converters have greatly reduced toxic exhaust emissions, the above precautions should still be observed.

If you are fortunate enough to have the use of an inspection pit, never drain or pour petrol, and never run the engine, while the vehicle is standing over it; the fumes, being heavier than air, will concentrate in the pit with possibly lethal results.

The battery

Batteries which are sealed for life require special precautions which are normally outlined on a label attached to the battery. Such precautions are primarily related to situations involving battery charging and jump starting from another vehicle.

With a conventional battery, never cause a spark, or allow a naked light, in close proximity to it. It will normally be giving off a certain amount of hydrogen gas, which is highly explosive.

Whenever possible disconnect the battery earth terminal before working on the fuel or electrical systems.

If possible, loosen the filler plugs or cover when charging the battery from an external source. Do not charge at an excessive rate or the battery may burst. Special care should be taken with the use of high charge-rate boost chargers to prevent the battery from overheating.

Take care when topping up and when carrying the battery. The acid electrolyte, even when diluted, is very corrosive and should not be allowed to contact clothing, eyes or skin.

Always wear eye protection when cleaning the battery to prevent the caustic deposits from entering your eyes.

Mains electricity and electrical equipment

When using an electric power tool, inspection light, diagnostic equipment, etc., which works from the mains, always ensure that the appliance is correctly connected to its plug and that, where necessary, it is properly earthed. Do not use such appliances in damp conditions and, again, beware of creating a spark or applying excessive heat in the vicinity of fuel or fuel vapour. Also ensure that the appliances meet the relevant national safety standards.

Ignition HT voltage

A severe electric shock can result from touching certain parts of the ignition system, such as the HT leads, when the engine is running or being cranked, particularly if components are damp or the insulation is defective. Where an electronic ignition system is fitted, the HT voltage is much higher and could prove fatal, especially to wearers of cardiac pacemakers.

Jacking and vehicle support

The jack provided with the vehicle is designed primarily for emergency wheel changing, and its use for servicing and overhaul work on the vehicle is best avoided. Instead, a more substantial workshop jack (trolley jack or similar) should be used. Whichever type is employed, it is essential that additional safety support is provided by means of axle stands designed for this purpose. Never use makeshift means such as wooden blocks or piles of house bricks, as these can easily topple or, in the case of bricks, disintegrate under the weight of the vehicle. Further information on the correct positioning of the jack and axle stands is provided in the *Jacking, towing and wheel changing* section.

If removal of the wheels is not required, the use of drive-on ramps is recommended. Caution should be exercised to ensure that they are correctly aligned with the wheels, and that the vehicle is not driven too far along them so that it promptly falls off the other ends or tips the ramps.

General repair procedures

Whenever servicing, repair or overhaul work is carried out on the car or its components, it is necessary to observe the following procedures and instructions. This will assist in carrying out the operation efficiently and to a professional standard of workmanship.

Joint mating faces and gaskets

When separating components at their mating faces, never insert screwdrivers or similar implements into the joint between the faces in order to prise them apart. This can cause severe damage which results in oil leaks, coolant leaks, etc., upon reassembly. Separation is usually achieved by tapping along the joint with a soft-faced hammer in order to break the seal. However, note that this method may not be suitable where dowels are used for component location.

Where a gasket is used between the mating faces of two components, ensure that it is renewed on reassembly and fit it dry unless otherwise stated in the repair procedure. Make sure that the mating faces are clean and dry with all traces of old gasket removed. When cleaning a joint face, use a tool which is not likely to score or damage the face, and remove any burrs or nicks with an oilstone or fine file.

Make sure that tapped holes are cleaned with a pipe cleaner and keep them free of jointing compound, if this is being used, unless specifically instructed otherwise.

Ensure that all orifices, channels or pipes are clear and blow through them, preferably using compressed air.

Oil seals

Oil seals can be removed by levering them out with a wide flat-bladed screwdriver or similar implement. Alternatively, a number of self-tapping screws may be screwed into the seal and these used as a purchase for pliers or some similar device in order to pull the seal free.

Whenever an oil seal is removed from its working location, either individually or as part of an assembly, it should be renewed.

The very fine sealing lip of the seal is easily damaged and will not seal if the surface it contacts is not completely clean and free from scratches, nicks or grooves. If the original sealing surface of the component cannot be restored, and the manufacturer has not made provision for slight relocation of the seal relative to the sealing surface, the component should be renewed.

Protect the lips of the seal from any surface which may damage them in the course of fitting. Use tape or a conical sleeve where possible. Lubricate the seal lips with oil before fitting and, on dual-lipped seals, fill the space between the lips with grease.

Unless otherwise stated, oil seals must be fitted with their sealing lips toward the lubricant to be sealed.

Use a tubular drift or block of wood of the appropriate size to install the seal and, if the seal housing is shouldered, drive the seal down to the shoulder. If the seal housing is unshouldered, the seal should be fitted with its face flush with the housing top face (unless otherwise instructed).

Screw threads and fastenings

Seized nuts, bolts and screws are quite a common occurrence where corrosion has set in, and the use of penetrating oil or releasing fluid will often overcome this problem if the offending item is soaked for a while before attempting to release it. The use of an impact driver may also provide a means of releasing such stubborn fastening devices when used in conjunction with the appropriate screwdriver bit or socket. If none of these methods works, it may be necessary to resort to the careful application of heat, or the use of a hacksaw or nut splitter device.

Studs are usually removed by locking two nuts together on the threaded part and then using a spanner on the lower nut to unscrew the stud. Studs or bolts which have broken off below the surface of the component in which they are mounted can sometimes be removed using a proprietary stud extractor. Always ensure that a blind tapped hole is completely free from oil, grease, water or other fluid before installing the bolt or stud. Failure to do this could cause the housing to crack due to the hydraulic action of the bolt or stud as it is screwed in.

When tightening a castellated nut to accept a split pin, tighten the nut to the specified torque, where applicable, and then tighten further to the next split pin hole. Never slacken the nut to align the split pin hole unless stated in the repair procedure.

When checking or retightening a nut or bolt to a specified torque setting, slacken the nut or bolt by a quarter of a turn, and then retighten to the specified setting. However, this should not be attempted where angular tightening has been used.

For some screw fastenings, notably cylinder head bolts or nuts, torque wrench settings are no longer specified for the latter stages of tightening, 'angle-tightening' being called up instead. Typically, a fairly low torque wrench setting will be applied to the bolts/nuts in the correct sequence, followed by one or more stages of tightening through specified angles.

Locknuts, locktabs and washers

Any fastening which will rotate against a component or housing in the course of tightening should always have a washer between it and the relevant component or housing.

Spring or split washers should always be renewed when they are used to lock a critical component such as a big-end bearing retaining bolt or nut. Locktabs which are folded over to retain a nut or bolt should always be renewed.

Self-locking nuts can be re-used in non-critical areas, providing resistance can be felt when the locking portion passes over the bolt or stud thread. However, it should be noted that self-locking stiffnuts tend to lose their effectiveness after long periods of use, and in such cases should be renewed as a matter of course.

Split pins must always be replaced with new ones of the correct size for the hole.

When thread-locking compound is found on the threads of a fastener which is to be re-used, it should be cleaned off with a wire brush and solvent, and fresh compound applied on reassembly.

Special tools

Some repair procedures in this Manual entail the use of special tools such as a press, two or three-legged pullers, spring compressors, etc. Wherever possible, suitable readily available alternatives to the manufacturer's special tools are described, and are shown in use. In some instances, where no alternative is possible, it has been necessary to resort to the use of a manufacturer's tool and this has been done for reasons of safety as well as the efficient completion of the repair operation. Unless you are highly skilled and have a thorough understanding of the procedures described, never attempt to bypass the use of any special tool when the procedure described specifies its use. Not only is there a very great risk of personal injury, but expensive damage could be caused to the components involved.

Environmental considerations

When disposing of used engine oil, brake fluid, antifreeze, etc, give due consideration to any detrimental environmental effects. Do not, for instance, pour any of the above liquids down drains into the general sewage system or onto the ground to soak away. Many local council refuse tips provide a facility for waste oil disposal as do some garages. If none of these facilities are available, consult your local Environmental Health Department for further advice.

With the universal tightening-up of legislation regarding the emission of environmentally harmful substances from motor vehicles, most current vehicles have tamperproof devices fitted to the main adjustment points of the fuel system. These devices are primarily designed to prevent unqualified persons from adjusting the fuel/air mixture with the chance of a consequent increase in toxic emissions. If such devices are encountered during servicing or overhaul, they should, wherever possible, be renewed or refitted in accordance with the vehicle manufacturer's requirements or current legislation.

Tools and working facilities

Introduction

A selection of good tools is a fundamental requirement for anyone contemplating the maintenance and repair of a motor vehicle. For the owner who does not possess any, their purchase will prove a considerable expense, offsetting some of the savings made by doing-it-yourself. However, provided that the tools purchased meet the relevant national safety standards and are of good quality, they will last for many years and prove an extremely worthwhile investment.

To help the average owner to decide which tools are needed to carry out the various tasks detailed in this Manual, we have compiled three lists of tools under the following headings: *Maintenance and minor repair, Repair and overhaul*, and *Special*. Newcomers to practical mechanics should start off with the *Maintenance and minor repair* tool kit and confine themselves to the simpler jobs around the vehicle. Then, as confidence and experience grow, more difficult tasks can be undertaken, with extra tools being purchased as, and when, they are needed. In this way, a *Maintenance and minor repair* tool kit can be built up into a *Repair and overhaul* tool kit over a considerable period of time without any major cash outlays. The experienced do-it-yourselfer will have a tool kit good enough for most repair and overhaul procedures and will add tools from the *Special* category when it is felt that the expense is justified by the amount of use to which these tools will be put.

Maintenance and minor repair tool kit

The tools given in this list should be considered as a minimum requirement if routine maintenance, servicing and minor repair operations are to be undertaken. We recommend the purchase of combination spanners (ring one end, open-ended the other); although more expensive than open-ended ones, they do give the advantages of both types of spanner.

Combination spanners:
Metric – 8, 9, 10, 11, 12, 13, 14, 15, 17 & 19 mm
Adjustable spanner – 35 mm jaw (approx)
Spark plug spanner (with rubber insert)
Spark plug gap adjustment tool
Set of feeler gauges
Brake pipe spanner
Screwdrivers:
Flat blade – approx 100 mm long x 6 mm dia
Cross blade – approx 100 mm long x 6 mm dia
Combination pliers
Hacksaw (junior)
Tyre pump
Tyre pressure gauge
Oil can
Oil filter removal tool
Fine emery cloth
Wire brush (small)
Funnel (medium size)

Repair and overhaul tool kit

These tools are virtually essential for anyone undertaking any major repairs to a motor vehicle, and are additional to those given in the *Maintenance and minor repair* list. Included in this list is a comprehensive set of sockets. Although these are expensive, they will be found invaluable as they are so versatile – particularly if various drives are included in the set. We recommend the 1/2 in square-drive type, as this can be used with most proprietary torque wrenches. If you cannot afford a socket set, even bought piecemeal, then inexpensive tubular box spanners are a useful alternative.

The tools in this list will occasionally need to be supplemented by tools from the *Special* list.

Sockets (or box spanners) to cover range in previous list
Reversible ratchet drive (for use with sockets) (photo)
Extension piece, 250 mm (for use with sockets)
Universal joint (for use with sockets)
Torque wrench (for use with sockets)
Self-locking grips
Ball pein hammer
Soft-faced mallet (plastic/aluminium or rubber)

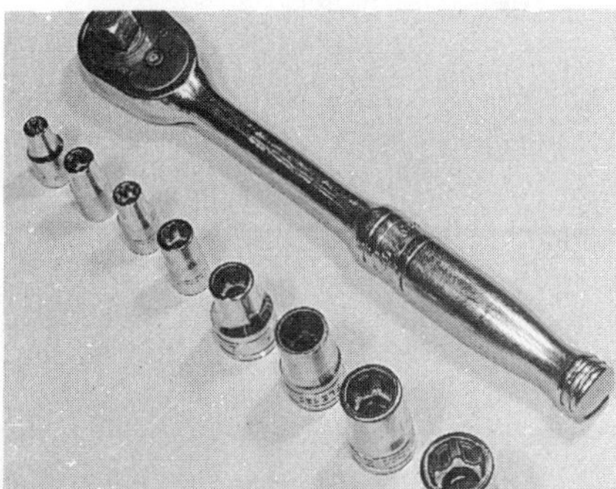

Sockets and reversible ratchet drive

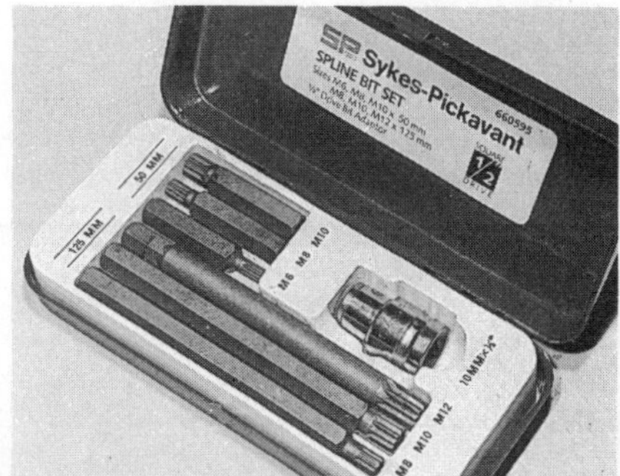

Spline bit set

Spline key set

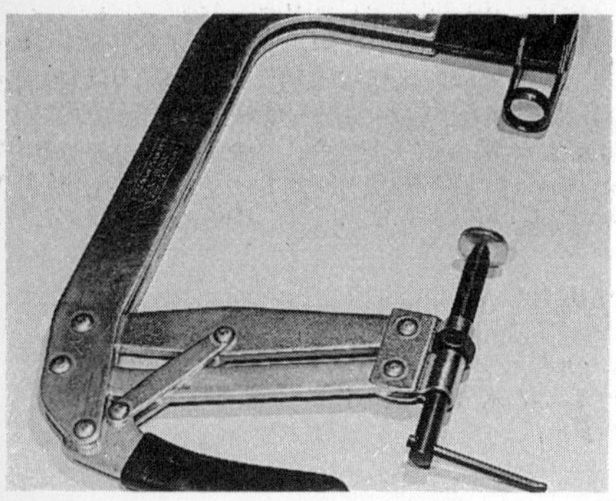
Valve spring compressor

Piston ring compressor

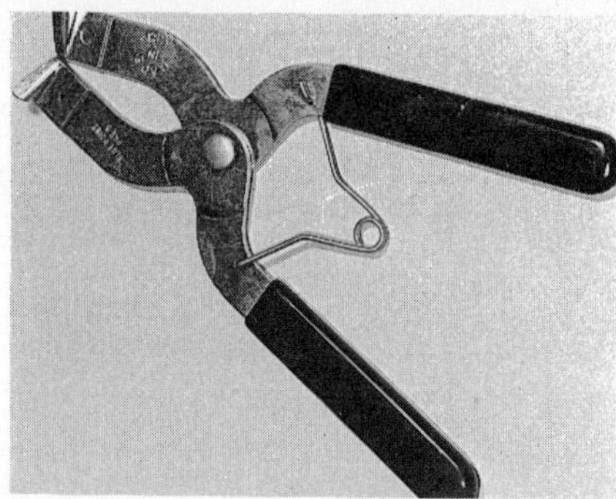
Piston ring removal/installation tool

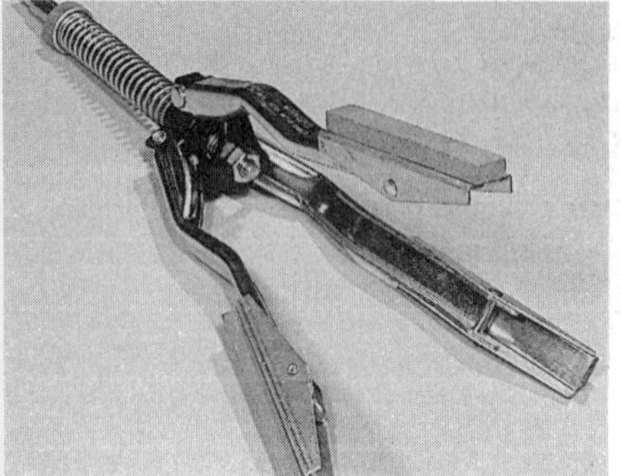
Cylinder bore hone

Three-legged hub and bearing puller

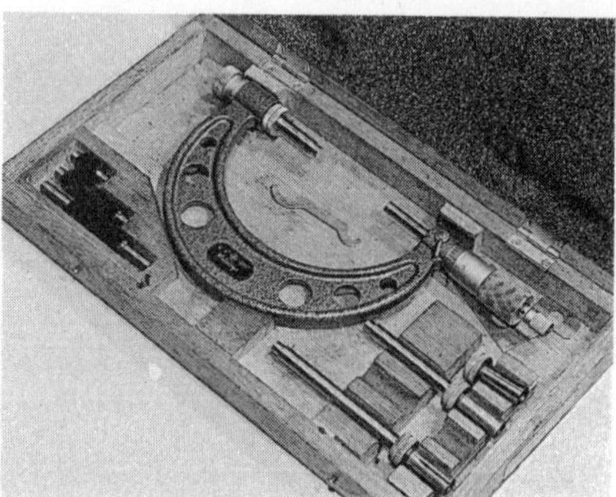
Micrometer set

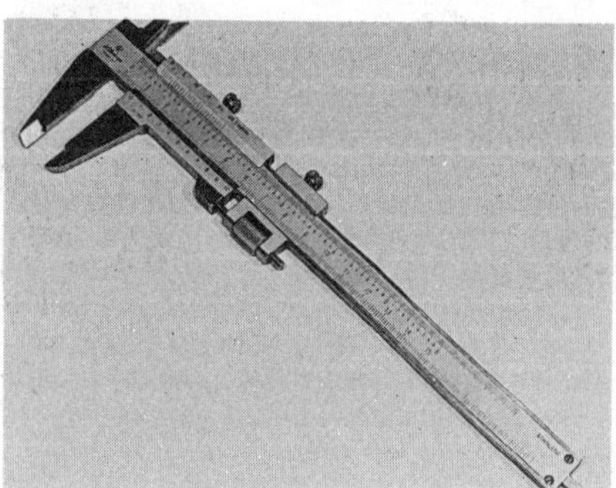
Vernier calipers

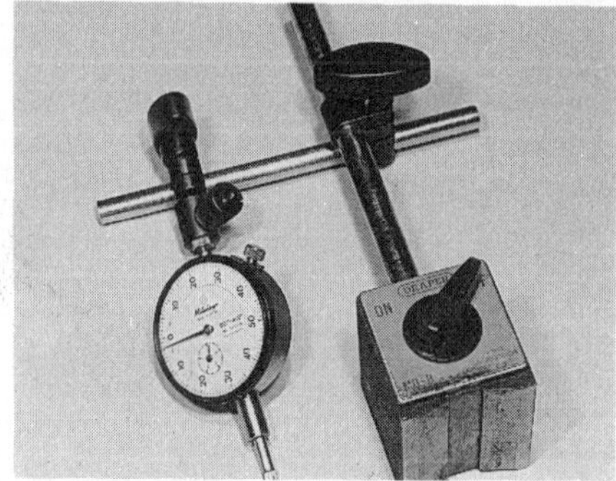
Dial test indicator and magnetic stand

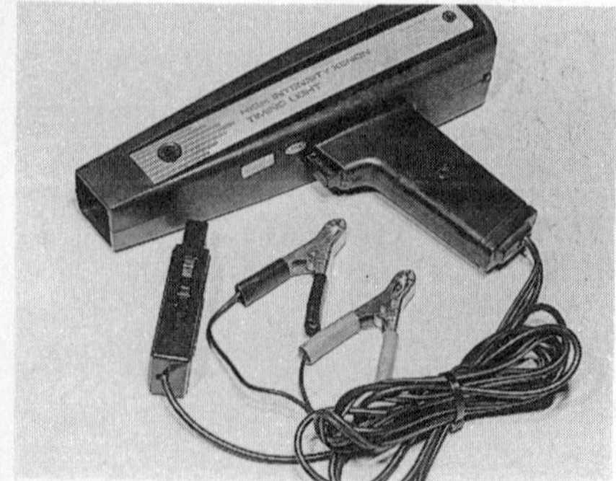
Stroboscopic timing light

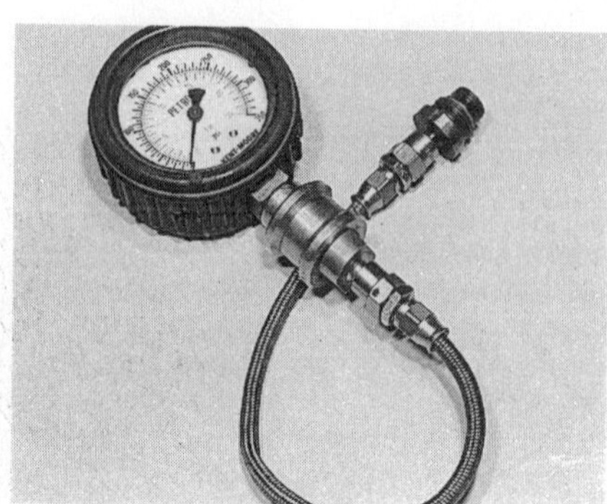
Compression testing gauge

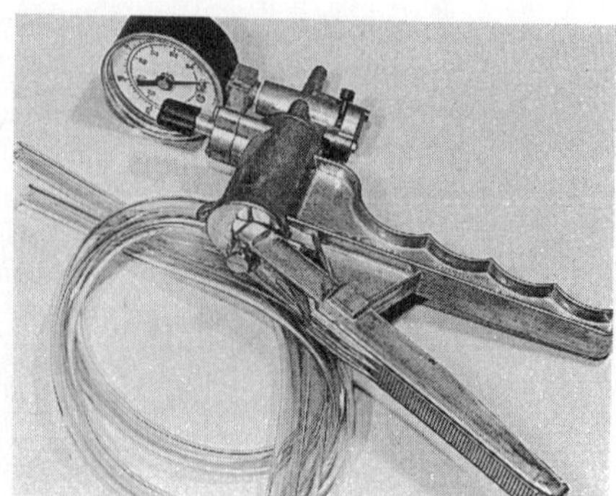
Vacuum pump and gauge

Screwdrivers:
Flat blade – long & sturdy, short (chubby), and narrow (electricians) types
Cross blade – Long & sturdy, and short (chubby) types
Pliers:
Long-nosed
Side cutters (electricians)
Circlip (internal and external)
Cold chisel – 25 mm
Scriber
Scraper
Centre punch
Pin punch
Hacksaw
Brake hose clamp
Brake bleeding kit
Selection of twist drills
Steel rule/straight-edge
Allen keys (inc. splined/Torx type) (photos)
Selection of files
Wire brush
Axle-stands
Jack (strong trolley or hydraulic type)
Light with extension lead

Special tools

The tools in this list are those which are not used regularly, are expensive to buy, or which need to be used in accordance with the manufacturer's instructions. Unless relatively difficult mechanical jobs are undertaken frequently, it will not be economic to buy many of these tools. Where this is the case, you could consider clubbing together with friends (or joining a motorists' club) to make a joint purchase, or borrowing the tools against a deposit from a local garage or tool hire specialist. It is worth noting that many of the larger DIY superstores now carry a large range of special tools for hire at modest rates.

The following list contains only those tools and instruments freely available to the public, and not those special tools produced by the vehicle manufacturer specifically for its dealer network. You will find occasional references to these manufacturer's special tools in the text of this Manual. Generally, an alternative method of doing the job without the vehicle manufacturer's special tool is given. However, sometimes there is no alternative to using them. Where this is the case and the relevant tool cannot be bought or borrowed, you will have to entrust the work to a franchised garage.

Valve spring compressor (photo)
Valve grinding tool
Piston ring compressor (photo)
Piston ring removal/installation tool (photo)
Cylinder bore hone (photo)
Balljoint separator
Coil spring compressors
Two/three-legged hub and bearing puller (photo)
Impact screwdriver
Micrometer and/or vernier calipers (photos)
Dial test indicator/dial gauge (photo)
Stroboscopic timing light (photo)
Dwell angle meter/tachometer
Universal electrical multi-meter
Cylinder compression gauge (photo)
Hand-operated vacuum pump and gauge (photo)
Clutch plate alignment set (photo)
Brake shoe steady spring cup removal tool (photo)
Bush and bearing removal/installation set (photo)
Stud extractors (photo)
Tap and die set (photo)
Lifting tackle
Trolley jack

Buying tools

For practically all tools, a tool factor is the best source since he will have a very comprehensive range compared with the average garage or accessory shop. Having said that, accessory shops often offer excellent

Clutch plate alignment set

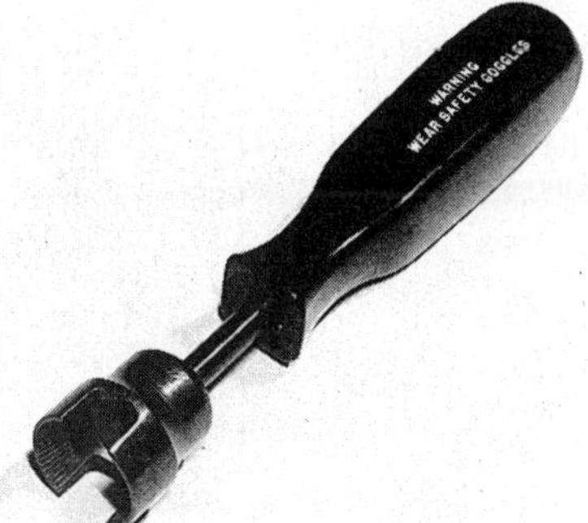

Brake shoe steady spring cup removal tool

Bush and bearing removal/installation set

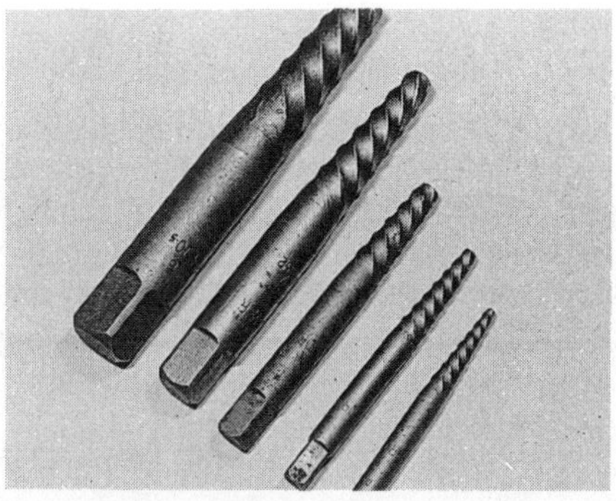

Stud extractor set

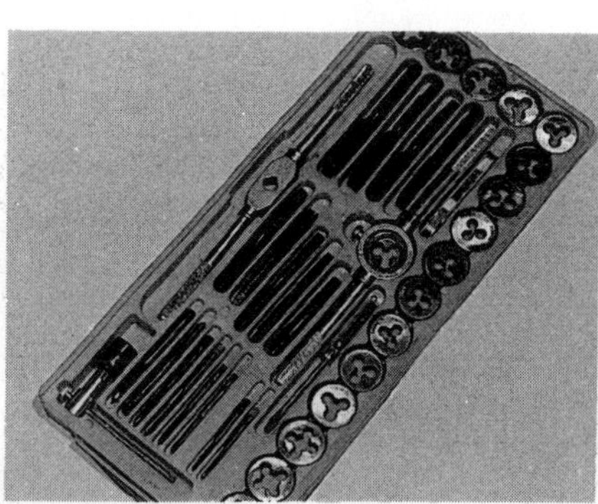

Tap and die set

quality tools at discount prices, so it pays to shop around.

Remember, you don't have to buy the most expensive items on the shelf but it is always advisable to steer clear of the very cheap tools. There are plenty of good tools around at reasonable prices, but always aim to purchase items which meet the relevant national safety standards. If in doubt, ask the proprietor or manager of the shop for advice before making a purchase.

Care and maintenance of tools

Having purchased a reasonable tool kit, it is necessary to keep the tools in a clean and serviceable condition. After use, always wipe off any dirt, grease and metal particles using a clean, dry cloth, before putting the tools away. Never leave them lying around after they have been used. A simple tool rack on the garage or workshop wall for items such as screwdrivers and pliers is a good idea. Store all normal spanners and sockets in a metal box. Any measuring instruments, gauges, meters, etc, must be carefully stored where they cannot be damaged or become rusty.

Take a little care when tools are used. Hammer heads inevitably become marked and screwdrivers lose the keen edge on their blades from time to time. A little timely attention with emery cloth or a file will soon restore items like this to a good serviceable finish.

Working facilities

Not to be forgotten when discussing tools is the workshop itself. If anything more than routine maintenance is to be carried out, some form of suitable working area becomes essential.

It is appreciated that many an owner mechanic is forced by circumstances to remove an engine or similar item without the benefit of a garage or workshop. Having done this, any repairs should always be done under the cover of a roof.

Wherever possible, any dismantling should be done on a clean, flat workbench or table at a suitable working height.

Any workbench needs a vice; one with a jaw opening of 100 mm (4 in) is suitable for most jobs. As mentioned previously, some clean dry storage space is also required for tools, as well as for any lubricants, cleaning fluids, touch-up paints and so on, which become necessary.

Another item which may be required, and which has a much more general usage, is an electric drill with a chuck capacity of at least 8 mm (5/16 in). This, together with a good range of twist drills, is virtually essential for fitting accessories.

Last, but not least, always keep a supply of old newspapers and clean, lint-free rags available, and try to keep any working area as clean as possible.

Spanner jaw gap and bolt size comparison table

Jaw gap – in (mm)	Spanner size	Bolt size
0.197 (5.00)	5 mm	M 2.5
0.216 (5.50)	5.5 mm	M 3
0.218 (5.53)	7/32 in AF	
0.236 (6.00)	6 mm	M 3.5
0.250 (6.35)	1/4 in AF	
0.275 (7.00)	7 mm	M 4
0.281 (7.14)	9/32 in AF	
0.312 (7.92)	5/16 in AF	
0.315 (8.00)	8 mm	M 5
0.343 (8.71)	11/32 in AF	
0.375 (9.52)	3/8 in AF	
0.394 (10.00)	10 mm	M 6
0.406 (10.32)	13/32 in AF	
0.433 (11.00)	11 mm	M 7
0.437 (11.09)	7/16 in AF	1/4 in SAE
0.468 (11.88)	15/32 in AF	
0.500 (12.70)	1/2 in AF	5/16 in SAE
0.512 (13.00)	13 mm	M8
0.562 (14.27)	9/16 in AF	3/8 in SAE
0.593 (15.06)	19/32 in AF	
0.625 (15.87)	5/8 in AF	7/16 in SAE
0.669 (17.00)	17 mm	M 10
0.687 (17.44)	11/16 in AF	
0.709 (19.00)	19 mm	M 12
0.750 (19.05)	3/4 in AF	1/2 in SAE
0.781 (19.83)	25/32 in AF	
0.812 (20.62)	13/16 in AF	
0.866 (22.00)	22 mm	M 14
0.875 (22.25)	7/8 in AF	9/16 in SAE
0.937 (23.79)	15/16 in AF	5/8 in SAE
0.945 (24.00)	24 mm	M 16
0.968 (24.58)	31/32 in AF	
1.000 (25.40)	1 in AF	11/16 in SAE
1.062 (26.97)	1 1/16 in AF	3/4 in SAE
1.063 (27.00)	27 mm	M 18
1.125 (28.57)	1 1/8 in AF	
1.182 (30.00)	30 mm	M 20
1.187 (30.14)	1 3/16 in AF	
1.250 (31.75)	1 1/4 in AF	7/8 in SAE
1.260 (32.00)	32 mm	M 22
1.312 (33.32)	1 5/16 in AF	
1.375 (34.92)	1 3/8 in AF	
1.418 (36.00)	36 mm	M 24
1.437 (36.49)	1 7/16 in AF	1 in SAE
1.500 (38.10)	1 1/2 in AF	
1.615 (41.00)	41 mm	M 27

Booster battery (jump) starting

When jump starting a car using a booster battery, observe the following precautions:

(a) *Before connecting the booster battery, make sure that the ignition is switched off.*
(b) *Ensure that all electrical equipment (lights, heater, wipers, etc.) is switched off.*
(c) *Make sure that the booster battery is the same voltage as the discharged one in the vehicle.*
(d) *If the battery is being jump started from the battery in another vehicle, the two vehicles MUST NOT TOUCH each other.*
(e) *Make sure that the transmission is in Neutral.*

Connect one jump lead between the positive (+) terminals of the two batteries. Connect the other jump lead first to the negative (–) terminal of the booster battery, and then to a good earthing point on the vehicle to be started, such as a bolt or bracket on the engine block, at least 45 cm (18 in) from the battery if possible. Make sure that the jump leads will not come into contact with the fan, drivebelts or other moving parts of the engine.

Start the engine using the booster battery, then with the engine running at idle speed, disconnect the jump leads in the reverse order of connection.

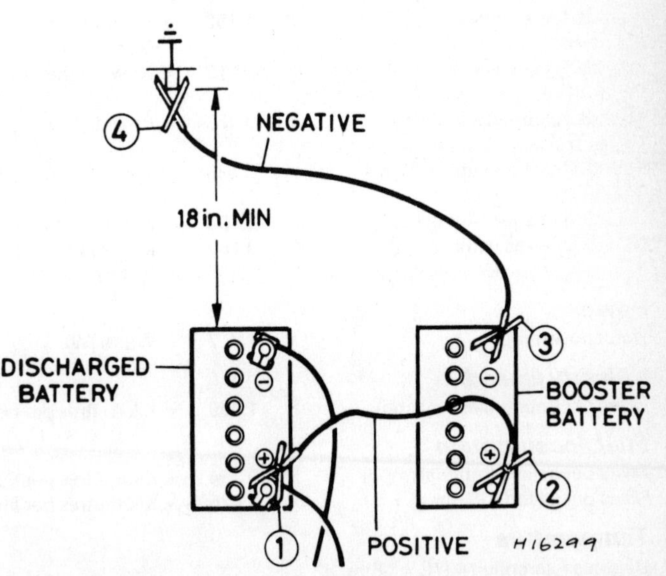

Jump start lead connections for negative-earth vehicles – connect leads in order shown

Conversion factors

Length (distance)

Inches (in)	X	25.4	= Millimetres (mm)	X	0.0394	= Inches (in)
Feet (ft)	X	0.305	= Metres (m)	X	3.281	= Feet (ft)
Miles	X	1.609	= Kilometres (km)	X	0.621	= Miles

Volume (capacity)

Cubic inches (cu in; in^3)	X	16.387	= Cubic centimetres (cc; cm^3)	X	0.061	= Cubic inches (cu in; in^3)
Imperial pints (Imp pt)	X	0.568	= Litres (l)	X	1.76	= Imperial pints (Imp pt)
Imperial quarts (Imp qt)	X	1.137	= Litres (l)	X	0.88	= Imperial quarts (Imp qt)
Imperial quarts (Imp qt)	X	1.201	= US quarts (US qt)	X	0.833	= Imperial quarts (Imp qt)
US quarts (US qt)	X	0.946	= Litres (l)	X	1.057	= US quarts (US qt)
Imperial gallons (Imp gal)	X	4.546	= Litres (l)	X	0.22	= Imperial gallons (Imp gal)
Imperial gallons (Imp gal)	X	1.201	= US gallons (US gal)	X	0.833	= Imperial gallons (Imp gal)
US gallons (US gal)	X	3.785	= Litres (l)	X	0.264	= US gallons (US gal)

Mass (weight)

Ounces (oz)	X	28.35	= Grams (g)	X	0.035	= Ounces (oz)
Pounds (lb)	X	0.454	= Kilograms (kg)	X	2.205	= Pounds (lb)

Force

Ounces-force (ozf; oz)	X	0.278	= Newtons (N)	X	3.6	= Ounces-force (ozf; oz)
Pounds-force (lbf; lb)	X	4.448	= Newtons (N)	X	0.225	= Pounds-force (lbf; lb)
Newtons (N)	X	0.1	= Kilograms-force (kgf; kg)	X	9.81	= Newtons (N)

Pressure

Pounds-force per square inch (psi; lbf/in^2; lb/in^2)	X	0.070	= Kilograms-force per square centimetre (kgf/cm^2; kg/cm^2)	X	14.223	= Pounds-force per square inch (psi; lbf/in^2; lb/in^2)
Pounds-force per square inch (psi; lbf/in^2; lb/in^2)	X	0.068	= Atmospheres (atm)	X	14.696	= Pounds-force per square inch (psi; lbf/in^2; lb/in^2)
Pounds-force per square inch (psi; lbf/in^2; lb/in^2)	X	0.069	= Bars	X	14.5	= Pounds-force per square inch (psi; lbf/in^2; lb/in^2)
Pounds-force per square inch (psi; lbf/in^2; lb/in^2)	X	6.895	= Kilopascals (kPa)	X	0.145	= Pounds-force per square inch (psi; lbf/in^2; lb/in^2)
Kilopascals (kPa)	X	0.01	= Kilograms-force per square centimetre (kgf/cm^2; kg/cm^2)	X	98.1	= Kilopascals (kPa)
Millibar (mbar)	X	100	= Pascals (Pa)	X	0.01	= Millibar (mbar)
Millibar (mbar)	X	0.0145	= Pounds-force per square inch (psi; lbf/in^2; lb/in^2)	X	68.947	= Millibar (mbar)
Millibar (mbar)	X	0.75	= Millimetres of mercury (mmHg)	X	1.333	= Millibar (mbar)
Millibar (mbar)	X	0.401	= Inches of water (inH_2O)	X	2.491	= Millibar (mbar)
Millimetres of mercury (mmHg)	X	0.535	= Inches of water (inH_2O)	X	1.868	= Millimetres of mercury (mmHg)
Inches of water (inH_2O)	X	0.036	= Pounds-force per square inch (psi; lbf/in^2; lb/in^2)	X	27.68	= Inches of water (inH_2O)

Torque (moment of force)

Pounds-force inches (lbf in; lb in)	X	1.152	= Kilograms-force centimetre (kgf cm; kg cm)	X	0.868	= Pounds-force inches (lbf in; lb in)
Pounds-force inches (lbf in; lb in)	X	0.113	= Newton metres (Nm)	X	8.85	= Pounds-force inches (lbf in; lb in)
Pounds-force inches (lbf in; lb in)	X	0.083	= Pounds-force feet (lbf ft; lb ft)	X	12	= Pounds-force inches (lbf in; lb in)
Pounds-force feet (lbf ft; lb ft)	X	0.138	= Kilograms-force metres (kgf m; kg m)	X	7.233	= Pounds-force feet (lbf ft; lb ft)
Pounds-force feet (lbf ft; lb ft)	X	1.356	= Newton metres (Nm)	X	0.738	= Pounds-force feet (lbf ft; lb ft)
Newton metres (Nm)	X	0.102	= Kilograms-force metres (kgf m; kg m)	X	9.804	= Newton metres (Nm)

Power

Horsepower (hp)	X	745.7	= Watts (W)	X	0.0013	= Horsepower (hp)

Velocity (speed)

Miles per hour (miles/hr; mph)	X	1.609	= Kilometres per hour (km/hr; kph)	X	0.621	= Miles per hour (miles/hr; mph)

Fuel consumption

Miles per gallon, Imperial (mpg)	X	0.354	= Kilometres per litre (km/l)	X	2.825	= Miles per gallon, Imperial (mpg)
Miles per gallon, US (mpg)	X	0.425	= Kilometres per litre (km/l)	X	2.352	= Miles per gallon, US (mpg)

Temperature

Degrees Fahrenheit = (°C x 1.8) + 32

Degrees Celsius (Degrees Centigrade; °C) = (°F − 32) x 0.56

** It is common practice to convert from miles per gallon (mpg) to litres/100 kilometres (l/100km), where mpg (Imperial) x l/100 km = 282 and mpg (US) x l/100 km = 235*

Fault diagnosis

Contents

Introduction

The vehicle owner who does his or her own maintenance according to the recommended service schedules should not have to use this section of the Manual very often. Modern component reliability is such that, provided those items subject to wear or deterioration are inspected or renewed at the specified intervals, sudden failure is comparatively rare. Faults do not usually just happen as a result of sudden failure, but develop over a period of time. Major mechanical failures in particular are usually preceded by characteristic symptoms over hundreds or even thousands of miles. Those components which do occasionally fail without warning are often small and easily carried in the vehicle.

With any fault finding, the first step is to decide where to begin investigations. Sometimes this is obvious, but on other occasions a little detective work will be necessary. The owner who makes half a dozen haphazard adjustments or replacements may be successful in curing a fault (or its symptoms), but will be none the wiser if the fault recurs and ultimately may have spent more time and money than was necessary. A calm and logical approach will be found to be more satisfactory in the long run. Always take into account any warning signs or abnormalities that may have been noticed in the period preceding the fault – power loss, high or low gauge readings, unusual smells, etc. – and remember that failure of components such as fuses or spark plugs may only be pointers to some underlying fault.

The pages which follow provide an easy reference guide to the more common problems which may occur during the operation of the vehicle. These problems and their possible causes are grouped under headings denoting various components or systems, such as Engine, Cooling system, etc. The Chapter and/or Section which deals with the problem is also shown in brackets. Whatever the fault, certain basic principles apply. These are as follows:

Verify the fault. This is simply a matter of being sure that you know what the symptoms are before starting work. This is particularly important if you are investigating a fault for someone else who may not have described it very accurately.

Don't overlook the obvious. For example, if the vehicle won't start, is there petrol in the tank? (Don't take anyone else's word on this particular point, and don't trust the fuel gauge either!) If an electrical fault is indicated, look for loose or broken wires before digging out the test gear.

Cure the disease, not the symptom. Substituting a flat battery with a fully charged one will get you off the hard shoulder, but if the underlying cause is not attended to, the new battery will go the same way. Similarly, changing oil-fouled spark plugs for a new set will get you moving again, but remember that the reason for the fouling (if it wasn't simply an incorrect grade of plug) will have to be established and corrected.

Don't take anything for granted. Particularly, don't forget that a 'new' component may itself be defective (especially if it's been rattling around in the boot for months), and don't leave components out of a fault diagnosis sequence just because they are new or recently fitted. When you do finally diagnose a difficult fault, you'll probably realise that all the evidence was there from the start.

1 Engine

Engine fails to rotate when attempting to start

- Battery terminal connections loose or corroded (Chapter 12).
- Battery discharged or faulty (Chapter 12).
- Broken, loose or disconnected wiring in the starting circuit (Chapter 12).
- Defective starter solenoid or switch (Chapter 12).
- Defective starter motor (Chapter 12).
- Starter pinion or flywheel ring gear teeth loose or broken (Chapter 12).
- Engine earth strap broken or disconnected (Chapter 12).

Engine rotates but will not start

- Fuel tank empty.
- Battery discharged (engine rotates slowly) (Chapter 12).
- Battery terminal connections loose or corroded (Chapter 12).
- Ignition components damp or damaged (Chapters 1 and 5).
- Broken, loose or disconnected wiring in the ignition circuit (Chapters 1 and 5).
- Worn, faulty or incorrectly gapped spark plugs (Chapter 1).
- Choke mechanism sticking, incorrectly adjusted, or faulty – carburettor models only (Chapter 4).
- Major mechanical failure (eg camshaft drive) (Chapter 2).

Engine difficult to start when cold

- Battery discharged (Chapter 12).
- Battery terminal connections loose or corroded (Chapter 12).
- Worn, faulty or incorrectly gapped spark plugs (Chapter 1).
- Choke mechanism sticking, incorrectly adjusted, or faulty – carburettor models only (Chapter 4).
- Other ignition system fault (Chapters 1 and 5).
- Low cylinder compressions (Chapter 2).

Engine difficult to start when hot

- Air filter element dirty or clogged (Chapter 1).
- Choke mechanism sticking, incorrectly adjusted, or faulty – carburettor engines only (Chapter 4).
- Carburettor float chamber flooding (Chapter 4).
- Low cylinder compressions (Chapter 2).

Starter motor noisy or excessively rough in engagement

- Starter pinion or flywheel ring gear teeth loose or broken (Chapter 12).
- Starter motor mounting bolts loose or missing (Chapter 12).
- Starter motor internal components worn or damaged (Chapter 12).

Engine starts but stops immediately

- Insufficient fuel reaching carburettor/throttle body (as applicable) (Chapter 4).
- Loose or faulty electrical connections in the ignition circuit (Chapters 1 and 5).
- Vacuum leak at the carburettor/throttle body (as applicable) or inlet manifold (Chapter 4).
- Blocked carburettor jet(s) or internal passages – carburettor models (Chapter 4).
- Blocked injector – fuel-injected models (Chapter 4)

Engine idles erratically

- Incorrectly adjusted idle speed and/or mixture settings – carburettor models only (Chapter 1).
- Air filter element clogged (Chapter 1).
- Vacuum leak at the carburettor/throttle body (as applicable), inlet manifold or associated hoses (Chapter 4).
- Worn, faulty or incorrectly gapped spark plugs (Chapter 1).
- Uneven or low cylinder compressions (Chapter 2).
- Camshaft lobes worn (Chapter 2).
- Timing belt incorrectly tensioned (Chapter 2).

Engine misfires at idle speed

- Worn, faulty or incorrectly gapped spark plugs (Chapter 1).
- Faulty spark plug HT leads (Chapter 1).
- Incorrectly adjusted idle mixture settings – carburettor models only (Chapter 1).
- Incorrect ignition timing – carburettor models only (Chapter 1).
- Vacuum leak at the carburettor/throttle body (as applicable), inlet manifold or associated hoses (Chapter 4).
- Distributor cap cracked or tracking internally (Chapter 1).
- Uneven or low cylinder compressions (Chapter 2).
- Disconnected, leaking or perished crankcase ventilation hoses (Chapters 1 and 4).

Engine misfires throughout the driving speed range

- Blocked carburettor jet(s) or internal passages – carburettor models only (Chapter 4).
- Blocked injector – fuel-injected models (Chapter 4).
- Carburettor worn or incorrectly adjusted (Chapters 1 and 4).
- Fuel filter choked – fuel-injected models only (Chapter 1).
- Fuel pump faulty or delivery pressure low (Chapter 4).
- Fuel tank vent blocked or fuel pipes restricted (Chapter 4).
- Vacuum leak at the carburettor/throttle body (as applicable), inlet manifold or associated hoses (Chapter 4).
- Worn, faulty or incorrectly gapped spark plugs (Chapter 1).
- Faulty spark plug HT leads (Chapter 1).
- Distributor cap cracked or tracking internally (Chapter 1).
- Faulty ignition coil (Chapter 5).
- Uneven or low cylinder compressions (Chapter 2).

Engine hesitates on acceleration

- Worn, faulty or incorrectly gapped spark plugs (Chapter 1).
- Carburettor accelerator pump faulty (Chapter 4).
- Blocked carburettor jets or internal passages – carburettor models only (Chapter 4).
- Blocked injector – fuel injected models only (Chapter 4).
- Vacuum leak at the carburettor/throttle body (as applicable), inlet manifold or associated hoses (Chapter 4).
- Carburettor worn or incorrectly adjusted (Chapters 1 and 4).

Engine stalls

- Incorrectly adjusted idle speed and/or mixture settings – carburettor models only (Chapter 1).
- Blocked carburettor jet(s) or internal passages – carburettor models only (Chapter 4).
- Blocked injector – fuel-injected models only (Chapter 4).
- Vacuum leak at the carburettor/throttle housing (as applicable), inlet manifold or associated hoses (Chapter 4).
- Fuel filter choked – fuel injected models only (Chapter 1).
- Fuel pump faulty or delivery pressure low (Chapter 4).
- Fuel tank vent blocked or fuel pipes restricted (Chapter 4).

Engine lacks power

- Incorrect ignition timing (Chapter 1).
- Carburettor worn or incorrectly adjusted (Chapter 1).
- Timing belt incorrectly fitted or tensioned (Chapter 2).
- Fuel filter choked – fuel injected models only (Chapter 1).
- Fuel pump faulty or delivery pressure low (Chapter 4).
- Uneven or low cylinder compressions (Chapter 2).

- Worn, faulty or incorrectly gapped spark plugs (Chapter 1).
- Vacuum leak at the carburettor/throttle housing (as applicable), inlet manifold or associated hoses (Chapter 4).
- Brakes binding (Chapters 1 and 9).
- Clutch slipping (Chapter 6).

Engine backfires

- Ignition timing incorrect (Chapter 1).
- Timing belt incorrectly fitted or tensioned (Chapter 2).
- Carburettor worn or incorrectly adjusted (Chapter 1).
- Vacuum leak at the carburettor/throttle body (as applicable), inlet manifold or associated hoses (Chapter 4).

Oil pressure warning light illuminated with engine running

- Low oil level or incorrect grade (Chapter 1).
- Faulty oil pressure transmitter (sender) unit (Chapter 2).
- Worn engine bearings and/or oil pump (Chapter 2).
- High engine operating temperature (Chapter 3).
- Oil pressure relief valve defective (Chapter 2).
- Oil pick-up strainer clogged (Chapter 2).

Engine runs-on after switching off

- Idle speed excessively high (Chapter 1).
- Faulty anti-run-on solenoid – carburettor models only (Chapter 4).
- Excessive carbon build-up in engine (Chapter 2).
- High engine operating temperature (Chapter 3).

Engine noises

Pre-ignition (pinking) or knocking during acceleration or under load

- Ignition timing incorrect (Chapter 1).
- Incorrect grade of fuel (Chapter 4).
- Vacuum leak at the carburettor/throttle body (as applicable), inlet manifold or associated hoses (Chapter 4).
- Excessive carbon build-up in engine (Chapter 2).
- Worn or damaged distributor or other ignition system component (Chapters 1 and 5).
- Carburettor worn or incorrectly adjusted (Chapter 1).

Whistling or wheezing noises

- Leaking inlet manifold or carburettor/throttle body gasket (as applicable) (Chapter 4).
- Leaking exhaust manifold gasket or pipe to manifold joint (Chapter 1).
- Leaking vacuum hose (Chapters 4, 5 and 9).
- Blowing cylinder head gasket (Chapter 2).

Tapping or rattling noises

- Incorrect valve clearances (Chapter 2).
- Worn valve gear or camshaft (Chapter 2).
- Ancillary component fault (water pump, alternator, etc.) (Chapters 3 and 12).

Knocking or thumping noises

- Worn big-end bearings (regular heavy knocking, perhaps less under load) (Chapter 2).
- Worn main bearings (rumbling and knocking, perhaps worsening under load) (Chapter 2).
- Piston slap (most noticeable when cold) (Chapter 2).
- Ancillary component fault (alternator, water pump etc) (Chapters 3 and 12).

2 Cooling system

Overheating

- Insufficient coolant in system (Chapter 3).
- Thermostat faulty (Chapter 3).
- Radiator core blocked or grille restricted (Chapter 3).
- Electric cooling fan or thermoswitch faulty (Chapter 3).
- Pressure cap faulty (Chapter 3).
- Timing belt worn, or incorrectly adjusted (Chapter 2).
- Ignition timing incorrect (Chapter 1).
- Inaccurate temperature gauge sender unit (Chapter 3).
- Air lock in cooling system (Chapter 1).

Overcooling

- Thermostat faulty (Chapter 3).
- Inaccurate temperature gauge sender unit (Chapter 3).

External coolant leakage

- Deteriorated or damaged hoses or hose clips (Chapter 1).
- Radiator core or heater matrix leaking (Chapter 3).
- Pressure cap faulty (Chapter 3).
- Water pump seal leaking (Chapter 3).
- Boiling due to overheating (Chapter 3).
- Core plug leaking (Chapter 2).

Internal coolant leakage

- Leaking cylinder head gasket (Chapter 2).
- Cracked cylinder head or cylinder bore (Chapter 2).

Corrosion

- Infrequent draining and flushing (Chapter 1).
- Incorrect antifreeze mixture or inappropriate type (Chapter 1).

3 Fuel and exhaust system

Excessive fuel consumption

- Air filter element dirty or clogged (Chapter 1).
- Carburettor worn or incorrectly adjusted (Chapter 4).
- Choke cable incorrectly adjusted or choke sticking – carburettor models only (Chapter 4).
- Ignition timing incorrect (Chapter 1).
- Tyres underinflated (Chapter 1).

Fuel leakage and/or fuel odour

- Damaged or corroded fuel tank, pipes or connections (Chapter 1).
- Carburettor float chamber flooding (Chapter 4).

Excessive noise or fumes from exhaust system

- Leaking exhaust system or manifold joints (Chapter 1).
- Leaking, corroded or damaged silencers or pipe (Chapter 1).
- Broken mountings causing body or suspension contact (Chapter 1).

4 Clutch

Pedal travels to floor – no pressure or very little resistance

- Broken clutch cable (Chapter 6).
- Faulty clutch cable self-adjust mechanism (Chapter 6).
- Broken clutch release bearing or fork (Chapter 6).
- Broken diaphragm spring in clutch pressure plate (Chapter 6).

Clutch fails to disengage (unable to select gears)

- Faulty clutch pedal self-adjust mechanism (Chapter 6).
- Clutch disc sticking on gearbox input shaft splines (Chapter 6).
- Clutch disc sticking to flywheel or pressure plate (Chapter 6).
- Faulty pressure plate assembly (Chapter 6).
- Gearbox input shaft seized in crankshaft spigot bearing (Chapter 2).
- Clutch release mechanism worn or incorrectly assembled (Chapter 6).

Clutch slips (engine speed increases with no increase in vehicle speed)

- Faulty clutch pedal self-adjust mechanism (Chapter 6).
- Clutch disc linings excessively worn (Chapter 6).
- Clutch disc linings contaminated with oil or grease (Chapter 6).
- Faulty pressure plate or weak diaphragm spring (Chapter 6).

Judder as clutch is engaged

- Clutch disc linings contaminated with oil or grease (Chapter 6).
- Clutch disc linings excessively worn (Chapter 6).
- Clutch cable sticking or frayed (Chapter 6).
- Faulty or distorted pressure plate or diaphragm spring (Chapter 6).
- Worn or loose engine/transmission mountings (Chapter 2).
- Clutch disc hub or gearbox input shaft splines worn (Chapter 6).

Noise when depressing or releasing clutch pedal

- Worn clutch release bearing (Chapter 6).
- Worn or dry clutch pedal bushes (Chapter 6).
- Faulty pressure plate assembly (Chapter 6).
- Pressure plate diaphragm spring broken (Chapter 6).
- Broken clutch disc cushioning springs (Chapter 6).

5 Transmission

Noisy in neutral with engine running

- Input shaft bearings worn (noise apparent with clutch pedal released but not when depressed) (Chapter 7).*
- Clutch release bearing worn (noise apparent with clutch pedal depressed, possibly less when released) (Chapter 6).

Noisy in one particular gear

- Worn, damaged or chipped gear teeth (Chapter 7).*

Difficulty engaging gears

- Clutch fault (Chapter 6).
- Worn or damaged gear linkage (Chapter 7).
- Incorrectly adjusted gear linkage (Chapter 7).
- Worn synchroniser units (Chapter 7).*

Jumps out of gear

- Worn or damaged gear linkage (Chapter 7).
- Incorrectly adjusted gear linkage (Chapter 7).
- Worn synchroniser units (Chapter 7).*
- Worn selector forks (Chapter 7).*

Vibration

- Lack of oil (Chapter 1).
- Worn bearings (Chapter 7).*

Lubricant leaks

- Leaking differential output oil seal (Chapter 7).
- Leaking housing joint (Chapter 7).*
- Leaking input shaft oil seal (Chapter 7).

** Although the corrective action necessary to remedy the symptoms described is beyond the scope of the home mechanic, the above information should be helpful in isolating the cause of the condition so that the owner can communicate clearly with a professional mechanic.*

6 Driveshafts

Clicking or knocking noise on turns (at slow speed on full lock)

- Lack of constant velocity joint lubricant (Chapter 8).
- Worn outer constant velocity joint (Chapter 8).

Vibration when accelerating or decelerating

- Worn inner constant velocity joint (Chapter 8).
- Bent or distorted driveshaft (Chapter 8).

7 Braking system

Note: *Before assuming that a brake problem exists, make sure that the tyres are in good condition and correctly inflated, the front wheel alignment is correct and the vehicle is not loaded with weight in an unequal manner. Apart from checking the condition of all pipe and hose connections, any faults occurring on the Anti-lock Braking System should be referred to a Rover dealer for diagnosis.*

Vehicle pulls to one side under braking

- Worn, defective, damaged or contaminated front or rear brake pads/shoes on one side (Chapter 1).
- Seized or partially seized front or rear brake caliper/wheel cylinder piston (Chapter 9).
- A mixture of brake pad/shoe lining materials fitted between sides (Chapter 1).
- Brake caliper mounting bolts loose (Chapter 9).
- Rear brake backplate mounting bolts loose – non ABS models only (Chapter 9).
- Worn or damaged steering or suspension components (Chapter 10).

Noise (grinding or high-pitched squeal) when brakes applied

- Brake pad or shoe friction lining material worn down to metal backing (Chapter 1).
- Excessive corrosion of brake disc or drum. (May be apparent after the vehicle has been standing for some time (Chapter 1).
- Foreign object (stone chipping, etc.) trapped between brake disc and dust shield (Chapter 1).

Excessive brake pedal travel

- Inoperative rear brake self-adjust mechanism – non ABS models only (Chapter 9).
- Faulty master cylinder (Chapter 9).
- Air in hydraulic system (Chapter 9).
- Faulty vacuum servo unit (Chapter 9).

Brake pedal feels spongy when depressed

- Air in hydraulic system (Chapter 9).
- Deteriorated flexible rubber brake hoses (Chapter 9).
- Master cylinder mounting nuts loose (Chapter 9).
- Faulty master cylinder (Chapter 9).

Excessive brake pedal effort required to stop vehicle

- Faulty vacuum servo unit (Chapter 9).
- Disconnected, damaged or insecure brake servo vacuum hose (Chapter 9).
- Primary or secondary hydraulic circuit failure (Chapter 9).
- Seized brake caliper or wheel cylinder piston(s) (Chapter 9).
- Brake pads or brake shoes incorrectly fitted (Chapter 1).
- Incorrect grade of brake pads or brake shoes fitted (Chapter 1).
- Brake pads or brake shoe linings contaminated (Chapter 1).

Judder felt through brake pedal or steering wheel when braking

- Excessive run-out or distortion of front discs or rear discs/drums (as applicable) (Chapter 9).
- Brake pad or brake shoe linings worn (Chapter 1).
- Brake caliper or rear brake backplate mounting bolts loose (Chapter 9).
- Wear in suspension or steering components or mountings (Chapter 10).

Brakes binding

- Seized brake caliper or wheel cylinder piston(s) (Chapter 9).
- Incorrectly adjusted handbrake mechanism or linkage (Chapter 1).
- Faulty master cylinder (Chapter 9).

Rear wheels locking under normal braking

- Rear brake shoe pads/linings contaminated (Chapter 1).
- Faulty brake pressure regulating valve (Chapter 9).

8 Suspension and steering systems

Note: *Before diagnosing suspension or steering faults, be sure that the trouble is not due to incorrect tyre pressures, mixtures of tyre types or binding brakes.*

Vehicle pulls to one side

- Defective tyre (Chapter 1).
- Excessive wear in suspension or steering components (Chapter 10).
- Incorrect front wheel alignment (Chapter 10).
- Accident damage to steering or suspension components (Chapter 10).

Wheel wobble and vibration

- Front roadwheels out of balance (vibration felt mainly through the steering wheel) (Chapter 10).
- Rear roadwheels out of balance (vibration felt throughout the vehicle) (Chapter 10).
- Roadwheels damaged or distorted (Chapter 1).
- Faulty or damaged tyre (Chapter 1).
- Worn steering or suspension joints, bushes or components (Chapter 10).
- Wheel bolts loose (Chapter 10).

Excessive pitching and/or rolling around corners or during braking

- Defective shock absorbers (Chapter 10).
- Broken or weak coil spring and/or suspension component (Chapter 10).
- Worn or damaged anti-roll bar or mountings (Chapter 10).

Wandering or general instability

- Incorrect front wheel alignment (Chapter 10).
- Worn steering or suspension joints, bushes or components (Chapter 10).
- Roadwheels out of balance (Chapter 10).
- Faulty or damaged tyre (Chapter 1).
- Wheel bolts loose (Chapter 10).
- Defective shock absorbers (Chapter 10).

Excessively stiff steering

- Lack of steering gear lubricant (Chapter 10).
- Seized tie-rod end balljoint or suspension balljoint (Chapter 10).
- Broken or incorrectly adjusted power steering pump drivebelt (where fitted) (Chapter 1).
- Incorrect front wheel alignment (Chapter 10).
- Steering rack or column bent or damaged (Chapter 10).

Excessive play in steering

- Worn steering column universal joint(s) or intermediate coupling (Chapter 10).
- Worn steering tie-rod end balljoints (Chapter 10).
- Worn rack and pinion steering gear (Chapter 10).
- Worn steering or suspension joints, bushes or components (Chapter 10).

Lack of power assistance

- Broken or incorrectly adjusted power steering pump drivebelt (Chapter 1).
- Incorrect power steering fluid level (Chapter 1).
- Restriction in power steering fluid hoses (Chapter 10).
- Faulty power steering pump (Chapter 10).
- Faulty rack and pinion steering gear (Chapter 10).

Tyre wear excessive

Tyres worn on inside or outside edges

- Tyres underinflated (wear on both edges) (Chapter 1).
- Incorrect camber or castor angles (wear on one edge only) (Chapter 10).
- Worn steering or suspension joints, bushes or components (Chapter 10).
- Excessively hard cornering.
- Accident damage.

Tyre treads exhibit feathered edges

- Incorrect toe setting (Chapter 10).

Tyres worn in centre of tread

- Tyres overinflated (Chapter 1).

Tyres worn on inside and outside edges

- Tyres underinflated (Chapter 1).

Tyres worn unevenly

- Tyres out of balance (Chapter 1).
- Excessive wheel or tyre run-out (Chapter 1).
- Worn shock absorbers (Chapter 10).
- Faulty tyre (Chapter 1).

9 Electrical system

Note: *For problems associated with the starting system, refer to the faults listed under the 'Engine' heading earlier in this Section.*

Battery will not hold a charge for more than a few days

- Battery defective internally (Chapter 12).
- Battery electrolyte level low (Chapter 1).
- Battery terminal connections loose or corroded (Chapter 12).
- Alternator drivebelt worn or incorrectly adjusted (Chapter 1).
- Alternator not charging at correct output (Chapter 12).
- Alternator or voltage regulator faulty (Chapter 12).
- Short-circuit causing continual battery drain (Chapter 12).

Ignition warning light remains illuminated with engine running

- Alternator drivebelt broken, worn, or incorrectly adjusted (Chapter 1).
- Alternator brushes worn, sticking, or dirty (Chapter 12).
- Alternator brush springs weak or broken (Chapter 12).
- Internal fault in alternator or voltage regulator (Chapter 12).
- Broken, disconnected, or loose wiring in charging circuit (Chapter 12).

Ignition warning light fails to come on

- Warning light bulb blown (Chapter 12).
- Broken, disconnected, or loose wiring in warning light circuit (Chapter 12).
- Alternator faulty (Chapter 12).

Lights inoperative

- Bulb blown (Chapter 12).
- Corrosion of bulb or bulbholder contacts (Chapter 12).
- Blown fuse (Chapter 12).
- Faulty relay (Chapter 12).
- Broken, loose, or disconnected wiring (Chapter 12).
- Faulty switch (Chapter 12).

Instrument readings inaccurate or erratic

Instrument readings increase with engine speed

- Faulty voltage regulator (Chapter 12).

Fuel or temperature gauge give no reading

- Faulty gauge sender unit (Chapters 3 or 4).
- Wiring open-circuit (Chapter 12).
- Faulty gauge (Chapter 12).

Fuel or temperature gauges give continuous maximum reading

- Faulty gauge sender unit (Chapters 3 or 4).
- Wiring short-circuit (Chapter 12).
- Faulty gauge (Chapter 12).

Horn inoperative or unsatisfactory in operation

Horn operates all the time

- Horn push either earthed or stuck down (Chapter 12).
- Horn cable to horn push earthed (Chapter 12).

Horn fails to operate

- Blown fuse (Chapter 12).
- Cable or cable connections loose, broken or disconnected (Chapter 12).
- Faulty horn (Chapter 12).

Horn emits intermittent or unsatisfactory sound

- Cable connections loose (Chapter 12).
- Horn mountings loose (Chapter 12).
- Faulty horn (Chapter 12).

Windscreen/tailgate wipers inoperative or unsatisfactory in operation

Wipers fail to operate or operate very slowly

- Wiper blades stuck to screen or linkage seized or binding (Chapter 12).
- Blown fuse (Chapter 12).
- Cable or cable connections loose, broken or disconnected (Chapter 12).
- Faulty relay (Chapter 12).
- Faulty wiper motor (Chapter 12).

Wiper blades sweep over too large or too small an area of the glass

- Wiper arms incorrectly positioned on spindles (Chapter 1).
- Excessive wear of wiper linkage (Chapter 1).
- Wiper motor or linkage mountings loose or insecure (Chapter 12).

Wiper blades fail to clean the glass effectively

- Wiper blade rubbers worn or perished (Chapter 1).
- Wiper arm tension springs broken or arm pivots seized (Chapter 1).
- Insufficient windscreen washer additive to adequately remove road film (Chapter 1).

Windscreen/tailgate washers inoperative or unsatisfactory in operation

One or more washer jets inoperative

- Blocked washer jet (Chapter 12).
- Disconnected, kinked or restricted fluid hose (Chapter 12).
- Insufficient fluid in washer reservoir (Chapter 1).

Washer pump fails to operate

- Broken or disconnected wiring or connections (Chapter 12).
- Blown fuse (Chapter 12).
- Faulty washer switch (Chapter 12).
- Faulty washer pump (Chapter 12).

Washer pump runs for some time before fluid is emitted from jets

- Faulty one-way valve in fluid supply hose (Chapter 12).

Electric windows inoperative or unsatisfactory in operation

Window glass will only move in one direction

- Faulty switch (Chapter 12).

Window glass slow to move

- Incorrectly adjusted door glass guide channels (Chapter 11).
- Regulator seized or damaged, or in need of lubrication (Chapter 11).
- Door internal components or trim fouling regulator (Chapter 11).
- Faulty motor (Chapter 12).

Window glass fails to move

- Incorrectly adjusted door glass guide channels (Chapter 11).
- Blown fuse (Chapter 12).
- Faulty relay (Chapter 12).
- Broken or disconnected wiring or connections (Chapter 12).
- Faulty motor (Chapter 12).
- Faulty control unit (Chapter 12).

Central locking system inoperative or unsatisfactory in operation

Complete system failure

- Blown fuse (Chapter 12).
- Faulty relay (Chapter 12).
- Faulty control unit (Chapter 12).
- Broken or disconnected wiring or connections (Chapter 12).

Latch locks but will not unlock, or unlocks but will not lock

- Faulty master switch (Chapter 12).
- Broken or disconnected latch operating rods or levers (Chapter 11).
- Faulty relay (Chapter 12).

One solenoid/motor fails to operate

- Broken or disconnected wiring or connections (Chapter 12).
- Faulty solenoid/motor (Chapter 12).
- Broken, binding or disconnected latch operating rods or levers (Chapter 11).
- Fault in door latch (Chapter 11).

MOT test checks

Introduction

Motor vehicle testing has been compulsory in Great Britain since 1960 when the Motor Vehicle (Tests) Regulations were first introduced. At that time testing was only applicable to vehicles ten years old or older, and the test itself only covered lighting equipment, braking systems and steering gear. Current vehicle testing is far more extensive and, in the case of private cars, is now an annual inspection commencing three years after the date of first registration.

This section is intended as a guide to getting your car through the MOT test. It lists all the relevant testable items, how to check them yourself, and what is likely to cause the vehicle to fail. Obviously it will not be possible to examine the vehicle to the same standard as the professional MOT tester who will be highly experienced in this work and will have all the necessary equipment available. However, working through the following checks will provide a good indication as to the condition of the vehicle and will enable you to identify any problem areas before submitting the vehicle for the test. Where a component is found to need repair or renewal, a cross reference is given to the relevant Chapter in the Manual where further information and the appropriate repair procedures will be found.

The following checks have been sub-divided into three categories as follows.

(a) Checks carried out from the driver's seat.
(b) Checks carried out with the car on the ground.
(c) Checks carried out with the car raised and with the wheels free to rotate.

In most cases the help of an assistant will be necessary to carry out these checks thoroughly.

Checks carried out from the driver's seat

Handbrake (Chapters 1 and 9)

Test the operation of the handbrake by pulling on the lever until the handbrake is in the normal fully-applied position. Ensure that the travel of the lever (the number of clicks of the ratchet) is not excessive before full resistance of the braking mechanism is felt. If so, this indicates incorrect adjustment of the rear brakes or incorrectly adjusted handbrake cables. With the handbrake fully applied, tap the lever sideways and make sure that it does not release, indicating wear in the ratchet and pawl. Release the handbrake and move the lever from side to side to check for excessive wear in the pivot bearing. Check the security of the lever mountings and make sure that there is no corrosion of any part of the body structure within 30 cm (12 in) of the lever mounting. If the lever mountings cannot be readily seen from inside the vehicle, carry out this check later when working underneath.

Footbrake (Chapters 1 and 9)

Check that the brake pedal is sound without visible defects such as excessive wear of the pivot bushes or a broken or damaged pedal pad. Check also for signs of fluid leaks on the pedal, floor or carpets, indicating failed seals in the brake master cylinder. Depress the brake pedal slowly at first, then rapidly until sustained pressure can be held. Maintain this pressure and check that the pedal does not creep down to the floor, indicating problems with the master cylinder. Release the pedal, wait a few seconds then depress it once until firm resistance is felt. Check that this resistance occurs near the top of the pedal travel. If the pedal travels nearly to the floor before firm resistance is felt, this indicates incorrect brake adjustment resulting in 'insufficient reserve travel' of the footbrake. If firm resistance cannot be felt, ie the pedal feels spongy, this indicates the presence of air in the hydraulic system, which will necessitate complete bleeding of the system. Check that the servo unit is operating correctly by depressing the brake pedal several times to exhaust the vacuum. Keep the pedal depressed and start the engine. As soon as the engine starts, the brake pedal resistance will be felt to alter. If this is not the case, there may be a leak from the brake servo vacuum hose, or the servo unit itself may be faulty.

Steering wheel and column (Chapter 10)

Examine the steering wheel for fractures or looseness of the hub, spokes or rim. Move the steering wheel from side to side and then up and down, in relation to the steering column. Check that the steering wheel is not loose on the column, indicating wear in the column splines or a loose steering wheel retaining nut. Continue moving the steering wheel as before, but also turn it slightly from left to right. Check that there is no abnormal movement of the steering wheel, indicating excessive wear in the column upper support bearing, universal joint(s) or flexible coupling.

Electrical equipment (Chapter 12)

Switch on the ignition and operate the horn. The horn must operate and produce a clear sound audible to other road users. Note that a gong, siren or two-tone horn fitted as an alternative to the manufacturer's original equipment is not acceptable.

Check the operation of the windscreen washers and wipers. The washers must operate with adequate flow and pressure and with the jets adjusted so that the liquid strikes the windscreen near the top of the glass.

Operate the windscreen wipers in conjunction with the washers and check that the blades cover their designed sweep of the windscreen without smearing. The blades must effectively clean the glass so that the driver has an adequate view of the road ahead and to the front nearside and offside of the vehicle. If the screen smears or does not clean adequately, it is advisable to renew the wiper blades before the MOT test.

Depress the footbrake with the ignition switched on and have your assistant check that both rear stop lights operate, and are extinguished when the footbrake is released. If one stop light fails to operate it is likely

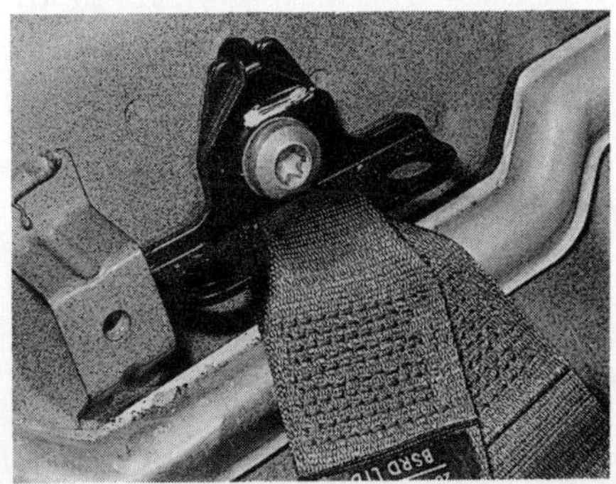

Check the security of all seat belt mountings

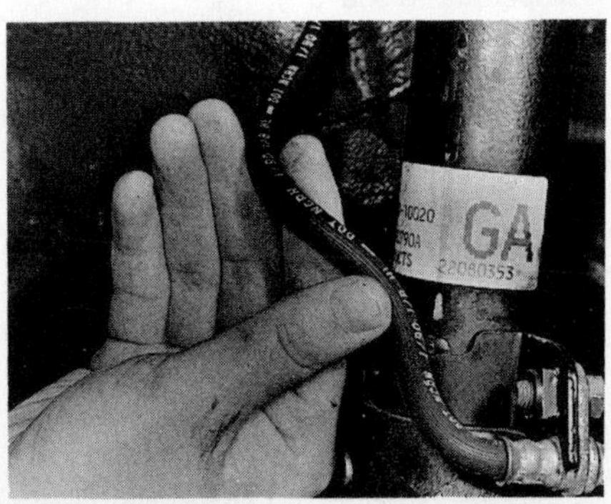

Check the flexible brake hoses for cracks or deterioration

Examine the steering rack rubber gaiters for condition and security

Check all rubber suspension mounting bushes for damage or deterioration

Shake the roadwheel vigorously to check for excess play in the wheel bearings and suspension components

Check the condition of the shock absorber mountings and bushes (arrowed)

that a bulb has blown or there is a poor electrical contact at, or near the bulbholder. If both stop lights fail to operate, check for a blown fuse, faulty stop light switch or possibly two blown bulbs. If the lights stay on when the brake pedal is released, it is possible that the switch is at fault.

Seat belts (Chapters 1 and 11)

Note: *The following checks are applicable to the seat belts provided for the driver's seat and front passenger's seat. Both seat belts must be of a type that will restrain the upper part of the body; lap belts are not acceptable.*

Carefully examine the seat belt webbing for cuts or any signs of serious fraying or deterioration. If the seat belt is of the retractable type, pull the belt all the way out and examine the full extent of the webbing.

Fasten and unfasten the belt ensuring that the locking mechanism holds securely and releases properly when intended. If the belt is of the retractable type, check also that the retracting mechanism operates correctly when the belt is released.

Check the security of all seat belt mountings and attachments which are accessible, without removing any trim or other components, from inside the car (photo). Any serious corrosion, fracture or distortion of the body structure within 30 cm (12 in) of any mounting point will cause the vehicle to fail. Certain anchorages will not be accessible, or even visible from inside the car and in this instance further checks should be carried out later, when working underneath. If any part of the seat belt mechanism is attached to the front seat, then the seat mountings are treated as anchorages and must also comply as above.

Checks carried out with the car on the ground

Electrical equipment (Chapter 12)

Switch on the side lights and check that both front and rear side lights are illuminated and that the lenses and reflectors are secure and undamaged. This is particularly important at the rear where a cracked or damaged lens would allow a white light to show to the rear, which is unacceptable. It is also worth noting that any lens that is excessively dirty, either inside or out, such that the light intensity is reduced, could also constitute a fail.

Switch on the headlamps and check that both dipped beam and main beam units are operating correctly and at the same light intensity. If either headlamp shows signs of dimness, this is usually attributable to a poor earth connection or severely corroded internal reflector. Inspect the headlamp lenses for cracks or stone damage. Any damage to the headlamp lens will normally constitute a fail, but this is very much down to the tester's discretion. Bear in mind that with all light units they must operate correctly when first switched on – it is not acceptable to tap a light unit to make it operate.

The headlamps must be aligned so as not to dazzle other road users when switched to dipped beam. This can only be accurately checked using optical beam setting equipment so if you have any doubts about the headlamp alignment, it is advisable to have this professionally checked and if necessary reset, before the MOT test.

With the ignition switched on, operate the direction indicators and check that they show a white or amber light to the front and red or amber light to the rear, that they flash at the rate of between one and two flashes per second and that the 'tell-tale' on the instrument panel also functions. Examine the lenses for cracks or damage as described previously.

Footbrake (Chapters 1 and 9)

From within the engine compartment examine the brake pipes for signs of leaks, corrosion, insecurity, chafing or other damage and check the master cylinder and servo unit for leaks, security of their mountings or excessive corrosion in the vicinity of the mountings.

Turn the steering as necessary so that the right-hand front brake flexible hose can be examined. Inspect the hose carefully for any sign of cracks or deterioration of the rubber (photo). This will be most noticeable if the hose is bent in half and is particularly common where the rubber portion enters the metal end fitting. Turn the steering onto full left then full right lock and ensure that the hose does not contact the wheel, tyre, or any part of the steering or suspension mechanism. While your assistant depresses the brake pedal firmly, check the hose for any bulges or fluid leaks under pressure. Now repeat these checks on the left-hand front hose. Should any damage or deterioration be noticed, renew the hose.

Steering mechanism and suspension (Chapters 1 and 10)

Have your assistant turn the steering wheel from side to side slightly, up to the point where the steering gear just begins to transmit this movement to the roadwheels. Check for excessive free play between the steering wheel and the steering gear, indicating wear in the steering column joints, wear or insecurity of the steering column to steering gear coupling, or insecurity, incorrect adjustment, or wear in the steering gear itself. Generally speaking, free play greater than 1.3 cm (0.5 in) should be considered excessive.

Have your assistant turn the steering wheel more vigorously in each direction up to the point where the roadwheels just begin to turn. As this is done, carry out a complete examination of all steering joints, linkages, fittings and attachments. Any component that shows signs of wear, damage, distortion, or insecurity should be renewed or attended to accordingly. On models equipped with power-assisted steering also check that the power steering pump is secure and the drivebelt is correctly adjusted. Also ensure that the system operates correctly with no signs of fluid leakage from any of the hose unions. Additional checks can be carried out later with the vehicle raised when there will be greater working clearance underneath.

Check that the vehicle is standing level and at approximately the correct ride height. Ensure that there is sufficient clearance between the suspension components and the bump stops to allow full suspension travel over bumps.

Shock absorbers (Chapter 10)

Depress each corner of the car in turn and then release it. If the suspension components are in good condition the corner of the car will rise and then settle in its normal position. If there is no noticeable damping effect and the car continues to rise and fall, then the suspension is defective.

Exhaust system (Chapter 1)

Start the engine and with your assistant holding a rag over the tailpipe, check the entire system for leaks which will appear as a

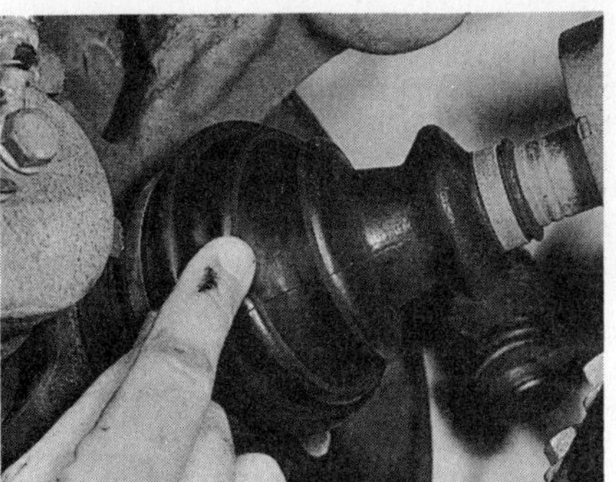
Inspect the constant velocity joint gaiters for splits or damage

Check the handbrake mechanism for signs of frayed or broken cables or insecurity of the linkage

Check the condition of the exhaust system paying particular attention to the mountings

rhythmic fluffing or hissing sound at the source of the leak. Check the effectiveness of the silencer by ensuring that the noise produced is of a level to be expected from a vehicle of similar type. Providing that the system is structurally sound, it is acceptable to cure a leak using a proprietary exhaust system repair kit or similar method.

Checks carried out with the car raised and with the wheels free to rotate

Jack up the front and rear of the car and securely support it on axle stands positioned at suitable load bearing points under the vehicle structure. Position the stands clear of the suspension assemblies and ensure that the wheels are clear of the ground and that the steering can be turned onto full right and left lock.

Steering mechanism (Chapter 10)

Examine the steering rack rubber gaiters for signs of splits, lubricant leakage or insecurity of the retaining clips (photo). Also check for excessive stiffness or binding of the steering, a missing split pin or locking device or any severe corrosion of the body structure within 30 cm (12 in) of any steering component attachment point.

Have your assistant turn the steering onto full left then full right lock. Check that the steering turns smoothly without undue tightness or roughness and that no part of the steering mechanism, including a wheel or tyre, fouls any brake flexible or rigid hose or pipe, or any part of the body structure.

Front and rear suspension and wheel bearings (Chapter 10)

Starting at the front right-hand side of the vehicle, grasp the roadwheel at the 3 o'clock and 9 o'clock positions and shake it vigorously. Check for any free play at the wheel bearings, suspension ball joints, or suspension mountings, pivots and attachments. Check also for any serious deterioration of the rubber or metal casing of any mounting bushes, or any distortion, deformation or severe corrosion of any components (photo). Look for missing split pins, tab washers or other locking devices on any mounting or attachment, or any severe corrosion of the vehicle structure within 30 cm (12 in) of any suspension component attachment point. If any excess free play is suspected at a component pivot point, this can be confirmed by using a large screwdriver or similar tool and levering between the mounting and the component attachment. This will confirm whether the wear is in the pivot bush, its retaining bolt or in the mounting itself (note that the bolt holes can often become elongated). Now grasp the wheel at the 12 o'clock and 6 o'clock positions, shake it vigorously and repeat the previous inspection (photo). Rotate the wheel and check for roughness or tightness of the front wheel bearing such that imminent failure of the bearing is indicated. Carry out all the above checks at the other front wheel and then at both rear wheels. Note, however, that the condition of the rear wheel bearings is not actually part of the MOT test, but if they are at all suspect, it is likely that this will be brought to the owner's attention at the time of the test.

Roadsprings and shock absorbers (Chapter 10)

On vehicles with strut type suspension units, examine the strut assembly for signs of fluid leakage, corrosion or severe pitting of the piston rod or damage to the casing. Check also for security of the mounting points (photo).

Check that the coil spring ends locate correctly in their spring seats, that there is no severe corrosion of the spring and that it is not cracked, broken or in any way damaged.

Driveshafts (Chapter 8)

With the steering turned onto full lock, rotate each front wheel in turn and inspect the constant velocity joint gaiters for splits or damage (photo). Also check the gaiter is securely attached to its respective housings by clips or other methods of retention.

Continue turning the wheel and check that each driveshaft is straight with no sign of damage.

Braking system (Chapters 1 and 9)

If possible, without dismantling, check for wear of the brake pads and the condition of the discs. Ensure that the friction lining material has not worn excessively and that the discs are not fractured, pitted, scored or worn excessively.

Carefully examine all the rigid brake pipes underneath the car and the flexible hoses at the rear. Look for signs of excessive corrosion, chafing or insecurity of the pipes and for signs of bulging under pressure, chafing, splits or deterioration of the flexible hoses.

Look for signs of hydraulic fluid leaks at the brake calipers or on the brake backplates, indicating failed hydraulic seals in the components concerned.

Slowly spin each wheel while your assistant depresses the footbrake then releases it. Ensure that each brake is operating and that the wheel is free to rotate when the pedal is released.

Examine the handbrake mechanism and check for signs of frayed or broken cables, excessive corrosion or wear or insecurity of the linkage (photo). Have your assistant operate the handbrake while you check that the mechanism works on each relevant wheel and releases fully without binding.

Exhaust system (Chapter 1)

Starting at the front, examine the exhaust system over its entire length checking for any damaged, broken or missing mountings, security of the pipe retaining clamps and condition of the system with regard to rust and corrosion (photo).

Wheels and tyres (Chapter 1)

Carefully examine each tyre in turn on both the inner and outer walls and over the whole of the tread area and check for signs of cuts, tears, lumps, bulges, separation of the tread and exposure of the ply or cord due to wear or other damage. Check also that the tyre bead is correctly seated on the wheel rim and that the tyre valve is sound and properly seated. Spin the wheel and check that it is not excessively distorted or damaged particularly at the bead rim. Check that the tyres are of the correct size for the car and that they are of the same size and type on each axle. They should also be inflated to the specified pressures.

Using a suitable gauge check the tyre tread depth. The current legal requirement states that the tread pattern must be visible over the whole tread area and must be of a minimum depth of 1.6 mm over at least three-quarters of the tread width. It is acceptable for some wear of the inside or outside edges of the tyre to be apparent but this wear must be in one even circumferential band and the tread must be visible. Any excessive wear of this nature may indicate incorrect front wheel alignment which should be checked before the tyre becomes excessively worn. See Chapters 1 and 10 for further information on tyre wear patterns and front wheel alignment.

Body corrosion

Check the condition of the entire vehicle structure for signs of corrosion in any load bearing areas. For the purpose of the MOT test all chassis box sections, side sills, subframes, crossmembers, pillars, suspension, steering, braking system and seat belt mountings and anchorages should all be considered as load bearing areas. As a general guide, any corrosion which has seriously reduced the metal thickness of a load bearing area to weaken it, is likely to cause the vehicle to fail. Should corrosion of this nature be encountered, professional repairs are likely to be needed.

Chapter 1 Routine maintenance and servicing

Contents

Lubricants, fluids and capacities
Maintenance schedule
Maintenance procedures

Specifications

Engine

Oil filter type	Champion B104

Cooling system

Antifreeze properties – 50% antifreeze (by volume):	
Commences freezing	– 36°C
Frozen solid	– 48°C

Fuel system

Air cleaner filter element:	
Carburettor engines	Champion W218
Fuel-injected engines	Champion W221
Idle speed:	
Carburettor engines	850 ± 50 rpm
Fuel-injected engines – nominal value given for reference purposes only	850 ± 50 rpm
CO level at idle speed – engine at normal operating temperature:	
Carburettor engines – without catalytic converter – at exhaust tailpipe	2.0 to 3.0%
Carburettor engines – with catalytic converter – at gas-sampling pipe	1.0 to 3.0%
Fuel-injected engines – without catalytic converter – at exhaust tailpipe	0.5 to 2.0%
Fuel-injected engines – with catalytic converter – at gas-sampling pipe	0.5 to 2.0%
Recommended fuel:	
Cars without catalytic converter	95 RON unleaded (ie unleaded Premium) or 97 RON leaded (ie 4-star)
Cars with catalytic converter	95 RON unleaded (ie unleaded Premium) **only**

Ignition system

Firing order	1–3–4–2 (No 1 cylinder at timing belt end)
Direction of crankshaft rotation	Clockwise (viewed from right-hand side of car)
Direction of distributor rotor arm rotation	Anti-clockwise (viewed from left-hand side of car)
Ignition timing:	
Carburettor engines – @ 1500 rpm (vacuum pipe disconnected)	9° ± 1° BTDC
Fuel-injected engines	See text
Spark plugs:	
Type	Champion RC9YCC
Electrode gap	0.8 mm
Spark plug (HT) leads:	
Resistance	25 k ohms per lead, maximum

Braking system

Front brake pad friction material minimum thickness	3.0 mm
Rear brake shoe friction material minimum thickness	2.0 mm
Rear brake pad friction material minimum thickness	3.0 mm

Suspension and steering

Power steering pump drivebelt deflection	7.5 to 8.5 mm @ 10 kg pressure

Tyre pressures – tyres cold

	Front	Rear
155 SR 13 tyres:		
Normal driving conditions	2.1 bars (30 lbf/in²)	2.1 bars (30 lbf/in²)
Loads in excess of four persons	2.1 bars (30 lbf/in²)	2.3 bars (34 lbf/in²)
Speeds in excess of 100 mph – all loads	2.2 bars (32 lbf/in²)	2.2 bars (32 lbf/in²)
175/65 TR 14 tyres:		
All loads – up to 100 mph	2.1 bars (30 lbf/in²)	2.1 bars (30 lbf/in²)
All loads – over 100 mph	2.2 bars (32 lbf/in²)	2.2 bars (32 lbf/in²)
185/60 HR 14 tyres:		
All loads – up to 100 mph	2.1 bars (30 lbf/in²)	2.1 bars (30 lbf/in²)
All loads – over 100 mph	2.5 bars (36 lbf/in²)	2.5 bars (36 lbf/in²)

Note: *Pressures apply only to original equipment tyres and may vary if any other make or type is fitted; check with the tyre manufacturer or supplier for correct pressures if necessary*

Electrical system

Alternator drivebelt deflection:	
Models equipped with air conditioning	9 to 10 mm @ 10 kg pressure
Models without air conditioning	6 to 8 mm @ 10 kg pressure
Wiper blades – front and rear	Champion X-4503

Torque wrench settings

	Nm	lbf ft
Air cleaner metal intake duct to cylinder head support bracket bolt – K16 engine	8	6
Spark plug cover screws – K16 engine	2	1.5
Spark plugs	25	19
Timing belt cover fasteners:		
Upper right-hand/outer cover	4	3
Lower and upper left-hand inner covers	9	6
Distributor cap screws	2	1.5
Distributor rotor arm grub screw – fuel-injected engines	10	7
Distributor mounting bolts – carburettor engines	25	19
Alternator mounting/pivot/adjusting arm bolts	25	19
Power steering/alternator drivebelt adjuster pulley nut and bolt	25	19
Engine oil drain plug	42	31
Transmission oil filler/level and drain plugs	25	19
Fuel system pressure release bolt – at fuel filter	12	9
Fuel filter inlet union	40	30
Fuel filter outlet union	35	26
Front brake caliper guide pin bolts	32	24
Rear brake drum retaining screws	10	7
Roadwheel nuts	100	74

Lubricants, fluids and capacities

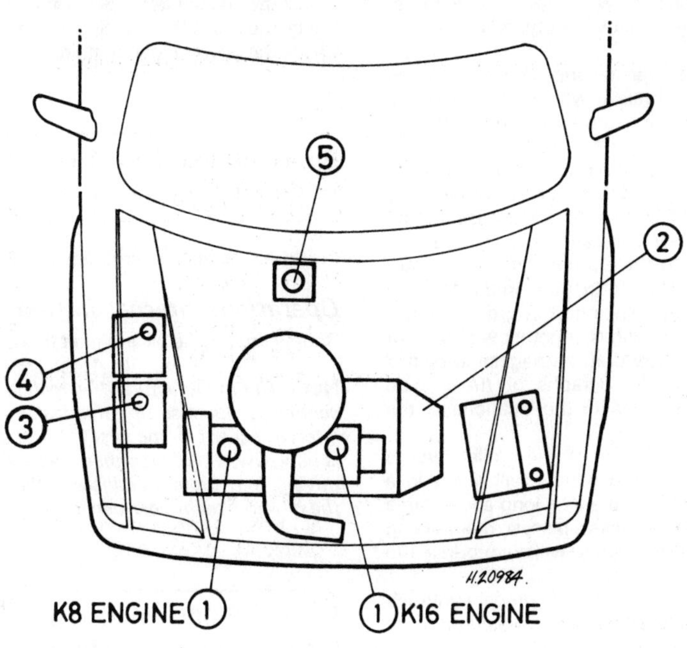

Lubricants and fluids

Component or system	Lubricant type/specification	Duckhams recommendation
1 Engine	SAE 10W/40 multigrade engine oil meeting specifications API-SG or SG/CD, CCMC G4, or RES.22.OL.G4	Duckhams QXR or 10W/40 Motor Oil
2 Transmission	Special transmission oil – refer to your Rover dealer	Duckhams Hypoid PT 75W/80 Gear Oil – for topping-up only
3 Cooling system	Ethylene glycol-based antifreeze with non-phosphate corrosion inhibitors, suitable for mixed-metal engines, containing no methanol and meeting specifications BS6580 and BS5117	Duckhams Universal Antifreeze & Summer Coolant
4 Power steering system	Automatic Transmission Fluid (ATF) meeting Dexron II D specification	Duckhams Uni-Matic or D-Matic Automatic Transmission Fluid
5 Braking system	Hydraulic fluid meeting specification SAE J1703 or DOT 4	Duckhams Universal Brake and Clutch Fluid
General greasing	Multi-purpose lithium-based grease, NLGI consistency No. 2	Duckhams LB10 Grease

Capacities

Engine oil

Total capacity (including filter) .... 4.5 litres
Difference between dipstick MAX and MIN marks .... 1 litre

Cooling system .... 5.8 litres

Power steering reservoir .... 1.2 litres

Fuel tank .... 55 litres

Transmission .... 2.0 litres

Washer system reservoir .... 3.1 litres

Maintenance schedule

Introduction

This Chapter is designed to help the DIY owner maintain the Rover 214/414 with the goals of maximum economy, safety, reliability and performance in mind.

On the following pages is a master maintenance schedule, listing the servicing requirements, and the intervals at which they should be carried out as recommended by the manufacturers. The operations are listed in the order in which the work can be most conveniently undertaken. For example, all the operations that are performed from within the engine compartment are grouped together, as are all those that require the car to be raised and supported for access to the suspension and underbody. Alongside each operation in the schedule is a reference which directs the reader to the Sections in this Chapter covering maintenance procedures or to other Chapters in the Manual, where the operations are described and illustrated in greater detail. Specifications for all the maintenance operations, together with a list of lubricants, fluids and capacities are provided at the beginning of this Chapter. Refer to the accompanying photographs of the engine compartment and the underbody of the car for the locations of the various components.

Servicing your car in accordance with the mileage/time maintenance schedule and step-by-step procedures will result in a planned maintenance programme that should give a long and reliable service life. Bear in mind that it is a comprehensive plan, so maintaining some items but not others at the specified intervals will not produce the same results.

The first step in this maintenance programme is to prepare yourself before the actual work begins. Read through all the procedures to be undertaken then obtain all the parts, lubricants and any additional tools needed.

Daily

Operations internal and external

Check the operation of the horn, all lamps, the direction indicators and the wipers and washers (Section 11)
Check the operation of the seat belts (Section 10)
Check the operation of the brakes (Section 8)
Check under the car for signs of fluid leaks on the ground

Every 250 miles (400 km) or weekly

Operations internal and external

Visually examine the tyres for tread depth and wear or damage (Section 9)
Check, and if necessary adjust, the tyre pressures (Section 9)

Operations in the engine compartment

Check the engine oil level (Section 1)
Check the washer system reservoir fluid level (Section 11)

Every 1000 miles (1500 km) or monthly – whichever comes first

Carry out the daily and weekly checks, then check the following:

Operations internal and external

Check the operation of all locks, hinges and latch mechanisms (Section 10)

Operations in the engine compartment

Check the coolant level (Section 2)
Check the brake fluid level (Section 8)
Check the power steering fluid level – where necessary (Section 9)

Every 6000 miles (10 000 km) or 6 months – whichever comes first

In addition to all the items listed above, carry out the following:

Operations internal and external

Renew the engine oil and filter (Section 1)

Note: *The manufacturer has recently (approx mid-1991) extended the service schedule so that this task need no longer be carried out at this interval, except for the First Lubrication Service, carried out when the car is new. Owners of high-mileage cars, or those who do a lot of stop-start driving, may prefer to adhere to the original recommendation, changing the oil and filter in-between the major services described below.*

Every 12 000 miles (20 000 km) or 12 months – whichever comes first

In addition to the items listed under the daily, weekly and monthly checks, carry out the following:

Operations internal and external

Renew the engine oil and filter (Section 1)
Check the operation of the clutch (Section 5)
Check the transmission oil level (Section 6)
Check the tightness of the roadwheel nuts (Section 9)
Check the exterior paintwork, the body panels and the underbody sealer (Section 10)
Check and lubricate all locks, hinges, latch mechanisms and the sunroof (Section 10)

Operations with the car raised and supported

Check the fuel tank hoses, pipes and connections (Section 3)
Check the exhaust system (Section 3)
Check the driveshaft gaiters and CV joints (Section 7)
Check the front brake pads, calipers and discs (Section 8)*
Check the rear brake shoes, check the wheel cylinders and drums – Non ABS models (Section 8)*
Check the rear brake pads, calipers and discs – ABS models (Section 8)*
Check the braking system master cylinder, flexible hoses and metal pipes (Section 8)*
Adjust and lubricate the handbrake (Section 8)
Check the front suspension (Section 9)
Check the steering gear, the rubber gaiters and the track rod balljoints (Section 9)
Check the rear suspension (Section 9)
** Every 60 000 miles/100 000 km or every THREE years – whichever comes first – the braking system master cylinder, the brake calipers and (where necessary) rear wheel cylinders must be overhauled and their seals renewed as a matter of course. Refer to Chapter 9 for overhaul procedures.*

Operations in the engine compartment

Check the cooling system hoses and connections (Section 2)
Check the operation of the radiator electric cooling fan (Section 2)
Drain, flush and refill the cooling system, renewing the antifreeze (Section 2)*
Top up the carburettor piston damper (Section 3)

Are your plugs trying to tell you something?

Normal.

Grey-brown deposits, lightly coated core nose. Plugs ideally suited to engine, and engine in good condition.

Heavy Deposits.

A build up of crusty deposits, light-grey sandy colour in appearance.
Fault: Often caused by worn valve guides, excessive use of upper cylinder lubricant, or idling for long periods.

Lead Glazing.

Plug insulator firing tip appears yellow or green/yellow and shiny in appearance.
Fault: Often caused by incorrect carburation, excessive idling followed by sharp acceleration. Also check ignition timing.

Carbon fouling.

Dry, black, sooty deposits.
Fault: over-rich fuel mixture.
Check: carburettor mixture settings, float level, choke operation, air filter.

Oil fouling.

Wet, oily deposits. Fault: worn bores/piston rings or valve guides; sometimes occurs (temporarily) during running-in period.

Overheating.

Electrodes have glazed appearance, core nose very white – few deposits. Fault: plug overheating. Check: plug value, ignition timing, fuel octane rating (too low) and fuel mixture (too weak).

Electrode damage.

Electrodes burned away; core nose has burned, glazed appearance. Fault: pre-ignition. Check: for correct heat range and as for 'overheating'.

Split core nose.

(May appear initially as a crack). Fault: detonation or wrong gap-setting technique. Check: ignition timing, cooling system, fuel mixture (too weak).

WHY DOUBLE COPPER IS BETTER FOR YOUR ENGINE.

Champion Double Copper plugs are the first in the world to have copper core in both centre <u>and</u> earth electrode. This innovative design means that they run cooler by up to 100°C – giving greater efficiency and longer life. These double copper cores transfer heat away from the tip of the plug faster and more efficiently. Therefore, Double Copper runs at cooler temperatures than conventional plugs giving improved acceleration response and high speed performance with no fear of pre-ignition.

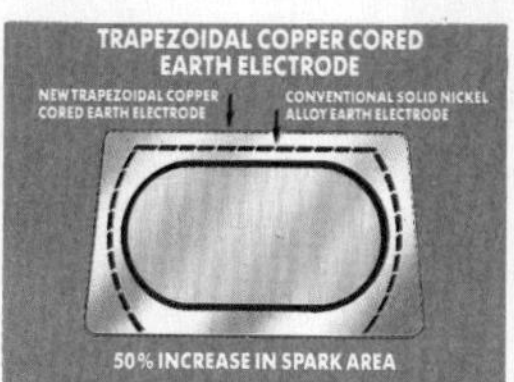

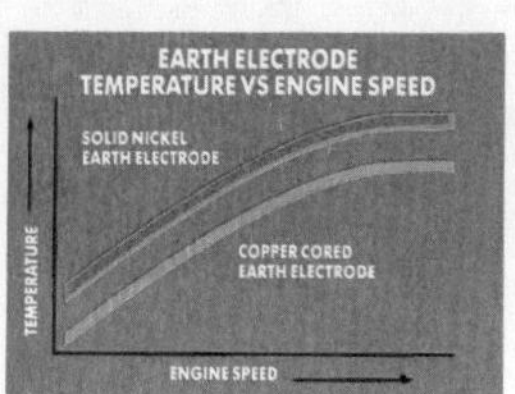

Champion Double Copper plugs also feature a unique trapezoidal earth electrode giving a 50% increase in spark area. This, together with the double copper cores, offers greatly reduced electrode wear, so the spark stays stronger for longer.

 **FASTER COLD STARTING**

 **FOR UNLEADED OR LEADED FUEL**

 **ELECTRODES UP TO 100°C COOLER**

 **BETTER ACCELERATION RESPONSE**

 **LOWER EMISSIONS**

 **50% BIGGER SPARK AREA**

 **THE LONGER LIFE PLUG**

Plug Tips/Hot and Cold.

Spark plugs must operate within well-defined temperature limits to avoid cold fouling at one extreme and overheating at the other.

Champion and the car manufacturers work out the best plugs for an engine to give optimum performance under all conditions, from freezing cold starts to sustained high speed motorway cruising.

Plugs are often referred to as hot or cold. With Champion, the higher the number on its body, the hotter the plug, and the lower the number the cooler the plug.

Plug Cleaning

Modern plug design and materials mean that Champion no longer recommends periodic plug cleaning. Certainly don't clean your plugs with a wire brush as this can cause metal conductive paths across the nose of the insulator so impairing its performance and resulting in loss of acceleration and reduced m.p.g.

However, if plugs are removed, always carefully clean the area where the plug seats in the cylinder head as grit and dirt can sometimes cause gas leakage.

Also wipe any traces of oil or grease from plug leads as this may lead to arcing.

DOUBLE COPPER

This photographic sequence shows the steps taken to repair the dent and paintwork damage shown above. In general, the procedure for repairing a hole will be similar; where there are substantial differences, the procedure is clearly described and shown in a separate photograph.

First remove any trim around the dent, then hammer out the dent where access is possible. This will minimise filling. Here, after the large dent has been hammered out, the damaged area is being made slightly concave.

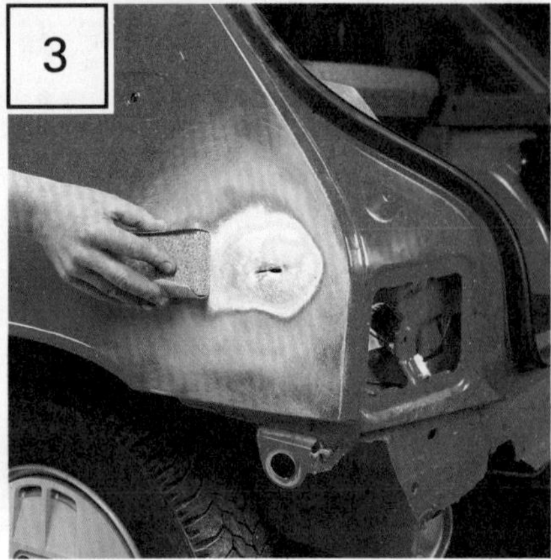

Next, remove all paint from the damaged area by rubbing with coarse abrasive paper or using a power drill fitted with a wire brush or abrasive pad. 'Feather' the edge of the boundary with good paintwork using a finer grade of abrasive paper.

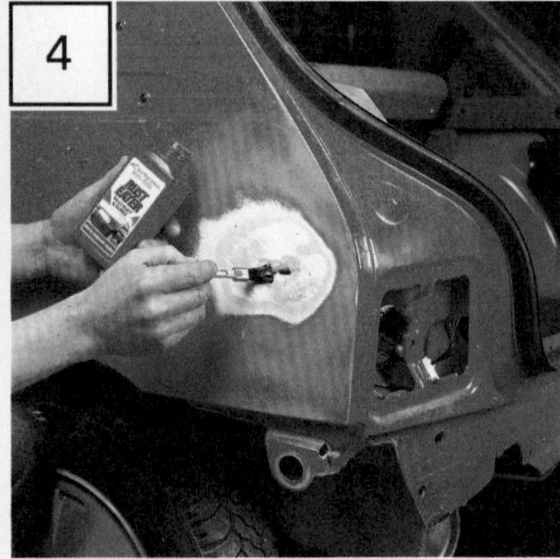

Where there are holes or other damage, the sheet metal should be cut away before proceeding further. The damaged area and any signs of rust should be treated with Turtle Wax Hi-Tech Rust Eater, which will also inhibit further rust formation.

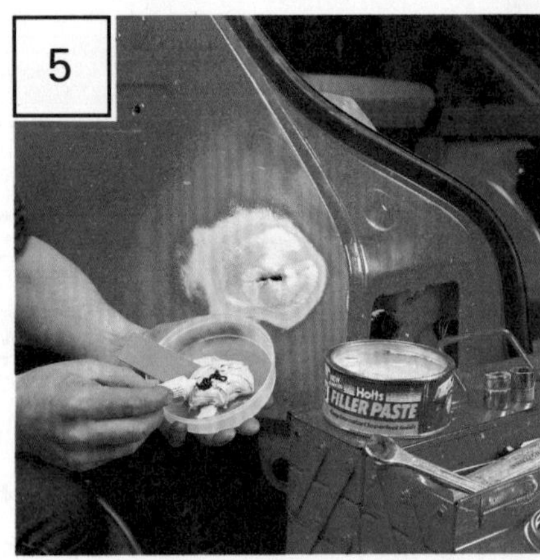

For a large dent or hole mix Holts Body Plus Resin and Hardener according to the manufacturer's instructions and apply around the edge of the repair. Press Glass Fibre Matting over the repair area and leave for 20-30 minutes to harden. Then ...

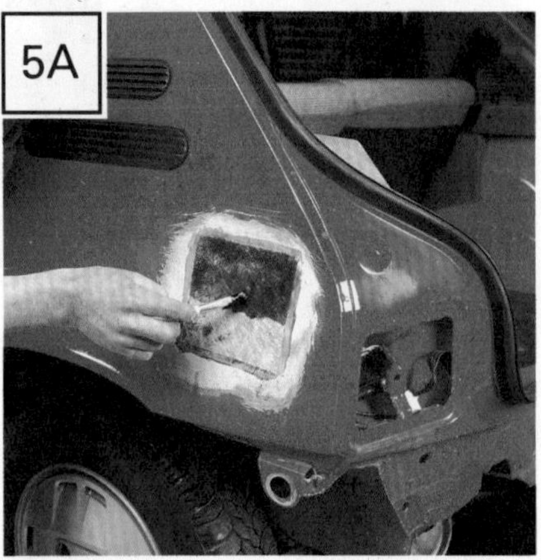

... brush more Holts Body Plus Resin and Hardener onto the matting and leave to harden. Repeat the sequence with two or three layers of matting, checking that the final layer is lower than the surrounding area. Apply Holts Body Plus Filler Paste as shown in Step 5B.

For a medium dent, mix Holts Body Plus Filler Paste and Hardener according to the manufacturer's instructions and apply it with a flexible applicator. Apply thin layers of filler at 20-minute intervals, until the filler surface is slightly proud of the surrounding bodywork.

For small dents and scratches use Holts No Mix Filler Paste straight from the tube. Apply it according to the instructions in thin layers, using the spatula provided. It will harden in minutes if applied outdoors and may then be used as its own knifing putty.

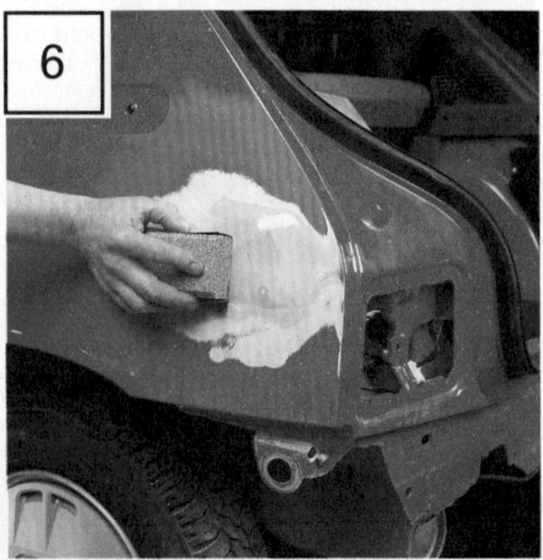

Use a plane or file for initial shaping. Then, using progressively finer grades of wet-and-dry paper, wrapped round a sanding block, and copious amounts of clean water, rub down the filler until glass smooth. 'Feather' the edges of adjoining paintwork.

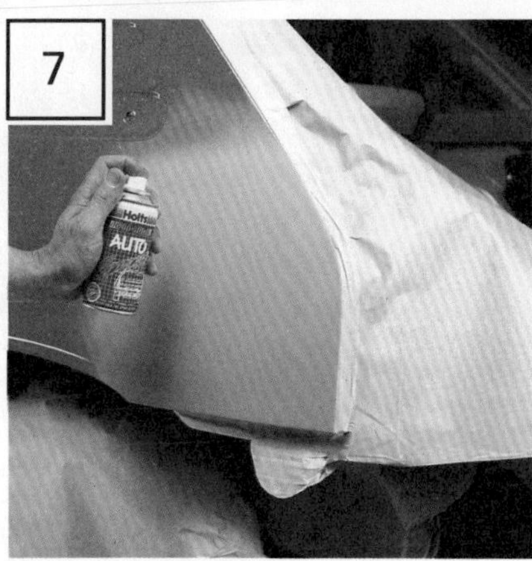

Protect adjoining areas before spraying the whole repair area and at least one inch of the surrounding sound paintwork with Holts Dupli-Color primer.

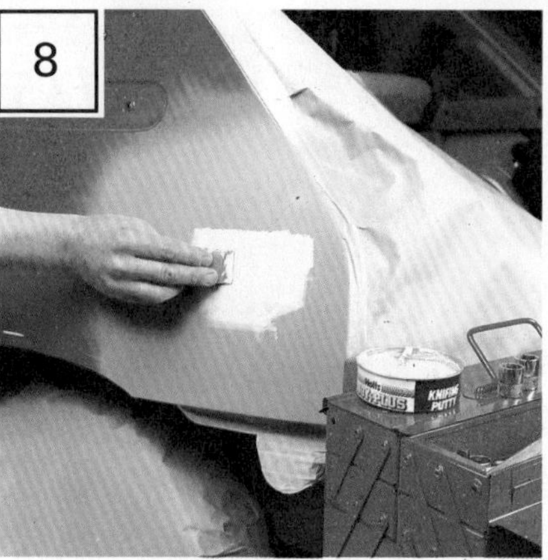

Fill any imperfections in the filler surface with a small amount of Holts Body Plus Knifing Putty. Using plenty of clean water, rub down the surface with a fine grade wet-and-dry paper – 400 grade is recommended – until it is really smooth.

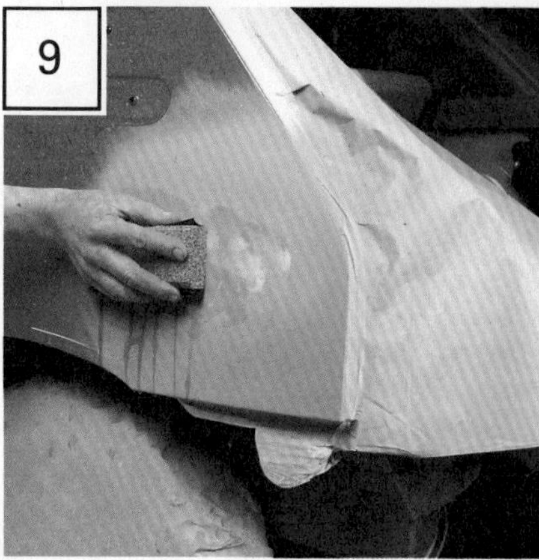

Carefully fill any remaining imperfections with knifing putty before applying the last coat of primer. Then rub down the surface with Holts Body Plus Rubbing Compound to ensure a really smooth surface.

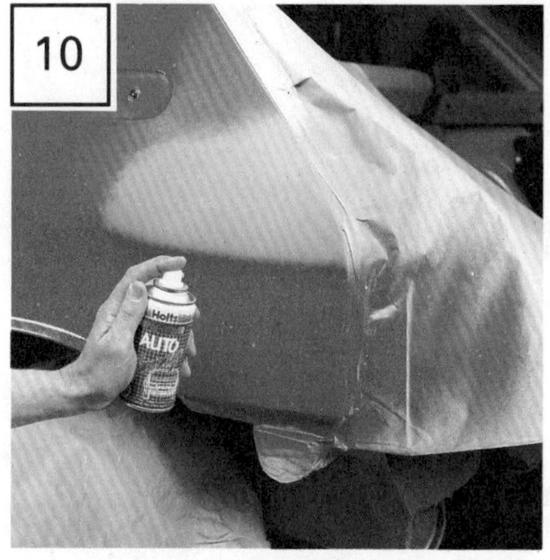

Protect surrounding areas from overspray before applying the topcoat in several thin layers. Agitate Holts Dupli-Color aerosol thoroughly. Start at the repair centre, spraying outwards with a side-to-side motion.

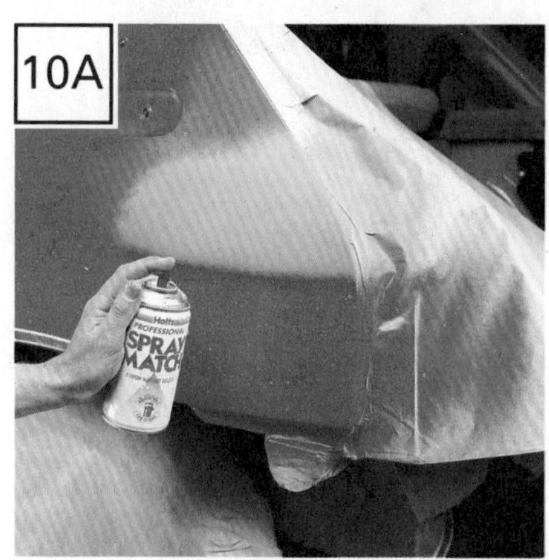

If the exact colour is not available off the shelf, local Holts Professional Spraymatch Centres will custom fill an aerosol to match perfectly.

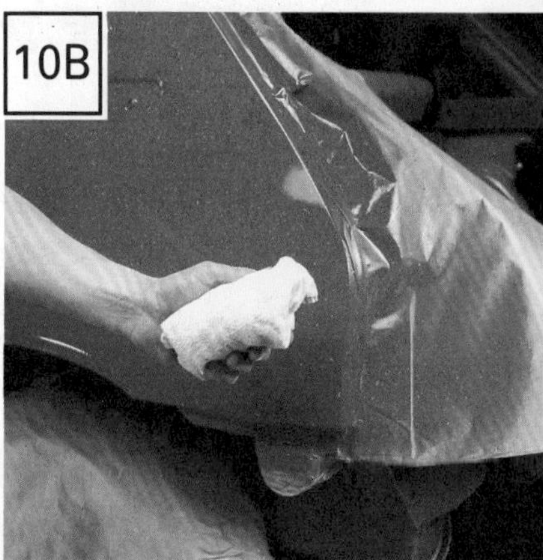

To identify whether a lacquer finish is required, rub a painted unrepaired part of the body with wax and a clean cloth.

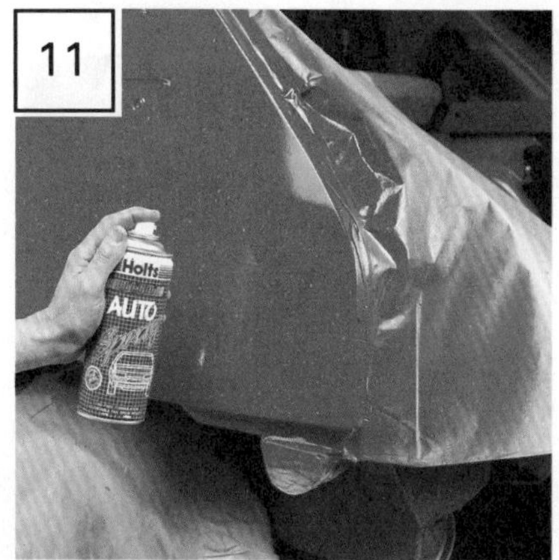

If *no* traces of paint appear on the cloth, spray Holts Dupli-Color clear lacquer over the repaired area to achieve the correct gloss level.

The paint will take about two weeks to harden fully. After this time it can be 'cut' with a mild cutting compound such as Turtle Wax Minute Cut prior to polishing with a final coating of Turtle Wax Extra.

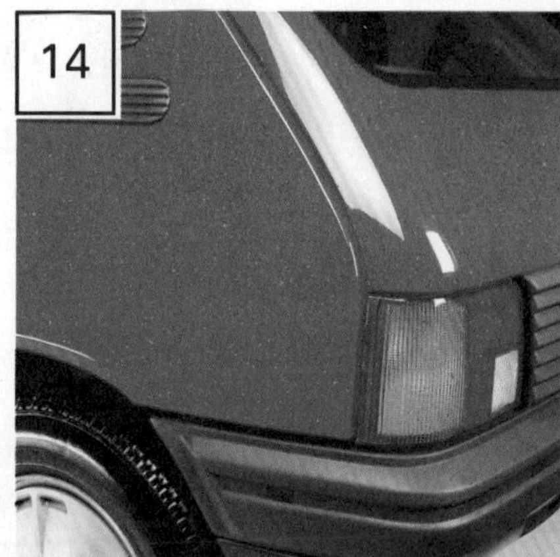

When carrying out bodywork repairs, remember that the quality of the finished job is proportional to the time and effort expended.

Check, where possible, the idle speed and mixture (Section 3)
Check the operation of the lambda sensor – where fitted (Chapter 4 and Section 3)
Check the distributor cap, ignition HT coil and the spark plug (HT) leads (Section 4)
Check the battery connections and electrolyte level (Section 11)
Check and adjust the alternator or alternator/air conditioner and power steering pump drivebelt(s) (Sections 11, 2 and 9 – as applicable)

** If Rover-recommended antifreeze is used, this task need only be carried out after the first three years of the car's life and every two years thereafter.*

Road test

Check that the engine starts and warms up properly, that the oil pressure and ignition/battery charging warning lamps go out, that the throttle pedal movement is correct and that the engine responds correctly to the throttle. When driving, check the operation of the clutch, gearchange and brakes and listen for noises, roughness or other faults from the engine and transmission, the steering and the suspension.

Every 24 000 miles (40 000 km) or 2 years – whichever comes first

In addition to all the items listed under the 12 000 mile service heading, carry out the following:

Operations with the car raised and supported

Renew the braking system hydraulic fluid (Section 8)

Operations in the engine compartment

Renew the air cleaner filter element (Section 3)
Renew the fuel filter – fuel injected models only (Section 3)
Check the crankcase breather hoses (Section 1)
Renew the spark plugs (Section 4)
Check and adjust the ignition timing – where possible (Section 4)
Check the operation of the air conditioning system – where fitted (Section 2)

Every 48 000 miles (80 000 km) or 4 years – whichever comes first

In addition to all the items listed under the 24 000 mile service heading, carry out the following:

Operations in the engine compartment

Check the timing belt (Section 1)

Every 60 000 miles (100 000 km) or 5 years – whichever comes first

In addition to all the items listed under the 12 000 mile service heading, carry out the following:

Operations in the engine compartment

Check the components of the evaporative emission control system – where fitted (Chapter 4 and Section 3)

Every 96 000 miles (160 000 km) or 8 years – whichever comes first

In addition to all the items listed under the 24 000 mile service heading, carry out the following:

Operations in the engine compartment

Renew the timing belt (Section 1)

Engine compartment component locations – K16 engine

1 *Engine oil level dipstick*
2 *Engine oil filler cap*
3 *Coolant expansion tank filler cap*
4 *Braking system fluid reservoir cap*
5 *Power steering fluid reservoir cap (where fitted)*
6 *Battery*
7 *Air cleaner housing*
8 *Distributor*
9 *Cooling system filler neck*
10 *Fuel filter – non catalyst model shown*
11 *Clutch cable*
12 *Speedometer cable*
13 *Washer fluid reservoir*
14 *Front suspension strut mounting nuts*
15 *Reverse gear interlock cable*
16 *Left-hand engine/transmission mounting*
17 *Engine management ECU*
18 *Intake air temperature control valve*
19 *Alternator*
20 *Windscreen wiper motor*
21 *Braking system pressure regulating valve*
22 *Engine compartment fusebox*
23 *Bonnet lock*

Front underbody view (undercover panel removed for clarity)

1 *Engine oil drain plug*
2 *Oil filter*
3 *Transmission oil drain plug*
4 *Transmission oil level plug*
5 *Rear engine/transmission mounting*
6 *Left-hand driveshaft inner constant velocity joint*
7 *Right-hand driveshaft inner constant velocity joint*
8 *Starter motor*
9 *Front towing eye*
10 *Front suspension tie bar*
11 *Front suspension lower arm*
12 *Anti-roll bar connecting link*
13 *Steering gear track rod balljoint*
14 *Anti-roll bar*
15 *Fuel lines*
16 *Gearchange lever mounting plate*
17 *Front exhaust pipe*
18 *Intermediate exhaust pipe*

Rear underbody view

1 Fuel tank
2 Left-hand handbrake cable
3 Fuel lines
4 Rear suspension left-hand front lateral link
5 Rear suspension left-hand trailing arm
6 Flexible brake hose
7 Rear suspension left-hand lower lateral link
8 Rear towing eye
9 Exhaust tailpipe
10 Rear suspension right-hand lower lateral link
11 Flexible brake hose
12 Rear suspension right-hand trailing arm
13 Right-hand handbrake cable
14 Rear suspension right-hand front lateral link
15 Intermediate exhaust pipe
16 Exhaust heatshield

Maintenance procedures

1 Engine

Engine oil level check

1 The engine oil level is checked with a dipstick that extends through a tube and into the sump at the bottom of the engine. The dipstick is located at the rear right-hand end of the engine, between the air cleaner assembly and the cooling system expansion tank.

2 The oil level should be checked with the car standing on level ground and before it is driven, or at least 5 minutes after the engine has been switched off. If the oil is checked immediately after driving the car, some of the oil will remain in the engine upper components and oil galleries, resulting in an inaccurate dipstick reading.

3 Withdraw the dipstick from the tube and wipe all the oil from the end with a clean rag or paper towel. Insert the clean dipstick back into the tube as far as it will go, then withdraw it once more. Note the oil level on the end of the dipstick. Add oil as necessary until the level is between the upper (MAX) and lower (MIN) marks on the dipstick (photo). Note that 1 litre of oil will be required to raise the level from the lower mark to the upper mark.

4 Always maintain the level between the two dipstick marks. If the level is allowed to fall below the lower mark, oil starvation may result which could lead to severe engine damage. If the engine is overfilled by adding too much oil, this may result in oil-fouled spark plugs, oil leaks or oil seal failures.

5 Oil is added to the engine after removing the filler cap (rotate it through a quarter-turn anti-clockwise and withdraw it) in the cylinder head cover. An oil can spout or funnel may help to reduce spillage. Always use the correct grade and type of oil as shown in *'Lubricants, fluids and capacities'* (photo).

Engine oil and filter renewal

6 Frequent oil and filter changes are the most important preventative maintenance procedures that can be undertaken by the DIY owner. As engine oil ages, it becomes diluted and contaminated, which leads to premature engine wear.

7 Before starting this procedure, gather together all the necessary tools and materials. Also make sure that you have plenty of clean rags and newspapers handy to mop up any spills. Ideally, the engine oil should be warm as it will drain better and more built-up sludge will be removed with it. Take care however, not to touch the exhaust or any other hot parts of the engine when working under the car. To avoid any possibility of scalding and to protect yourself from possible skin irritants and other harmful contaminants in used engine oils, it is advisable to wear gloves when carrying out this work.

8 The engine oil drain plug is located on the front of the sump and can be reached easily, without having to raise the car. Remove the oil filler cap and use a spanner, or preferably a suitable socket and bar, to slacken the drain plug about half a turn (photo). Position the draining container under the drain plug, then remove the plug completely. If possible, try to keep the plug pressed into the sump while unscrewing it by hand the last couple of turns. As the plug releases from the threads, move it away sharply so the stream of oil issuing from the sump runs into the container, not up your sleeve!

9 Allow some time for the old oil to drain, noting that it may be necessary to reposition the container as the flow of oil slows to a trickle; work can be speeded-up by removing the oil filter, as described below, while the oil is draining.

10 After all the oil has drained, wipe off the drain plug with a clean rag and renew its sealing washer. Clean the area around the drain plug opening and refit the plug. Tighten the plug securely, preferably to the

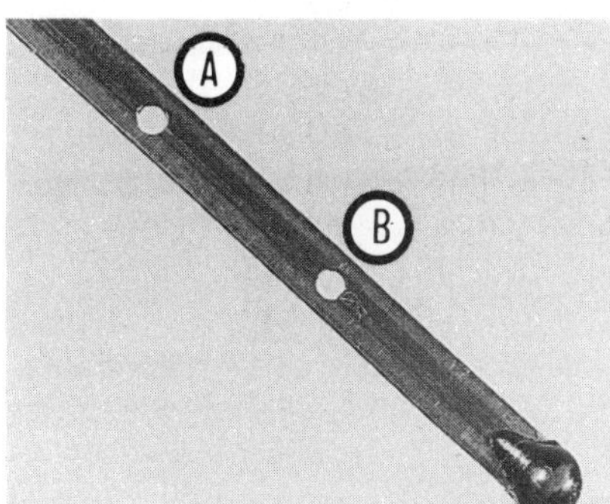

1.3 Engine oil dipstick marks MAX (A) and MIN (B) marks

1.5 Use only good quality oil of the specified grade when topping up the engine

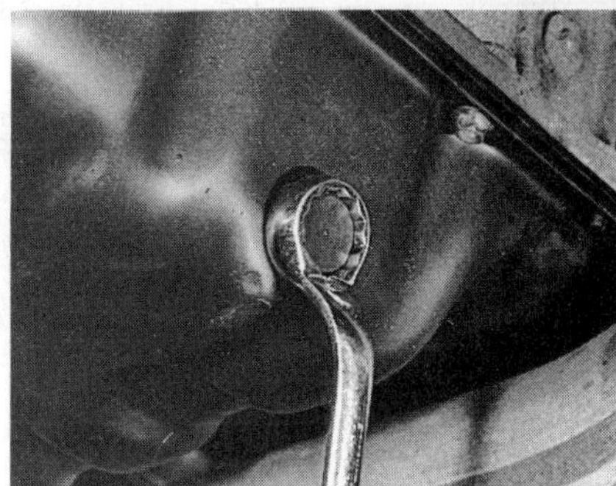
1.8 Unscrewing the engine oil drain plug

1.12 Using an oil filter removal tool to slacken the filter

1.14 Apply a light coat of clean oil to the oil filter sealing ring before fitting

specified torque using a torque wrench.

11 Move the container into position under the oil filter, which is located next to the drain plug on the front of the engine.

12 Using an oil filter removal tool, slacken the filter initially then unscrew it by hand the rest of the way (photo). Empty the oil in the old filter into the container and allow any residual oil to drain out of the engine.

13 Use a clean rag to remove all oil, dirt and sludge from the filter sealing area on the engine. Check the old filter to make sure that the rubber sealing ring has not stuck to the engine. If it has, carefully remove it.

14 Apply a light coating of clean engine oil to the new filter's sealing ring and screw the filter into position on the engine until it seats, then tighten it through a further half-turn **only**; tighten the filter by hand only, do not use any tools (photo).

15 Remove the old oil and all tools from under the car.

16 Refill the engine with fresh oil, using the correct grade and type of oil, as described earlier in this Section. Pour in half the specified quantity of oil first, then wait a few minutes for the oil to fall to the sump. Continue adding oil a small quantity at a time until the level is up to the lower mark on the dipstick. Adding a further 1 litre will bring the level up to the upper mark on the dipstick.

17 Start the engine and run it for a few minutes while checking for leaks around the oil filter seal and the sump drain plug.

18 Switch off the engine and wait a few minutes for the oil to settle in the sump once more. With the new oil circulated and the filter now completely full, recheck the level on the dipstick and add more oil as necessary.

19 Dispose of the used engine oil safely with reference to *'Tools and working facilities'* in the preliminary Sections of this Manual.

Timing belt check

20 Working as described in Chapter 2, Section 6, remove the timing belt upper right-hand (outer) cover.

21 Apply the handbrake and ensure that the transmission is in neutral, then jack up the front of the car and support it on axle stands. Remove the right-hand roadwheel.

22 From underneath the front of the car, slacken and remove the three bolts securing the bumper flange to the body. Remove the seven bolts securing the front undercover panel to the body and remove the panel to gain access to the crankshaft pulley.

23 Using a spanner or socket and extension bar applied to the crankshaft pulley bolt, rotate the crankshaft in a clockwise direction so that the full length of the timing belt can be checked. Examine the belt carefully for any signs of uneven wear, splitting or oil contamination and renew it if there is the slightest doubt about its condition (see below).

24 Note that Rover state that there is no need to adjust the belt's tension once it has been installed. If, however, the belt is thought to be incorrectly tensioned, especially if it has been disturbed for other servicing/repair work, the tensioner can be reset following the procedure outlined in Chapter 2, Section 7 (under 'Adjustment – general').

25 Refit all removed components and lower the car to the ground once the check is complete.

Timing belt renewal

26 The timing belt **must** be renewed as a matter of course at the specified interval, following the procedure given in Section 7 of Chapter 2. If the belt is not renewed as directed, it may break while the engine is running, which will result in serious and expensive engine damage.

General engine checks

Valve clearances – general

27 It is necessary for a clearance to exist between the tip of each valve stem and the valve operating mechanism, to allow for the expansion of the various engine components as the engine reaches normal operating temperature.

28 On most older engine designs, this meant that the valve clearances (also known as 'tappet' clearances) had to be checked and adjusted regularly. If the clearances were too slack, the engine would be very noisy, its power output would suffer and its fuel consumption would increase; conversely, if the clearances were too tight, the engine's power output would be reduced and the valves and their seats could be severely damaged.

29 The engines covered in this Manual, however, employ hydraulic tappets which use the lubricating system's oil pressure automatically to take up the clearance between each camshaft lobe and its respective valve stem. Therefore there is no need for regular checking and inspection of the valve clearances, but it is essential that **only** good quality oil of the recommended viscosity and specification is used in the engine and that this oil is scrupulously changed at the recommended intervals. If this advice is not followed, the oilways and tappets may become clogged with particles of dirt or deposits of burnt engine oil (resulting from the use of an inferior oil) so that the system cannot work properly; ultimately one or more of the tappets may fail and expensive repairs may be required.

30 On starting the engine from cold, there will be a slight delay while full oil pressure builds up in all parts of the engine, especially in the tappets; the valve clearances, therefore, may well 'rattle' for about 10 seconds or so and then quieten. This is a normal state of affairs and is nothing to worry about, provided that all tappets quieten quickly and stay quiet.

31 After the car has been standing for several days, the valve clearances may 'rattle' for longer than usual as nearly all the oil will have drained away from the engine's top end components and bearing surfaces; while this is only to be expected, care must be taken not to damage the engine by running it at high speed until all the tappets are refilled with oil and operating normally. With the car stationary, hold the engine at no more than a fast idle speed (maximum 2000 to 2500 rpm)

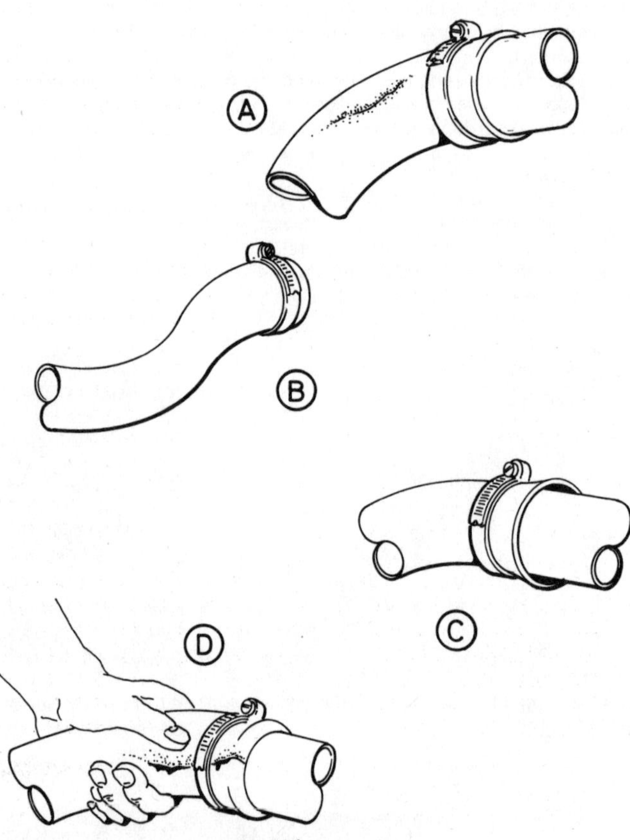

Fig. 1.1 Coolant hose inspection (Sec 2)

A Check hose for chafed or burned areas; these may lead to sudden and costly failure
B A soft hose indicates inside deterioration, leading to contamination of the cooling system and clogging of the radiator
C A hardened hose can fail at any time; tightening the clamps will not seal the joint or prevent leaks
D A swollen hose or one with oil-soaked ends indicates contamination from oil or grease. Cracks and breaks can be easily seen by squeezing the hose

for 10 to 15 minutes or until the noise ceases. **Do not** run the engine at more than 3000 rpm until the tappets are fully recharged with oil and the noise has ceased.

32 If the valve clearances are thought to be noisy, or if a light rattle persists from the engine's top end after it has reached normal operating temperature, take the car to a Rover dealer for expert advice. Depending on the mileage covered and the usage to which each car has been put, some cars may be noisier than others; only a good mechanic experienced in these engines can tell if the noise level is typical for the car's mileage or if a genuine fault exists. If any tappet's operation is faulty, it must be renewed as described in Chapter 2, Section 10.

General engine checks

33 Visually inspect the engine joint faces, gaskets and seals for any signs of water or oil leaks. Pay particular attention to the areas around the cylinder head cover, cylinder head, oil filter and sump joint faces. Bear in mind that over a period of time some very slight seepage from these areas is to be expected, but what you are really looking for is any indication of a serious leak. Should a leak be found, renew the offending gasket or oil seal by referring to the appropriate Chapters in this Manual.

34 Also check the security and condition of all the engine related pipes and hoses, particularly the crankcase breather hose(s) from the cylinder head cover. Ensure that all cable ties or securing clips are in place and in good condition. Clips which are broken or missing can lead to chafing of the hoses pipes or wiring which could cause more serious problems in the future.

2 Cooling, heating and ventilation systems

Coolant level check

Warning: *DO NOT attempt to remove the expansion tank filler cap when the engine is hot, as there is a very great risk of scalding.*

1 All models are equipped with a sealed cooling system. A translucent expansion tank located in the front right-hand corner of the engine compartment is connected by hoses to the cooling system (see Chapter 3) so that a continual flow of coolant passes through it to purge any air from the system.

2 The coolant level in the expansion tank should be checked regularly. The level in the tank varies with the temperature of the engine. When the engine is cold, the coolant level should be between the COOLANT LEVEL (MAX) mark on the front of the of the expansion tank and the expansion tank ridge (MIN); when the engine is hot, the level will be slightly higher (photo).

3 If topping-up is necessary, wait until the engine is cold, then cover the expansion tank with a thick layer of rag and unscrew the filler cap anti-clockwise until a hissing sound is heard; wait until the hissing ceases, indicating that all pressure is released, then slowly unscrew the filler cap until it can be removed. If more hissing sounds are heard, wait until they have stopped before unscrewing the cap completely. At all times keep well away from the filler opening.

4 Add a mixture of water and antifreeze (see below) through the expansion tank filler neck until the coolant is up to the level mark (photo). Refit the cap, tightening it securely.

5 With this type of cooling system, the addition of coolant should only be necessary at very infrequent intervals. If frequent topping-up is required, it is likely there is a leak in the system. Check the radiator, all hoses and joint faces for any sign of staining or actual wetness and rectify as necessary. If no leaks can be found, it is advisable to have the expansion tank filler cap and the entire system pressure-tested by a dealer or suitably-equipped garage as this will often show up a small leak not previously visible.

Coolant draining

Warning: *Wait until the engine is cold before starting this procedure. Do not allow antifreeze to come in contact with your skin or painted surfaces of the car. Rinse off spills immediately with plenty of water. Never leave antifreeze lying around in an open container or in a puddle in the driveway or on the garage floor. Children and pets are attracted by its sweet smell. Antifreeze is fatal if ingested.*

6 To drain the system, remove the expansion tank filler cap as described above, then move the heater air temperature control to the maximum heat position.

7 Place a large drain tray beneath the coolant drain tap fitted to the bottom right-hand corner of the radiator then open up the tap and allow the coolant to drain into the container. Once the system had drained completely, securely close the tap.

System flushing

8 With time, the cooling system may gradually lose its efficiency due to the radiator core having become choked with rust, scale deposits from the water and other sediment. To minimise this, as well as using only good quality antifreeze and clean soft water the system should be flushed as follows whenever the coolant is renewed.

9 With the coolant drained, ensure the drain tap is closed then refill the system with fresh water. Refit the expansion tank filler cap, start the engine and warm it up to normal operating temperature, then stop it and (after allowing it to cool down completely) drain the system again. Repeat as necessary until only clean water can be seen to emerge, then refill finally with the specified coolant mixture.

10 If the specified coolant mixture has been used and has been renewed at the specified intervals, the above procedure will be sufficient to keep clean the system for a considerable length of time. If, however, the system has been neglected, a more thorough operation will be required, as follows:

11 First drain the coolant, then disconnect the radiator top and bottom hoses from the radiator. Insert a garden hose into the radiator top hose outlet and allow water to circulate through the radiator until it runs clean from the bottom outlet.

12 To flush the engine, insert the garden hose into the top hose and allow water to circulate until it runs clear from the bottom hose. If, after a reasonable period, the water still does not run clear, the cooling system should be flushed with a good proprietary cleaning agent such as Holts Radflush or Holts Speedflush.

13 In severe cases of contamination, reverse-flushing of the radiator may be necessary. To do this, remove the radiator as described in Chapter 3, invert it and insert a garden hose into the bottom outlet. Continue flushing until clear water runs from the top hose outlet. If

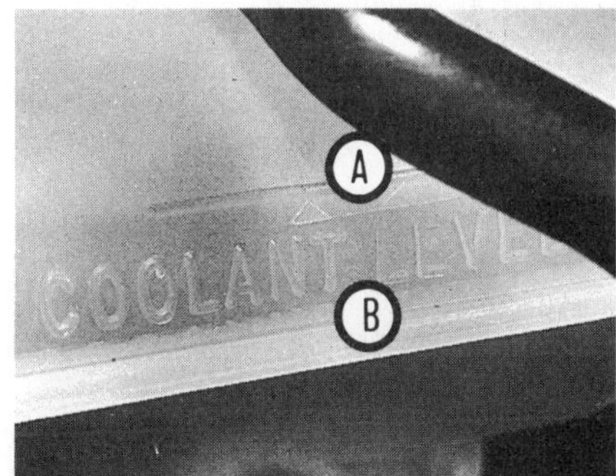

2.2 Coolant level must be between expansion tank MAX (A) and MIN (B) level marks

2.4 Use only the specified mixture to top up the cooling system

2.17A Unscrew the cooling system bleed screw to allow trapped air to escape

2.17B Unscrew the filler cap bolt whilst retaining the filler stem with an open-ended spanner...

2.18 ...then fill the system slowly via the filler stem

necessary, a similar procedure can be used to flush the heater matrix.
14 The use of chemical cleaners should be necessary only as a last resort; the regular renewal of the coolant will prevent excessive contamination of the system.

Coolant filling

15 With the cooling system drained and flushed, ensure that the drain tap is securely closed and that all disturbed hose unions are correctly secured.
16 Prepare a sufficient quantity of the specified coolant mixture (see below); allow for a surplus so as to have a reserve supply for topping-up.
17 Slacken the bleed screw from the coolant rail situated underneath the distributor to allow the escape of air trapped during refilling, then remove the cooling system filler cap bolt which is situated directly behind the distributor. Use a suitable open-ended spanner to retain the filler stem neck whilst the cap bolt is removed to prevent any strain being placed on the hose (photos).
18 Fill the system slowly through the filler stem (photo). When coolant can be seen emerging from the bleed screw in a steady stream, tighten the bleed screw securely. Continue filling until the coolant reaches the neck of the filler stem. Refit the filler stem cap bolt and tighten it securely whilst retaining the neck with an open-ended spanner. Top up the expansion tank to the correct level, then refit the filler cap.
19 Start the engine and run it at no more than idle speed until it has warmed up to normal operating temperature and the radiator electric cooling fan has cut in; watch the temperature gauge to check for signs of overheating.
20 Stop the engine and allow it to cool down **completely**, then remove the expansion tank filler cap and top up the tank to the correct level. Refit the filler cap and wash off all the spilt coolant from the engine compartment and bodywork.
21 After refilling, always check carefully all components of the system (but especially any unions disturbed during draining and flushing) for signs of coolant leaks; fresh antifreeze has a searching action which will rapidly expose any weak points in the system.

Note: *If, after draining and refilling the system, symptoms of overheating are found which did not occur previously, then the fault is almost certainly due to trapped air at some point in the system causing an air-lock and restricting the flow of coolant; usually the air is trapped because the system was refilled too quickly. In some cases air-locks can be released by tapping or squeezing the various hoses. If the problem persists, stop the engine and allow it to cool down completely before unscrewing the bleed screw to allow the trapped air to escape.*

Antifreeze mixture

22 The antifreeze should always be renewed at the specified intervals. This is necessary not only to maintain the antifreeze properties, but also to prevent corrosion which would otherwise occur as the corrosion inhibitors become progressively less effective.
23 Always use an ethylene glycol-based antifreeze which is suitable for use in mixed-metal cooling systems.
24 The type of antifreeze and levels of protection afforded are indicated in the Specifications. To give the recommended 50% concentration, 2.9 litres of antifreeze must be mixed with 2.9 litres of clean, soft water; this should provide enough to refill the complete system, but it is best to make up a larger amount so that a supply is available for subsequent topping-up.
25 Before adding antifreeze the cooling system should be completely drained, preferably flushed and all hoses checked for condition and security; fresh antifreeze has a searching action which will rapidly find any weaknesses in the system.
26 After filling with antifreeze, a label should be attached to the radiator or expansion tank stating the type and concentration of antifreeze used and the date installed. Any subsequent topping-up should be made with the same type and concentration of antifreeze.
27 Do not use engine antifreeze in the screen washer system, as it will damage the car's paintwork. A screen wash such as Turtle Wax High Tech Screen Wash should be added to the washer system in the recommended quantities.

General cooling system checks

28 The engine should be cold for the cooling system checks, so perform the following procedure before driving the car or after it has been shut off for at least three hours.
29 Remove the expansion tank filler cap (see above) and clean it thoroughly inside and out with a rag. Also clean the filler neck on the expansion tank. The presence of rust or corrosion in the filler neck indicates that the coolant should be changed. The coolant inside the expansion tank should be relatively clean and transparent. If it is rust-coloured, drain and flush the system and refill with a fresh coolant mixture.
30 Carefully check the radiator hoses and heater hoses along their entire length. Renew any hose which is cracked, swollen or deteriorated. Cracks will show up better if the hose is squeezed. Pay close attention to the hose clips that secure the hoses to the cooling system components. Hose clips can pinch and puncture hoses, resulting in cooling system leaks. If wire type hose clips are used, it may be a good idea to replace them with screw-type clips.
31 Inspect all the cooling system components (hoses, joint faces, etc.) for leaks. A leak in the cooling system will usually show up as white or rust-coloured deposits on the area adjoining the leak. Where any problems of this nature are found on system components, renew the component or gasket with reference to Chapter 3.
32 Clean the front of the radiator with a soft brush to remove all insects, leaves, etc., imbedded in the radiator fins. Be extremely careful not to damage the radiator fins or cut your fingers on them.

Air conditioning system compressor drivebelt check, adjustment and renewal

33 On models equipped with air conditioning, the air conditioning system compressor is belt driven by the crankshaft via the same belt as the alternator. Refer to Section 11 of this Chapter for details of drivebelt check, adjustment and renewal procedures.

Air conditioner refrigerant check

34 The refrigerant condition and level is checked via the sightglass on the top of the receiver drier. The receiver drier is situated in the engine compartment where it is located just to the left of the radiator.
35 Start the engine then switch on the air conditioning system and

allow the engine to idle for a couple of minutes whilst observing the sightglass. If the air conditioning system is operating normally occasional bubbles should be visible through the sightglass.
36 If a constant stream of bubbles is visible the refrigerant level is low and must be topped up. If the sightglass has become clouded or streaked there is a fault in the system. If either condition is present, the car must be taken to a Rover dealer or suitable professional refrigeration specialist for the air conditioning system to be checked further and overhauled.

3 Fuel, exhaust and emission control systems

Warning: *Certain procedures in this Section require the removal of fuel lines and connections which may result in some fuel spillage. Before carrying out any operation on the fuel system refer to the precautions given in Safety first! at the beginning of this Manual and follow them implicitly. Petrol is a highly dangerous and volatile liquid and the precautions necessary when handling it cannot be overstressed.*

Air cleaner filter element renewal

1 Release the clips securing the air cleaner assembly cover, then unscrew the retaining screws and carefully unclip the cover from the assembly. If the assembly is dislodged, lift it carefully and check that none of the vacuum pipes, hoses or wiring (as applicable) connected to its underside have been damaged or disconnected (photos).
2 Lift out the air cleaner filter element and discard it. Wipe clean the inside of the assembly and the cover, then check that there is no foreign matter visible either in the air cleaner intake duct or in the inlet tract.
3 Place the new element in the air cleaner assembly, ensure that it is correctly seated and clip the cover back onto the assembly (photo). Refit the retaining screws and the clips to secure the cover.

Fuel filter renewal – fuel injected models

4 Depressurise the fuel system as described in Chapter 4. Place wads of rag beneath the fuel filter unions to catch any spilled fuel.
5 Using two spanners to prevent damage to any of the fuel system pipes or components, disconnect the fuel filter inlet and outlet unions then remove the filter mounting clamp bolt and withdraw the filter from its mounting (photo).
6 Fit the new filter with the arrows indicating fuel flow pointing in the direction of the fuel flow, ie. to the right of the car on models not equipped with a catalytic converter, and downwards on models equipped with catalytic converters.
7 Tighten the filter mounting clamp bolt, connect the fuel pipes to the filter and tighten their unions securely, to the specified torque wrench settings if possible. Start the engine and check carefully for any signs of fuel leaks from any of the disturbed components.
8 Dispose safely of the old filter; it will be highly inflammable and may explode if thrown on a fire.

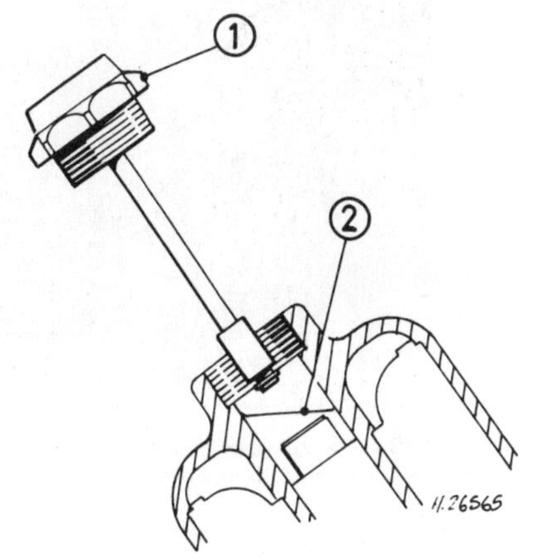

Fig. 1.2 Topping up the carburettor piston damper (Sec 3)

1 Piston damper *2 Oil level*

3.1A Release the air cleaner assembly cover retaining clips...

3.1B ...then remove the retaining screws and lift off the cover (carburettor model shown)

3.3 Ensure new filter element is correctly seated on refitting

3.5 Use two spanners when slackening fuel filter unions (non-catalyst model shown)

3.10A Unscrew the piston damper from the carburettor suction chamber...

3.10B ...and top up the carburettor damper chamber with engine oil – note carburettor's metal identification tag (arrowed)

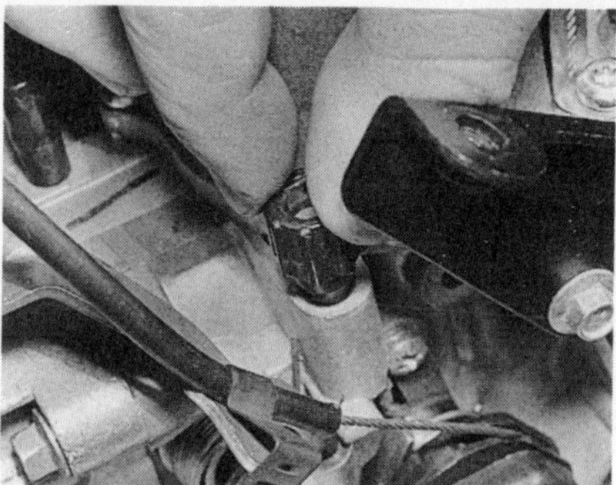

3.16 Turn the idle speed adjusting knob to alter engine idle speed

3.18 Adjusting the idle mixture (air cleaner removed for clarity)

Topping-up the carburettor piston damper – carburettor models

9 Remove the air cleaner housing as described in Chapter 4.

10 Unscrew the piston damper from the top of the carburettor suction chamber and top up the damper chamber to the top of the damper cylinder (Fig. 1.2) with the specified type and viscosity of engine oil (photos). Note that since the advent of modern low-viscosity multigrade engine oils there is no need to use a special carburettor oil in SU carburettors.

11 Raise and lower the carburettor piston, ensuring that it moves smoothly and without sticking, then refit and tighten (very carefully, but securely) the piston damper.

12 Refit the air cleaner assembly, ensuring that the vacuum pipes are correctly reconnected.

Idle speed and mixture adjustment

Carburettor engines

13 Before beginning any form of carburettor adjustment, always check the following first.

(a) *Check that the ignition timing is accurate (Section 4).*
(b) *Check that the spark plugs are in good condition and correctly gapped (Section 4).*
(c) *Check that the accelerator and choke cables are correctly adjusted (Chapter 4).*
(d) *Check that the carburettor idle bypass system is functioning correctly (Chapter 4).*
(e) *Check that the piston damper is topped-up.*
(f) *Check that the crankcase breather hose(s), the float chamber vent hose and the full load air bleed hose are clear.*
(g) *Check that the air cleaner filter element is clean and that the exhaust system is in good condition.*
(h) *If the engine is running very roughly, check the compression pressures as described in Chapter 2, bearing in mind the possibility that one of the hydraulic tappets might be faulty, producing an incorrect valve clearance.*

14 Take the car on a journey of sufficient length to warm it up to normal operating temperature.

Note: *Adjustment should be completed within two minutes of return, without stopping the engine. If this cannot be achieved, or if the radiator electric cooling fan operates, wait for the cooling fan to stop and clear any excess fuel from the inlet manifold by racing the engine two or three times to between 2000 and 3000 rpm, then allow it to idle again.*

15 Ensure all electrical loads are switched off; if the car is not equipped with a tachometer, connect one following the manufacturer's instructions. Note the idle speed, comparing it with that specified.

16 The idle speed adjusting knob is under the air cleaner assembly, on the rear right-hand corner of the carburettor; screw it in or out as necessary to obtain the specified speed (photo).

17 The idle mixture is set at the factory and should require no further adjustment. If, due to a change in engine characteristics (carbon build-up, bore wear, etc.) or after a major carburettor overhaul, the mixture becomes incorrect it can be reset. Note, however, that an exhaust gas analyser (CO meter) will be required to check the mixture and to set it with the necessary standard of accuracy; if this is not available, the car must be taken to a Rover dealer for the work to be carried out.

18 If an exhaust gas analyser is available, follow the manufacturer's instructions to check the CO level. If adjustment is required, it is made by turning the idle air bypass screw, which is set in a deep recess on the carburettor left-hand side, beneath the breather hose (photo). Using a Torx-type screwdriver, size TX10, turn the screw in very small increments until the level is correct; screwing it in (clockwise) richens the idle mixture and increases the CO level.

19 When adjustments are complete, disconnect any test equipment and refit any components removed for access.

Fuel-injected engines

20 While experienced home mechanics with a considerable amount of skill and equipment (including a good-quality tachometer and a good-quality, carefully-calibrated exhaust gas analyser) may be able to check the exhaust CO level and the idle speed, if these are found to be in need of adjustment the car **must** be taken to a suitably-equipped Rover dealer; adjustments can be made only by re-programming the fuel-injection/ignition system ECU using Rover diagnostic equipment connected to the system by the diagnostic connector. For most owners the best solution will be to carry out those maintenance operations that they feel able to undertake, with the car then being taken to a Rover dealer for expert attention to the remaining items.

Lambda sensor operational check

21 This task (outlined in Chapter 4, Part C) can only be carried out using Rover diagnostic equipment; see the preceding paragraph. Do not neglect to have this check made at the specified intervals, especially as the car's mileage increases, as it is the only means of checking (in conjunction with a CO level check) whether the catalytic converter's closed-loop control system is working properly or not. Lambda sensors are delicate components working under arduous conditions and do not last for ever; if the sensor is no longer effective, it must be renewed.

General fuel system checks

22 The fuel system is most easily checked with the car raised on a hoist or suitably supported on axle stands so the components underneath are readily visible and accessible.

23 If the smell of petrol is noticed while driving or after the car has been parked in the sun, the system should be thoroughly inspected immediately.

24 Remove the petrol tank filler cap and check for damage, corrosion and an unbroken sealing imprint on the gasket. Renew the cap if necessary.

25 With the car raised, inspect the petrol tank and filler neck for punctures, cracks and other damage. The connection between the filler neck and tank is especially critical. Sometimes a rubber filler neck or connecting hose will leak due to loose retaining clips or deteriorated rubber.

26 Carefully check all rubber hoses and metal fuel lines leading away from the petrol tank. Check for loose connections, deteriorated hoses, crimped lines and other damage. Pay particular attention to the vent pipes and hoses which often loop up around the filler neck and can become blocked or crimped. Follow the lines to the front of the car carefully inspecting them all the way. Renew damaged sections as necessary.

27 From within the engine compartment, check the security of all fuel hose attachments and inspect the fuel hoses and vacuum hoses for kinks, chafing and deterioration. Where an evaporative emission control system is fitted, check the hoses and the security of the purge control valve wiring as well as checking the physical condition of the charcoal canister.

28 Check the operation of the throttle linkage and lubricate the linkage components with a few drops of light oil.

Exhaust system check

29 With the engine cold (or at least an hour after the car has been driven), check the complete exhaust system from the engine to the end of the tailpipe. Ideally the inspection should be carried out with the car on a hoist to permit unrestricted access. If a hoist is not available, raise and support the car on axle stands.

30 Check the exhaust pipes and connections for evidence of leaks, severe corrosion and damage. Make sure that all brackets and mountings are in good condition and tight. Leakage at any of the joints or in other parts of the system will usually show up as a black sooty stain in the vicinity of the leak. Holts Flexiwrap and Holts Gun Gum exhaust repair systems can be used for effective repairs to exhaust pipes and silencer boxes, including ends and bends. Holts Flexiwrap is an MOT approved permanent exhaust repair. Holts Firegum is suitable for the assembly of all exhaust system joints.

31 Rattles and other noises can often be traced to the exhaust system, especially the brackets and mountings. Try to move the pipes and silencers. If the components can come into contact with the body or suspension parts, secure the system with new mountings or if possible, separate the joints and twist the pipes as necessary to provide additional clearance.

4 Ignition system

Warning: *Voltages produced by an electronic ignition system are considerably higher than those produced by conventional ignition systems. Extreme care must be taken when working on the system with the ignition switched on. Persons with surgically-implanted cardiac pacemaker devices should keep well clear of the ignition circuits, components and test equipment.*

Ignition timing check and adjustment

Carburettor engines

1 Firmly apply the handbrake then jack up the front of the car and support it on axle stands. From underneath the front of the car, slacken and remove the three bolts securing the bumper flange to the body. Remove the seven bolts securing the front undercover panel to the body and remove the panel. Remove the right-hand roadwheel.

2 Before the ignition timing can be checked, the crankshaft pulley timing marks must be clarified. When looking at a brand-new pulley, the only obvious timing mark is the straight line (emphasised by the factory with white paint) cut radially in the pulley's outer (right-hand) face; this is, however, an engine assembly mark **only** which when aligned with the single, separate mark (at the 12 o'clock position) on the timing belt lower cover sets the crankshaft to 90° BTDC. The **ignition** timing mark is a tiny notch cut in the rim of the pulley's inner (left-hand) rim at approximately 100° anti-clockwise from the engine assembly mark; it is virtually invisible and care is required to identify it.

3 Rotate the pulley so that the engine assembly mark points vertically downwards, whereupon the ignition timing mark can be seen clearly enough to scribe a line squarely across the pulley rims. A hacksaw can then be used to enlarge the mark in the pulley outer (right-hand) rim and white paint can be used to highlight it (photos).

4 Start the engine and warm it up to normal operating temperature, then stop the engine and connect a timing light, according to the manufacturer's instructions. Disconnect the vacuum pipe from the distributor and plug it temporarily.

5 Start the engine and have an assistant increase engine speed to the specified amount, then aim the timing light at the timing marks; the highlighted mark should stand out clearly. Check that the crankshaft pulley mark aligns with the correct cover reference mark, or within the specified tolerance (see Specifications).

6 If adjustment is required, slacken the distributor mounting bolts until the distributor body is just able to rotate, then turn the body clockwise (viewed from the car's left-hand side) to advance the ignition

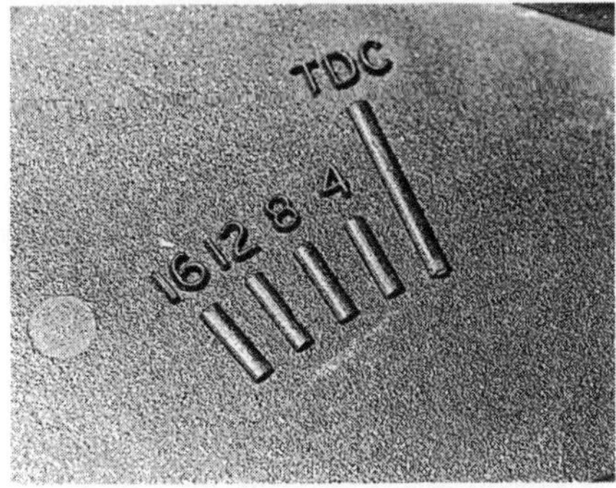

4.3A Ignition timing reference marks are on the timing belt lower cover

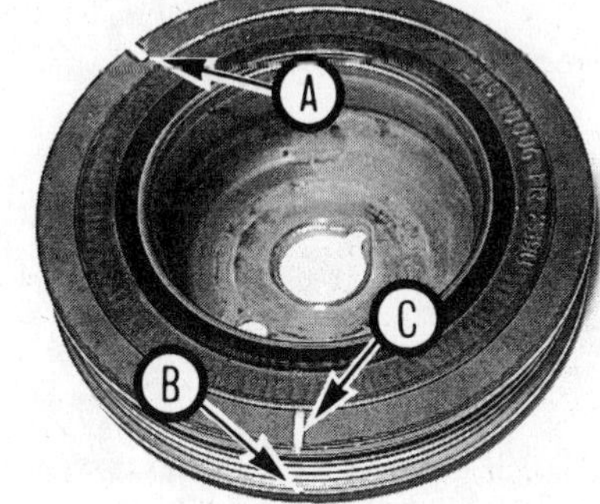

4.3B Crankshaft pulley engine assembly mark (A), factory ignition timing mark (B) and home-made ignition timing mark (C)

4.3C Ignition timing marks on pulley (arrowed) must be clarified as described before ignition timing can be checked

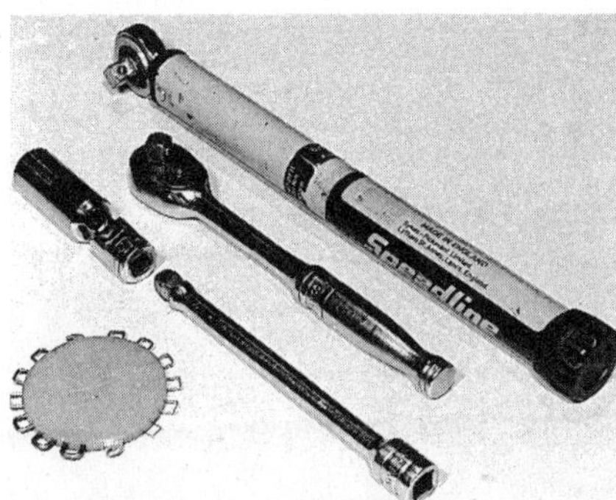

4.11 Tools required for removing, refitting and adjusting spark plugs

4.12A Spark plugs are easily accessed on K8 engines

4.12B On K16 engines remove air cleaner intake duct and spark plug cover...

timing, or anti-clockwise to retard it. Tighten the bolts to the specified torque wrench setting when the correct position is found, then recheck the ignition timing to ensure that it has not altered.

7 Increase engine speed and check that the pulley mark advances to beyond the beginning of the cover reference marks, returning to close to the TDC mark when the engine is allowed to idle; this shows that the centrifugal advance mechanism is functioning, but a detailed check must be left to a Rover dealer who has the necessary equipment.

8 Unplug and reconnect the vacuum pipe; the ignition timing should advance as the pipe is reconnected, retarding again when it is disconnected. If the ignition timing does not alter, check that the pipe is clear of blockages or kinks and that it is not leaking. Suck on the carburettor end of the pipe; if there is no effect on the ignition timing, then the vacuum diaphragm unit is faulty and must be renewed. On models equipped with a catalytic converter, the thermostatically-operated vacuum switch may be at fault (refer to Chapter 5 for further information). This can be eliminated by connecting a vacuum pipe directly from the carburettor to the distributor; if the vacuum advance is then restored to normal the switch is faulty and must be renewed. Again, more detailed tests must be left to a Rover dealer.

9 When the ignition timing is correct, stop the engine and disconnect the timing light and tachometer, then reconnect the vacuum pipe. Refit the undercover and the roadwheel.

Fuel-injected engines

10 While home mechanics with a timing light and a good-quality tachometer may be able to check the ignition timing (the procedure being as described in paragraphs 1 to 5 above, except that the check should be made at idle speed and there is no vacuum pipe to disconnect), if it is found to be in need of adjustment the car **must** be taken to a suitably-equipped Rover dealer; adjustments can be made only by re-programming the fuel-injection/ignition system ECU using Rover diagnostic equipment connected to the system by the diagnostic connector. Note also that the timing and idle speed are under ECU control and may, therefore, vary significantly from the nominal values given in Chapters 4 and 5; without full equipment, any check is therefore nothing more than a rough guide.

Spark plug renewal

11 The correct functioning of the spark plugs is vital for the correct running and efficiency of the engine. It is essential that the plugs fitted are appropriate for the engine (the suitable type is specified at the beginning of this Chapter). If this type is used and the engine is in good condition, the spark plugs should not need attention between scheduled replacement intervals. Spark plug cleaning is rarely necessary and should not be attempted unless specialised equipment is available as damage can easily be caused to the firing ends (photo).

12 To gain access to the plugs, first remove the air cleaner housing metal intake duct as described in Chapter 4. On K8 (carburettor) engines the plugs are then easily reached along the front of the engine. On K16 (fuel-injected) engines, undo the two retaining screws and remove the spark plug cover from the centre of the cylinder head cover (photos).

13 If the marks on the original-equipment spark plug (HT) leads cannot be seen, mark the leads one to four to correspond to the cylinder the lead serves (number one cylinder is at the timing belt end of the engine). Pull the leads from the plugs by gripping the end fitting, not the lead, otherwise the lead connection may be fractured (photo).

14 It is advisable to remove the dirt from the spark plug recesses using a clean brush, vacuum cleaner or compressed air before removing the plugs, to prevent dirt dropping into the cylinders.

15 Unscrew the plugs using a spark plug spanner, suitable box spanner or a deep socket and extension bar (photo). Keep the socket aligned with the spark plug, otherwise if it is forcibly moved to one side, the ceramic insulator may be broken off. As each plug is removed, examine it as follows.

16 Examination of the spark plugs will give a good indication of the condition of the engine. If the insulator nose of the spark plug is clean and white, with no deposits, this is indicative of a weak mixture or too hot a plug (a hot plug transfers heat away from the electrode slowly, a cold plug transfers heat away quickly).

17 If the tip and insulator nose are covered with hard black-looking

4.13 ...then disconnect the HT leads from the spark plugs

4.15 Remove spark plugs as described in text

4.20A Measuring the spark plug electrode gap using a feeler gauge

4.20B Measuring the spark plug electrode gap using a wire gauge

4.21 Adjusting the spark plug electrode gap using a special tool

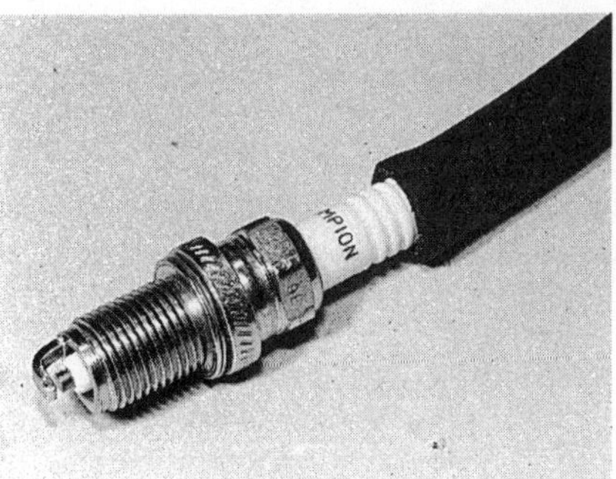

4.23 Use a short length of rubber hose to guide spark plugs into position on refitting

4.32A Distributor cap is retained by two offset screws

4.32B Removing distributor rotor arm grub screw – fuel-injected engines

deposits, then this is indicative that the mixture is too rich. Should the plug be black and oily, then it is likely that the engine is fairly worn, as well as the mixture being too rich.

18 If the insulator nose is covered with light tan to greyish brown deposits, then the mixture is correct and it is likely that the engine is in good condition.

19 The spark plug electrode gap is of considerable importance as, if it is too large or too small, the size of the spark and its efficiency will be seriously impaired. The gap should be set to the value given in the Specifications at the beginning of this Chapter.

20 To set it, measure the gap with a feeler gauge and then bend open, or close, the outer plug electrode until the correct gap is achieved (photos). The centre electrode should never be bent, as this may crack the insulator and cause plug failure, if nothing worse.

21 Special spark plug electrode gap adjusting tools are available from most motor accessory shops (photo).

22 Before refitting the spark plugs check that the threaded connector sleeves are tight and that the plug exterior surfaces and threads are clean.

23 It is very often difficult to insert spark plugs into their holes without cross-threading them. To avoid this possibility, fit a short length of 5/16 inch internal diameter rubber hose over the end of the spark plug (photo). The flexible hose acts as a universal joint to help align the plug with the plug hole. Should the plug begin to cross-thread, the hose will slip on the spark plug, preventing thread damage to the aluminium cylinder head. Remove the rubber hose and tighten the plug to the specified torque using the spark plug socket and a torque wrench. Refit the remaining spark plugs in the same manner.

24 Check the spark plug (HT) leads as described below then reconnect them in their correct order and refit all components removed for access.

Spark plug (HT) leads, distributor cap and rotor arm check and renewal

25 The spark plug (HT) leads should be checked whenever new spark plugs are installed in the engine.

26 Ensure that the leads are numbered before removing them, to avoid confusion when refitting. Pull the leads from the plugs by gripping the end fitting, not the lead, otherwise the lead connection may be fractured.

27 Check inside the end fitting for signs of corrosion, which will look like a white crusty powder. Push the end fitting back onto the spark plug ensuring that it is a tight fit on the plug. If not, remove the lead again and use pliers to carefully crimp the metal connector inside the end fitting until it fits securely on the end of the spark plug.

28 Using a clean rag, wipe the entire length of the lead to remove any built-up dirt and grease. Once the lead is clean, check for burns, cracks and other damage. Do not bend the lead excessively or pull the lead lengthwise – the conductor inside might break.

29 Disconnect the other end of the lead from the distributor cap. Again, pull only on the end fitting. Check for corrosion and a tight fit in the same manner as the spark plug end. If an ohmmeter is available, check the resistance of the lead by connecting the meter between the spark plug end of the lead and the segment inside the distributor cap. Refit the lead securely on completion.

30 Check the remaining leads one at a time, in the same way.

31 If new spark plug (HT) leads are required, purchase a set for your specific car and engine.

32 Unscrew the two screws and remove the distributor cap, wipe it clean and carefully inspect it inside and out for signs of cracks, carbon tracks (tracking) and worn, burned or loose contacts; check that the cap's carbon brush is unworn, free to move against spring pressure and making good contact with the rotor arm. Similarly inspect the rotor arm; on fuel-injected engines it is retained by a small grub screw – if checking components with a meter, note that the rotor arm has an in-built resistor (photos). Renew any components which are found to be faulty. It is common practice to renew the cap and rotor arm whenever new spark plug (HT) leads are fitted. When fitting a new cap, remove the leads from the old cap one at a time and fit them to the new cap in exactly the same location – do not simultaneously remove all the leads from the old cap or firing order confusion may occur – note that the screw locations are offset so that the cap may be refitted only one way. Tighten the cap retaining screws and, where necessary the rotor arm grub screw, to complete.

33 Even with the ignition system in first class condition, some engines may still occasionally experience poor starting attributable to damp ignition components. To disperse moisture Holts Wet Start can be very effective. Holts Damp Start should be used for providing a sealing coat to exclude moisture from the ignition system, and in extreme difficulty, Holts Cold Start will help to start a car when only a very poor spark occurs.

5 Clutch

General check

1 Check that the clutch pedal moves smoothly and easily through its full travel and that the clutch itself functions correctly, with no trace of slip or drag. If excessive effort is required to operate the clutch, check first that the cable is correctly routed and undamaged, then remove the pedal to ensure that its pivot is properly greased before suspecting a fault in the cable itself; if the cable is worn or damaged, or if its self-adjusting mechanism is no longer effective, renew it as described in Chapter 6.

2 No adjustment is possible of the cable or of the clutch release; if any fault develops in the clutch, the transmission must be removed so that the clutch can be overhauled. Refer to Chapter 6 for further information.

6 Transmission

Oil level check

1 Even though this makes access awkward, the oil level must be checked with the car standing on its wheels on level ground. Also, the level must be checked before the car is driven, or at least 5 minutes after the engine has been switched off. If the oil is checked immediately after driving the car, some of the oil will remain distributed around the

6.3 Transmission oil level is correct when oil has just stopped trickling from filler/level plug hole

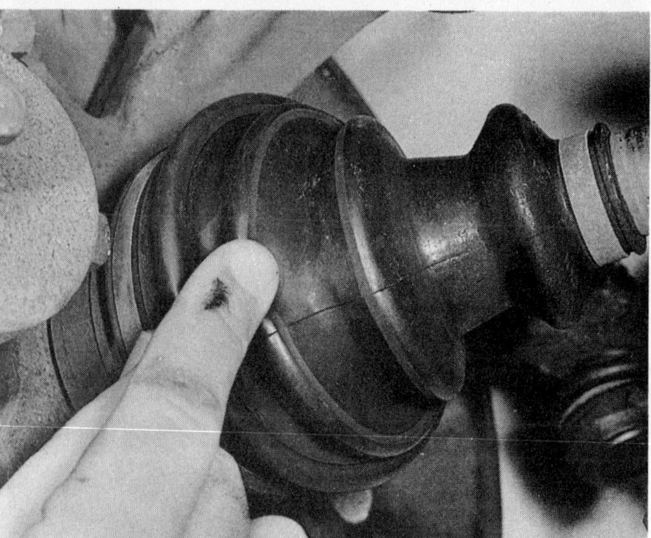

7.1 Checking driveshaft outer CV joint rubber gaiter

transmission components, resulting in an inaccurate level reading.

2 Wipe clean the area around the filler/level plug, which is located at the rear of the transmission, next to the left-hand driveshaft inner constant velocity joint. Unscrew the plug and clean it; discard the sealing washer. To avoid rounding-off the corners of the plug hexagon, use only good quality, close-fitting, single-hexagon or surface drive spanners or sockets.

3 The oil level should reach the lower edge of the filler/level hole. A certain amount of oil will have gathered behind the filler/level plug and will trickle out when it is removed; this does **not** necessarily indicate that the level is correct (photo).

4 To ensure that a true level is established, wait until the initial trickle has stopped, then add oil as necessary until a trickle of new oil can be seen emerging. The level will be correct when the flow ceases; use only good quality oil of the specified type.

Note: *Refilling the transmission is an extremely awkward operation; above all, allow plenty of time for the oil level to settle properly before checking it. If a large amount had to be added to the transmission and a large amount flows out on checking the level, refit the filler/level plug and take the car on a short journey so that the new oil is distributed fully around the transmission components, then recheck the level when it has settled again.*

5 If the transmission has been overfilled so that oil flows out as soon as the filler/level plug is removed, check that the car is completely level (front to rear and side to side) and allow the surplus to drain off into a suitable container.

6 When the level is correct, fit a new sealing washer and refit the filler/level plug, tightening it to the specified torque wrench setting. Wash off any spilt oil.

Oil renewal

7 The manufacturer specifies that, provided only the recommended oils are used (see a Rover dealer for details) the transmission is filled for life and the oil does not require regular changes; this operation does not, therefore, appear in the manufacturer's service schedule.

8 If the transmission oil is to be drained and refilled for any other reason, the operation is described in Chapter 7, Section 2.

7 Driveshafts

Driveshaft rubber gaiter and CV joint check

1 With the car raised and securely supported on axle stands, turn the steering onto full lock then slowly rotate the roadwheel. Inspect the condition of the outer constant velocity (CV) joint rubber gaiters while squeezing the gaiters to open out the folds (photo). Check for signs of cracking, splits or deterioration of the rubber which may allow the grease to escape and lead to the entry of water and grit into the joint. Also check the security and condition of the retaining clips. Repeat these checks on the inner CV joints. If any damage or deterioration is found, the gaiters should be renewed as described in Chapter 8.

2 At the same time check the general condition of the CV joints themselves by first holding the driveshaft and attempting to rotate the roadwheel. Repeat this check by holding the inner joint and attempting to rotate the driveshaft. Any appreciable movement indicates wear in the joints, in the driveshaft splines, or a loose driveshaft nut.

8 Braking system

Hydraulic fluid level check

1 The brake master cylinder and fluid reservoir is mounted on top of the vacuum servo unit in the engine compartment. The MAX and MIN level marks are indicated on the side of the reservoir and the fluid level should be maintained between these marks at all times (photo).

2 If topping-up is necessary, wipe the area around the filler cap with a clean rag. Unscrew the cap and remove it from the reservoir taking care not to damage the sender unit. When adding fluid, pour it carefully into the reservoir to avoid spilling it on surrounding painted surfaces. Be sure to use only the specified brake hydraulic fluid since mixing different types of fluid can cause damage to the system. See *'Lubricants, fluids and capacities'* at the beginning of this Chapter (photo).

Warning: *Brake hydraulic fluid can harm your eyes and damage painted surfaces, so use extreme caution when handling and pouring it. Do not use fluid that has been standing open for some time as it absorbs moisture from the air. Excess moisture can cause a dangerous loss of braking effectiveness.*

3 When adding fluid it is a good idea to inspect the reservoir for contamination. The system should be drained and refilled if deposits, dirt particles or contamination are seen in the fluid.

4 After filling the reservoir to the proper level, make sure that the cap is refitted securely to avoid leaks and the entry of foreign matter and reconnect the fluid level wiring connector.

5 The fluid level in the master cylinder reservoir will drop slightly as the brake pads and shoes wear down during normal operation. If the reservoir requires repeated topping-up to maintain the proper level, this is an indication of an hydraulic leak somewhere in the system which should be investigated immediately.

Hydraulic fluid renewal

6 The procedure is similar to that for the bleeding of the hydraulic

system as described in Chapter 9, except that the brake fluid reservoir should be emptied by syphoning, using a clean poultry baster or similar before starting, and allowance should be made for the old fluid to be expelled when bleeding a section of the circuit.

7 Working as described in Chapter 9, open the first bleed nipple in the sequence and pump the brake pedal gently until nearly all the old fluid has been emptied from the master cylinder reservoir. Top up to the 'MAX' level with new fluid and continue pumping until only the new fluid remains in the reservoir and new fluid can be seen emerging from the bleed nipple. Tighten the nipple and top the reservoir level up to the 'MAX' level line.

8 Old hydraulic fluid is invariably much darker in colour than the new, making it easy to distinguish the two.

9 Work through all the remaining nipples in the sequence until new fluid can be seen at all of them. Be careful to keep the master cylinder reservoir topped up to above the 'MIN' level at all times or air may enter the system and greatly increase the length of the task.

10 When the operation is complete, check that all nipples are securely tightened and that their dust caps are refitted. Wash off all traces of spilt fluid and recheck the master cylinder reservoir fluid level.

11 Check the operation of the brakes before taking the car on the road.

General system check

12 Check that the brake pedal pivot is properly greased and that the pedal moves smoothly and easily through its full travel. When the engine is switched off, the pedal should have a small amount of free play, then firm resistance. If the pedal feels spongy or if it has a long travel, the system should be checked further, as described in Chapter 9.

13 The brake hydraulic system consists of a number of metal hydraulic pipes which run from the master cylinder around the engine compartment to the front brakes and pressure regulating valves and along the underbody to the rear brakes. Flexible hoses are fitted at front and rear to cater for steering and suspension movement.

14 When checking the system, first look for signs of leakage at the pipe or hose unions, then examine the flexible hoses for signs of cracking, chafing or deterioration of the rubber. Bend them sharply between the fingers (but do not actually bend them double or the casing may be damaged) and check that this does not reveal previously hidden cracks, cuts or splits. Check that all pipes and hoses are securely fastened in their clips.

15 Carefully work along the length of the metal hydraulic pipes looking for dents, kinks, damage of any sort or corrosion. Corrosion should be polished off; if the depth of pitting is significant the pipe must be renewed.

Front brake pad, caliper and disc check

16 Firmly apply the handbrake then jack up the front of the car and support it securely on axle stands. Remove the front roadwheels.

17 For a quick check, the thickness of friction material remaining on each brake pad can be measured through the slot in the caliper body (photo). If any pad's friction material is worn to the specified thickness or less, all four pads must be renewed as a set.

18 For a comprehensive check, the brake pads should be removed and cleaned. This will permit the operation of the caliper to be checked and the condition of the brake disc itself to be fully examined on both sides. Refer to Chapter 9 for further information.

Rear brake shoe, wheel cylinder and drum check

19 Chock the front wheels then jack up the rear of the car and support it on axle stands.

20 For a quick check, the thickness of friction material remaining on one of the brake shoes can be measured through the slot in the brake backplate that is exposed by prising out its sealing grommet (photo). If a rod of the same diameter as the specified minimum thickness is placed against the shoe friction material, the amount of wear can quickly be assessed; if any shoe's friction material is worn to the specified thickness or less, all four shoes must be renewed.

21 For a comprehensive check, the brake drums should be removed and cleaned. This will permit the wheel cylinders to be checked and the condition of the brake drum itself to be fully examined. Refer to Chapter 9 for further information.

Rear brake pad, caliper and disc check

22 Chock the front wheels then jack up the rear of the car and support it on axle stands.

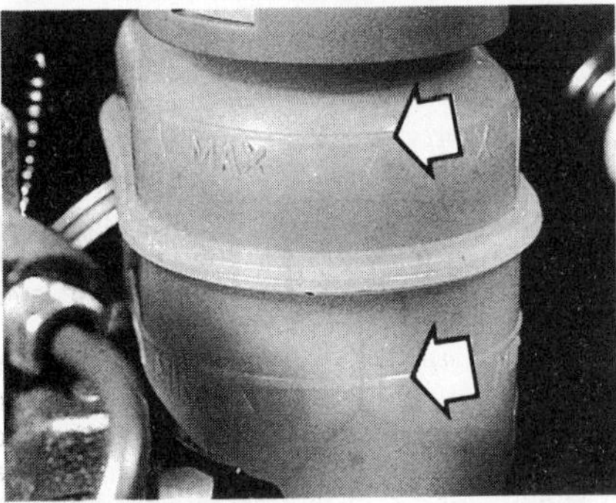

8.1 Brake fluid level must be maintained between the reservoir MAX and MIN level marks (arrowed)

8.2 Use only good quality brake fluid of the specified type when topping up brake system fluid reservoir

8.17 Front brake pad friction material can be checked through slot in caliper body

8.20 Remove grommet to check rear brake shoe friction material thickness on non-ABS models

8.28A Remove the ashtray from the centre console...

8.28B ...to gain access to the handbrake cable adjuster nut and equalizer mechanism

Condition	Probable cause	Corrective action	Condition	Probable cause	Corrective action
Shoulder wear	• Underinflation (wear on both sides) • Incorrect wheel camber (wear on one side) • Hard cornering	• Check and adjust pressure • Repair or renew suspension parts • Reduce speed	Feathered edge Toe wear	• Incorrect toe setting	• Adjust front wheel alignment
Centre wear	• Overinflation	• Measure and adjust pressure	Uneven wear	• Incorrect camber or castor • Malfunctioning suspension • Unbalanced wheel • Out-of-round brake disc/drum	• Repair or renew suspension parts • Repair or renew suspension parts • Balance tyres • Machine or renew disc/drum

Fig. 1.3 Tyre tread wear patterns and causes (Sec 9)

23 For a quick check, the thickness of friction material remaining on each brake pad can be measured through the slot in the caliper body. If any pad's friction material is worn to the specified thickness or less, all four pads must be renewed as a set.

24 For a comprehensive check, the brake pads should be removed and cleaned. This will permit the operation of the caliper to be checked and the condition of the brake disc itself to be fully examined on both sides. Refer to Chapter 9 for further information.

Handbrake check and adjustment

25 The handbrake should be capable of holding the parked car stationary, even on steep slopes, when applied with moderate force. The mechanism should be firm and positive in feel with no trace of stiffness or sponginess from the cables, and should release immediately the handbrake lever is released. If the mechanism is faulty in any of these respects it must be checked immediately.

26 To check the setting, first apply the footbrake firmly several times to establish correct shoe to drum clearance. Applying normal, moderate pressure, pull the handbrake lever to the fully-applied position whilst counting the number of clicks emitted from the handbrake ratchet mechanism. If adjustment is correct there should be between 8 and 10 clicks before the handbrake is fully applied, if this is not the case adjustment is required.

27 To adjust the handbrake, chock the front wheels then jack up the rear of the car and support it on axle stands.

28 Lift out the ashtray, situated between the two front seats, from the rear of the centre console to gain access to the handbrake adjusting nut (photos). Apply the handbrake and check that the equalizer and cables move freely and smoothly then set the lever on the first notch of the ratchet mechanism. With the lever in this position, rotate the handbrake lever adjusting nut until only a slight drag can be felt when the rear wheels are turned. Once this is so, fully release the handbrake lever and check that the wheels rotate freely. Check the adjustment by applying the handbrake fully whilst counting the clicks emitted from the handbrake ratchet and, if necessary, re-adjust.

29 Once adjustment is correct refit the ashtray and lower the car to the ground.

9 Suspension and steering

Front suspension and steering check

1 Raise the front of the car and securely support it on axle stands.

2 Visually inspect the balljoint dust covers and the steering gear rubber gaiters for splits, chafing or deterioration (photo). Any wear of these components will cause loss of lubricant together with dirt and water entry, resulting in rapid deterioration of the balljoints or steering gear.

3 On cars equipped with power steering, check the fluid hoses for chafing or deterioration and the pipe and hose unions for fluid leakage. Also check for signs of fluid leakage under pressure from the steering gear rubber gaiters which would indicate failed fluid seals within the steering gear.

4 Grasp the roadwheel at the 12 o'clock and 6 o'clock positions and try to rock it (photo). Very slight free play may be felt, but if the movement is appreciable further investigation is necessary to determine the source. Continue rocking the wheel while an assistant depresses the brake pedal. If the movement is now eliminated or significantly reduced, it is likely that the hub bearings are at fault. If the free play is still evident with the brake pedal depressed, then there is wear in the suspension joints or mountings.

5 Now grasp the roadwheel at the 9 o'clock and 3 o'clock positions and try to rock it as before. Any movement felt now may again be caused by wear in the hub bearings, or in the track rod balljoints. If a balljoint is worn the visual movement will be obvious. If the inner joint is suspect it can be felt by placing a hand over the steering gear rubber gaiter and gripping the track rod. If the wheel is now rocked, movement will be felt at the inner joint if wear has taken place.

6 Using a large screwdriver or flat bar check for wear in the suspension mounting bushes by levering between the relevant suspension component and its attachment point. Some movement is to be expected as the mountings are made of rubber, but excessive wear should be obvious. Also check the condition of any visible rubber bushes, looking for splits, cracks or contamination of the rubber.

7 With the car standing on its wheels, have an assistant turn the

9.2 Checking one of the steering gear rubber gaiters

9.4 Rocking the roadwheel to check steering/suspension wear

9.10 Power steering fluid level must be between the MAX and MIN level marks on the side of the reservoir

steering wheel back and forth about an eighth of a turn each way. There should be very little, if any, lost movement between the steering wheel and the roadwheels. If this is not the case, closely observe the joints and mountings previously described, but in addition check for wear of the steering column universal joint and the steering gear itself.

Power steering fluid level check

8 The power steering fluid reservoir is located on the right-hand side of the engine compartment, just behind the cooling system expansion tank.

9 For the check, the car should be parked on level ground with the front wheels pointing straight-ahead and the engine should be stopped. Note that for the check to be accurate the steering **must** not be operated once the engine has been stopped.

10 The fluid level is visible through the translucent material of the reservoir and should be between the MAX and MIN level lines cast on the side of the reservoir (photo).

11 If necessary, wipe the area around the reservoir cap clean then remove the cap and top up to the MAX mark using the specified type of fluid (photo). Take great care not to allow any dirt or foreign matter to enter the hydraulic system and do not overfill the reservoir. When the level is correct refit the cap. Note that the need for frequent topping up of the system indicates a leak which should be investigated immediately.

Power steering pump drivebelt check, adjustment and renewal

General

12 On models equipped with power-assisted steering, the power steering pump is situated on the rear right-hand end of the engine and is driven by the crankshaft pulley via a belt. Due to its function and material makeup, the drivebelt is prone to failure after a period of time and should therefore be inspected and adjusted periodically.

Check and adjustment

13 Apply the handbrake then jack up the front of the car and support it on axle stands. Remove the right-hand front roadwheel.

14 From underneath the front of the car, slacken and remove the three bolts securing the bumper flange to the body. Remove the seven bolts securing the front undercover panel to the body and remove the panel.

15 Check the drivebelt for cracks, splitting, fraying or damage, whilst rotating the crankshaft using a suitable spanner applied to the crankshaft pulley bolt, so that the entire length of the belt is examined. Check also for signs of glazing (shiny patches) and for separation of the belt plies. Renew the belt if worn or damaged.

16 The drivebelt's tension is checked by measuring the amount of deflection that takes place when a pressure of 10 kg is applied (using a spring balance, or similar) midway between the crankshaft and power steering pump pulleys on the belt's upper run. If the deflection measured is any more or less than that specified, the drivebelt must be adjusted as follows.

17 Slacken the drivebelt adjuster (idler) pulley spindle nut and bolt, then rotate the adjuster bolt, situated on the underside of the pulley assembly, clockwise or anti-clockwise as required to obtain the correct belt tension (photos).

18 When the correct tension is achieved, tighten the adjuster pulley spindle bolt and nut to the specified torque setting and rotate the crankshaft several times to settle the drivebelt. Recheck the belt tension, repeating the adjustment procedure if necessary.

19 Refit the undercover and roadwheel and lower the car to the ground.

Renewal

20 Carry out the operations in paragraphs 13 and 14.

21 Slacken the drivebelt adjuster (idler) pulley spindle nut and bolt and slacken the adjuster bolt until the drivebelt can be slipped off the pulleys and removed from the car.

22 Clean the belt pulleys carefully, removing all traces of oil or grease and checking that the grooves are clear, then fit the new belt to the pulleys and tighten the adjuster bolt until the tension is approximately correct, then check and adjust the tension as described above.

23 Start the engine and allow it to idle at the specified speed for approximately 10 minutes to settle the drivebelt in position. Stop the engine then recheck the drivebelt tension as described above and, if necessary, repeat the adjustment procedure.

24 Refit the undercover and roadwheel then lower the car to the ground.

Rear suspension check

25 Chock the front wheels then jack up the rear of the car and support it on axle stands.

26 Working as described above for the front suspension, check the rear hub bearings and the trailing arm and lateral link bushes for wear.

Wheel and tyre maintenance and tyre pressure checks

27 Periodically remove the wheels and clean any dirt or mud from the inside and outside surfaces. Examine the wheel rims for signs of rusting, corrosion or other damage. Light alloy wheels are easily damaged by 'kerbing' whilst parking, and similarly steel wheels may become dented or buckled. Renewal of the wheel is very often the only course of remedial action possible.

28 To check that the roadwheel nuts are securely fastened, remove the roadwheel trim (where fitted), then slacken each nut in turn through

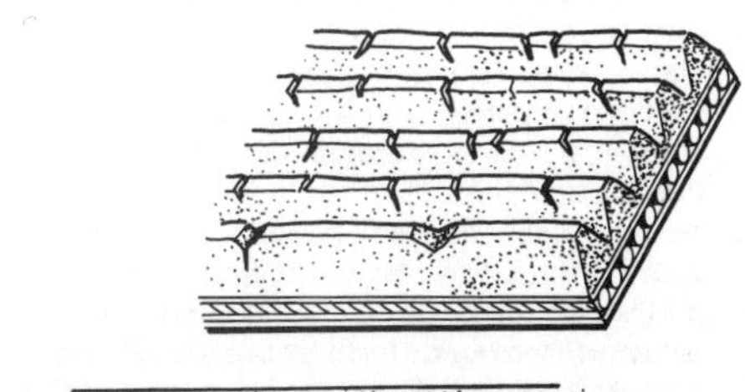

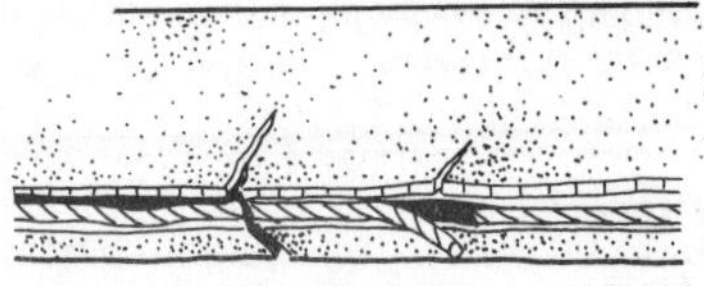

Fig. 1.4 Check the multi-ribbed drivebelt(s) for signs of wear like shown and renew if necessary (Secs 9 and 11)

9.11 Top up the power steering fluid with a good quality fluid of the specified type

9.17A Slacken the adjuster pulley spindle nut...

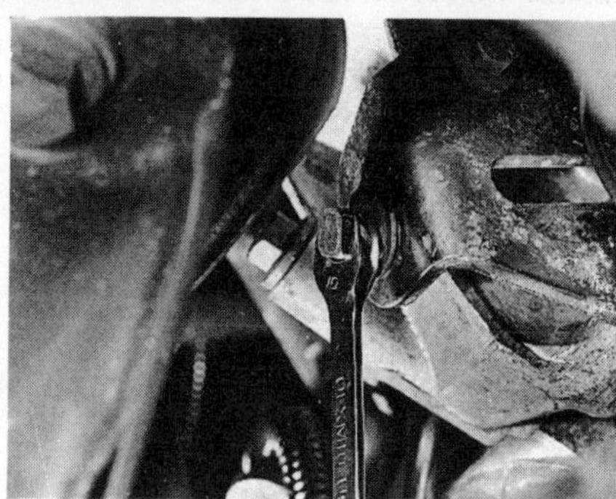

9.17B ...and rotate the adjuster bolt until power steering pump drivebelt tension is correct

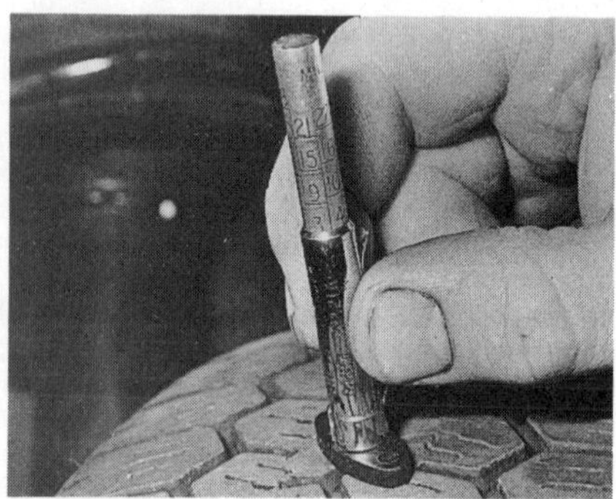

9.29 Checking tyre tread depth with a depth gauge

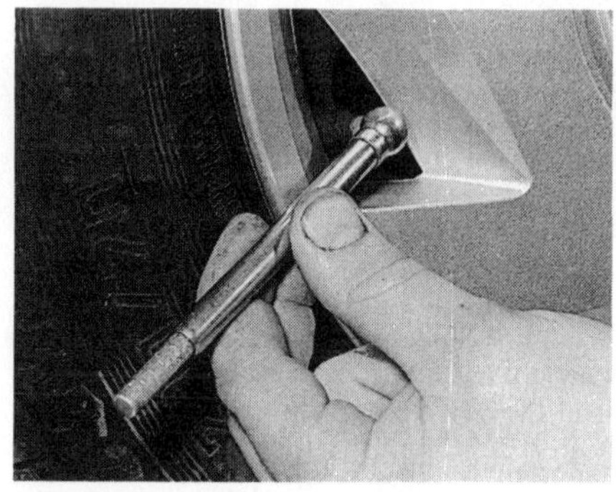

9.34 Checking the tyre pressures with a tyre pressure gauge

one-quarter of a turn and tighten it to the specified torque wrench setting. Refit the trim, where applicable.

29 The tyres originally fitted are equipped with tread wear indicators which will appear flush with the surface of the tread, thus producing the effect of a continuous band of rubber across the width of the tyre, when the tread depth is reduced to approximately 1.6 mm (0.063 in); **at this point, the tyre must be renewed immediately**. Tread wear can be monitored with a simple inexpensive device, known as a tread depth indicator gauge (photo).

30 Note any abnormal tread wear with reference to Fig. 1.3. Tread pattern irregularities such as feathering, flat spots and more wear on one side than the other are indications of front wheel alignment and/or balance problems. If any of these conditions are noted, they should be rectified as soon as possible.

31 General tyre wear is influenced to a large degree by driving style – harsh braking and acceleration or fast cornering will all produce more rapid tyre wear. Interchanging of tyres may result in more even wear, however it is worth bearing in mind that if this is completely effective, the added expense is incurred of replacing simultaneously a complete set of tyres, which may prove financially restrictive for many owners.

32 Front tyres may wear unevenly as a result of wheel misalignment. The front wheels should always be correctly aligned according to the settings specified. Refer to Chapter 10 for further information.

33 Regularly check the tyres for damage in the form of cuts or bulges, especially in the sidewalls. Remove any nails or stones embedded in the tread before they penetrate the tyre to cause deflation. If removal of a nail does reveal that the tyre has been punctured, refit the nail so that its point of penetration is marked, then immediately change the wheel and have the tyre repaired by a tyre dealer. Do not drive on a tyre in such a condition. In many cases a puncture can be simply repaired by the use of an inner tube of the correct size and type. If in any doubt as to the possible consequences of any damage found, consult your local tyre dealer for advice.

34 Ensure that tyre pressures are checked regularly and maintained correctly (photo). Checking should be carried out with the tyres cold and not immediately after the car has been in use. If the pressures are checked with the tyres hot, an apparently high reading will be obtained owing to heat expansion. Under no circumstances should an attempt be made to reduce the pressures to the quoted cold reading in this instance, or effective underinflation will result.

35 Underinflation will cause overheating of the tyre owing to excessive flexing of the casing, and the tread will not sit correctly on the road surface. This will cause a consequent loss of adhesion and excessive wear, not to mention the danger of sudden tyre failure due to heat build-up.

36 Overinflation will cause rapid wear of the centre part of the tyre tread coupled with reduced adhesion, harsher ride, and the danger of shock damage occurring in the tyre casing.

37 The balance of each wheel and tyre assembly should be maintained to avoid excessive wear, not only to the tyres but also to the steering and suspension components. Wheel imbalance is normally signified by vibration through the car's bodyshell, although in many cases it is particularly noticeable through the steering wheel. Conversely, it should be noted that wear or damage in suspension or steering components may cause excessive tyre wear. Out-of-round or out-of-true tyres, damaged wheels and wheel bearing wear also fall into this category. Balancing will not usually cure vibration caused by such wear.

38 Wheel balancing may be carried out with the wheel either on or off the car. If balanced on the car, ensure that the wheel to hub relationship is marked in some way prior to subsequent wheel removal so that it may be refitted in its original position.

39 Legal restrictions apply to many aspects of tyre fitting and usage and in the UK this information is contained in the Motor Vehicle Construction and Use Regulations. It is suggested that a copy of these regulations is obtained from your local police if in doubt as to current legal requirements with regard to tyre type and condition, minimum tread depth, etc.

10 Bodywork and fittings

Cleaning the car's exterior

1 The general condition of a car's bodywork is the one thing that significantly affects its value. Maintenance is easy but needs to be

regular. Neglect, particularly after minor damage, can lead quickly to further deterioration and costly repair bills. It is important also to keep watch on those parts of the car not immediately visible, for instance the underbody, inside all the wheel arches and the lower part of the engine compartment.

2 The basic maintenance routine for the bodywork is washing – preferably with a lot of water, from a hose. This will remove all the loose solids which may have stuck to the car. It is important to flush these off in such a way as to prevent grit from scratching the finish. The wheel arches and underbody need washing in the same way to remove any accumulated mud which will retain moisture and tend to encourage rust, particularly in winter when it is essential that any salt (from that put down on the roads) is washed off. Paradoxically enough, the best time to clean the underbody and wheel arches is in wet weather when the mud is thoroughly wet and soft. In very wet weather the underbody is usually cleaned automatically of large accumulations; this is therefore a good time for inspection.

3 If the car is very dirty, especially underneath or in the engine compartment, it is tempting to use one of the pressure washers or steam cleaners available on garage forecourts; while these are quick and effective, especially for the removal of the accumulation of oily grime which sometimes is allowed to become thick in certain areas, their usage does have some disadvantages. If caked-on dirt is simply blasted off the paintwork, its finish soon becomes scratched and dull and the pressure can allow water to penetrate door and window seals and the lock mechanisms; if the full force of such a jet is directed at the car's underbody the wax-based protective coating can easily be damaged and water (with whatever cleaning solvent is used) could be forced into crevices or components that it would not normally reach. Similarly, if such equipment is used to clean the engine compartment water can be forced into the components of the fuel and electrical systems and the protective coating can be removed that is applied to many small components during manufacture; this may therefore actually promote corrosion (especially inside electrical connectors) and initiate engine problems or other electrical faults. Also, if the jet is pointed directly at any of the oil seals, water can be forced past the seal lips and into the engine or transmission. Great care is required, therefore, if such equipment is used and, in general, regular cleaning by such methods should be avoided.

4 A much better solution in the long term is just to flush away as much loose dirt as possible using a hose alone, even if this leaves the engine compartment looking 'dirty'. If an oil leak has developed, or if any other accumulation of oil or grease is to be removed, there are one or two excellent grease solvents available, such as Holts Engine Cleaner or Holts Foambrite, which can be brush applied. The dirt can then be simply hosed off. Take care to replace the wax-based protective coat, if this was affected by the solvent.

5 Normal washing of the car's bodywork is best carried out using cold or warm water with a proprietary car shampoo such as Holts Turtle Wax Zipwax or Turtle Extra Car Wash and Wax. Remove dead insects with products such as Holts Fly Squash Remover; tar spots can be removed either by using white spirit, followed by soapy water to remove all traces of spirit, or by using Holts Body + Plus Tar Remover. Try to keep water out of the bonnet air intakes and check afterwards that the heater air inlet box drain tube is clear so that any water has drained out of the box.

6 After washing the paintwork, wipe off with a chamois leather to give an unspotted clear finish. A coat of clear protective wax polish, such as one of the many excellent Turtle Wax polishes, will give added protection against chemical pollutants in the air. If the paintwork sheen has dulled or oxidised, use a cleaner/polisher combination such as Turtle Extra to restore the brilliance of the shine. This requires a little effort, but such dulling is usually caused because regular washing has been neglected. Care needs to be taken with metallic paintwork, as special non-abrasive cleaner/polisher is required to avoid damage to the finish.

7 Brightwork should be treated in the same way as paintwork.

8 Windscreens and windows can be kept clear of the smeary film which often appears, by the use of proprietary glass cleaner like Holts Mixra. Never use any form of wax or other body or chromium polish on glass.

Exterior paintwork and body panels check

9 Once the car has been washed and all tar spots and other surface blemishes have been cleaned off, check carefully all paintwork, looking closely for chips or scratches; check with particular care vulnerable areas such as the front (bonnet and spoiler) and around the wheel arches. Any damage to the paintwork must be rectified as soon as possible to comply with the terms of the manufacturer's cosmetic and anti-corrosion warranties; check with a Rover dealer for details.

10 If a chip or (light) scratch is found that is recent and still free from rust, it can be touched-up using the appropriate touch-up pencil; these can be obtained from Rover dealers or from the Holts Dupli-Color Color Touch range. Any more serious damage, or rusted stone chips, can be repaired as described in the relevant sub-section of Chapter 11, Section 2, but if damage or corrosion is so severe that a panel must be renewed, seek professional advice as soon as possible.

11 Always check that the door and ventilator opening drain holes and pipes are completely clear so that water can be drained out.

Underbody sealer check

12 The wax-based underbody protective coating should be inspected annually, preferably just prior to winter, when the underbody should be washed down as thoroughly but gently as possible (see paragraph 3 above concerning steam cleaners, etc.) and any damage to the coating repaired using Holts Undershield; if any of the body panels are disturbed for repair or renewed, do not forget to replace the coating and to inject wax into door panels, sills, box sections, etc., to maintain the level of protection provided by the car's manufacturer.

13 Check carefully that the wheel arch liners and undercover panel are in place and securely fastened and that there is no sign of underbody damage or of developing corrosion; if any is found, seek immediate professional advice.

Hinge and lock check and lubrication

14 Lubricate the hinges of the bonnet, doors and tailgate with a light machine oil (Duckhams Home Oil).

15 Lightly lubricate the bonnet release mechanism and cable with the specified type of grease.

16 The door and tailgate latches, strikers and locks must be lubricated using only the special Rover Door Lock and Latch Lubricant supplied in 25 gram sachets under Part Number VWN 10075; inject 1 gram into each lock and wipe off any surplus, then apply a thin film to the latches and strikers. **Do not** lubricate the steering lock mechanism with oil or any other lubricant which might foul the ignition switch contacts; if the lock is stiff, try to introduce a graphite-based powder into the mechanism.

17 Check carefully the security and operation of all hinges, latches and locks, adjusting them where required. Check the operation of the central locking system (if fitted).

18 Check the condition and operation of the tailgate struts, renewing them if either is leaking or no longer able to support the tailgate securely when raised.

19 If a sunroof is fitted, lubricate very sparingly the seal lip with Rover's Non-Staining Grease (Corning No. 7) available under Part Number BAU 5812.

Seat belt check

20 All models are fitted with three-point lap and diagonal inertia reel seat belts at both front and the rear outer seats. The rear centre seat has a two-point lap-type belt which is fixed (ie not inertia reel).

21 Belt maintenance is limited to regular inspection. Check the webbing for signs of fraying, cuts or other damage, pulling the belt out to its full extent to check its entire length. Check the operation of the buckles by fitting the belt tongue plate and pulling hard to ensure that it remains locked, then check the retractor mechanism (inertia reel only) by pulling out the belt to the halfway point and jerking hard; the mechanism must lock immediately to prevent any further unreeling, but must allow free movement during normal driving. Finally, ensure that all mounting bolts are securely tightened. Note that the bolts are shouldered so that the belt anchor points are free to rotate.

22 If there is any sign of damage, or any doubt about a belt's condition, it must be renewed. If the car has been involved in a collision any belts in use at the time must be renewed as a matter of course and all other belts should be checked carefully.

23 Use only warm water and non-detergent soap to clean the belts. Never use any chemical cleaners, strong detergents, dyes or bleaches. Keep the belts fully extended until they have dried naturally; do not apply heat to dry them.

Cleaning the car's interior

24 Mats and carpets should be brushed or vacuum cleaned regularly to keep them free of grit. If they are badly stained remove them from the

car for scrubbing or sponging and make quite sure they are dry before refitting.

25 Where leather upholstery is fitted it should be cleaned only if necessary, using either a mild soap (such as saddle soap) or a proprietary leather cleaner; **do not** use strong soaps, detergents or chemical cleaners. If the leather is very stained, seek the advice of a Rover dealer. Fabric-trimmed seats and interior trim panels can be kept clean by wiping with a damp cloth and Turtle Wax Carisma. If they do become stained (which can be more apparent on light coloured upholstery) use a little liquid detergent and a soft nail brush to scour the grime out of the grain of the material. Do not forget to keep the headlining clean in the same way as the (fabric) upholstery.

26 When using liquid cleaners of any sort inside the car do not over-wet the surfaces being cleaned. Excessive damp could get into the seams and padded interior causing stains, offensive odours or even rot. If the inside of the car gets wet accidentally it is worthwhile taking some trouble to dry it out properly, particularly where carpets are involved. *Do not leave oil or electric heaters inside the car for this purpose.*

11 Electrical system

Battery check and maintenance

Caution: *Before carrying out any work on the car battery, read through the precautions given in Safety first! at the beginning of this Manual.*

1 A 'maintenance-free' (sealed for life) battery is standard equipment on all cars covered by this Manual. Although this type of battery has many advantages over the older re-fillable type and should never require the addition of distilled water, it should still be routinely checked according to the following procedure.

2 The battery is located on the left-hand side of the engine compartment. The exterior of the battery should be inspected periodically for damage such as a cracked case or cover and should be kept clean and dry.

3 The electrolyte level can be seen through the battery's translucent case; although it should not alter in normal use, if the level has lowered (for example, due to electrolyte having boiled away as a result of overcharging) it is permissible to gently prise up the cell cover(s) and to top up the level as described in paragraphs 10 and 11 below.

4 If regular topping-up becomes necessary and the battery case is not fractured, the battery is being over-charged and the voltage regulator will have to be checked. Refer to Chapter 12 for further information.

5 Check the tightness of the battery terminal clamps to ensure good electrical connections and check the entire length of each cable for cracks and frayed conductors. Remove the fusible link box cover and check the security of the link connections, then refit the cover.

6 If corrosion (visible as white, fluffy deposits) is evident, remove the cables from the battery terminals, clean them with a small wire brush then refit them. Corrosion can be kept to a minimum by applying a layer of petroleum jelly to the clamps and terminals after they are reconnected.

7 Make sure that the battery tray is in good condition and the retaining clamp is tight.

8 Corrosion on the retaining clamp and the battery itself can be removed with a solution of water and baking soda. Thoroughly rinse all cleaned areas with plain water.

9 Any metal parts of the car damaged by corrosion due to contact with battery electrolyte should be treated with a water/baking soda solution or with household ammonia to neutralise the acid. The area should then be flushed with plain water, dried thoroughly and coated with a zinc-based primer before repainting.

10 If a conventional battery has been fitted as a replacement, the electrolyte level of each cell should be checked every month and, if necessary, topped up until the separators are just covered. On some batteries the case is translucent and incorporates minimum and maximum level marks. The check should be made more often if the car is operated in high ambient temperature conditions.

11 If necessary, top up the level with distilled or de-ionized water after removing the cell plug(s) or cover(s) from the top of the casing, although it should be noted that this should not be necessary often under normal operating conditions.

12 Further information on the battery, charging and jump starting can be found in Chapter 12 and in the preliminary sections of this Manual.

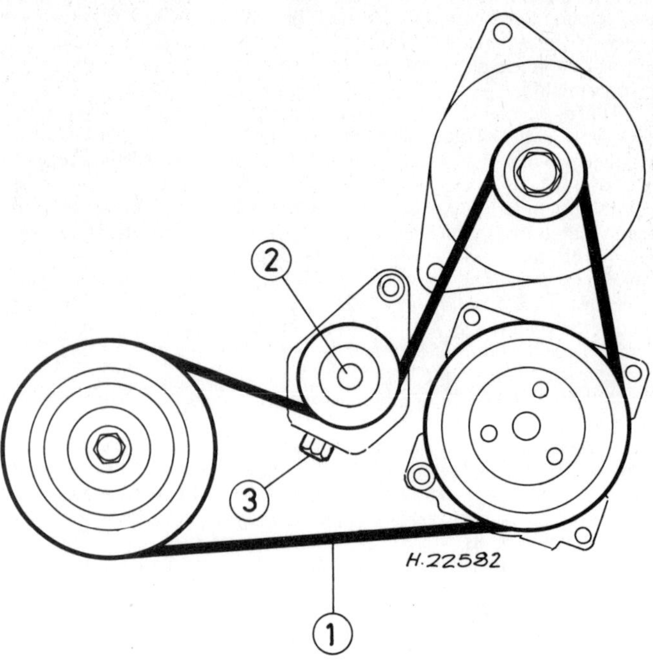

Fig. 1.5 Alternator drivebelt adjustment – models equipped with air conditioning (Sec 11)

1 *Drivebelt tension checking point*
2 *Adjuster pulley spindle bolt*
3 *Adjuster bolt*

Alternator drivebelt check, adjustment and renewal

General

13 The alternator is located on the front right-hand side of the engine unit, just above the engine oil filter, and is driven by the crankshaft pulley via a belt. On models equipped with air conditioning an extended alternator drivebelt is fitted which also drives the air conditioning compressor; the compressor being situated just below the alternator. Due to the drivebelt's function and construction it is subject to wear and will cause poor battery charging, or may even break, if not checked and adjusted at regular intervals.

Drivebelt check

14 Apply the handbrake then jack up the front of the car and support it on axle stands. Remove the right-hand front roadwheel.

15 From underneath the front of the car, slacken and remove the three bolts securing the bumper flange to the body. Remove the seven bolts securing the front undercover panel to the body and remove the panel.

16 Check the drivebelt for cracks, splitting, fraying or damage, whilst rotating the crankshaft clockwise using a suitable spanner applied to the crankshaft pulley bolt, so that the entire length of the belt is examined. Check also for signs of glazing (shiny patches) and for separation of the belt plies. Renew the belt if worn or damaged.

Drivebelt adjustment – models equipped with air conditioning

17 Carry out the operations described in paragraphs 14 and 15, if not already having done so.

18 The drivebelt's tension is checked by measuring the amount of deflection that takes place when a pressure of 10 kg is applied (using a spring balance, or similar) midway between the crankshaft and air conditioning pulleys on the belt's lower run. If the deflection measured is any more or less than that specified, the drivebelt must be adjusted as follows.

19 Slacken the drivebelt adjuster (idler) pulley spindle nut and bolt, then rotate the adjuster bolt, situated on the underside of the pulley

11.24A On models without air conditioning, slacken the alternator upper pivot mounting bolts (arrowed)...

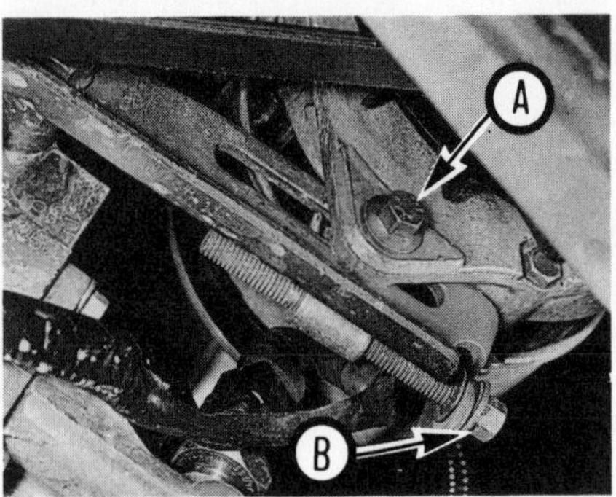

11.24B ...and the lower adjusting arm bolt (A) then rotate the adjuster bolt (B) to obtain the correct drivebelt tension

11.28 Power steering pump drivebelt (where fitted) must first be removed to permit alternator drivebelt renewal

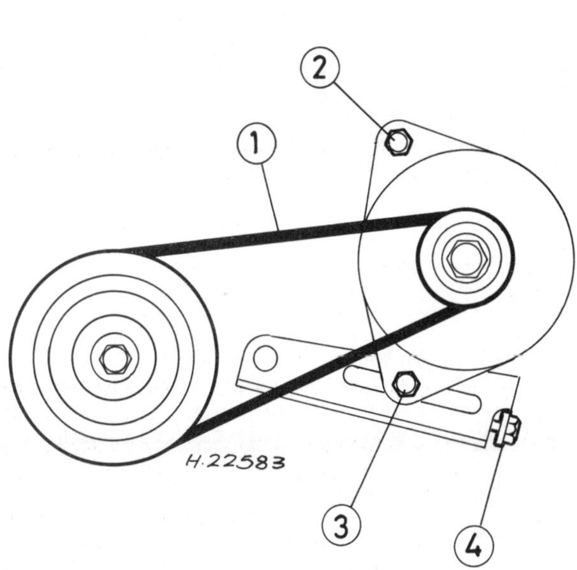

Fig. 1.6 Alternator drivebelt adjustment – models without air conditioning (Sec 11)

1 *Drivebelt tension checking point*
2 *Upper pivot bolt*
3 *Adjusting arm mounting bolt*
4 *Adjuster bolt*

assembly, clockwise or anti-clockwise as required to obtain the correct belt tension.

20 When the correct tension is achieved, tighten the adjuster pulley spindle bolt and nut to the specified torque setting and rotate the crankshaft several times to settle the drivebelt. Recheck the belt tension, repeating the adjustment procedure if necessary.

21 Refit the undercover and roadwheel and lower the car to the ground.

Drivebelt adjustment – models without air conditioning

22 Carry out the operations described in paragraphs 14 and 15, if not already having done so.

23 The drivebelt's tension is checked by measuring the amount of deflection that takes place when a pressure of 10 kg is applied (using a spring balance, or similar) midway between the crankshaft and alternator pulleys on the belt's upper run. If the deflection measured is any more or less than that specified, the drivebelt must be adjusted as follows.

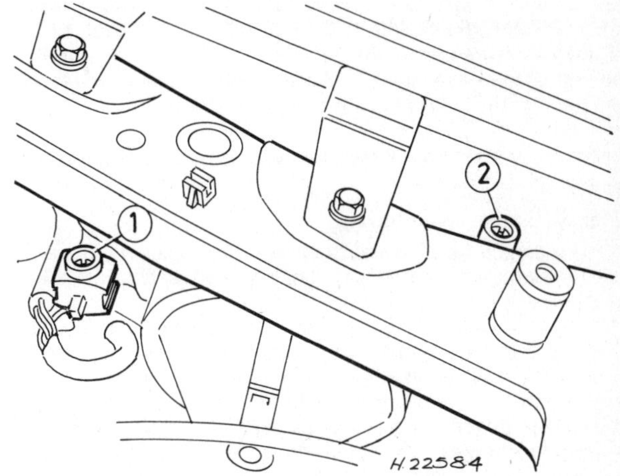

Fig. 1.7 Headlamp unit adjusters (Sec 11)

1 *Vertical adjuster*
2 *Horizontal adjuster*

24 Slacken both the alternator upper pivot mounting bolts and the lower adjusting arm mounting bolt. Rotate the adjuster bolt clockwise or anti-clockwise as required to obtain the correct belt tension (photos).

25 When the correct tension is achieved, tighten the alternator adjusting arm and pivot bolts to the specified torque and rotate the crankshaft several times to settle the drivebelt. Recheck the belt tension and re-adjust if necessary.

26 Refit the undercover and roadwheel and lower the car to the ground.

Drivebelt renewal

27 Carry out the operations in paragraphs 14 and 15, if not already having done so.

28 If the car is equipped with power steering, remove the power steering pump drivebelt as described in Section 9 (photo).

29 Slacken the drivebelt adjuster (idler) pulley spindle nut and bolt (models equipped with air conditioning), or the alternator pivot and adjusting arm mounting bolts (models without air conditioning) and slacken the adjuster bolt until the drivebelt can be slipped off the pulleys and removed from the car.

30 Clean the belt pulleys carefully, removing all traces of oil or grease and checking that the grooves are clear, then fit the new belt to the pulleys and tighten the adjuster bolt until the tension is approximately correct, then check and adjust the tension as described above.

31 Where necessary, refit the power steering pump drivebelt as described in Section 9.

32 Start the engine and allow it to idle at the specified speed for

approximately 10 minutes to settle the drivebelt in position. Stop the engine then recheck the drivebelt tension as described above and, if necessary, repeat the adjustment procedure.
33 Refit the undercover and roadwheel then lower the car to the ground.

Lamps, horn and direction indicators operational check

34 Check the operation of all the electrical equipment, ie lamps, direction indicators, horn, etc. Refer to the appropriate Sections of Chapter 12 for details if any of the circuits are found to be inoperative.
35 Note that stop lamp switch adjustment is described in Chapter 9.
36 Visually check all accessible wiring connectors, harnesses and retaining clips for security and for signs of chafing or damage. Rectify any faults found.

Headlamp beam alignment – general information

37 Accurate adjustment of the headlamp beam is only possible using optical beam setting equipment, and this work should therefore be carried out by a Rover dealer or workshop with the necessary facilities.
38 For reference the headlamps can be adjusted by using a suitably sized crosshead screwdriver to rotate the two adjuster assemblies fitted to the rear of the lamp (Fig. 1.7). Access to the lower adjuster can be gained through the hole in the bonnet lock platform.

Windscreen and rear window washer/wiper system check

Washer system reservoir top-up

39 The reservoir for the windscreen and rear window (where fitted) washer systems is located on the left-hand side of the engine compartment.
40 Check, and if necessary top up, the washer fluid level in the reservoir. When topping-up the reservoir, a screenwash such as Turtle Wax High Tech Screen Wash should be added in the recommended quantities. It is permissible to use only clean water in summer, though this is best mixed with a screenwash additive of the type recommended. In winter mix the water either with methylated spirit or with a combined screenwash additive and antifreeze. Follow the manufacturer's instructions for the mixing ratio.
41 **Never** use strong detergents (washing-up liquids, etc.) or engine antifreeze in the washer fluid. Not only can they cause smearing of the glass, but they can also damage the car's paintwork.

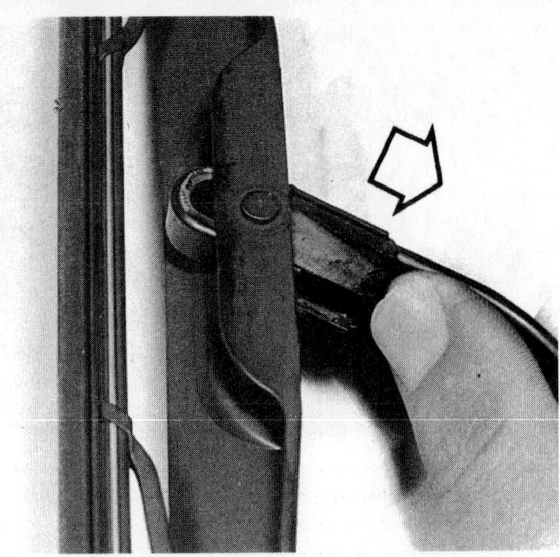

11.45 Depress the locking tab and slide out wiper blade in direction of arrow

42 Check the security of the pump wires and the washer tubing; if any of the jets are blocked, clear the obstruction using a thin wire probe.

Washer jet adjustment

43 Check the operation of the windscreen and rear window washers. Adjust the nozzles using a pin if necessary, aiming the spray to a point slightly above the centre of the swept area.

Wiper blade check and renewal

44 Check the condition of the wiper blades; if they are cracked or show any signs of deterioration, or if the glass swept area is smeared, renew them. For maximum clarity of vision wiper blades should be renewed annually, as a matter of course.
45 To remove a wiper blade, pull the arm fully away from the glass until it locks. Swivel the blade through 90°, press the locking tab with the finger nail and slide the blade out of the arm's hooked end (photo). On refitting, ensure that the blade locks securely into the arm.

Chapter 2 Engine

Contents

Specifications

Engine (general)

Type	Four-cylinder in-line, four-stroke, liquid-cooled
Designation:	
1.4 8-valve sohc	K8
1.4 16-valve dohc	K16
Bore	75.00 mm
Stroke	79.00 mm
Capacity	1396 cc
Firing order	1-3-4-2 (No 1 cylinder at timing belt end)
Direction of crankshaft rotation	Clockwise (seen from right-hand side of car)
Compression ratio:	
K8	9.75 : 1
K16	9.50 : 1
Minimum compression pressure	10.3 bars
Maximum compression pressure difference between cylinders	1.4 bars
Maximum power (EEC):	
1.4 - K8	76 ps (56 kW) @ 5700 rpm
1.4 - K8 (with catalytic converter)	75 ps (55 kW) @ 5500 rpm
1.4 - K16	95 ps (70 kW) @ 6250 rpm
1.4 - K16 (with catalytic converter)	90 ps (66 kW) @ 6250 rpm
Maximum torque (EEC):	
1.4 - K8	117 Nm (86 lbf ft) @ 3500 rpm
1.4 - K16	124 Nm (91 lbf ft) @ 4000 rpm
1.4 - K16 (with catalytic converter)	120 Nm (89 lbf ft) @ 4000 rpm

Cylinder block/crankcase

Material	Aluminium alloy
Cylinder liner bore diameter - 60 mm from top of bore:	
Standard - grade A (Red)	74.975 to 74.985 mm
Standard - grade B (Blue)	74.986 to 74.995 mm
Service limit	75.045 mm

Note: *Service liners are Grade B*

Crankshaft

Number of main bearings	5
Main bearing journal diameter	47.979 to 48.000 mm
Main bearing journal size grades:	
Grade A	47.993 to 48.000 mm
Grade B	47.986 to 47.993 mm
Grade C	47.979 to 47.986 mm
Crankpin journal diameter	42.986 to 43.007 mm
Crankpin journal size grades:	
Grade A	43.000 to 43.007 mm
Grade B	42.993 to 43.000 mm
Grade C	42.986 to 42.993 mm
Main bearing and crankpin journal maximum ovality	0.010 mm
Main bearing and big-end bearing running clearance	0.021 to 0.049 mm
Crankshaft endfloat:	
Standard	0.10 to 0.30 mm
Service limit	0.50 mm
Thrustwasher thickness	2.61 to 2.65 mm

Pistons and piston rings

Piston diameter - K8:	
Grade A	74.940 to 74.955 mm
Grade B	74.956 to 74.970 mm
Piston diameter - K16:	
Grade A	74.945 to 74.960 mm
Grade B	74.960 to 74.975 mm

Note: *Service pistons are Grade B*

Piston to bore clearance:	
K8 - standard	0.015 to 0.045 mm
K16 - standard	0.010 to 0.040 mm
Service limit - all	0.080 mm
Piston ring end gaps (fitted 20 mm from top of bore):	
Top compression ring:	
K8	0.25 to 0.45 mm
K16	0.30 to 0.50 mm
Second compression ring - all models	0.30 to 0.50 mm
Oil control ring:	
K8 - standard	0.25 to 1.00 mm
K16 - standard	0.25 to 0.50 mm
K16 - service limit	0.60 mm
Piston ring to groove clearance:	
Top compression ring:	
K8	0.04 to 0.09 mm
K16	0.04 to 0.07 mm
Second compression ring:	
K8	0.04 to 0.08 mm
K16	0.04 to 0.07 mm
Oil control ring - all models	0.02 to 0.06 mm

Gudgeon pins

Diameter	18 mm
Fit in connecting rod	Interference

Cylinder head

Material	Aluminium alloy
Height	118.95 to 119.05 mm
Reface limit	0.20 mm
Maximum acceptable gasket face distortion	0.05 mm
Valve seat angle	45°
Valve seat width	1.5 mm
Seat cutter correction angle:	
Upper	30°
Lower	60°
Valve stem installed height:	
K8 - new	38.95 to 40.81 mm
K8 - service limit	41.06 mm
K16 - new	38.93 to 39.84 mm
K16 - service limit	40.10 mm

Camshaft

Drive	Toothed belt
Number of bearings	6
Bearing journal running clearance:	
Standard	0.060 to 0.094 mm
Service limit	0.150 mm
Camshaft endfloat:	
Standard	0.060 to 0.190 mm
Service limit	0.500 mm
Valve lift:	
K8	9.0 mm
K16	8.2 mm
Hydraulic tappet outside diameter	32.959 to 32.975 mm

Valves

Seat angle:	
Inlet	45°
Exhaust	44° 30′
Head diameter:	
Inlet – K8	34 mm
Inlet – K16	28 mm
Exhaust – K8	31 mm
Exhaust – K16	24 mm
Stem outside diameter:	
Inlet – K8	6.967 to 6.975 mm
Inlet – K16	5.952 to 5.967 mm
Exhaust – K8	6.952 to 6.967 mm
Exhaust – K16	5.947 to 5.962 mm
Guide inside diameter:	
K8	7.000 to 7.025 mm
K16	6.000 to 6.025 mm
Stem to guide clearance:	
Inlet – standard	0.03 to 0.04 mm
Inlet – service limit	0.07 mm
Exhaust – standard	0.07 to 0.08 mm
Exhaust – service limit	0.11 mm
Valve timing – K8:	
Inlet opens	13° BTDC
Inlet closes	47° ABDC
Exhaust opens	53° BBDC
Exhaust closes	7° ATDC
Valve timing – K16:	
Inlet opens	15° BTDC
Inlet closes	45° ABDC
Exhaust opens	55° BBDC
Exhaust closes	5° ATDC
Valve spring free length:	
K8	46.2 mm
K16	50.0 mm
Valve guide fitted height	6.0 mm

Lubrication system

System pressure – @ idle speed	1.0 bar
Oil pump type	Trochoidal, eccentric-rotor
Oil pump clearances:	
Rotor endfloat	0.02 to 0.06 mm
Outer rotor to body clearance	0.28 to 0.36 mm
Rotor lobe clearance	0.05 to 0.13 mm
Pressure relief valve operating pressure	4.1 bars
Oil pressure warning lamp lights at	Below 0.3 to 0.5 bar

Torque wrench settings

	Nm	lbf ft
Spark plug (HT) lead clip screws – K8	9	6
Air intake duct support bracket to cylinder head screws – K16	4	3
Spark plug cover screws – K16	2	1.5
Cylinder head cover bolts	9	6
Camshaft bearing cap/carrier to cylinder head bolts	9	6
Cylinder head bolts:		
1st stage	20	15
2nd stage	Tighten through 180°	Tighten through 180°
3rd stage	Tighten through (a further) 180°	Tighten through (a further) 180°
Timing belt cover fasteners:		
Upper right-hand (outer) cover	4	3
Lower and upper left-hand (inner) covers	9	6

Torque wrench settings (continued)	Nm	lbf ft
Timing belt tensioner backplate clamp bolt	25	19
Timing belt tensioner pulley Allen screw	45	33
Camshaft sprocket bolt	33	24
Crankshaft pulley bolt	160	118
Oil pump to cylinder block/crankcase bolt and screws	9	6
Alternator mounting bracket to cylinder block/crankcase bolts	45	33
Dipstick tube to cylinder block/crankcase bolts	9	6
Flywheel bolts	85	63
Transmission to engine bolts	85	63
Flywheel cover plate screws	9	6
Flywheel rear cover plate bolt and nut	38	28
Big-end bearing cap bolts*:		
1st stage	20	15
2nd stage	Tighten through 45°	Tighten through 45°
Main bearing ladder to cylinder block/crankcase bolts	10	7
Oil rail to main bearing ladder nuts	9	6
Oil pump pick-up/strainer pipe bolts	9	6
Sump bolts	10	7
Engine oil drain plug	42	31
Engine/transmission right-hand mounting:		
Bracket to cylinder block/crankcase bolts	45	33
Mounting to bracket nuts	100	74
Mounting to body through-bolt and nut	85	63
Engine/transmission left-hand mounting:		
Mounting to body bolts	45	33
Mounting to transmission bracket bolts	60	44
Transmission bracket bolts	100	74
Engine/transmission rear mounting:		
Mounting bracket to transmission bolt	85	63
Connecting link to transmission bracket bolt	60	44
Connecting link to body bolt	85	63
Anti-beaming bracket to support bracket bolt	45	33

Part A: In-car engine repair procedures

1 General information

How to use this Chapter

This Part of Chapter 2 describes those repair procedures that can reasonably be carried out on the engine while it remains in the car. If the engine has been removed from the car and is being dismantled as described in Part B, any preliminary dismantling procedures can be ignored.

Note that while it may be possible physically to overhaul items such as the piston/connecting rod assemblies while the engine is in the car, such tasks are not usually carried out as separate operations and usually require the execution of several additional procedures (not to mention the cleaning of components and of oilways); for this reason all such tasks are classed as major overhaul procedures and are described in Part B of this Chapter.

Part B describes the removal of the engine/transmission unit from the car and the full overhaul procedures that can then be carried out.

For ease of reference, all specifications are given in the one Specifications Section at the beginning of the Chapter.

Engine description

The engine is of four-cylinder, in-line type, mounted transversely at the front of the car with the clutch and transmission on its left-hand end. The engine is available in two forms; the K8 engine which is the eight-valve single overhead camshaft engine fitted to the carburettor equipped 214 S model, and the K16 which is a sixteen-valve double overhead camshaft engine which is fitted to all fuel-injected 214 and 414 models. Apart from the different cylinder head designs, both engines are of an identical construction.

Apart from the pressed steel sump, the plastic timing belt covers and the aluminium alloy cylinder head cover, the engine consists of three major castings (the cylinder head, the cylinder block/crankcase and the crankshaft main bearing ladder); there is also an oil rail underneath the main bearing ladder and the camshaft carrier/bearing caps (see below). All these castings are of aluminium alloy, the three major ones being clamped together by ten long through-bolts which perform the dual role of cylinder head bolts and crankshaft main bearing fasteners. Since these bolts pass through the cylinder block/crankcase and the main bearing ladder, the oil rail is secured also to the main bearing ladder (by two nuts) and the main bearing ladder is secured also to the cylinder block/crankcase (by ten smaller bolts) so that the cylinder head can be removed without disturbing the rest of the engine. The passages provided for the bolts in the major castings are used as breather passages or as returns for the oil to the sump.

Note: *A side-effect of this design is that the crankshaft cannot be rotated once the through-bolts have been slackened. During any servicing or overhaul work the crankshaft must always be rotated to the desired position before the bolts are disturbed.*

The crankshaft runs in five main bearings. Thrustwashers are fitted to the centre main bearing (upper half) to control crankshaft endfloat.

The connecting rods rotate on horizontally-split bearing shells at their big-ends. The pistons are attached to the connecting rods by gudgeon pins which are an interference fit in the connecting rod small-end eyes. The aluminium alloy pistons are fitted with three piston rings, comprising two compression rings and an oil control ring.

The cylinder bores are formed by replaceable wet liners that are located from their top ends; two sealing O-rings are fitted at the base of each liner to prevent the escape of coolant into the sump.

The inlet and exhaust valves are each closed by coil springs and operate in guides pressed into the cylinder head; the valve seat inserts are pressed into the cylinder head and can be renewed separately if worn.

On the K8 engine, the camshaft is driven by a toothed timing belt and operates the eight valves via self-adjusting hydraulic tappets, thus

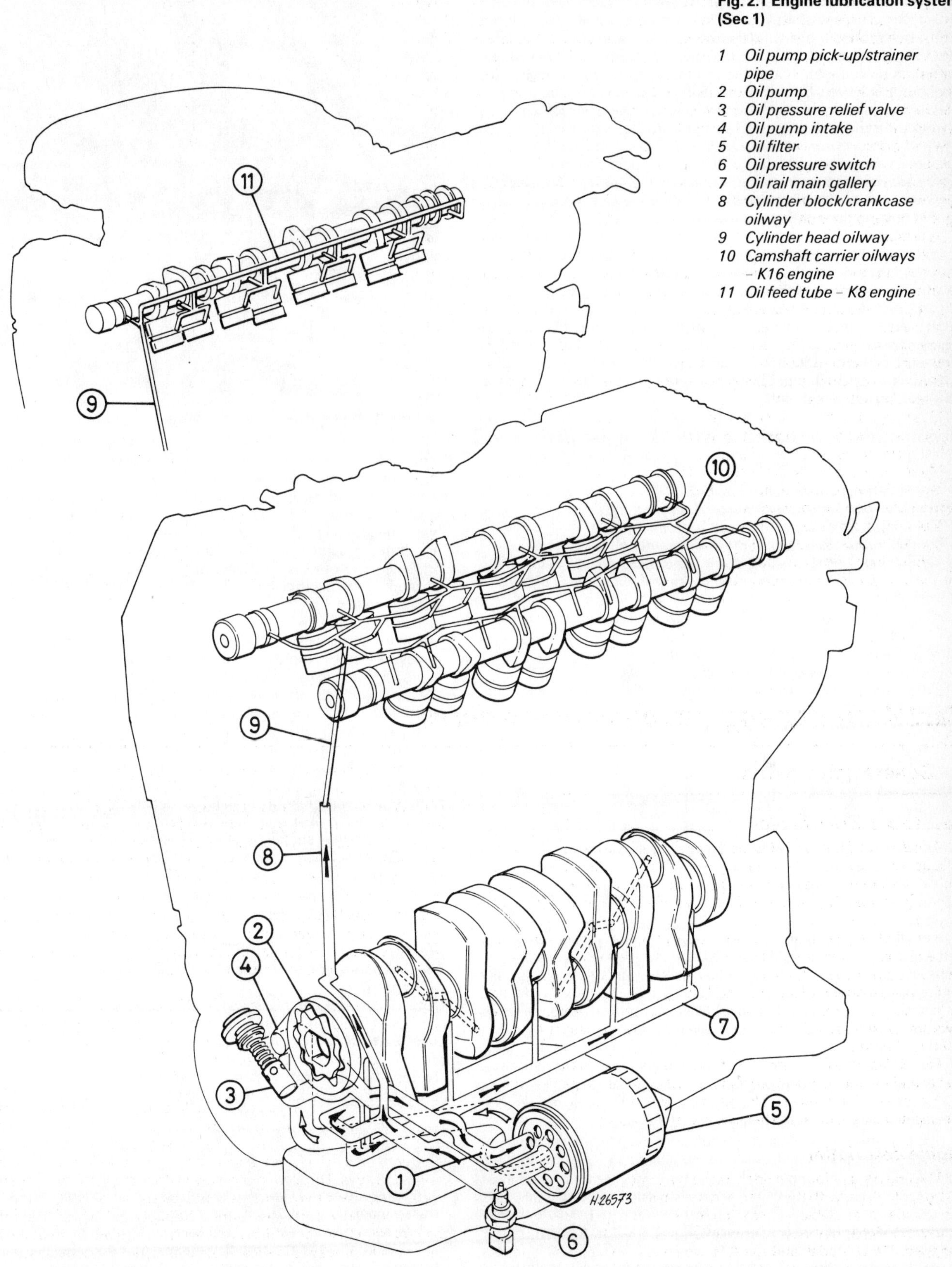

Fig. 2.1 Engine lubrication system (Sec 1)

1 *Oil pump pick-up/strainer pipe*
2 *Oil pump*
3 *Oil pressure relief valve*
4 *Oil pump intake*
5 *Oil filter*
6 *Oil pressure switch*
7 *Oil rail main gallery*
8 *Cylinder block/crankcase oilway*
9 *Cylinder head oilway*
10 *Camshaft carrier oilways – K16 engine*
11 *Oil feed tube – K8 engine*

eliminating the need for routine checking and adjustment of the valve clearances. The camshaft rotates in six bearings that are line-bored direct in the cylinder head and the (bolted-on) bearing caps; this means that the bearing caps are not available separately from the cylinder head and must not be interchanged with others from another engine. The distributor is driven from the left-hand end of the camshaft and the mechanical fuel pump is operated by an eccentric on the camshaft.

Apart from the fact that it has two camshafts, one inlet and one exhaust, each controlling eight valves and both retained by a single camshaft carrier, the same applies to the K16 engine; on the K16 engine the distributor is driven from the left-hand end of the inlet camshaft (the fuel pump is electrically operated).

On both engine types, the water pump is driven by the timing belt.

Lubrication is by means of an eccentric-rotor trochoidal pump mounted on the crankshaft right-hand end. It draws oil through a strainer located in the sump and then forces it through an externally-mounted full-flow cartridge-type filter into galleries in the oil rail and cylinder block/crankcase, from where it is distributed to the crankshaft (main bearings) and camshaft(s). The big-end bearings are supplied with oil via internal drillings in the crankshaft, while the camshaft bearings and the hydraulic tappets receive a pressurised supply. The camshaft lobes and valves are lubricated by splash, as are all other engine components.

Repair operations possible with the engine in the car

The following work can be carried out with the engine in the car.

- (a) *Compression pressure – testing.*
- (b) *Cylinder head cover – removal and refitting.*
- (c) *Crankshaft pulley – removal and refitting.*
- (d) *Timing belt covers – removal and refitting.*
- (e) *Timing belt – removal, refitting and adjustment.*
- (f) *Timing belt tensioner and sprockets – removal and refitting.*
- (g) *Camshaft oil seal(s) – renewal.*
- (h) *Camshaft(s) and hydraulic tappets – removal, inspection and refitting.*
- (i) *Cylinder head – removal and refitting.*
- (j) *Cylinder head and pistons – decarbonising.*
- (k) *Sump – removal and refitting.*
- (l) *Oil pump – removal, overhaul and refitting.*
- (m) *Crankshaft oil seals – renewal.*
- (n) *Engine/transmission mountings – inspection and renewal.*
- (o) *Flywheel – removal, inspection and refitting.*

2 Compression test – description and interpretation

1 When engine performance is down, or if misfiring occurs which cannot be attributed to the ignition or fuel systems, a compression test can provide diagnostic clues as to the engine's condition. If the test is performed regularly it can give warning of trouble before any other symptoms become apparent.

2 The engine must be fully warmed up to normal operating temperature, the battery must be fully charged and the spark plugs must be removed (Chapter 1). The aid of an assistant will be required also.

3 Disable the ignition system by disconnecting the ignition HT coil lead from the distributor cap and earthing it on the cylinder block. Use a jumper lead or similar wire to make a good connection.

4 Fit a compression tester to the number 1 cylinder spark plug hole – the type of tester which screws into the plug thread is to be preferred (photo).

5 Have the assistant hold the throttle wide open and crank the engine on the starter motor; after one or two revolutions the compression pressure should build up to a maximum figure and then stabilise. Record the highest reading obtained.

6 Repeat the test on the remaining cylinders, recording the pressure in each.

7 All cylinders should produce very similar pressures; any difference greater than that specified indicates the existence of a fault. Note that the compression should build up quickly in a healthy engine; low compression on the first stroke, followed by gradually increasing pressure on successive strokes, indicates worn piston rings. A low compression reading on the first stroke, which does not build up during successive strokes, indicates leaking valves or a blown head gasket (a cracked head could also be the cause). Deposits on the undersides of the valve heads can also cause low compression.

2.4 Measuring compression pressure

8 If the pressure in any cylinder is reduced to the specified minimum or less, carry out the following test to isolate the cause. Introduce a teaspoonful of clean oil into that cylinder through its spark plug hole and repeat the test.

9 If the addition of oil temporarily improves the compression pressure, this indicates that bore or piston wear is responsible for the pressure loss. No improvement suggests that leaking or burnt valves, or a blown head gasket may be to blame.

10 A low reading from two adjacent cylinders is almost certainly due to the head gasket having blown between them; the presence of coolant in the engine oil will confirm this.

11 If one cylinder is about 20 per cent lower than the others and the engine has a slightly rough idle, a worn camshaft lobe could be the cause.

12 If the compression reading is unusually high, the combustion chambers are probably coated with carbon deposits. If this is the case, the cylinder head should be removed and decarbonised.

13 On completion of the test, refit the spark plugs and reconnect the ignition system.

3 Top Dead Centre (TDC) for number one piston – locating

General

Note: *The crankshaft pulley, crankshaft and camshaft sprockets are provided by the factory with clear marks which align only at 90° BTDC; this positions the pistons half-way up the bores so that there is no risk of damage as the engine is reassembled. These marks do not indicate TDC; use only the ignition timing marks, as described in this Section, to find TDC.*

1 Top dead centre (TDC) is the highest point in its travel up-and-down the cylinder bore that each piston reaches as the crankshaft rotates. While each piston reaches TDC both at the top of the compression stroke and again at the top of the exhaust stroke, for the purpose of timing the engine, TDC refers to the piston position (usually number 1) at the top of its compression stroke.

2 While all engine reassembly procedures use the factory timing marks (90° BTDC), it is useful for several other servicing procedures to be able to position the engine at TDC.

3 Number 1 piston and cylinder is at the right-hand (timing belt) end of

the engine. Note that the crankshaft rotates clockwise when viewed from the right-hand side of the car.

Locating TDC

4 Disconnect the battery negative lead and remove all the spark plugs as described in Chapter 1.

5 Trace number 1 spark plug (HT) lead from the plug back to the distributor cap and use chalk or similar to mark the distributor body or engine casting nearest to the cap's number 1 terminal. Undo the distributor cap retaining screws and remove the cap.

6 Apply the handbrake and ensure that the transmission is in neutral, then jack up the front of the vehicle and support it on axle stands. Remove the right-hand roadwheel.

7 From underneath the front of the vehicle, slacken and remove the three bolts securing the bumper flange to the body. Remove the seven bolts securing the front undercover panel to the body and remove the panel to gain access to the crankshaft pulley and ignition timing marks.

8 Using a spanner, or socket and extension bar, applied to the crankshaft pulley bolt rotate the crankshaft clockwise until the notch on the crankshaft pulley's inboard (left-hand) rim is aligned with the TDC mark on the timing belt lower cover (see Chapter 1, *Ignition timing check and adjustment*, for details of the ignition timing marks).

9 With the crankshaft in this position Numbers 1 and 4 cylinders are now at TDC, one of them on the compression stroke. If the distributor rotor arm is pointing at (the previously-marked) number 1 terminal, then number 1 cylinder is correctly positioned; if the rotor arm is pointing at number 4 terminal, rotate the crankshaft one full turn (360°) clockwise until the arm points at the marked terminal. Number 1 cylinder will then be at TDC on the compression stroke.

10 Once number 1 cylinder has been positioned at TDC on the compression stroke, TDC for any of the other cylinders can then be located by rotating the crankshaft clockwise 180° at a time and following the firing order (see Specifications).

4 Cylinder head cover – removal and refitting

Removal

1 Disconnect the battery negative lead.

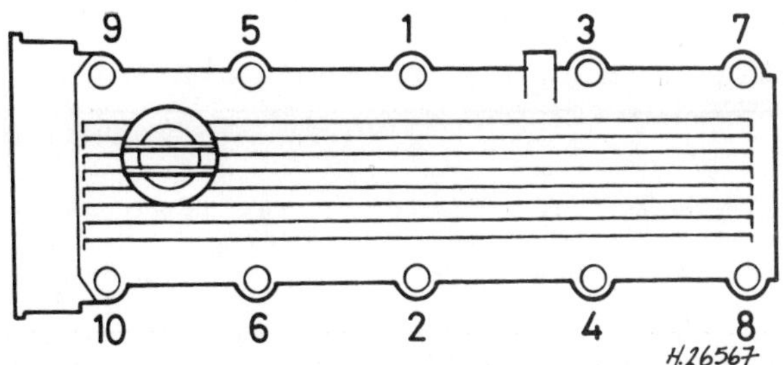

Fig. 2.2 Cylinder head cover bolt tightening sequence – K8 engine (Sec 4)

2 Remove the air cleaner assembly and metal intake duct as described in Chapter 4.

3 Using a suitable pair of pliers, release the retaining clip(s) and disconnect the breather hose(s) from the cylinder head cover (photos).

K8 engines

4 Undo the bolts securing the HT lead mounting and air intake support brackets to the cylinder head cover, then remove the brackets and position the HT leads clear of the cover.

5 Remove the two uppermost retaining screws securing the timing belt upper right-hand/outer cover to the cylinder head cover, then slacken the remaining screws and bolts, referring to Section 6 for further information, as necessary until the timing belt cover can be prised clear of the cylinder head cover without damaging it.

6 Working progressively and in the **reverse** of the sequence shown in Fig. 2.2, slacken and remove the cylinder head cover retaining bolts.

7 Remove the cover, peel off the rubber seal and check it for cuts, other damage or distortion; renew it if necessary.

K16 engines

8 Undo the two spark plug cover retaining screws and lift off the cover. Disconnect the HT leads from the plugs and withdraw them from the cylinder head along with the clip plate and the grommet which is fitted to the left-hand end of the cylinder head cover.

9 Working progressively and in the **reverse** of the sequence shown in photo 4.22, slacken and remove the cylinder head cover retaining bolts, noting the correct fitted position of the air intake duct support bracket.

10 Carefully lift off the cylinder head cover taking care not to damage the gasket. Check that the gasket sealing path is undamaged and is attached to the gasket all around its periphery. If the sealing path is undamaged the gasket is re-usable and should remain in place on the cover until reassembly, unless its removal is necessary for other servicing work.

Refitting

K8 engines

11 On reassembly, carefully clean the cylinder head mating surfaces and the cover seal's groove and remove all traces of oil.

12 Seat the seal in its groove in the cover and refit the bolts, pushing each through the seal, then apply a smear of silicone-RTV sealant to each corner of the seal (photos).

13 Refit the cover to the cylinder head, ensuring that the seal remains seated in its groove, and start all bolts finger-tight.

14 Working in the sequence shown in Fig. 2.2, tighten the cylinder head cover bolts to the specified torque wrench setting.

15 Refit the timing belt upper right-hand/outer cover to the cylinder head cover and tighten all the disturbed screws and bolts to the specified torque setting.

16 Refit the HT lead mounting clips and air cleaner intake support brackets to the cylinder head and tighten the retaining bolts to the specified torque. Ensure the HT leads are correctly routed.

17 Connect the breather hose to the cylinder head cover and secure it in position with the retaining clip.

18 Refit the air cleaner housing as described in Chapter 4 and reconnect the battery negative lead.

4.3A Disconnecting breather hose from cylinder head cover – K8 engines

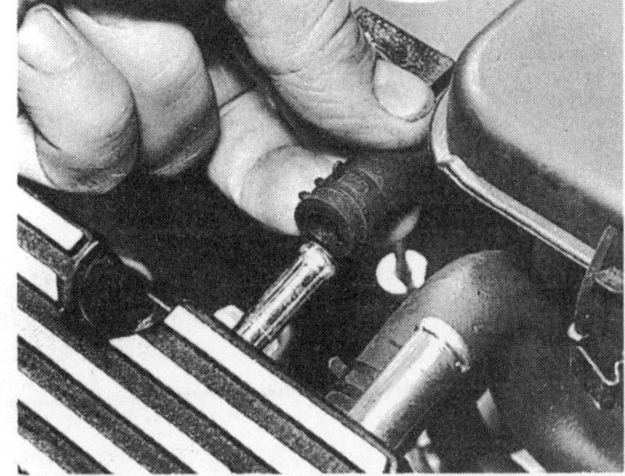

4.3B Disconnecting breather hoses from cylinder head cover – K16 engines

4.12A Ensure the cylinder head cover seal is seated correctly in cover groove...

4.12B ...then refit the bolts and apply sealant at locations arrowed – K8 engines

4.20A Fit gasket to cylinder head cover dowels (arrowed) so that...

4.20B ...stamped markings would appear as shown if gasket were placed on camshaft carrier

4.22 Cylinder head cover bolt tightening sequence – K16 engine

5.7 Ensure notch in crankshaft pulleys centre fits over crankshaft timing belt sprocket locating lug (arrowed)

K16 engines

19 On reassembly, carefully clean the mating surfaces, removing all traces of oil. If the gasket has been removed, the oil separator elements can be cleaned by removing them from the cover and washing them in solvent. Use compressed air to blow dry the elements before refitting them to the cover.

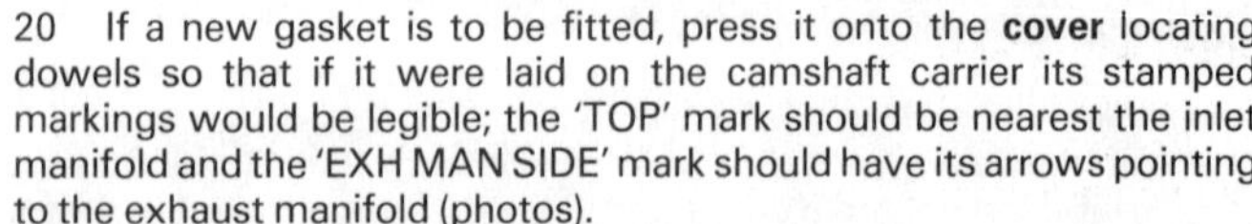

20 If a new gasket is to be fitted, press it onto the **cover** locating dowels so that if it were laid on the camshaft carrier its stamped markings would be legible; the 'TOP' mark should be nearest the inlet manifold and the 'EXH MAN SIDE' mark should have its arrows pointing to the exhaust manifold (photos).

21 Lower the cover onto the cylinder head, ensuring that the gasket is not damaged or displaced. Install the cover retaining bolts, not forgetting to refit the air intake duct support bracket to its original position, and tighten them finger-tight.

22 Working in the sequence shown, tighten the cylinder head cover retaining bolts to the specified torque setting (photo).

23 Reconnect the HT leads to the spark plugs, and locate the clip plate and grommet in the left-hand end of the cylinder head cover. Ensure the HT leads are correctly routed then refit the spark plug cover.

24 Connect both the breather hoses to the cylinder head cover.

25 Refit the air cleaner housing as described in Chapter 4 and reconnect the battery negative lead.

5 Crankshaft pulley – removal and refitting

Removal

1 Apply the handbrake then jack up the front of the car and support it on axle stands. Remove the right-hand roadwheel.

2 From underneath the front of the vehicle, slacken and remove the three bolts securing the bumper flange to the body. Remove the seven bolts securing the front undercover panel to the body and remove the panel.

3 If necessary, rotate the crankshaft until the relevant timing marks align.

4 Referring to Chapter 1 for further information, remove the power steering pump and/or alternator drivebelt(s) (as applicable).

5 To prevent crankshaft rotation while the pulley bolt is unscrewed, select top gear and have an assistant apply the brakes firmly. If the engine has been removed from the car, lock the flywheel using the arrangement shown in photo 34.30C.

6 Unscrew the pulley bolt, noting the special washer behind it, then remove the pulley from the crankshaft.

Refitting

7 Align the crankshaft pulley centre notch with the locating lug on the crankshaft timing belt sprocket then refit the washer, ensuring that its flat surface is facing the pulley, and retaining bolt (photo).

8 Lock the crankshaft by the method used on removal and tighten the pulley retaining bolt to the specified torque setting.

9 Refit the power steering pump and/or alternator drivebelt(s) (as applicable) and adjust them as described in Chapter 1.

10 Refit the undercover panel and roadwheel then lower the car to the ground.

6 Timing belt covers – removal and refitting

Removal

Upper right-hand (outer) cover

1 Slacken the bolt situated at the cover's bottom corner, immediately behind the engine/transmission right-hand mounting bracket.
2 Unscrew the remaining cover retaining bolts and withdraw the cover, noting the rubber seal fitted to the mounting bracket edge. Note that if the cover is not slotted at the bottom corner screw's location, the screw will have to be removed fully; if this is the case the cover can be slotted to ease future removal and refitting (photo).

Lower cover

3 Remove the crankshaft pulley as described in Section 5.
4 Remove the cover retaining screws, including the one which also secures the upper cover's bottom front corner and remove the cover, noting the rubber seal fitted to its mounting bracket edge (photo).

Upper left-hand (inner) cover

5 Remove the timing belt as described in Section 7.
6 Remove the camshaft sprocket(s) and the timing belt tensioner, referring to Section 8 for further information.
7 Unscrew the bolt securing the cover to the water pump.
8 On K16 engines unbolt the engine/transmission right-hand mounting bracket from the cylinder block/crankcase.
9 Remove the remaining cover retaining bolts and withdraw the cover (photos).

Refitting

Upper right-hand (outer) cover

10 Refitting is the reverse of the removal procedure; ensure that the

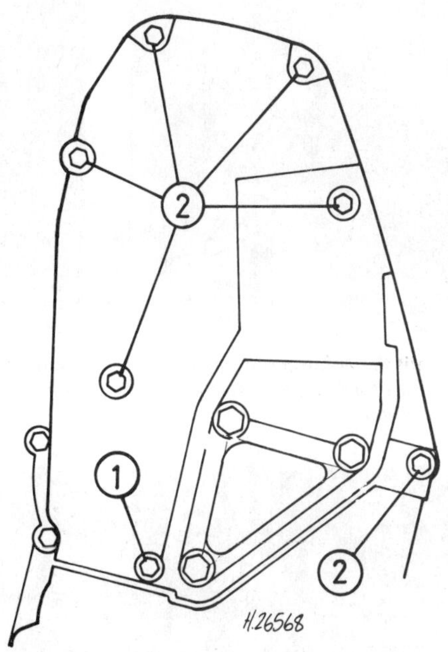

Fig. 2.3 Location of K8 engine timing belt upper right-hand (outer) cover fasteners (Sec 6)

1 Slacken screw – cover should be slotted
2 Remove fasteners

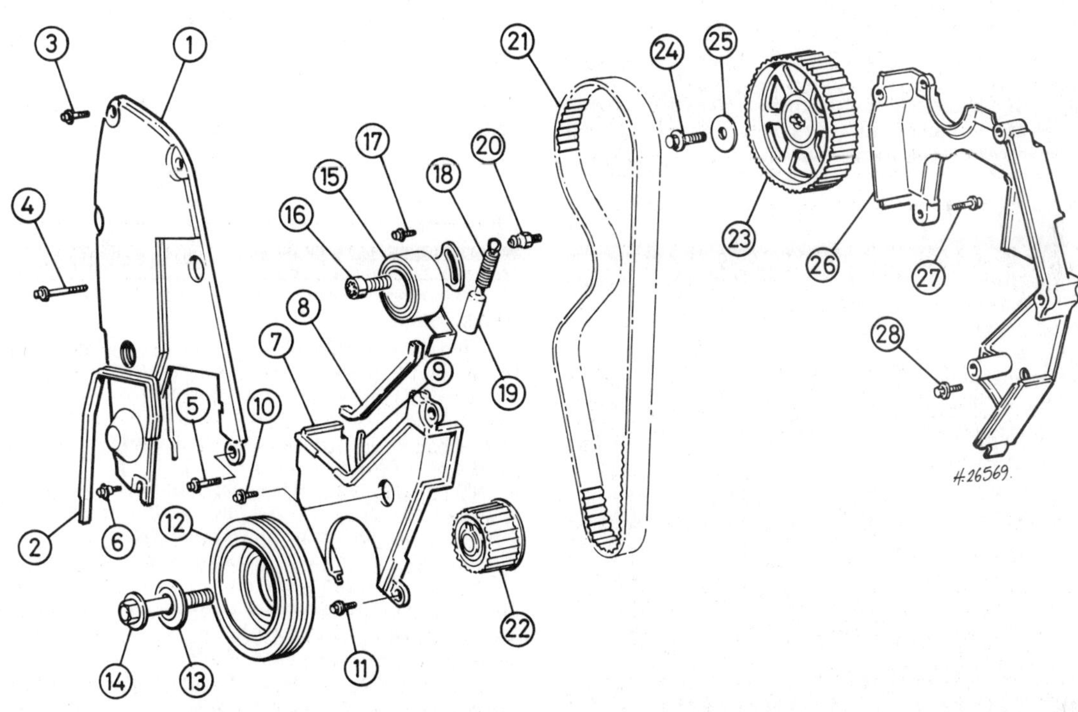

Fig. 2.4 Timing belt, sprockets and covers – K8 engine (Secs 6, 7 and 8)

1 Timing belt upper right-hand (outer) cover
2 Seal
3 Bolt
4 Bolt
5 Bolt
6 Shouldered bolt
7 Timing belt lower cover
8 Seal
9 Seal
10 Bolt
11 Bolt
12 Crankshaft pulley
13 Washer
14 Crankshaft pulley bolt
15 Timing belt tensioner pulley assembly
16 Tensioner pulley Allen screw
17 Tensioner backplate clamp bolt
18 Tensioner pulley spring
19 Sleeve
20 Pillar bolt
21 Timing belt
22 Crankshaft sprocket
23 Camshaft sprocket
24 Camshaft sprocket bolt
25 Washer
26 Timing belt upper left-hand (inner) cover
27 Bolt – cover to water pump
28 Bolt

6.2 Location of K16 engine timing belt upper right-hand/outer cover fasteners (arrowed) – engine raised for clarity

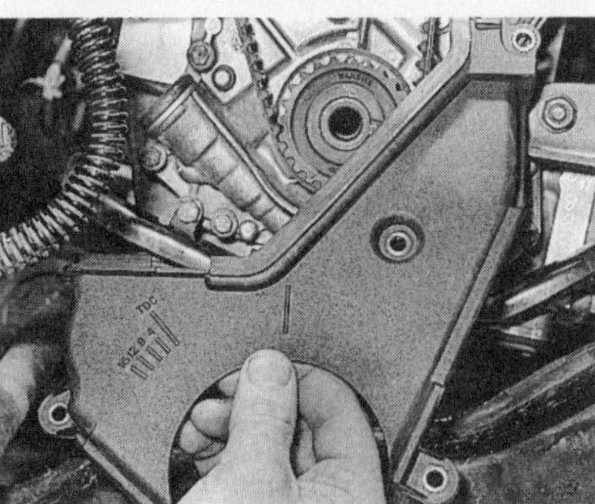
6.4 Removing timing belt lower cover

6.9A Location of K8 engine timing belt upper left-hand (inner) cover fasteners (arrowed)

6.9B Location of K16 engine timing belt upper left-hand (inner) cover fasteners (arrowed)

6.9C Removing K16 engine timing belt upper left-hand (inner) cover

6.10 Ensure timing belt upper right-hand (outer) cover engages correctly with cylinder head cover – K8 engine

seal fits correctly between the cover and the mounting bracket and that the cover edges mate correctly with those of the inner cover and (K8 engines only) cylinder head cover (photo).

11 Tighten the cover fasteners to the specified torque setting.

Lower cover

12 Refitting is the reverse of the removal procedure; ensure that the seal fits correctly between the cover and the mounting bracket and tighten the cover fasteners to the specified torque setting.

13 Refit the crankshaft pulley as described in Section 5.

Upper left-hand (inner) cover

14 Refitting is the reverse of the removal procedure tightening all disturbed fasteners to their specified torque wrench settings.

7 Timing belt – removal, refitting and adjustment

Removal

1 Disconnect the battery negative lead.

2 To improve access to the timing belt, remove the three expansion tank mounting bolts then free the coolant hose from any relevant retaining clips and position the tank clear of the engine. On models equipped with power-assisted steering, undo all the power steering hose retaining clip bolts then slide the fluid reservoir out of its retaining clip and position it clear of the timing belt covers. Take great care not to place any undue strain on the coolant/hydraulic hoses and mop up any spilt coolant/hydraulic fluid immediately (as applicable).

3 Remove the timing belt upper right-hand (outer) cover as described in Section 6.

4 Firmly apply the handbrake then jack up the front of the car and support it on axle stands.

5 From underneath the front of the vehicle, slacken and remove the three bolts securing the bumper flange to the body. Remove the seven bolts securing the front undercover panel to the body and remove the panel to gain access to the crankshaft pulley bolt.

6 Using a suitable spanner or socket on the crankshaft pulley bolt, rotate the crankshaft in a clockwise direction until the long white-painted mark on the crankshaft pulley's outboard (right-hand) face is aligned with the single, separate mark on the timing belt lower cover so that the crankshaft is in the 90° BTDC position (see Chapter 1, *Ignition timing check and adjustment*, for full details of the pulley/cover marks) (photo).

7 Check that the camshaft sprocket mark(s) align as described in paragraph 15 below, showing that numbers 1 and 4 cylinders are at 90° BTDC so that there is no risk of the valves contacting the pistons during dismantling and reassembly. If the camshaft sprocket mark(s) are 180° out rotate the crankshaft through one complete turn (360°) to align the marks as described (photo).

8 On K16 engines use the tool described in Section 8 to lock up the camshaft sprockets so that they cannot move under valve spring pressure when the timing belt is removed.

9 Remove the crankshaft sprocket and timing belt lower cover as described in Sections 5 and 6.

10 Position a trolley jack with a wooden spacer beneath the sump then gently jack it up to take the weight of the engine.

11 Slacken and remove the engine/transmission right-hand mounting through-bolt and nut and the mounting to bracket nuts. Remove the mounting along with the two rubber washers which are fitted on each side of the mounting. On K8 engines only, unscrew the retaining bolts securing the bracket to cylinder block/crankcase and remove it from the engine unit (photo).

12 Slacken both the timing belt tensioner pulley Allen screw and the tensioner backplate clamp bolt through half a turn each, then push the pulley assembly downwards to remove all the tension from the timing belt. Hold the tensioner pulley in this position and re-tighten the backplate clamp bolt securely (photo).

13 If the timing belt is to be re-used, use white paint or similar to mark the direction of rotation on the belt, then slip the belt off the sprockets (photo). **Do not** rotate the crankshaft until the timing belt has been refitted.

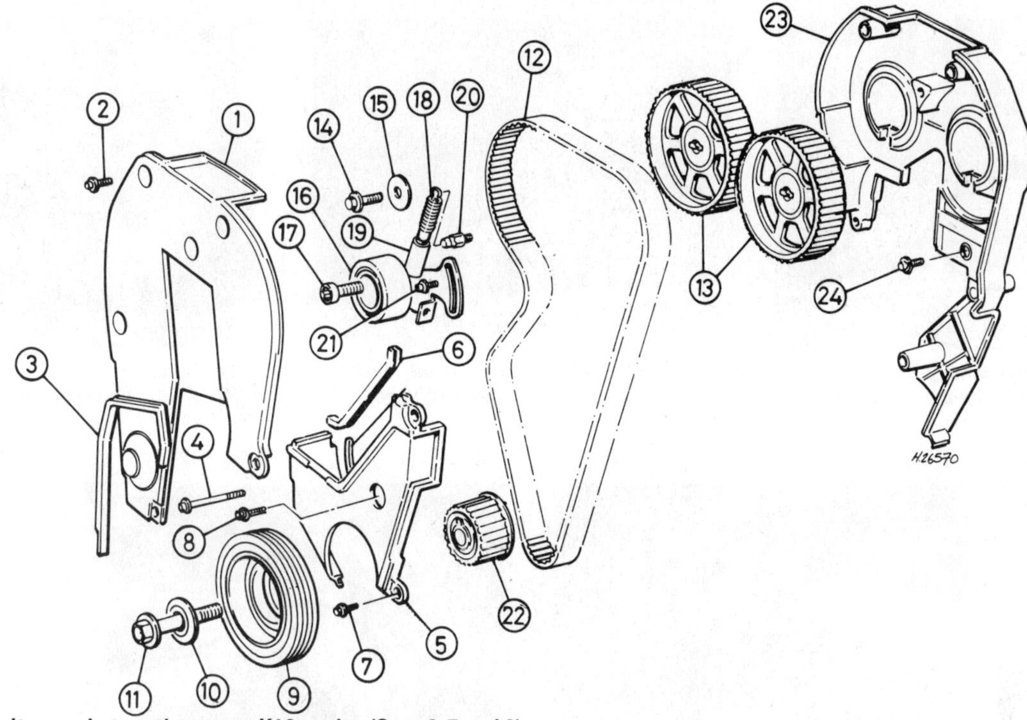

Fig. 2.5 Timing belt, sprockets and covers – K16 engine (Secs 6, 7 and 8)

1 *Timing belt upper right-hand (outer) cover*
2 *Bolt*
3 *Seal*
4 *Bolt*
5 *Timing belt lower cover*
6 *Seal*
7 *Bolt*
8 *Bolt*
9 *Crankshaft pulley*
10 *Washer*
11 *Crankshaft pulley bolt*
12 *Timing belt*
13 *Camshaft sprockets*
14 *Bolt*
15 *Washer*
16 *Timing belt tensioner pulley assembly*
17 *Tensioner pulley Allen screw*
18 *Tensioner pulley spring*
19 *Sleeve*
20 *Pillar bolt*
21 *Tensioner backplate clamp bolt*
22 *Crankshaft sprocket*
23 *Timing belt upper left-hand (inner) cover*
24 *Bolt*

7.6 Crankshaft pulley mark aligned with timing belt lower cover mark at 90° BTDC

7.7 Camshaft sprocket marks 'A' aligned with timing belt upper left-hand (inner) cover mark 'B' – K16 engine

7.11 Removing engine/transmission right-hand mounting bracket – K8 engine

14 Check the timing belt carefully for any signs of uneven wear, splitting or oil contamination and renew it if there is the slightest doubt about its condition. If the engine is undergoing an overhaul and has covered more than 48 000 miles (80 000 km) since the original belt was fitted, renew the belt as a matter of course, regardless of its apparent condition. If signs of oil contamination are found, trace the source of the oil leak and rectify it, then wash down the engine timing belt area and all related components to remove all traces of oil.

Refitting

15 On reassembly, thoroughly clean the timing belt sprockets and check that they are aligned as follows (photos):

(a) *Camshaft sprocket – K8 engine – the 'EX' line and the mark stamped on the sprocket rim must be at the front (looking at the sprocket from the right-hand side of the car) and aligned exactly with the cylinder head top surface.*

(b) *Camshaft sprockets – K16 engine – both 'EXHAUST' arrow marks must point to the rear (looking at the sprockets from the right-hand side of the car) with the 'IN' lines and the sprocket rim marks aligned exactly with the line on the timing belt upper left-hand/inner cover (representing the cylinder head top surface); see photo 7.7.*

(c) *Crankshaft sprocket – the two dots must be positioned on each side of the raised rib on the oil pump body.*

It is most important that these marks are aligned exactly as this sets the valve timing, but note that in this position numbers 1 and 4 cylinders are at 90° BTDC so that there is no risk of the valves contacting the pistons during dismantling and reassembly.

16 Fit the timing belt over the crankshaft and camshaft sprockets,

7.12 Timing belt tensioner pulley Allen bolt 'A', tensioner backplate clamp bolt 'B'

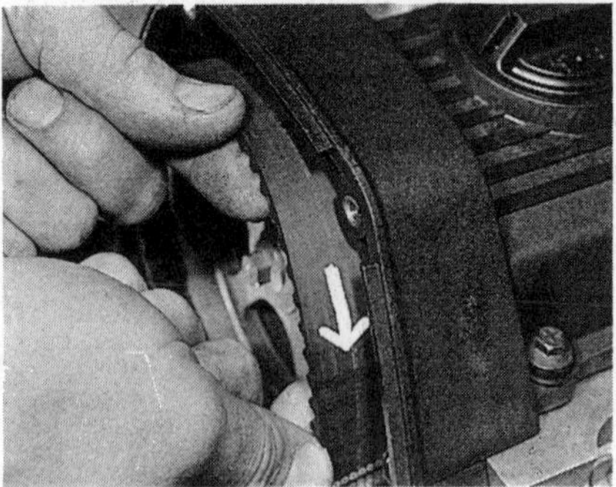

7.13 If timing belt is to be re-used, mark direction of rotation as shown before removal

7.15A Camshaft sprocket marks 'A' aligned with cylinder head top surface 'B' - K8 engine

7.15B Crankshaft sprocket dots 'A' aligned on each side of oil pump raised rib 'B'

7.16 Refitting the timing belt - K16 engine

ensuring that the belt front run (and, on K16 engines, the top run) is taut ie, all slack is on the tensioner pulley side of the belt, then over the water pump sprocket and tensioner pulley. Do not twist the belt sharply while refitting it, ensure that the belt teeth are correctly seated centrally in the sprockets and that the timing marks remain in alignment (photo). If a used belt is being refitted, ensure that the arrow mark made on removal points in the normal direction of rotation as before.

17 Slacken the tensioner backplate clamp bolt and check that the tensioner pulley moves to tension the belt; if the tensioner assembly is not free to move under spring tension, rectify the fault or the timing belt will not be correctly tensioned.

18 On K16 engines remove the camshaft sprocket locking tool.

19 On K8 engines refit the engine/transmission right-hand mounting bracket, tightening its bolts to the specified torque wrench setting.

20 On all engines, refit the timing belt lower cover and the crankshaft pulley as described in Sections 6 and 5 of this Chapter.

21 Using a suitable spanner or socket, rotate the crankshaft two full turns clockwise to settle and tension the belt. Realign the crankshaft pulley (90° BTDC) mark and check that the sprocket timing mark(s) are still correctly aligned.

22 If all is well, first tighten the tensioner pulley backplate clamp bolt to the specified torque, then tighten the tensioner pulley Allen screw to the specified torque.

23 Reassemble the engine/transmission right-hand mounting, ensuring that the rubber washers are correctly located, and tighten the mounting nuts and bolts to their specified torque settings. Remove the jack from underneath the engine unit.

24 Refit the front undercover panel and roadwheel, then lower the car to the ground.

25 Refit the timing belt upper right-hand (outer) cover as described in Section 6.

26 Where necessary, refit the power steering fluid reservoir to the mounting bracket and secure the hydraulic hose clamps in position with the retaining bolts.

27 Refit the coolant expansion tank and tighten the mounting bolts securely. Secure the coolant hose in position with any necessary retaining clips and reconnect the battery negative lead.

Adjustment - general

28 As the timing belt is a 'fit-and-forget' type, the manufacturer states that tensioning need be carried out only after a new belt has been fitted (although tensioning is obviously required if the existing belt has been disturbed for other servicing/overhaul work); no re-tensioning is recommended once a belt has been fitted and therefore this operation is not included in the manufacturer's maintenance schedule.

29 If the timing belt is thought to be incorrectly tensioned, adjust the tension as described in paragraphs 1 to 7, 17, 21, 22 and 24 to 27 above.

30 If the timing belt has been disturbed, adjust its tension following the same procedure, omitting as appropriate the irrelevant preliminary dismantling/reassembly steps.

8 Timing belt tensioner and sprockets - removal, inspection and refitting

Note: *This Section describes as individual operations the removal and refitting of the components concerned - if more than one of them are to be removed at the same time, start by removing the timing belt as described in Section 7, then remove the actual component as described below, ignoring the preliminary dismantling steps.*

Removal

1 Disconnect the battery negative lead.

2 To improve access to the timing belt components, remove the three expansion tank mounting bolts then free the coolant hose from any relevant retaining clips and position the tank clear of the engine. On models equipped with power-assisted steering, undo all the power steering hose retaining clip bolts then slide the fluid reservoir out of its retaining clip and position it clear of the timing belt covers. Take great care not to place any undue strain on the coolant/hydraulic hoses and mop up any spilt coolant/hydraulic fluid immediately (as applicable).

3 Remove the timing belt upper right-hand (outer) cover as described in Section 6.

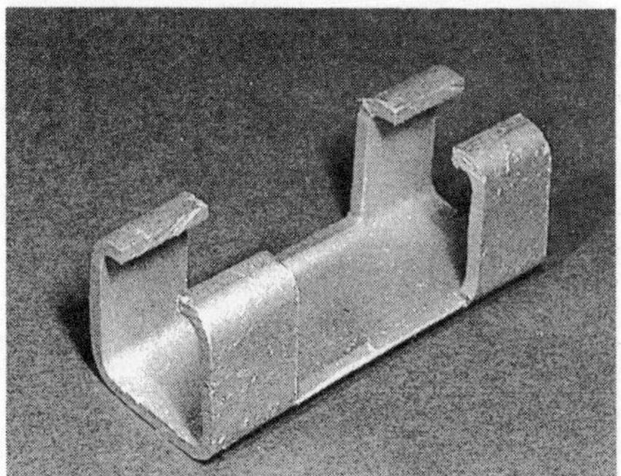
8.11A K16 engine camshaft locking tool cut from steel tube...

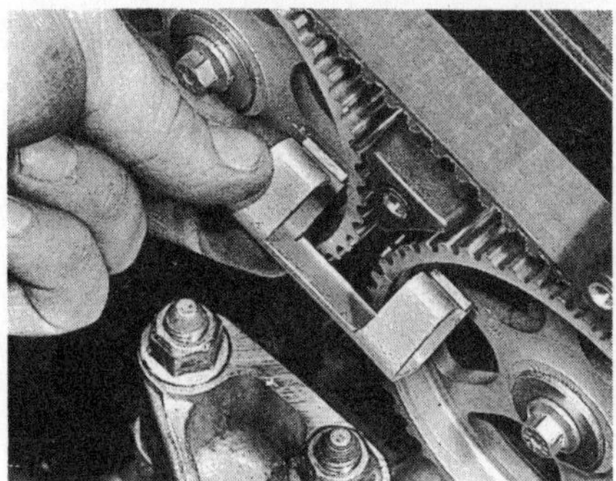
8.11B ...to fit sprocket spokes as closely as possible, as shown

8.12 Removing camshaft sprocket - K8 engine - note roll pin (arrowed)

4 Apply the handbrake then jack up the front of the vehicle and support it on axle stands. Remove the right-hand roadwheel.
5 From underneath the front of the vehicle, slacken and remove the three bolts securing the bumper flange to the body. Remove the seven bolts securing the front undercover panel to the body and remove the panel.
6 Using a suitable spanner or socket on the crankshaft pulley bolt, rotate the crankshaft in a clockwise direction until the long white-painted mark on the crankshaft pulley's outboard (right-hand) face is aligned with the single, separate mark on the timing belt lower cover so that the crankshaft is in the 90° BTDC position (see Chapter 1, *Ignition timing check and adjustment*, for full details of the pulley/cover marks).
7 Check that the camshaft sprocket mark(s) align as described in Section 7, paragraph 15 then proceed as described under the relevant sub heading.

Camshaft sprocket(s)

8 Slacken through half a turn each the timing belt tensioner pulley Allen screw and the tensioner backplate clamp bolt, push the pulley assembly down to release all the tension from the timing belt, then re-tighten the backplate clamp bolt securely.
9 Remove the belt from the camshaft sprocket(s), taking care not to twist it too sharply; use the fingers only to handle the belt. **Do not** rotate the crankshaft until the timing belt is refitted.
10 On K8 engines, slacken the camshaft sprocket retaining bolt and remove it, along with its washer. To prevent the camshaft from rotating, use Rover service tool 18G 1521 to retain the sprocket. If this is not available an acceptable substitute can be fabricated from two lengths of steel strip (one long, the other short) and three nuts and bolts; one nut and bolt forming the pivot of a forked tool with the remaining two nuts and bolts at the tips of the 'forks' to engage with the sprocket spokes as shown in photo 8.23A.
11 On K16 engines, unscrew the appropriate camshaft sprocket retaining bolt and remove it, along with its washer. To prevent a camshaft from rotating, lock together both sprockets using Rover service tool 18G 1570; this is a metal sprag shaped on both sides to fit the sprocket teeth and is inserted between the sprockets. If this tool is not available an acceptable substitute can be cut from a length of steel tube or similar to fit as closely as possible around the sprocket spokes (photos). If both sprockets are to be removed, it is good practice to mark them (inlet or exhaust) so that they can be returned to their original locations on reassembly.
12 On all engines, remove the sprocket(s) from the camshaft end(s), noting the locating roll pin(s) (photo). If a roll pin is a loose fit in the camshaft end, remove it and store it with the sprocket for safe-keeping.

Crankshaft sprocket

13 On K16 engines use the tool described in paragraph 11 above to lock together the camshaft sprockets so that they cannot move under valve spring pressure when the timing belt is removed.
14 Remove the crankshaft pulley and timing belt lower cover as described in Sections 5 and 6 of this Chapter.
15 Slacken through half a turn each the timing belt tensioner pulley Allen screw and the tensioner backplate clamp bolt, push the pulley assembly down to release all the tension from the timing belt, then re-tighten the backplate clamp bolt securely.
16 Work the belt clear of the crankshaft sprocket, taking care not to twist it too sharply; use the fingers only to handle the belt. **Do not** rotate the crankshaft until the timing belt is refitted.
17 Remove the sprocket from the crankshaft.

Tensioner assembly

18 On K16 engines use the tool described in paragraph 11 above to lock together the camshaft sprockets so that they cannot move under valve spring pressure when the timing belt is removed.
19 Using a suitable pair of pliers, unhook the tensioner spring from the pillar bolt. Unscrew the tensioner pulley Allen screw and the tensioner backplate clamp bolt then withdraw the tensioner assembly from the engine unit. **Do not** rotate the crankshaft until the timing belt is re-tensioned.

Inspection

20 Clean thoroughly the camshaft/crankshaft sprockets and renew any that show signs of wear, damage or cracks.
21 Clean the tensioner assembly but do not use any strong solvent which may enter the pulley bearing. Check that the pulley rotates freely on the backplate, with no sign of stiffness or of free play. Renew the assembly if there is any doubt about its condition or if there are any obvious signs of wear or damage; the same applies to the tensioner spring, which should be checked with great care as its condition is critical for the correct tensioning of the timing belt.

Refitting

Camshaft sprocket(s)

22 If removed, refit the roll pin to the camshaft end, ensuring that its split is facing the centre of the camshaft, then refit the sprocket so that the timing marks are facing outwards (to the right). On K16 engines ensure that the appropriate sprocket keyway engages with the camshaft locating pin (ie, if refitting the inlet camshaft sprocket, engage its 'IN' keyway with the roll pin and so on) then refit the sprocket retaining bolt and washer (photo). Where necessary, repeat the procedure for the second sprocket.
23 Prevent the sprocket(s) from rotating using the method employed on removal and tighten the sprocket retaining bolt(s) to the specified torque setting. Check that the sprocket timing marks align as described in Section 7, paragraph 15 (photos).
24 Fit the timing belt over the camshaft sprockets, ensuring that the belt front run (and, on K16 engines, the top run) is taut ie, all slack is on the tensioner pulley side of the belt. Do not twist the belt sharply while refitting it and ensure that the belt teeth are correctly seated centrally in the sprockets and that the timing marks remain in alignment.
25 Slacken the tensioner backplate clamp bolt and check that the tensioner pulley moves to tension the belt; if the tensioner assembly is not free to move under spring tension, rectify the fault or the timing belt will not be correctly tensioned.
26 On K16 engines remove the camshaft sprocket locking tool.
27 Using a suitable spanner or socket, rotate the crankshaft two full turns clockwise to settle and tension the belt. Realign the crankshaft pulley (90° BTDC) mark and check that the sprocket timing mark(s) are still correctly aligned.

8.22 K16 engine camshaft sprockets have two keyways - engage 'EX' keyway with exhaust camshaft roll pin, 'IN' keyway with inlet camshaft roll pin

8.23A On K8 engines use fabricated tool shown to hold pulley while bolt is tightened to the specified torque

8.23B On K16 engines lock camshafts with fabricated tool while sprocket bolt is tightened to the specified torque

28 If all is well, first tighten the tensioner pulley backplate clamp bolt to the specified torque, then tighten the tensioner pulley Allen screw to the specified torque.
29 Refit the front undercover panel and roadwheel, then lower the car to the ground.
30 Refit the timing belt upper right-hand (outer) cover as described in Section 6.
31 Where necessary, refit the power steering fluid reservoir to the mounting bracket and secure the hydraulic hose clamps in position with the retaining bolts.
32 Refit the coolant expansion tank and tighten the mounting bolts securely. Secure the coolant hose in position with any necessary retaining clips and reconnect the battery negative lead.

Crankshaft sprocket

33 Refit the sprocket to the crankshaft so that it locates correctly on the crankshaft's flattened section, noting that the sprocket flange must be innermost so that the two timing marks are on the outside (right-hand side) of the sprocket. Check that the sprocket timing marks align as described in Section 7, paragraph 15.
34 Fit the timing belt over the crankshaft sprocket, ensuring that the belt front run (and, on K16 engines, the top run) is taut, ie, all slack is on the tensioner pulley side of the belt. Do not twist the belt sharply while refitting it and ensure that the belt teeth are correctly seated centrally in the sprockets and that the timing marks remain in alignment.
35 Slacken the tensioner backplate clamp bolt and check that the tensioner pulley moves to tension the belt; if the tensioner assembly is not free to move under spring tension, rectify the fault or the timing belt will not be correctly tensioned.
36 On K16 engines remove the camshaft sprocket locking tool.
37 Refit the lower timing belt cover and the crankshaft pulley as described in Sections 6 and 5 of this Chapter.
38 Carry out the operations described above in paragraphs 27 to 32.

Tensioner pulley

39 Refit the tensioner pulley assembly and tighten the pulley Allen screw and the backplate clamp bolt lightly. Hook the tensioner spring over the pillar bolt and check that the tensioner is free to move under spring tension and that the pulley bears correctly against the timing belt (photo).
40 On K16 engines remove the camshaft sprocket locking tool.
41 Carry out the operations described above in paragraphs 27 to 32.

8.39 Ensure timing belt tensioner spring is correctly hooked onto pillar bolt

9 Camshaft oil seal(s) - renewal

Note: *If a right-hand oil seal is to be renewed with the timing belt still in place, check that the belt is free from oil contamination (renew the belt as a matter of course if signs of oil contamination are found; see Section 7), then cover the belt to protect it from contamination by oil while work is in progress and ensure that all traces of oil are removed from the area before the belt is refitted.*

Right-hand seal(s)

1 Remove the camshaft sprocket(s) as described in Section 8.
2 Punch or drill two small holes opposite each other in the oil seal. Screw a self-tapping screw into each and pull on the screws with pliers to extract the seal.
3 Clean the seal housing and polish off any burrs or raised edges which may have caused the seal to fail in the first place.
4 Lubricate the lips of the new seal with clean engine oil and drive it into position until it seats on its locating shoulder, using a suitable tubular drift, such as a socket, which bears only on the hard outer edge of the seal (photo). Take care not to damage the seal lips during fitting. Note that the seal lips should face inwards.
5 Refit the camshaft sprocket as described in Section 8.

Left-hand seals - K16 engines

6 Disconnect the battery negative lead.
7 To reach the inlet camshaft seal, remove the distributor as described in Chapter 5.
8 To reach the exhaust camshaft seal, unfasten the rubber strap securing the air intake duct to its support bracket, disconnect the vacuum pipe from the air temperature control valve and unclip the pipe from the support bracket. Undo the bracket's retaining bolts and remove the bracket from the cylinder head (photo).
9 Remove the old seal and install the new one as described above in paragraphs 2 to 4.
10 On the inlet camshaft, refit the distributor as described in Chapter 5.

9.4 Fitting a new camshaft right-hand oil seal – K16 engine

9.8 On K16 engine remove air intake duct support bracket to reach exhaust camshaft left-hand oil seal

11 On the exhaust camshaft, refit the air intake duct support bracket, tightening its screws to the specified torque wrench setting, then reconnect and secure the air temperature control valve vacuum pipe and refit the rubber strap to secure the air intake duct.

12 Connect the battery negative lead.

10 Camshaft(s) and hydraulic tappets – removal, inspection and refitting

Note: *Prior to removing camshaft(s) obtain the Rover sealant kit LVV 10002 which also contains a plastic scraper. If difficulty is experienced with removal of hardened sealant from mating surfaces it may also be necessary to use a foam action gasket remover. Carefully read the instructions supplied with the sealant kit, and take care not to allow the sealant to contact the fingers as it will bond human skin.*

Removal

K8 engines

1 Remove the cylinder head cover as described in Section 4.

2 Remove the distributor as described in Chapter 5.

3 Remove the camshaft sprocket as described in Section 8.

4 Carefully prise up the oil feed tube away from the camshaft bearing caps and remove it from the head assembly. Remove the O-rings from the oil rail and discard them; they must be renewed as a matter of course whenever they are disturbed.

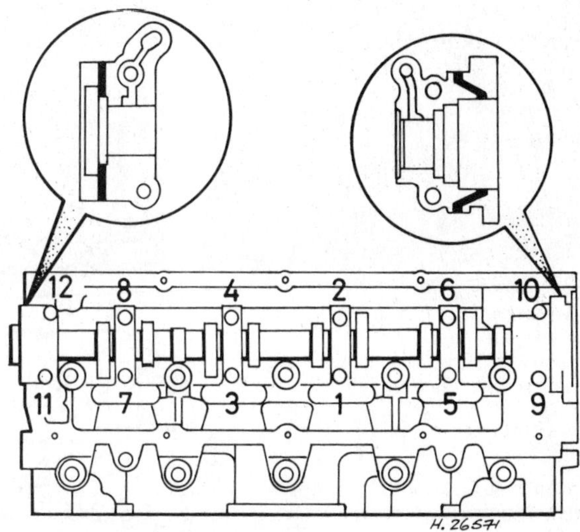

Fig. 2.6 Camshaft bearing cap bolt tightening sequence – K8 engine (Sec 10)

Note: *Apply thin bead of sealant to end bearing cap mating surfaces along paths shown by heavy black lines*

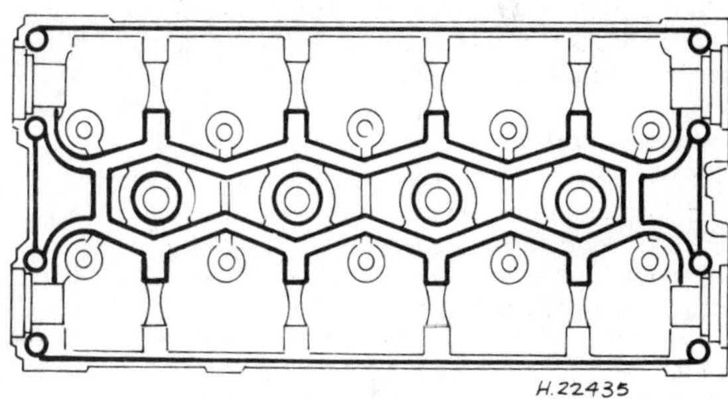

Fig. 2.7 Apply thin bead of sealant to camshaft carrier mating surfaces along paths shown by heavy black lines – K16 engine (Sec 10)

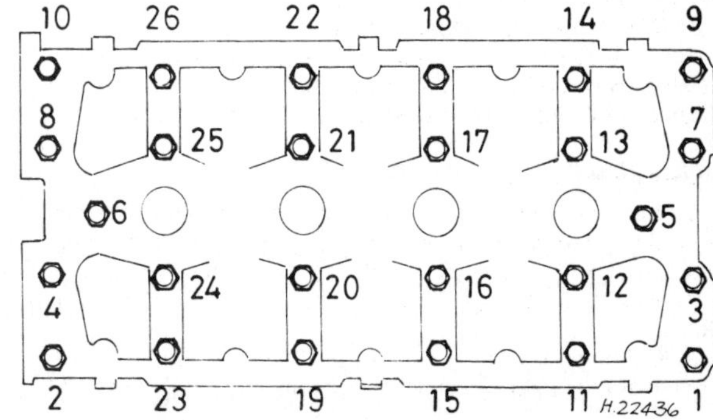

Fig. 2.8 Camshaft carrier bolt tightening sequence – K16 engine (Sec 10)

5 The camshaft right- and left-hand end bearing caps are noticeably different and cannot be confused; the intermediate bearing caps (which are all similar) are marked by the manufacturer with a number (1, 2, 3, or 4) stamped in the boss next to the oil feed hole. Before unbolting any of the caps, make written notes to ensure that each can be easily identified and refitted in its original location.

Fig. 2.9 Top end components – K8 engine (Secs 10 and 11)

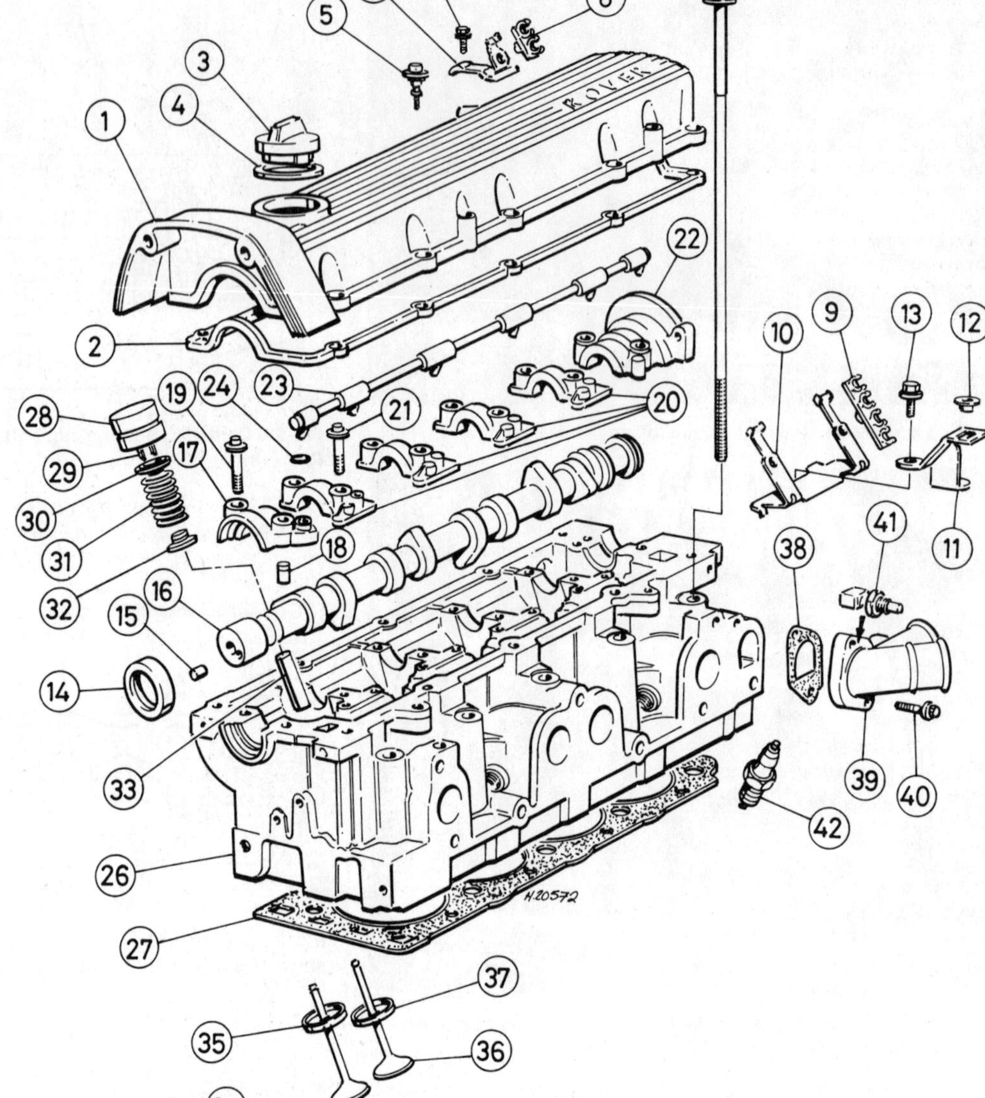

1 *Cylinder head cover*
2 *Seal*
3 *Engine oil filler cap*
4 *Seal*
5 *Bolt*
6 *HT lead retaining clip bracket*
7 *Screw*
8 *HT lead retaining clip*
9 *HT lead retaining clip*
10 *HT lead retaining clip bracket*
11 *Air intake duct support bracket*
12 *Fastener insert*
13 *Bolt*
14 *Oil seal*
15 *Roll pin*
16 *Camshaft*
17 *Camshaft right-hand bearing cap **
18 *Dowel*
19 *Bolt*
20 *Camshaft intermediate bearing cap **
21 *Bolt*
22 *Camshaft left-hand bearing cap **
23 *Oil feed tube*
24 *O-ring*
25 *Cylinder head bolt*
26 *Cylinder head*
27 *Cylinder head gasket*
28 *Hydraulic tappet*
29 *Split collets*
30 *Spring retainer*
31 *Valve spring*
32 *Valve stem seal/spring lower seat*
33 *Valve guide*
34 *Inlet valve*
35 *Valve seat insert*
36 *Exhaust valve*
37 *Valve seat insert*
38 *Gasket*
39 *Coolant outlet elbow*
40 *Bolt*
41 *Coolant temperature gauge sender unit*
42 *Spark plug*

* **Note:** *Camshaft bearing caps shown for reference only – not available separately from cylinder head*

6 Working in the **reverse** of the sequence shown in Fig. 2.6, slacken the camshaft bearing cap bolts progressively, and by one turn at a time. Work only as described to release the pressure of the valve springs on the bearing caps gradually and evenly.

7 Withdraw the bearing caps, noting the presence of the locating dowels on the end caps, then remove the camshaft and withdraw the oil seal.

8 Obtain eight small, clean plastic containers and number them 1 to 8. Using a rubber sucker, withdraw each hydraulic tappet in turn, invert it to prevent oil loss and place it in its respective container, which should then be filled with clean engine oil. Do not interchange the hydraulic tappets or the rate of wear will be much increased and do not allow them to lose oil or they will take a long time to refill with oil on restarting the engine, resulting in incorrect valve clearances.

K16 engines

9 Remove both the camshaft sprockets as described in Section 8, then unscrew the inner cover's upper retaining bolts (see Section 6 and photos for details) so that the cover can be pulled away from the cylinder head just far enough for adequate working clearance; take care not to distort or damage the cover or the timing belt (photo).

10 Remove the cylinder head cover as described in Section 4.

11 Remove the distributor as described in Chapter 5.

12 Unclip the air temperature control valve vacuum pipe from the air intake duct support bracket, then unbolt the bracket from the cylinder head.

13 Working in the **reverse** of the sequence shown in Fig. 2.8, evenly and progressively slacken the camshaft carrier bolts by one turn at a time. Once all valve spring pressure has been relieved, remove the bolts.

14 Withdraw the camshaft carrier, noting the presence of the locating dowels, then remove the camshafts and slide off the oil seals. The inlet camshaft can be identified by the distributor rotor arm drive spindle (or its location); therefore there is no need to mark the camshafts.

15 Obtain sixteen small, clean plastic containers and number them 1 to 16. Using a rubber sucker, withdraw each hydraulic tappet in turn, invert it to prevent oil loss and place it in its respective container, which should then be filled with clean engine oil. Do not interchange the hydraulic tappets or the rate of wear will be much increased and do not

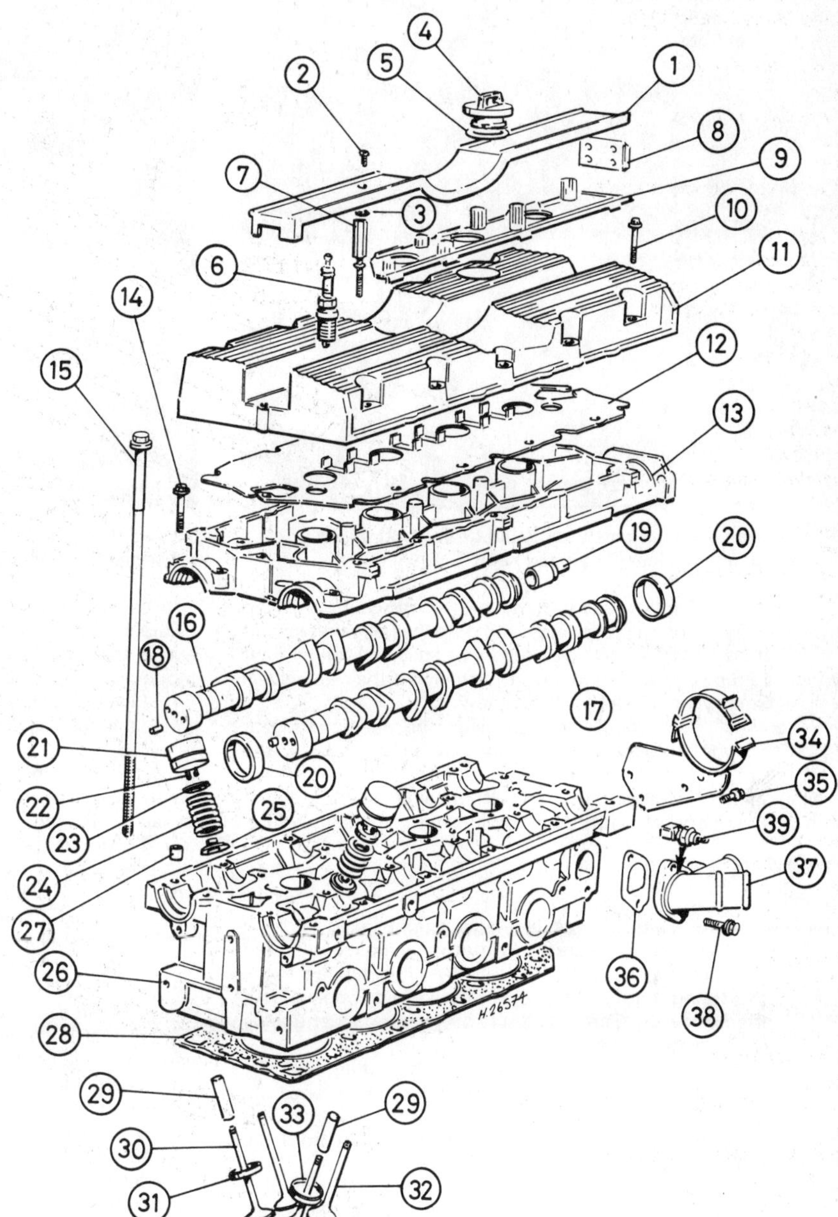

Fig. 2.10 Top end components – K16 engines (Secs 10 and 11)

1 *Spark plug cover*
2 *Screw*
3 *Retaining washer*
4 *Engine oil filler cap*
5 *Seal*
6 *Spark plug*
7 *Pillar bolt*
8 *HT lead grommet*
9 *HT lead clip plate*
10 *Bolt*
11 *Cylinder head cover*
12 *Gasket*
13 *Camshaft carrier **
14 *Bolt*
15 *Cylinder head bolt*
16 *Inlet camshaft*
17 *Exhaust camshaft*
18 *Roll pin*
19 *Rotor arm drive spindle*
20 *Oil seal*
21 *Hydraulic tappet*
22 *Split collets*
23 *Spring retainer*
24 *Valve spring*
25 *Valve stem seal/spring lower seat*
26 *Cylinder head*
27 *Dowel*
28 *Cylinder head gasket*
29 *Valve guide*
30 *Inlet valves*
31 *Valve seat insert*
32 *Exhaust valves*
33 *Valve seat insert*
34 *Air intake duct support bracket*
35 *Bolt*
36 *Gasket*
37 *Coolant outlet elbow*
38 *Bolt*
39 *Coolant temperature gauge sender unit*

* **Note:** *Camshaft carrier shown for reference only – not available separately from cylinder head*

allow them to lose oil or they will take a long time to refill with oil on restarting the engine, resulting in incorrect valve clearances.

Inspection

16 Remove the camshaft(s) and tappets for inspection as described above in the relevant sub-section.

17 With the hydraulic tappets removed, check each for signs of obvious wear (scoring, pitting, etc.) and for ovality; renew if necessary.

18 If the engine's valve clearances have sounded noisy, particularly if the noise persists after initial start-up from cold, there is reason to suspect a faulty hydraulic tappet. Only a good mechanic experienced in these engines can tell whether the noise level is typical, or if renewal is warranted of one or more of the tappets. If faulty tappets are diagnosed and the engine's service history is unknown, it is always worth trying the effect of renewing the engine oil and filter, using **only** good quality engine oil of the recommended viscosity and specification (Chapter 1), before going to the expense of renewing any of the tappets. If any tappet's operation is faulty, it must be renewed.

19 Carefully remove all traces of old sealant from the mating surfaces of the bearing caps or camshaft carrier and cylinder head (see Figs. 2.6 and 2.7) using the plastic scraper supplied with the sealant kit. Examine the camshaft bearing journals and the cylinder head bearing surfaces for signs of obvious wear or pitting. If any such signs are evident, renew the component concerned.

20 To check the bearing journal running clearance, remove the hydraulic tappets, clean carefully the bearing surfaces and refit the camshaft(s) and carrier/bearing caps with a strand of Plastigage (see Section 34 for instructions on usage) across each journal. Tighten the carrier/bearing cap bolts to the specified torque wrench setting whilst taking great care not to rotate the camshaft(s), then remove the carrier/bearing caps and use the scale provided with the Plastigage kit to measure the width of each compressed strand.

21 If the running clearance of any bearing is found to be worn to the specified service limit or beyond, fit a new camshaft and repeat the check; if the clearance is still excessive the cylinder head must be renewed.

22 To check camshaft endfloat, remove the hydraulic tappets, clean carefully the bearing surfaces and refit the camshaft(s) and carrier/bearing caps. Tighten to the specified torque wrench setting the carrier/bearing cap bolts, then measure the endfloat using a DTI (Dial Test Indicator, or dial gauge) mounted on the cylinder head so that its tip bears on the camshaft right-hand end.

10.9 On K16 engine secure partly-removed timing belt upper left-hand (inner) cover clear of cylinder head

10.34 K16 engine camshaft roll pin locations at TDC position (for refitting camshaft carrier)

23 Tap the camshaft fully towards the gauge, zero the gauge, then tap the camshaft fully away from the gauge and note the gauge reading. If the endfloat measured is found to be worn to the specified service limit or beyond, fit a new camshaft and repeat the check; if the clearance is still excessive the cylinder head must be renewed.
24 The camshaft itself should show no signs of marks, pitting or scoring on the lobe surfaces; if such marks are evident, renew the camshaft.
25 If a camshaft is renewed, extract the roll pin from the old one and fit the pin to the new camshaft with its split towards the camshaft's centre.

Refitting

K8 engines

26 Liberally oil the cylinder head hydraulic tappet bores and the tappets. Note that if new tappets are being fitted, they must be charged with clean engine oil before installation. Carefully refit the tappets to the cylinder head, ensuring that each tappet is refitted to its original bore and is the correct way up. Some care will be required to enter the tappets squarely into their bores.
27 Liberally oil the camshaft bearings and lobes then refit the camshaft. Position the shaft so that its number 1 cylinder lobes are pointing away from their valves and the roll pin in the camshaft's right-hand end is in the 4 o'clock position when viewed from the right-hand end of the engine.
28 Ensure that the locating dowels are pressed firmly into their recesses, check that the mating surfaces are completely clean, unmarked and free from oil, then apply a thin bead of the special Rover sealant to the mating surfaces of the front and rear bearing caps as shown in Fig. 2.6. Carefully follow the instructions supplied with the sealant kit. Refit the bearing caps, using the notes made on removal to ensure that each is installed correctly and in its original location.
29 Working in the sequence shown in Fig. 2.6, progressively tighten the camshaft bearing cap bolts by one turn at a time until the caps touch the cylinder head evenly, then go round again, working in the same sequence, and tighten all the bolts to the specified torque setting. Work only as described to impose the pressure of the valve springs gradually and evenly on the bearing caps. Wipe off all surplus sealant so that none is left to find its way into any oilways.
30 Squirt clean engine oil into each camshaft bearing cap oil hole and fit new sealing O-rings to each of the oil feed tube stubs. Refit the oil feed tube to the cylinder head and press it firmly into position in the camshaft bearing caps.
31 Fit a new camshaft oil seal as described in Section 9, then refit the cylinder head cover and camshaft sprocket as described in Sections 4 and 8 of this Chapter.
32 Refit the distributor as described in Chapter 5.

K16 engines

33 Liberally oil the cylinder head hydraulic tappet bores and the tappets. Note that if new tappets are being fitted, they must be charged with clean engine oil before installation. Carefully refit the tappets to the cylinder head, ensuring that each tappet is refitted to its original bore and is the correct way up. Some care will be required to enter the tappets squarely into their bores.
34 Liberally oil the camshaft bearings and lobes and refit them to the cylinder head. Position each shaft so that its number 1 cylinder lobes are pointing away from their valves. With the shafts in this position, the roll pin in the inlet camshaft's right-hand end will be in the 4 o'clock position when viewed from the right-hand end of the engine, while that of the exhaust camshaft will be in the 8 o'clock position (photo).
35 Ensure that the locating dowels are pressed firmly into their recesses, check that the mating surfaces are completely clean, unmarked and free from oil, then apply a thin bead of the special Rover sealant to the mating surfaces of the camshaft carrier as shown in Fig. 2.7. Carefully follow the instructions supplied with the sealing kit. Refit the carrier.
36 Working in the sequence shown in Fig. 2.8, progressively tighten the camshaft carrier bolts by one turn at a time until the carrier touches the cylinder head evenly, then go round again, working in the same sequence, and tighten all the bolts to the specified torque setting. Work only as described to impose the pressure of the valve springs gradually and evenly on the carrier. Wipe off all surplus sealant so that none is left to find its way into any oilways.
37 Fit new camshaft oil seals as described in Section 9, then refit the cylinder head cover, inner timing cover retaining bolts and camshaft sprockets as described in Sections 4, 6 and 8 of this Chapter.
38 Refit the distributor as described in Chapter 5.
39 Refit the air intake duct support bracket, tightening its screws to their specified torque wrench setting, then reconnect and secure the air temperature control valve vacuum pipe and refit the rubber strap to secure the air intake duct.

11 Cylinder head - removal and refitting

Note: *Due to the design of the engine, it will become very difficult, almost impossible, to turn the crankshaft once the cylinder head bolts have been slackened. The manufacturer accordingly states that the crankshaft will be 'tight' and should not be rotated more than absolutely necessary once the head has been removed; if the crankshaft cannot be rotated, it must be removed for overhaul work to proceed. With this in mind, during any servicing or overhaul work the crankshaft always must be rotated to the desired position before the bolts are disturbed.*

Removal

1 Disconnect the battery negative lead.
2 Drain the cooling system as described in Chapter 1.
3 Remove the camshaft sprocket(s) as described in Section 8.
4 Unscrew the bolts securing the timing belt upper left-hand (inner)

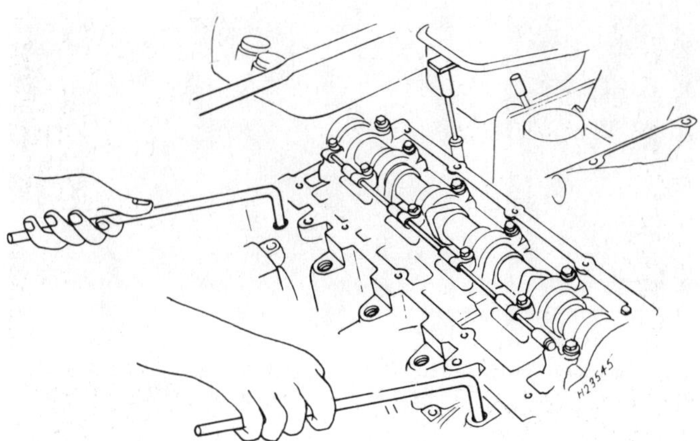

Fig. 2.11 Using two cranked bars to break the cylinder head joint by rocking (Sec 11)

cover to the cylinder head so that the cover can be pulled away from the cylinder head just far enough for adequate working clearance; take care not to distort or damage the cover or the timing belt. Refer to Section 6 for further information.

5 Remove the cylinder head cover as described in Section 4.

6 Working as described in Chapter 4, disconnect the exhaust system front pipe from the manifold and, where fitted, disconnect or release the lambda sensor wiring so that it is not strained by the weight of the exhaust.

7 Note that the following text assumes that the cylinder head will be removed with both inlet and exhaust manifolds attached; this is easier, but makes it a bulky and heavy assembly to handle. If it is wished first to remove the manifolds, proceed as described in the relevant Sections of Chapter 4.

8 On carburettor engines, disconnect the following from the carburettor and inlet manifold as described in the relevant sections of Chapter 4:

- *(a) Fuel pump feed hose (plug both openings to prevent loss of fuel and the entry of dirt into the system).*
- *(b) Carburettor idle bypass solenoid wires.*
- *(c) Accelerator cable.*
- *(d) Choke cable.*
- *(e) Vacuum servo unit vacuum hose.*
- *(f) Inlet manifold PTC heater wire.*
- *(g) Inlet manifold heater temperature switch wiring.*

9 On fuel-injected engines, carry out the following operations as described in the relevant sections of Chapter 4:

- *(a) Depressurise the fuel system and disconnect the fuel feed and return hoses from the throttle body pipes – plug both openings of each pipe to prevent loss of fuel and the entry of dirt into the system.*
- *(b) Disconnect the accelerator cable.*
- *(c) Disconnect the three electrical connector plugs from the throttle body.*
- *(d) Disconnect the vacuum servo unit vacuum hose from the inlet manifold; discard the sealing washers.*
- *(e) Disconnect the inlet manifold PTC heater wire.*
- *(f) Disconnect the inlet manifold coolant temperature sensor connector plug.*

10 Working as described in the relevant Sections of Chapter 3, disconnect the connector plug from the coolant temperature sensor screwed into the coolant outlet elbow, then disconnect the coolant hoses from the (three) inlet manifold unions and from the coolant outlet elbow.

11 Unclip the engine wiring harness from the inlet manifold or its support stays, slacken the bolts securing the stays to the manifold, then unbolt the support stays and the carburettor metal overflow pipes from the cylinder block/crankcase.

12 Working as described in Chapter 1, remove the distributor cap complete with the spark plug HT leads, and spark plugs.

13 On K16 engines which are equipped with air conditioning, undo the nuts and bolts securing the heat shields to the rear of the alternator and air conditioning compressor and remove both heat shields. Slacken the two lower alternator mounting bolts then remove the upper mounting bolt and pivot the alternator away from the cylinder head.

14 Working in the **reverse** of the sequence shown in photo 11.29A (K8 engines) or 11.29B (K16 engines), progressively slacken the ten cylinder head bolts by one turn at a time; a female Torx-type socket (No. 12 size) will be required. Remove each bolt in turn and store it in its correct fitted order by pushing it through a clearly-marked cardboard template.

15 The joint between the cylinder head and gasket and the cylinder block/crankcase must now be broken without disturbing the wet liners; although these liners are better located and sealed than some wet liner engines, there is still a risk of coolant and foreign matter leaking into the sump if the cylinder head is lifted carelessly. If care is not taken and the liners are moved, there is also a possibility of the bottom seals being disturbed, causing leakage after refitting the head.

16 To break the joint, obtain two L-shaped metal bars which fit into the cylinder head bolt holes and gently 'rock' the cylinder head free towards the front of the car; see Fig. 2.11. Do not try to swivel the head on the cylinder block/crankcase; it is located by dowels as well as by the tops of the liners.

17 When the joint is broken lift the cylinder head away; use assistance if possible as it is a heavy assembly, especially if it is complete with the manifolds. Remove the gasket, noting the two locating dowels, and discard it.

18 Note that, further to the warnings given in the note at the beginning of this Section, **do not** attempt to rotate the crankshaft with the cylinder head removed, otherwise the wet liners may be displaced. Operations that would normally require the rotation of the crankshaft (eg cleaning the piston crowns), must be carried out with great care to ensure that no particles of dirt or foreign matter are left behind. If cylinder liner clamps are to be used, they must be clamped in place using spacers fitted under the heads of the cylinder head bolts.

19 If the cylinder head is to be dismantled, remove the camshaft(s) as described in Section 10, then refer to the relevant Sections of Part B of this Chapter.

Refitting

20 Check the condition of the cylinder head bolts and particularly their threads whenever they are removed (see also Section 26). Keeping all the bolts in their correct fitted order, wash them and wipe dry, then check each for any sign of visible wear or damage, renewing any bolt if necessary. Lightly oil the threads of each bolt, carefully enter it into its original hole (**do not drop**) and screw it in, by hand only until finger-tight. Measure the distance from the cylinder block/crankcase gasket surface to under the bolt's head (photo).

21 If the distance measured is up to 97 mm, the bolt may be re-used. If the distance measured is more than 97 mm, the bolt **must** be renewed. Considering the task these bolts perform and the pressures they must withstand, owners should consider renewing all the bolts as a matched set if more than one of the originals fail inspection or are close to the limit set.

22 The mating faces of the cylinder head and cylinder block/crankcase must be perfectly clean before refitting the head. Use a hard plastic or wood scraper to remove all traces of gasket and carbon; also clean the piston crowns. Take particular care as the soft aluminium alloy is damaged easily. Also, make sure that the carbon is not allowed to enter the oil and water passages – this is particularly important for the lubrication system, as carbon could block the oil supply to any of the engine's components. Using adhesive tape and paper, seal the water, oil and bolt holes in the cylinder block/crankcase. To prevent carbon entering the gap between the pistons and bores, smear a little grease in the gap. After cleaning each piston, use a small brush to remove all traces of grease and carbon from the gap, then wipe away the remainder with a clean rag. Clean all the pistons in the same way.

23 Check the mating surfaces of the cylinder block/crankcase and the cylinder head for nicks, deep scratches and other damage. If slight, they may be removed carefully with a file, but if excessive, machining may be the only alternative to renewal.

24 If warpage is suspected of the cylinder head gasket surface, use a straight-edge to check it for distortion. Refer to Part B of this Chapter if necessary.

25 Wipe clean the mating surfaces of the cylinder head and cylinder block/crankcase. Check that the two locating dowels are in position at each end of the cylinder block/crankcase surface.

26 Position a new gasket on the cylinder block/crankcase surface so

11.20 Checking condition of cylinder head bolt threads – cylinder head removed

11.26A Fit new cylinder head gasket on two locating dowels (arrowed)...

11.26B ...so that 'TOP' mark is upwards and 'FRONT' arrow points to timing belt end

11.27 Refitting the cylinder head

11.29A Cylinder head bolt tightening sequence – K8 engine

11.29B Cylinder head bolt tightening sequence – K16 engine

11.29C Tightening cylinder head bolts – first stage...

11.29D ...second and third stages use alignment of bolt head radial marks with cylinder head to establish angles (arrowed)

that the 'TOP' mark is uppermost and the 'FRONT' arrow points to the timing belt end (photos).

27 Refit the cylinder head, locating it on the dowels (photo).

28 Keeping all the cylinder head bolts in their correct fitted order, wash them and wipe dry, then lightly oil under the head and on the threads of each bolt, carefully enter it into its original hole (**do not drop**) and screw it in, by hand only until finger-tight.

29 Working progressively and in the sequence shown in photo 11.29A (K8 engines) or photo 11.29B (K16 engines), use first a torque wrench, then an ordinary socket extension bar to tighten the cylinder head bolts in the stages given in the Specifications Section of this Chapter. To tighten the bolts through the angles specified, simply use a felt-tip pen or similar to mark the position on the cylinder head of each bolt head's radial mark; the second stage then tightens each bolt through half a turn so that the marks face away from each other and the third stage tightens them through another half-turn so that all the bolt-head marks will then align again with their cylinder head counterparts. If any bolt is overtightened past its mark, slacken it through 90°, then re-tighten until the marks align (photos).

30 Refit and tighten the inlet manifold support stay bolts, then secure the engine wiring harness using the clips provided.

31 On K16 engines which are equipped with air conditioning, refit the alternator mounting bolts and tighten them to the specified torque setting. Refit the compressor and alternator heatshields and tighten their retaining bolts and nuts securely.

32 Connect all disturbed coolant hoses, securing them in position with their retaining clips, and reconnect the coolant temperature sensor wiring.

33 Working as described in the relevant Sections of Chapter 4, connect or refit all disturbed wiring, hoses and control cable(s) to the inlet manifold and fuel system components, then adjust the choke and or accelerator cable(s).

34 Working as described in Chapter 4, reconnect the exhaust system front pipe to the manifold and (if applicable) reconnect the lambda sensor wiring.

35 Refit the cylinder head cover, inner timing cover retaining bolts

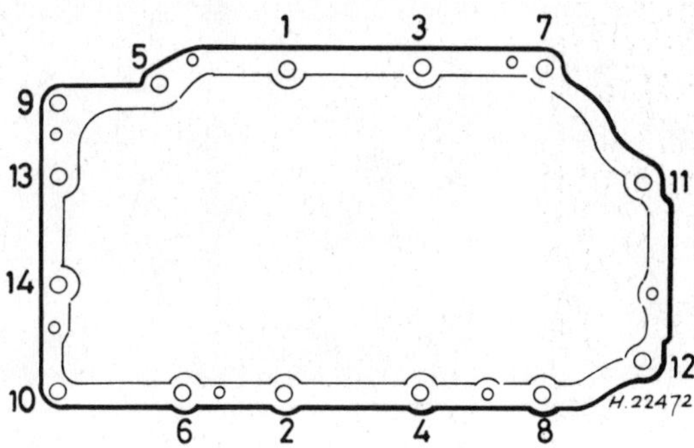

Fig. 2.12 Sump bolt tightening sequence (Sec 12)

and the camshaft sprocket(s) as described in Sections 4, 6 and 8 of this Chapter.

36 Refit the spark plugs and distributor cap as described in Chapter 1 and reconnect the battery negative lead.

37 Refill the cooling system as described in Chapter 1.

12 Sump - removal and refitting

Note: *It is essential that new sump bolts of the Patchlok type are used during the refitting operation.*

Removal

1 Disconnect the battery negative lead.

2 Drain the engine oil, then clean and refit the engine oil drain plug, tightening it to the specified torque wrench setting. If the engine is nearing its service interval when the oil and filter are due for renewal, it is recommended that the filter is also removed and a new one fitted. After reassembly, the engine can then be replenished with fresh engine oil. Refer to Chapter 1 for further information.

3 Apply the handbrake then jack up the front of the car and support it on axle stands.

4 From underneath the front of the vehicle, slacken and remove the three bolts securing the bumper flange to the body. Remove the seven bolts securing the front undercover panel to the body and remove the panel.

5 Working as described in Chapter 4, disconnect the exhaust system front pipe from the manifold and, where fitted, disconnect or release the lambda sensor wiring so that it is not strained by the weight of the exhaust.

6 Unscrew the three retaining bolts and remove the flywheel lower cover plate (photo).

7 Slacken and remove the bolts securing the anti-beaming bracket to the engine and transmission and remove the bracket.

8 Progressively slacken the sump retaining bolts then remove them along with the anti-beaming bracket support. Make a note of the correct fitted position of the support and the longer bolts at positions 4, 8 and 12 (Fig. 2.12) to ensure correct fitment on reassembly.

9 Break the joint by striking the sump with the palm of the hand, then lower the sump and withdraw it (photo).

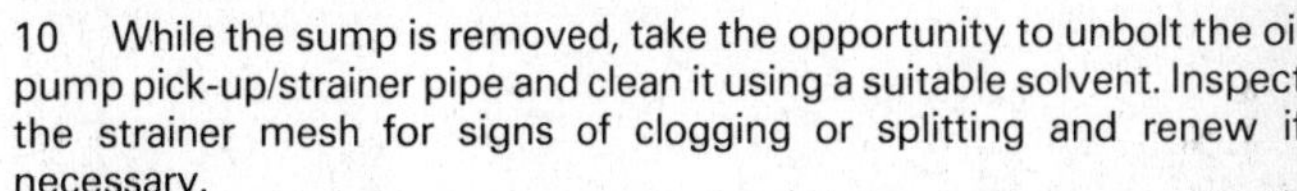

10 While the sump is removed, take the opportunity to unbolt the oil pump pick-up/strainer pipe and clean it using a suitable solvent. Inspect the strainer mesh for signs of clogging or splitting and renew if necessary.

Refitting

11 Clean all traces of gasket from the mating surfaces of the cylinder block/crankcase and sump, then use a clean rag to wipe out the sump and the engine's interior. If the oil pump pick-up/strainer pipe was removed, fit a new sealing O-ring to its end and refit the pipe, tightening its retaining bolts to the specified torque setting.

12 If the sump gasket is damaged or shows signs of deterioration it must be renewed; otherwise it can be re-used. Fit it to the sump mating surface so that the gasket's seven locating pegs fit into the sump holes (photo).

13 Offer up the sump to the cylinder block/crankcase then refit the new sump retaining bolts, not forgetting the anti-beaming bracket support, and tighten them finger-tight only.

14 Working in the sequence shown in Fig. 2.12, tighten the sump bolts to the specified torque setting.

15 Refit the anti-beaming bracket and tighten the mounting bolts to the specified torque setting.

16 Install the flywheel lower cover plate and tighten the retaining bolts to the specified torque wrench setting.

17 Reconnect the exhaust system front pipe to the manifold and, where necessary, reconnect the lambda sensor wiring, referring to Chapter 4.

18 Refit the undercover panel then lower the vehicle to the ground and reconnect the battery negative lead.

19 Replenish the engine oil as described in Chapter 1.

13 Oil pump - removal and refitting

Note: *The oil pressure relief valve can be dismantled, if required, without removing the oil pump from the car; see Section 14 for details.*

Removal

1 Remove the crankshaft sprocket as described in Section 8 and secure the timing belt clear of the working area so that it cannot be contaminated with oil.

2 Drain the engine oil, then clean and refit the engine oil drain plug, tightening it to the specified torque wrench setting. If the engine is nearing its service interval when the oil and filter are due for renewal, it is recommended that the filter is also removed and a new one fitted. After reassembly, the engine can then be replenished with fresh engine oil. Refer to Chapter 1 for further information.

3 Where necessary, unscrew the alternator adjuster link retaining nut and unbolt the engine wiring harness guide retaining screws, then move the link and guide clear of the oil pump.

4 Unscrew the oil pump retaining bolts, noting the fitted position of the special bolt and withdraw the oil pump (photo). Recover the pump gasket and discard it, then carefully lever the crankshaft right-hand oil seal out of the oil pump; the oil seal should be renewed whenever it is disturbed. If necessary, the pump can be dismantled and inspected as described in Section 14.

12.6 Remove flywheel lower cover plate to reach sump bolts

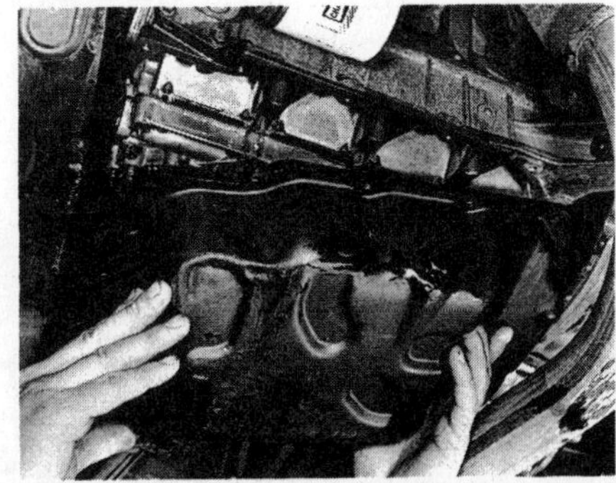

12.9 Removing the sump

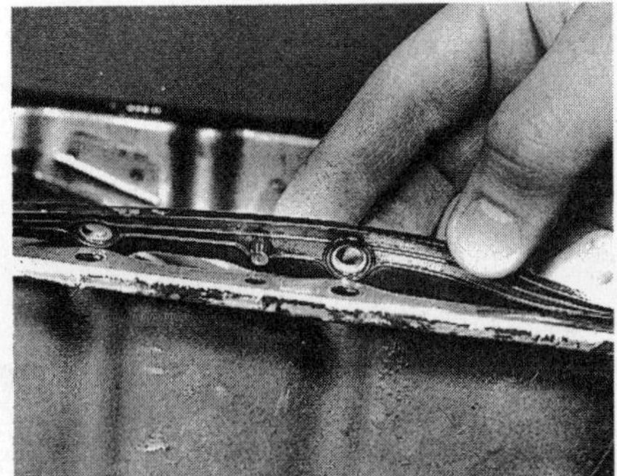

12.12 Sump gasket pegs must engage with sump mating surface holes

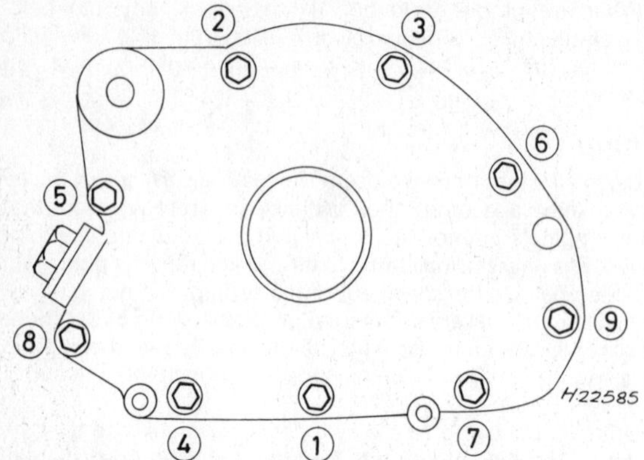

Fig. 2.13 Oil pump bolt tightening sequence (Sec 13)

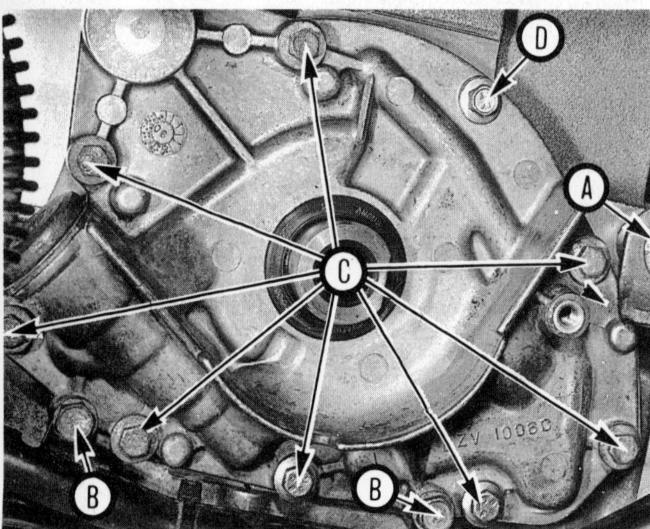

13.4 Alternator adjuster link nut 'A', wiring guide screws 'B', oil pump bolts 'C', and special oil pump bolt 'D'

Refitting

5 Thoroughly clean the mating faces of the oil pump and cylinder block/crankcase. Use grease to stick a new gasket in place.

6 Note that whether the original pump is refitted or a new pump is installed, it is essential that the pump is primed before installation by injecting oil into it and turning it by hand.

7 Offer up the pump, ensuring that its inner gear engages fully on the crankshaft flats, then push the pump fully into position.

8 Refit the pump retaining bolts, ensuring that the special bolt is refitted to its original position, and tighten them to the specified torque setting in the order shown in Fig. 2.13.

9 If removed, refit the alternator adjuster link and the engine wiring harness guide, then tighten securely the retaining nut and screws.

10 Fit a new crankshaft right-hand oil seal as described in Section 15.

11 Remove all traces of surplus oil then refit the crankshaft sprocket as described in Section 8.

12 Replenish the engine oil as described in Chapter 1.

14 Oil pump – dismantling, inspection and reassembly

Note: *If oil pump wear is suspected, check the cost and availability of new parts (only available in the form of repair kit LQX 10001) against the cost of a new pump. Examine the pump as described in this Section and then decide whether renewal or repair is the best course of action.*

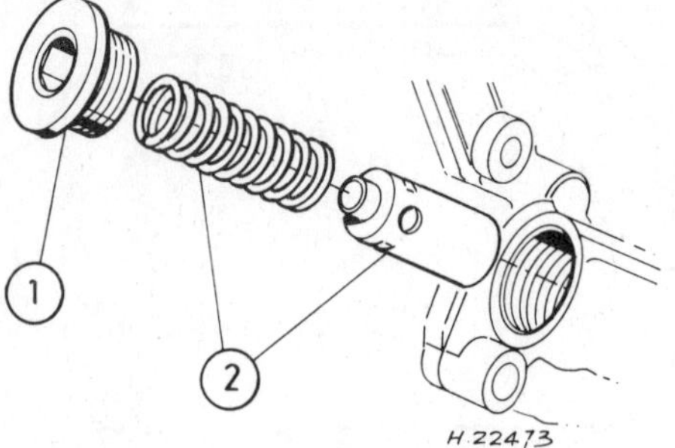

Fig. 2.14 Oil pressure relief valve components (Sec 14)

1 *Threaded plug* 2 *Valve spring and plunger*

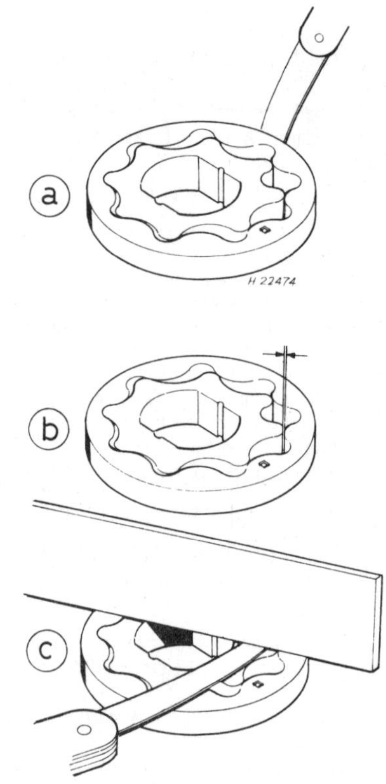

Fig. 2.15 Checking oil pump rotors for wear – see text for details (Sec 14)

Dismantling

1 Remove the oil pump as described in Section 13.

2 Unscrew the Torx screws (size T25) and remove the pump cover plate; discard the sealing O-ring.

3 Note the identification marks on the outer rotor then remove both the rotors from the body.

4 The oil pressure relief valve can be dismantled, if required, without disturbing the pump. If this is to be done with the pump in position on the engine unit and the engine still installed in the vehicle, it will first be necessary to jack up the front of the vehicle and remove the right-hand roadwheel to gain access to the valve (photo).

5 To dismantle the valve, unscrew the threaded plug and recover the valve spring and plunger (Fig. 2.14). Discard the plug's sealing washer.

Inspection

6 Inspect the rotors for obvious signs of wear or damage and renew if necessary; if the pump body or cover plate are scored or damaged, the complete oil pump assembly must be renewed.

7 Using feeler gauge blades of the appropriate thickness, measure the clearance between the outer rotor and the pump body and between the

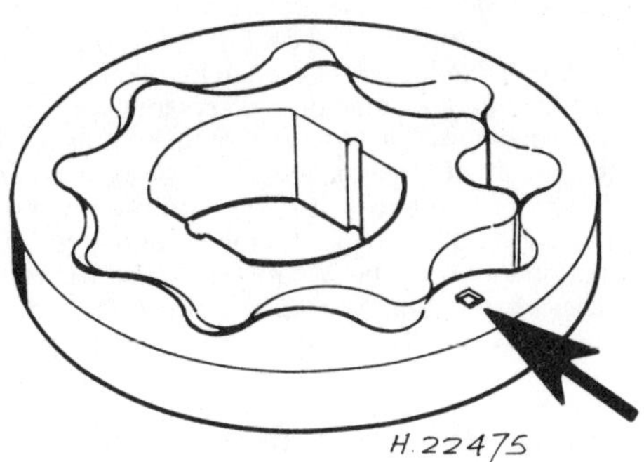

Fig. 2.16 Oil pump outer rotor outside face identifying mark (arrowed) (Sec 14)

tips of the inner and outer rotor lobes ('a' and 'b' respectively, Fig. 2.15).
8 Using feeler gauge blades and a straight-edge placed across the top of the pump body and the rotors, measure the rotor endfloat ('c' Fig. 2.15).
9 If any measurement is outside the specified limits, the complete pump assembly must be renewed.
10 If the pressure relief valve plunger is scored, or if it does not slide freely in the pump body bore, it must be renewed, using all the components from the repair kit.
11 To complete a thorough inspection of the oil pump components, the sump should be removed and the oil pump pick-up/strainer pipe removed and cleaned. Refer to Section 12 for further information.

Reassembly

12 Lubricate the rotors with clean engine oil and refit them to the pump body, ensuring that the outer rotor's identification mark faces outwards (Fig. 2.16).
13 Fit a new sealing O-ring to the pump body and refit the cover plate. Apply thread-locking compound to the threads of the cover plate Torx screws and tighten them securely.
14 Check that the pump rotates freely, then prime it by injecting oil into its passages and rotating it; if a long time elapses before the pump is refitted to the engine, prime it again before installation.
15 Refit the oil pressure relief valve plunger, ensuring that it is the correct way up (Fig. 2.14), and install the spring. Fit a new sealing washer to the threaded plug and tighten the plug securely.

15 Crankshaft oil seals – renewal

Right-hand oil seal

1 Remove the crankshaft sprocket as described in Section 8 and secure the timing belt clear of the working area so that it cannot be contaminated with oil.
2 Punch or drill two small holes opposite each other in the seal. Screw a self-tapping screw into each and pull on the screws with pliers to extract the seal.
3 Clean the seal housing and polish off any burrs or raised edges which may have caused the seal to fail in the first place.
4 Lubricate the lips of the new seal with clean engine oil and drive it into position until it seats on its locating shoulder, using a suitable tubular drift, such as a socket, which bears only on the hard outer edge of the seal. Take care not to damage the seal lips during fitting; use either grease or a thin layer of insulating tape to protect the seal lips from the edges of the crankshaft flats, but be careful to remove all traces of tape and to lubricate the seal lips if the second method is used. Note that the seal lips should face inwards.
5 Wash off any traces of oil, then refit the crankshaft sprocket as described in Section 8.

Left-hand oil seal

6 Remove the flywheel as described in Section 16.

14.4 Unscrewing oil pressure relief valve threaded plug – in car

7 Taking care not to mark either the crankshaft or any part of the cylinder block/crankcase, lever the seal evenly out of its housing.
8 Clean the seal housing and polish off any burrs or raised edges which may have caused the seal to fail in the first place.
9 Lubricate with grease the lips of the new seal and the crankshaft shoulder, then offer up the seal to the cylinder block/crankcase.
10 Ease the sealing lip of the seal over the crankshaft shoulder by hand only, and press the seal evenly into its housing until its outer flange seats evenly on the housing lip. If necessary, a soft-faced mallet can be used to tap the seal gently into place.
11 Wash off any traces of oil, then refit the flywheel as described in Section 16.

16 Flywheel – removal, inspection and refitting

Removal

1 Remove the transmission as described in Chapter 7, then remove the clutch assembly as described in Chapter 6.
2 Prevent the flywheel from turning by locking the ring gear teeth as shown in photo 34.30C, or by bolting a strap between the flywheel and the cylinder block/crankcase.
3 Slacken and remove the flywheel retaining bolts and discard them; they must be renewed whenever they are disturbed.
4 Remove the flywheel. Do not drop it, as it is very heavy.

Inspection

5 If the flywheel's clutch mating surface is deeply scored, cracked or otherwise damaged, the flywheel must be renewed, unless it is possible to have it surface ground; seek the advice of a Rover dealer or engine reconditioning specialist.
6 If the ring gear is badly worn or has missing teeth it must be renewed, but this job is best left to a Rover dealer or engine reconditioning specialist. The temperature to which the new ring gear must be heated for installation (350°C, shown by an even light blue colour) is critical and, if not done accurately, the hardness of the teeth will be destroyed.
7 Examine the reluctor ring, which is fitted to the rear of the flywheel, for signs of damage and check that it is securely fastened by the two retaining screws. If the reluctor ring is damaged, it must be renewed as described in Chapter 5, Part B.

Refitting

8 Clean the mating surfaces of the flywheel and crankshaft. Clean any remaining adhesive from the threads of the crankshaft threaded holes by making two saw cuts at opposite points along the (carefully-cleaned) threads of one of the original flywheel bolts and screwing it into each

hole in turn. **Do not** use a tap to clean the threads in this way.
9 Position the flywheel over the crankshaft's locating dowel, press it into place and fit six **new** bolts.
10 Lock the flywheel using the method employed on dismantling and tighten the retaining bolts to the specified torque wrench setting.
11 Refit the clutch as described in Chapter 6, then remove the locking tool and refit the transmission as described in Chapter 7.

17 Engine/transmission mountings - inspection and renewal

Inspection

1 If improved access is required, raise the front of the car and support it securely on axle stands.
2 Check the mounting rubber to see if it is cracked, hardened or separated from the metal at any point; renew the mounting if any such damage or deterioration is evident.
3 Check that all the mounting's fasteners are securely tightened; use a torque wrench to check if possible.
4 Using a large screwdriver or a pry bar, check for wear in the mounting by carefully levering against it to check for free play; where this is not possible, enlist the aid of an assistant to move the engine/transmission unit back and forth or from side to side while you watch the mounting. While some free play is to be expected even from new components, excessive wear should be obvious. If excessive free play is found, check first that the fasteners are correctly secured, then renew any worn components as described below.

Renewal

Right-hand mounting

5 Disconnect the battery negative lead.
6 To improve access to the mounting, remove the three expansion tank mounting bolts then free the coolant hose from any relevant retaining clips and position the tank clear of the engine. On models equipped with power-assisted steering, undo all the power steering hose retaining clamp bolts then slide the fluid reservoir out of its retaining clip and position it clear of the timing belt covers. Take great care not to place any undue strain on the coolant/hydraulic hoses and mop up any spilt coolant/hydraulic fluid immediately (as applicable).
7 Support the weight of the engine/transmission using a trolley jack, with a wooden spacer to prevent damage to the sump, then unscrew the mounting through-bolt and nut and the mounting to bracket nuts. Remove the mounting, noting the two rubber washers (photos).
8 Where necessary, also unscrew the retaining bolts and remove the bracket from the cylinder block/crankcase.
9 Check carefully for signs of wear or damage on all components and renew them where necessary.
10 On reassembly, refit the bracket to the cylinder block/crankcase and tighten the retaining bolts to the specified torque setting.
11 Locate the rubber washers on the mounting, one on each side of its centre boss, then refit the mounting to the bracket and tighten the retaining nuts finger-tight only.
12 Using the trolley jack to position the engine unit at the correct height, refit from rear to front the mounting to body through-bolt, ensuring that the rubber washers are correctly seated, and refit the nut (photo).
13 Tighten the mounting to bracket nuts and the through-bolt to the specified torque wrench settings then lower and remove the jack.
14 Where necessary, refit the power steering fluid reservoir to its mounting bracket and secure the hydraulic hose clamps in position with the retaining bolts.
15 Refit the coolant expansion tank and tighten the mounting bolts securely. Secure the coolant hose in position with any necessary retaining clips and reconnect the battery negative lead.

Left-hand mounting

16 Disconnect the battery negative lead then disconnect the clutch cable as described in Chapter 6.
17 To improve access to the mounting, unclip the engine wiring

17.7A Use trolley jack (with wooden spacer to prevent damage) to adjust height of engine/transmission while mountings are renewed

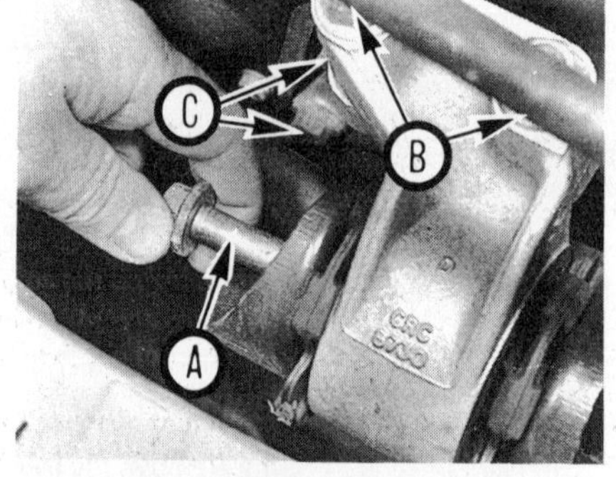

17.7B Right-hand mounting through-bolt 'A', mounting to bracket nuts 'B', bracket to cylinder block/crankcase bolts (two arrowed) 'C'

17.12 Check rubber washers are correctly installed before tightening through-bolt nut

17.18 Slacken and remove the transmission bracket to mounting bolts...

17.19A ...then lower the transmission and remove the four left-hand mounting to body bolts (arrowed)...

17.19B ...and manoeuvre the mounting out of position

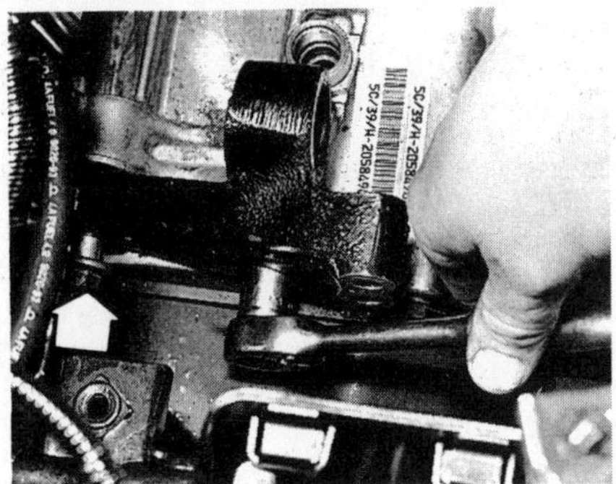

17.19C Transmission bracket is retained by two bolts (one arrowed)

17.26A Unbolt the rear mounting to transmission bolts (arrowed)...

17.26B ...then undo the connecting link to underbody bracket bolt and remove the mounting

harness and position it clear of the mounting.

18 Support the weight of the engine/transmission using a trolley jack, with a wooden spacer to prevent damage to the transmission casing, then slacken and remove the two bolts securing the transmission bracket to the mounting (photo).

19 Lower the engine/transmission unit, then remove the four bolts securing the mounting to the body and manoeuvre the mounting out of position. If required, slacken and remove the two bolts which secure the bracket to the transmission and remove the bracket (photos).

20 Although the mounting's rubber is secured by two nuts to a metal outer section, the two parts can be renewed only as a complete assembly. Check all components carefully for signs of wear or damage, and renew them where necessary.

21 On reassembly, refit the bracket to the transmission and tighten the retaining bolts to the specified torque setting.

22 Manoeuvre the mounting into position then refit the retaining bolts and tighten them to the specified torque setting.

23 Use the trolley jack to raise the transmission to the correct height then refit the mounting bracket to mounting bolts and tighten them to the specified torque setting. Refit the wiring harness to its retaining clip.

24 Refit the clutch cable as described in Chapter 6 and reconnect the battery negative lead.

Rear mounting

25 Apply the handbrake then jack up the front of the car and support it securely on axle stands.

26 Support the weight of the engine/transmission using a trolley jack, with a wooden spacer to prevent damage to the transmission casing, then unbolt the mounting bracket from the transmission and the connecting link from the underbody bracket and remove the mounting (photos).

27 Unscrew the through-bolt to separate the connecting link from the bracket. Check carefully for signs of wear or damage, paying particular attention to the connecting link rubber bushes, and renew as necessary.

28 Reassembly is the reverse of the removal procedure, tightening all the mounting bolts to the specified torque settings.

Part B: Engine removal and general overhaul procedures

18 General information

Included in this part of Chapter 2 are details of removing the engine/transmission unit from the car and general overhaul procedures for the cylinder head, cylinder block/crankcase and all other engine internal components.

The information given ranges from advice concerning preparation for an overhaul and the purchase of replacement parts, to detailed step-by-step procedures covering removal, inspection, renovation and refitting of engine internal components.

After Section 22, all instructions are based on the assumption that the engine has been removed from the car. For information concerning in-car engine repair, as well as the removal and refitting of those external components necessary for full overhaul, refer to Part A of this Chapter and to Section 22. Ignore any preliminary dismantling operations described in Part A that are no longer relevant once the engine has been removed from the car.

All specifications relating to engine overhaul are at the beginning of this Chapter.

19 Engine overhaul – general information

It is not always easy to determine when, or if, an engine should be completely overhauled, as a number of factors must be considered.

High mileage is not necessarily an indication that an overhaul is needed, while low mileage does not preclude the need for an overhaul. Frequency of servicing is probably the most important consideration; an engine which has had regular and frequent oil and filter changes, as well as other required maintenance, should give many thousands of miles of reliable service. Conversely, a neglected engine may require an overhaul very early in its life.

Excessive oil consumption is an indication that piston rings, valve seals and/or valve guides are in need of attention. Make sure that oil leaks are not responsible before deciding that the rings and/or guides are worn. Perform a compression test, as described in Section 2, to determine the likely cause of the problem.

Check the oil pressure with a gauge fitted in place of the oil pressure switch and compare it with that specified. If it is extremely low, the main and big-end bearings and/or the oil pump are probably worn out.

Loss of power, rough running, knocking or metallic engine noises, excessive valve gear noise and high fuel consumption may also point to the need for an overhaul, especially if they are all present at the same time. If a complete service does not remedy the situation, major mechanical work is the only solution.

An engine overhaul involves restoring all internal parts to the specification of a new engine. During an overhaul, the cylinder liners, the pistons and the piston rings are renewed. New main and big-end bearings are generally fitted and if necessary, the crankshaft may be renewed to restore the journals. The valves are also serviced as well, since they are usually in less than perfect condition at this point. While the engine is being overhauled, other components, such as the distributor, starter and alternator, can be overhauled as well. The end result should be an as-new engine that will give many trouble-free miles.

Note: *Critical cooling system components such as the hoses, thermostat*

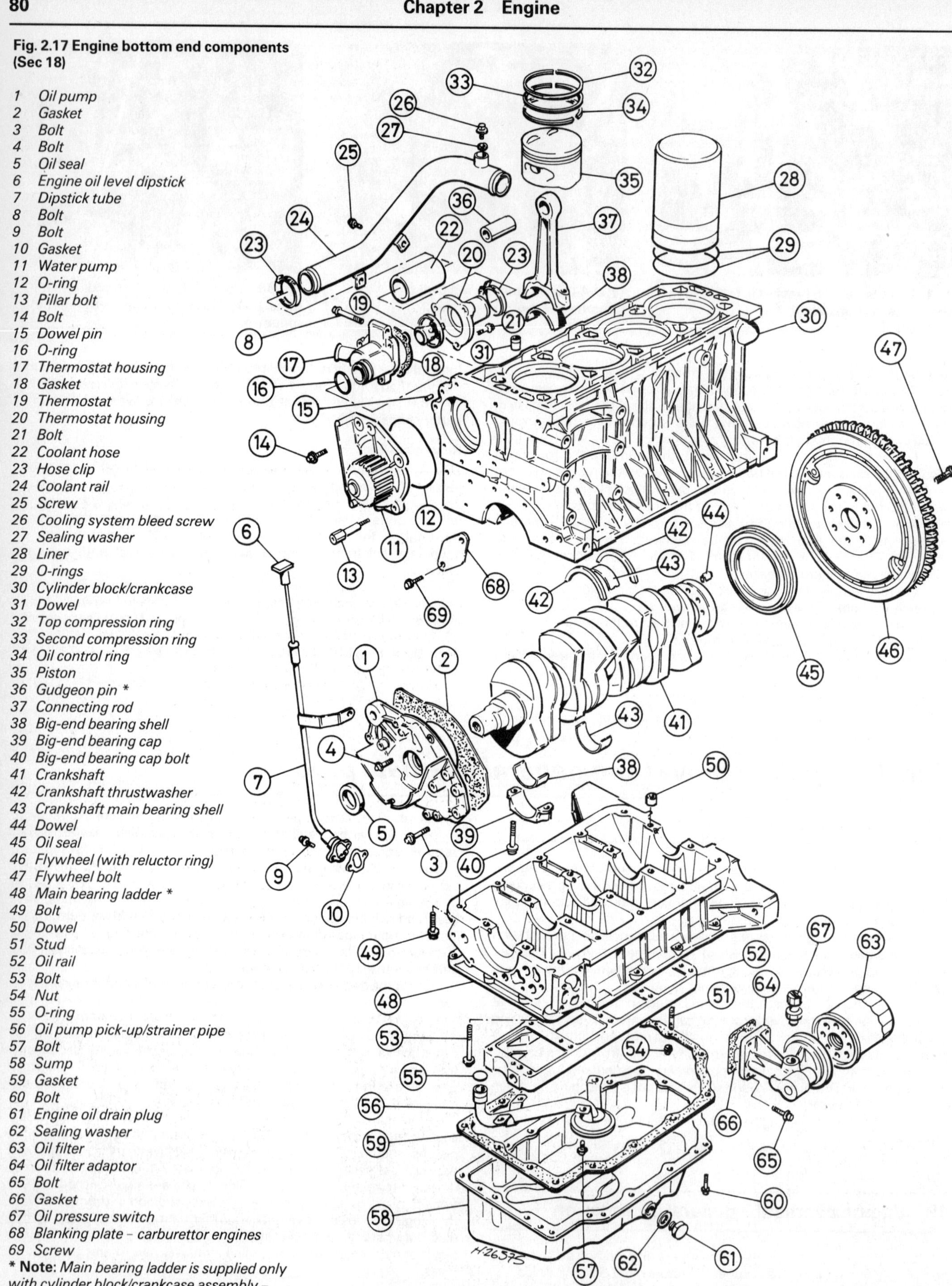

Fig. 2.17 Engine bottom end components (Sec 18)

1 Oil pump
2 Gasket
3 Bolt
4 Bolt
5 Oil seal
6 Engine oil level dipstick
7 Dipstick tube
8 Bolt
9 Bolt
10 Gasket
11 Water pump
12 O-ring
13 Pillar bolt
14 Bolt
15 Dowel pin
16 O-ring
17 Thermostat housing
18 Gasket
19 Thermostat
20 Thermostat housing
21 Bolt
22 Coolant hose
23 Hose clip
24 Coolant rail
25 Screw
26 Cooling system bleed screw
27 Sealing washer
28 Liner
29 O-rings
30 Cylinder block/crankcase
31 Dowel
32 Top compression ring
33 Second compression ring
34 Oil control ring
35 Piston
*36 Gudgeon pin **
37 Connecting rod
38 Big-end bearing shell
39 Big-end bearing cap
40 Big-end bearing cap bolt
41 Crankshaft
42 Crankshaft thrustwasher
43 Crankshaft main bearing shell
44 Dowel
45 Oil seal
46 Flywheel (with reluctor ring)
47 Flywheel bolt
*48 Main bearing ladder **
49 Bolt
50 Dowel
51 Stud
52 Oil rail
53 Bolt
54 Nut
55 O-ring
56 Oil pump pick-up/strainer pipe
57 Bolt
58 Sump
59 Gasket
60 Bolt
61 Engine oil drain plug
62 Sealing washer
63 Oil filter
64 Oil filter adaptor
65 Bolt
66 Gasket
67 Oil pressure switch
68 Blanking plate – carburettor engines
69 Screw

*** Note:** *Main bearing ladder is supplied only with cylinder block/crankcase assembly – gudgeon pin is supplied only with piston assembly* *and water pump should be renewed when an engine is overhauled. The radiator should be checked carefully to ensure that it is not clogged or leaking. Also it is a good idea to renew the oil pump whenever the engine is overhauled.*

Before beginning the engine overhaul, read through the entire procedure to familiarize yourself with the scope and requirements of the job. Overhauling an engine is not difficult if you follow carefully all of the instructions, have the necessary tools and equipment and pay close attention to all specifications; however, it can be time consuming. Plan on the car being off the road for a minimum of two weeks, especially if parts must be taken to an engineering works for repair or reconditioning. Check on the availability of parts and make sure that any necessary special tools and equipment are obtained in advance. Most work can be done with typical hand tools, although a number of precision measuring tools are required for inspecting parts to determine if they must be renewed. Often the engineering works will handle the inspection of parts and offer advice concerning reconditioning and renewal.

Note: *Always wait until the engine has been completely dismantled and all components, especially the cylinder block/crankcase, the cylinder liners and the crankshaft have been inspected before deciding what service and repair operations must be performed by an engineering works. Since the condition of these components will be the major factor to consider when determining whether to overhaul the original engine or buy a reconditioned unit, do not purchase parts or have overhaul work done on other components until they have been thoroughly inspected.*

As a general rule, time is the primary cost of an overhaul, so it does not pay to fit worn or substandard parts.

As a final note, to ensure maximum life and minimum trouble from a reconditioned engine, everything must be assembled with care in a spotlessly clean environment.

20 Engine/transmission removal - methods and precautions

If you have decided that the engine must be removed for overhaul or major repair work, several preliminary steps should be taken.

Locating a suitable place to work is extremely important. Adequate work space, along with storage space for the car, will be needed. If a shop or garage is not available, at the very least a flat, level, clean work surface is required.

Cleaning the engine compartment and engine/transmission before beginning the removal procedure will help keep tools clean and organized.

An engine hoist or A-frame will also be necessary. Make sure the equipment is rated in excess of the combined weight of the engine and transmission (290 lb/130 kg approximately). Safety is of primary importance, considering the potential hazards involved in lifting the engine/transmission out of the car.

If the engine/transmission is being removed by a novice, a helper should be available. Advice and aid from someone more experienced would also be helpful. There are many instances when one person cannot simultaneously perform all of the operations required when lifting the engine out of the car.

Plan the operation ahead of time. Before starting work, arrange for the hire of or obtain all of the tools and equipment you will need. Some of the equipment necessary to perform engine/transmission removal and installation safely and with relative ease are (in addition to an engine hoist) a heavy duty trolley jack, a complete sets of spanners and sockets as described in the front of this Manual, wooden blocks and plenty of rags and cleaning solvent for mopping up spilled oil, coolant and fuel. If the hoist must be hired, make sure that you arrange for it in advance, and perform all of the operations possible without it beforehand. This will save you money and time.

Plan for the car to be out of use for quite a while. An engineering works will be required to perform some of the work which the do-it-yourselfer cannot accomplish without special equipment. These places often have a busy schedule, so it would be a good idea to consult them before removing the engine in order to accurately estimate the amount of time required to rebuild or repair components that may need work.

Always be extremely careful when removing and refitting the engine/transmission. Serious injury can result from careless actions. Plan ahead, take your time and a job of this nature, although major, can be accomplished successfully.

21 Engine/transmission - removal and refitting

Removal

Note: *The engine can be removed from the car only as a complete unit with the transmission; the two are then separated for overhaul.*

1 Park the vehicle on firm, level ground then remove the bonnet as described in Chapter 11.

2 If the engine is to be dismantled, working as described in Chapter 1, drain the oil and remove the oil filter then clean and refit the drain plug, tightening it to its specified torque setting.

3 Firmly apply the handbrake then jack up the front of the car and support it securely on axle stands. Remove both front roadwheels.

4 From underneath the front of the vehicle, slacken and remove the three bolts securing the bumper flange to the body. Remove the seven bolts securing the front undercover panel to the body and remove the panel.

5 Drain the transmission oil, then clean and refit the drain plug tightening it to its specified torque setting as described in Chapter 7.

6 Drain the cooling system as described in Chapter 1.

7 Working as described in Chapter 12, remove the battery followed by the battery tray and support bracket.

8 Remove the complete air cleaner assembly including the intake duct and mounting bracket, intake hose and resonator as described in Chapter 4.

9 Disconnect the ignition coil HT lead from the distributor cap (photo).

10 Undo the nut and disconnect the battery positive lead from the main starter motor solenoid terminal then carefully disconnect the spade connector from the solenoid.

11 Undo the two bolts securing the engine compartment fusebox to

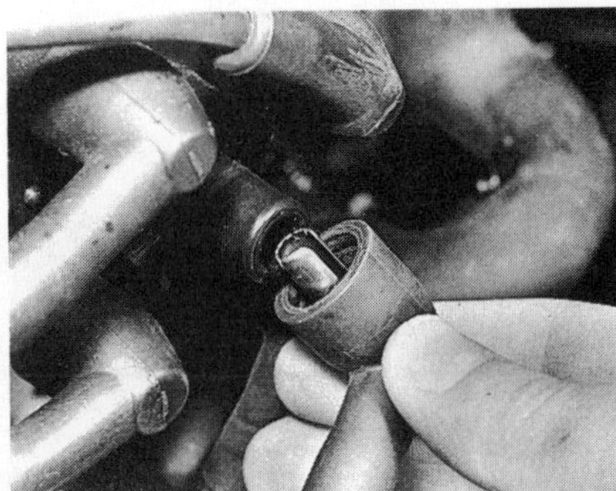

21.9 Disconnect the ignition coil HT lead from the distributor

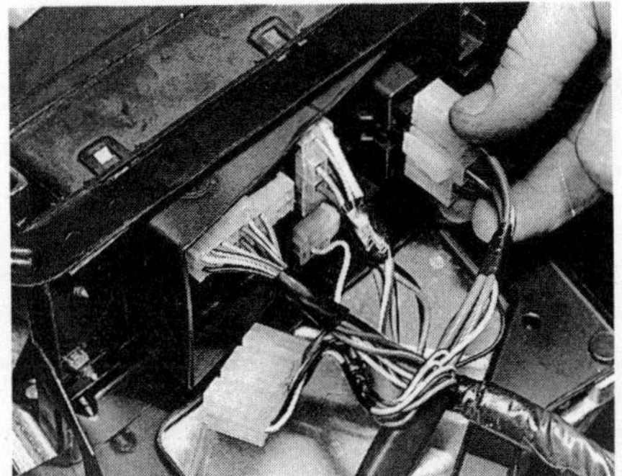

21.11A Disconnect the engine harness wiring connectors from the underside of the fusebox...

21.11B ...and the ignition coil LT wiring connector

21.11C On fuel-injected engines disconnect the vacuum pipe from the engine management ECU

21.16 Disconnect all the necessary cooling system hoses

the body, then disconnect the two engine wiring harness block connectors from the underside of the fusebox. Undo the bolt securing the wiring harness earth lead to the bonnet platform and disconnect the LT wiring connector from the ignition coil. On fuel-injected engines, also disconnect the wiring connector and vacuum pipe from the engine management ECU. Free the engine wiring harness from any relevant clips or ties so that it is free to be removed with the engine/transmission unit (photos).

12 Trace the clutch cable back from the clutch release lever to the bulkhead and remove the C-clip which retains the outer cable spring in position. Unhook the inner cable from the release lever and free the outer cable from its mounting bracket and position it clear of the transmission.

13 From underneath the car, pull out the rubber retaining pin which secures the lower end of the speedometer cable to the transmission housing. Withdraw the cable from the speedometer drive and remove the O-rings from the cable lower end. Discard the O-rings and renew then regardless of their apparent condition.

14 In the absence of the special gearchange linkage balljoint separator (Rover service tool number 18G 1592), use a suitable flat-bladed screwdriver to carefully lever the link rod balljoints off the transmission upper and lower selector levers, taking care not to damage the balljoint gaiters.

15 Unscrew the reverse interlock cable nut from the top of the transmission housing. In the absence of the special spanner (Rover service tool number 18G 1591), use a close fitting spanner to unscrew the plastic nut noting that it is easily damaged. Plug the transmission orifice to prevent the entry of dirt.

16 Working as described in the relevant Sections of Chapter 3, disconnect the coolant hose from the bottom of the expansion tank, the expansion tank hose from the inlet manifold union, both heater hoses from the heater matrix unions and the radiator top hose from the coolant outlet elbow. Either remove the radiator bottom hose or secure it so that it will not hinder engine/transmission removal (photo).

17 Slacken and remove the union bolt which secures the vacuum servo unit vacuum hose to the inlet manifold; discard the sealing washers as they must be renewed whenever they are disturbed.

18 On carburettor engines, working as described in Chapter 4, Part A, disconnect the feed hose from the fuel pump, and disconnect the accelerator and choke cables from the carburettor.

19 On fuel-injected engines, working as described in Chapter 4, Part B, depressurise the fuel system and disconnect the fuel feed and return hoses from the throttle body pipes. Disconnect the accelerator cable from the throttle housing.

20 Remove the three expansion tank mounting bolts and position the tank clear of the engine unit.

21 Remove the alternator as described in Chapter 12.

22 On models equipped with power-assisted steering, remove the power steering pump as described in Chapter 10.

23 On models equipped with air conditioning, slacken and remove the two compressor heatshield retaining bolts then remove the heatshield and disconnect the compressor wiring connector. Undo the four bolts securing the compressor to the mounting bracket and the single bolt securing the air conditioning pipe to the mounting bracket and position the compressor clear of the engine unit. Secure it to the body to avoid placing any strain on the air conditioning pipes and hoses.

24 Working as described in Chapter 4, disconnect the exhaust system front pipe from the manifold and, where necessary, disconnect the lambda sensor wiring connector.

25 Slacken and remove the bolt and washer securing the anti-roll bar connecting link to the left-hand lower suspension arm, and the two bolts securing the tie bar to the lower suspension arm.

26 Extract the split pins and undo the nuts securing the steering gear track rod end balljoint and the left-hand lower suspension arm balljoint to the swivel hub. Remove the nuts and release the balljoint tapered shanks using a universal balljoint separator.

27 Insert a suitable flat bar in between the left-hand inner constant velocity joint and transmission housing, then carefully lever the joint out of position, whilst taking great care not to damage the transmission housing.

28 Withdraw the left-hand inner constant velocity joint from the transmission and support the driveshaft to avoid damaging the constant velocity joints or gaiters. Repeat the operations described in paragraphs 25 to 28 for the right-hand driveshaft.

29 On K8 engines, the cylinder head has a tapped hole provided at the right-hand rear end (above the dipstick tube) and at the left-hand front

21.29A Right-hand engine lifting bracket...

21.29B ...and left-hand engine lifting bracket attached to points described in text – K16 engine

21.34 Lifting out engine/transmission unit

end (behind the spark plug lead clips). On K16 engine cylinder heads the right-hand end hole is in the same place, but at the left-hand end the air intake duct support bracket mounting points must be used. Attach lifting brackets to the engine at these points (photos). Take the weight of the engine/transmission on the engine hoist.
30 From underneath the car, unscrew the two bolts securing the rear engine/transmission mounting bracket to the transmission, then slacken the connecting link to body through bolt and pivot the mounting away from the transmission.
31 Slacken and remove the two bolts securing the left-hand transmission bracket to the mounting. Lower the transmission slightly then undo the four bolts securing the mounting to the body and manoeuvre the mounting out of position.
32 Raise the transmission again then slacken and remove the right-hand engine/transmission mounting through bolt and nut. Unscrew the two nuts securing the mounting to the engine bracket and remove it, noting the rubber washers which are fitted on each side of the bracket.
33 Make a final check that all components have been removed or disconnected that will prevent the removal of the engine/transmission from the car and ensure that components such as the gearchange linkage link rods are secured so that they cannot be damaged on removal.
34 Lift the engine/transmission out of the car, ensuring that nothing is trapped or damaged. Once the engine is high enough, lift it out over the front of the body and lower the unit to the ground (photo).
35 To separate the engine and transmission first remove the starter motor, referring to Chapter 12 for further information.
36 Unbolt the flywheel front, lower and rear cover plates, then unscrew the four bolts securing the transmission to the engine and gently prise the transmission off the two locating dowels (at the front and rear of the main bearing ladder). Move the transmission squarely away from the engine, ensuring that the clutch components are not damaged.
37 If the engine is to be overhauled, remove the clutch as described in Chapter 6.

Refitting

38 Refitting is the reverse of removal, following where necessary the instructions given in the other Chapters of this Manual. Note the following additional points:

- *(a) Overhaul and lubricate the clutch components, as described in Chapter 6, before refitting.*
- *(b) When the transmission, starter motor and flywheel cover plates have been refitted, lift the engine/transmission unit and lower it into the engine compartment so that it is slightly tilted (transmission down); engage both driveshafts then return the unit to the horizontal and refit the engine/transmission mountings.*
- *(c) Remove the lifting brackets and refit any components removed to enable them to be fitted.*
- *(d) Tighten all nuts and bolts to the specified torque wrench settings.*
- *(e) Adjust the choke and/or accelerator cable(s) as described in Chapter 4.*
- *(f) Refill the engine and transmission with oil. Referring to Chapters 1 and 7.*
- *(g) Refill the cooling system as described in Chapter 1.*

22 Engine overhaul - dismantling sequence

1 It is much easier to dismantle and work on the engine if it is mounted on a portable engine stand. These stands can often be hired from a tool hire shop. Before the engine is mounted on a stand, the flywheel should be removed, as described in Section 16, so that the stand bolts can be tightened into the end of the cylinder block/crankcase (**not** the main bearing ladder).
2 If a stand is not available, it is possible to dismantle the engine with it blocked up on a sturdy workbench or on the floor. Be extra careful not to tip or drop the engine when working without a stand.
3 If you are going to obtain a reconditioned engine, all external components must be removed first to be transferred to the replacement engine (just as they will if you are doing a complete engine overhaul yourself). These components include the following:

- *(a) Alternator mounting brackets (Chapter 12).*
- *(b) Power steering pump and air conditioning compressor brackets (where fitted) (Chapter 10).*
- *(c) Distributor, HT leads and spark plugs (Chapter 5).*
- *(d) Thermostat and housing, coolant rail, coolant outlet elbow (Chapter 3).*
- *(e) Dipstick tube.*
- *(f) Carburettor/fuel-injection system components (Chapter 4).*
- *(g) All electrical switches and sensors.*
- *(h) Inlet and exhaust manifolds (Chapter 4).*
- *(i) Oil filter (Chapter 1).*
- *(j) Fuel pump (Chapter 4).*
- *(k) Engine mountings (Section 17).*
- *(l) Flywheel (Section 16).*

Note: *When removing the external components from the engine, pay close attention to details that may be helpful or important during refitting. Note the fitted position of gaskets, seals, spacers, pins, washers, bolts and other small items.*

4 If you are obtaining a short motor (which consists of the engine cylinder block/crankcase and main bearing ladder, crankshaft, pistons and connecting rods all assembled), then the cylinder head, sump, oil pump, and timing belt will have to be removed also.
5 If you are planning a complete overhaul, the engine can be dismantled and the internal components removed in the following order:

- *(a) Inlet and exhaust manifolds (Chapter 4).*
- *(b) Timing belt, sprockets, tensioner and timing belt inner cover (Sections 6, 7 and 8).*
- *(c) Cylinder head (Section 11).*
- *(d) Flywheel (Section 16).*
- *(e) Sump (Section 12).*
- *(f) Oil pump (Section 13).*
- *(g) Piston/connecting rod assemblies (Section 26).*
- *(h) Crankshaft (Section 27).*

6 Before beginning the dismantling and overhaul procedures, make sure that you have all of the correct tools necessary. Refer to the introductory pages at the beginning of this Manual for further information.

23 Cylinder head - dismantling

Note: *New and reconditioned cylinder heads are available from the manufacturer and from engine overhaul specialists. Due to the fact that some specialist tools are required for the dismantling and inspection procedures, and new components may not be readily available, it may be more practical and economical for the home mechanic to purchase a reconditioned head rather than dismantle, inspect and recondition the original head.*

1 Remove the camshaft(s) and hydraulic tappets as described in Section 10, being careful to store the hydraulic tappets as described (photos).
2 Remove the cylinder head as described in Section 11.
3 Using a valve spring compressor, compress each valve spring in turn until the split collets can be removed. Release the compressor and lift off the spring retainer and spring, then use a pair of pliers to extract the spring bottom seat/stem seal (photos).
4 If, when the valve spring compressor is screwed down, the spring retainer refuses to free and expose the split collets, gently tap the top of the tool, directly over the retainer with a light hammer. This will free the retainer.
5 Withdraw the valve through the combustion chamber.
6 It is essential that each valve is stored together with its collets, retainer and spring, and that all valves are in their correct sequence unless they are so badly worn that they are to be renewed. If they are going to be kept and used again, place each valve assembly in a labelled

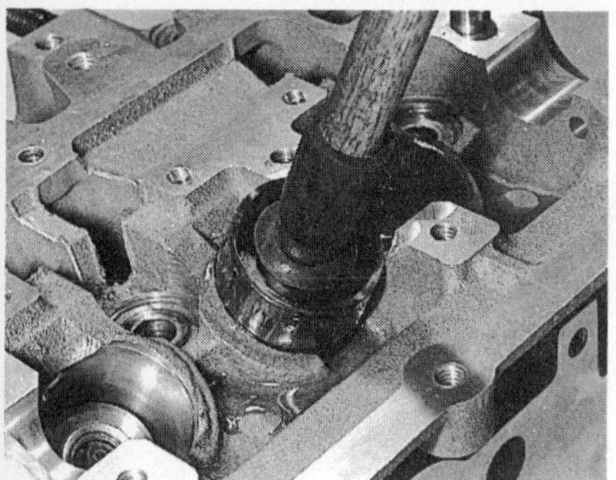

23.1A Use a valve-grinding sucker to extract hydraulic tappets...

23.1B ...and store in clearly-marked containers filled with oil to prevent oil loss

23.3A Using a valve spring compressor to release split collets

23.3B Extracting a valve spring bottom seat/stem seal

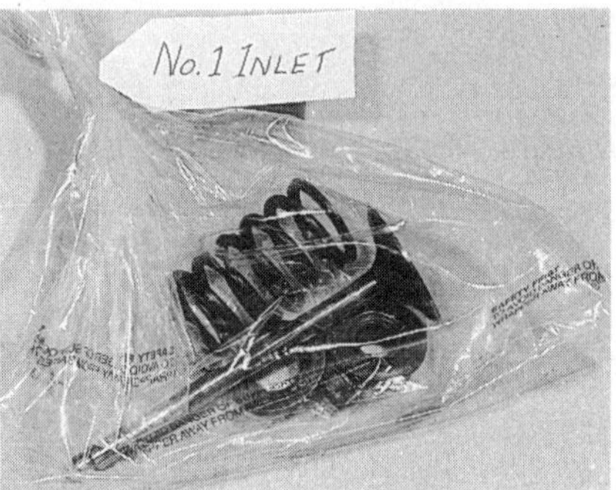

23.6 Use a labelled plastic bag to keep together and identify valve components

polythene bag or similar small container (photo). Note that No 1 valve is nearest to the timing belt end of the engine.

24 Cylinder head and valves – cleaning and inspection

1 Thorough cleaning of the cylinder head and valve components, followed by a detailed inspection, will enable you to decide how much valve service work must be carried out during the engine overhaul.

Note: *If the engine has been severely overheated, it is best to assume that the cylinder head is warped and to check carefully for signs of this.*

Cleaning

2 Scrape away all traces of old gasket material and sealing compound from the cylinder head; see Section 11 for details.
3 Scrape away the carbon from the combustion chambers and ports, then wash the cylinder head thoroughly with paraffin or a suitable solvent.
4 Scrape off any heavy carbon deposits that may have formed on the valves, then use a power-operated wire brush to remove deposits from the valve heads and stems.

Inspection

Note: *Be sure to perform all the following inspection procedures before concluding that the services of a machine shop or engine overhaul specialist are required. Make a list of all items that require attention.*

Cylinder head

5 Inspect the head very carefully for cracks, evidence of coolant leakage and other damage. If cracks are found, a new cylinder head should be obtained.
6 Use a straight-edge (placed as shown in Fig. 2.18) and feeler gauge

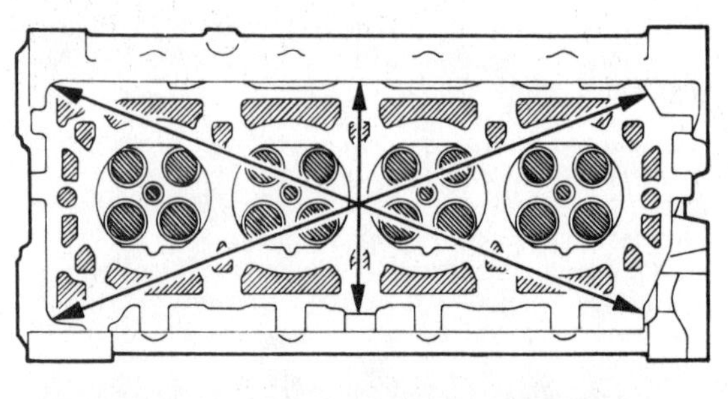

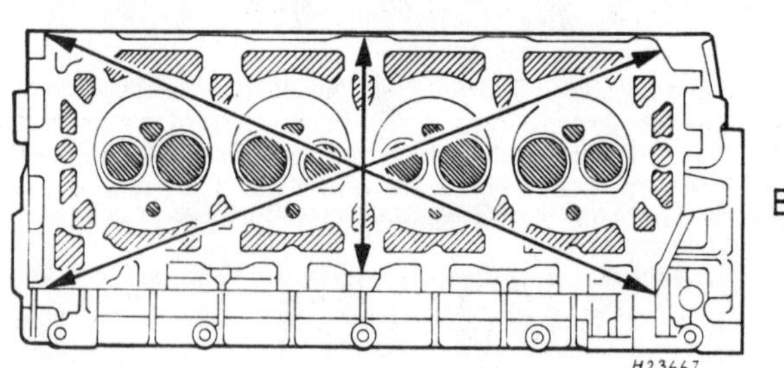

Fig. 2.18 Check the cylinder head gasket surface for warpage along the paths shown (Sec 24)

A K16 engine *B K8 engine*

blade to check that the cylinder head surface is not distorted (photo). If it is, it may be possible to resurface it, provided that the specified reface limit is not exceeded in so doing, or that the cylinder head is not reduced to less than the specified height.
7 Examine the valve seats in each of the combustion chambers. If they are severely pitted, cracked or burned then they will need to be renewed or re-cut by an engine overhaul specialist. If they are only slightly pitted, this can be removed by grinding-in the valve heads and

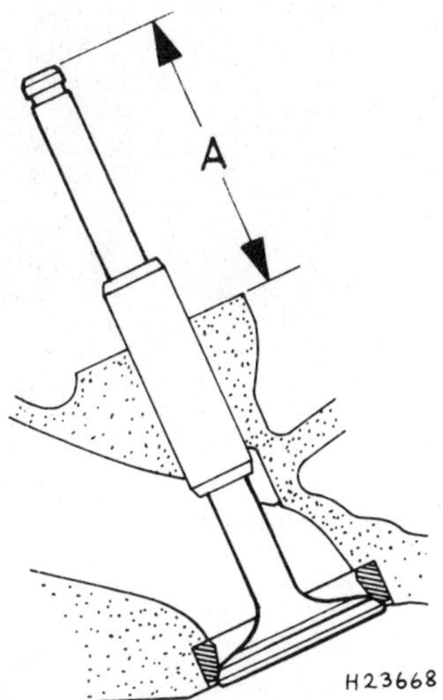

Fig. 2.19 Check valve seat wear by measuring valve stem installed height 'A' (Sec 24)

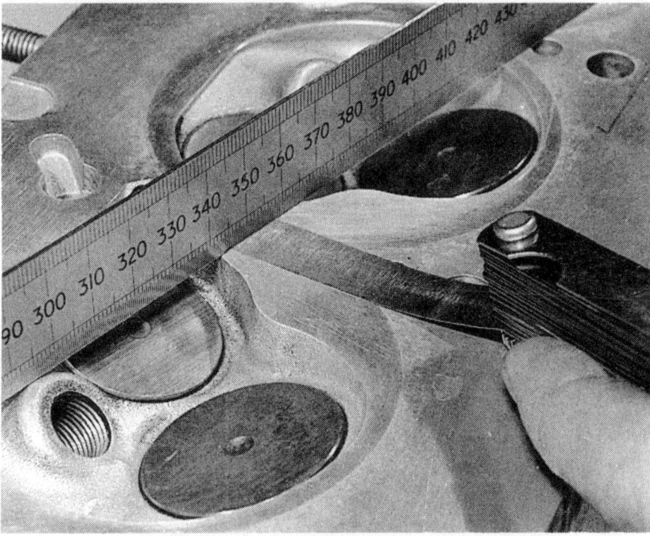

24.6 Checking a cylinder head gasket surface for warpage

seats with fine valve-grinding compound as described below. To check whether they are excessively worn, refit the valve and measure the installed height of the stem tip above the cylinder head upper surface (Fig. 2.19); if the measurement is above the specified limit, repeat the test using a new valve. If the measurement is still excessive, renew the seat insert.

8 If the valve guides are worn, indicated by a side to side motion of the valve, new guides must be fitted. Measure the diameter of the existing valve stems (see below) and the bore of the guides, then calculate the clearance and compare the result with the specified value; if the clearance is excessive, renew the valves or guides as necessary.

9 The renewal of valve guides is best carried out by an engine overhaul specialist. If the work is to be carried out at home, however, use a stepped, double-diameter drift to drive out the worn guide towards the combustion chamber. On fitting the new guide, place it first in a deep-freeze for one hour, then drive it into the cylinder head bore from the camshaft side until it projects the specified amount above the spring bottom seat/stem seal surface.

10 If the valve seats are to be re-cut, this must be done **only after** the guides have been renewed.

Valves

11 Examine the head of each valve for pitting, burning, cracks and general wear and check the valve stem for scoring and wear ridges. Rotate the valve and check for any obvious indication that it is bent. Look for pits and excessive wear on the tip of each valve stem. Renew any valve that shows any such signs of wear or damage.

12 If the valve appears satisfactory at this stage, measure the valve stem diameter at several points using a micrometer (photo). Any significant difference in the readings obtained indicates wear of the valve stem. Should any of these conditions be apparent, the valve(s) must be renewed.

13 If the valves are in satisfactory condition they should be ground (lapped) into their respective seats to ensure a smooth gas-tight seal. If the seat is only lightly pitted, or if it has been re-cut, fine grinding compound **only** should be used to produce the required finish. Coarse valve-grinding compound should **not** be used unless a seat is badly burned or deeply pitted; if this is the case the cylinder head and valves should be inspected by an expert to decide whether seat re-cutting or even the renewal of the valve or seat insert is required.

14 Valve grinding is carried out as follows. Place the cylinder head upside down on a bench.

15 Smear a trace of (the appropriate grade of) valve-grinding compound on the seat face and press a suction grinding tool onto the valve head. With a semi-rotary action, grind the valve head to its seat, lifting the valve occasionally to redistribute the grinding compound (photo). A light spring placed under the valve head will greatly ease this operation.

16 If coarse grinding compound is being used, work only until a dull, matt even surface is produced on both the valve seat and the valve, then wipe off the used compound and repeat the process with fine compound. When a smooth unbroken ring of light grey matt finish is produced on both the valve and seat, the grinding operation is complete. **Do not** grind in the valves any further than absolutely necessary, or the seat will be prematurely sunk into the cylinder head.

17 To check that the seat has not been over-ground, measure the valve stem installed height, as described in paragraph 7 above.

18 When all the valves have been ground-in, carefully wash off **all** traces of grinding compound using paraffin or a suitable solvent before reassembly of the cylinder head.

Valve components

19 Examine the valve springs for signs of damage and discoloration

24.12 Measuring valve stem diameter

24.15 Grinding-in a valve seat

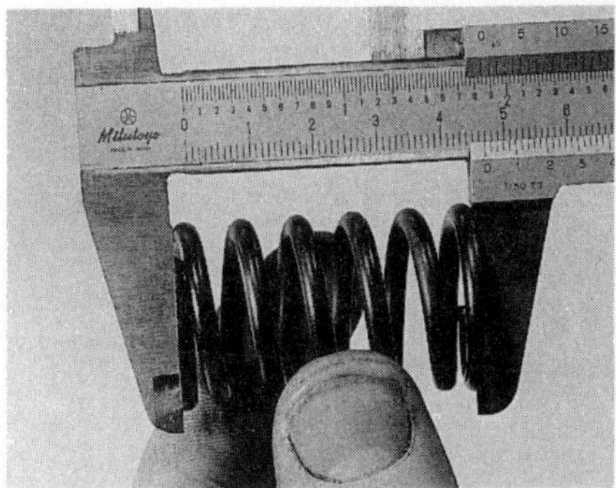

24.19 Measuring valve spring free length

25.2 Using a socket to install a valve stem seal

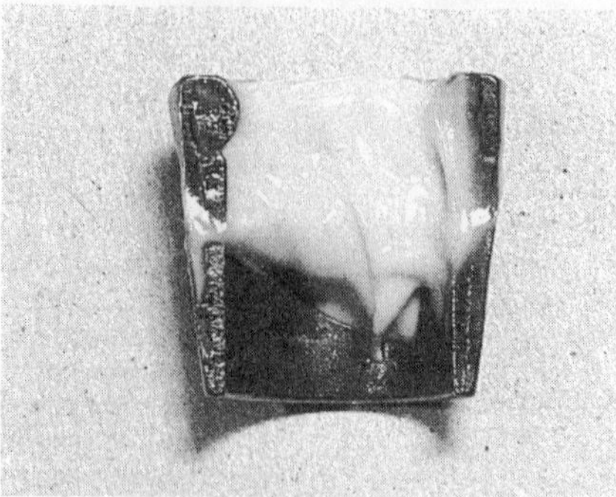
25.4 Use a little grease to hold the collets in place

25.6 Lubricate the hydraulic tappets thoroughly and refit the correct way up

25.7A Apply sealant (arrowed) to camshaft bearing caps as directed in Fig. 2.6 - K8 engines

25.7B Fill oil holes with clean oil - note cap stamped identifying number

25.7C Renew O-rings (arrowed) before refitting oil feed tube

25.7D K8 engine camshaft roll pin location at TDC position (for refitting camshaft bearing caps)

25.7E Fitting a new camshaft right-hand oil seal - K8 engine

and also measure their free length using vernier calipers or by comparing the existing spring with a new component (photo).

20 Stand each spring on a flat surface and check it for squareness. If any of the springs are damaged, distorted or have lost their tension, obtain a complete new set of springs.

21 Check the hydraulic tappets as described in Section 10.

25 Cylinder head - reassembly

1 Lubricate the stems of the valves and insert them into their original locations. If new valves are being fitted, insert them into the locations to which they have been ground.

2 Working on the first valve, dip the spring bottom seat/stem seal in fresh engine oil then carefully locate it over the valve and onto the guide. Take care not to damage the seal as it is passed over the valve stem. Use a suitable socket or metal tube to press the seal firmly onto the guide (photo).

3 Locate the spring on the seat, followed by the spring retainer.

4 Compress the valve spring and locate the split collets in the recess in the valve stem. Use a little grease to hold the collets in place (photo). Release the compressor, then repeat the procedure on the remaining valves.

5 With all the valves installed, place the cylinder head flat on the bench and, using a hammer and interposed block of wood, tap the end of each valve stem to settle the components.

6 Refit the hydraulic tappets as described in Section 10 (photo).

7 Refit the camshaft(s) as described in Section 10 (photos).

26 Piston/connecting rod assembly - removal

Note: *Due to the design of the engine, it will become very difficult, almost impossible, to turn the crankshaft once the cylinder head bolts have been slackened. The manufacturer accordingly states that the crankshaft will*

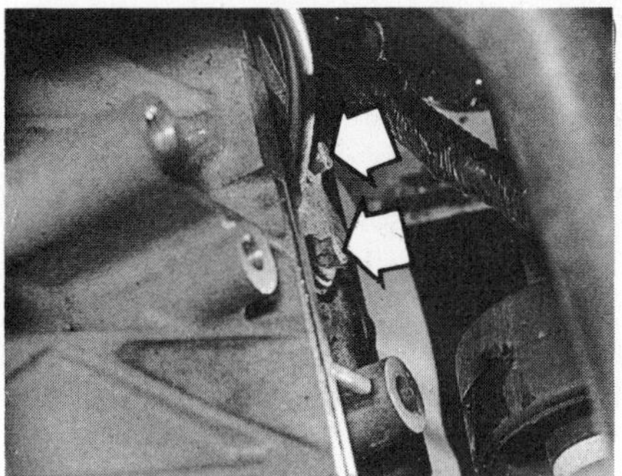

26.6 Dipstick tube mounting bolts (arrowed)

26.7 Removing oil pump pick-up/strainer pipe from oil rail – always renew sealing O-ring (arrowed)

26.8 Oil rail must be removed to reach connecting rod big-end bearings

26.9 Always mark big-end bearing caps before removal (see text) – number 4 cylinder cap shown

26.16 Checking condition of cylinder head bolt threads – cylinder head and oil rail removed

be 'tight' and should not be rotated more than absolutely necessary once the head has been removed; if the crankshaft cannot be rotated, it must be removed for overhaul work to proceed. With this in mind, during any servicing or overhaul work the crankshaft must always be rotated to the desired position before the bolts are disturbed.

Removal – without removing crankshaft

1 Remove the timing belt, the camshaft sprocket(s) and tensioner, and the timing belt inner cover as described in Sections 6, 7 and 8.

2 Remove the camshaft(s) and hydraulic tappets as described in Section 10, being careful to store the hydraulic tappets as described.

3 If the flywheel has been removed, temporarily refit the crankshaft pulley and apply a spanner to the bolt to rotate the crankshaft.

4 Rotate the crankshaft until numbers 2 and 3 cylinder pistons are at the bottom of their stroke.

5 Remove the cylinder head as described in Section 11; the crankshaft cannot now be rotated.

6 Slacken and remove the two dipstick tube retaining bolts and remove it from the cylinder block/crankcase (photo).

7 Remove the sump as described in Section 12 and unbolt the oil pump pick-up/strainer pipe from the oil rail; discard the sealing O-ring (photo).

8 Unscrew the two retaining nuts and remove the oil rail (photo).

9 Using a hammer and centre punch, paint or similar, mark each connecting rod big-end bearing cap with its respective cylinder number on the flat, machined surface provided; if the engine has been dismantled before, note carefully any identifying marks made previously (photo). Note that No 1 cylinder is at the timing belt end of the engine.

10 Unscrew and remove the big-end bearing cap bolts and withdraw the cap, complete with bearing shell, from the connecting rod. If only the bearing shells are being attended to, push the connecting rod up and off the crankpin, ensuring that the connecting rod big-ends do not mark the cylinder bore walls, then remove the upper bearing shell. Keep the cap, bolts and (if they are to be refitted) the bearing shells together in their correct sequence.

11 With numbers 2 and 3 cylinder big-ends disconnected, repeat the procedure (exercising great care to prevent damage to any of the components) to remove numbers 1 and 4 cylinder bearing caps.

12 Push each piston/connecting rod assembly up and remove it from the top of the bore. Remove the ridge of carbon from the top of each cylinder bore and ensure that the connecting rod big-ends do not mark the cylinder bore walls. Immediately refit the bearing cap, shells and bolts to each piston/connecting rod assembly so that they are all kept together as a matched set.

13 Note that the number stamped by you on each bearing cap should match the cylinder number stamped on the front (alternator bracket side) of each connecting rod; if any connecting rod number does not match its correct cylinder, mark or label it immediately so that each piston/connecting rod assembly can be refitted to its original bore. Keep each assembly together with the cap, bolts and bearing shells at all times.

Removal – alternative methods

14 If the engine is being completely dismantled and the cylinder head has been removed, either unbolt the main bearing ladder, as described in Section 27, so that the crankshaft can be rotated with care, or remove the crankshaft completely and then remove the connecting rods and pistons.

Checking the condition of the cylinder head bolts

15 Check the condition of the cylinder head bolts and particularly their threads whenever they are removed. If the cylinder head only is removed, check the bolts as described in Section 11, but if the cylinder head and the oil rail are removed, check as follows.

16 Keeping all the bolts in their correct fitted order, wash them and wipe dry, then check each for any sign of visible wear or damage, renewing any bolt if necessary. Lightly oil the threads of each bolt, carefully enter it into the original hole and screw it in, by hand only until finger-tight. If the full length of thread is engaged, the bolt may be re-used. If the full length of thread is not engaged, measure the distance from the oil rail gasket surface to under the bolt's head (photo).

17 If the distance measured is up to 378 mm, the bolt may be re-used. If the distance measured is more than 378 mm, the bolt **must** be renewed. Considering the task these bolts perform and the pressures they must withstand, owners should consider renewing all the bolts as a

matched set if more than one of the originals fail inspection or are close to the limit set.

18 Note that if any of the cylinder head bolt threads in the oil rail are found to be damaged, the oil rail must be renewed; thread inserts (eg Helicoils) are not an acceptable repair in this instance.

27 Crankshaft - removal

Note: *The following procedure assumes that the crankshaft alone is being removed and therefore uses a slightly different sequence of operations to that given in Section 26; depending on the reason for dismantling, either sequence may be adapted as necessary. If the crankshaft endfloat is to be checked (Section 30), this must be done when the crankshaft is free to move; if a dial gauge is to be used, check after paragraph 1 below, but if feeler gauges are to be used, check after paragraph 9.*

1 Remove the timing belt, sprocket(s) and tensioner, and the timing belt inner cover as described in Sections 6, 7 and 8.

2 Slacken and remove the two dipstick tube retaining bolts and remove it from the cylinder block/crankcase.

3 Remove the cylinder head as described in Section 11; the crankshaft cannot now be rotated.

4 Remove the oil pump as described in Section 13.

5 Remove the crankshaft left-hand oil seal as described in Section 15.

6 Remove the sump as described in Section 12 and unbolt the oil pump pick-up/strainer pipe from the oil rail; discard the sealing O-ring.

7 Unscrew the two retaining nuts and remove the oil rail.

8 Working in the sequence shown in Fig. 2.20, progressively unscrew the main bearing ladder retaining bolts by a turn at a time, then withdraw the ladder. Note the two locating dowels and the main bearing shells, which should be removed from the ladder and stored in their correct fitted order (photo).

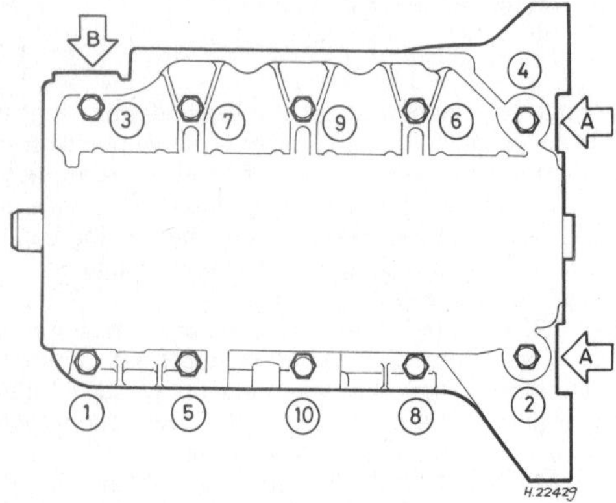

Fig. 2.20 Crankshaft main bearing ladder bolt slackening sequence (Sec 27)

A Bolts hidden in ladder flanges
B Location of single longer bolt

9 Mark the big-end bearing caps as described in Section 26, paragraph 9, then unscrew and remove the big-end bearing cap bolts and withdraw the cap, complete with the lower bearing shell, from each of the four connecting rods (photo). Push the connecting rods up and off their crankpins, then remove the upper bearing shell. Keep the cap, bolts and (if they are to be refitted) the bearing shells together in their correct sequence.

10 Remove the crankshaft; withdraw the two thrustwashers from the number 3 main bearing upper location (photo). Noting the position of the grooved shells, remove the upper main bearing shells, which must be kept with their correct respective partners from the main bearing ladder so that all shells can be identified and (if necessary) refitted in their original locations.

11 Check the condition of the cylinder head bolts as described in Section 26, paragraphs 15 to 18.

28 Cylinder block/crankcase, bearing ladder and oil rail - cleaning and inspection

Note: *During any cleaning operations take care not to score mating surfaces of the cylinder block/crankcase, bearing ladder and oil rail. A scraper is provided with the sealant kit specified in Section 32, but it may also be necessary to use a foam action gasket remover.*

Cleaning

1 For complete cleaning, remove the liners (see below), all external components and electrical switches/sensors.

2 Scrape all traces of gasket from the cylinder block/crankcase, bearing ladder and oil rail, taking care not to damage the gasket/sealing surfaces.

3 Remove all oil gallery plugs (where fitted). The plugs are usually very tight - they may have to be drilled out and the holes re-tapped. Use new plugs when the engine is reassembled.

4 If any of the castings are extremely dirty, all should be steam cleaned.

5 After the castings are returned, clean all oil holes and oil galleries one more time. Flush all internal passages with warm water until the water runs clear, then dry thoroughly and apply a light film of oil to all liner surfaces to prevent rusting. If you have access to compressed air, use it to speed up the drying process and to blow out all the oil holes and galleries.

Warning: *Wear eye protection when using compressed air!*

6 If the castings are not very dirty, you can do an adequate cleaning job with hot (as hot as you can stand!), soapy water and a stiff brush. Take plenty of time and do a thorough job. Regardless of the cleaning method used, be sure to clean all oil holes and galleries very thoroughly and to dry all components well; protect the liners as described above to prevent rusting.

7 All threaded holes must be clean to ensure accurate torque readings during reassembly. To clean all threads **except** those of the flywheel retaining bolts, run the proper size tap into each of the holes to remove

27.8 Removing main bearing ladder - note two locating dowels (arrowed)

27.9 Removing (number 1 cylinder) big-end bearing cap and lower bearing shell

27.10 Removing the crankshaft

rust, corrosion, thread sealant or sludge and to restore damaged threads. If possible, use compressed air to clear the holes of debris produced by this operation; a good alternative is to inject aerosol-applied water-dispersant lubricant into each hole, using the long spout usually supplied.

Warning: *Wear eye protection when cleaning out these holes in this way!*

Note: *The flywheel retaining bolt threads must be cleaned using the procedure described in Section 16.*

Now is a good time to check the condition of the cylinder head bolts, using the method described in Section 26.

8 Apply suitable sealant to the new oil gallery plugs and insert them into the holes in the block. Tighten them securely.

9 If the engine is not going to be reassembled right away, cover it with a large plastic bag to keep it clean; protect the liners as described above to prevent rusting.

Inspection

10 Visually check the castings for cracks and corrosion. Look for stripped threads in the threaded holes. If there has been any history of internal water leakage, it may be worthwhile having an engine overhaul specialist check the cylinder block/crankcase with special equipment. If defects are found have them repaired, if possible, or renew the assembly.

11 Check the bore of each cylinder liner for scuffing and scoring.

12 Measure the diameter of each cylinder liner bore 60 mm from the top of the bore, both parallel to the crankshaft axis and at right angles to it.

13 Compare the results with the Specifications at the beginning of this Chapter; if any measurement exceeds the service limit specified the liner must be renewed.

14 Measure the piston diameter at right angles to the gudgeon pin axis, 16 mm up from the bottom of the skirt; compare the results with the Specifications at the beginning of this Chapter.

15 To measure the piston to bore clearance, either measure the bore and piston skirt as described above and subtract the skirt diameter from the bore measurement, or insert each piston into the original bore, select a feeler gauge blade and slip it into the bore along with the piston. The piston must be aligned exactly in its normal attitude and the feeler gauge blade must be between the piston and bore on one of the thrust faces, 20 mm up from the bottom of the bore.

16 If the clearance is excessive a new piston will be required. If the piston binds at the lower end of the bore and is loose towards the top, the bore is tapered. If tight spots are encountered as the piston/feeler gauge blade is rotated in the bore, the bore is out-of-round.

17 Repeat this procedure for the remaining pistons and cylinder liners.

18 If the cylinder liner walls are badly scuffed or scored, or if they are excessively worn, out-of-round or tapered, obtain new cylinder liners; new pistons will also be required.

19 If the bores are in reasonably good condition and not worn to the specified limits and if the piston to bore clearances can be maintained properly, then it may only be necessary to renew the piston rings.

20 If this is the case, the bores should be honed to allow the new rings to bed in correctly and provide the best possible seal. The conventional type of hone has spring-loaded stones and is used with a power drill. You will also need some paraffin or honing oil and rags. The hone should be moved up and down the bore to produce a crosshatch pattern and plenty of honing oil should be used. Ideally the crosshatch lines should intersect at approximately a 60° angle. Do not take off more material than is necessary to produce the required finish. If new pistons are being fitted, the piston manufacturers may specify a finish with a different angle, so their instructions should be followed. Do not withdraw the hone from the bore while it is still being turned, but stop it first. After honing a bore, wipe out all traces of the honing oil. If equipment of this type is not available, or if you are not sure whether you are competent to undertake the task yourself, an engine overhaul specialist will carry out the work at moderate cost.

21 To remove the liners, invert the cylinder block/crankcase and support it on blocks of wood, then use a hard wood drift to tap out each liner from the crankshaft side. When all the liners are released, tip the cylinder block/crankcase on its side and remove each liner from the cylinder head side; discard the two sealing O-rings from the base of each. If the liners are to be re-used, mark each one by sticking masking

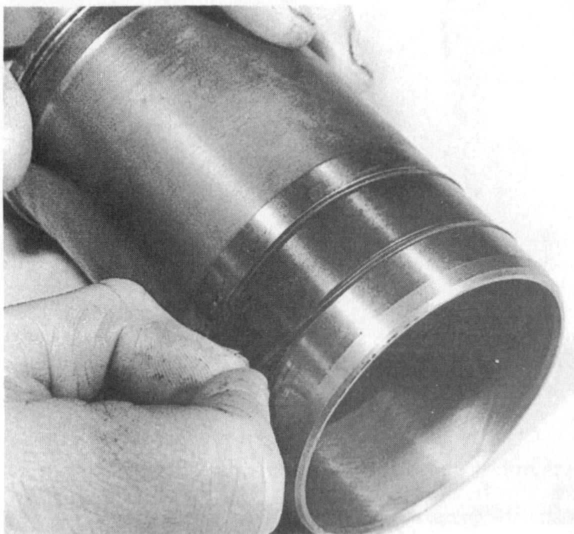

28.22 Always renew liner O-rings whenever liners are removed – oil before refitting

28.23 Ensuring O-rings are not displaced, tap liner as shown onto locating shoulder

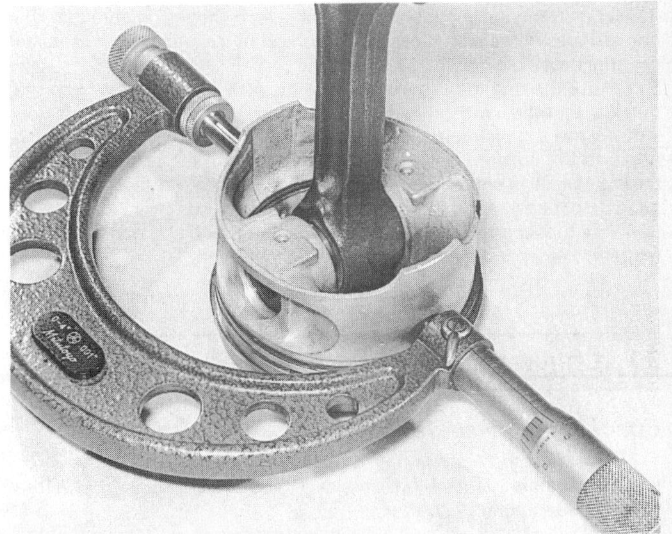

29.1 Measuring piston diameter

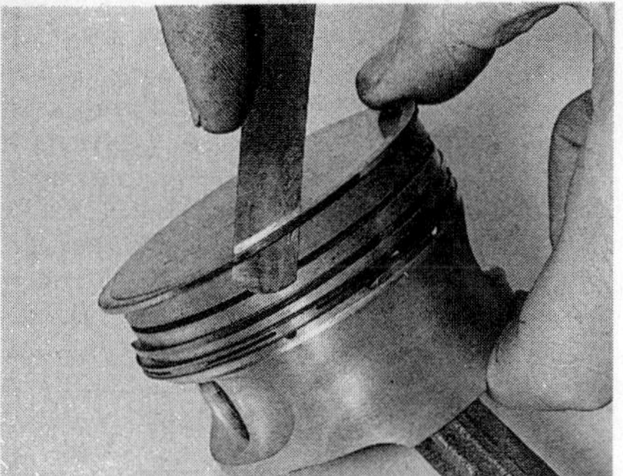

29.3 Removing piston rings using feeler gauge blades

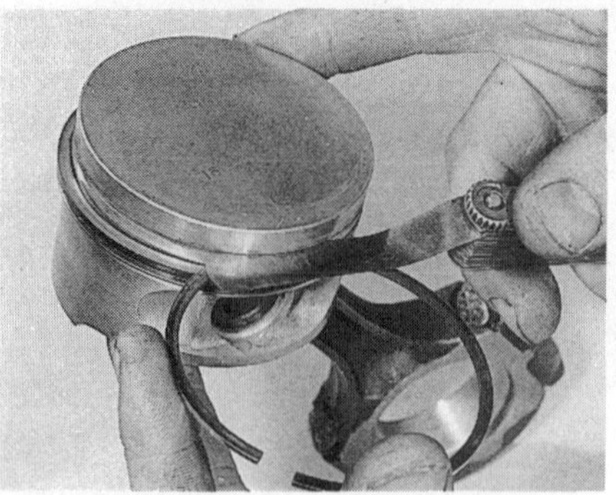

29.5A Measuring piston ring to groove clearance

29.5B Measuring piston ring end gap

tape on its right-hand (timing belt) face and writing the cylinder number on the tape.

22 To install the liners, thoroughly clean the liner mating surfaces in the cylinder block/crankcase and use fine abrasive paper to polish away any burrs or sharp edges which might damage the liner O-rings. Clean the liners and wipe dry, then fit new sealing O-rings to the two grooves at the base of each liner and apply a thin film of oil to the O-rings and to the liner surface on each side of the O-rings (photo).

23 If the original liners are being refitted, use the marks made on removal to ensure that each is refitted the same way round into its original bore. Insert each liner into the cylinder block/crankcase taking great care not to displace or damage the O-rings and press it home as far as possible by hand. Using a hammer and a block of wood, tap each liner lightly but fully onto its locating shoulder (photo). Wipe clean, then lightly oil all exposed liner surfaces to prevent rusting.

29 Piston/connecting rod assembly – inspection

1 Examine the pistons for ovality, scoring and scratches, and for wear of the piston ring grooves. Use a micrometer to measure the pistons (photo).

2 If the pistons or connecting rods are to be renewed, it is necessary to have this work carried out by a Rover dealer or suitable engine overhaul specialist who will have the necessary tooling to remove and install the gudgeon pins.

3 If new rings are to be fitted to the original pistons, expand the old rings over the top of the pistons. The use of two or three old feeler gauge blades will be helpful in preventing the rings dropping into empty grooves (photo).

4 When the original piston rings have been removed, ensure that the ring grooves in the piston are free of carbon by cleaning them using an old ring. Break the ring in half to do this.

5 Check the ring to groove clearance by inserting each ring from the outside together with a feeler gauge blade between the ring's top surface and the piston land. Check the ring end gaps by inserting each ring into the cylinder bore and pushing it in with the piston crown to ensure that it is square in the bore, 20 mm from the top; use feeler gauges to measure the gap (photos).

6 Note that each piston should be considered as being matched to its respective liner and they must not be interchanged.

30 Crankshaft – inspection

Checking crankshaft endfloat

1 If the crankshaft endfloat is to be checked, this must be done when the crankshaft is still installed in the cylinder block/crankcase, but is free to move (see Section 27).

2 Check the endfloat using a dial gauge in contact with the end of the crankshaft. Push the crankshaft fully one way and then zero the gauge. Push the crankshaft fully the other way and check the endfloat. The result can be compared with the specified amount and will give an indication as to whether new thrustwashers are required.

3 If a dial gauge is not available, feeler gauges can be used. First push the crankshaft fully towards the flywheel end of the engine, then use feeler gauges to measure the gap between the web of number 3 crankpin and the thrustwasher.

Inspection

4 Clean the crankshaft and dry it with compressed air, if available.

Warning: *Wear eye protection when using compressed air!*

Be sure to clean the oil holes with a pipe cleaner or similar probe.

5 Check the main and crankpin (big-end) bearing journals for uneven wear, scoring, pitting and cracking.

6 Rub a penny across each journal several times. If a journal picks up copper from the penny, it is too rough (photo).

7 Remove any burrs from the crankshaft oil holes with a stone, file or scraper.

8 Using a micrometer, measure the diameter of the main bearing and crankpin (big-end) journals and compare the results with the Specifications at the beginning of this Chapter (photo). Check carefully that each journal's diameter is within the tolerances of the size grade corresponding to the code number on the crankshaft right-hand web (main bearing) or indicated by the code letter on the left-hand web (crankpin/big-end bearing); see Section 34 or 35 as appropriate. If any diameter measured is incorrect for the grade indicated, re-check the measurement carefully; if the journal is fit for further service the correct grade code should be substituted when selecting new bearing shells.

9 By measuring the diameter at a number of points around each journal's circumference, you will be able to determine whether or not

30.6 Using a penny to check the condition of a crankshaft journal

30.8 Measuring the diameter of a crankshaft journal

the journal is out-of-round. Take the measurement at each end of the journal (near the webs) to determine if the journal is tapered.

10 If the crankshaft journals are damaged, tapered, out-of-round or worn beyond the limits specified in this Chapter, the crankshaft must be renewed unless an engine overhaul specialist can be found who will regrind it and supply the necessary undersize bearing shells.

11 Check the oil seal journals at each end of the crankshaft for wear and damage. If either seal has worn an excessive groove in its journal, consult an engine overhaul specialist who will be able to advise whether a repair is possible or whether a new crankshaft is necessary.

31 Main and big-end bearings - inspection

1 Even though the main and big-end bearings should be renewed during the engine overhaul, the old bearings should be retained for close examination, as they may reveal valuable information about the condition of the engine. The bearing shells are graded by thickness, the grade of each shell being indicated by the colour code marked on it.

2 Bearing failure occurs because of lack of lubrication, the presence of dirt or other foreign particles, overloading the engine and corrosion. Regardless of the cause of bearing failure, it must be corrected before the engine is reassembled to prevent it from happening again.

3 When examining the bearing shells, remove them from the cylinder block/crankcase, the main bearing ladder, the connecting rods and the connecting rod big-end bearing caps and lay them out on a clean surface in the same general position as their location in the engine. This will enable you to match any bearing problems with the corresponding crankshaft journal. **Do not** touch any shell's bearing surface with your fingers while checking it, or the delicate surface may be scratched.

4 Dirt and other foreign particles get into the engine in a variety of ways. It may be left in the engine during assembly, or it may pass through filters or the crankcase ventilation system. It may get into the oil and from there into the bearings. Metal chips from machining operations and normal engine wear are often present. Abrasives are sometimes left in engine components after reconditioning, especially when parts are not thoroughly cleaned using the proper cleaning methods. Whatever the source, these foreign objects often end up embedded in the soft bearing material and are easily recognized. Large particles will not embed in the bearing and will score or gouge the bearing and journal. The best prevention for this cause of bearing failure is to clean all parts thoroughly and keep everything spotlessly clean during engine assembly. Frequent and regular engine oil and filter changes are also recommended.

5 Lack of lubrication (or lubrication breakdown) has a number of interrelated causes. Excessive heat (which thins the oil), overloading (which squeezes the oil from the bearing face) and oil leakage (from excessive bearing clearances, worn oil pump or high engine speeds) all contribute to lubrication breakdown. Blocked oil passages, which usually are the result of misaligned oil holes in a bearing shell, will also oil starve a bearing and destroy it. When lack of lubrication is the cause of bearing failure, the bearing material is wiped or extruded from the steel backing of the bearing. Temperatures may increase to the point where the steel backing turns blue from overheating.

6 Driving habits can have a definite effect on bearing life. Full throttle, low speed operation (labouring the engine) puts very high loads on bearings, which tends to squeeze out the oil film. These loads cause the bearings to flex, which produces fine cracks in the bearing face (fatigue failure). Eventually the bearing material will loosen in pieces and tear away from the steel backing. Short-distance driving leads to corrosion of bearings because insufficient engine heat is produced to drive off the condensed water and corrosive gases. These products collect in the engine oil, forming acid and sludge. As the oil is carried to the engine bearings, the acid attacks and corrodes the bearing material.

7 Incorrect bearing installation during engine assembly will lead to bearing failure as well. Tight fitting bearings leave insufficient bearing running clearance and will result in oil starvation. Dirt or foreign particles trapped behind a bearing shell result in high spots on the bearing which lead to failure. **Do not** touch any shell's bearing surface with your fingers during reassembly; there is a risk of scratching the delicate surface or of depositing particles of dirt on it.

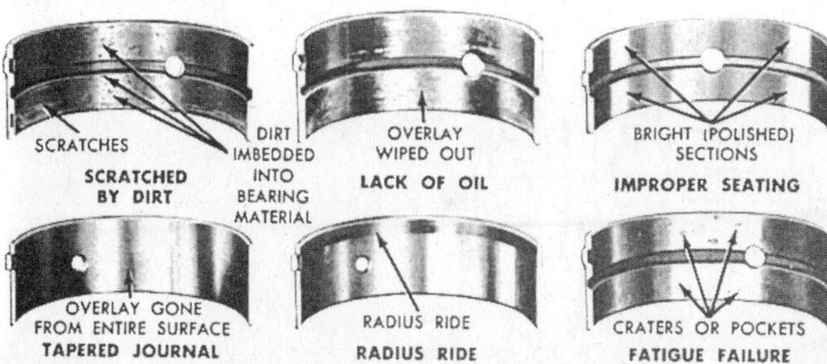

Fig. 2.21 Typical bearing shell failures (Sec 31)

32 Engine overhaul - reassembly sequence

1 Before reassembly begins ensure that all new parts have been obtained and that all necessary tools are available. Read through the entire procedure to familiarise yourself with the work involved, and to ensure that all items necessary for reassembly of the engine are at hand. In addition to all normal tools and materials, it will also be necessary to obtain the Rover sealant kit LVV 10002. Carefully read the instructions supplied with the sealant kit, and take care not to allow the sealant to contact the fingers as it will bond human skin.

2 In order to save time and avoid problems, engine reassembly can be carried out in the following order:

- *(a) Crankshaft (Section 34).*
- *(b) Piston/connecting rod assemblies (Section 35).*
- *(c) Oil pump (Section 13).*
- *(d) Sump (Section 12).*
- *(e) Flywheel (Section 16).*
- *(f) Cylinder head (Section 11).*
- *(g) Timing belt inner cover, tensioner and sprockets, and timing belt (Sections 6, 7 and 8).*
- *(h) Engine external components.*

3 At this stage, all engine components should be absolutely clean and dry, with all faults repaired and should be laid out (or in individual containers) on a completely clean work surface.

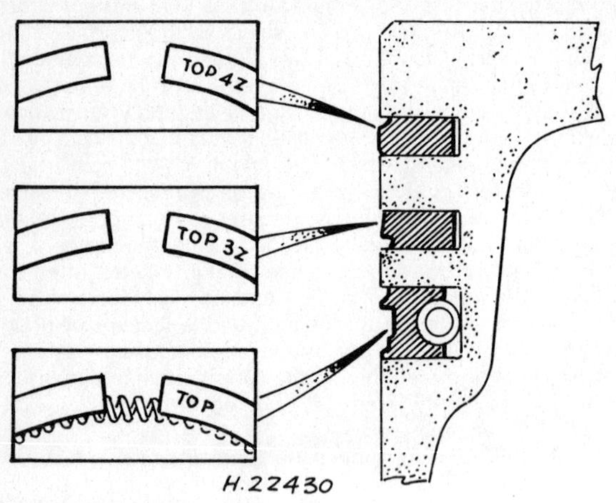

Fig. 2.22 Piston ring fitting details and top surface markings (Sec 33)

33 Piston rings – refitting

1 Before installing new piston rings, check the ring end gaps and the ring to groove clearance as described in Section 29.
2 When measuring new rings, lay out each piston set with a piston/connecting rod assembly and keep them together as a matched set from now on.
3 If the end gap of a new ring is found to be too large or too small, double-check to ensure that you have the correct rings before proceeding. If the end gap is still too small, it must be opened up by careful filing of the ring ends using a fine file; if it is too large, this is not as serious unless the specified service limit is exceeded, in which case very careful checking is required of the dimensions of all components as well as of the new parts.
4 Once all rings have been checked, they can be installed; ensure that each ring is refitted only to its matched piston and bore.
5 Install the new rings by fitting them over the top of the piston, starting with the oil control ring spring. Note that all the rings must be fitted with the word 'TOP' uppermost – see Fig. 2.22.
6 With all the rings in position, space the ring gaps as shown in Fig. 2.23, noting that the 'FRONT' marking shown is usually in fact an arrow mark on the piston crown and indicates the timing belt end of the engine.

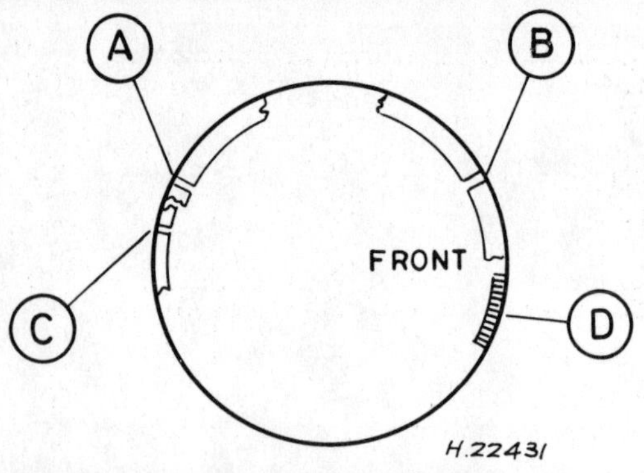

Fig. 2.23 Piston ring end gap locations (Sec 33)

A Top compression ring
B Second compression ring
C Oil control ring
D Oil control ring spring

34 Crankshaft – refitting and main bearing running clearance check

Selection of bearing shells

1 The main bearing running clearance is controlled in production by selecting one of three grades of bearing shell. The grades are indicated by a colour-coding marked on the edge of each shell which governs the shell's thickness, as follows:

(a) Green – Thin.
(b) Blue – Intermediate.
(c) Red – Thick.

2 If shells of differing grades are to be fitted to the same journal, the

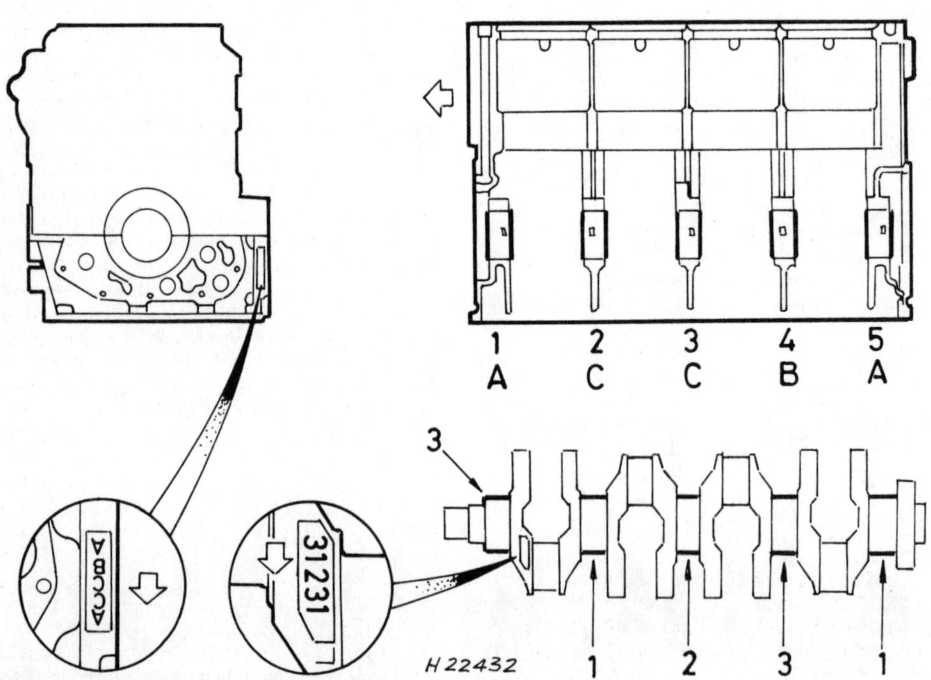

Fig. 2.24 Crankshaft main bearing size code locations (Sec 34)

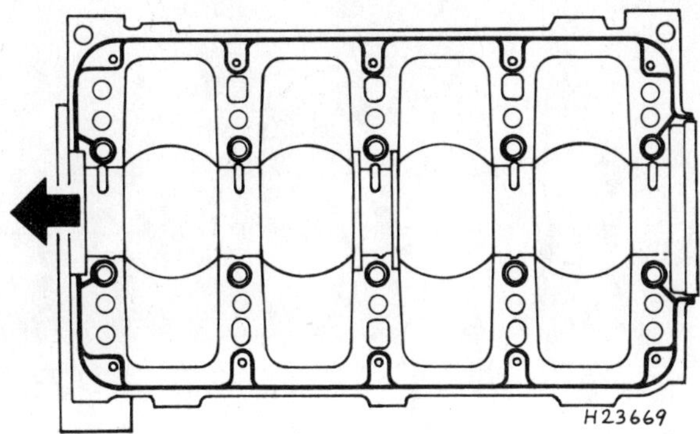

Fig. 2.25 Apply thin bead of sealant to cylinder block/crankcase mating surface along paths shown by heavy black lines, then spread to an even film (Sec 34)

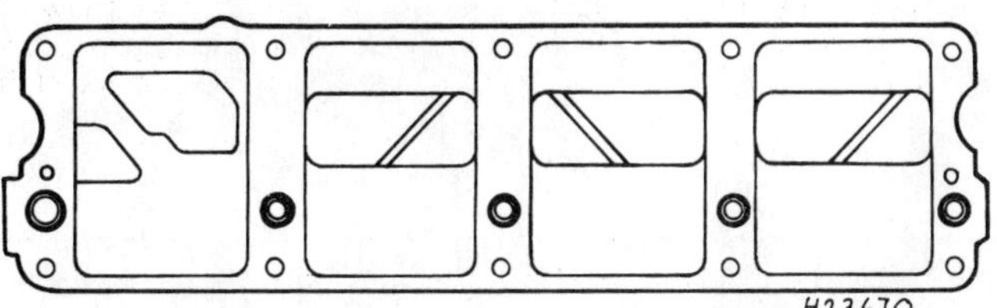

Fig. 2.27 Apply thin bead of sealant to oil rail mating surface as shown by heavy black lines, then spread to an even film (Sec 34)

thicker shell **must always** be fitted to the main bearing ladder location; bear this carefully in mind when ordering replacement shells for numbers 2, 3 and 4 bearings.

3 If the bearing shells are to be renewed, first check and record the main bearing code letters stamped on the right-hand front face of the main bearing ladder (Fig. 2.24); the letters are read with the ladder inverted, number 1 bearings code letter then being at the top and the remainder following in order from the engine's timing belt end.

4 Secondly, check and record the crankshaft journal code numbers stamped on the crankshaft's right-hand web (Fig. 2.24); number 1 journals code number being the first. If the original crankshaft is to be re-used, the size grade can be checked by direct measurement as described in Section 30.

5 Note that if the crankshaft is found to be excessively worn it must be renewed and the code numbers of the new component must be used instead to select a new set of bearing shells.

6 Matching the codes noted to the following table, select a new set of bearing shells.

Ladder code letter	Crankshaft code number	Shells
A	1	Blue, Blue
A	2	Red, Blue
A	3	Red, Red
B	1	Blue, Green
B	2	Blue, Blue
B	3	Red, Blue
C	1	Green, Green
C	2	Blue, Green
C	3	Blue, Blue

Main bearing running clearance check

7 Clean the backs of the bearing shells and the bearing locations in both the cylinder block/crankcase and the main bearing ladder.

8 Press the bearing shells into their locations, ensuring that the tab on each shell engages in the notch in the cylinder block/crankcase or main bearing ladder location, and taking care not to touch any shell's bearing surface with your fingers.

9 Press the bearing shells with the oil grooves into the upper locations (in the cylinder block/crankcase). Note the following points (photo):

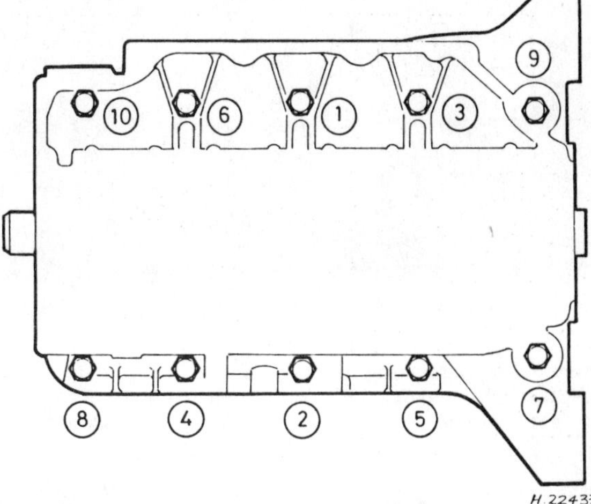

Fig. 2.26 Crankshaft main bearing ladder bolt tightening sequence (Sec 34)

(a) *On all engines grooved bearing shells are fitted to numbers 2, 3 and 4 upper bearing locations; note the central locating tabs of the grooved shells.*

(b) *On early engines grooved bearing shells were fitted only to numbers 2 and 4 upper bearing locations at the factory; on reassembly of one of these units, a grooved shell must be fitted at number 3 upper bearing location as well, instead of the plain item originally used. Note, however, that this will require a grooved shell with an offset locating tab instead of the central tab that is used on all other grooved shells; see your Rover dealer for details.*

(c) *If bearing shells of differing grades are to be fitted to the same journal, the thicker shell must always be fitted to the main bearing ladder location (see paragraph 1 above).*

(d) *On all engines, if the original main bearing shells are being re-used these must be refitted to their original locations in the cylinder block/crankcase and main bearing ladder.*

10 The main bearing running clearance should be checked if there is any doubt about the amount of crankshaft wear that has taken place, if the crankshaft has been reground and is to be refitted with non-genuine undersized bearing shells, or if non-genuine bearing shells are to be fitted. If the original crankshaft or a genuine Rover replacement part is to be installed, the shell selection procedure given above will produce the correct clearances and a further check will not be necessary. If the clearance is to be checked, it can be done in either of two ways.

11 One method (which will be difficult to achieve without a range of internal micrometers or internal/external expanding calipers) is to refit the main bearing ladder to the cylinder block/crankcase, with bearing shells in place. With the ladder retaining bolts tightened to the specified torque, refit the oil rail and the cylinder head, tightening the cylinder head bolts as described in Section 11, then measure the internal diameter of each assembled pair of bearing shells. If the diameter of each corresponding crankshaft journal is measured and then subtracted from the bearing internal diameter, the result will be the main bearing running clearance.

12 The second (and more accurate) method is to use an American product known as Plastigage. This consists of a fine thread of perfectly round plastic which is compressed between the bearing shell and the journal. When the shell is removed, the plastic is deformed and can be measured with a special card gauge supplied with the kit. The running clearance is determined from this gauge. Plastigage is sometimes difficult to obtain but enquiries at one of the larger specialist quality motor factors should produce the name of a stockist in your area. The procedure for using Plastigage is as follows.

13 With the main bearing upper shells in place, carefully lay the crankshaft in position. Do not use any lubricant; the crankshaft journals and bearing shells must be perfectly clean and dry.

14 Cut several lengths of the appropriate size Plastigage (they should be slightly shorter than the width of the main bearings) and place one length on each crankshaft journal axis (photo).

34.9 Ensure grooved bearing shells (arrowed) are installed exactly as described in text - early engine shown

34.14 Lay the length of Plastigage on the journal to be measured, parallel to the crankshaft centre-line

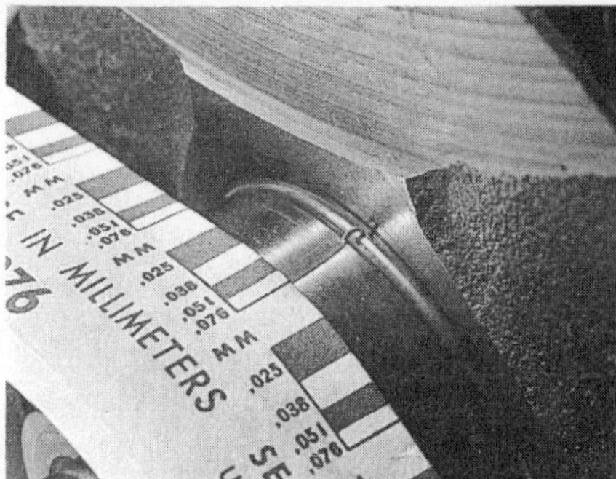

34.18 Using the scale on the envelope provided to check (at its widest point) the width of the crushed Plastigage and measure the bearing running clearance

34.24A If piston/connecting rod assemblies are refitted before the main bearing ladder is installed...

34.24B ...care is required to hold the crankshaft steady while the connecting rod big-end cap bolts are tightened...

34.24C ...but crankshaft can be rotated to required position

34.28 Tighten oil rail nuts to specified torque wrench setting

34.30A Fitting a new crankshaft left-hand oil seal

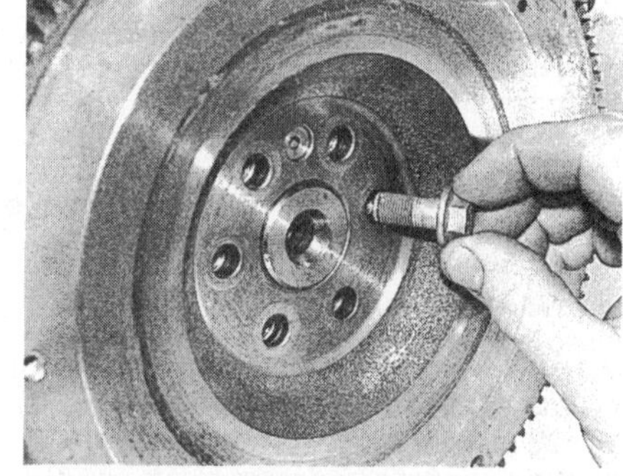

34.30B Always use new bolts when refitting flywheel

15 With the main bearing lower shells in position, refit the main bearing ladder (see below) and the oil rail, tightening their fasteners to the specified torque wrench settings. Take care not to disturb the Plastigage.
16 Refit the cylinder head (using the original gasket, to save over-compressing the new one) and tighten the bolts as described in Section 11. **Do not** rotate the crankshaft at any time during this operation.
17 Remove the cylinder head, the oil rail and the main bearing ladder. **Do not** disturb the Plastigage or rotate the crankshaft.
18 Compare the width of the crushed Plastigage on each journal to the scale printed on the Plastigage envelope to obtain the main bearing running clearance (photo).
19 If the clearance is not as specified, the bearing shells may be the wrong grade (or excessively worn if the original shells are being re-used). Before deciding that different grade shells are needed, make sure that no dirt or oil was trapped between the bearing shells and the ladder or cylinder block/crankcase when the clearance was measured. If the Plastigage was wider at one end than at the other, the journal may be tapered.
20 Carefully scrape away all traces of the Plastigage material from the crankshaft and bearing shells using a fingernail or other object which is unlikely to score the shells.

Final crankshaft refitting

21 Carefully lift the crankshaft out of the cylinder block once more.
22 Using a little grease, stick the thrustwashers to each side of the number 3 main bearing upper location; ensure that the oilway grooves on each thrustwasher face outwards.
23 Place the bearing shells in their locations as described in paragraphs 7 to 9 above. If new shells are being fitted, ensure that all traces of the protective grease are cleaned off using paraffin. Wipe dry the shells and connecting rods with a lint-free cloth. Liberally lubricate each bearing shell in the cylinder block/crankcase, then lower the crankshaft into position so that numbers 2 and 3 cylinder crankpins are at TDC.
24 Refit the piston/connecting rod assemblies as described in Section 35; the crankshaft should now be at the (number 1 and 4 cylinders) TDC position (photos).

34.30C Use fabricated tool as shown to lock flywheel while slackening or tightening flywheel bolts

34.31A Use grease to stick new gasket in place when refitting oil pump

34.31B Fitting a new crankshaft right-hand oil seal

25 Thoroughly degrease the mating surfaces of the cylinder block/crankcase and the main bearing ladder. Apply the special Rover sealant to the mating surface of the cylinder block/crankcase as shown in Fig. 2.25. Carefully follow the instructions supplied with the sealant kit.

26 Lubricate the bearing shells, then refit the main bearing ladder, ensuring that the shells are not displaced and that the locating dowels engage correctly. Working progressively, by a turn at a time and in the sequence shown in Fig. 2.26, tighten the ladder bolts to the specified torque wrench setting; the crankshaft cannot now be rotated.

27 Thoroughly degrease the mating surfaces of the oil rail and the main bearing ladder. Apply the special Rover sealant to the oil rail mating surface as shown in Fig. 2.27. Again, carefully follow the instructions supplied with the sealant kit.

28 Refit the oil rail, tightening the nuts to the specified torque wrench setting (photo).

29 Using a new sealing O-ring, refit the oil pump pick-up/strainer pipe to the oil rail, then refit the sump as described in Section 12; tighten all nuts and bolts to the specified torque wrench settings.

30 Fit a new crankshaft left-hand oil seal as described in Section 15, then refit the flywheel as described in Section 16 (photos).

31 Refit the oil pump and install a new crankshaft right-hand oil seal as described in Sections 13 and 15 (photos).

32 Refit the cylinder head as described in Section 11. Rotate the crankshaft to the 90° BTDC position so that the crankshaft sprocket timing marks align as described in Section 7, paragraph 15.

33 Refit the dipstick tube to the cylinder block/crankcase, tightening the bolts to the specified torque wrench setting.

34 Refit the timing belt inner cover, the sprocket(s) and tensioner, and the belt itself as described in Sections 6, 7 and 8.

35 Using a torque wrench, check that the amount of force required to rotate the crankshaft does not exceed 31 Nm; if the effort required is greater than this, the engine must be dismantled again to trace and rectify the cause. This value takes into account the increased friction of a new engine and is much higher than the actual pressure required to rotate a run-in engine, so do not make allowances for 'tight' components; if excessive pressure is required to rotate the crankshaft, the engine has not been rebuilt to the required standard and **must** be dismantled again.

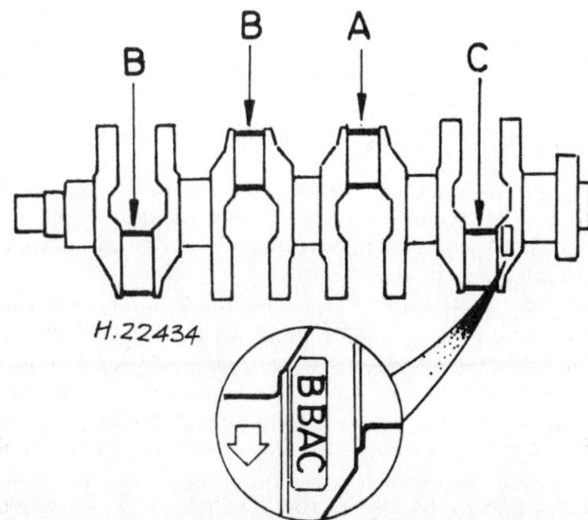

Fig. 2.28 Crankpin (big-end) journal size code location (Sec 35)

35 Piston/connecting rod assembly – refitting and big-end bearing running clearance check

Selection of bearing shells

1 The big-end bearing running clearance is controlled in production by selecting one of three grades of bearing shell. The grades are indicated by a colour-coding marked on the edge of each shell which governs the shell's thickness, as follows.

(a) Yellow – Thin.
(b) Blue – Intermediate.
(c) Red – Thick.

2 If shells of differing grades are to be fitted to the same journal, the thicker shell **must always** be fitted to the big-end bearing cap location.

3 If the bearing shells are to be renewed, first check and record the codes stamped on the front face of each big-end bearing cap and connecting rod; the number stamped on the big-end bearing cap is the bearing size code, the number stamped on the connecting rod is the piston/rod assembly's cylinder number and the letter stamped on the connecting rod is the weight code (photo).

4 Secondly, check and record the crankpin/big-end journal code letters stamped on the crankshaft's left-hand web (Fig. 2.28); number 1 journal's code letter being the first. If the original crankshaft is to be re-used, the code letter can be checked by direct measurement as described in Section 30.

5 Note that if the crankshaft is found to be excessively worn it must be renewed and the code letters of the new component must be used instead to select a new set of bearing shells.

6 Matching the codes noted to the following table, select a new set of bearing shells.

Cap code number	Crankshaft code letter	Shells
5	A	Blue, Blue
5	B	Red, Blue
5	C	Red, Red
6	A	Blue, Yellow
6	B	Blue, Blue
6	C	Red, Blue
7	A	Yellow, Yellow
7	B	Blue, Yellow
7	C	Blue, Blue

Big-end bearing running clearance check

7 Refer to Section 34, paragraph 10. If the clearance is to be checked, it can be done in either of two ways.

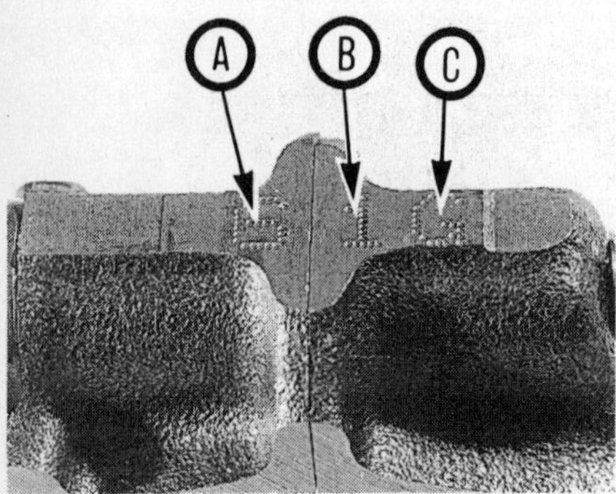

35.3 Big-end bearing size code number 'A' (on cap), piston/connecting rod assembly's cylinder number 'B', connecting rod weight code letter 'C'

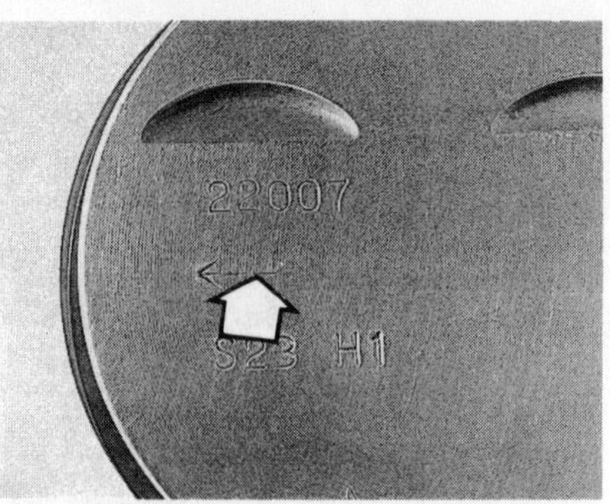

35.15A Arrow (or 'FRONT' marking) (arrowed) on piston crown must point to timing belt end of engine

35.15B Using a piston ring compressor to clamp piston rings while piston/connecting rod assembly is refitted to cylinder bore

35.17A Tighten connecting rod big-end bearing cap bolts to specified torque wrench setting (first stage)...

35.17B ...then use angular torque gauge to tighten bolts through angle specified (second stage)

8 One method is to refit the big-end bearing cap to the connecting rod, with bearing shells in place. With the cap retaining bolts tightened to the specified torque, use an internal micrometer or vernier caliper to measure the internal diameter of each assembled pair of bearing shells. If the diameter of each corresponding crankshaft journal is measured and then subtracted from the bearing internal diameter, the result will be the big-end bearing running clearance.

9 The second method is to use Plastigage as described in Section 34, paragraphs 12 to 20. Place a strand of Plastigage on each (cleaned) crankpin journal and refit the (clean) piston/connecting rod assemblies, shells and big-end bearing caps, tightening the bolts to the specified torque wrench settings. Take care not to disturb the Plastigage. Dismantle the assemblies without rotating the crankshaft and use the scale printed on the Plastigage envelope to obtain the big-end bearing running clearance. On completion of the measurement, carefully scrape off all traces of Plastigage from the journal and shells using a fingernail or other object which will not score the components.

Final piston/connecting rod assembly refitting

10 Note that the following procedure assumes that the cylinder liners have been refitted to the cylinder block/crankcase as described in Section 28, and that the crankshaft and main bearing ladder are in place. It is of course possible to refit the piston/connecting rod assemblies to the cylinder bores, to refit the crankshaft and to reassemble the piston/connecting rods on the crankshaft before refitting the main bearing ladder (see Section 34).

11 Clean the backs of the bearing shells and the bearing recesses in both the connecting rod and the big-end bearing cap. If new shells are being fitted, ensure that all traces of the protective grease are cleaned off using paraffin. Wipe dry the shells and connecting rods with a lint-free cloth.

12 Press the bearing shells into their locations, ensuring that the tab on each shell engages in the notch in the connecting rod or big-end bearing cap and taking care not to touch any shell's bearing surface with your fingers. Note the following points:

(a) If bearing shells of differing grades are to be fitted to the same journal, the thicker shell must always be fitted to the big-end bearing cap location (see paragraph 1 above).

(b) On all engines, if the original big-end bearing shells are being re-used these must be refitted to their original locations in the connecting rod and big-end bearing cap.

13 Lubricate the cylinder bores, the pistons and piston rings then lay out each piston/connecting rod assembly in its respective position.

14 Starting with assembly number 1, make sure that the piston rings are still spaced as shown in Fig. 2.23, then clamp them in position with a piston ring compressor.

15 Insert the piston/connecting rod assembly into the top of liner number 1, ensuring that the arrow (or 'FRONT' marking) on the piston crown faces the timing belt end of the engine; note that the stamped marks on the connecting rod and big-end bearing cap should face the front (alternator bracket side) of the engine. Using a block of wood or hammer handle against the piston crown, tap the assembly into the liner until the piston crown is flush with the top of the liner (photos).

16 Ensure that the bearing shell is still correctly installed. Taking care not to mark the liner bores, liberally lubricate the crankpin and both bearing shells, then pull the piston/connecting rod assembly down the bore and onto the crankpin. Noting that the faces with the stamped marks must match (which means that the bearing shell locating tabs abut each other), refit the big-end bearing cap, tightening the bolts finger-tight at first.

17 Use a torque wrench to tighten the bolts evenly to the (first stage) torque wrench setting specified, then use an angular torque gauge to tighten the bolts evenly through the (second stage) angle specified (photos).

18 Repeat the procedure for the remaining three piston/connecting rod assemblies.

19 Thoroughly degrease the mating surfaces of the oil rail and the main bearing ladder. Apply the special Rover sealant to the oil rail mating surface as shown in Fig. 2.27. Carefully follow the instructions supplied with the sealant kit.

20 Refit the oil rail, tightening the nuts to the specified torque wrench setting.
21 Refit the oil pump pick-up/strainer pipe and sump as described in Section 12.
22 Refit the cylinder head as described in Section 11. Rotate the crankshaft to the 90° BTDC position so that the crankshaft sprocket timing marks align as described in Section 7, paragraph 15.
23 Refit the dipstick tube to the cylinder block/crankcase, tightening the bolts to the specified torque wrench setting.
24 Refit the hydraulic tappets and camshaft(s) as described in Section 10.
25 Refit the timing belt inner cover, sprocket(s) and tensioner, and the belt itself as described in Sections 6, 7 and 8.
26 Using a torque wrench, check that the amount of force required to rotate the crankshaft does not exceed 31 Nm; if the effort required is greater than this, the engine must be dismantled again to trace and rectify the cause. This value takes into account the increased friction of a new engine and is much higher than the actual pressure required to rotate a run-in engine, so do not make allowances for 'tight' components; if excessive pressure is required to rotate the crankshaft, the engine has not been rebuilt to the required standard and **must** be dismantled again.

36 Engine – initial start-up after overhaul

1 With the engine refitted in the car, double-check the engine oil and coolant levels. Make a final check that everything has been reconnected and that there are no tools or rags left in the engine compartment.
2 With the spark plugs removed and the ignition system disabled by earthing the ignition HT coil distributor spark plug (HT) lead with a jumper lead, turn the engine over on the starter until the oil pressure warning lamp goes out.
3 Refit the spark plugs and connect all the spark plug (HT) leads, referring to Chapter 1 for further information.
4 Start the engine, noting that this may take a little longer than usual due to the fuel system components being empty.
5 While the engine is idling, check for fuel, water and oil leaks. Don't be alarmed if there are some odd smells and smoke from parts getting hot and burning off oil deposits. If the hydraulic tappets have been disturbed, some valve gear noise may be heard at first; this should disappear as the oil circulates fully around the engine and normal pressure is restored in the tappets.
6 Keep the engine idling until hot water is felt circulating through the top hose, check the ignition timing and idle speed and mixture (as appropriate), then switch it off.
7 After a few minutes, recheck the oil and coolant levels as described in Chapter 1 and top up as necessary.
8 If they were tightened as described, there is no need to re-tighten the cylinder head bolts once the engine has first run after reassembly.
9 If new pistons, rings or crankshaft bearings have been fitted, the engine must be run-in for the first 500 miles (800 km). Do not operate the engine at full throttle or allow it to labour in any gear during this period. It is recommended that the oil and filter be changed at the end of this period.

Chapter 3
Cooling, heating and ventilation systems

Contents

Specifications

System type .... Pressurised, pump-assisted thermo-syphon with front mounted radiator and thermostatically-controlled electric cooling fan

Thermostat

Type	Wax
Start to open temperature	76 to 80°C
Fully open temperature	82 or 88°C (actual value stamped in unit end)
Full lift height	9.0 mm

Expansion tank cap pressure .... 0.9 to 1.0 bar

Cooling fan operating temperature .... 88 to 92°C

System capacity .... 5.8 litres

Antifreeze properties and quantities

50% antifreeze (by volume):	
Commences freezing	-36°C
Frozen solid	-48°C
Quantities (system refill)	2.9 litres antifreeze, 2.9 litres water
Antifreeze type	Ethylene glycol-based antifreeze with non-phosphate corrosion inhibitors, suitable for mixed-metal engines, containing no methanol and meeting specifications BS6580 and BS5117 (Duckhams Universal Antifreeze & Summer Coolant)

Torque wrench settings

Torque wrench settings	Nm	lbf ft
Radiator cooling fan motor nuts	5	3.5
Coolant temperature gauge sender unit	15	11
Thermostat housing cover bolts	9	6
Thermostat housing/dipstick tube to cylinder block/crankcase bolt	9	6
Coolant rail to cylinder block/crankcase bolts	9	6

Torque wrench settings (continued)

	Nm	lbf ft
Water pump fastenings:		
Pump to timing belt upper left-hand (inner) cover bolt	9	6
Pump to cylinder block/crankcase bolts	10	7
Heater lower mounting nut	21	15
Heater blower motor mounting bolts	10	7
Air conditioning compressor mounting bolts	45	33
Air conditioning pipe union nuts:		
Condenser unions	17	13
Evaporator inlet union (from receiver drier)	17	13
Evaporator outlet union	33	24
Receiver drier union	17	13
Trinary switch	12	9

1 General information

The cooling system is of the pressurised, pump-assisted thermo-syphon type. It consists of the front-mounted radiator (which is of copper/brass, with moulded plastic side tanks), a translucent expansion tank mounted on the right-hand inner wing, a thermostatically-controlled electric cooling fan mounted on the rear of the radiator, a thermostat and a centrifugal water pump, as well as the connecting hoses. The water pump is driven by the engine's timing belt.

The location of the system's components and the direction of coolant flow are shown in Figs. 3.1 and 3.2.

The system is of the by-pass type, allowing coolant to circulate around the engine while the thermostat is closed. Whilst the engine is cold, the thermostat closes off the coolant feed from the bottom radiator hose. The coolant is then drawn into the engine via the heater matrix, inlet manifold and from the top of the cylinder block. This allows some heat transfer, by convection, to the radiator through the top hose whilst retaining the majority of heat within the cylinder block.

The siting of the thermostat in the intake rather than the outlet side of the system ensures that the engine warms up quickly by circulating a

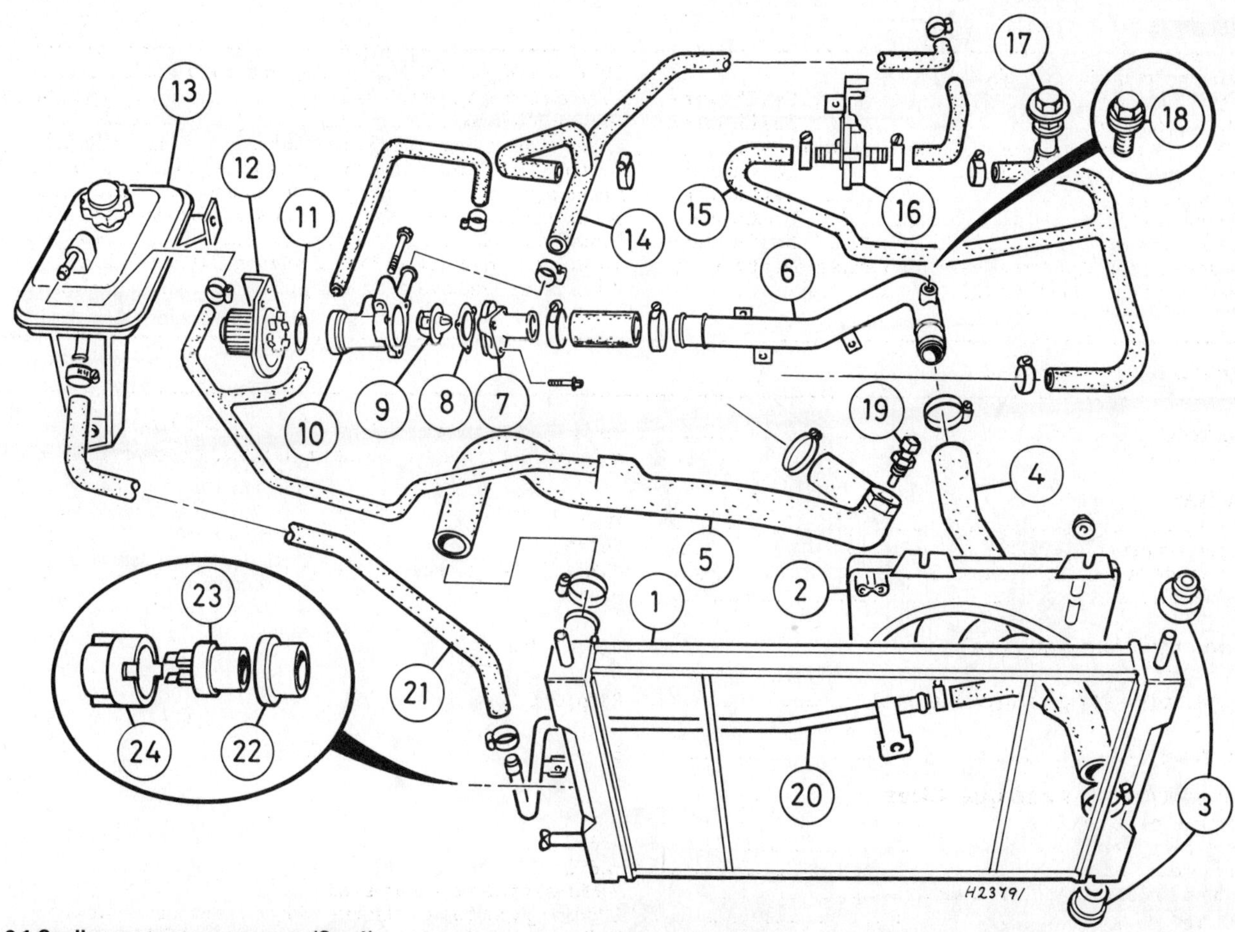

Fig. 3.1 Cooling system components (Sec 1)

1 Radiator
2 Cooling fan and cowling
3 Radiator mounting rubbers
4 Bottom hose
5 Top hose
6 Coolant pipe – bottom hose to thermostat housing
7 Thermostat housing cover
8 Gasket
9 Thermostat
10 Thermostat housing
11 O-ring
12 Water pump
13 Expansion tank
14 Hose – heater matrix and manifold return
15 Hose – heater matrix and manifold feed
16 Heater temperature control valve
17 Coolant filler stem
18 Cooling system bleed screw
19 Engine overheat switch – where fitted
20 Coolant pipe – expansion tank to bottom hose
21 Hose – expansion tank return
22 Sealing ring
23 Cooling fan thermostatic switch
24 Locking ring

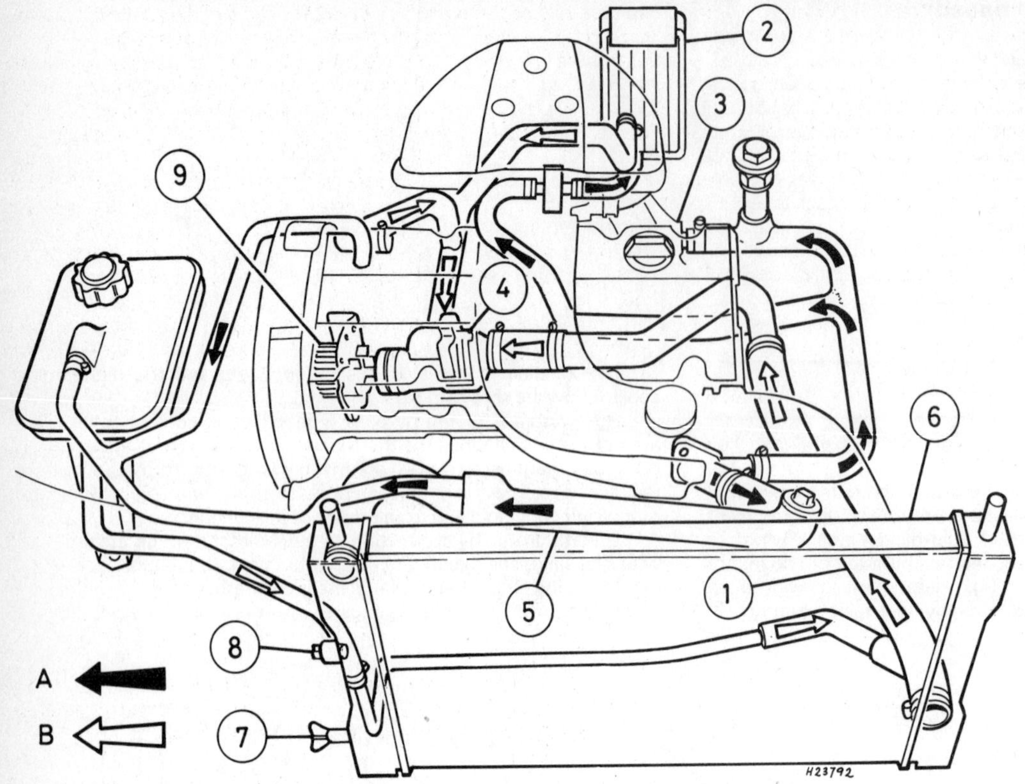

Fig. 3.2 Direction of coolant flow (Sec 1)

1 *Bottom hose*
2 *Heater matrix*
3 *Inlet manifold*
4 *Thermostat housing*
5 *Top hose*
6 *Radiator*
7 *Radiator drain tap*
8 *Cooling fan thermostatic switch*
9 *Water pump*
A *Engine hot*
B *Engine cold*

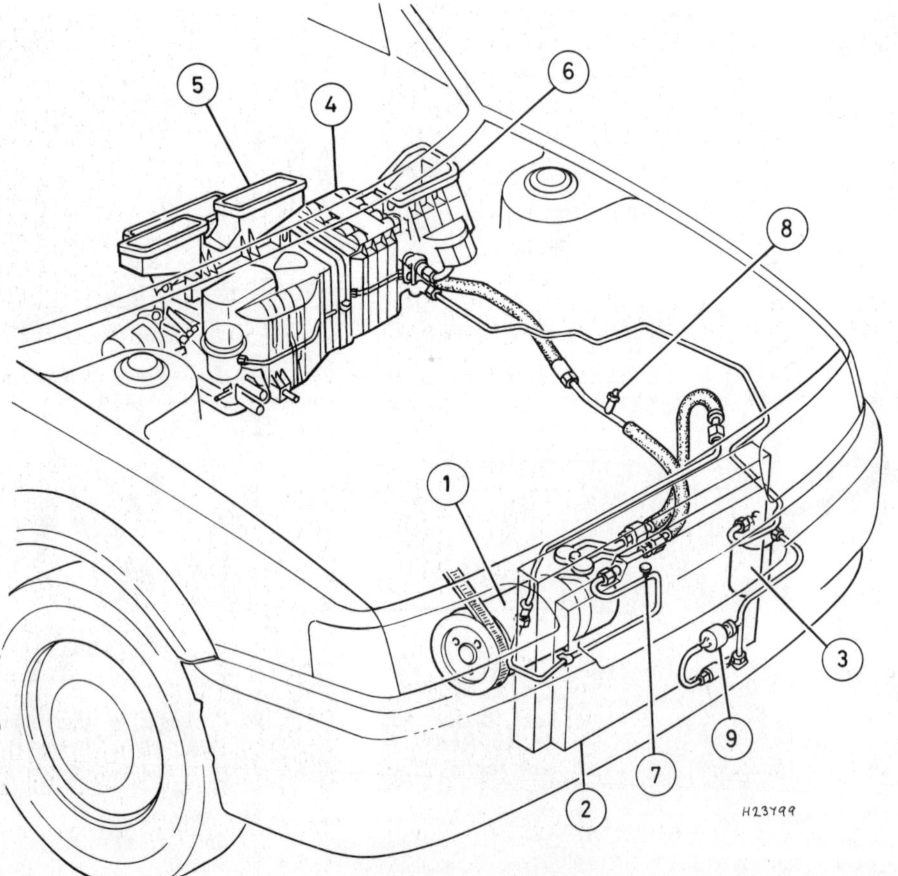

Fig. 3.3 Air conditioning system component layout (Sec 1)

1 *Compressor*
2 *Condenser*
3 *Receiver drier*
4 *Evaporator*
5 *Heater unit*
6 *Blower unit*
7 *High pressure servicing connection*
8 *Low pressure servicing connection*
9 *Trinary switch*

small amount of coolant around a shorter tract. This also prevents temperature build up in the cylinder head prior to the thermostat opening.

When the coolant reaches a predetermined temperature, the thermostat opens and the coolant is allowed to flow freely through the top hose to the radiator. As the coolant circulates through the radiator it is cooled by the inrush of air when the car is in forward motion. Airflow is supplemented by the action of the electric cooling fan when necessary. Upon reaching the bottom of the radiator, the coolant is now cooled and the cycle is repeated.

When the engine is at normal operating temperature the coolant expands and some of it is displaced into the expansion tank. This coolant collects in the tank and is returned to the radiator when the system cools.

The electric cooling fan mounted behind the radiator is controlled by a thermostatic switch located in the radiator side tank. At a predetermined coolant temperature the switch contacts close, thus actuating the fan.

On models equipped with an air conditioning system, it is necessary to observe special precautions whenever dealing with any part of the system, its associated components and any items which necessitate disconnection of the system. If for any reason the system must be disconnected, entrust this task to your Rover dealer or a refrigeration engineer. The layout of the air conditioning system is shown in Fig. 3.3.

Warning: *The refrigeration circuit contains a liquid refrigerant (Freon) and it is therefore dangerous to disconnect any part of the system without specialised knowledge and equipment.*

The refrigerant must not be allowed to come in contact with a naked flame otherwise a poisonous gas will be created. Do not allow the fluid to come in contact with the skin or eyes.

Warning: *Do not attempt to remove the expansion tank filler cap or to disturb any part of the cooling system while it or the engine is hot, as there is a very great risk of scalding. If the expansion tank filler cap must be removed before the engine and radiator have fully cooled down (even though this is not recommended) the pressure in the cooling system must first be released. Cover the cap with a thick layer of cloth, to avoid scalding, and slowly unscrew the filler cap until a hissing sound can be heard. When the hissing has stopped, showing that pressure is released, slowly unscrew the filler cap until it can be removed; if more hissing sounds are heard, wait until they have stopped before unscrewing the cap completely. At all times keep well away from the filler opening.*

Warning: *Do not allow antifreeze to come in contact with your skin or painted surfaces of the vehicle. Rinse off spills immediately with plenty of water. Never leave antifreeze lying around in an open container or in a puddle in the driveway or on the garage floor. Children and pets are attracted by its sweet smell. Antifreeze is fatal if ingested.*

Warning: *If the engine is hot, the electric cooling fan may start rotating even if the engine is not running, so be careful to keep hands, hair and loose clothing well clear when working in the engine compartment.*

2 Radiator and expansion tank – removal, inspection and refitting

Note: *Refer to the warnings given in Section 1 before proceeding further.*

Removal

Radiator

1 Drain the cooling system as described in Chapter 1.

2 On models equipped with air conditioning, remove the condenser fan as described in Section 11, then undo the two bolts securing the air conditioning pipes to the bonnet platform.

3 Remove the air cleaner metal intake duct and intake hose, referring to Chapter 4 for further information.

4 Disconnect the radiator cooling fan wiring connector, then slacken and remove the bolt securing the earth leads to the bonnet platform. Disconnect the wiring from the thermostatic switch(es) which are fitted to the right-hand side of the radiator (photos).

2.4A Disconnect the cooling fan wiring connector then remove the earth lead retaining bolt (arrowed)

2.4B Disconnect the wiring connector from the radiator switch

2.6A Slacken the clips and disconnect the top hose from the radiator...

2.6B ...and engine coolant elbow

2.7A Undo the radiator mounting bolts...

2.7B ...remove the mounting brackets...

2.7C ...and manoeuvre the radiator out of the engine compartment

2.13 Inspect the radiator mounting rubbers for signs of wear and renew if necessary

2.18 On refitting ensure radiator hose clips are securely tightened

5 Slacken the bottom hose retaining clip and disconnect the hose from the radiator.
6 Slacken the retaining clips and disconnect the top hose from both the radiator and engine coolant elbow (photos). Position the hose clear of the radiator so that it does not hinder removal.
7 Undo the two bolts securing the upper mounting brackets to the bonnet platform and remove the brackets from the radiator. Disengage the radiator from its lower mounting points and carefully manoeuvre it out of the engine compartment (photos).

Expansion tank

8 Slacken and remove the three bolts securing the expansion tank to the body. Unscrew the expansion tank cap and tip out its contents into a suitable container.
9 Slacken the retaining clips then disconnect both the hoses from the expansion tank and remove the tank from the vehicle.

Inspection

Radiator

10 If the radiator was removed because of clogging (causing overheating) then try reverse flushing or, in severe cases, use a radiator cleanser strictly in accordance with the manufacturer's instructions; ensure that the cleanser is suitable for use in a copper/brass radiator. Refer to Chapter 1 for further information.
11 Use a soft brush and an air line or garden hose to clear the radiator matrix of leaves, insects, etc.
12 Minor leaks from the radiator can be cured using Holts Radweld. Major leaks or extensive damage should be repaired by a specialist, or the radiator should be renewed or exchanged for a reconditioned unit.
13 Examine the mounting rubbers for signs of damage or deterioration and renew if necessary (photo).

Expansion tank

14 Empty any remaining coolant from the tank and flush it with fresh water to clean it. If the tank is leaking it must be renewed, but it is worth first attempting a repair using a proprietary sealant or suitable adhesive.
15 The expansion tank cap should be cleaned and checked whenever it is removed. Check that its sealing surfaces and threads are clean and undamaged and that they mate correctly with those of the expansion tank.
16 The cap's performance can be checked only using a cap pressure-tester (cooling system tester) with a suitable adaptor. On applying pressure, the cap's pressure relief valve should hold until the specified pressure is reached, at which point the valve should open.
17 If there is any doubt about the cap's performance, it must be renewed; ensure that the replacement is of the correct type and rating.

Refitting

Radiator

18 Refitting is the reverse of the removal procedure, noting the following points (photo):

(a) *Ensure that the radiator is seated correctly and without strain on its mountings.*
(b) *Ensure that the radiator hoses are securely held by the retaining clips.*
(c) *Ensure that all wiring connectors are correctly routed so that they are clear of the cooling fan and are retained by any necessary clips or ties.*
(d) *Refill the cooling system as described in Chapter 1.*

Expansion tank

19 Refitting is the reverse of the removal procedure, noting the following points:

(a) *Ensure that the hoses, especially that between the tank and the radiator, are correctly routed with no kinks or sharp bends and are securely held by the retaining clips.*
(b) *Top up the expansion tank as described in Chapter 1.*

3 Thermostat - removal, testing and refitting

Note: *Refer to the warnings given in Section 1 before proceeding further.*

Removal

1 Note that access to the thermostat is very limited; depending on the

3.1 The thermostat can be removed without disturbing the housing if the inlet manifold is first removed

3.3 Disconnect the coolant rail and heater/inlet manifold hoses (arrowed)...

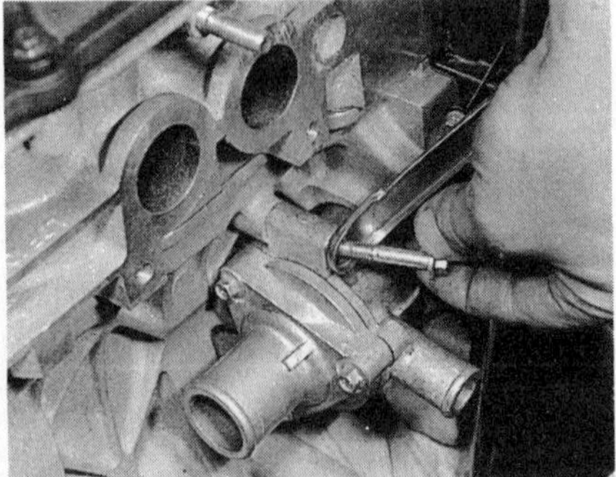
3.4A ...then unscrew the dipstick tube retaining bolt...

3.4B ...and withdraw the thermostat housing noting the O-ring (arrowed) – inlet manifold removed for clarity

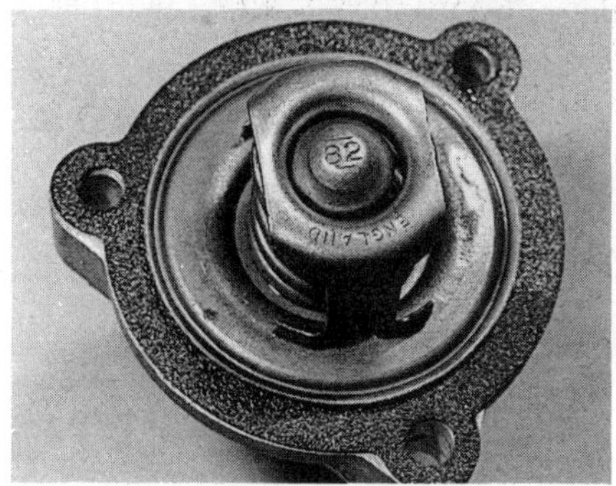

3.8 Note temperature specification stamped in thermostat end

3.10 Thermostat housing refitted and coolant hoses correctly secured

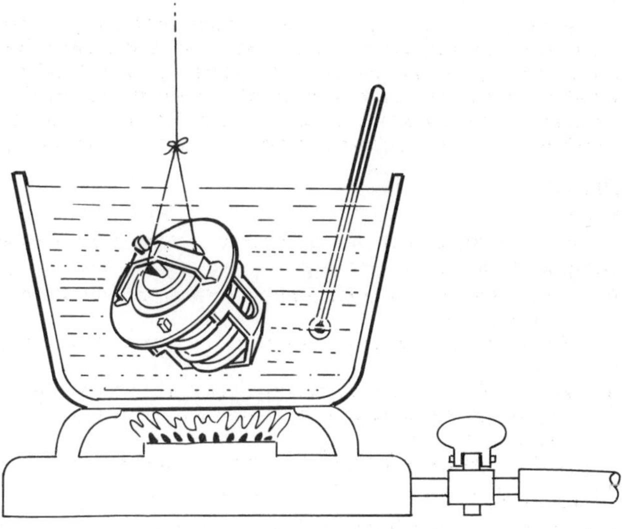

Fig. 3.4 Testing the thermostat (Sec 3)

tools available, it may be easier to raise the front of the car and to work from underneath – ensure the car is securely supported on axle stands. In most cases, however, access is better if the air cleaner and carburettor/throttle body (as appropriate) are removed first and is best if the complete inlet manifold is removed (Chapter 4). If the inlet manifold is removed, the thermostat housing cover can be unbolted to remove the thermostat without disturbing the housing itself (photo). Whichever method is used, first drain the cooling system as described in Chapter 1.

2 On carburettor models equipped with a catalytic converter, either remove the thermostatically-operated vacuum switch, as described in Chapter 5, or disconnect the vacuum pipes from the switch so that it can be removed with the thermostat housing.

3 Unbolt the coolant rail from the rear of the cylinder block/crankcase, then slacken the clips and disconnect the coolant rail hose and heater/inlet manifold return hose from the thermostat housing (photo).

4 Undo the thermostat housing/dipstick tube to cylinder block/crankcase bolt and remove the thermostat housing from the cylinder block/crankcase. Remove the housing O-ring; this must be renewed whenever it is disturbed (photos).

5 Slacken and remove the three thermostat housing cover bolts and lift off the housing cover. Discard the gasket and remove the thermostat.

Testing

6 If the thermostat remains in the open position at room temperature it is faulty and must be renewed as a matter of course.

7 To test it fully, suspend the (closed) thermostat on a length of string in a container of cold water, with a thermometer beside it; ensure that neither touches the side of the container (Fig. 3.4).

8 Heat the water and check the temperature at which the thermostat begins to open; compare this value with that specified. Continue to heat the water until the thermostat is fully open; the temperature at which this should happen is stamped in the unit's end (photo). Remove the thermostat and measure the height of the fully opened valve, then allow the thermostat to cool down and check that it closes fully.

9 If the thermostat does not open and close as described, if it sticks in either position, or if it does not open at the specified temperature, it must be renewed.

Refitting

10 Refitting is the reverse of the removal procedure, noting the following points (photo):

(a) *Clean the thermostat housing, housing cover and cylinder block/crankcase mating surfaces thoroughly.*
(b) *Always fit a new housing cover gasket and O-ring – smear the O-ring with grease to aid refitting.*
(c) *Tighten all bolts to their specified torque wrench settings (where given).*
(d) *Ensure the coolant hose clips are positioned so that they do not foul any other component, then tighten them securely.*
(e) *Refit any components removed for improved access.*
(f) *Refill the cooling system as described in Chapter 1.*

4 Electric cooling fan – testing, removal and refitting

Testing

Note: *On models equipped with air conditioning there are two switches fitted to the right-hand side of the radiator; the lower one of these being the cooling fan switch.*

1 The cooling fan motor is supplied with current via the ignition switch, fuse 4 and the cooling fan relay. The relay is energised by the radiator-mounted thermostatic switch which is fed via fuse number 15.

2 If the fan does not appear to work, first check that both fuses are in good condition and have not blown. Run the engine until normal operating temperature is reached, then allow it to idle. If the fan does not cut in within a few minutes, switch off the ignition and disconnect the two wires from the thermostatic switch. Bridge these two wires with a length of spare wire and switch on the ignition. If the fan now operates, the thermostatic switch is probably faulty and must be tested further as described in Section 5.

3 If the fan still fails to operate check that full battery voltage is available at the switch's light green and grey wire terminal; if not, check the feed for a blown fuse or other fault such as a broken wire. If the feed is good, check the cooling fan relay as described in Chapter 12. If the relay operates correctly check for continuity between the fan motor's black wire terminal and a good earth point on the body; if not, then the earth connection is faulty and must be remade. The circuit earth connection is one of those at earth header 1, attached to the left-hand inner wing panel next to the battery.

4.10A Undo the cooling fan cowling retaining nuts...

4.10B ...and remove the fan assembly from the engine compartment

4.11 Cooling fan motor retaining nuts

4 If the switch and wiring are in good condition, the fault must be in the motor itself. This can be checked by disconnecting it from the wiring loom and connecting a 12 volt supply directly to it. If the motor does not work it must be renewed.

Removal

Note: *Refer to the warnings given in Section 1 of this Chapter before starting work.*

5 Drain the cooling system as described in Chapter 1, then jack up the front of the car and support it securely on axle stands.
6 From underneath the front of the vehicle, slacken and remove the three bolts securing the bumper flange to the body. Remove the seven bolts securing the front undercover panel to the body and remove the panel.
7 Remove the air cleaner metal intake duct and intake hose, referring to Chapter 4 for further information.
8 Slacken the retaining clips and disconnect the top hose from both the radiator and engine. Position the hose clear of the radiator so that it does not hinder removal.
9 Disconnect the radiator cooling fan wiring connector.
10 Undo the four nuts securing the cooling fan cowling to the rear of the radiator and manoeuvre the fan assembly out of the engine compartment (photos).
11 To dismantle the assembly, first prise off the fan retaining circlip, then lift the fan off the motor spindle. Undo the three nuts which secure the motor assembly to the cowling then release the motor wiring and connector and separate the motor and cowling (photo).

Refitting

12 Refitting is a reverse of the removal procedure noting the following points:

- (a) *If necessary, reassemble the fan motor, cowling and fan and tighten the motor retaining nuts to the specified torque. Ensure that the motor wiring is securely retained by the cowling clips.*
- (b) *Ensure that the radiator hose is securely held by its retaining clips.*
- (c) *On completion refill the cooling system as described in Chapter 1.*

5 Cooling system electrical switches – testing, removal and refitting

Note: *Refer to the warnings given in Section 1 before proceeding further.*

Testing

Electric cooling fan thermostatic switch

Note: *On models equipped with air conditioning there are two switches fitted to the right-hand side of the radiator; the lower one of these being the cooling fan switch.*

1 Refer to Section 4 for details of a quick test which should eliminate most faulty switches. If the switch is to be renewed, or to be tested thoroughly, it must be removed.

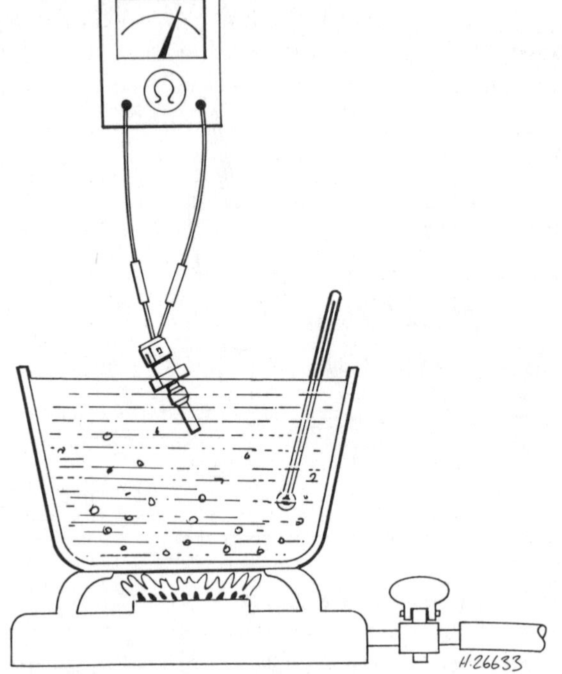

Fig. 3.5 Testing the cooling system electrical switches (Sec 5)

2 To carry out a thorough test of the switch, use two spare wires to connect to it either a multimeter (set to the resistance function) or a battery and bulb test circuit. Suspend the switch in a pan of water which is being heated. Measure the temperature of the water with a thermometer. Do not let either the switch or the thermometer touch the pan itself (Fig. 3.5).
3 The switch contacts should close to the 'On' position (ie, continuity should exist) when the water reaches the temperature specified. Stop heating the water and allow it to cool down; the switch contacts should open at the same temperature or just below.
4 If the switch's performance is significantly different from that specified, or if it does not work at all, it must be renewed.

Coolant temperature gauge sender unit

5 The coolant temperature gauge mounted in the instrument panel is fed with a stabilised 10 volt supply from the instrument panel feed (via the ignition switch and fuse 1), its earth being controlled by the sender unit.
6 The sender unit is screwed into the coolant outlet elbow mounted on the left-hand end of the cylinder head, underneath the distributor (photo). It contains a thermistor, which is an element whose electrical resistance decreases at a predetermined rate as its temperature rises; thus when the coolant is cold, the sender's resistance is high, current

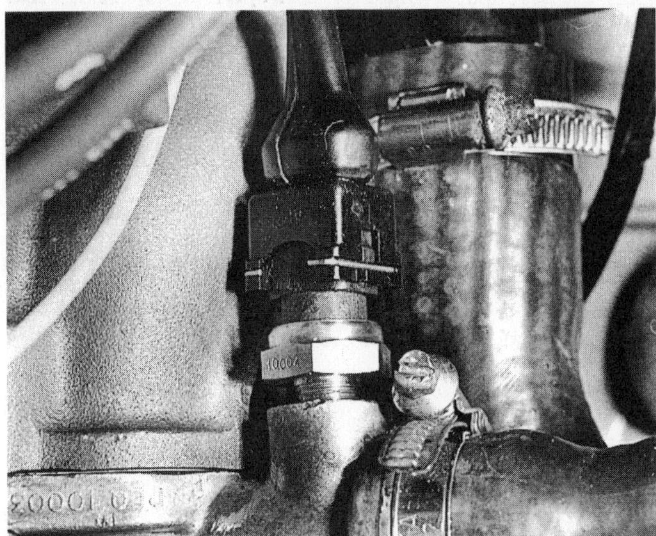

5.6 Coolant temperature gauge sender unit

flow through the gauge is reduced and the gauge needle points to the 'C' (cold) end of the scale. If the unit is faulty it must be renewed.

7 If the gauge develops a fault, check first the other instruments; if they do not work at all, check the instrument panel feed. If the readings are erratic, there may be a fault in the voltage stabiliser which will necessitate the renewal of the gauge unit or printed circuit (see Chapter 12). If the fault is in the temperature gauge alone, check it as follows.

8 If the gauge needle remains at the 'C' end of the scale, disconnect the sender unit wire and earth it to the cylinder head; if the needle then deflects when the ignition is switched on the sender unit is proven faulty and must be renewed. If the needle still does not move, remove the instrument panel as described in Chapter 12 and check the continuity of the green/blue wire between the gauge and the sender unit and the feed to the gauge unit. If continuity is shown, and the fault still exists, then the gauge is faulty and the gauge unit must be renewed.

9 If the gauge needle remains at the 'H' end of the scale, disconnect the sender unit wire; if the needle then returns to the 'C' end of the scale when the ignition is switched on the sender unit is proven faulty and must be renewed. If the needle still does not move, check the remainder of the circuit as described above.

Inlet manifold pre-heater temperature switch – carburettor engines

10 The switch screwed into the underside of the inlet manifold on carburettor engines controls the inlet manifold heater circuit; refer to Chapter 4 for details (photo).

11 The switch contacts should be closed to the 'On' position (ie, continuity should exist) only at temperatures below 50°C; remove the switch and test it as described in paragraphs 2 to 4 above.

Thermostatically-operated vacuum switch – carburettor engines equipped with catalytic converters

12 The switch is screwed into the thermostat housing, refer to Chapter 5, Part A for details.

13 To test the switch, fit two suitable lengths of hose to the switch and suspend the switch in a pan of water which is being heated. Measure the temperature of the water with a thermometer. Do not let either the switch or the thermometer touch the pan itself.

14 Blow down one of the hoses which is attached to the switch; the switch should be closed (ie, passes no air) when the water temperature is below 70°C. Above 70°C the switch should open and air should flow freely through the hoses. Stop heating the water then allow the water to cool down and check that the switch closes at 70°C or just below.

15 If the switch's performance is significantly different from that specified, or if it does not work at all, it must be renewed.

Coolant temperature sensor – fuel-injected engines

16 The sensor screwed into the underside of the inlet manifold is a thermistor (see paragraph 6 above) which is supplied with approximately 5 volts by the engine management system ECU; the ECU also controls the sensor's earth path and, by measuring the amount of current in the sensor circuit, determines the engine's temperature. This information is used, in conjunction with other inputs, to control idle speed, injector opening time duration and ignition timing.

17 If the sensor circuit should fail to provide adequate information, the ECU's back-up facility assumes a value corresponding to 60°C. The sensor itself can be tested only by having a Rover dealer check the complete system using the correct diagnostic equipment; **do not** attempt to 'test' the circuit using any other equipment, or the ECU will be damaged.

Removal

Electric cooling fan thermostatic switch

18 When the engine and radiator are cold, either drain the cooling system as described in Chapter 1, or unscrew the expansion tank filler cap to release any remaining pressure, and have ready a suitable plug that can be used temporarily to stop the escape of coolant while the switch is removed. If the latter method is used, take care not to damage the radiator and do not use anything which will leave foreign matter inside the radiator.

19 Disconnect the battery negative lead.

20 Disconnect the wiring connector from the switch then rotate the locking ring to release it, and withdraw the switch and sealing ring from the radiator (photo).

Coolant temperature gauge sender unit

21 When the engine and radiator are cold, either drain the cooling system as described in Chapter 1, or unscrew the expansion tank filler cap to release any remaining pressure, and have ready a suitable plug that can be used temporarily to stop the escape of coolant while the unit is removed. If the latter method is used, take care not to damage the threads and do not use anything which will leave foreign matter inside the cooling system.

22 Disconnect the battery negative lead.

23 Disconnect the unit's wiring connector and unscrew the unit from the coolant outlet elbow.

Inlet manifold pre-heater temperature switch – carburettor engines

24 Refer to Chapter 4, Section 15.

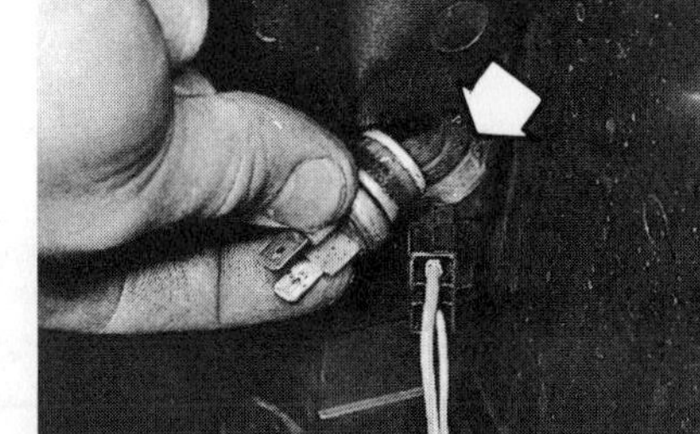

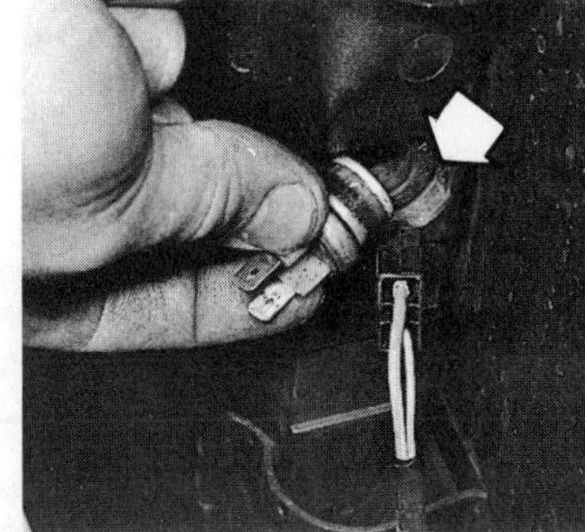

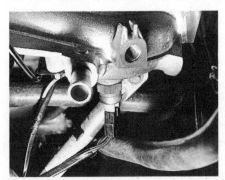

5.10 Inlet manifold pre-heater temperature switch (carburettor engines)

5.20 Remove the cooling fan thermostatic switch and withdraw the sealing ring (arrowed)

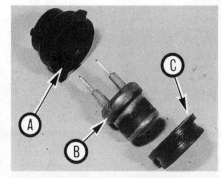

5.27 Cooling fan switch locking ring 'A', thermostatic switch 'B' and sealing ring 'C'

Thermostatically-operated vacuum switch - carburettor engines equipped with catalytic converters

25 Refer to Chapter 5, Section 6.

Coolant temperature sensor - fuel-injected engines

26 Refer to Chapter 4, Section 33.

Refitting

Electric cooling fan thermostatic switch

27 On refitting, renew the sealing ring if it is worn or compressed and clean carefully the radiator seat before pressing in the sealing ring and switch (photo). Refit the locking ring and rotate it to tighten it securely. Reconnect the switch and battery, then refill the cooling system or check the coolant level (as applicable) as described in Chapter 1.

Coolant temperature gauge sender unit

28 On refitting, apply a suitable sealant to the unit threads and tighten it to its specified torque wrench setting. Reconnect the unit and battery, then refill the cooling system or check the coolant level, (as applicable) as described in Chapter 1.

Inlet manifold pre-heater temperature switch - carburettor engines

29 Refer to Chapter 4, Section 15.

Thermostatically-operated vacuum switch - carburettor engines equipped with catalytic converters

30 Refer to Chapter 5, Section 6.

Coolant temperature sensor - fuel-injected engines

31 Refer to Chapter 4, Section 33.

6 Water pump - removal and refitting

Note: *Refer to the warnings given in Section 1 before proceeding further.*

Removal

1 Water pump failure is usually indicated by coolant leaking from the gland behind the pump's bearing, or by rough and noisy operation, usually accompanied by excessive pump spindle play. If the pump shows any of these symptoms it must be renewed as follows.
2 Drain the cooling system as described in Chapter 1.
3 Remove the timing belt as described in Chapter 2, Section 7.
4 Noting the location of the pillar bolt(s), unscrew the five bolts securing the water pump to the cylinder block/crankcase, then unscrew the single bolt securing the pump to the timing belt upper left-hand (inner) cover.
5 Withdraw the water pump and discard its sealing O-ring; this should be renewed whenever it is disturbed. Carefully clean the cylinder block/crankcase mating surface and the pump socket (photo).

6.5 Removing the water pump

Refitting

6 On refitting, install the pump using a new sealing O-ring and tighten the bolts to the specified torque wrench settings. The remainder of the refitting procedure is the reverse of removal; refer to the relevant sections of Chapters 1 and 2.

7 Cooling system hoses - renewal

Note: *Refer to the warnings given in Section 1 before proceeding further.*

1 If the checks described in Chapter 1 reveal a faulty hose, it must be renewed as follows.
2 First drain the cooling system as described in Chapter 1; if the antifreeze is not due for renewal, the drained coolant may be re-used if it is collected in a clean container.
3 To disconnect any hose, use a screwdriver to slacken the clips, then move them along the hose clear of the outlet. Carefully work the hose off its outlets. While the hoses can be removed with relative ease when new or warm, **do not** attempt to disconnect any part of the system when it is still hot (Section 1).
4 Note that the radiator hose outlets are fragile; do not use excessive force when attempting to remove the hoses. If a hose proves stubborn try to release it by rotating it on its outlets before attempting to work it off. If all else fails, cut the hose with a sharp knife then slit it so that it can be peeled off in two pieces. While expensive, this is preferable to buying a new radiator.
5 When refitting a hose first slide the clips onto the hose, then work the hose onto its outlets. If the hose is stiff, use soap as a lubricant or soften it by first soaking it in boiling water, but take care to prevent scalding.
6 Work each hose end fully onto its outlet, check that the hose is settled correctly and is properly routed, then slide each clip along the hose until it is behind the outlet flared end before tightening it securely.
7 Refill the system with coolant as described in Chapter 1.
8 Check carefully for leaks as soon as possible after disturbing any part of the cooling system.

8 Heater components - removal and refitting

Note: *Refer to the warnings given in Section 1 before proceeding further.*

Removal

Heater unit

1 Drain the cooling system as described in Chapter 1.
2 Working in the engine compartment, slacken the hose clips and disconnect the heater feed and return hoses from the matrix outlets on the bulkhead. Disconnect the inner cable from the heater valve and free the outer cable from its retaining clip. Slacken and remove the heater lower mounting nut which is situated just to the left of the matrix outlets (photos).
3 Remove the facia as described in Chapter 11.
4 Slacken and remove the two retaining screws and remove the blower motor to heater unit duct (photo).

Note: *On models equipped with air conditioning, the evaporator unit is fitted in place of the duct. It may be possible to gain the necessary clearance required to disengage the evaporator from the heater unit by removing the mounting brackets and nuts, if not, the evaporator must be removed. Refer to Section 11 for further information.*

5 Undo the screw securing the right-hand heater duct to the mounting bracket, then move the duct to the right to disengage it from the heater unit (photos).
6 Undo the inertia switch retaining nut and disengage the switch from the steering column support bracket.
7 Release the wiring block connector from the right-hand end of the steering column support bracket and undo the fusebox retaining nut. Slacken and remove the five support bracket retaining bolts and remove the bracket from the car (photos).

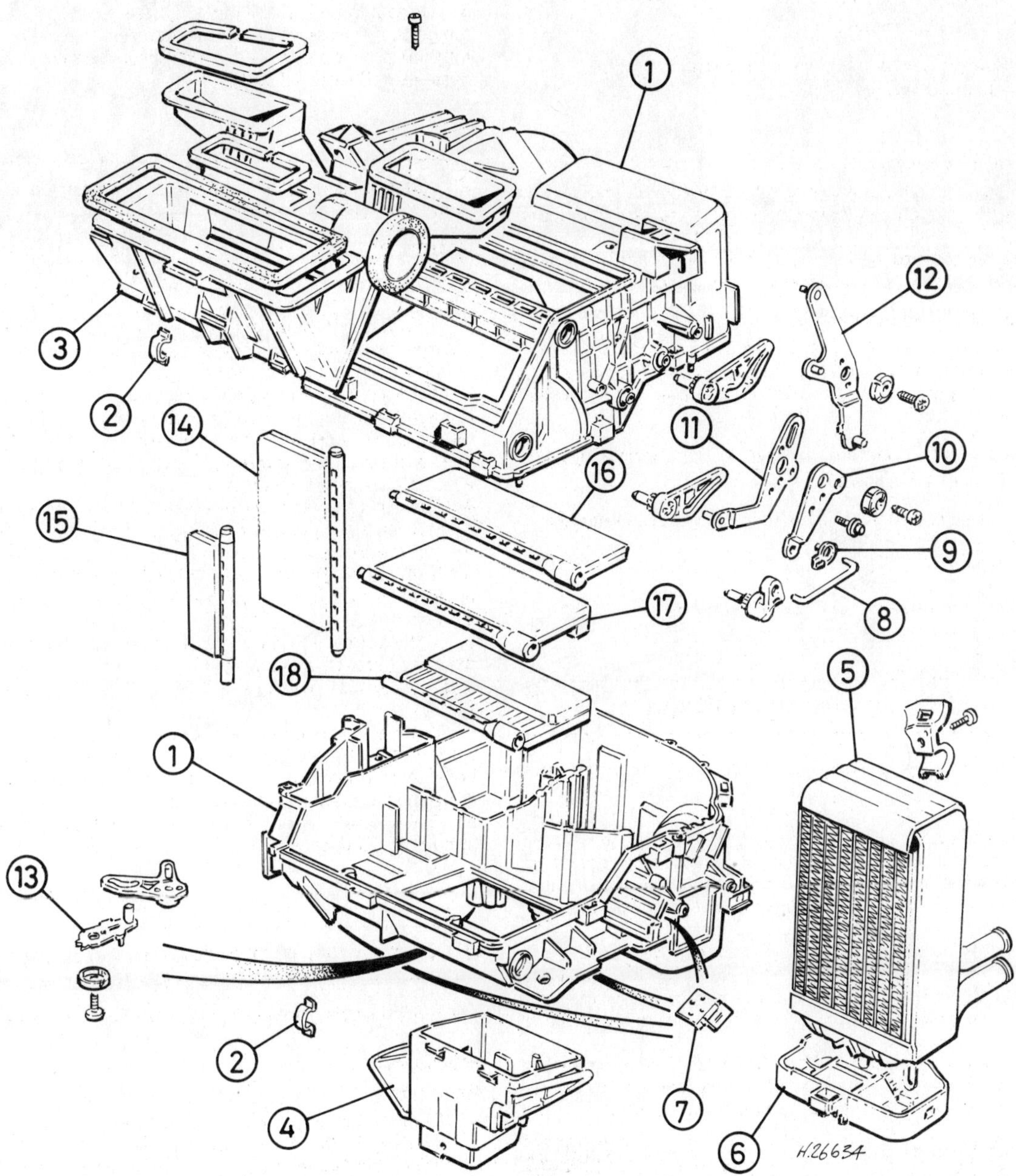

Fig. 3.6 Heater unit components (Sec 8)

1 Heater case
2 Heater case clip
3 Face level/windscreen duct
4 Floor level duct
5 Heater matrix
6 Heater matrix cover
7 Cable retaining clip
8 Floor level flap operating lever
9 Clip
10 Floor level flap idler lever
11 Face level flap idler lever
12 Flap operating lever
13 Air mix flap operating lever
14 Air mix flap
15 Ambient air flap – centre console vents
16 Distribution flap – windscreen
17 Distribution flap – face level vents
18 Distribution flap – floor level vents

8 Disconnect the air recirculation inner cable from the flap and free the outer cable from the blower motor.

9 Prise out the stud securing the rear heater duct sleeve to the bottom of the heater unit, and slide the sleeve down to disengage it from the unit (photo).

10 Disconnect the wiring connectors from the heater control panel, then remove the two upper heater unit retaining nuts and carefully manoeuvre the heater unit out of the car (photos).

Heater matrix

11 Remove the heater unit as described above.

12 Undo the screw securing the matrix outlet pipe bracket to the heater unit and remove the bracket (photo).

13 Slacken and remove the two matrix cover retaining screws then remove the cover and withdraw the matrix from the heater unit (photos).

14 If the matrix is leaking it is best to obtain a new or reconditioned unit; home repairs are seldom successful. If it is blocked it can sometimes be cleared by reverse flushing using a garden hose, using a proprietary radiator cleaning product if absolutely necessary. Refer to Chapter 1 for further information.

Heater blower motor

15 Undo the two glovebox retaining screws then partially withdraw

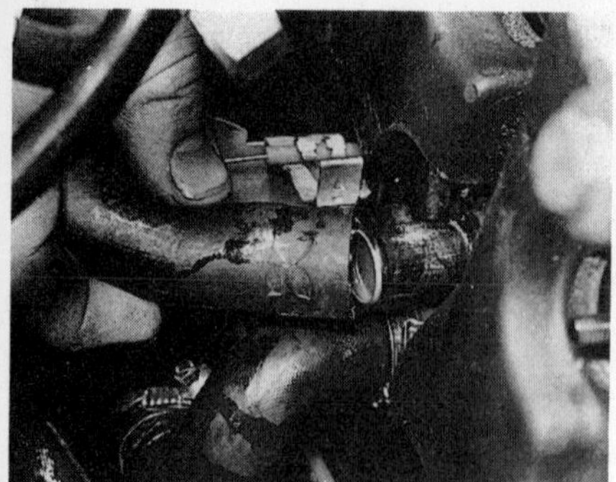

8.2A Disconnect the heater feed and return hoses...

8.2B ...and free the heater valve cable from the retaining clip

8.2C Slacken and remove the heater unit lower mounting nut

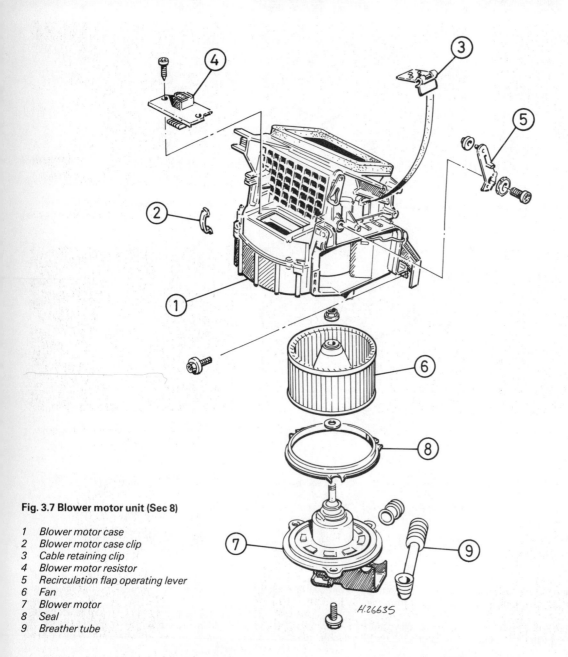

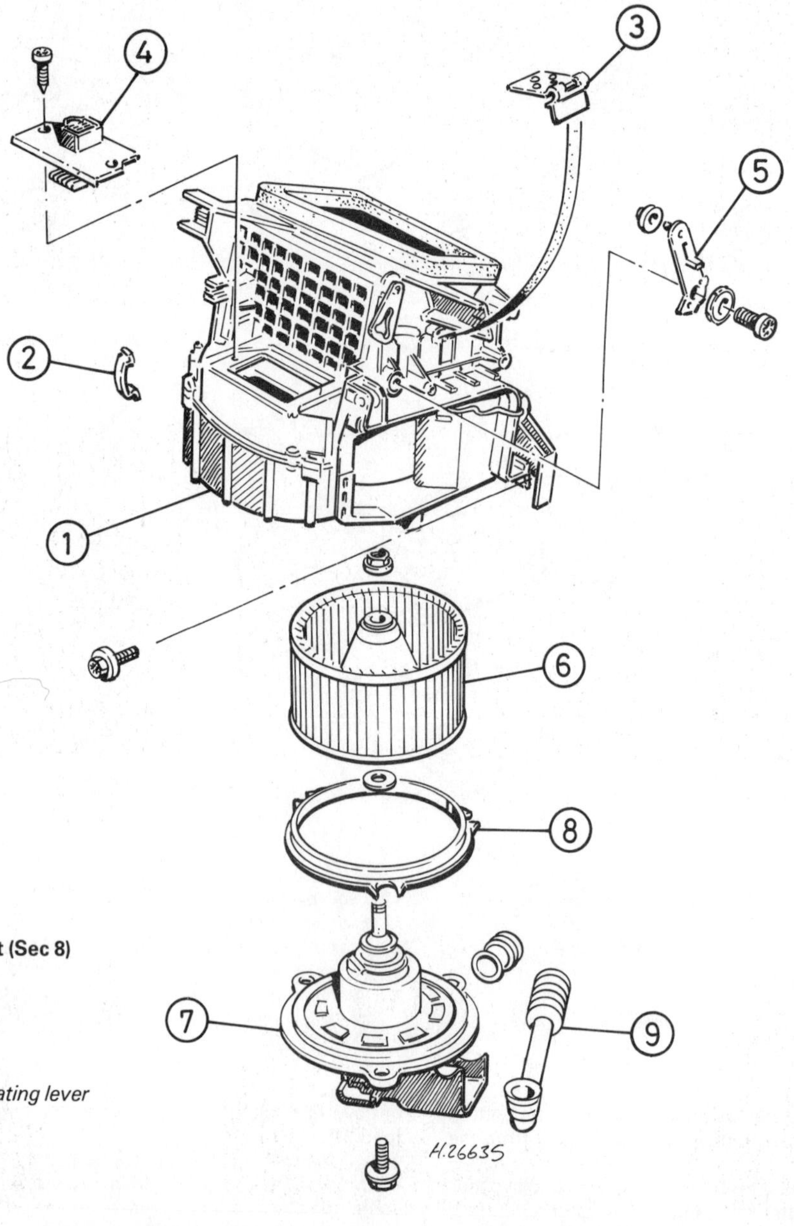

Fig. 3.7 Blower motor unit (Sec 8)

1 *Blower motor case*
2 *Blower motor case clip*
3 *Cable retaining clip*
4 *Blower motor resistor*
5 *Recirculation flap operating lever*
6 *Fan*
7 *Blower motor*
8 *Seal*
9 *Breather tube*

8.4 Remove the blower motor to heater unit duct

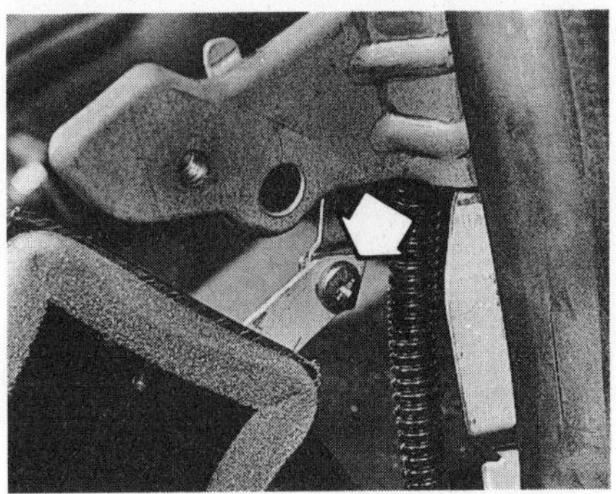

8.5A Undo the right-hand duct retaining screw (arrowed)...

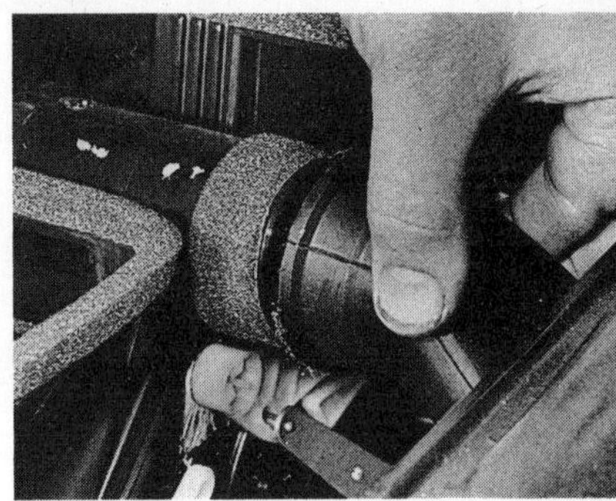

8.5B ...and disengage the duct from the heater unit

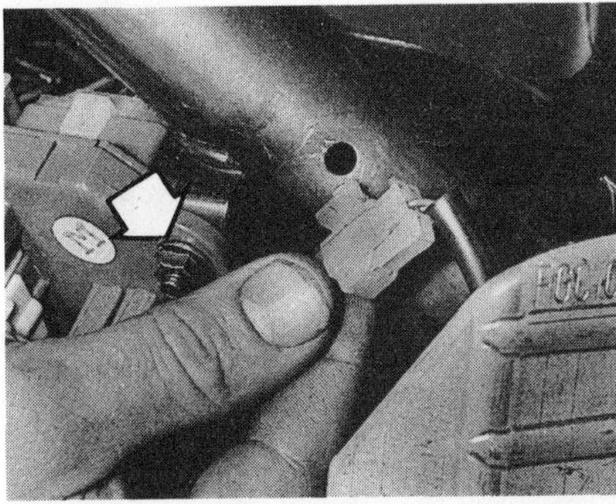

8.7A Release the wiring connector from the steering column support bracket and remove the fusebox nut (arrowed)

8.7B Remove the mounting bolts and manoeuvre the steering column mounting bracket out of position

8.9 Remove the retaining stud and disengage the rear heater duct sleeve from the heater unit

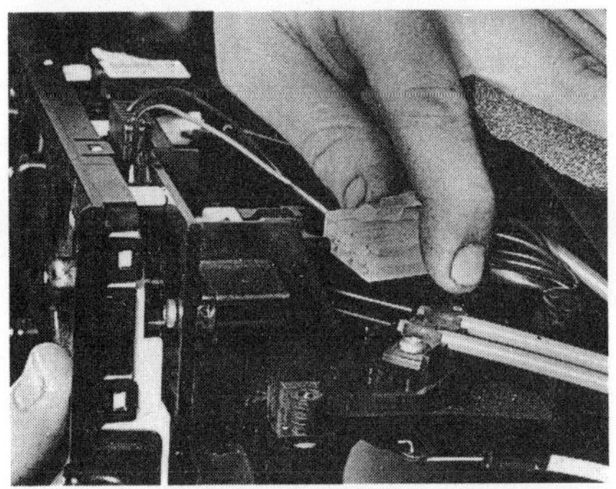

8.10A Disconnect the wiring from the heater control panel...

8.10B ...and remove the heater retaining nuts

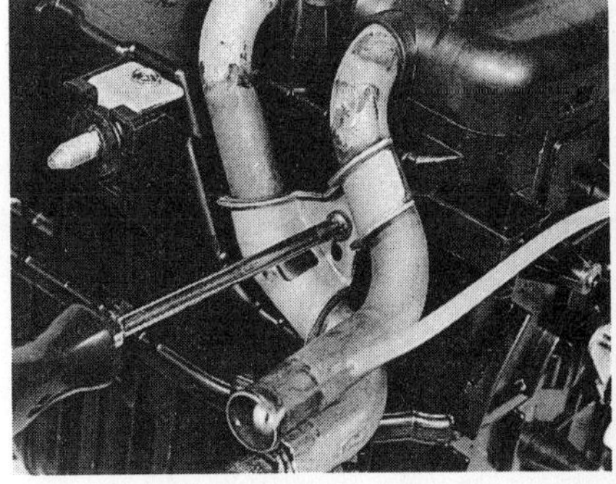

8.12 Undo the retaining screw and remove the matrix outlet pipe bracket

8.13A Undo the two matrix cover retaining screws...

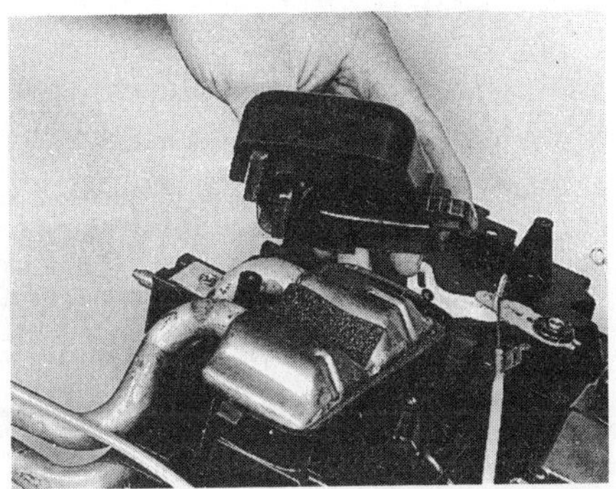

8.13B ...then remove the cover...

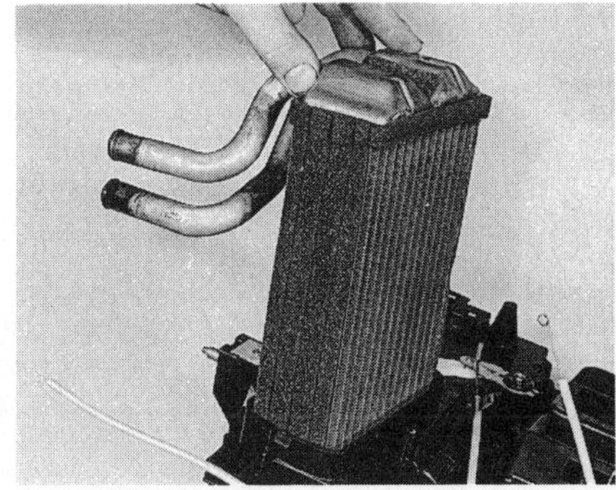

8.13C ...and withdraw the matrix from the heater unit

8.15 Glovebox damper retaining screw (arrowed)

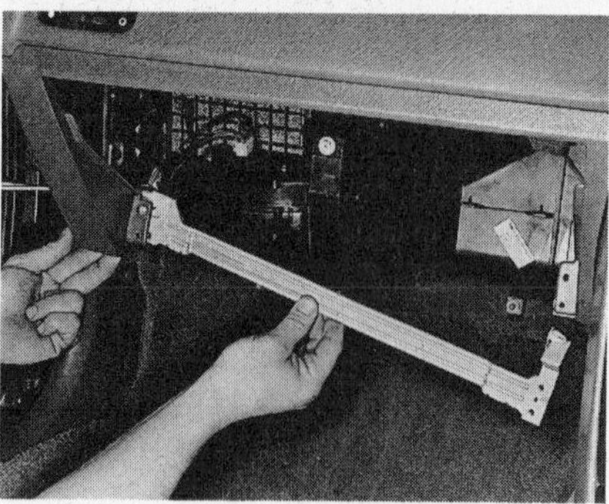
8.16 Remove the glovebox support rail...

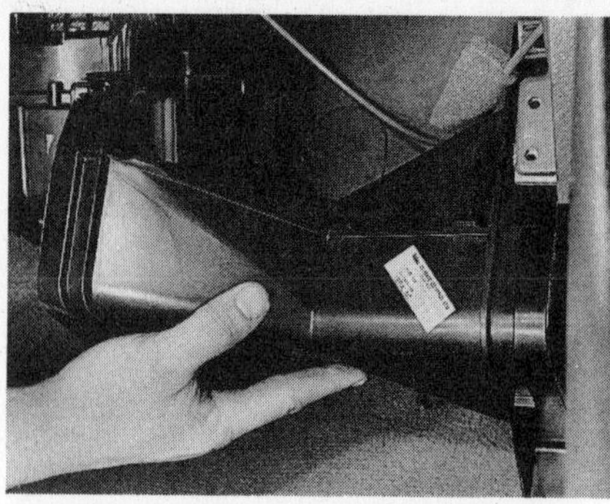
8.17 ...then remove the blower motor to heater unit duct

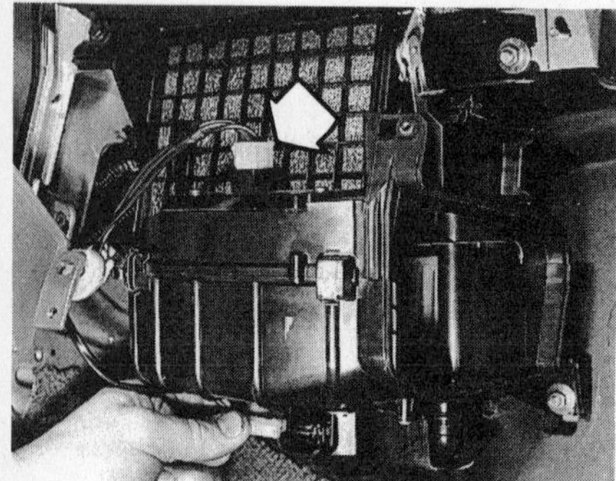
8.18 Disconnect the air recirculation cable and the motor wiring connectors (arrowed)

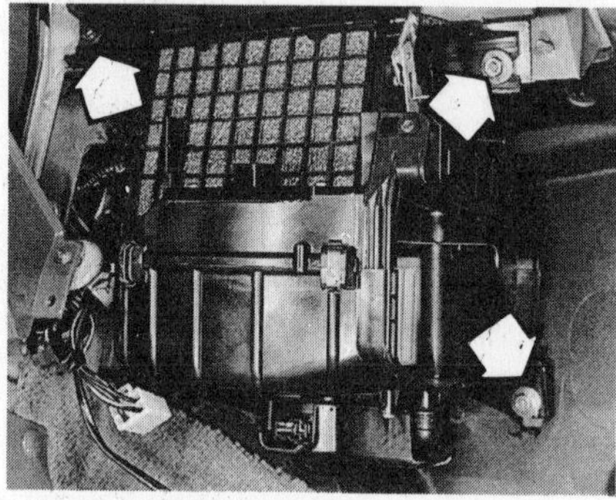
8.19A Undo the three blower motor mounting bolts (arrowed)...

8.19B ...and remove the unit from behind the facia

8.20A Remove the motor cover retaining screws (arrowed)...

8.20B ...and disconnect the breather hose

8.20C Undo the motor retaining bolts and withdraw the motor from the unit

the glovebox until access can be gained to the glovebox damper to facia screw. Undo the damper screw and remove the glovebox and damper (photo).

16 Slacken and remove the four glovebox support rail mounting bolts and remove the rail (photo).

17 Slacken and remove the two retaining screws and remove the blower motor to heater unit duct (photo).

Note: *On models equipped with air conditioning, the evaporator unit is fitted in place of the duct. It may be possible to gain the necessary clearance required to disengage the evaporator and remove the blower motor by removing the mounting brackets and nuts, if not, the evaporator must be removed. Refer to Section 11 for further information.*

18 Disconnect the air recirculation inner cable from the flap and free the outer cable from the blower motor. Disconnect the two blower motor wiring connectors (photo).

19 Slacken and remove the three blower motor mounting bolts and manoeuvre the blower unit out from underneath the facia (photos).

20 To remove the motor from the unit, undo the four motor cover retaining screws, then disconnect the breather hose and lift off the cover. Slacken and remove the three motor retaining bolts and withdraw the motor assembly from the blower unit. Undo the fan retaining nut and separate the fan and motor noting the seal which is fitted between the two components (photos).

Heater blower motor resistor

21 Remove the glovebox as described in paragraphs 15 and 16.

22 Disconnect the wiring connector, then undo the two retaining screws and remove the resistor from the front of the motor assembly.

Heater valve

23 Working in the engine compartment, disconnect the inner cable from the heater valve and free the outer cable from the retaining clip.

24 Slacken and remove the bolt securing the heater valve mounting bracket to the engine compartment bulkhead.

8.20D Remove the fan retaining nut...

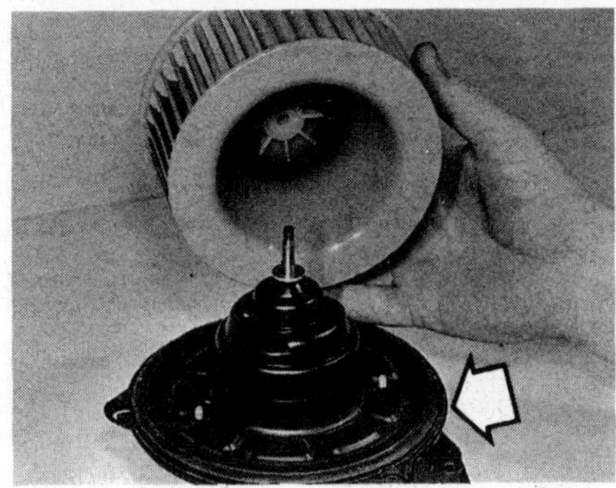
8.20E ...and lift off the fan noting the seal (arrowed)

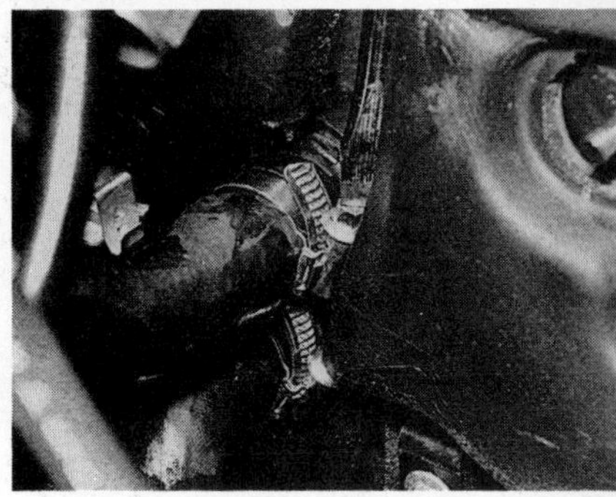
8.27 Ensure heater feed and return hose clips are securely tightened

25 Either drain the cooling system as described in Chapter 1, or clamp the coolant hoses on each side of the coolant valve to minimise the loss of coolant.
26 Slacken the hose retaining clips, then disconnect both hoses from the coolant valve and remove the valve from the engine compartment. Mop up any spilt coolant immediately.

Refitting

Heater unit

27 Refitting is a reverse of the removal procedure noting the following points (photo):

- *(a) Ensure that the heater ducts are securely connected to the unit so that there are no air leaks or gaps.*
- *(b) Check the operation of all heater cables before refitting the facia, ensuring that the relevant component moves smoothly from the fully open to the fully closed position. If necessary adjustments can be made by releasing the relevant retaining clip and repositioning the outer cable.*
- *(c) Ensure that the heater hoses are correctly reconnected and are securely held by the retaining clips.*
- *(d) Tighten the lower heater mounting nut to the specified torque setting.*
- *(e) Refill the cooling system as described in Chapter 1.*

Heater matrix

28 Refitting is a reverse of the removal procedure.

Heater blower motor

29 Refitting is a reversal of the removal sequence, noting the following points:

- *(a) Ensure that the foam rubber seal is refitted correctly so that the blower motor to bulkhead aperture is closed off.*
- *(b) Tighten the blower motor mounting bolts to the specified torque setting.*
- *(c) Ensure that the air recirculation cable and flap functions correctly before refitting the glovebox. If necessary, adjust by releasing the cable retaining clip and repositioning the outer cable.*

Heater blower motor resistor

30 Refitting is a reverse of the removal procedure.

Heater valve

31 Refitting is a reversal of the removal procedure. On completion check the heater cable operates smoothly and top up or refill (as applicable) the cooling system as described in Chapter 1.

9 Heater ducts and vents – removal and refitting

Removal

Facia ducts

1 Remove the facia as described in Chapter 11.
2 The ducts are mounted onto the facia assembly and can be removed individually once the retaining screws have been removed.

Heater unit ducts

3 The left-hand heater unit to blower motor duct is removed as described in paragraphs 15 to 17 of Section 8.
4 To remove the right-hand duct, remove the facia as described in Chapter 11. Slacken and remove the retaining screw which secures the right-hand end of the duct to the mounting bracket and release the radio aerial from the retaining clips on the underside of the duct. The duct can then be manoeuvred out of position.
5 Removal of the lower ducts which supply air to the rear passenger footwells is a complex job, requiring the removal of the front seats, centre console and the various trim panels so that the floor carpet can be peeled back, and is therefore not recommended.

Centre console vents

6 Remove the centre console as described in Chapter 11.
7 The vents can then be unclipped from the rear of the front console section and removed.

Facia vents

8 The adjustable face-level vents can be removed by prising them gently out of the facia until the clips are released, taking care not to mark the facia.
9 The door window demister vents, fitted to the sides of the facia, can also be prised out of position once the relevant door has been opened.

Refitting

10 Refitting is a reverse of the removal procedure.

10 Heater controls – removal, refitting and adjustment

Removal

1 Remove the heater unit as described in Section 8.
2 Disconnect the heater control cables from the heater unit and unclip the control panel. Remove the panel assembly complete with cables (photos).

Refitting and adjustment

3 Refit the heater control panel to the heater unit and reconnect the necessary control cables to their original positions.
4 Check the operation of the control cables, ensuring that they operate smoothly and move the necessary component from the fully open to the fully closed position. Adjustments can be made by releasing the cable retaining clip and repositioning the outer cable.
5 Once the necessary control cables are functioning correctly refit the heater unit as described in Section 8.

10.2A Disconnect the control cables from the heater unit...

10.2B ...and remove the heater control panel and cables as an assembly

11 Air conditioning system components – removal and refitting

Warning: *The system should be professionally discharged before carrying out any of the following work. Cap or plug the pipe lines as soon as they are disconnected to prevent the entry of moisture. Refer to the precautions given in Section 1 before proceeding.*

Compressor

Removal

1 Remove the alternator/air conditioning compressor drivebelt as described in Chapter 1.

2 Disconnect the air conditioning pipes from the compressor.

3 Slacken and remove the four bolts securing the compressor to the mounting bracket and manoeuvre it downwards and away from the engine.

Refitting

4 Refitting is a reverse of the removal sequence, tightening the compressor mounting bolts to the specified torque setting. Ensure that the compressor pipe unions are securely tightened then refit and adjust the drivebelt as described in Chapter 1. On completion have the air conditioning system recharged by a refrigeration specialist or suitably equipped Rover dealer.

Condenser

Removal

5 Remove the front bumper as described in Chapter 11.

6 Slacken and remove the bolts securing the power steering oil cooler to the body, then undo the bonnet lock mounting bracket bolts and position the lock assembly clear of the condenser unit.

7 Unscrew the air conditioning pipe union nuts from the condenser unit then disconnect the pipes. Discard the union pipe O-rings as these must be renewed whenever they are disturbed.

8 Slacken and remove the four retaining bolts and withdraw both the condenser upper mounting brackets. Release the condenser from its lower mounting points and manoeuvre it away from the car.

Refitting

9 Prior to refitting check the condenser lower mounting rubbers for signs of damage or deterioration and renew as necessary. Renew the pipe union O-rings as a matter of course.

10 Refitting is a direct reversal of the removal procedure, tightening the pipe union nuts to the specified torque setting. On completion have the air conditioning system recharged by a refrigeration specialist or a suitably equipped Rover dealer.

Condenser cooling fan

Removal

11 Drain the cooling system as described in Chapter 1.

12 Disconnect the wiring connector from the engine overheat switch, located in the top coolant hose, then slacken the clips securing the hose to the radiator and engine. Disconnect the hose from the radiator and engine and position it clear of the condenser so that it does not hinder removal.

13 Disconnect the condenser fan electrical wiring connector then undo the four fan cowling retaining nuts and manoeuvre the assembly out of the engine compartment.

14 To dismantle the assembly, first undo the fan retaining nut then lift the fan off the motor spindle. Undo the two screws which secure the motor assembly to the cowling then release the motor wiring and connector and separate the motor and cowling.

Refitting

15 Refitting is a reverse of the removal procedure noting the following points:

(a) Ensure that the motor wiring is securely retained by the cowling clips and is clear of the condenser fan.
(b) Ensure that the radiator hose is securely held by its retaining clips.
(c) On completion refill the cooling system as described in Chapter 1.

Evaporator

Removal

16 Undo the three bolts which secure the washer system reservoir to the engine compartment bulkhead and move the reservoir to gain access to the two evaporator union nuts. Slacken both the union nuts and disconnect the pipes from the evaporator. Remove the O-rings from the union nuts and discard them.

17 Working from inside the car, undo the two glovebox retaining screws, then partially withdraw the glovebox until access can be gained to the glovebox damper to facia screw. Undo the damper screw and remove the glovebox and damper.

18 Slacken and remove the four glovebox support rail mounting bolts and remove the rail.

19 Undo the two evaporator bracket retaining bolts and remove both the brackets.

20 Disconnect the wiring connector from the right-hand side of the evaporator.

21 Slacken and remove the two evaporator mounting nuts and manoeuvre the unit out of position.

Refitting

22 Refitting is a reverse of the removal procedure noting the following points:

- *(a) Ensure that the evaporator is correctly joined to the heater unit and blower motor, so that there are no air leaks or gaps, then tighten the retaining nuts and bracket bolts securely.*
- *(b) Fit new O-rings to the pipe unions and tighten the union nuts to the specified torque setting.*
- *(c) On completion have the system recharged by a refrigeration specialist or a suitably equipped Rover dealer.*

Receiver drier

Note: *The receiver drier unit unions must be capped immediately after they are disconnected and must remain capped until they are to be reconnected. If the receiver drier unit is left uncapped for any period of time it must be renewed.*

Removal

23 Remove the left-hand headlamp and the battery and battery tray as described in the relevant Sections of Chapter 12.

24 Undo the two screws securing the air intake grille to the body. Disengage the grille from the resonator and remove it from the vehicle. Move the resonator to one side to gain access to the receiver drier.

25 Slacken the union nuts and disconnect the pipes from the receiver drier noting the O-rings which are fitted to the pipe unions; discard the O-rings as they must be renewed whenever they are disturbed.

26 Slacken the receiver drier clamp bolt then slide the unit out of the retaining clamp and remove it from the engine compartment.

Refitting

27 Refitting is a direct reversal of the removal sequence, tightening the pipe union nuts to the specified torque setting. On completion have the system recharged by a refrigeration specialist or suitably equipped Rover dealer.

Trinary switch

Removal

28 Remove the front bumper as described in Chapter 11.

29 Disconnect the wiring connector and unscrew the switch from the air conditioning pipe. Remove the O-ring from the switch and discard it.

Refitting

30 Refitting is a reverse of the removal procedure. Fit a new O-ring to the switch and tighten it to the specified torque setting. On completion have the system recharged by a refrigeration specialist or suitably equipped Rover dealer.

Chapter 4
Fuel, exhaust and emission control systems

Contents

Specifications

Part A: Carburettor engines

Fuel pump

Type	Mechanical, driven by eccentric on camshaft

Carburettor (general)

Type	Hobourn-SU constant-depression/variable choke
Designation	KIF 44
Choke type	Manual

Carburettor data

Carburettor number:	
Without catalytic converter	MAC 10004 or 10025
With catalytic converter	MAC 10011 or 10027
Throttle bore diameter	44 mm
Piston spring colour code	Red
Damper	LZX 2337
Jet size	ZX 2237 (0.100 in)

Carburettor data (continued)

Needle identification	BGZ
Needle valve seat	LZX 1756
Fast idle speed – at choke control first detent	1200 rpm
Idle speed	850 ± 50 rpm
CO level at idle speed – engine at normal operating temperature:	
Without catalytic converter	2.0 to 3.0 %
With catalytic converter – at gas sampling pipe	1.0 to 3.0 %

Recommended fuel

Minimum octane rating:	
Without catalytic converter	95 RON unleaded (ie unleaded Premium) or 97 RON leaded (ie 4-star)
With catalytic converter	95 RON unleaded (ie unleaded Premium) **only**

Part B: Fuel-injected engines

System type

Rover/Motorola Modular Engine Management System, using ECU-controlled single-point injection (MEMS-SPi) and speed/density method of airflow measurement

MEMS-SPi system data

Fuel pump type	Electric, immersed in fuel tank
Fuel pump pressure:	
Maximum – at 16 volts	2.7 bars
Regulated constant pressure	1.0 to 1.2 bars
Injector/pressure regulator assembly	JZX 3028
Throttle potentiometer voltage:	
Throttle closed	0 to 1 volt
Throttle open	4 to 5 volts
Idle speed – nominal value given for reference purposes only	850 ± 50 rpm
CO level at idle speed – engine at normal operating temperature:	
Without catalytic converter – at tailpipe	0.5 to 2.0 %
With catalytic converter – at gas-sampling pipe	0.5 to 2.0 %

Recommended fuel

Minimum octane rating:	
Without catalytic converter	95 RON unleaded (ie unleaded Premium) or 97 RON leaded (ie 4-star)
With catalytic converter	95 RON unleaded (ie unleaded Premium) **only**

Part C: All models

Torque wrench settings

	Nm	lbf ft
Carburettor models		
Fuel pump mounting nuts	10	7
Fuel tank hose retaining clip and union nuts	9	6
Carburettor retaining screws	10	7
Needle retaining (grub) screw	1.7 to 2.3	1.3 to 1.7
Throttle disc retaining screws	0.80 to 1.14	0.6 to 0.8
Carburettor vent and air bleed pipe mounting nuts and bolts	9	6
Manifold temperature sensor	15	11
Fuel injected models		
Fuel system pressure release bolt – models without catalytic converter	12	9
Fuel pump retaining nuts	9	6
Vent valve and hose retaining nuts	9	6
Injector housing fuel pipe union nuts	24	18
Injector housing fuel pipe adaptors	24	18
Throttle housing retaining nuts	18	13
Injector housing screws	5	3.5
ECU retaining nuts	9	6
Intake air temperature sensor	7	5
Coolant temperature sensor	15	11
Lambda sensor	55	41
All models		
Inlet manifold nuts and bolts	25	18
Inlet manifold support stay bolts	25	18
Exhaust manifold retaining nuts	45	33
Exhaust manifold shroud screws	6	4
Exhaust system flange nuts:		
Manifold to front pipe joint	50	37
All other joints	45	33
Exhaust front pipe mounting bolts	15	11

Part A: Carburettor engines

1 General information and precautions

The fuel system consists of a fuel tank mounted under the rear of the car, a mechanical fuel pump and a carburettor. The fuel pump is operated by an eccentric on the camshaft and is mounted on the rear of the cylinder head. The air cleaner contains a disposable paper filter element and incorporates a flap valve air temperature control system which allows cold air from the outside of the car and warm air from the exhaust manifold to enter the air cleaner in the correct proportions.

The carburettor is the Hobourn SU-manufactured KIF type, a development by Rover of the previous HIF instrument. To reduce emissions and to improve driveability when the engine is cold, the inlet manifold is heated by the cooling system coolant and by an electric

Fig. 4.1 Location of fuel and ignition system components – carburettor engines (Sec 1)

1 *Carburettor*
2 *Accelerator pedal switch*
3 *Choke control lever*
4 *Inlet manifold PTC heater relay*
5 *Engine compartment fusebox*
6 *Ignition HT coil*
7 *Distributor*
8 *Inlet manifold PTC heater switch*
9 *Inlet manifold PTC heater*
10 *Idle bypass solenoid*
11 *Vacuum diaphragm unit*
12 *Ignition amplifier unit*
13 *Fuel pump*

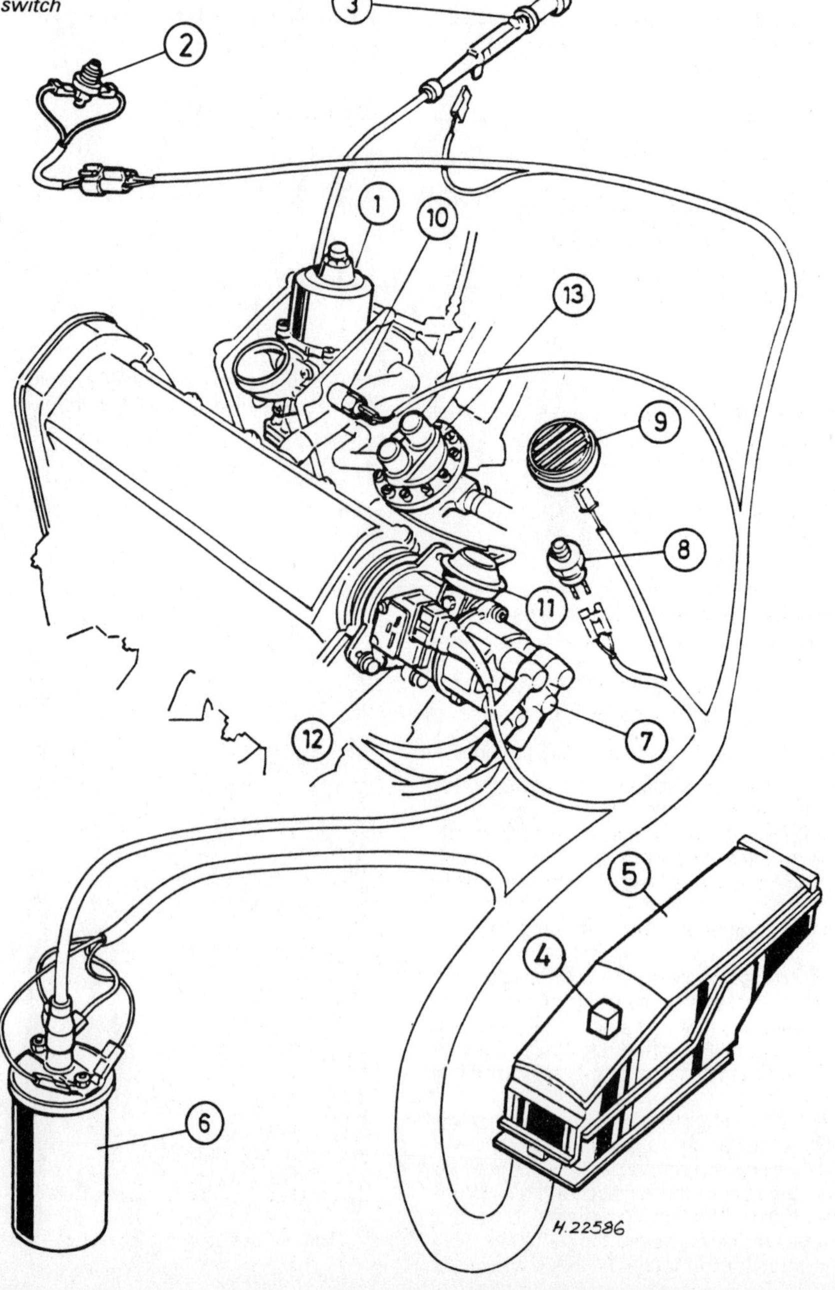

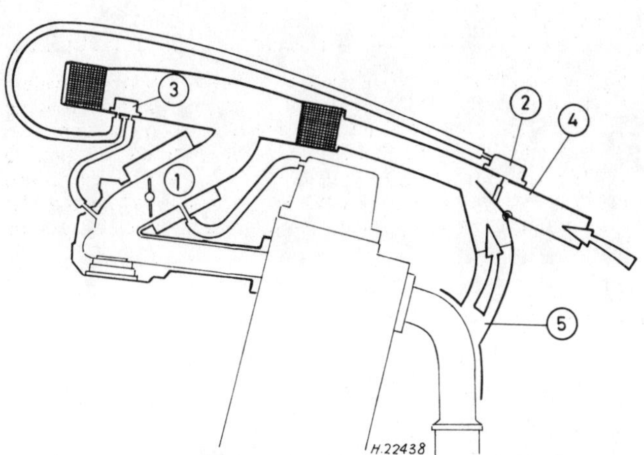

Fig. 4.2 Air cleaner air temperature control system components – carburettor engines (Secs 2 and 3)

1 *Carburettor*
2 *Air temperature control valve*
3 *Thermac switch*
4 *Air cleaner intake duct*
5 *Hot air intake*

2.2 Note colour-coding of thermac switch vacuum pipes before disconnecting

2.4 Slacken clamp to disconnect intake hose from air cleaner assembly metal intake duct

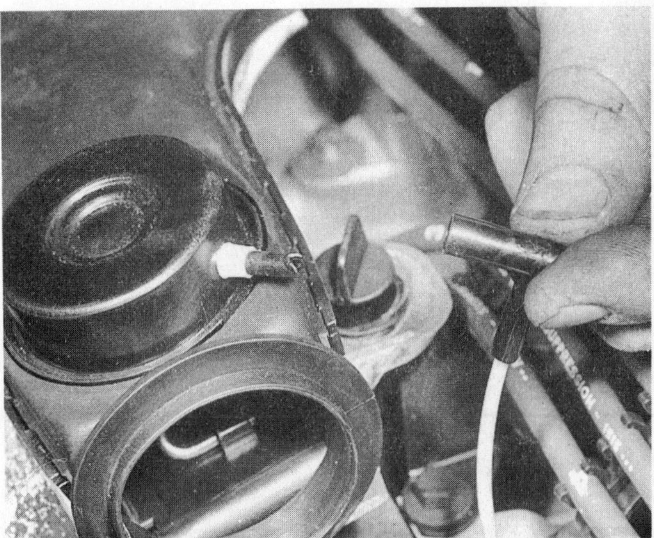

3.4 Disconnect vacuum pipe from control valve to check operation of system components

pre-heater system. Mixture enrichment for cold starting is by a manually-operated choke control.

The exhaust system consists of three sections; the front pipe and front silencer box, the intermediate pipe and middle silencer box, and the tailpipe and main silencer box. The system is suspended throughout its entire length by rubber mountings. If a catalytic converter is fitted, the exhaust system consists of four sections, the catalytic converter being situated between the front pipe and the (much shorter) intermediate pipe.

Warning: *Many of the procedures in this Chapter require the removal of fuel lines and connections which may result in some fuel spillage. Before carrying out any operation on the fuel system refer to the precautions given in Safety first! at the beginning of this Manual and follow them implicitly. Petrol is a highly dangerous and volatile liquid and the precautions necessary when handling it cannot be overstressed.*

2 Air cleaner assembly – removal and refitting

Removal

1 Release the two clips securing the air intake duct to the assembly, then undo the four screws securing the assembly to its mounting bracket.

2 Release the assembly from the intake duct and withdraw it until the thermac switch vacuum pipes can be reached. Make a note of the correct fitted positions of the pipes to ensure that they are correctly connected on refitting (yellow to the temperature control valve, red to the inlet manifold) then disconnect them and withdraw the air cleaner assembly (photo).

3 Check the condition of the O-ring around the carburettor inlet and renew it if worn or damaged.

4 To remove the metal intake duct, disconnect the vacuum pipe from the air temperature control valve and slacken the intake hose retaining clamp (photo). Undo the fastener securing the duct to its mounting bracket and remove the metal duct taking care not to lose the hot air intake connector hose which connects the duct to the exhaust manifold shroud.

5 To remove the air intake hose it will first be necessary to remove the left-hand headlamp assembly (Chapter 12), to gain access to the two retaining screws. Remove the retaining screws securing the front of the hose to the body front panel then release the clip securing the ignition HT lead to the hose. If the metal intake duct is still in position, slacken the hose clamp then remove the hose from the engine compartment.

6 A resonator chamber is fitted to the intake hose to reduce the

3.9 Thermac switch is clipped into air cleaner assembly

3.11 Disconnecting vacuum pipe from air temperature control valve – note clamp (arrowed) securing intake hose to the metal intake duct

3.12 Do not lose hot air intake connector hose when removing air cleaner metal intake duct

amount of induction noise. To remove the chamber first remove the battery and battery tray (Chapter 12). Disconnect the intake hose and release any relevant retaining clips from the resonator then remove the resonator from the engine compartment.

Refitting

7 Refitting is the reverse of the removal procedure; ensure that the vacuum pipes are correctly reconnected and are not trapped as the assembly is refitted, then check that the assembly sits properly on the carburettor inlet before tightening the screws securely.

3 Air cleaner air temperature control system – general information and component renewal

General information

1 The system is controlled by a thermac switch mounted in the air cleaner assembly; when the engine is started from cold, the switch is closed to allow inlet manifold depression to act on the air temperature control valve in the intake duct. This raises a vacuum servo in the valve assembly and draws a flap valve across the cold air intake, thus allowing only (warmed) air from the exhaust manifold to enter the air cleaner.
2 As the temperature rises of the exhaust-warmed air in the air cleaner, a bi-metallic strip in the thermac switch deforms and opens the switch to shut off the depression in the air temperature control valve assembly; the flap is lowered gradually across the hot air intake until, when the engine is fully warmed up to normal operating temperature, only cold air from the front of the car is entering the air cleaner.
3 To check the system, allow the engine to cool down completely, then slacken the intake hose retaining clamp and disconnect the hose from the metal intake duct; the flap valve in the duct should be securely seated across the hot air intake. Start the engine; the flap should immediately rise to close off the cold air intake and should then lower steadily as the engine warms up until it is eventually seated across the hot air intake again.
4 To check the thermac switch, disconnect the vacuum pipe from the control valve when the engine is running and place a finger over the pipe end (photo). When the engine is cold, full inlet manifold vacuum should be present in the pipe, and when the engine is at normal operating temperature there should be no vacuum in the pipe.
5 To check the air temperature control valve, slacken the intake hose retaining clamp and disconnect the hose from the metal intake duct; the flap valve should be securely seated across the hot air intake. Disconnect the vacuum pipe and suck hard at the control valve stub; the flap should rise to shut off the cold air intake.
6 If either component is faulty, it must be renewed.

Thermac switch – renewal

7 Remove the air cleaner assembly as described in Section 2.
8 Release the lid retaining clips then remove the lid and withdraw the air cleaner filter element.
9 Bend up the tags on the switch clip and remove the clip, then withdraw the switch and its seal (photo).
10 Refitting is the reverse of the removal procedure; ensure that the switch mating surfaces are clean and that the switch and seal are correctly located before fastening the clip.

Air temperature control valve – renewal

11 Disconnect the vacuum pipe from the air temperature control valve, then slacken the intake hose retaining clamp and disconnect the hose from the metal intake duct (photo).
12 Release the two clips securing the air intake duct to the air cleaner assembly and undo the fastener securing the duct to its mounting bracket. Withdraw the duct, taking care not to lose the hot air intake connector hose which connects the duct to the manifold shroud (photo).
13 The air temperature control valve can be renewed only with the complete intake duct assembly. If a new intake duct assembly is being fitted, undo the four screws securing the hot air intake adaptor plate to the bottom of the duct and transfer the adaptor plate to the new duct.
14 Refitting is the reverse of the removal procedure.

4 Fuel pump – testing, removal and refitting

Note: *Refer to the warning note in Section 1 before proceeding.*

Testing

1 To test the fuel pump on the engine, temporarily disconnect the outlet pipe which leads to the carburettor, and hold a wad of rag over the pump outlet while an assistant spins the engine on the starter. *Keep the hands away from the electric cooling fan.* Regular spurts of fuel should be ejected as the engine turns.
2 The pump can also be tested by removing it. With the pump outlet pipe disconnected but the inlet pipe still connected, hold the wad of rag

4.3 Plug fuel hoses when disconnecting them – pump inlet hose disconnected, outlet hose arrowed

4.5 Removing fuel pump and insulating block

by the outlet. Operate the pump lever by hand, moving it in and out; if the pump is in a satisfactory condition a strong jet of fuel should be ejected.

Removal

3 Identify the pump inlet and outlet hoses then, using a pair of pliers, release the retaining clips and disconnect them from the pump. Place wads of rag beneath the hose unions to catch any spilled fuel and plug the hose ends to minimise fuel loss (photo).

4 Slacken and remove the nuts and washers securing the pump to the cylinder head.

5 Withdraw the fuel pump from the engine and remove the insulating block (photo).

Refitting

6 Refitting is the reverse of the removal procedure; clean the mating surfaces and renew the insulating block if its sealing surfaces are marked or damaged. Tighten the pump mounting nuts to the specified torque wrench setting.

5 Fuel gauge sender unit – removal and refitting

Note: *Refer to the warning note in Section 1 before proceeding.*

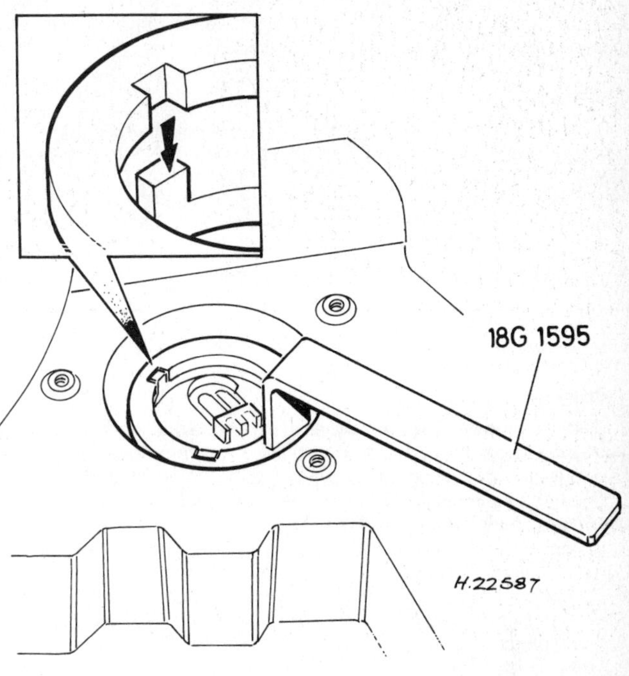

Fig. 4.3 Using Rover special tool to remove fuel gauge sender unit (Sec 5)

Removal

1 Disconnect the battery negative lead.

2 On 214 models, open the tailgate and remove the parcel tray shelf. Fold the rear seats fully forwards then raise the luggage compartment carpet to gain access to the fuel sender unit access cover.

3 On 414 models, open the boot lid and lift up the luggage compartment carpet to gain access to the fuel sender unit access cover.

4 On all models undo the three screws and remove the access cover from the floor (photos).

5 Remove the sender unit wiring connector rubber cover and disconnect the connector from the sender.

6 Unscrew the sender unit retaining ring by turning it in an anti-clockwise direction and remove it from the fuel tank. In the absence of the special Rover ring spanner, Service tool number 18G 1595, a pair

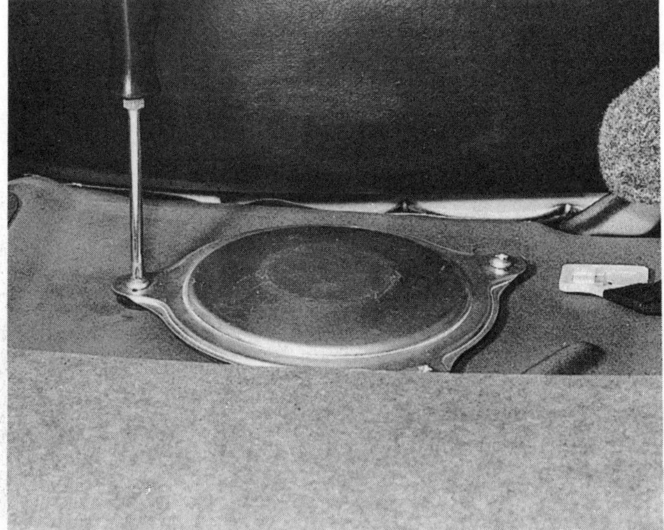

5.4A Undo the three screws...

5.4B ...and remove the access cover to reach fuel gauge sender unit

of slip-jointed pliers will serve as an adequate substitute to slacken the ring.
7 Carefully lift the sender unit, taking great care not to bend or damage the sender float, and remove the sealing ring. Examine the sealing ring and renew it if it is worn or damaged.

Refitting

8 Refitting is the reverse of the removal procedure, ensuring that the tab on the sender unit is correctly engaged with the cutout in the fuel tank.

6 Fuel tank – removal and refitting

Note: *Refer to the warning note in Section 1 before proceeding.*

Removal

1 Before removing the fuel tank all fuel must be drained from the tank. Since a fuel tank drain plug is not provided, it is therefore preferable to carry out the removal operation when the tank is nearly empty. Before proceeding, disconnect the battery negative lead and syphon or hand pump the remaining fuel from the tank.
2 Chock the front wheels, then jack up the rear of the car and support it on axle stands. Remove the left-hand rear roadwheel.
3 Undo the bolt then slacken and remove the two screws securing the cover fitted to the left-hand side of the fuel tank. Prise out the screw retaining plugs and remove the cover to gain access to the fuel tank feed and return pipes (photo).
4 Using a suitable pair of pliers, release the retaining clip and disconnect the small section of return pipe hose from the fuel tank (photo).
5 Slacken the fuel feed pipe union nut and disconnect the pipe from the union. Undo the two union mounting bolts and free the union from the body (photo).
6 Disconnect the fuel tank wiring block connector from the main wiring harness. If the block connector cannot yet be reached it may be disconnected as the tank is lowered out of position.
7 Slacken the clamp securing the filler neck hose to the tank and use a pair of pliers to release the filler neck breather pipe retaining clip (photo). Disconnect both the filler neck hose and breather pipe from the fuel tank.
8 Release the fuel tank breather, situated directly above the filler neck hose, from the vehicle body.
9 Slacken the tank retaining strap locknuts then unscrew the lower locknuts and remove the straps whilst supporting the tank (photo).
10 Lower the fuel tank out of position and remove it from under the car.
11 If the tank is contaminated with sediment or water, remove the sender unit (Section 5) and swill the tank out with clean fuel. If the tank is damaged or leaks, it should be repaired by a specialist or alternatively renewed. *Do not under any circumstances attempt to solder or weld a fuel tank.*

Refitting

12 Refitting is the reverse of the removal procedure; tighten all nuts and bolts to their specified torque wrench settings and ensure that all hoses are correctly routed and securely fastened so that there can be no risk of fuel leakage.

7 Accelerator cable – removal, refitting and adjustment

Removal

1 Unscrew the four windscreen wiper motor mounting bolts to free the motor from the engine compartment bulkhead.
2 Slacken the accelerator cable locknuts and free the outer cable from its mounting bracket on the carburettor. Release the inner cable from the accelerator cam (photo).

6.3 Remove cover retaining bolt and screw retaining plugs and remove the fuel tank cover

6.4 Fuel tank return pipe retaining clip 'A' and feed pipe union nut 'B'

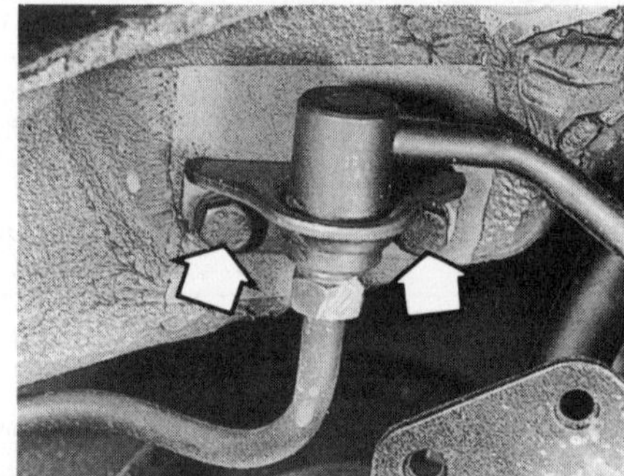

6.5 Feed pipe union mounting nuts (arrowed)

6.7 Slacken the filler neck hose retaining clamp and disconnect the breather pipe (arrowed)

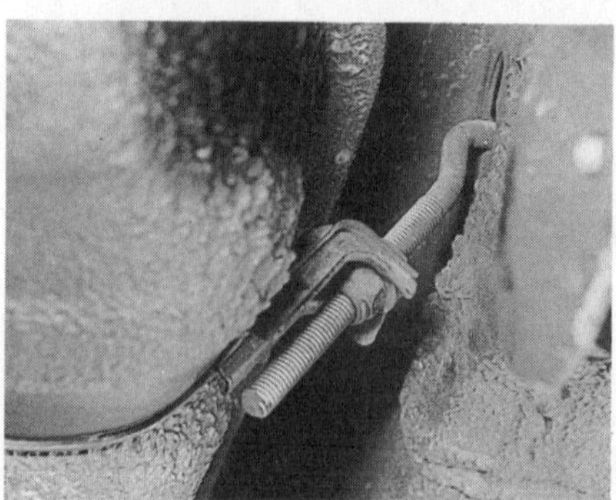

6.9 Fuel tank mounting strap retaining locknut

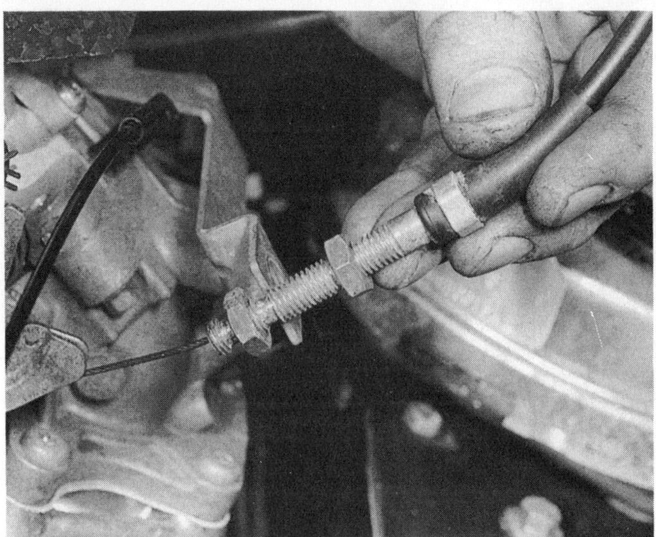

7.2 Disconnecting the accelerator cable from the carburettor

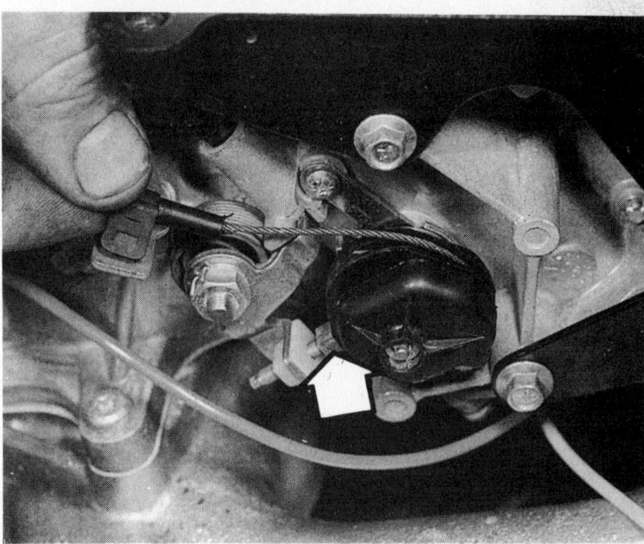

9.2 Release clip to disconnect choke cable from carburettor – note fast idle adjusting screw (arrowed)

3 Work back along the outer cable and release it from any relevant retaining clamps and ties and the engine compartment bulkhead.
4 Working from inside the car, undo the five right-hand lower facia panel retaining screws and remove the panel.
5 Release the cable from the upper end of the accelerator pedal and withdraw from cable from the engine compartment.

Refitting and adjustment

6 Refitting is the reverse of the removal procedure, tighten the windscreen wiper motor retaining bolts to the specified torque (Chapter 12). Prior to tightening the cable locknuts adjust the cable as follows.
7 Slacken both the locknuts then gently pull up on the outer cable until all free play is removed from the cable and the accelerator cam just starts to move. Holding the cable in this position, screw the upper locknut down until there is a gap of approximately 5 mm between the lower edge of the nut and the cable mounting bracket. Release the cable then have an assistant depress the accelerator pedal fully and check that the throttle opens fully and returns to the at-rest position when the pedal is released. If the throttle operation is correct, hold the upper locknut stationary and tighten the lower locknut securely.

8 Accelerator pedal – removal and refitting

Removal

1 Working from inside the car, undo the five right-hand lower facia panel retaining screws and remove the panel.
2 Release the accelerator cable from the upper end of the pedal and, using a pair of pliers, unhook the accelerator pedal return spring.
3 Prise off the circlip from the pedal pivot and withdraw the accelerator pedal from the mounting bracket.

Refitting

4 Refitting is a reverse of the removal procedure applying a smear of multi-purpose grease to the pedal pivot. On completion adjust the accelerator cable as described in Section 7.

9 Choke cable – removal, refitting and adjustment

Removal

1 Remove the air cleaner assembly as described in Section 2.
2 Free the choke outer cable from its retaining clip on the carburettor and disconnect the inner cable from the choke cam (photo).
3 Work back along the outer cable and release it from any relevant retaining clamps and ties and prise the cable grommet out of the engine compartment bulkhead.
4 Working from inside the car, undo the five right-hand lower facia panel retaining screws and remove the panel.
5 Using a suitable small screwdriver, slacken and remove the choke knob grub screw then pull the knob off the cable.
6 Unscrew the choke cable retaining nut then release the cable from the facia and disconnect the choke switch wiring connectors. The cable can then be withdrawn from the engine compartment and removed from the car.

Refitting and adjustment

7 Refitting is a reverse of the removal procedure. On completion adjust as follows.
8 Have an assistant pull the choke control knob fully out and check that the choke cam opens fully. Push the choke knob fully in and check that the choke cam returns to the fully-off position so that there is clearance between the cam and the fast idle adjusting screw. Providing that the choke cam returns fully, there should be no free play present in the cable.
9 The cable is adjusted by releasing the carburettor clip and repositioning the outer cable as necessary.

10 Unleaded petrol – general information and usage

Note: *The information given in this Chapter is correct at the time of writing and applies only to petrols currently available in the UK. If updated information is thought to be required check with a Rover dealer. If travelling abroad consult one of the motoring organisations (or a similar authority) for advice on the petrols available and their suitability for your vehicle.*

1 The fuel recommended by Rover for the 214/414 models is given in the Specifications Section of this Chapter, followed by the equivalent petrol currently on sale in the UK.
2 RON and MON are different testing standards; RON stands for Research Octane Number (also written as RM), while MON stands for Motor Octane Number (also written as MM).
3 All Rover 214/414 models are designed to run on 95 (RON) octane petrol. Super/Super Plus (unleaded) petrols can be used without modification, if nothing else is available; 4-star (leaded) petrol can **only** be used if the car is **not** fitted with a catalytic converter.

Note: *The only cars which MUST use unleaded petrol at all times are those with catalytic converters; see Section 40.*

Fig. 4.4 Carburettor idle bypass system (Sec 11)

1 *Carburettor piston*
2 *Plunger*
3 *Idle bypass screw*
4 *Accelerator pedal switch*
5 *Idle bypass solenoid*

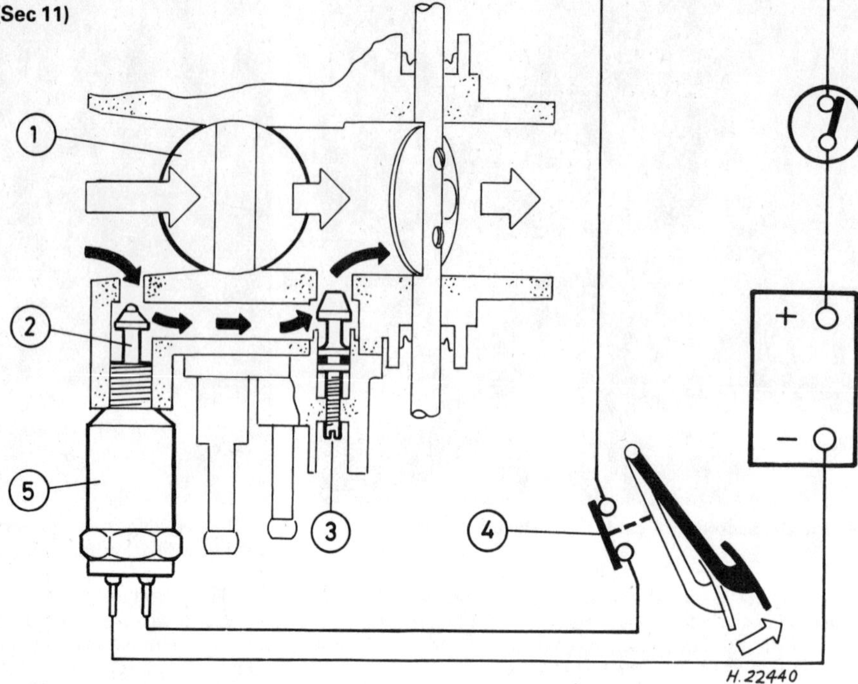

11 Carburettor – general information

The carburettor features an electrically-controlled idle bypass system that is separate from the main fuel/air mixture circuit provided by the piston, jet and metering needle, a manual choke, an overrun valve and a full load enrichment device.

The idle bypass system is described in Section 13; see also Fig. 4.4.

The manual choke (Fig. 4.5) uses the constant manifold depression to draw fuel and air into a fixed orifice; a helical groove in the spindle keyed to the choke cam is arranged so that extra fuel/air mixture can pass from the orifice only when the choke cam is rotated slightly from the at-rest position; the amount of extra fuel delivered increases to a maximum point when the choke cam is rotated through 60°.

The full load enrichment device also uses manifold depression. At light engine loads, with the accelerator partially closed (idling, cruising or decelerating) a high depression is generated in the manifold, downstream of the throttle disc. A passage connects the space behind a diaphragm to this point so that the diaphragm is sucked off its seat against spring pressure; the air passing through the air bleed hose can then enter through two passages which means that the depression across the fuel pick-up is too low for fuel to be drawn from the float chamber into the system (Fig. 4.6, *'Engine under light load'*).

At high engine loads, with the accelerator fully open (acceleration, full-throttle running) manifold depression drops to the point where the diaphragm is seated by its spring and the air can enter only through a small jet; this increases air speed and raises the depression over the fuel pick-up to the point where additional fuel is drawn up from the float chamber, mixed with the air bleed and passed into the carburettor venturi downstream of the piston (Fig. 4.6, *'Engine under full load'*).

Some models are fitted with a spring-loaded poppet valve in the throttle disc, so that when the accelerator is closed at high engine speeds the high manifold depression sucks the valve open, admitting enough air to burn completely the small amount of fuel that is sucked through the jet under these conditions, thus reducing exhaust emissions.

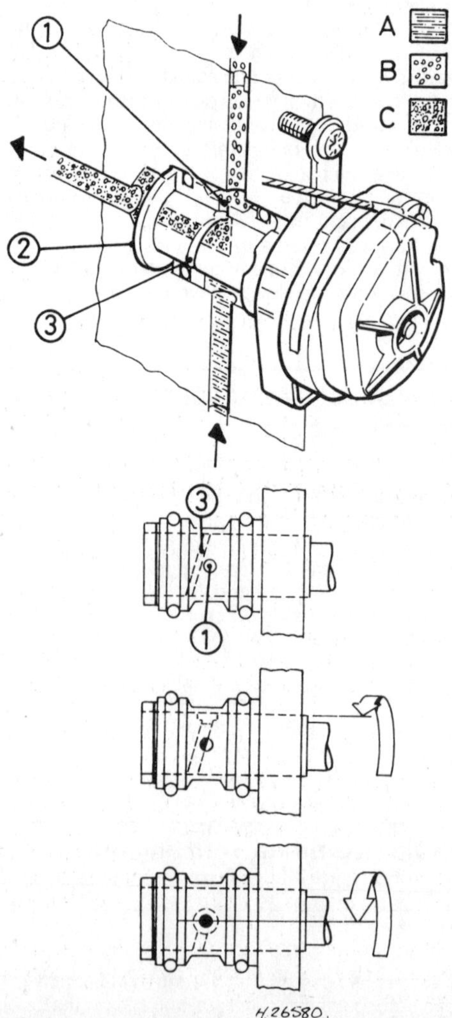

Fig. 4.5 Operation of the carburettor choke assembly (Sec 11)

A	*Path of fuel*	1	*Fixed orifice*
B	*Path of air*	2	*Choke spindle*
C	*Path of fuel/air mixture*	3	*Helical groove*

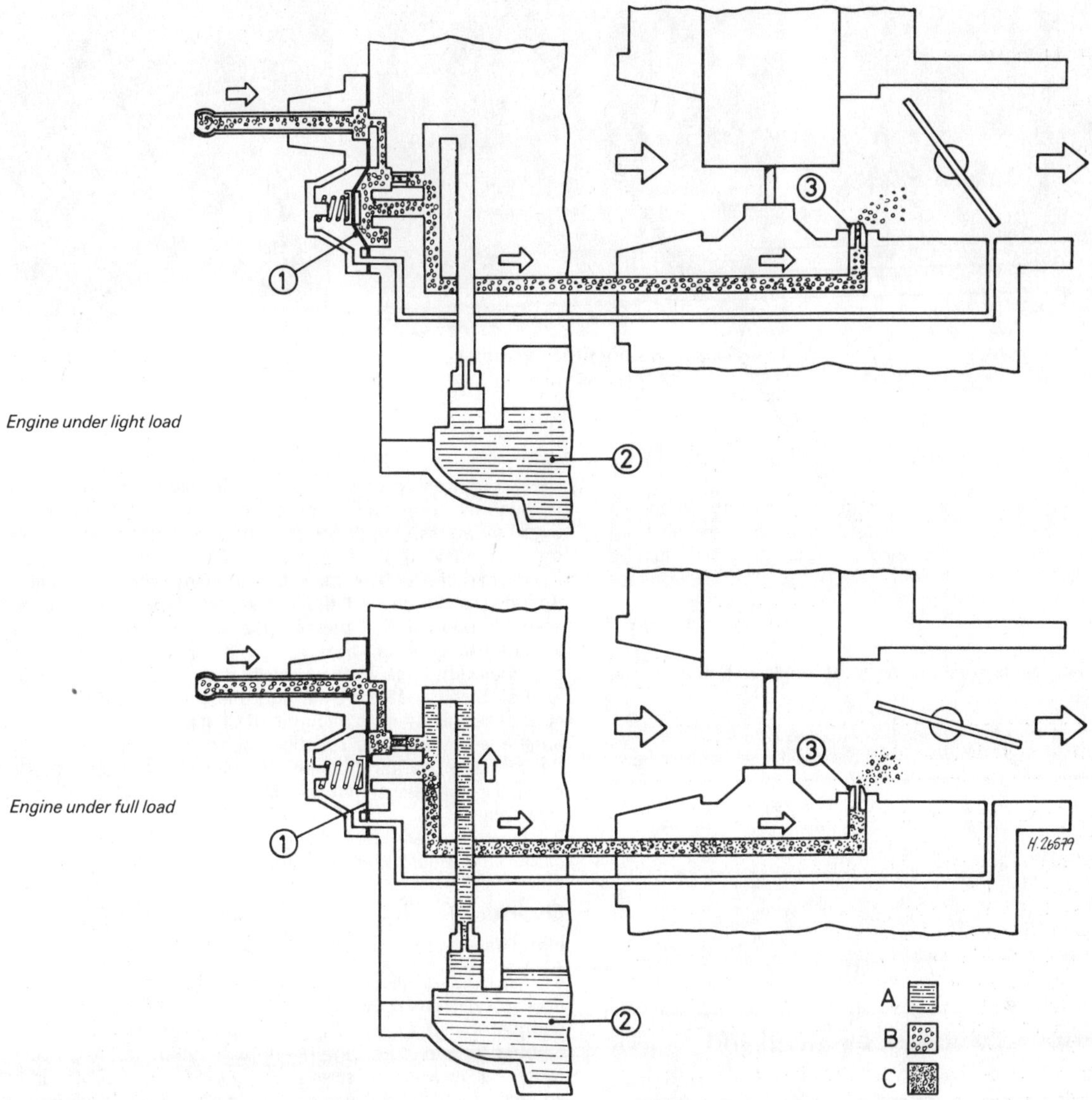

Engine under light load

Engine under full load

H.26579

A
B
C

Fig. 4.6 Carburettor full load enrichment device (Sec 11)

1 Diaphragm
2 Float chamber
3 Jet
A Path of fuel
B Path of air
C Path of fuel/air mixture

12 Carburettor – removal and refitting

Note: *Refer to the warning note in Section 1 before proceeding.*

Removal

1 Remove the air cleaner assembly as described in Section 2.

2 Slacken the accelerator cable locknuts and free the outer cable from its mounting bracket on the carburettor. Release the inner cable from the accelerator cam.

3 Free the choke outer cable from its retaining clip on the carburettor and disconnect the inner cable from the choke cam.

4 Make a note of the correct fitted positions of the two small bore vacuum pipes, to ensure they are correctly positioned on refitting, then disconnect them from the carburettor (photo).

5 Using pliers, release the retaining clip and disconnect the fuel feed hose from the carburettor. Place wads of rag around the union to catch any spilled fuel and plug the hose as soon as it is disconnected to minimise fuel loss.

6 Make a note of the correct fitted positions of the breather hoses then, where necessary, release the retaining clips and disconnect the three breather hoses from the carburettor.

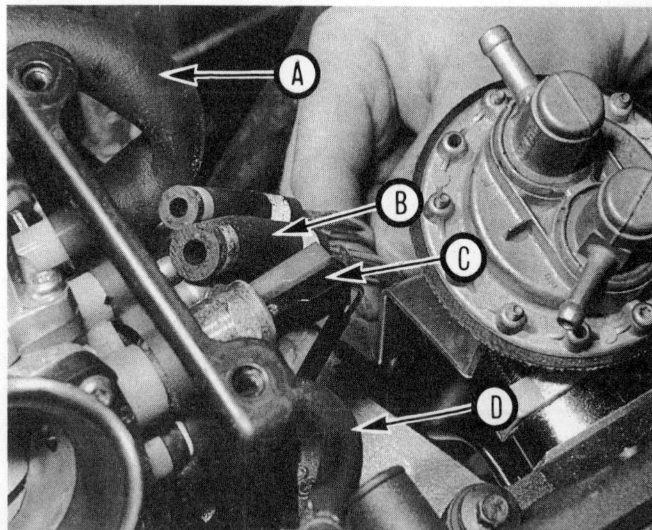

12.4 Breather hose 'A', float chamber vent and full load air bleed hoses 'B', idle bypass solenoid wiring 'C', fuel pump outlet hose 'D'

12.7 Note connections before disconnecting idle bypass solenoid wiring

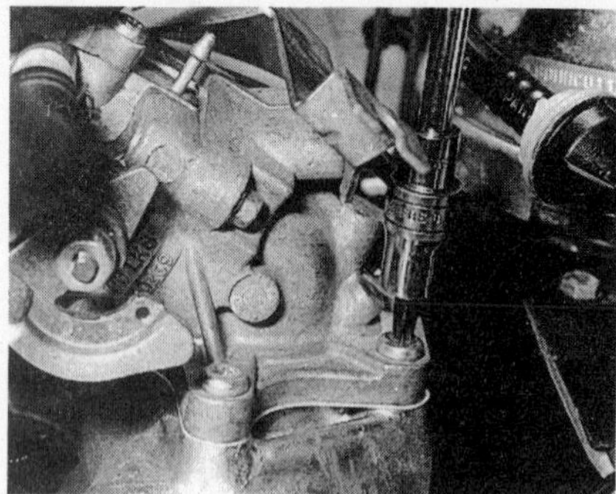

12.8A Unscrew upper to lower inlet manifold Torx screws...

12.8B ...and remove carburettor assembly

7 Disconnect the wiring connector from the carburettor idle bypass solenoid (photo).

8 Unscrew the four Torx screws securing the carburettor manifold adaptor to the inlet manifold and remove the carburettor assembly from the car (photos). Remove the gasket and discard it; a new one must be used on refitting. Plug the inlet port with a wad of clean cloth to prevent the possible entry of foreign matter.

Refitting

9 Refitting is the reverse of the removal procedure noting the following points:

- (a) *Ensure the carburettor and inlet manifold sealing faces are clean and flat. Fit a new gasket and tighten the carburettor retaining screws to the specified torque.*
- (b) *Use the notes made on dismantling to ensure all hoses are refitted to their original positions and, where necessary, are securely held by their retaining clips.*
- (c) *Refit and adjust the choke cable and accelerator cables as described in Sections 7 and 9.*
- (d) *Refit the air cleaner assembly as described in Section 2.*
- (e) *On completion check and, if necessary, adjust the idle speed and mixture settings as described in Chapter 1.*

13 Carburettor – diagnosis, overhaul and adjustments

Diagnosis

1 The SU carburettor does not usually suffer from jet blockages and wear is usually only found between the needle and jet, although it is worth checking the fit of the piston in the suction chamber whenever the carburettor is dismantled. If the idle speed is too high and cannot be reduced by normal adjustment, it is worth checking the throttle disc overrun valve spring (if fitted); if this has weakened, the throttle disc must be renewed.

2 If a carburettor fault is suspected, always check first that the ignition timing is accurate and the spark plugs are in good condition and correctly gapped, that the accelerator and choke cables are correctly adjusted, that the carburettor piston damper is topped-up, that the float chamber vent hose and (especially if the mixture is very rich) the full load air bleed hose are clear and that the air cleaner filter element is clean; see the relevant Sections of Chapter 1 or of this Chapter. If the engine is running very roughly, check the compression pressures as described in Chapter 2 bearing in mind the possibility that one of the hydraulic tappets might be faulty, producing an incorrect valve clearance.

3 If careful checking of all of the above produces no improvement, the carburettor must be removed for cleaning and overhaul.

Overhaul

Note: *Refer to the warning note in Section 1 before proceeding.*

4 Note that in the rare event of a complete carburettor overhaul being necessary, it may prove more economical to renew the carburettor as a complete unit. Check the price and availability of a replacement carburettor and of its component parts before starting work; note that most sealing washers, screws and gaskets are available in kits, as are some of the major sub-assemblies. In most cases it will be sufficient to dismantle the carburettor and to clean the jets and passages.

5 Remove the carburettor and unbolt the two air cleaner assembly support brackets from the side of the carburettor. Remove the three screws securing the air cleaner adaptor to the carburettor and the three

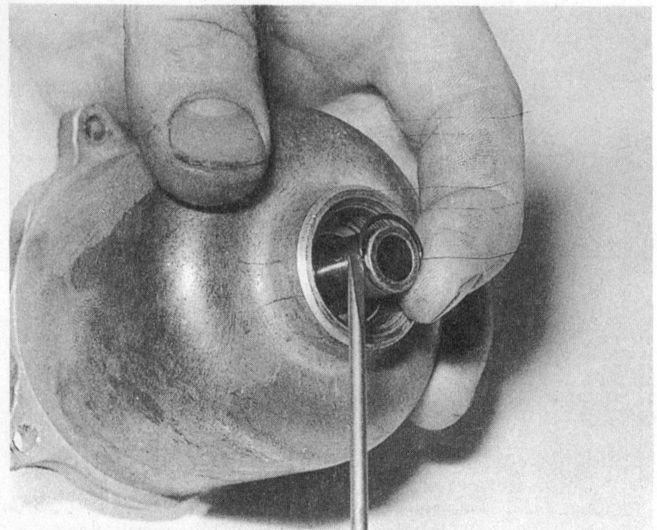

13.7 Prise C-clip from piston upper end...

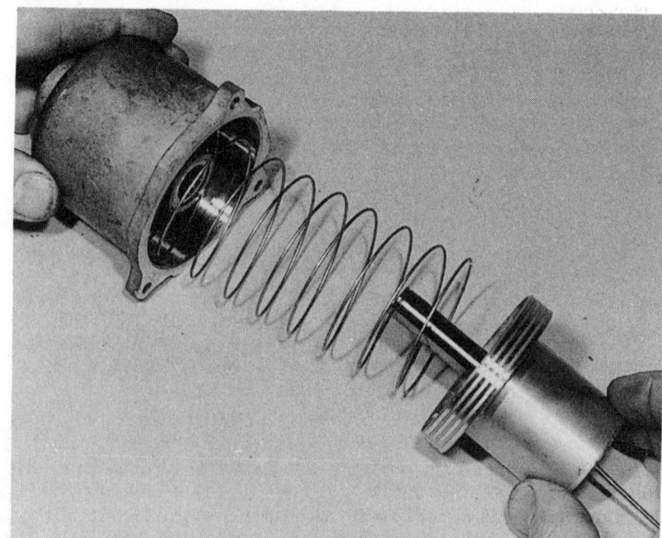

13.8 ...to separate piston (and piston spring) from suction chamber

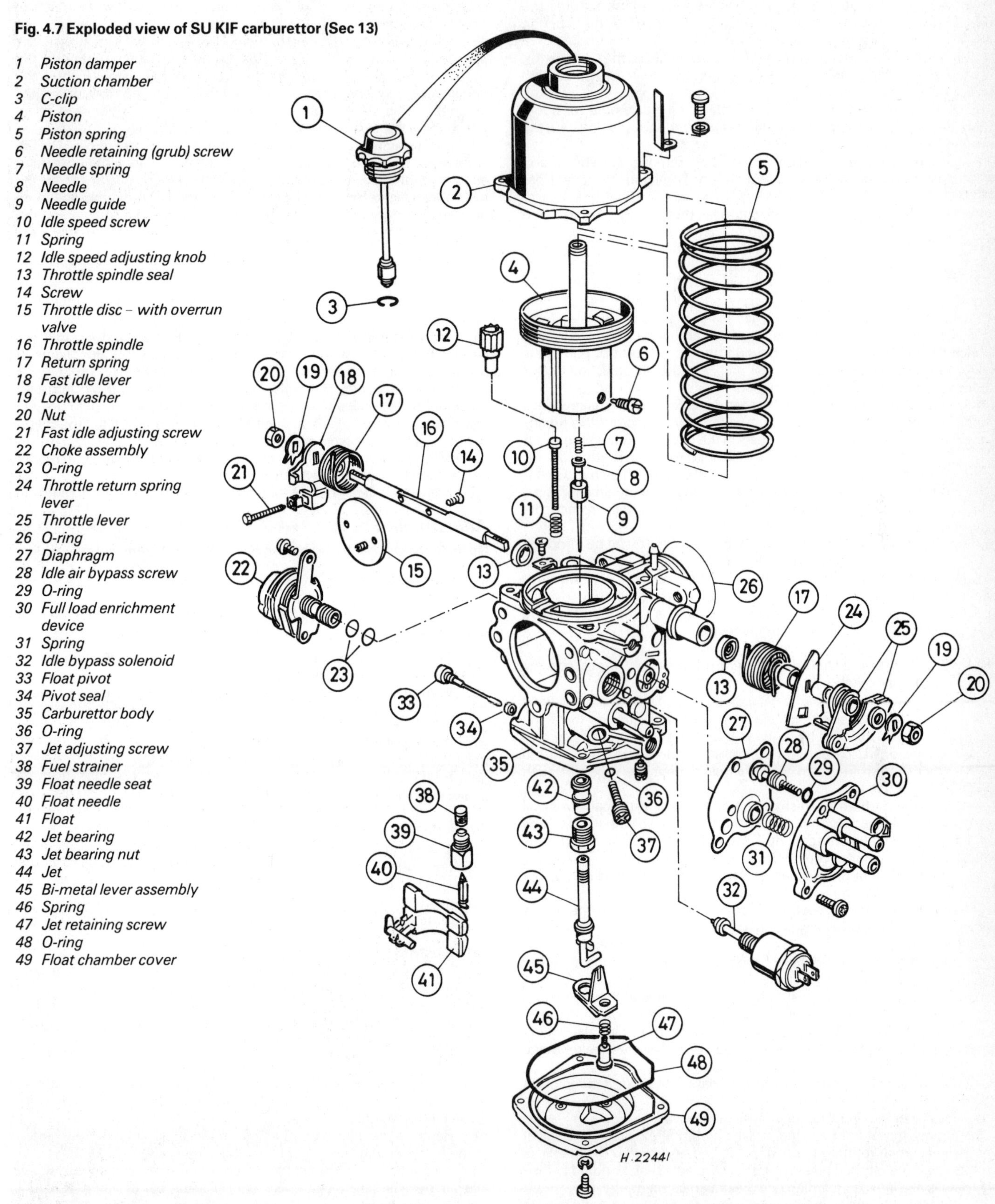

Fig. 4.7 Exploded view of SU KIF carburettor (Sec 13)

1 *Piston damper*
2 *Suction chamber*
3 *C-clip*
4 *Piston*
5 *Piston spring*
6 *Needle retaining (grub) screw*
7 *Needle spring*
8 *Needle*
9 *Needle guide*
10 *Idle speed screw*
11 *Spring*
12 *Idle speed adjusting knob*
13 *Throttle spindle seal*
14 *Screw*
15 *Throttle disc – with overrun valve*
16 *Throttle spindle*
17 *Return spring*
18 *Fast idle lever*
19 *Lockwasher*
20 *Nut*
21 *Fast idle adjusting screw*
22 *Choke assembly*
23 *O-ring*
24 *Throttle return spring lever*
25 *Throttle lever*
26 *O-ring*
27 *Diaphragm*
28 *Idle air bypass screw*
29 *O-ring*
30 *Full load enrichment device*
31 *Spring*
32 *Idle bypass solenoid*
33 *Float pivot*
34 *Pivot seal*
35 *Carburettor body*
36 *O-ring*
37 *Jet adjusting screw*
38 *Fuel strainer*
39 *Float needle seat*
40 *Float needle*
41 *Float*
42 *Jet bearing*
43 *Jet bearing nut*
44 *Jet*
45 *Bi-metal lever assembly*
46 *Spring*
47 *Jet retaining screw*
48 *O-ring*
49 *Float chamber cover*

inlet manifold adaptor retaining screws. Remove both adaptors and discard the air cleaner adaptor gasket and the inlet manifold adaptor O-ring; a new gasket and O-ring must be used on reassembly.

6 Make a note of the correct fitted positions of any remaining vacuum pipes or breather hoses then, where necessary, releasing their retaining clips and disconnect them from the carburettor. Clean away all traces of external dirt from the carburettor body.

7 Unscrew the piston damper and tip out the oil, then push the piston upwards until the C-clip can be prised out of its upper end (photo).

8 Mark the suction chamber in relation to the carburettor body.

Remove the three retaining screws (noting that one also secures the carburettor's metal identification tag) and withdraw the suction chamber, noting the piston spring (photo).

9 Carefully lift the piston and needle assembly out of the carburettor, unscrew the needle retaining grub screw and withdraw the needle with its spring and guide.

10 Mark the float chamber cover in relation to the carburettor body, then remove its retaining screws and withdraw the cover along with the sealing O- ring.

11 Unscrew the jet retaining screw, then remove the spring and withdraw the jet and bi-metal lever assembly. Disengage the lever from the jet.

12 Unscrew the float pivot, noting its seal, then remove the float and the float needle. Unscrew the needle seat and tip out the fuel strainer.

13 If required, unscrew the jet bearing nut and withdraw the bearing.

14 Unscrew the idle bypass solenoid.

15 **Do not** alter the setting of the idle speed adjusting knob, the idle air bypass screw or the jet adjusting screw; once disturbed these can only be reset correctly using an exhaust gas analyser and a tachometer. Note that the idle air bypass screw cannot be removed until the full load enrichment device has been removed from the carburettor body (it is secured by four Torx-type screws) and that the jet adjusting screw recess is sealed by a tamperproof plug.

16 If any of these screws are to be removed for cleaning, screw each in until it seats lightly (in the case of the idle air bypass screw, this means screwing it anti-clockwise until it seats in the cover), counting the **exact** number of turns required to do this, then unscrew it. On refitting, screw each screw in until it seats lightly, then back the screw off by the number of turns noted on removal, to return the screw to its original location. Have the carburettor settings checked by a Rover dealer once the engine is running.

17 If the choke assembly is thought to be blocked it can be removed from the carburettor body so that the passages can be blown clear with compressed air; if this is not available a blast of commercial carburettor cleaner (applied from an aerosol via the thin plastic tube usually supplied) will serve to clear most obstructions. The same approach can be applied to the full load enrichment device.

Note: *Be careful to wear full eye protection when using compressed air or chemicals in such a way.*

18 Check the accelerator linkage for wear, especially the fit of the spindle in the carburettor body. If wear is found, seek the advice of a Rover dealer or SU carburettor specialist; at the time of writing, no replacement parts are listed which would permit the repair of such faults.

19 With the carburettor dismantled as far as is practicable and all components cleaned carefully, check them for signs of wear or damage and renew any faulty component. Renew all seals, gaskets and O-rings disturbed as a matter of course.

20 Check the float needle seat and tip, renewing them if they show wear ridges. Renew the float if it appears to be leaking.

21 Check the tapered needle, jet and jet bearing; renew them as a matched set if they show any sign of wear, or if there is any doubt about their condition.

22 Clean the mating surfaces of the piston and the suction chamber with methylated spirit, then wipe them dry; *do not use any form of abrasive cleaner.* Insert the piston (without the spring and damper) into the suction chamber, hold them horizontally and spin the piston; it should rotate freely in the suction chamber without sticking or touching the chamber walls. The piston and suction chamber must be renewed as a matched pair if either is worn or damaged.

23 On reassembly, refit the idle bypass solenoid, tightening it securely but not overtightening it.

24 Fit the jet bearing and bearing nut, if removed.

25 Do not forget the fuel strainer when refitting the float needle seat or the seal when refitting the float pivot, and ensure that the needle is refitted with its tapered tip engaged in the needle seat; as noted below, no data is available concerning float height adjustment.

26 Fit the jet to the bi-metal lever, ensuring that the jet head moves freely in the lever cut-out, then refit the assembly to the carburettor, ensuring that the lever engages correctly with the jet adjusting screw. Refit the spring and tighten the jet retaining screw securely; see below for details of jet adjustment.

27 Fit a new sealing O-ring to the float chamber cover. Refit the float chamber cover, aligning the marks made on dismantling; it will fit correctly only one way. Tighten securely, but do not overtighten, the cover screws.

28 Fit the needle and spring to the guide, then fit the assembly to the piston so that the guide cut-out faces the grub screw hole and the bottom of the guide is flush with the bottom of the piston. Tighten the needle retaining grub screw carefully (note the specified torque wrench setting); if this is overtightened, it will distort the guide and make subsequent needle removal and refitting very difficult.

29 Temporarily refit the piston and needle assembly to the carburettor body, engaging the piston slot on its locating projection and ensuring that the needle enters the jet. Fit the suction chamber over the piston and align it on its mounting screws (or use the marks made on dismantling). Mark the correct relative positions of the piston and the suction chamber with a soft pencil, then remove them from the carburettor.

30 Fit the piston spring to the piston, then offer up the assembly to the suction chamber, aligning the pencil marks so that the piston spring is not 'wound up'. Push the piston fully up into the suction chamber and refit the C-clip to secure the assembly.

31 Ensuring that the pencil marks remain in alignment (so that the piston spring is not 'wound up' by the piston being rotated relative to the suction chamber) refit the piston/suction chamber assembly to the carburettor, engaging the piston slot on its locating projection and ensuring that the needle enters the jet. Do not forget the identification tag when refitting the suction chamber screws; tighten securely, but do not overtighten, the screws.

32 Fill the piston damper chamber with oil as described in Chapter 1 and tighten the damper securely.

33 The remainder of the refitting procedure is the reverse of removal.

Adjustments

Note: *Refer to the warning note in Section 1 before proceeding.*

Idle speed and mixture

34 Refer to Chapter 1.

Fast idle speed

35 Check the accelerator and choke cables are correctly adjusted as described in Sections 7 and 9.

36 Warm the engine up to normal operating temperature and check that the idle speed and mixture are correctly set as described in Chapter 1.

37 Pull out the choke control to the first detent position and check that the engine speed increases to the specified amount.

38 If adjustment is required, screw in or out the fast idle adjusting screw until the engine speed is correct.

Fuel level

39 The carburettor fuel level is adjusted by bending the float arm to alter the float height, usually measured with the carburettor inverted; however since the necessary information is not provided by the manufacturer, the car should be taken to a Rover dealer or SU carburettor specialist if the fuel level is thought to be incorrect.

Jet adjustment

Note: *Accurate jet adjustment is not easy for the inexperienced and can only be carried out using an exhaust gas analyser. If the jet adjustment is thought to be incorrect or is to be checked, owners without the required equipment and the skill to use it are advised to have the work carried out by a Rover dealer or SU carburettor specialist.*

40 Warm the engine up to normal operating temperature and check that the ignition timing, idle speed and mixture are correctly set and that the carburettor piston damper is topped-up, referring to Chapter 1 for further information.

41 Remove the tamperproof cap from the jet adjusting screw recess at the front left-hand corner of the carburettor body.

42 Counting the exact number of turns required to do so, screw the idle air bypass screw clockwise until it seats lightly, then start the engine, switch on the headlamps, heated rear window and heater blower motor (first speed only) and adjust the idle speed to 700 to 750 rpm.

43 Connect the exhaust gas analyser following its manufacturer's instructions.

44 Turning the jet adjusting screw either way (clockwise to richen the mixture) by half a turn at a time and waiting for the analyser reading to

respond and stabilise before making a further alteration, set the mixture to a base CO level of 5.5 % ± 0.5 %. When the analyser reading is steady at the correct level, switch off all electrical loads.

45 Screw the idle air bypass screw anti-clockwise by the number of turns previously noted to return it to its original setting, then set the true idle mixture to the specified value, as described in Chapter 1.

46 Stop the engine when the adjustment is correct, disconnect the test equipment and fit a new tamperproof cap to the jet adjusting screw recess.

Idle bypass system

47 As well as the carburettor idle air bypass passage and screw, the system incorporates the solenoid and the accelerator pedal switch.

48 When the accelerator is closed and the ignition is switched on the solenoid is energised, its plunger being retracted to open the bypass passage (Fig. 4.4); this allows air to bypass the carburettor piston and thus makes the idle mixture independent of the needle metering. Screwing in (clockwise) the idle air bypass screw reduces the amount of air bypassing the piston and richens the idle mixture.

49 As soon as the accelerator pedal is depressed, the accelerator pedal switch opens, the solenoid is de-energised and the bypass passage is shut off.

50 To check the system, listen closely by the carburettor while an assistant switches on the ignition and depresses and releases the accelerator pedal several times; the solenoid should be heard to be clicking in and out.

51 If no clicking can be heard, remove the air cleaner assembly as described in Section 2 and use a meter or similar to check the solenoid earth and feed, referring to Chapter 12 for further information. Use a meter to check that the accelerator pedal switch contacts open and close as described. If the solenoid or switch is faulty it must be renewed. Note that if trouble is encountered with an ignition system fuse blowing repeatedly, and the fault cannot otherwise be traced, the solenoid may be at fault.

52 Refer to Section 14 for details of accelerator pedal switch removal and refitting.

14 Accelerator pedal switch – removal and refitting

Removal

1 Working from inside the car, undo the five right-hand lower facia panel retaining screws and remove the panel.

2 Using a suitable pair of pliers, unhook the accelerator pedal return spring from the pedal then disconnect the accelerator cable from the pedal.

3 Disconnect the wiring connectors from the accelerator pedal switch then prise off the C-clip and remove the switch from the mounting bracket noting the wave washer which is fitted between the switch and bracket.

Refitting

4 Refitting is a reversal of the removal procedure.

15 Inlet manifold pre-heater – general information, removal and refitting

General information

1 The system incorporates the manifold PTC (Positive Temperature Coefficient) heater, the relay and the manifold temperature switch.

2 When the ignition is switched on and the engine is cold (coolant below 50°C), the relay-energising current flows through the closed manifold temperature switch contacts, which then closes the relay contacts and allows current to flow from the battery to the heater. This ensures that the inlet manifold is warm enough, even before the effect of the coolant heating becomes apparent, to prevent fuel droplets condensing in the manifold, thus improving driveability and reducing exhaust emissions when the engine is cold.

3 As soon as the engine warms up to temperatures above 50°C, the switch contacts open and the relay cuts off the power supply to the manifold heater.

4 If the engine suddenly develops flat spots when cold, the system may be faulty.

Manifold PTC heater – removal and refitting

Removal

5 Drain the cooling system as described in Chapter 1.

6 Apply the handbrake then jack up the front of the car and support it on axle stands. Access to the PTC heater can then be gained from underneath the vehicle, via the gap between the engine and engine compartment bulkhead.

7 Disconnect the wiring connector from the heater terminal then extract the heater retaining circlip. Withdraw the heater from the underside of the manifold (photos). Inspect the heater rubber seal for signs of damage or deterioration and renew if necessary.

Refitting

8 Refitting is the reverse of the removal procedure ensuring that the heater locating projection is correctly engaged in the manifold recess. On completion, lower the car to the ground and fill the cooling system as described in Chapter 1.

Manifold pre-heater temperature switch

Removal

9 The pre-heater temperature switch is fitted to the underside of the inlet manifold (photo). Either drain the cooling system as described in Chapter 1, or be prepared for some loss of coolant as the switch is unscrewed.

10 Release the wire retaining clip and disconnect the wiring connector from the switch.

11 Unscrew the switch from the manifold and withdraw it, then plug the opening to prevent the entry of dirt; if the cooling system has not been drained, work quickly to minimise coolant loss.

Refitting

12 Wipe clean the threads of the switch and of the thermostat

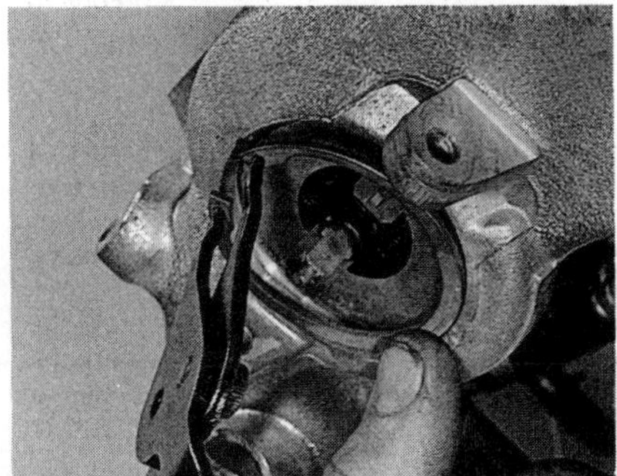

15.7A Extract the circlip...

15.7B ...and remove the PTC heater from the inlet manifold – manifold removed for clarity

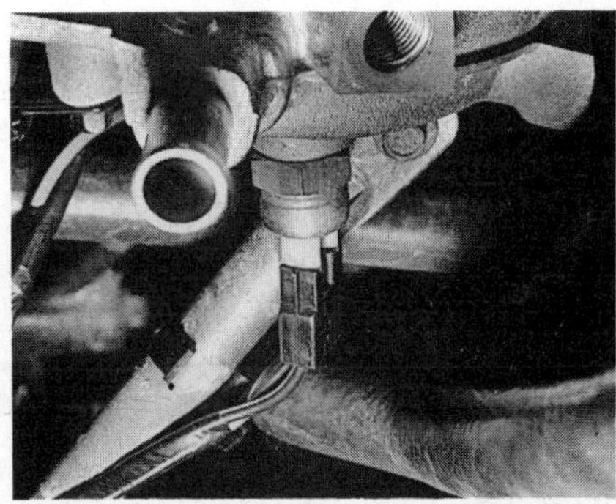

15.9 Location of inlet manifold pre-heater temperature switch

16.11A Inlet manifold support stay upper end bolt (arrowed)

16.11B Inlet manifold support stay lower end bolt (arrowed)

16.13A Always fit a new manifold gasket

16.13B Refitting the inlet manifold - less carburettor

16.13C Tighten manifold nuts and bolts in sequence to specified torque wrench setting

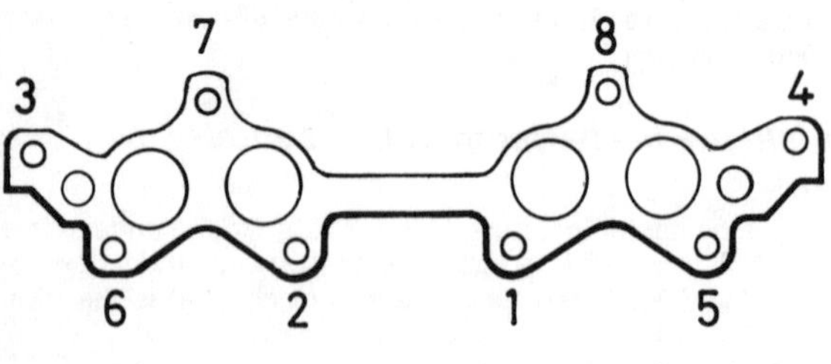

Fig. 4.8 Inlet manifold tightening sequence - K8 engines (Sec 16)

housing. If a sealing washer is fitted, renew it whenever it is disturbed to prevent leaks; if no sealing washer is fitted, apply a smear of sealant to the switch threads.

13 Refit the switch, working quickly if the cooling system was not drained, and tighten it to the specified torque. Reconnect the wiring connector.

14 Refill or top up the cooling system as described in Chapter 1.

Manifold heater relay - general

15 Refer to Chapter 12 for details.

16 Inlet manifold - removal and refitting

Removal

Note: *The following procedure describes the removal of the manifold with the carburettor. Access to some of the components concerned is, however, much better if the carburettor is first removed separately as described in Section 12; if this is done, the following procedure should be amended as required.*

Note: *Refer to the warning note in Section 1 before proceeding.*

1 Disconnect the battery negative terminal.

2 Remove the air cleaner assembly as described in Section 2.

3 Drain the cooling system as described in Chapter 1.

4 Disconnect the accelerator and choke cables as described in Sections 7 and 9.

5 Slacken the retaining clamps and disconnect the coolant hoses from the inlet manifold.

6 Trace the float chamber vent hose and the full load air bleed hose from the carburettor down to their metal pipes then unscrew the nut and bolts securing the pipes to the cylinder block/crankcase.

7 Using pliers, release the retaining clip and disconnect the fuel feed hose from the carburettor. Place wads of rag around the union to catch any spilled fuel and plug the hose as soon as it is disconnected to minimise fuel loss.

8 Disconnect the vacuum pipe from the distributor vacuum diaphragm unit and disconnect the breather hose from the cylinder head cover.

9 Slacken and remove the brake vacuum servo unit hose union bolt and disconnect the hose. Discard the hose union sealing washers; these must be renewed whenever they are disturbed.

10 Disconnect the idle bypass solenoid wiring, making notes of the connections so that they can be correctly reconnected, then disconnect the wiring from the manifold pre-heater switch and heater which are situated on the underside of the manifold.

11 Undo the single bolt which secures each manifold support stay to the cylinder block/crankcase and slacken the bolts which secure the stays to the inlet manifold (photos).

12 Make a final check that all the necessary fuel/breather hoses have been disconnected from the carburettor/manifold then unscrew the nuts and bolts securing the manifold to the cylinder head. Manoeuvre the manifold out of the engine compartment and discard the manifold gasket.

17.8A Refitting exhaust manifold - always renew gasket

17.8B Exhaust manifold nut tightening sequence - K8 engines

Refitting

13 Refitting is the reverse of the removal procedure, noting the following points (photos):

- (a) *Ensure that the manifold and cylinder head mating surfaces are clean and dry and fit a new manifold gasket.*
- (b) *Working in the sequence shown in Fig. 4.8, tighten the manifold retaining nuts and bolts evenly, to the specified torque wrench setting.*
- (c) *Ensure all relevant hoses are reconnected to their original positions and are securely held (where necessary) by their retaining clips.*
- (d) *Renew the vacuum servo unit vacuum hose banjo union sealing washers and tighten the union bolt to the specified torque (Chapter 9).*
- (e) *Refit and adjust the accelerator and choke cables as described in Sections 7 and 9.*
- (f) *On completion, refill the cooling system as described in Chapter 1.*

17 Exhaust manifold - removal and refitting

Removal

1 Disconnect the battery negative terminal.
2 Remove the air cleaner metal intake duct assembly as described in Section 3, paragraphs 11 and 12.
3 Firmly apply the handbrake then jack up the front of the car and support it on axle stands.
4 Unscrew the nuts securing the exhaust front pipe to the manifold then disconnect the pipe and collect the gasket.
5 Remove the four exhaust manifold shroud retaining screws and remove the shroud.
6 Unscrew the nuts securing the manifold to the cylinder head then manoeuvre it out of the engine compartment; remove the manifold gasket and discard it.
7 Examine all the exhaust manifold studs for signs of damage and corrosion; remove all traces of corrosion and repair or renew any damaged studs.

Refitting

8 Refitting is the reverse of the removal procedure, noting the following points (photos):

- (a) *Ensure that the manifold and cylinder head sealing faces are clean and flat and fit a new manifold gasket.*
- (b) *Working in the sequence shown in photo 17.8B, tighten the manifold retaining nuts evenly to the specified torque wrench setting.*
- (c) *Tighten all other disturbed nuts and bolts to their specified torque wrench settings (where given).*

18 Exhaust system - general information, removal and refitting

Note: *If a catalytic converter is fitted, remember that it is FRAGILE - do not use hammers, mallets, etc., to strike any part of the system and take care not to drop it or strike it against anything else while handling it.*

General information

1 The exhaust system components are shown in Figs. 4.8 and 4.9. On models not equipped with a catalytic converter the exhaust system is in three sections; the front pipe and front silencer box, the intermediate pipe and middle silencer boxes and the tailpipe and main silencer box. All exhaust sections are joined by a flanged joint. If a catalytic converter is fitted, it is situated between the front pipe and the (much shorter) intermediate pipe, with a flanged joint at each end; the front pipe then has a gas-sampling take off point which is fitted to permit mixture checks using an exhaust gas analyser.
2 The system is suspended throughout its entire length by rubber mountings (photo).

Removal

3 Each exhaust section can be removed individually or, alternatively, the complete system can be removed as a unit once the front pipe has been unbolted from the manifold, as described in paragraph 4, and the system has been freed from all its mounting rubbers.
4 To remove the system or part of the system, first jack up the front or rear of the car and support it on axle stands. Alternatively position the car over an inspection pit or on car ramps.

Front pipe

5 Remove the three nuts securing the front pipe flange joint to the manifold and, where necessary, the two bolts securing the front pipe to its mounting bracket. Separate the flange joint and collect the gasket (photo).
6 Free the pipe from its mounting rubber then undo the three nuts securing the front pipe to the intermediate pipe/catalytic converter (as applicable) and manoeuvre the front pipe out from under the vehicle (photo).

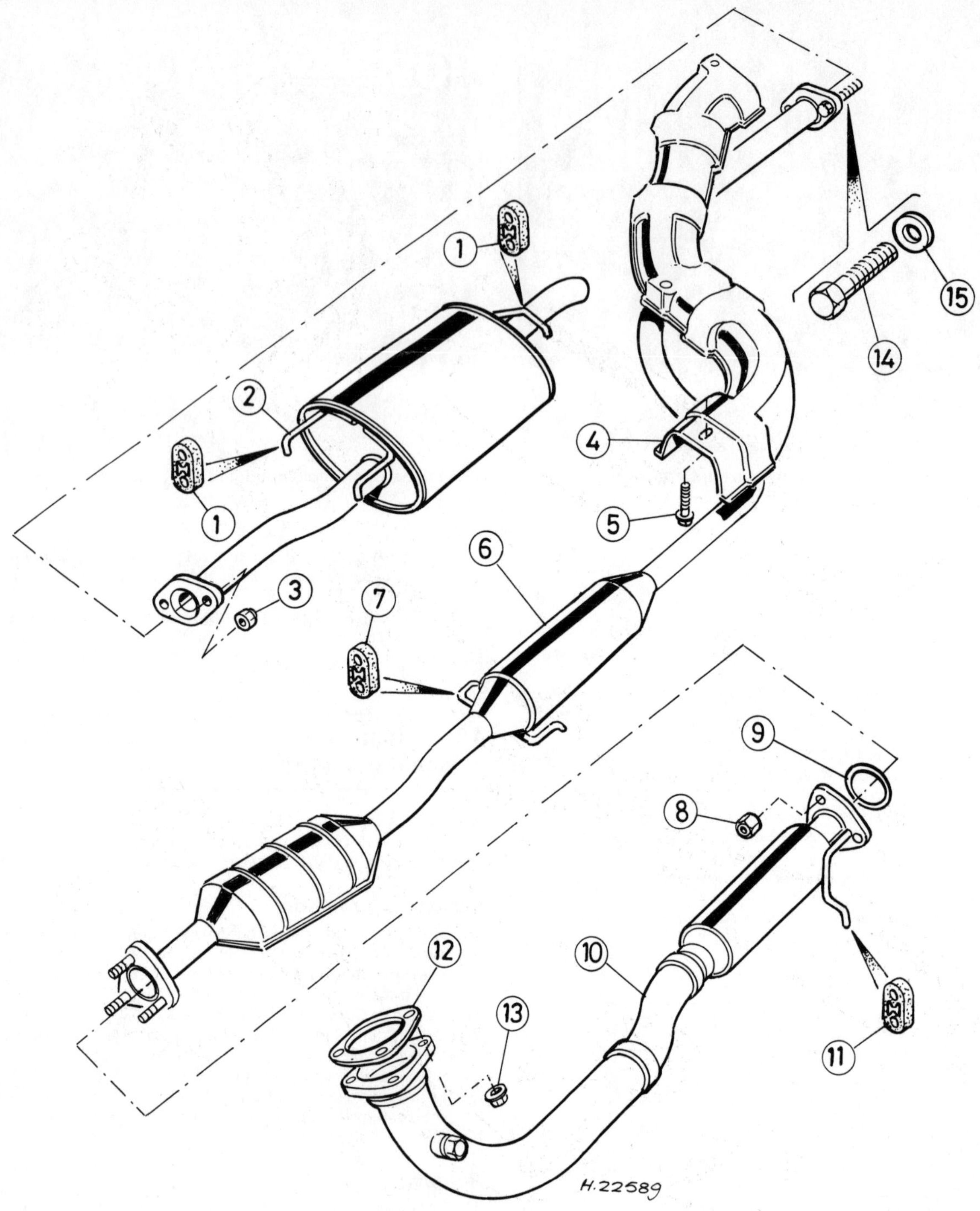

Fig. 4.9 Exhaust system components – models without catalytic converter (Sec 18)

1 *Mounting rubber*
2 *Tailpipe*
3 *Nut*
4 *Heatshield*
5 *Bolt*
6 *Intermediate pipe*
7 *Mounting rubber*
8 *Nut*
9 *Gasket – front pipe to intermediate pipe*
10 *Front pipe*
11 *Mounting rubber*
12 *Gasket – front pipe to exhaust manifold*
13 *Nut*
14 *Bolt (stud replacement)*
15 *Plain washer*

Catalytic converter (where fitted)

7 Slacken and remove the two nuts securing the catalytic converter to the intermediate pipe then separate the flange joint and recover the gasket.

8 Undo the three nuts securing the converter to the front pipe then remove it from the vehicle.

Intermediate pipe

9 Slacken the two nuts securing the tailpipe flange joint to the intermediate pipe and separate the flange joint.

10 Undo the three nuts securing the intermediate pipe to the front pipe or the two nuts securing the pipe to the catalytic converter (as applicable).

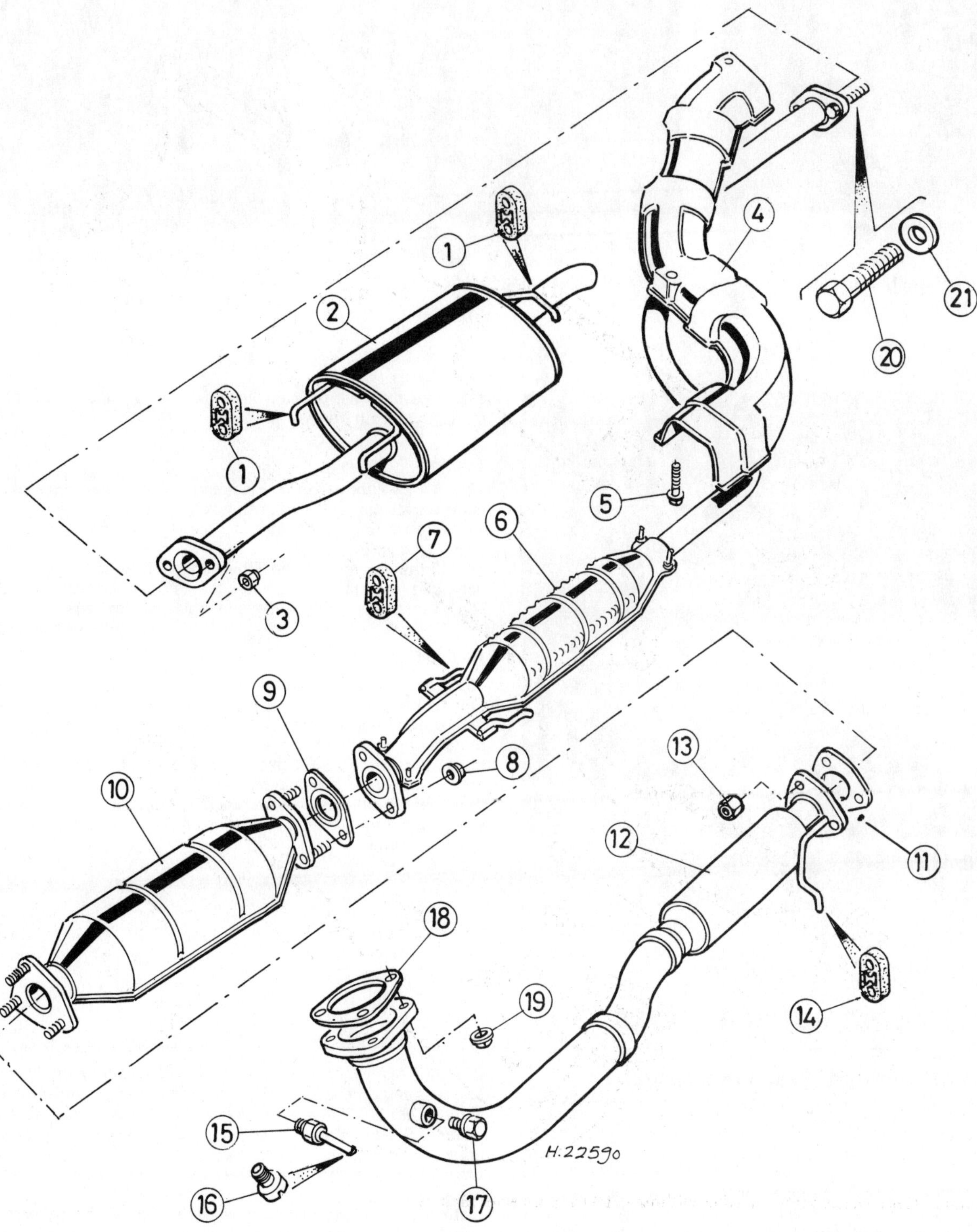

Fig. 4.10 Exhaust system components – models with catalytic converter (Sec 18)

1 *Mounting rubber*
2 *Tailpipe*
3 *Nut*
4 *Heatshield*
5 *Bolt*
6 *Intermediate pipe*
7 *Mounting rubber*
8 *Nut*
9 *Gasket – catalytic converter to intermediate pipe*
10 *Catalytic converter*
11 *Gasket – front pipe to catalytic converter*
12 *Front pipe*
13 *Nut*
14 *Mounting rubber*
15 *Gas sampling pipe – open loop system*
16 *Gas sampling pipe sealing screw – open loop system*
17 *Blanking plug – closed loop system*
18 *Gasket – front pipe to exhaust manifold*
19 *Nut*
20 *Bolt (stud replacement)*
21 *Plain washer*

18.2 Exhaust system is suspended on rubber mountings

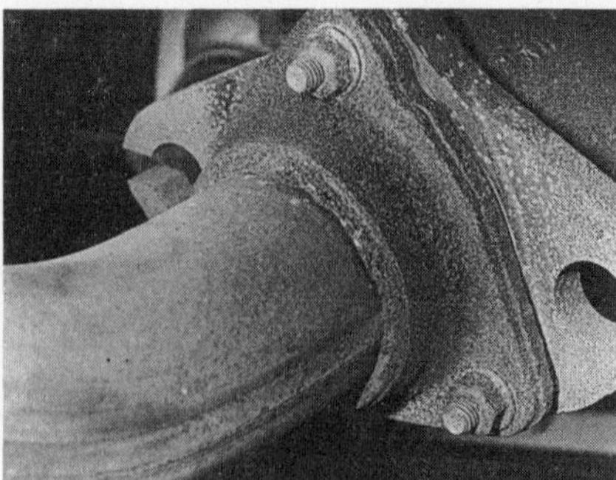
18.5 Front pipe to manifold flange joint

18.6 Front pipe to intermediate pipe flange joint and mounting rubber

18.12 Tailpipe to intermediate flange joint

11 Free the intermediate pipe from all its mounting rubbers and manoeuvre it out from under the car.

Tailpipe

12 Remove the two nuts securing the tailpipe flange joint to the intermediate pipe and separate the joint (photo).
13 Unhook the tailpipe from its three mounting rubbers and remove it from the vehicle.
14 If the threads of the intermediate pipe to tailpipe studs are damaged or the studs snap when the nuts are being undone, the studs can be knocked out of position and replaced with bolts.

Refitting

15 Each section is refitted by a reverse of the removal sequence. Ensure that all traces of corrosion have been removed from the flanges and renew all necessary gaskets. Inspect the rubber mountings for signs of damage or deterioration and renew as necessary. Tighten all flange nuts by hand only to locate the disturbed section in position, then ensure all exhaust system rubber mountings are correctly seated. Check that there is adequate clearance between the exhaust system and vehicle underbody before tightening all the disturbed flange nuts to the specified torque.

Part B: Fuel-injected engines

19 General information and precautions

The fuel system consists of a fuel tank mounted under the rear of the car with an electric fuel pump immersed in it, a fuel filter, fuel feed and return lines and the throttle body assembly (which incorporates the single fuel injector and the fuel pressure regulator), as well as the Engine Management Electronic Control Unit (ECU) and the various sensors, electrical components and related wiring. The air cleaner contains a disposable paper filter element and incorporates a flap valve air temperature control system which allows cold air from the outside of the car and warm air from the exhaust manifold to enter the air cleaner in the correct proportions.

To reduce emissions and to improve driveability when the engine is cold, the inlet manifold is heated by the cooling system coolant and by an electric pre-heater system. Mixture enrichment for cold starting is a pre-programmed function of the system.

The ECU fully controls both the ignition system and the fuel injection system, integrating the two in a complete engine management system; refer to Chapter 5 for information on the ignition side of the system.

The exhaust system is as described in Section 1 of this Chapter.

Warning: *Many of the procedures in this Chapter require the removal of fuel lines and connections which may result in some fuel spillage. Before carrying out any operation on the fuel system refer to the precautions given in Safety first! at the beginning of this Manual and follow them implicitly. Petrol is a highly dangerous and volatile liquid and the precautions necessary when handling it cannot be overstressed.*

Note: *Residual pressure will remain in the fuel lines long after the vehicle was last used, before disconnecting any fuel line depressurise the fuel system as described in Section 26.*

20 Air cleaner assembly – removal and refitting

Removal

1 Release the two clips securing the air intake duct to the assembly, then undo the three screws securing the assembly to the throttle body (photo).
2 Release the assembly from the intake duct and withdraw it,

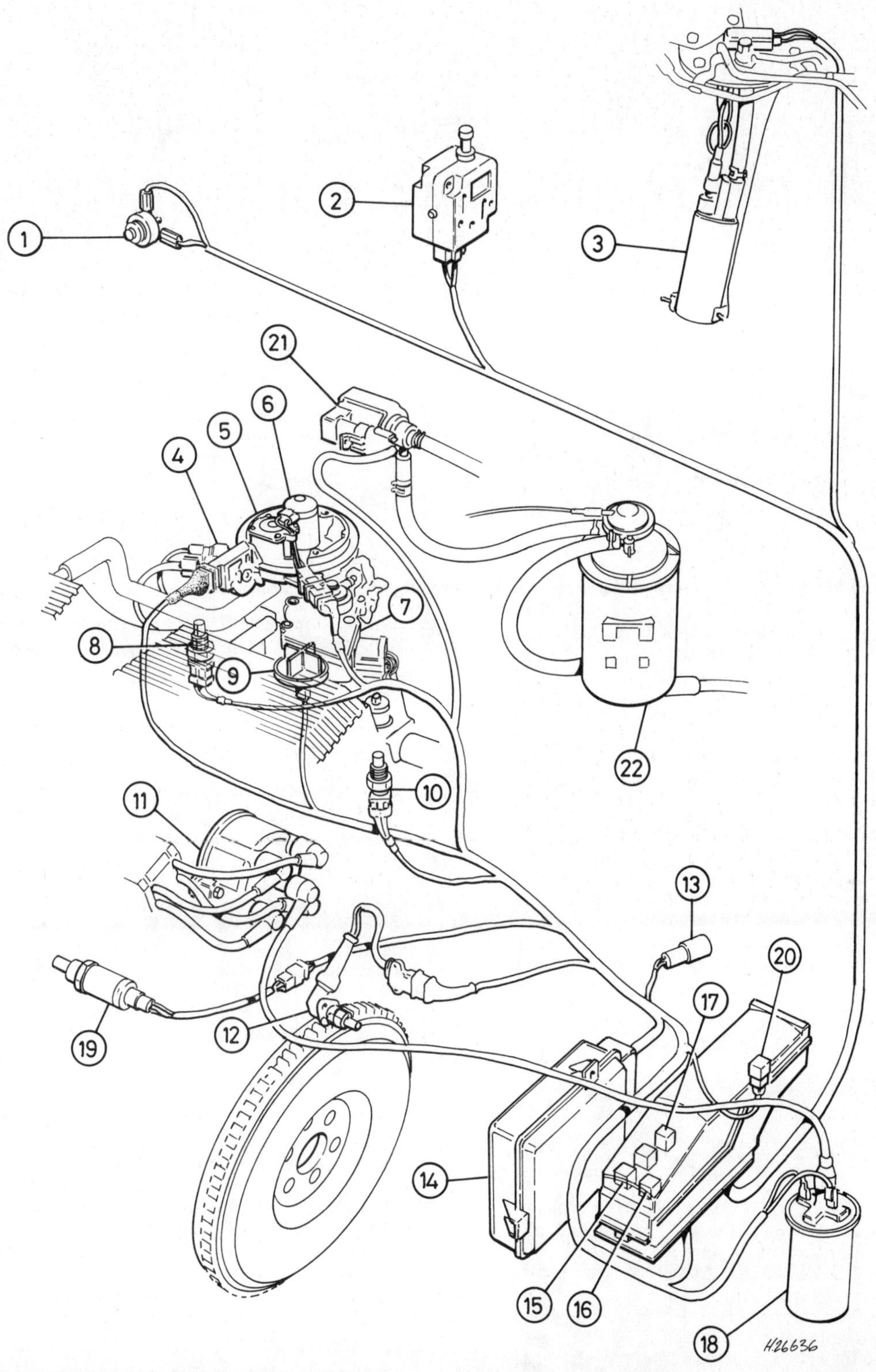

Fig. 4.11 Location of the fuel and ignition system components – fuel-injected engines (Sec 19)

1 Accelerator pedal switch
2 Fuel cut-out inertia switch
3 Fuel pump
4 Throttle potentiometer
5 Fuel pressure regulator
6 Injector
7 Stepper motor
8 Intake air temperature sensor
9 Inlet manifold PTC heater
10 Coolant temperature sensor
11 Distributor
12 Crankshaft sensor
13 Diagnostic connector
14 Engine management ECU
15 Main relay
16 Fuel pump relay
17 Inlet manifold PTC heater relay
18 Ignition HT coil
19 Lambda sensor – models equipped with catalytic converter
20 Lambda sensor relay – models equipped with catalytic converter
21 Purge valve (where fitted)
22 Charcoal canister (where fitted)

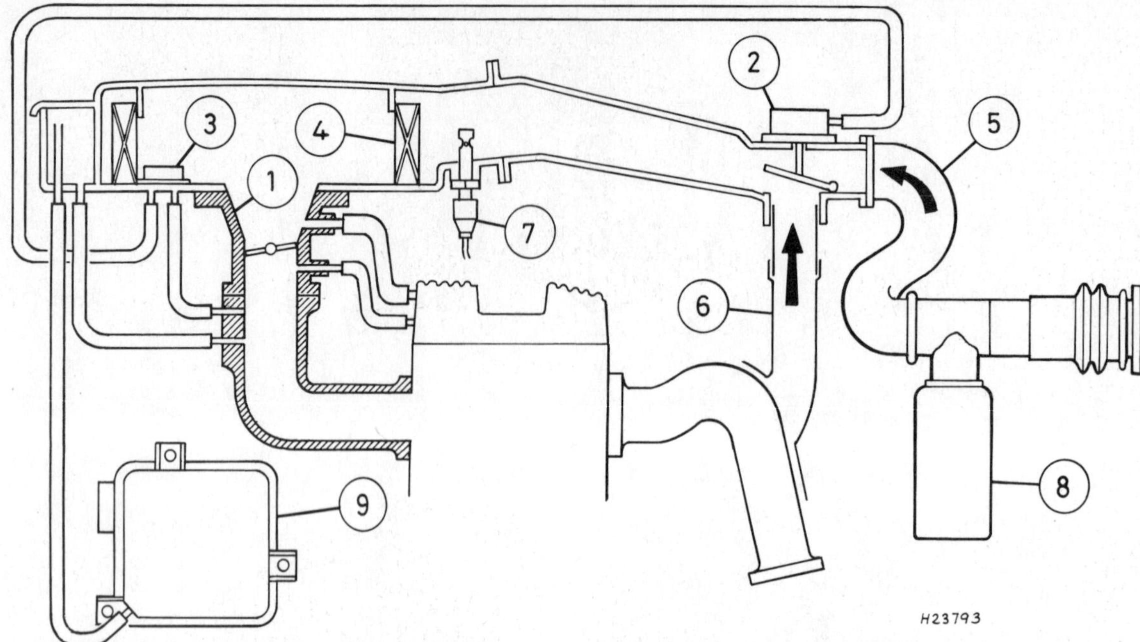

Fig. 4.12 Air cleaner air temperature control system components – fuel-injected engines (Secs 20 and 21)

1 *Throttle housing*
2 *Air temperature control valve*
3 *Thermac switch*
4 *Air filter element*
5 *Air intake duct*
6 *Hot air intake*
7 *Intake air temperature sensor*
8 *Resonator*
9 *Engine management ECU*

collecting the throttle housing seal and the intake duct sealing O-ring (where fitted), then disconnect the following (photo):

(a) *Disconnect the thermac switch vacuum pipes; note that these are colour-coded (yellow to the temperature control valve, red to the inlet manifold) to ensure correct reconnection.*
(b) *Disconnect the ECU manifold absolute pressure sensor fuel trap vacuum hoses; note that these are colour-coded (green to the ECU, white to the inlet manifold) to ensure correct reconnection.*
(c) *Release the wire clip and disconnect the intake air temperature sensor wiring.*

3 Check the condition of the throttle housing seal and the intake duct O- ring (where fitted); renew either if worn or damaged.

20.1 Releasing clips to separate intake duct from air cleaner assembly

4 To remove the metal intake duct, refer to Section 21, paragraphs 3 and 4.

5 To remove the air intake hose it will first be necessary to remove the left-hand headlamp assembly (Chapter 12), to gain access to the two retaining screws. Remove the two retaining screws and disconnect the duct from the body front panel, release the clip securing the ignition HT lead, then slacken the retaining clamp and unfasten the rubber strap to separate the cold air duct from the intake duct. Release the intake hose from the resonator T-piece and remove it from the engine compartment.

6 A resonator chamber is fitted to the intake hose to reduce the amount of induction noise. To remove the chamber first remove the battery and battery tray (Chapter 12). Disconnect the intake hose from the T-piece then remove the resonator T-piece. Release any relevant retaining clips from resonator then remove the resonator from the engine compartment (photos).

Refitting

7 Refitting is the reverse of the removal procedure; ensure that the vacuum pipes and hoses are correctly reconnected and are not trapped as the assembly is refitted, then check that the assembly sits properly on the throttle body before tightening the screws securely.

21 Air cleaner air temperature control system – general information and component renewal

General information

1 Refer to Part A: Section 3.

Thermac switch – renewal

2 Refer to Part A: Section 3 noting that the air cleaner assembly must be removed as described in Section 20.

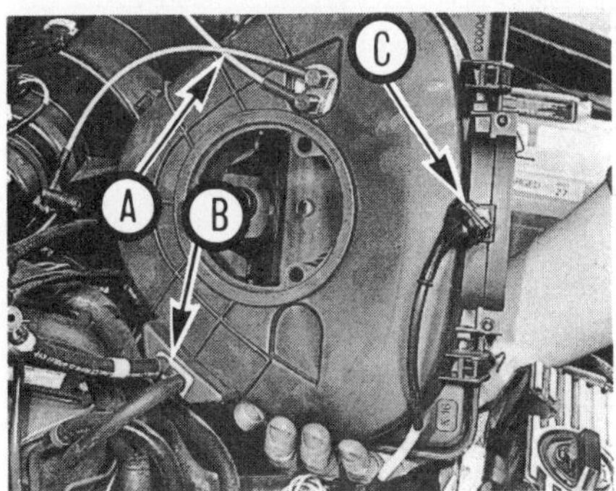

20.2 Thermac switch vacuum pipes 'A', fuel trap vacuum hoses 'B', intake air temperature sensor wiring 'C'

20.6A Remove the T-piece...

20.6B ...then manoeuvre the resonator out of position

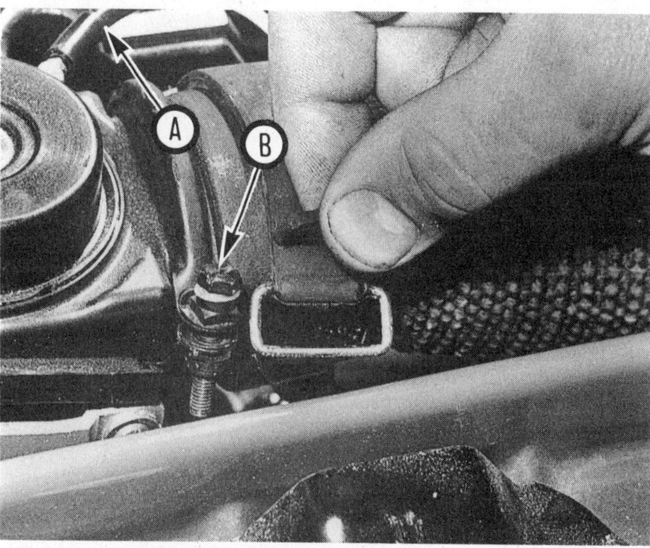

21.3 Unfastening cold air intake duct rubber strap – note vacuum pipe 'A' and clamp screw 'B'

21.4 Unfastening screw securing intake duct to support bracket

Air temperature control valve – renewal

3 Disconnect the vacuum pipe from the air temperature control valve, then slacken the intake hose retaining clamp. Release the intake hose rubber retaining strap and disconnect the hose from the metal intake duct (photo).

4 Release the two clips securing the air intake duct to the air cleaner assembly and undo the bolt securing the duct to its mounting bracket (photo). Withdraw the duct, taking care not to lose the hot air intake connector hose which connects the duct to the exhaust manifold shroud.

5 The air temperature control valve can be renewed only with the complete intake duct assembly. If a new intake duct assembly is being fitted, undo the three screws securing the hot air intake adaptor plate to the bottom of the duct and transfer the adaptor plate to the new duct.

6 Refitting is the reverse of the removal procedure.

22 Accelerator cable – removal, refitting and adjustment

Removal

1 Remove the four windscreen wiper motor mounting bolts to free the motor from the engine compartment bulkhead.

2 Slacken the accelerator cable locknuts and free the outer cable from its mounting bracket. Release the inner cable from the throttle cam (photo).

22.2 Disconnecting the accelerator cable from the throttle cam pulley

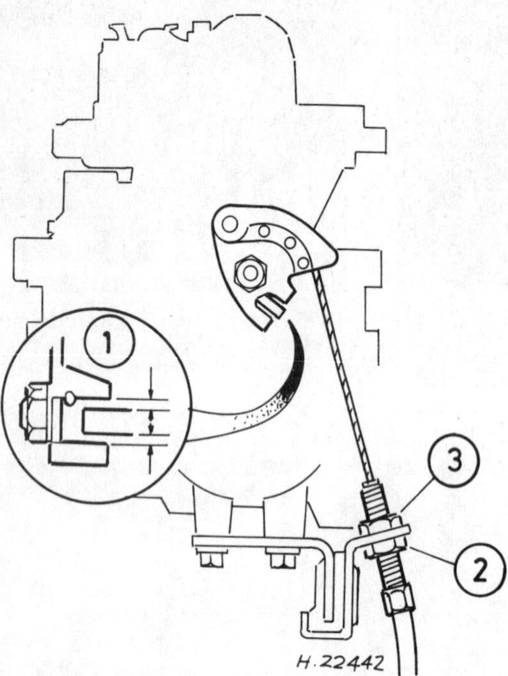

Fig. 4.13 Accelerator cable adjustment – fuel-injected engines (Sec 22)

1 Throttle lever to lost motion link clearance should be equal on each side
2 Adjuster nut
3 Adjuster locknut

3 Work back along the outer cable and release it from any relevant retaining clamps and ties and the engine compartment bulkhead.

4 Working from inside the car, undo the five right-hand lower facia panel retaining screws and remove the panel.

5 Release the cable from the upper end of the accelerator pedal and withdraw the cable from the engine compartment.

Refitting and adjustment

6 Refitting is the reverse of the removal procedure, tighten the windscreen wiper motor retaining bolts to the specified torque (Chapter 12). Prior to tightening the cable locknuts adjust the cable as follows.

7 With the pedal fully released, check that there is equal clearance on each side of the throttle lever at the lost motion link (Fig. 4.13) and no slack in the cable. Have an assistant fully depress the pedal and check that the throttle cam opens fully, then check that it returns to the at-rest position when released.

8 To adjust the cable, switch on the ignition and position the stepper motor by **moving the cam only** to open, and fully close the throttle. Note that it is essential for accurate positioning of the stepper motor that the accelerator pedal switch contacts remain closed, so that the ECU recognises the throttle movement as a command and indexes the stepper motor to 25 steps.

9 Slacken the adjuster locknut (upper nut), then tighten the adjuster (lower) nut until the clearance is equal on each side of the throttle lever at the lost motion link; tighten the locknut without disturbing this setting. Recheck the adjustment and switch off the ignition.

23 Accelerator pedal – removal and refitting

Refer to Part A: Section 8

24 Unleaded petrol – general information and usage

Refer to Part A: Section 10

25 Fuel injection system – general information

The Rover/Motorola Modular Engine Management System uses ECU-controlled single-point injection (MEMS-Spi) and the speed/density method of airflow measurement. The whole system is best explained if considered as three sub-systems; the fuel delivery, air metering and electrical control systems.

The fuel delivery system (Fig. 4.14) incorporates the fuel tank with an electric fuel pump, immersed in a swirl pot to prevent aeration of the fuel, inside it. When the ignition is switched on, the pump is supplied with current via the fuel pump relay, under the control of the ECU; the pump feeds petrol via a non-return valve (to prevent fuel draining out of the system components and back to the tank when the pump is not working) to the fuel filter and from the filter to the injector. Fuel pressure is controlled by the pressure regulator, which lifts to allow excess fuel to return to the tank swirl pot, where a venturi causes the returning fuel to draw cool fuel from the tank into the swirl pot. In the event of sudden deceleration (ie, an accident) an inertia switch cuts off the power to the pump so that the risk of fire is minimised from fuel spraying out of broken fuel lines under pressure.

The air metering system includes the intake air temperature control system (Sections 3 and 21; see Fig. 4.12) and the air cleaner, but the main components are in the throttle body assembly. This incorporates the injector, which sprays fuel onto the back of the throttle disc, the throttle potentiometer, which is linked to the throttle disc spindle and sends the ECU information on the rate of throttle opening by transmitting a varying voltage, and the stepper motor, which is controlled by the ECU and operates the throttle disc spindle lever via a cam and pushrod to provide idle speed control.

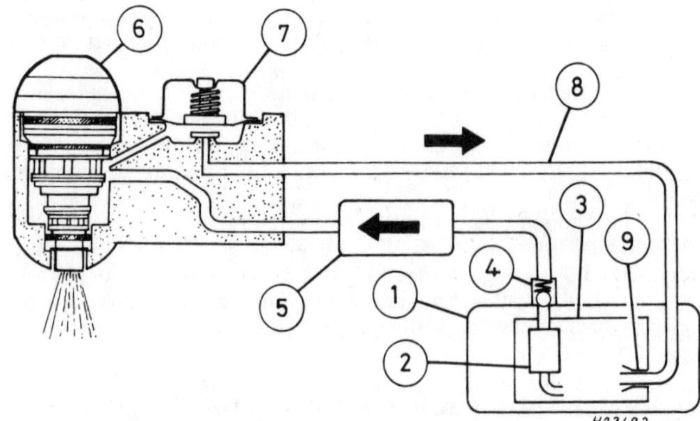

Fig. 4.14 Fuel delivery system – fuel-injected engines (Sec 25)

1 Fuel tank
2 Fuel pump
3 Swirl pot
4 Non-return valve
5 Fuel filter
6 Fuel injector
7 Fuel pressure regulator
8 Fuel return line
9 Venturi

Note: *There is no provision for the adjustment or alteration of the idle speed except by reprogramming the ECU using Rover diagnostic equipment; if checking the idle speed, remember that it will vary constantly under ECU control.*

The electrical control system consists of the ECU, with all the sensors that provide it with information and the actuators by which it controls the whole system's operation. The ECU's manifold absolute pressure sensor is connected, by hoses and a fuel (vapour) trap mounted in the air cleaner assembly, to the inlet manifold (Fig. 4.12); variations in manifold pressure are converted into graduated electrical signals which are used by the ECU to determine the load on the engine. The intake air temperature sensor is self-explanatory, the crankshaft sensor gives it the engine speed and crankshaft position, the coolant temperature sensor gives it the engine temperature, the accelerator pedal switch tells it when the accelerator is closed; the throttle potentiometer is explained above and the lambda sensor (where fitted) in Part C: Section 38. In addition, the ECU senses battery voltage (adjusting the injector pulse width to suit and using the stepper motor to increase the idle speed and, therefore, the alternator output if it is too low), incorporates short-circuit protection and diagnostic capabilities and can both receive and transmit information via the diagnostic connector, thus permitting engine diagnosis and tuning by Rover diagnostic equipment. If either the coolant temperature sensor, the intake air temperature sensor or the manifold absolute pressure sensor circuits should fail to provide adequate information, the ECU has a back-up facility which assumes a value corresponding to a coolant temperature of 60°C, an intake air temperature of 35°C and an engine load based on the engine speed and throttle position; these are used to implement a back-up air/fuel mixture ratio.

All these signals are compared by the ECU, using digital techniques, with set values pre-programmed (mapped) into its memory; based on this information, the ECU selects the response appropriate to those values and controls the ignition HT coil (varying the ignition timing as required), the fuel injector (varying its pulse width – the length of time the injector is held open – to provide a richer or weaker mixture, as appropriate), the stepper motor (controlling the idle and fast idle speeds), the fuel pump relay (controlling the fuel delivery), the manifold heater relay (controlling the inlet manifold pre-heater system) and the main relay, the purge control valve (where fitted) and the lambda sensor and relay (where fitted) accordingly. The mixture, idle speed and ignition timing are constantly varied by the ECU to provide the best settings for cranking, starting and engine warm-up (with either a hot or cold engine), idle, cruising and acceleration. A rev-limiter circuit is built into the ECU which switches off the injector earth (ie, the fuel supply) if engine speed exceeds 6860 rpm, switching it back on at 6820 rpm. The injector earth is also switched off on the overrun (coolant temperature above 80°C, throttle pedal switch contacts closed, engine speed above 1500 rpm) to improve fuel economy and reduce exhaust emissions.

The ECU idle control is an adaptive system; it learns the engine load and wear characteristics over a period of time and adjusts the idle speed to suit. If the ECU is renewed, or one from another car is fitted, it will take a short period of normal driving for the new ECU to learn the engine's characteristics and restore full idle control.

26 Fuel system – depressurisation

Note: *Refer to the warning note in Section 19 before proceeding.*

Warning: *The following procedure will merely relieve the pressure in the fuel system – remember that fuel will still be present in the system components and take precautions accordingly before disconnecting any of them.*

1 The fuel system referred to in this Section is defined as the tank-mounted fuel pump, the fuel filter, the fuel injector and the pressure regulator in the injector housing, and the metal pipes and flexible hoses of the fuel lines between these components. All these contain fuel which will be under pressure while the engine is running and/or while the ignition is switched on. The pressure will remain for some time after the ignition has been switched off and must be relieved before any of these components are disturbed for servicing work.

26.5 Slackening pressure release bolt to depressurise fuel system – non-catalyst model shown

Models equipped with a catalytic converter

2 On models equipped with a catalytic converter, the system is depressurised as follows via the small bolt fitted to the fuel filter inlet (feed) union nut.

3 Position wads of rag around the union to catch the spilled fuel and slowly slacken the bolt. Once all the pressure has been released remove the bolt. Inspect the sealing washer for signs of wear or damage and renew if necessary. Refit the bolt and sealing washer to the union nut and tighten it securely.

Models without a catalytic converter

4 On models not fitted with a catalytic converter, the system is depressurised as follows via the bolt in the metal fuel filter outlet pipe.

5 Position wads of rag around the pipe to catch the spilled fuel as the bolt is removed. Carefully slacken the bolt whilst holding the fuel pipe boss with an open-ended spanner to prevent any undue strain being placed on the fuel pipe (photo). Once all the pressure has been relieved remove the bolt and inspect the sealing washer for signs of wear or damage and renew if necessary. Refit the bolt and washer to the fuel pipe and tighten it to the specified torque wrench whilst using a spanner to counter-hold the pipe boss, to prevent the pipe or filter or filter being damaged.

27 Fuel system pressure check

Note: *Refer to the warning note in Section 19 before proceeding.*

1 The following procedure is based on the use of the Rover pressure gauge and adaptor (Service tool numbers 18G 1500 and 18G 1500/3).

2 Depressurise the fuel system as described in Section 26.

3 Unscrew the pressure release bolt and screw in the adaptor, then connect the pressure gauge.

4 Turn the engine over on the starter motor; the pressure should reach the specified value. Stop cranking the engine and watch the gauge; the pressure drop in the first minute should not exceed 0.7 bar.

5 If the pressure first recorded was too high, renew the pressure regulator; this means renewing the complete injector housing assembly.

6 If the pressure first recorded was too low or if it falls too quickly, check the system carefully for leaks. If no leaks are found check the pump by substituting a new one and recheck the pressure. If the pressure does not improve, the fault is in the pressure regulator and the complete injector housing assembly must be renewed; if this is the case

it is worth dismantling the regulator to check that the fault is not due to its being jammed open with dirt, or similar.

28 Fuel pump - removal and refitting

Note: *Refer to the warning note in Section 19 before proceeding.*

Removal

1 Remove the fuel tank as described in Section 30.
2 Release the clips securing the tank vent hose to the fuel tank breather and fuel cut-off valve and disconnect the hose. Undo the vent hose and valve retaining nuts, then disconnect the vent valve hose from the fuel pump and remove the vent hose and valve assembly from the tank.
3 Disconnect the wiring connector from the fuel pump.
4 Slacken and remove the six fuel pump retaining nuts then carefully withdraw the fuel pump assembly from the tank and remove the pump seal.

Refitting

5 Refitting is a reversal of the removal sequence, noting the following points:

(a) *Renew the pump seal if there is any doubt as to its condition.*
(b) *Tighten all the retaining nuts to the specified torque setting.*
(c) *Ensure that the vent hoses are correctly connected and are securely held by any necessary retaining clips.*

29 Fuel gauge sender unit - removal and refitting

Refer to Part A: Section 5

30 Fuel tank - removal and refitting

Refer to Part A: Section 6, noting that the fuel system must be depressurised as described in Section 26 before any fuel hose is disconnected.

31 Throttle housing - removal and refitting

Note: *Refer to the warning note in Section 19 before proceeding.*

Removal

1 Depressurise the fuel system as described in Section 26.
2 Disconnect the battery negative terminal and remove the air cleaner assembly as described in Section 20.
3 Examine the injector housing fuel pipe feed and return unions for signs of leakage, then wipe them clean.
4 Using a spanner to hold each adaptor, unscrew the pipe union nuts and release the fuel feed and return pipes from the adaptors. Plug each pipe and adaptor to minimise the loss of fuel and prevent the entry of dirt into the system.
5 Release the wire retaining clips and disconnect the wiring connectors from the injector housing, the throttle potentiometer and the stepper motor.
6 Slacken the accelerator cable locknuts and free the outer cable from its mounting bracket. Release the inner cable from the throttle cam.
7 Using a suitable pair of pliers, release the retaining clips and disconnect the breather hoses from the throttle housing (photo).
8 Slacken and remove the four nuts securing the throttle housing to the inlet manifold then remove the throttle housing from the car. Remove the throttle housing insulating spacer and examine it for signs of wear or damage, renewing it if necessary (photos).
9 If leakage was detected from the feed and return pipes or their union nuts, check the sealing surfaces of the nuts and adaptors and renew the adaptor or the pipe assembly as necessary. If leakage is detected from the adaptors, unscrew each through one turn with a spanner, then through two turns by hand; if the adaptor is still a tight fit in the housing, the threads are damaged and the housing and adaptors must be renewed as a set. If the threads are sound, fit new sealing washers to the adaptors and refit them, tightening them to their specified torque wrench setting.

Refitting

10 Refitting is a reverse of the removal sequence, noting the following points:

(a) *Ensure that the mating surfaces of the throttle housing and inlet manifold are clean then fit the insulating spacer.*
(b) *Tighten the throttle housing and fuel pipe union nuts to their specified torque settings.*
(c) *On completion, reconnect the accelerator cable and adjust it as described in Section 22.*

32 Fuel injection system components - testing

1 If a fault appears in the engine management (ignition/fuel injection) system first ensure that the fault is not due to poor maintenance; ie, check that the air cleaner filter element is clean, the spark plugs are in good condition and correctly gapped, that the engine breather hoses are clear and undamaged, referring to Chapter 1 for further information. Also check that the throttle cable is correctly adjusted as described in Section 22. If the engine is running very roughly, check the compression pressures as described in Chapter 2, bearing in mind that possibly one of the hydraulic tappets might be faulty, producing an incorrect valve clearance.
2 If these checks fail to reveal the cause of the problem the vehicle should be taken to a suitably equipped Rover dealer for testing. A wiring block connector is incorporated in the engine management circuit into

31.7 Disconnecting breather hoses from throttle housing

31.8A Lift the throttle body assembly away from the inlet manifold...

31.8B ...and remove the throttle body gasket spacer

33.1 Disconnecting fuel feed and return pipes from injector housing

33.2 Disconnect wiring connector from injector housing

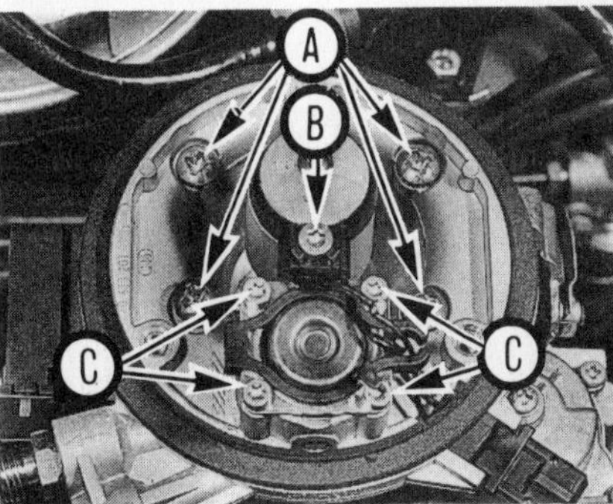

33.3A Injector housing to throttle body screws 'A', injector connector cap screw 'B', pressure regulator screws 'C'

33.3B Remove injector housing from throttle body noting its gasket

33.8A Remove screw then lift off the injector connector cap...

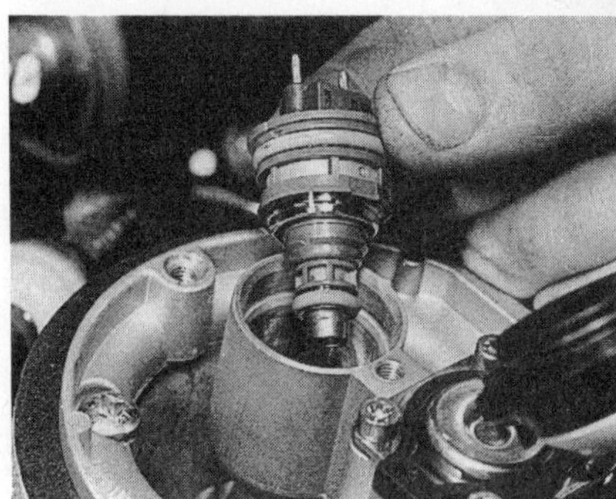

33.8B ...and withdraw injector

which a special electronic diagnostic tester can be plugged. The tester will locate the fault quickly and simply, alleviating the need to test all the system components individually which is a time consuming operation that carries a high risk of damaging the ECU.

3 If necessary, the system wiring and wiring connectors can be checked as described in Chapter 12 ensuring that the ECU wiring connectors have first been disconnected.

33 Fuel injection system components - removal and refitting

Note: *Refer to the warning note in Section 19 before proceeding.*

Injector housing

Removal

1 Carry out the operations described in paragraphs 1 to 4 of Section 31 (photo).

2 Release the wire retaining clip and disconnect the wiring connector from the injector housing (photo).

3 Remove the four screws securing the injector housing to the throttle body then lift off the injector housing and remove the gasket (photos).

4 If leakage was detected from the fuel feed and/or return pipes perform the checks described in paragraph 9 of Section 31.

Refitting

5 Refitting is a reversal of the removal procedure noting the following points:

(a) *Ensure the injector and throttle housing mating surfaces are clean and fit a new gasket.*
(b) *Apply thread locking compound (Rover recommend Loctite Screwlock or Nutlock) to the threads of the injector housing screws then tighten them to the specified torque.*
(c) *Tighten the fuel pipe union nuts to the specified torque setting.*

Fuel injector

Note: *As a Rover replacement part, the injector is available only as part of the injector housing. Note, however that it is a Bosch-manufactured component and can be obtained separately through Bosch agents.*

Removal

6 Depressurise the fuel system as described in Section 26.

7 Disconnect the battery negative terminal then remove the air cleaner assembly as described in Section 20.

8 Slacken and remove the injector connector cap retaining screw and lift off the connector cap. The injector can then be lifted out of the housing (photos).

Refitting

9 Refitting is the reverse of the removal procedure, ensuring that the connector cap makes good contact with the injector pins.

Fuel pressure regulator

10 The fuel pressure regulator is available only as part of the injector housing assembly. Refer to paragraphs 1 to 5 for details on removal and refitting.

Stepper motor

Removal

11 Remove the injector housing as described in paragraphs 1 to 4.

12 Release the retaining clip and disconnect the stepper motor wiring connector (photo).

13 Remove the four stepper motor retaining screws and remove the stepper motor assembly from the throttle housing (photos). Do not attempt to dismantle the assembly.

Refitting

14 Refitting is the reverse of the removal procedure ensuring that the throttle housing and motor mating surfaces are clean. On completion adjust the throttle cable as described in Section 22 to ensure that the stepper motor is correctly indexed.

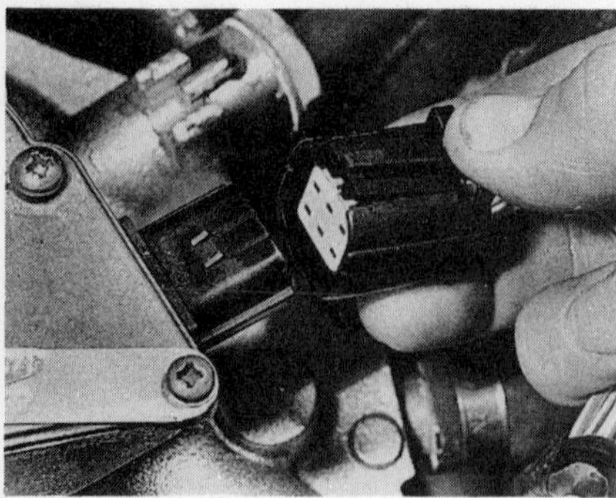
33.12 Disconnecting stepper motor wiring connector

33.13A Undo the four stepper motor retaining screws...

33.13B ...and remove the stepper motor assembly

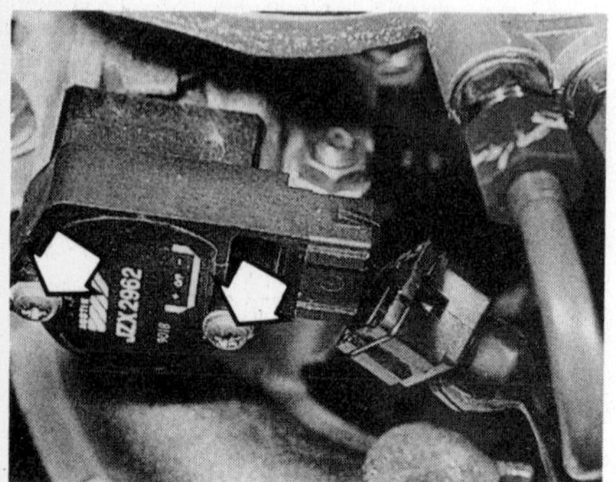
33.17 Disconnecting throttle potentiometer wiring connector – note mounting screws (arrowed)

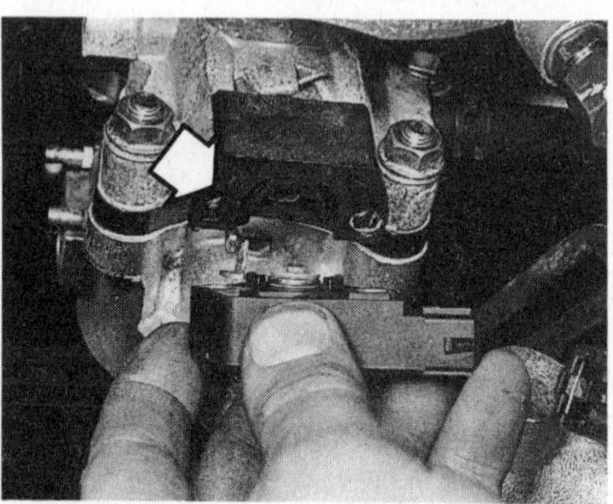
33.19 Ensure potentiometer tongue engages correctly with throttle lever – note spacer (arrowed)

33.20 Disconnect the wiring connector...

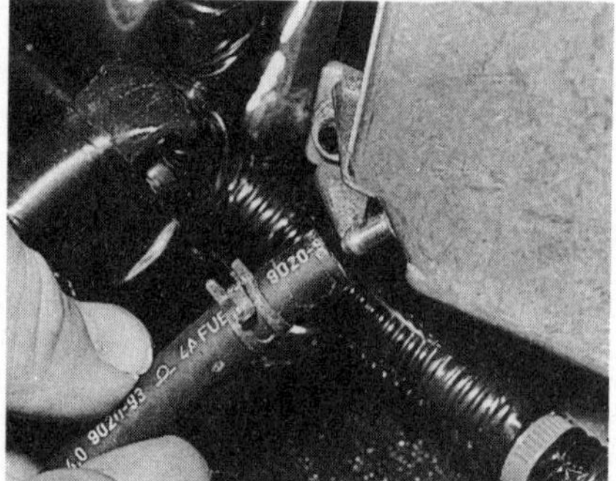
33.21A ...and the absolute pressure sensor vacuum hose from the ECU...

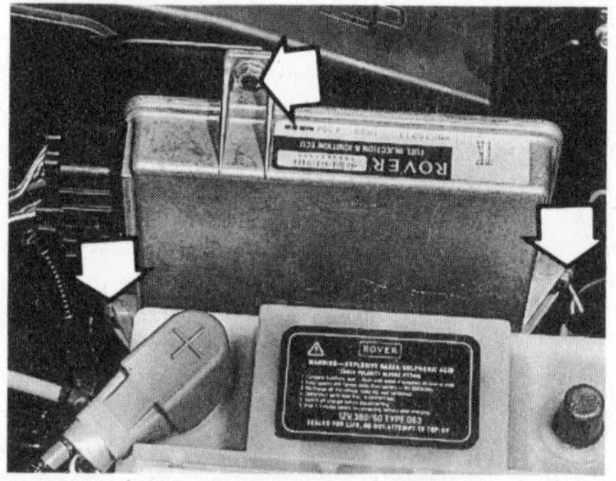

33.21B ...then undo the ECU mounting nuts (arrowed) and remove the unit

Throttle potentiometer

Removal

15 Although not strictly necessary, access is greatly improved if the air cleaner assembly is first removed as described in Section 20.
16 Disconnect the battery negative lead.
17 Release the wire retaining clip and disconnect the potentiometer wiring connector (photo).
18 Remove the two screws and remove the potentiometer from the throttle housing, noting how its tongue engages with the throttle disc spindle lever. Withdraw the spacer if required.

Refitting

19 Refitting is the reverse of the removal procedure, noting the following points (photo):

(a) *Carefully clean the mating surfaces of the throttle body, the spacer and the potentiometer, then refit the spacer.*
(b) *Refit the potentiometer so that its tongue engages FORWARD of (ie 'inside') the throttle disc spindle lever, then rotate the throttle cam to check the action of the lever and tongue.*
(c) *Securely tighten the potentiometer screws then recheck the potentiometer operation before reconnecting the wiring connector.*

Engine management (ignition/fuel injection) ECU

Removal

20 Disconnect the battery negative terminal and unplug the wiring connector(s) from the ECU (photo).
21 Disconnect the absolute pressure sensor vacuum hose from the unit, then undo the three retaining nuts and remove the ECU from the engine compartment (photos).

Refitting

22 Refitting is a reverse of the removal sequence; tighten the ECU

33.26 Absolute pressure sensor fuel trap hoses are colour-coded to ensure correct refitting

33.28 Remove the air cleaner metal intake duct to gain access to intake air temperature sensor

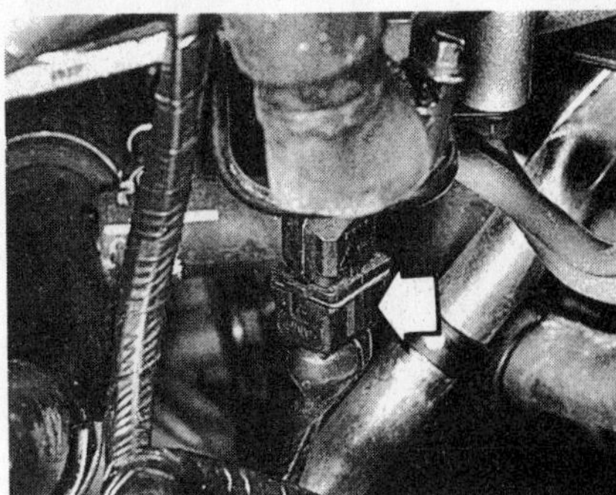

33.32 Location of coolant temperature sensor (arrowed)

33.39 Reset fuel cut-off inertia switch by depressing plunger

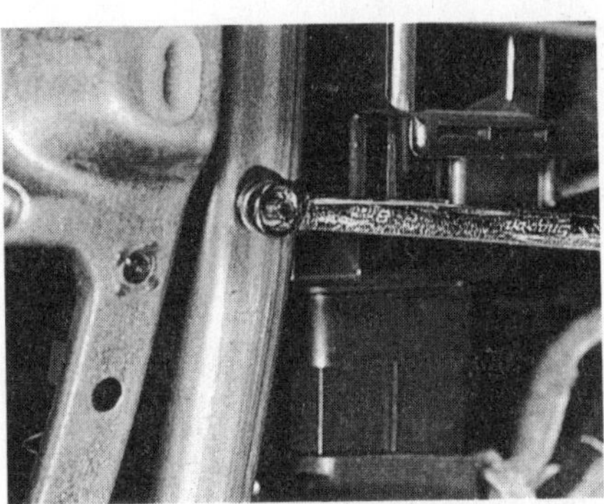

33.41A Undo the inertia switch retaining nut...

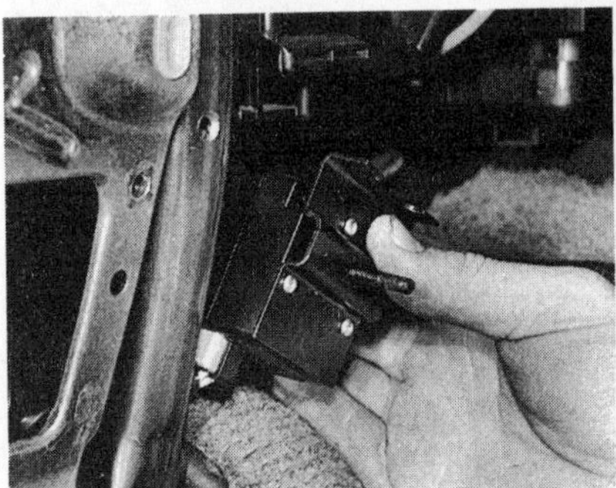

33.41B ...and remove the switch

retaining nuts to the specified torque. Due to the nature of the ECU, if a new or different ECU has been fitted, it may take a short while for full idle control to be restored (See Section 25 for further information).

Manifold absolute pressure sensor

23 This is part of the ECU and is removed and refitted as described above.

24 The sensor's vacuum hose runs from the inlet manifold to the ECU via a fuel (vapour) trap mounted in the air cleaner assembly.

25 To remove the fuel trap, remove the air cleaner assembly cover (Chapter 1), release the clips and disconnect the hoses, then remove the single retaining screw and withdraw the trap.

26 On refitting, note that the hoses are colour-coded (green to the ECU, white to the inlet manifold) to ensure correct reconnection (photo).

Intake air temperature sensor

Removal

27 Disconnect the battery negative lead.

28 Remove the air cleaner metal intake duct as described in Section 21, paragraphs 3 and 4 (photo).

29 Release the wire clip and disconnect the sensor wiring.

30 Unscrew the sensor and remove it from the air cleaner housing.

Refitting

31 Refitting is the reverse of the removal procedure; tighten the sensor to its specified torque wrench setting.

Coolant temperature sensor

Removal

32 The coolant temperature switch is fitted to the underside of the inlet manifold (photo). Either drain the cooling system as described in Chapter 1, or be prepared for some loss of coolant as the switch is unscrewed.

33 Release the wire retaining clip and disconnect the wiring connector from the switch.

34 Unscrew the switch from the manifold and withdraw it, then plug the opening to prevent the entry of dirt; if the cooling system has not been drained, work quickly to minimise coolant loss.

Refitting

35 Wipe clean the threads of the switch and of the thermostat housing. If a sealing washer is fitted, renew it whenever it is disturbed to prevent leaks; if no sealing washer is fitted, apply a smear of sealant to the switch threads.

36 Refit the switch, working quickly if the cooling system was not drained, and tighten it to the specified torque. Reconnect the wiring connector.

37 Refill or top up the cooling system as described in Chapter 1.

Accelerator pedal switch

38 Refer to Part A: Section 14.

Fuel cut-off inertia switch

39 The fuel cut-off inertia switch is located behind the centre console where it is mounted onto the steering column support bracket. If the switch has tripped it can be reset by pressing in the plunger situated at the top of the switch (photo).

Removal

40 Remove the centre console as described in Chapter 11.

41 Disconnect the wiring connector then undo the switch mounting bracket retaining nut and remove the switch (photos).

Refitting

42 Refitting is a reverse of the removal sequence. Before installing the centre console, reset the inertia switch by pressing in the plunger.

Relays

43 Refer to Chapter 12 for further information.

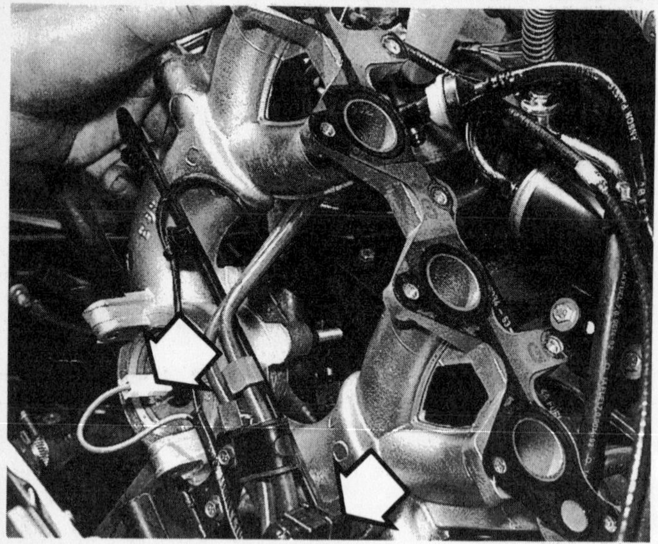

34.1 Inlet manifold partially removed to show manifold PTC heater and coolant temperature sensor (arrowed)

34 Inlet manifold pre-heater - general information, removal and refitting

The system is as described in Part A: Section 15, noting that there is no separate manifold pre-heater temperature switch; the ECU uses the information sent from the coolant temperature sensor (See Section 33) (photo).

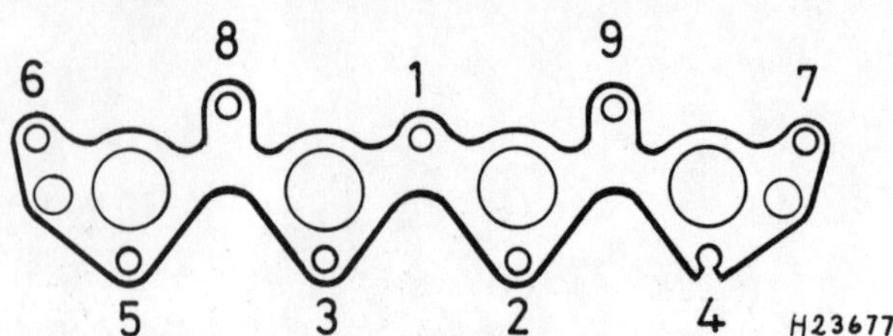

Fig. 4.15 Inlet manifold tightening sequence - K16 engines (Sec 35)

35 Inlet manifold - removal and refitting

Note: *Refer to the warning note in Section 1 before proceeding.*

Removal

1 Remove the throttle housing as described in Section 31.
2 Drain the cooling system as described in Chapter 1.
3 Slacken the retaining clamps and disconnect the coolant hoses from the inlet manifold (photo).
4 Slacken and remove the brake vacuum servo unit hose union bolt and disconnect the hose (photo). Discard the hose union sealing washers; these must be renewed whenever they are disturbed.
5 Undo the single bolt which secure each manifold support stay to the cylinder block/crankcase and slacken the bolts which secure the stays to the inlet manifold.
6 Make a final check that all the necessary vacuum hoses have been disconnected from the manifold then unscrew the nuts and bolts securing the manifold to the cylinder head. Manoeuvre the manifold out of the engine compartment and discard the manifold gasket (photos).

35.3 Disconnect coolant hoses (arrowed)...

35.4 ...and brake servo vacuum hose from inlet manifold

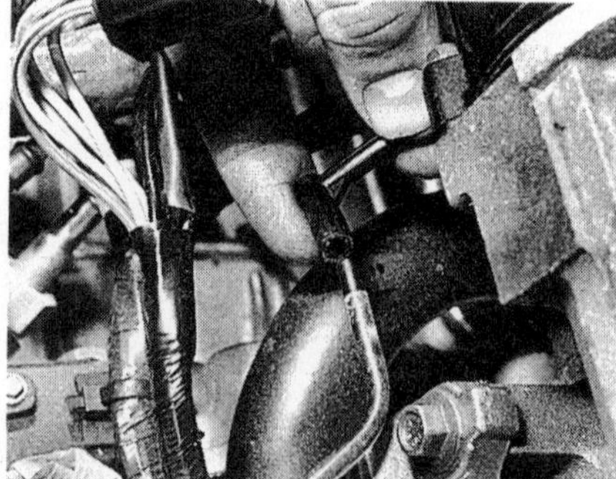

35.6A Ensure all vacuum pipes and hoses are disconnected

35.6B Remove the inlet manifold and withdraw the gasket

35.7A Always renew gasket when refitting manifold

35.7B Ensure coolant hoses are securely held by the retaining clamps

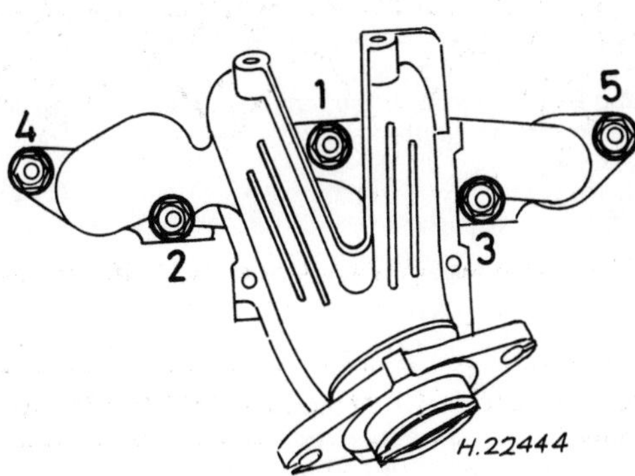

Fig. 4.16 Exhaust manifold tightening sequence – K16 engines (Sec 36)

Refitting

7 Refitting is the reverse of the removal procedure, noting the following points (photos):

- (a) *Ensure that the manifold and cylinder head mating surfaces are clean and dry and fit a new manifold gasket.*
- (b) *Working in the sequence shown in Fig. 4.15, tighten the manifold retaining nuts and bolts evenly, to the specified torque wrench setting.*
- (c) *Ensure all relevant hoses are reconnected to their original positions and are securely held (where necessary) by the retaining clips.*
- (d) *Renew the vacuum servo unit vacuum hose banjo union sealing washers and tighten the union bolt to the specified torque (Chapter 9).*
- (e) *Refit the throttle housing as described in Section 31.*
- (f) *On completion, refill the cooling system as described in Chapter 1.*

36 Exhaust manifold – removal and refitting

Removal

1 Disconnect the battery negative lead. Firmly apply the handbrake then jack up the front of the car and support it on axle stands.
2 Remove the air cleaner metal intake duct as described in Section 21, paragraphs 3 and 4. Undo the two bolts securing the duct mounting bracket to the cylinder head cover and remove the bracket.
3 Undo the two bolts securing the upper radiator mountings to the bonnet platform, then remove the mountings and tilt the radiator forward to gain the clearance necessary to remove the manifold.
4 Unscrew the nuts securing the exhaust front pipe to the manifold, then disconnect the pipe and collect the gasket.
5 Undo the five nuts securing the exhaust manifold to the cylinder head then carefully manoeuvre the manifold out of the engine compartment. Remove the manifold gasket and discard it.
6 Examine all the exhaust manifold studs for signs of damage and corrosion; remove all traces of corrosion and repair or renew any damaged studs.

Refitting

7 Refitting is the reverse of the removal procedure, noting the following points:

- (a) *Ensure that the manifold and cylinder head sealing faces are clean and flat and fit a new manifold gasket.*
- (b) *Working in the sequence shown in Fig. 4.16, tighten the manifold retaining nuts evenly to the specified torque wrench setting.*
- (c) *Tighten all other disturbed nuts and bolts to their specified torque wrench settings (where given).*

37 Exhaust system – general information, removal and refitting

Refer to Part A: Section 18, noting that on models fitted with closed-loop catalytic converters the lambda sensor must be removed, referring to Section 39 for further information, or its wiring must be disconnected whenever the exhaust system front pipe is disconnected from the manifold or removed.

Part C: Emission control systems

38 General information

Apart from their ability to use unleaded petrol and the various features which help to minimise emissions and are built into the fuel system, all models have at least the crankcase emission-control system described below. Models equipped with a catalytic converter are also fitted with the exhaust and evaporative emission control system.

Crankcase emission control

To reduce the emission of unburned hydrocarbons from the crankcase into the atmosphere, the engine is sealed and the blow-by gases and oil vapour are drawn from the crankcase, through a wire mesh oil separator in the cylinder head cover, into the inlet tract to be burned by the engine during normal combustion. On carburettor engines a single breather hose connects the cylinder head cover to the carburettor continuous-depression area. On fuel-injected engines a small-bore breather hose connects the cylinder head cover to the throttle body downstream of the throttle disc, while a larger-bore hose is connected above the throttle disc so that the same effect is obtained at all states of manifold depression.

Under conditions of high manifold depression (idling, deceleration) the gases will be sucked positively out of the crankcase. Under conditions of low manifold depression (acceleration, full-throttle running) the gases are forced out of the crankcase by the (relatively) higher crankcase pressure; if the engine is worn, the raised crankcase pressure (due to increased blow-by) will cause some of the flow to return under all manifold conditions.

Evaporative emission control

To minimise the escape into the atmosphere of unburned hydrocarbons, an evaporative emissions control system is fitted to models equipped with a catalytic converter. The fuel tank filler cap is sealed and a charcoal canister is mounted in the engine compartment to collect the petrol vapours generated in the tank when the car is parked. It stores them until they can be cleared from the canister (under the control of the fuel-injection/ignition system ECU via the purge control valve) into the inlet tract to be burned by the engine during normal combustion.

To ensure that the engine runs correctly when it is cold and/or idling and to protect the catalytic converter from the effects of an over-rich mixture, the purge control valve is not opened by the ECU until the engine has warmed up to above 70°C, the engine speed exceeds 1500 rpm and manifold absolute pressure is below 30 kPa; the valve solenoid is then modulated on and off to allow the stored vapour to pass into the inlet tract.

Exhaust emission control

To minimise the amount of pollutants which escape into the atmosphere, some models are fitted with a catalytic converter in the exhaust system. Either an open-loop control system, which has no feedback from the converter to the fuel system, or a closed-loop control system, in which the lambda sensor in the exhaust system provides the fuel-injection/ignition system ECU with constant feedback (which enables it to adjust the mixture to provide the best possible conditions for the converter to operate) may be fitted.

If a lambda sensor is fitted, it has a heating element built-in that is controlled by the ECU through the lambda sensor relay to quickly bring the sensor's tip to an efficient operating temperature. The sensor's tip is sensitive to oxygen and sends the ECU a varying voltage depending on the amount of oxygen in the exhaust gases; if the intake air/fuel mixture is too rich, the exhaust gases are low in oxygen so the sensor sends a low-voltage signal, the voltage rising as the mixture weakens and the amount of oxygen rises in the exhaust gases. Peak conversion efficiency of all major pollutants occurs if the intake air/fuel mixture is maintained at the chemically-correct ratio for the complete combustion of petrol of 14.7 parts (by weight) of air to 1 part of fuel (the 'stoichiometric' ratio). The sensor output voltage alters in a large step at this point, the ECU using the signal change as a reference point and correcting the intake air/fuel mixture accordingly by altering the fuel injector pulse width.

39 Emission control system components – testing and renewal

Crankcase emission control

1 Apart from the checks described in Chapter 1, the components of this system require no attention other than to check that the hose(s) are clear and that the wire mesh oil separators are flushed clean with a suitable solvent whenever the cylinder head cover is removed, as described in Chapter 2 (photo).

Evaporative emission control

Testing

2 If the system is thought to be faulty, disconnect the hoses from the charcoal canister and purge control valve and check that they are clear by blowing through them. If the purge control valve or charcoal canister are thought to be faulty, they must be renewed.

39.1 Always clean oil separators whenever cylinder head cover is removed

Charcoal canister – renewal

3 Disconnect the battery negative lead.

4 Make a note of the correct fitted positions of the canister hoses then use a suitable pair of pliers to release the retaining clips (where fitted) and disconnect all the hoses from the canister.

5 Lift the canister up to free it from its mounting bracket then remove it from the engine compartment.

6 Refitting is the reverse of the removal procedure ensuring that all the hoses are correctly refitted and, where necessary, securely held by their retaining clips.

Purge valve – renewal

7 Disconnect the battery negative terminal then disconnect the wiring connector from the purge valve.

8 Release the retaining clips and disconnect the inlet and outlet hoses from the valve.

9 Prise out the C-clip which secures the inlet hose adaptor to the mounting bracket, then withdraw the adaptor, noting the O-ring which is fitted between the adaptor and purge valve. Discard the O-ring; it must be renewed as a matter of course.

10 Undo the bolt securing the purge valve to its mounting bracket and remove the valve from the car.

11 Refitting is a reverse of the removal procedure using a new inlet hose adaptor O-ring.

Exhaust emission control

Note: *If the CO level reading is too high (or if any other symptom is encountered which causes you to suspect a fault in the exhaust emission control system), always check first that the air cleaner filter element is clean, the spark plugs are in good condition and correctly gapped, that the engine breather and vacuum hoses are clear and undamaged, referring to Chapter 1 for further information, and that the accelerator cable is correctly adjusted as described in Part A: Section 7 for carburettor-engines, or Part B: Section 22 for fuel-injected engines. If the engine is running very roughly, check the compression pressures as described in Chapter 2, bearing in mind the possibility that one of the hydraulic tappets might be faulty, producing an incorrect valve clearance.*

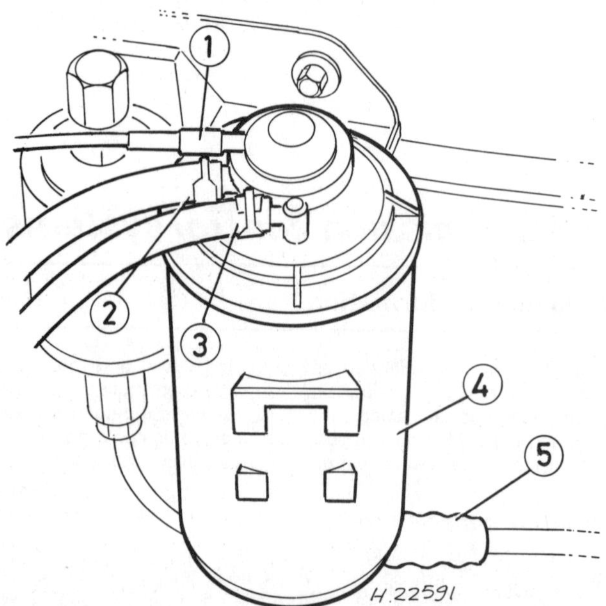

Fig. 4.17 Charcoal canister assembly and hose connections – models equipped with catalytic converter (Sec 39)

1 *Vacuum hose*
2 *Outlet hose – charcoal canister to purge valve*
3 *Inlet hose – fuel tank to charcoal canister*
4 *Charcoal canister*
5 *Drain hose*

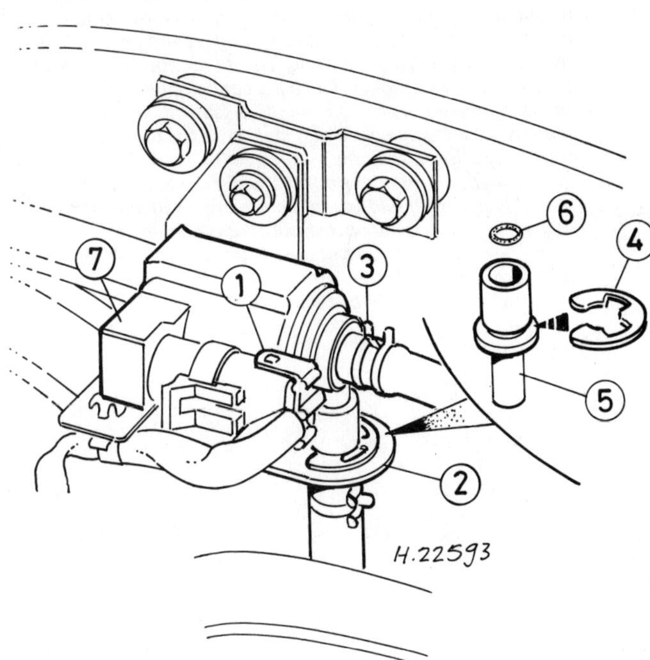

Fig. 4.18 Purge control valve and connections – models equipped with catalytic converter (Sec 39)

1 *Wiring connector*
2 *Inlet hose – charcoal canister to purge valve*
3 *Outlet hose – purge valve to throttle housing*
4 *C-clip*
5 *Inlet hose connector*
6 *O-ring*
7 *Purge valve*

Check also that all wiring is in good condition, with securely-fastened connectors, that the fuel filter (fuel-injected engines only) has been renewed at the recommended intervals and that the exhaust system is entirely free of air leaks which might upset the operation of the catalytic converter. Only when all these have been checked and found to be in serviceable condition should the converter be suspected.

Testing – open-loop system

12 The performance of the catalytic converter can be checked only using a good-quality, carefully-calibrated exhaust gas analyser.

13 Check that the CO level is as specified at the gas-sampling pipe when the engine is fully warmed up to normal operating temperature; if not, check the fuel and ignition systems until the fault is found and the level is restored to its correct value. Refer to Chapter 1 for further information.

14 Once the CO level is known to be correct upstream of the catalytic converter, take the car on a brisk 4-mile road test and check the CO level at the tailpipe **immediately** on return; it should be significantly lower than the level at the gas-sampling pipe (below 0.5 % approximately on fuel-injected engines, slightly higher on carburettor engines).

15 If the tailpipe CO level is little different from that at the gas-sampling pipe, repeat the check ensuring that it is made **immediately** on return from road test or the converter may not be at normal operating temperature and will not have reached its peak conversion efficiency. If the results are the same, the catalytic converter is proven faulty and must be renewed as described in Part A: Section 18.

Testing – closed-loop system

16 The performance of the catalytic converter can be checked only using a good-quality, carefully-calibrated exhaust gas analyser.

17 Where a gas-sampling pipe is fitted, the test described above can be carried out; if the CO level at the tailpipe is little different from that at the gas-sampling pipe, the catalytic converter is probably faulty and must be renewed, once the fuel-injection and ignition systems have been checked thoroughly using Rover diagnostic equipment and are known to be free from faults.

18 If a gas-sampling pipe is not fitted and the CO level at the tailpipe is too high, the complete fuel-injection and ignition systems must be checked thoroughly using Rover diagnostic equipment. Once these have been checked and are known to be free from faults, the fault must be in the catalytic converter, which must be renewed as described in Part A: Section 18.

Catalytic converter – renewal

19 Refer to Part A: Section 18.

Lambda sensor – operational check

20 The manufacturer's maintenance schedule calls for regular checks of the lambda sensor's operation. This can be done only by attaching Rover diagnostic equipment to the sensor wiring and checking that the voltage varies from low to high values when the engine is running; **do not** attempt to 'test' any part of the system with anything other than the correct test equipment.

Lambda sensor – renewal

Note: *The lambda sensor is delicate and will not work if it is dropped or knocked, if its power supply is disrupted, or if any cleaning materials are used on it.*

21 Release the sensor's wiring connector from the bracket on the transmission and unplug it to disconnect the sensor.

22 Raising and supporting the front of the car, if required, to remove the sensor from underneath, unscrew the sensor from the exhaust system front pipe; collect the sealing washer.

23 On refitting, clean the sealing washer and renew it if it is damaged or worn, then refit the sensor, tightening it to its specified torque wrench setting. Reconnect the wiring and refit the connector plug.

Lambda sensor relay – general

24 Refer to Chapter 12.

40 Catalytic converters – general information and precautions

The catalytic converter is a reliable and simple device which needs no maintenance in itself, but there are some facts of which an owner should be aware if the converter is to function properly for its full service life.

(a) *DO NOT use leaded petrol in a car equipped with a catalytic converter – the lead will coat the precious metals, reducing their converting efficiency and will eventually destroy the converter.*

(b) *Always keep the ignition and fuel systems well-maintained in accordance with the manufacturer's schedule – particularly, ensure that the air cleaner filter element, the fuel filter (where fitted) and the spark plugs are renewed at the correct interval – if the intake air/fuel mixture is allowed to become too rich due to neglect, the unburned surplus will enter and burn in the catalytic converter, overheating the element and eventually destroying the converter.*

(c) *If the engine develops a misfire, do not drive the car at all (or at least as little as possible) until the fault is cured – the misfire will allow unburned fuel to enter the converter, which will result in its overheating, as noted above.*

(d) *DO NOT push- or tow-start the car – this will soak the catalytic converter in unburned fuel, causing it to overheat when the engine does start – see (b) above.*

(e) *DO NOT switch off the ignition at high engine speeds – if the ignition is switched off at anything above idle speed, unburned fuel will enter the (very hot) catalytic converter, with the possible risk of its igniting on the element and damaging the converter.*

(f) *DO NOT use fuel or engine oil additives – these may contain substances harmful to the catalytic converter.*

(g) *DO NOT continue to use the car if the engine burns oil to the extent of leaving a visible trail of blue smoke – the unburned carbon deposits will clog the converter passages and reduce its efficiency; in severe cases the element will overheat.*

(h) Remember that the catalytic converter operates at very high temperatures – hence the heat shields on the car's underbody – and the casing will become hot enough to ignite combustible materials which brush against it. DO NOT, therefore, park the car in dry undergrowth, over long grass or piles of dead leaves.

(i) Remember that the catalytic converter is FRAGILE – do not strike it with tools during servicing work, take great care when working on the exhaust system, ensure that the converter is well clear of any jacks or other lifting gear used to raise the car and do not drive the car over rough ground, road humps, etc. in such a way as to 'ground' the exhaust system.

(j) In some cases, particularly when the car is new and/or is used for stop/start driving, a sulphurous smell (like that of rotten eggs) may be noticed from the exhaust. This is common to many catalytic converter-equipped cars and seems to be due to the small amount of sulphur found in some petrols reacting with hydrogen in the exhaust to produce hydrogen sulphide (H_2S) gas; while this gas is toxic, it is not produced in sufficient amounts to be a problem. Once the car has covered a few thousand miles the problem should disappear – in the meanwhile a change of driving style or of the brand of petrol used may effect a solution.

(k) The catalytic converter, used on a well-maintained and well-driven car, should last for between 50 000 and 100 000 miles – from this point on, careful checks should be made at all specified service intervals of the CO level to ensure that the converter is still operating efficiently – if the converter is no longer effective it must be renewed.

Chapter 5 Ignition system

Contents

Specifications

Carburettor engines

General

System type	Lucas constant energy inductive
Firing order	1–3–4–2 (No 1 cylinder at timing belt end)
Direction of crankshaft rotation	Clockwise (viewed from right-hand side of car)

Distributor

Type	Lucas 67 DM4, incorporating centrifugal and vacuum advance mechanisms and externally-mounted amplifier module
Identification:	
With catalytic converter	NJC 10026
Without catalytic converter	NJC 10033
Direction of rotor arm rotation	Anti-clockwise (viewed from left- hand side of car)
Pick-up coil resistance	950 to 1150 ohms
Vacuum diaphragm unit identification:	
With catalytic converter	80–200–8
Without catalytic converter	80–200–6
Vacuum advance commences	107 mbar (80 mm Hg)
Maximum vacuum advance:	
With catalytic converter	16° @ 267 mbar (200 mm Hg)
Without catalytic converter	12° @ 267 mbar (200 mm Hg)
Deceleration check – vacuum disconnected	4° to 8° @ 2500 rpm

Note: *Degree and speed values to be measured at crankshaft*

Ignition HT coil

Type	AUU 1326 or ADU 8779
Manufacturer	Bosch, Ducellier or Rudi Cajavec
Current consumption – average	0.25 to 0.75 amps @ idle speed
Winding resistances:	
Primary	0.3 to 0.5 ohms @ 20°C
Secondary	5 to 15 K ohms @ 20°C

Ignition timing

At 1500 rpm (vacuum pipe disconnected)	9° ± 1° BTDC

Torque wrench settings

	Nm	lbf ft
Spark plugs	25	19
Distributor cap screws	2	2
Amplifier module to distributor body (hex-head) screws	5	4
Distributor mounting bolts	25	19
Ignition HT coil mounting bolts	7	5

Fuel-injected engines

General

System type	Rover/Motorola Modular Engine Management System (MEMS), fully electronic, controlled by ECU
Firing order	1-3-4-2 (No 1 cylinder at timing belt end)
Direction of crankshaft rotation	Clockwise (viewed from right-hand side of car)

Distributor

Type	Spark distribution only (ignition timing controlled by ECU)
Direction of rotor arm rotation	Anti-clockwise (viewed from left-hand side of car)
Distributor cap	AUU 1186
Rotor arm	AUU 1641 (resistive type)

Engine management Electronic Control Unit (ECU)

With catalytic converter	MNE 10008, MNE 10023 or MNE 10042
Without catalytic converter	MNE 10011, MNE 10013 or MNE 10051

Ignition timing @ idle speed (ECU-controlled)

With catalytic converter – by ECU number (vacuum pipe connected):	
MNE 10008	13° ± 2° BTDC
MNE 10023, MNE 10042	14° ± 2° BTDC
Without catalytic converter – by ECU number (vacuum pipe connected):	
MNE 10011	13 ± 2° BTDC
MNE 10013, MNE 10051	14 ± 2° BTDC

Note: *Nominal value given for checking purposes only – not adjustable and may vary under ECU control*

Crankshaft sensor

Type	ADU 7340

Ignition HT coil

Type	NEC 10002 or NEC 10003
Manufacturer	Bosch, Ducellier or Rudi Cajavec
Current consumption – average	0.25 to 0.75 amps @ idle speed
Winding resistances:	
Primary	0.3 to 0.5 ohms @ 20°C
Secondary	5 to 15 k ohms @ 20°C

Torque wrench settings

	Nm	lbf ft
Spark plugs	25	19
Distributor cap screws	2	2
Distributor rotor arm grub screw	10	7
Reluctor ring to flywheel setscrews	3	2
Ignition HT coil mounting screws	7	5
Crankshaft sensor mounting screws	6	4
Crankshaft sensor lead to flywheel cover plate screw	6	4

Part A: Carburettor engines

1 General information and precautions

The ignition system is fully-electronic in operation and of the inductive type, incorporating a contact-less distributor (driven off the camshaft left-hand end) and an amplifier module as well as the spark plugs, HT leads, ignition HT coil and associated wiring. The system is divided into two circuits; primary (low tension/LT) and secondary (high tension/HT). The primary circuit consists of the battery, ignition switch, ignition HT coil primary windings, amplifier module and distributor pick-up coil and wiring. The secondary circuit consists of the ignition HT coil secondary windings, the distributor cap and rotor arm, the spark plugs and HT leads connecting these.

The distributor incorporates features which advance the ignition timing both mechanically and by vacuum operation. Its shaft, driven by the camshaft, incorporates a reluctor which has four shaped poles and is mounted on the centre of a centrifugal advance assembly whose two weights move outwards under centrifugal force as engine speed rises, thus rotating the reluctor on the shaft and advancing or retarding the spark; the amount of movement being controlled by light springs. A pick-up coil generates a weak magnetic field whenever the ignition is switched on; as the engine rotates the reluctor poles pass the coil, disturbing the field each time and sending a signal current to the amplifier module. Whenever this signal exceeds a threshold level determined by engine speed a high-voltage transistor in the amplifier is switched on, thus allowing HT coil current to flow; when this current has reached the required level it is held constant until the transistor is switched off, thus triggering the spark. The pick-up coil is clamped to a stator pack that is able to rotate under the control of the vacuum diaphragm unit mounted on the side of the distributor. The unit consists of a diaphragm, one side of which is connected via a small-bore pipe to the carburettor and the other side to the stator pack; inlet manifold depression, which varies with engine speed and throttle position, causes the diaphragm to move thus rotating the stator pack and advancing or retarding the spark.

Warning: *The voltages produced by the electronic ignition system are considerably higher than those produced by conventional systems. Extreme care must be taken when working on the system with the ignition switched on. Persons with surgically-implanted cardiac pacemaker devices should keep well clear of the ignition circuits, components and test equipment.*

2 Ignition system – testing

Note: *Refer to the warning given in Section 1 of this Chapter before starting work. Always switch off the ignition before disconnecting or connecting any component and when using a multi-meter to check resistances. Any voltmeter or multi-meter used to test ignition system components must have an impedance of 10 M ohms or greater.*

General

1 The components of electronic ignition systems are normally very reliable; most faults are far more likely to be due to loose or dirty connections or to 'tracking' of HT voltage due to dirt, dampness or damaged insulation than to the failure of any of the system's components. **Always** check all wiring thoroughly before condemning an electrical component and work methodically to eliminate all other possibilities before deciding that a particular component is faulty.

2 The old practice of checking for a spark by holding the live end of an HT lead a short distance away from the engine is not recommended; not only is there a high risk of a powerful electric shock, but the HT coil or amplifier module will be damaged. Similarly, **never** try to 'diagnose' misfires by pulling off one HT lead at a time.

Engine will not start

3 If the engine either will not turn over at all, or only turns very slowly, check the battery and starter motor. Connect a voltmeter across the battery terminals (meter positive probe to battery positive terminal), disconnect the ignition coil HT lead from the distributor cap and earth it, then note the voltage reading obtained while turning over the engine on the starter for (no more than) ten seconds. If the reading obtained is less than approximately 9.5 volts, check the battery, starter motor and charging system as described in Chapter 12.

4 If the engine turns over at normal speed but will not start, check the HT circuit by connecting a timing light (following the manufacturer's instructions) and turning the engine over on the starter motor; if the light flashes, voltage is reaching the spark plugs, so these should be checked first. If the light does not flash, check the HT leads themselves followed by the distributor cap, carbon brush and rotor arm using the information given in Chapter 1.

5 If there is a spark, check the fuel system for faults referring to Chapter 4 for further information.

6 If there is still no spark, check the voltage at the ignition HT coil '+' terminal; it should be the same as the battery voltage (ie, at least 11.7 volts). If the voltage at the coil is more than 1 volt less than that at the battery, check the feed back through the fusebox and ignition switch to the battery and its earth until the fault is found.

7 If the feed to the HT coil is sound, check the coil's primary and secondary winding resistance as described in Section 4; renew the coil if faulty, but be careful to check carefully the condition of the LT connections themselves before doing so, to ensure that the fault is not due to dirty or poorly-fastened connectors.

8 If the HT coil is in good condition, the fault is probably within the amplifier module or distributor pick-up coil. So that the operation of these two can be checked quickly, Rover dealers have a Neon indicator, which when connected across the HT coil's LT terminals, flashes every time the amplifier triggers an HT pulse in the coil if the ignition is switched on and the engine is turned over on the starter. Owners can substitute a low-wattage bulb; if the bulb flickers or flashes when the engine is turned over, the amplifier and distributor are sound.

9 If the amplifier and distributor are sound, and the entire LT circuit is in good condition, the fault, if it lies in the ignition system, must be in the HT circuit components. These should be checked carefully, as outlined above.

10 If the indicator or bulb does not flash, the fault is in either the distributor pick-up coil or the amplifier module; owners should note, however, that by far the commonest cause of 'failure' of either of these is a poor connection, either between the amplifier module and the distributor body or in the LT circuit wiring connections themselves. If a voltmeter or multi-meter is available, check the feed to the amplifier (the voltage reading obtained should be the same as that measured at the HT coil LT '+' terminal), then check that there is no measurable resistance between the amplifier module fixing screws and engine earth and that there is no continuity between either module terminal and earth. If any doubt exists as to the condition of the connections, remove the module, clean and check carefully the module earth and the connections and, if necessary, improve their fit as described in Section 5. If these checks fail to correct the fault, measure the resistance of the pick-up coil, comparing it with the specified value; renew the coil if the reading obtained differs significantly from that given. If the fault still exists, the only solution is to try the effect of renewing the amplifier module.

Engine misfires

11 An irregular misfire suggests either a loose connection or intermittent fault on the primary circuit, or an HT fault on the coil side of the rotor arm.

12 With the ignition switched off, check carefully through the system ensuring that all connections are clean and securely fastened. If the equipment is available, check the LT circuit as described in paragraphs 6 to 10 above.

13 Check that the HT coil, the distributor cap and the HT leads are clean and dry. Check the leads themselves and the spark plugs (by substitution, if necessary), then check the distributor cap, carbon brush and rotor arm as described in Chapter 1.

14 Regular misfiring is almost certainly due to a fault in the distributor cap, HT leads or spark plugs. Use a timing light (paragraph 4 above) to check whether HT voltage is present at all leads.

15 If HT voltage is not present on any particular lead, the fault will be in that lead or in the distributor cap. If HT is present on all leads, the fault will be in the spark plugs; check and renew them if there is any doubt about their condition.

16 If no HT is present, check the HT coil; its secondary windings may be breaking down under load.

3 Distributor – removal, overhaul and refitting

Removal

1 Disconnect the battery negative terminal.

2 Release the wire retaining clip and unplug the wiring connector from the ignition amplifier module (photo).

3 Disconnect the vacuum pipe from the vacuum diaphragm unit (photo).

4 Position the engine so that number 1 cylinder is at TDC on the compression stroke as described in Chapter 2.

5 Mark the relationship of the distributor body to the cylinder head, using a scriber or similar to use as a guide on refitting (photo).

6 Unscrew the distributor mounting bolts and withdraw the distributor (photo). Do not disturb the crankshaft setting while the distributor is removed.

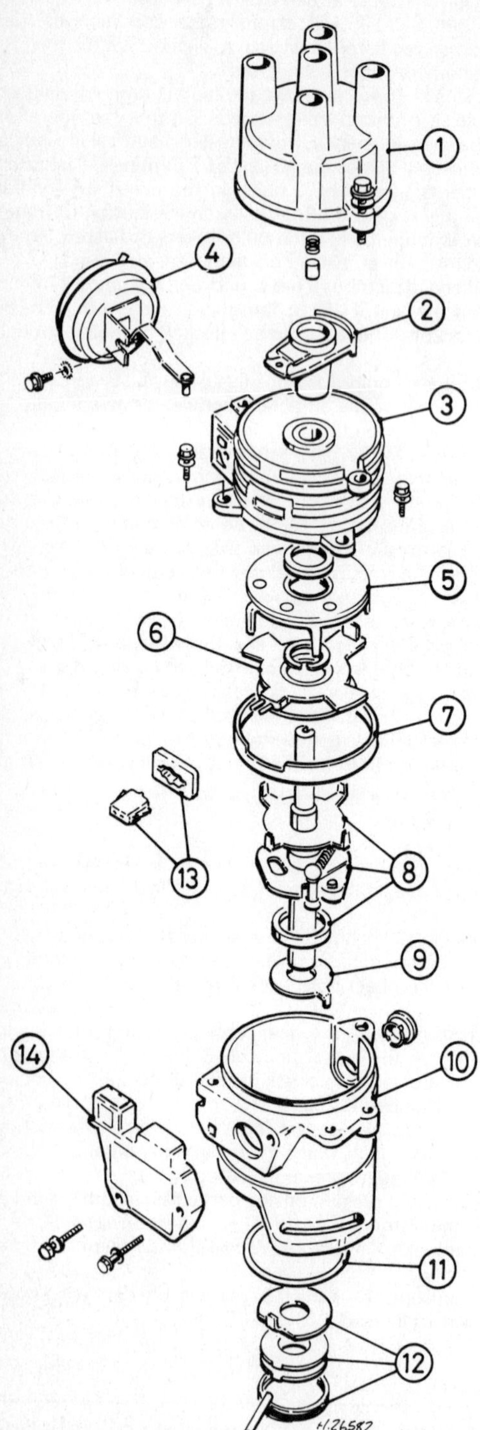

Fig. 5.1 Exploded view of the Lucas 67 DM4 distributor – carburettor engines (Secs 1 and 3)

1 Distributor cap
2 Rotor arm
3 Upper housing
4 Vacuum diaphragm unit
5 Stator pack including thrustwasher(s) and circlip
6 Pick-up coil
7 Clamp ring
8 Distributor shaft, including reluctor and advance assembly
9 Thrustwasher
10 Lower housing
11 O-ring
12 Drive coupling, including thrustwasher, spring and roll pin
13 Connector and gasket
14 Amplifier module

7 Remove the distributor body sealing O-ring; this must be renewed whenever it is disturbed (photo).

Overhaul

8 Remove the distributor cap and withdraw the rotor arm, if not already removed.
9 Undo the two bolts securing the amplifier module to the body, then carefully remove the gasket and withdraw the connector.
10 Remove the screws and separate the upper housing from the lower.
11 Remove the clamp ring and pick-up coil from the upper housing.
12 Remove the circlip (and first thrustwasher, if fitted) from the underside of the upper housing, disengage the stator pack from the vacuum diaphragm unit arm and withdraw the stator pack, followed by the (second) thrustwasher.
13 Remove the retaining screw and withdraw the vacuum diaphragm unit from the distributor.
14 Check the distributor shaft endfloat; if it seems excessive, seek expert advice.
15 Remove the spring from the distributor drive coupling, then use a scriber or similar to mark the relationship of the coupling to the shaft; it is essential that the coupling is refitted correctly in relationship to the rotor arm on refitting. Release the distributor shaft by driving out the retaining roll pin and removing the coupling, noting the toothed thrustwasher which is fitted behind it.
16 Withdraw the shaft, noting the toothed thrustwasher underneath the centrifugal advance assembly. Be very careful not to bend any of the reluctor poles and do not attempt to remove it from the shaft.
17 The advance assembly and shaft can be lubricated, but if any part of the assembly is found to be worn or damaged the complete distributor must be renewed; individual replacement parts are not available.
18 Clean and examine all components; if any are found to be worn or damaged, seek expert advice. A repair kit of sundry parts is available separately, also the coupling assembly, the pick-up coil and vacuum diaphragm unit, as well as the rotor arm and the distributor cap; if any other parts are worn or damaged, the complete distributor must be renewed.
19 In addition to the checks described in Chapter 1, use an ohmmeter or continuity tester to check that there is no continuity between any of the cap's terminal segments. Similarly, check that there is no continuity between the rotor arm body and its brass segment; note that the arm has a built-in resistance.
20 Reassembly is the reverse of the dismantling procedure, noting the following points:

(a) *Apply a few drops of suitable oil to the advance assembly pivots and springs and to the shaft, upper housing and stator pack bearing surfaces.*
(b) *Using the marks made on dismantling, be very careful to ensure that the coupling is located correctly on the shaft end (in relationship to the rotor arm) before driving in the roll pin to secure it, then ensure that the spring is fitted over the roll pin ends.*
(c) *Grease the vacuum diaphragm unit arm before refitting it, use grease to stick the thrustwasher to the underside of the upper housing. Refit the stator pack, ensuring it engages correctly with the vacuum diaphragm unit arm peg, followed by the (remaining thrustwasher, if fitted, and) circlip; tighten the unit retaining screw securely.*
(d) *Refit the pick-up coil to the upper housing and centre its terminals in the aperture before fitting the clamp ring so that its cut-out is over the aperture.*
(e) *Refit the upper housing to the lower, tighten the screws lightly and check that the shaft is free to rotate – there must be no sign of the reluctor poles touching the stator pack arms, as either can easily be bent – before tightening the screws securely.*
(f) *Refit the connector and its gasket.*
(g) *Refit the amplifier module, referring to Section 5 for further information, and the rotor arm.*
(h) *Fit a new sealing O-ring to the distributor body.*

Refitting

Original distributor

21 Ensure that number 1 cylinder is at TDC, referring to Chapter 2 for further information, then rotate the rotor arm to align with the distributor cap's number 1 terminal. Fit a new sealing O-ring to the

3.2 Disconnect the wiring connector from the ignition amplifier module

3.3 Disconnect the vacuum pipe from the distributor vacuum diaphragm unit

3.5 Make alignment marks on the distributor body and cylinder head to use as a guide on refitting

3.6 Unscrew the distributor mounting bolts (remaining bolt arrowed)...

3.7 ...then remove the distributor noting its O-ring (arrowed)

distributor body and lubricate it with a smear of engine oil.

22 Align the marks made on removal and refit the distributor to the cylinder head. If necessary, rotate the rotor arm very slightly to help the distributor drive dogs locate in the camshaft slots; they are offset and so will fit only one way. Refit the distributor mounting bolts and tighten them to the specified torque.

23 Refit the spark plugs as described in Chapter 1.

24 Refit the distributor cap, ensuring it is correctly located, and tighten its retaining screws to the specified torque. Reconnect the HT leads to the relevant spark plugs.

25 Reconnect the vacuum pipe to the vacuum diaphragm unit and the wiring connector to the ignition amplifier module.

26 Check and, if necessary, adjust the ignition timing as described in Chapter 1.

New distributor

27 If a new distributor is to be fitted (or no marks were made on removal), the following procedure will produce a basic setting which will enable the engine to start and run while the ignition timing is accurately set.

28 Place a finger over number 1 spark plug hole (nearest the timing belt/right-hand end of the engine) and turn the engine in the normal direction of rotation (clockwise, viewed from the right-hand end of the engine) using a suitable socket applied to the crankshaft pulley bolt until pressure is felt in number 1 cylinder. This indicates that the piston is commencing its compression stroke. Continue turning the engine until the notch on the inner rim of the crankshaft pulley is aligned with the TDC mark on the lower timing belt cover. The engine is now at TDC with number 1 cylinder on compression.

29 Rotate the crankshaft slightly anti-clockwise until the pulley notch is positioned in the 9° BTDC position (between the 8 and 12 marks on the timing scale).

30 Rotate the distributor rotor arm to align with the distributor cap's number 1 terminal; the terminal is marked with a 'K' which is cast on the outside of the distributor cap. Fit a new sealing O-ring to the distributor body and lubricate it with a smear of engine oil.

31 Fit the distributor to the cylinder head and refit its mounting bolts. Positioning the distributor body so that the mounting bolts are in the middle of their respective slots then tighten the bolts finger tight only.

32 Perform the operations listed above in paragraphs 23 to 25.

33 Check and adjust the ignition timing as described in Chapter 1.

4 Ignition HT coil – removal, testing and refitting

Removal

1 The coil is mounted on the left-hand side of the engine compartment, between the battery and the left-hand headlamp unit.

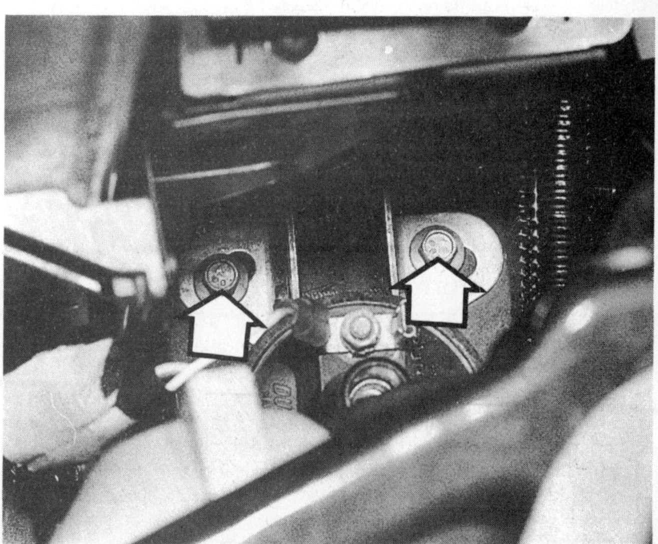
4.5 Ignition HT coil mounting bolts (arrowed)

2 Disconnect the battery negative terminal.
3 To improve access to the coil, remove the headlamp bulb cover.
4 Peel back the rubber cover, then disconnect the HT lead. Note which terminals they are connected to and disconnect the two pairs of LT wires from the coil.
5 Remove the two coil mounting bolts and withdraw the coil from the engine compartment (photo). If necessary, slacken the clamp screw and separate the coil from its mounting bracket.

Testing

6 Testing the coil consists of using a multimeter set to its resistance function, to check the primary (LT '+' to '–' terminals) and secondary (LT '+' to HT lead terminal) windings for continuity. If the meter is used the resistance of either winding can be checked and compared with the specified value. Note the resistance of the coil windings will vary slightly according to the coil temperature, the results in the Specifications are accurate only when the coil is at 20°C.
7 Using an ohmmeter or continuity tester, check that there is no continuity between the HT lead terminal and the coil body.
8 If the coil is faulty it must be renewed.

Refitting

9 Refitting is the reverse of the removal procedure.

5 Ignition amplifier module – removal and refitting

Warning: *Do not attempt to open or repair the module; if it is faulty, it must be renewed.*

Removal

1 Disconnect the battery negative terminal.
2 Releasing its wire clip, unplug the wiring connector from the amplifier module.
3 Remove the two bolts and withdraw the module, taking care not to damage the terminal pins.
4 Check carefully that the mating surfaces of the module and distributor are completely clean and unmarked and that the pick-up coil terminal pins are clean and a secure fit in the module; if in doubt, it is permissible to remove the connector and its gasket and to **gently** squeeze together the female terminals to improve the fit. The pick-up coil to connector and connector to module connections must be checked with particular care if the module is thought to be faulty; similarly, check, clean and tighten (if necessary) the distributor wiring connector to module terminals. It is **essential** that there is good electrical contact between the module and the distributor and at all four LT wiring connections mentioned above.

Refitting

5 On refitting, apply a smear of heat-conducting silicone grease to the mating surfaces of the module and the distributor; the correct grease can be obtained from Rover dealers under Part Number BAU 5812, but if this is not available either a heat-sink compound, or an anti-seize compound (such as Holt's Copaslip), will serve as an adequate substitute.
6 Check that the terminal pins are not bent or damaged and that they engage correctly with the module's connections.
7 Tighten the module retaining bolts to the specified torque wrench setting, then reconnect the distributor wiring and battery.

6 Thermostatically-operated vacuum switch – removal and refitting

General information

1 Models fitted with catalytic converters have a thermostatically-operated vacuum switch screwed into the cooling system thermostat housing; the switch is connected into the vacuum hose linking the carburettor to the distributor vacuum diaphragm unit. At coolant temperatures below 70°C the switch cuts off the vacuum supply to the diaphragm and prevents the unit from advancing the ignition timing. This then causes the exhaust gas temperatures to rise, due to the retarded ignition timing, and brings the catalytic converter swiftly up to its efficient operating temperature. Once coolant temperatures rise above 70°C, the switch opens and allows the vacuum to reach the diaphragm unit, thus restoring normal advance and retard of the ignition timing.

Removal

2 Either drain the cooling system as described in Chapter 1, or be prepared for some loss of coolant as the switch is unscrewed.
3 As noted in Chapter 3, access to the thermostat housing is possible with the inlet manifold and carburettor in place, but is made much easier if these are first removed (Chapter 4).
4 Disconnect and plug the switch vacuum pipes.
5 Unscrew the switch and withdraw it, then plug the opening to prevent the entry of dirt; if the cooling system has not been drained, work quickly to minimise coolant loss.
6 If required the switch can be tested as described in Chapter 3, Section 5.

Refitting

7 Refitting is the reverse of the removal procedure, noting the following points.

- *(a) Wipe clean the threads of the switch and the thermostat housing.*
- *(b) If a sealing washer is fitted, renew it whenever it is disturbed to prevent leaks; if no sealing washer is fitted, apply a smear of sealant to the switch threads.*
- *(c) Tighten the switch securely and reconnect the vacuum pipes.*
- *(d) Refit any components removed to improve access.*
- *(e) Refill or top up the cooling system as described in Chapter 1.*

Part B: Fuel injected engines

7 General information and precautions

The ignition system is fully electronic in operation, incorporating the Electronic Control Unit (ECU) mounted on the engine compartment bulkhead, a distributor (driven off the inlet camshaft left-hand end) and a crankshaft sensor mounted in the left-hand rear end of the engine's cylinder block/crankcase to register with the reluctor ring fixed to the flywheel, as well as the spark plugs, HT leads, ignition HT coil and associated wiring. The system is divided into two circuits; primary (low tension/LT) and secondary (high tension/HT). The primary circuit consists of the battery, ignition switch, ignition HT coil primary windings, ECU and wiring. The secondary circuit consists of the ignition HT coil secondary windings, the distributor cap and rotor arm, the spark plugs and the HT leads connecting these.

The ECU controls both the ignition system and the fuel injection system, integrating the two in a complete engine management system; refer to Part B of Chapter 4 for information on any part of the system not given here.

As far as the ignition system is concerned, the ECU receives information in the form of electrical impulses or signals from the crankshaft sensor (which gives it the engine speed and crankshaft position), from the coolant temperature sensor (which gives it the engine temperature), from the throttle pedal switch (which tells it when the throttle is closed) and from the manifold absolute pressure sensor (which gives it the load on the engine). All these signals are compared by the ECU, using digital techniques, with set values pre-programmed (mapped) into its memory; based on this information, the ECU selects the ignition timing appropriate to those values and controls the ignition HT coil accordingly.

Note that this means that the distributor is just that, a distributor of the HT pulse to the appropriate spark plug; it has no effect whatsoever on the ignition timing. Also, the system is so sensitive that, at idle speed, the ignition timing may be constantly changing; this should be remembered if trying to check the ignition timing (see Chapter 1, Ignition timing check and adjustment).

8 Ignition system – testing

1 If a fault appears in the engine management (ignition/fuel) system first ensure that the fault is not due to poor maintenance; ie, check that the air cleaner filter element is clean, the spark plugs are in good condition and correctly gapped, that the engine breather hoses are clear and undamaged, referring to Chapter 1 for further information. Also check that the accelerator cable is correctly adjusted as described in Chapter 4, Part B. If the engine is running very roughly, check the compression pressures as described in Chapter 2, bearing in mind that possibly one of the hydraulic tappets might be faulty, producing an incorrect valve clearance.

2 If these checks fail to reveal the cause of the problem, the vehicle should be taken to a suitably equipped Rover dealer for testing. A wiring block connector is incorporated in the engine management circuit into which a special electronic diagnostic tester can be plugged. The tester will locate the fault quickly and simply, alleviating the need to test all the system components individually which is a time consuming operation that carries a high risk of damaging the ECU.

3 The only ignition system checks which can be carried out by the home mechanic are those described in Chapter 1, relating to the spark plugs, HT leads, rotor arm and distributor cap, and the ignition HT coil test described in this Chapter. If necessary, the system wiring and wiring connectors can be checked as described in Chapter 12 ensuring that the ECU wiring connectors have first been disconnected.

9 Distributor – removal and refitting

Removal

1 Disconnect the HT leads from the spark plugs then undo the two distributor cap retaining screws and remove the cap and leads as an assembly.

2 Slacken and remove the grub screw securing the rotor arm to the camshaft end then pull off the rotor arm.

3 Remove the distributor cap insulating plate from the cylinder head.

4 Examine the components for signs of wear or damage as described in Chapter 1 and renew as necessary.

Refitting

5 Refitting is a reverse of the removal procedure, tightening the rotor arm grub screw and distributor cap screws to the specified torque settings.

10 Ignition HT coil – removal, testing and refitting

Refer to Part A: Section 4

11 Crankshaft sensor and reluctor ring – removal and refitting

Removal

Crankshaft sensor

1 Disconnect the battery negative terminal.

2 Disconnect the sensor wiring at its connector plug on the flywheel rear cover plate, then undo the retaining screw to release the wiring lead.

3 Remove the two retaining screws and withdraw the sensor from the cylinder block/crankcase (photo).

4 Inspect the sensor for obvious signs of wear or damage and renew it if necessary. No data is available to enable the sensor to be tested, so if it is thought to be faulty it can be checked only by the substitution of a new component.

Reluctor ring

5 Remove the flywheel as described in Chapter 2.

6 Undo the two screws securing the reluctor ring to the rear of the flywheel and withdraw it (photo).

7 Check the ring for obvious signs of wear or damage and renew it if necessary.

Refitting

Crankshaft sensor

8 Ensure that the sensor and cylinder block/crankcase mating surfaces are clean then refit the sensor and tighten its retaining screws to the specified torque.

9 Connect the sensor wiring connector and tighten the connector mounting screw to the specified torque.

10 Reconnect the battery negative terminal.

Reluctor ring

11 Refitting is a reversal of the removal procedure tightening the reluctor retaining screws to the specified torque.

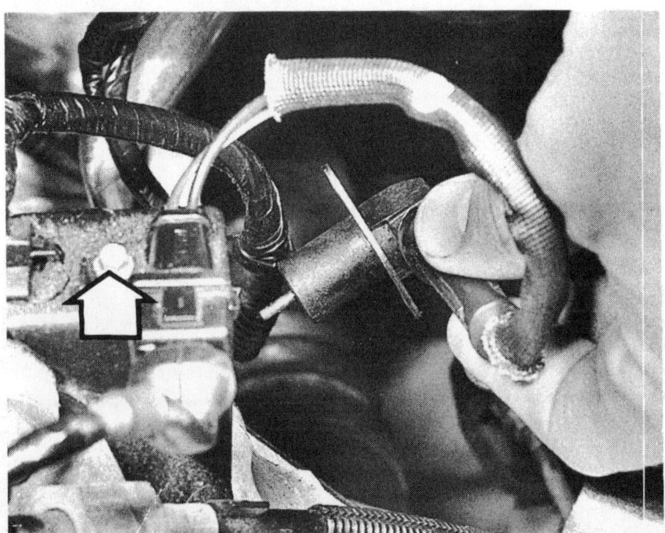

11.3 Removing crankshaft sensor – wiring lead screw arrowed

11.6 Reluctor ring-to-flywheel screws (arrowed)

Chapter 6 Clutch

Contents

Specifications

Type	Single dry plate with diaphragm spring, cable- operated, self-adjusting	
Friction plate		
Diameter	190 mm	
Friction material total thickness - AP plate only:		
New plate	8.00 to 8.40 mm	
Service limit	6.30 mm	
Rivet depth - distance from friction material surface to rivet heads:		
New plate - AP	1.3 mm minimum	
Service limit - AP	0.2 mm	
New plate - Valeo	0.9 mm minimum	
Service limit - Valeo	0.1 mm	
Maximum run-out - at outer edge of friction material:		
AP	1.3 mm	
Valeo	1.0 mm	
Pressure plate		
Diaphragm spring finger maximum clearance:		
AP	0.65 mm	
Valeo	1.00 mm	
Diaphragm spring finger height above flywheel surface:		
New plate - AP	27.6 to 33.1 mm	
Service limit - AP	39.4 mm	
New plate - Valeo	29.1 to 32.0 mm	
Service limit - Valeo	36.5 mm	
Maximum warpage of machined surface:		
AP	0.08 mm	
Valeo	0.20 mm	
Torque wrench settings	**Nm**	**lbf ft**
Pressure plate to flywheel bolts	18	13
Release bearing guide sleeve to bellhousing bolts	5	4

1 General information

The clutch consists of a friction plate, a pressure plate assembly, a release bearing and the release mechanism; all of these components are contained in the large cast aluminium alloy bellhousing, sandwiched between the engine and the transmission. The release mechanism is mechanical, being operated by a cable.

The friction plate is fitted between the engine flywheel and the clutch pressure plate and is allowed to slide on the transmission input shaft splines. It consists of two circular facings of friction material riveted in position to provide the clutch bearing surface, and a spring-cushioned hub to damp out transmission shocks.

The pressure plate assembly is bolted to the engine flywheel and is located by three dowel pins; it comprises the clutch cover, the diaphragm spring and the pressure plate. When the engine is running, drive is transmitted from the crankshaft via the flywheel and clutch cover to the friction plate (these last three components being clamped securely together by the pressure plate and diaphragm spring) and from the friction plate to the transmission input shaft.

To interrupt the drive the spring pressure must be relaxed. This is achieved by a sealed release bearing fitted concentrically around the transmission input shaft; when the driver depresses the clutch pedal the release bearing is pressed against the fingers at the centre of the diaphragm spring. Since the spring is held by rivets between two annular fulcrum rings the pressure at its centre causes it to deform so

Fig. 6.1 Clutch components (Sec 1)

1 *Flywheel*
2 *Flywheel bolt*
3 *Friction plate*
4 *Pressure plate assembly*
5 *Pressure plate bolt*
6 *Release bearing*
7 *Release fork*
8 *Release lever*
9 *Upper bush*
10 *Lower bush*

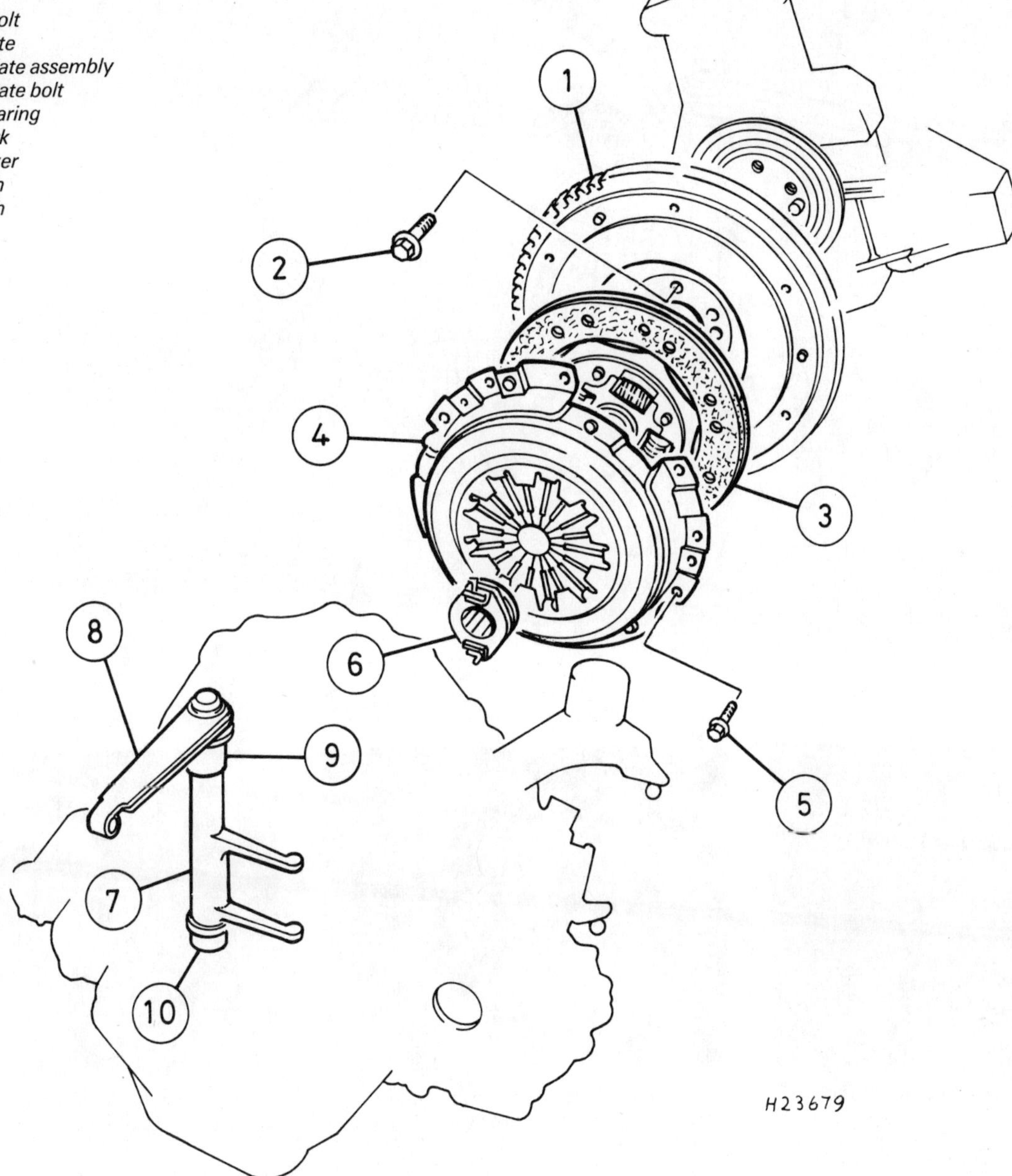

that it flattens and thus releases the clamping force it exerts, at its periphery, on the pressure plate.

Depressing the clutch pedal pulls the control cable inner wire and this in turn rotates the release fork by acting on the lever at the fork's upper end, above the bellhousing. The fork itself is clipped to the left of the release bearing.

As the friction plate facings wear, the pressure plate moves towards the flywheel; this causes the diaphragm spring fingers to push against the release bearing, thus reducing the clearance which must be present in the mechanism. To ensure correct operation, the clutch cable incorporates a spring-loaded self-adjusting mechanism, eliminating the need for periodic adjustments.

Note: *The clutch friction and pressure plates are manufactured by two suppliers, AP (Automotive Products) and Valeo. Both the friction plate and the pressure plate must come from the same supplier; they are not interchangeable between the two. Apart from the manufacturer's name which may be stamped on either component, AP components can be identified by the part number being applied with white paint, while on Valeo components the part number is applied either with green paint or with black paint with a green spot. All other clutch components are the same, irrespective of supplier.*

2 Clutch cable – removal, inspection and refitting

Removal

1 Working in the engine compartment, compress the cable spring and remove the C-clip, then unhook the cable end fitting from the release fork lever (photos).

2 Release the cable from the transmission bracket(s) and free it from

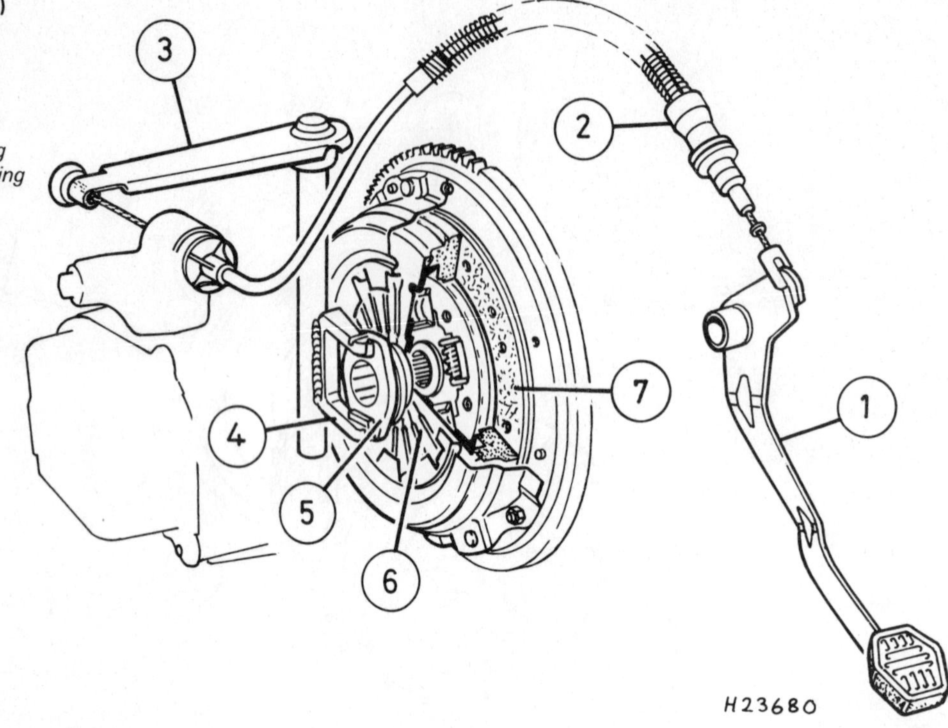

Fig. 6.2 Clutch release mechanism (Sec 1)

1 *Clutch pedal*
2 *Clutch cable*
3 *Release lever*
4 *Release fork*
5 *Release bearing*
6 *Diaphragm spring*
7 *Friction plate*

2.1A Compress clutch cable spring then remove the C-clip

2.1B Unhook the cable from the clutch release lever and withdraw the cable from the transmission bracket

2.4 Disconnect the clutch cable from the clutch pedal hook

any relevant cable ties or clamps.

3 Working inside the car, undo the five retaining screws and remove the right-hand lower facia panel.

4 Unhook the cable from the pedal upper end (photo).

5 Return to the engine compartment and withdraw the cable through the bulkhead.

Inspection

6 Examine the cable, looking for worn end fittings or a damaged outer casing and for signs of fraying of the inner wire. Check the cable's operation; the inner wire should move smoothly and easily through the outer casing, but remember that a cable that appears serviceable when tested off the car may well be much heavier in operation when compressed into its working position. Renew the cable if it shows any signs of excessive wear or of damage.

Refitting

7 Refitting is the reverse of the removal procedure, but apply a thin smear of multi-purpose grease to the cable end fittings. Align the slot in the inner wire's end with the pedal hook and smear petroleum jelly on the cable outer's rubber bush before hooking the cable onto the pedal; press the bush firmly into the bulkhead so that the steel washer butts firmly against the bulkhead boss.

8 Ensure that the cable is routed correctly, with no sharp bends or kinks, also that it is retained by any necessary clamps or ties.

9 When the cable is refitted, depress the pedal several times through its full travel, releasing it fully at each stroke, to enable the self-adjusting mechanism to set itself. Check that the clutch operation is correct.

3 Clutch pedal – removal, inspection and refitting

Removal

1 Disconnect the clutch cable from the pedal (Section 2).

3.2 Clutch pedal return spring and pivot nut (arrowed)

2 Using a pair of pliers, carefully unhook the clutch pedal return spring from the pedal and remove it (photo).
3 Slacken and remove the clutch pedal pivot nut and slide the pedal off the pivot.

Inspection

4 Carefully clean all components and renew any that are worn or damaged; check the bearing surfaces of the pivot bushes and shaft with particular care; the bushes can be renewed separately if worn.

Refitting

5 Refitting is the reverse of the removal procedure, but apply a thin smear of multi-purpose grease to the pedal pivot bearing surfaces.

4 Clutch assembly – removal, inspection and refitting

Warning: *Dust created by clutch wear and deposited on the clutch components may contain asbestos, which is a health hazard. DO NOT blow it out with compressed air or inhale any of it. DO NOT use petrol or petroleum-based solvents to clean off the dust. Brake system cleaner or methylated spirit should be used to flush the dust into a suitable receptacle. After the clutch components are wiped clean with rags, dispose of the contaminated rags and cleaner in a sealed, marked container.*

Note: *Although some friction materials may no longer contain asbestos it is safest to assume that they do and to take precautions accordingly.*

Removal

1 Unless the complete engine/transmission unit is to be removed from the car and separated for major overhaul (see Chapter 2), the clutch can be reached by removing the transmission as described in Chapter 7.
2 Before disturbing the clutch use chalk or a felt-tip pen to mark the relationship of the pressure plate assembly to the flywheel.
3 Working in a diagonal sequence, slacken by half a turn at a time the pressure plate bolts until the spring pressure is released and the bolts can be unscrewed by hand.
4 Prise the pressure plate assembly off its locating dowels and collect the friction plate, noting which way round the friction plate is fitted (photo).

Inspection

Note: *Due to the amount of work necessary to remove and refit clutch components, it is usually considered good practice to renew the clutch friction plate, pressure plate assembly and release bearing as a matched set, even if only one of these is actually worn enough to require renewal.*

5 Remove the clutch assembly.
6 When cleaning clutch components, first read the warning at the beginning of this Section; remove dust using a clean, dry cloth and working in a well-ventilated atmosphere.
7 Check the friction plate facings for signs of wear, damage or oil contamination. If the friction material is cracked, burnt, scored or damaged, or if it is contaminated with oil or grease (shown by shiny black patches), the friction plate must be renewed.
8 If the depth from the friction material surface to any of the rivets is worn to the service limit specified or less, the friction plate must be renewed (photo).
9 If the friction plate is an AP item (see Section 1 for identification details), the total thickness of friction material can be measured and compared with the Specifications at the beginning of this Chapter (photo). If the plate is excessively worn, or even close to the service limit, it must be renewed.
10 If the friction material is still serviceable, check that the centre boss splines are unworn, that the torsion springs are in good condition and securely fastened and that all the rivets are tightly fastened. If any wear or damage is found, the friction plate must be renewed.
11 If the friction material is fouled with oil, this must be due to an oil leak from the crankshaft left-hand oil seal, from the sump to main bearing ladder joint, from the main bearing ladder to cylinder block/crankcase joint or from the transmission input shaft; renew the seal or repair the joint, as appropriate, as described in Chapters 2 or 7.
12 Check the pressure plate assembly for obvious signs of wear or damage; shake it to check for loose rivets or worn or damaged fulcrum rings and check that the drive straps securing the pressure plate to the cover do not show signs (such as a deep yellow or blue discoloration) of overheating. If the diaphragm spring is worn or damaged, or if its pressure is in any way suspect, the pressure plate assembly should be renewed.
13 To check the condition of the diaphragm spring, place a circular piece of flat plate across the tips of the spring fingers and use feeler gauges to measure the clearance between each finger's tip and the plate. If any finger is distorted so that the clearance between its tip and the plate is at the specified service limit or greater, the pressure plate must be renewed.

4.4 Note locating dowels (two arrowed) and which way around friction plate is fitted on removing clutch components

4.8 Measuring friction plate rivet depth

4.9 Measuring friction plate total thickness

4.18 Check friction plate for markings on refitting – this side must face the flywheel

4.21 Using a clutch aligning tool to centralise the friction plate

4.22 Once friction plate is centralised tighten pressure plate bolts to the specified torque

14 To check the condition of the complete pressure plate assembly, first check that the friction plate is within tolerances (paragraphs 8 and/or 9 above), then refit the clutch assembly to the flywheel as described below. Measure the height of each diaphragm spring finger from the flywheel's machined bearing surface; if any finger's height is at the service limit specified or greater, the pressure plate assembly must be renewed.

15 Examine the machined bearing surfaces of the pressure plate and of the flywheel; they should be clean, completely flat and free from scratches or scoring. If either is discoloured from excessive heat or shows signs of cracks it should be renewed, although minor damage of this nature can sometimes be polished away using emery paper. Use a straight-edge, placed across the pressure plate surface at four different points, and feeler gauges to check the pressure plate surface, comparing any warpage found with the specified service limit.

16 Check the release bearing as described in Section 5 of this Chapter.

Refitting

17 On reassembly, ensure that the bearing surfaces of the flywheel and pressure plate are completely clean, smooth and free from oil or grease. Use solvent to remove any protective grease from new components.

18 Fit the friction plate so that the longer part of its central, splined, boss is towards the flywheel and so that its spring hub assembly faces away from the flywheel; there may also be a marking showing which way round the plate is to be refitted (photo).

19 Refit the pressure plate assembly, aligning the marks made on dismantling (if the original pressure plate is re-used) and locating the pressure plate on its three locating dowels. Fit the pressure plate bolts, but tighten them only finger-tight so that the friction plate can still be moved.

20 The friction plate must now be centralised so that when the transmission is refitted its input shaft will pass through the splines at the centre of the friction plate.

21 Centralisation can be achieved by passing a screwdriver or other long bar through the friction plate and into the hole in the crankshaft; the friction plate can then be moved around until it is centred on the crankshaft hole. Alternatively, a clutch aligning tool can be used to eliminate the guesswork; these can be obtained from most accessory shops or can be made up from a length of metal rod or wooden dowel which fits closely inside the crankshaft hole, and has insulating tape wound around it to match the diameter of the friction plate splined hole (photo).

22 When the friction plate is centralised, tighten the pressure plate bolts evenly and in a diagonal sequence to the specified torque setting (photo).

23 Apply a thin smear of molybdenum disulphide grease to the splines of the friction plate and the transmission input shaft, also to the release bearing bore and release fork shaft.

24 Refit the transmission as described in Chapter 7.

5 Clutch release mechanism – removal, inspection and refitting

Note: *Refer to the warning concerning the dangers of asbestos dust at the beginning of Section 4.*

Removal

1 Unless the complete engine/transmission unit is to be removed from the car and separated for major overhaul (see Chapter 2), the clutch release mechanism can be reached only by removing the transmission as described in Chapter 7.

2 Disengaging the release bearing from the fork ends, pull the release bearing off its guide sleeve.

3 Drive out the roll pin from the top of the release fork using a hammer and a parallel punch then remove the lever (photo).

4 Using a suitable flat-bladed screwdriver, carefully prise the release fork upper bush out of the transmission housing. Withdraw the release fork then prise out the lower bush (photos).

5.3 Drive out the roll pin and remove the release fork lever

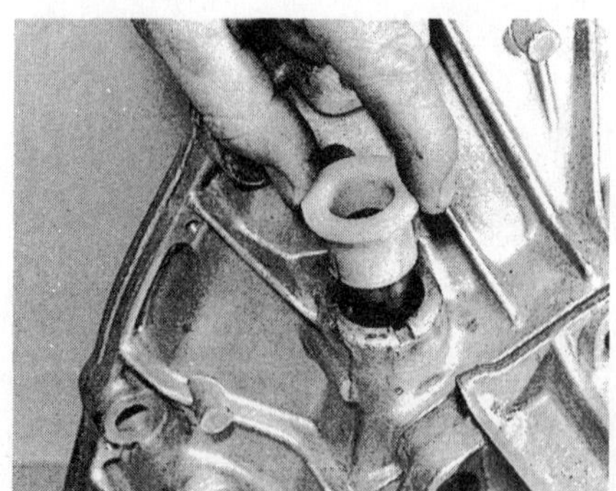
5.4A Remove the release fork upper bush...

5.4B ...then manoeuvre the release fork out of position

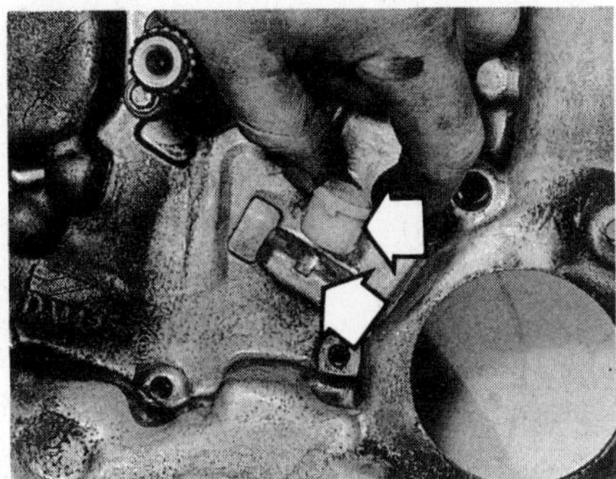

5.8A On refitting align bush locating tabs with the bellhousing slots (arrowed)...

5.8B ...and ensure the release bearing hooks are correctly engaged with the fork

Inspection

5 Check the release mechanism, renewing any component which is worn or damaged. Carefully check all bearing surfaces and points of contact.

6 When checking the release bearing itself, note that it is often considered worthwhile to renew it as a matter of course. Check that the contact surface rotates smoothly and easily, with no sign of noise or roughness and that the surface itself is smooth and unworn, with no signs of cracks, pitting or scoring. If there is any doubt about its condition the bearing must be renewed.

7 Note that when cleaning clutch components, **do not** use solvents on the release bearing; it is packed with grease which may be washed out if care is not taken.

Refitting

8 Reassembly is the reverse of the dismantling procedure, noting the following points (photos):

(a) When refitting the release fork bushes, ensure that each bush's locating tags engage in the bellhousing slots. Apply a smear of molybdenum disulphide grease to the release fork shaft's bearing surfaces before refitting it and use a new roll pin if required to secure the release fork lever.

(b) Clean the release bearing bore and guide sleeve, then apply a smear of molybdenum disulphide grease to both bearing surfaces before engaging the bearing on the fork ends and sliding it onto the sleeve.

(c) Move the fork up and down to check that it fits correctly against the bearing, then move the release lever to check that the fork and bearing operate properly before refitting the transmission as described in Chapter 7.

Chapter 7 Transmission

Contents

Specifications

General

Type	Manual, five forward speeds and reverse. Synchromesh on all forward speeds
Designation	Rover R65
Transmission code	5C 39W

Reduction ratios

Final drive	3.937 : 1
1st	3.417 : 1
2nd	1.947 : 1
3rd	1.333 : 1
4th	1.054 : 1
5th	0.857 : 1
Reverse	3.583 : 1

Lubrication

Recommended oil	Special gearbox oil - refer to your Rover dealer (Duckhams Hypoid PT 75W/80 Gear Oil - for topping-up only)
Capacity	2.0 litres
Recommended gearchange linkage grease	Rover Grease containing 3% molybdenum disulphide - Part Number AFU 1500.1509 (Duckhams LBM 10 Grease)

Torque wrench settings

Torque wrench settings	Nm	lbf ft
Oil filler/level and drain plugs	25	19
Clutch release bearing guide sleeve bolts	5	4
Transmission to engine bolts	85	63
Flywheel cover plate bolts	8	6
Engine/transmission left-hand mounting:		
Mounting to body bolts	45	33
Mounting to transmission bracket bolts	60	44
Transmission bracket bolts	100	74
Engine/transmission rear mounting:		
Mounting bracket to transmission bolts	100	74
Connecting link to transmission bracket bolt	60	44
Connecting link to subframe bracket bolt	85	63
Subframe mounting bracket bolts	63	47
Anti-beaming bracket to support bracket bolt	45	33

2.3 Transmission oil filler/level plug 'A' and drain plug 'B'

1 General information

The transmission is contained in a cast aluminium alloy casing bolted to the engine's left-hand end and consists of the gearbox and final drive differential, often called a transaxle.

Drive is transmitted from the crankshaft via the clutch to the input shaft, which has a splined extension to accept the clutch friction plate and rotates in sealed ball-bearings; from the input shaft drive is transmitted to the output shaft, which rotates in a roller bearing at its right-hand end and a sealed ball-bearing at its left-hand end. From the output shaft the drive is transmitted to the differential crownwheel, which rotates with the differential case and planetary gears, thus driving the sun gears and driveshafts. The rotation of the planetary gears on their shaft allows the inner roadwheel to rotate at a slower speed than the outer roadwheel when the car is cornering.

The input and output shafts are arranged side by side, parallel to the crankshaft and driveshafts, so that their gear pinion teeth are in constant mesh. In the neutral position the output shaft gear pinions rotate freely so that drive cannot be transmitted to the crownwheel.

Gear selection is by a floor-mounted lever acting through a remote control linkage on the selector mechanism. The selector mechanism causes the appropriate selector fork to move its respective synchro-sleeve along the shaft to lock the gear pinion to the synchro-hub. Since the synchro-hubs are splined to the output shaft, this locks the pinion to the shaft so that drive can be transmitted. To ensure that gear changing can be made quickly and quietly a synchromesh system is fitted to all forward gears, consisting of baulk rings and spring-loaded fingers as well as the gear pinions and synchro-hubs; the synchromesh cones are formed on the mating faces of the baulk rings and gear pinions.

2 Transmission oil – renewal

1 This operation is much quicker and more efficient if the car is first taken on a journey of sufficient length to warm the engine/transmission up to normal operating temperature.

2 Park the car on level ground, switch off the ignition and apply the handbrake firmly. For improved access, jack up the front of the car and support it securely on axle stands. Note that the car must be lowered to the ground and level, to ensure accuracy, when refilling and checking the oil level.

3 Unscrew the filler/level plug, then position a suitable container under the drain plug at the rear of the transmission, below the left-hand driveshaft inner constant velocity joint, and unscrew the plug (photo).

4 Allow the oil to drain completely into the container. If the oil is hot, take precautions against scalding. Clean both the filler/level and the drain plugs, being especially careful to wipe any metallic particles off the magnetic inserts. Discard the original sealing washers; they should be renewed whenever they are disturbed.

5 When the oil has finished draining, clean the drain plug threads and those of the transmission casing, fit a new sealing washer and refit the drain plug, tightening it to the specified torque wrench setting. If the car was raised for the draining operation, now lower it to the ground.

6 Refilling the transmission is an extremely awkward operation. Above all, allow plenty of time for the oil level to settle properly before checking it. Note that the car must be parked on flat level ground when checking the oil level.

7 Refill the transmission with the exact amount of the specified type of oil, noting that only a few oils are recommended by Rover for refilling. Allow time for the oil to settle.

8 Check the oil level as described in Chapter 1; if the correct amount was poured into the transmission and a large amount flows out on checking the level, refit the filler/level plug and take the car on a short journey so that the new oil is distributed fully around the transmission components, then check the level again.

9 Dispose of the old oil safely; **do not** pour it down a drain (see *'General repair procedures'* at the beginning of this Manual).

3 Reverse interlock cable – removal and refitting

Note: *On later models (from VIN XW 408115 onwards) or earlier models which have been fitted with a Unipart replacement gearbox and/or gearbox housing, there is no provision for the reverse interlock cable. Therefore the reverse interlock cable is no longer needed and, if already fitted, it can be removed.*

Removal

1 Working from within the engine compartment, unscrew the reverse interlock cable nut from the top of the transmission housing (photo). In the absence of the special spanner (Rover service tool number 18G 1591), use a close fitting spanner to unscrew the plastic nut noting that it is easily damaged. Plug the transmission orifice to prevent the entry of dirt.

2 Firmly apply the handbrake then jack up the front of the car and support it on axle stands.

3 From underneath the car, trace the cable back along its entire length and free it from all the retaining clips securing it to the subframe and gearchange linkage control rod.

4 From inside the car remove the centre console assembly as described in Chapter 11.

5 With the console removed, prise off the rubber cover from the base

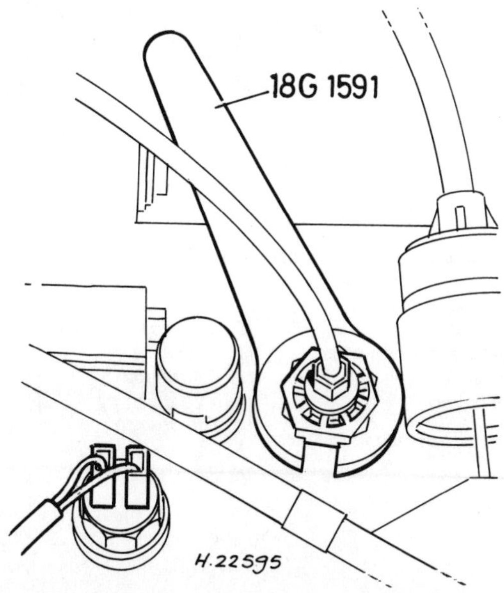

Fig. 7.1 Using Rover service tool to unscrew the reverse interlock cable from the transmission (Sec 3)

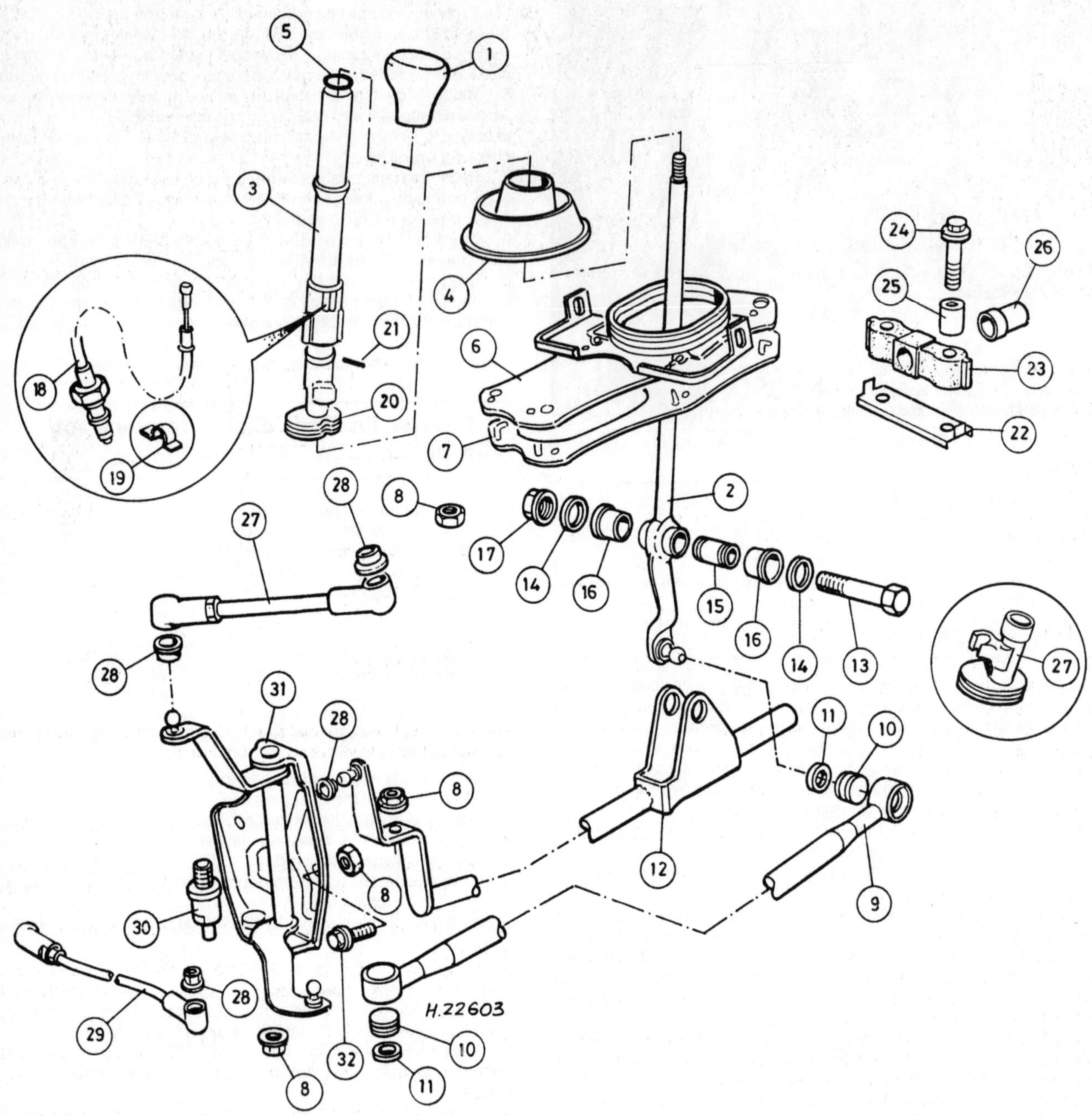

Fig. 7.2 Gearchange linkage components (Secs 3 to 5)

1 *Gearchange lever knob*
2 *Gearchange lever*
3 *Gearchange lever reverse selector slide*
4 *Rubber cover*
5 *Retaining clip*
6 *Mounting plate*
7 *Seal*
8 *Nut*
9 *Selector rod*
10 *Ball housing*
11 *Rubber seal*
12 *Control rod*
13 *Pivot bolt*
14 *Thrustwasher*
15 *Spacer*
16 *Bush*
17 *Nut*
18 *Reverse interlock cable*
19 *Retaining clip*
20 *Reverse interlock cable abutment*
21 *Roll pin*
22 *Mounting plate*
23 *Mounting rubber*
24 *Bolt*
25 *Spacer*
26 *Bush*
27 *Upper link rod*
28 *Dust cover*
29 *Lower link rod*
30 *Bucket joint*
31 *Bellcrank assembly*
32 *Bolt*

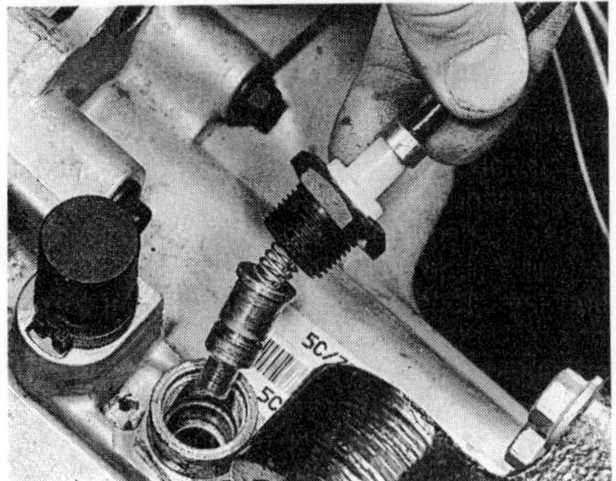
3.1 Unscrew the reverse interlock cable from the transmission

3.5 Remove the rubber cover...

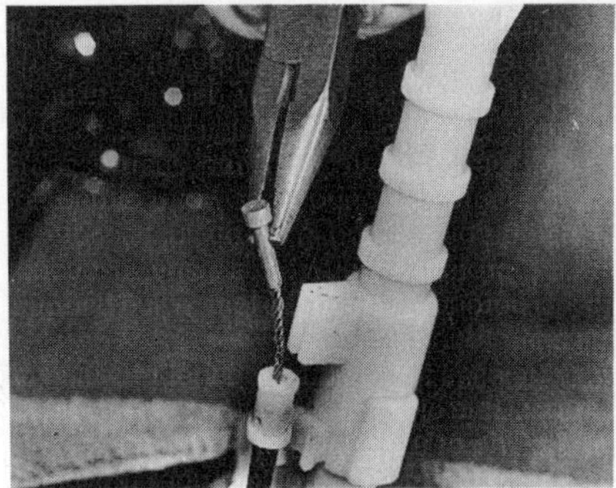
3.6 ...and disconnect the cable from the gearchange lever

of the gearchange lever and slide the cover off the lever (photo).
6 Release the outer cable from its abutment and disconnect the inner cable from the gearchange lever reverse slide (photo). The reverse interlock cable can then be removed from underneath the vehicle.

Refitting

7 Refitting is the reverse of the removal procedure ensuring that the cable is securely retained by all the necessary ties. On completion check that the reverse interlock cable functions correctly before taking the car on the road.

4 Gearchange linkage – adjustment

1 If a stiff, sloppy or imprecise gearchange leads you to suspect that a fault exists within the linkage, first dismantle it completely and check it for wear or damage as described in Section 5, then reassemble it, applying a smear of grease to all bearing surfaces.
2 If this does not cure the fault, the car should be examined by an expert, as the fault must lie within the transmission itself. There is no adjustment as such in the linkage; note that while the length of the link rods can be altered, this is for initial setting-up only and is not intended to provide a form of compensation for wear.
3 If the link rods have been renewed, or if the length of the originals is incorrect, adjust them as follows.
4 Ensure that the car is parked on level ground, with the ignition switched off, the handbrake firmly applied and neutral selected. Remembering that the selector mechanism is spring-loaded so that the gearchange lever rests naturally between the third and fourth gear positions, have an assistant hold the gearchange lever in its normal position in relation to the front seats.
5 Working in (or under) the engine compartment, slacken the locknut at the bellcrank end of the rod to be adjusted; if not already done, disconnect the rod from the transmission selector levers.
6 Check that the selector lever concerned is in its neutral position, with no signs of free play or damage, then hold the rod end socket over the lever ball and alter the length of the rod by screwing the rod end socket in or out (as applicable).
7 When the length of the rod is correct, tighten the locknut securely whilst retaining the socket.
8 Press the link rod socket firmly onto the selector lever and check that all gears can be selected, with the gearchange lever returning properly to its correct at-rest position.

5 Gearchange linkage – removal, overhaul and refitting

Removal

1 Park the car on level ground, switch off the ignition, check that the transmission is in neutral and apply the handbrake firmly. Jack up the front of the car and support it securely on axle stands.
2 Although not strictly necessary, access to the gearchange linkage is greatly improved if the exhaust front pipe is first removed as described in Chapter 4.

18 G 1592

H.22448

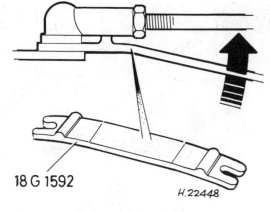

Fig. 7.3 Using Rover special tool to disconnect gearchange linkage link rod balljoint from transmission (Sec 5)

3 In the absence of the special gearchange linkage balljoint separator (Rover service tool number 18G 1592), use a suitable flat-bladed screwdriver to carefully lever the link rod balljoints off the transmission upper and lower selector levers, taking care not to damage the balljoint gaiters.
4 Unscrewing the nuts and/or releasing the balljoints as necessary, disconnect the gearchange control and selector rods from the bellcrank assembly. Release the balljoint connecting the selector rod to gearchange lever and remove the selector rod (photos).
5 If necessary, remove the three bolts securing the bellcrank assembly to the suspension front subframe and remove it from the vehicle.
6 Working from inside the car, remove the centre console assembly as described in Chapter 11.
7 With the console removed, carefully prise the rubber cover off the base of the gearchange lever and slide the cover off the lever to gain access to the control rod pivot bolt. Slacken the nut and remove the pivot bolt and thrustwashers (photo).
8 From underneath the car, release all the ties securing the reverse interlock cable (where fitted) to the control rod, then undo the two bolts securing the control rod rear mounting to the body (photo). Remove the mounting assembly and control rod from underneath the car.
9 If necessary, slacken and remove the six gearchange lever housing retaining nuts and remove the seal, mounting plate and lever assembly from the car noting that it will be necessary to disconnect the reverse interlock cable (where fitted) from gearchange lever (photo).

Overhaul

10 Thoroughly clean all components and check them for wear or damage, renewing all worn or faulty items. Note that the gearchange lever to control rod pivot bushes can be renewed separately if necessary.

5.4A Disconnect the gearchange linkage rods from the bellcrank...

5.4B ...and the selector rod from the gearchange lever

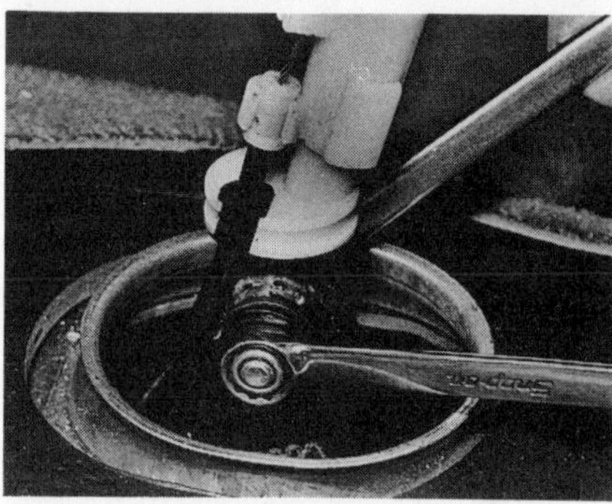

5.7 Removing the control rod pivot bolt

5.8 Remove control rod rear mounting retaining bolts (remaining one arrowed)

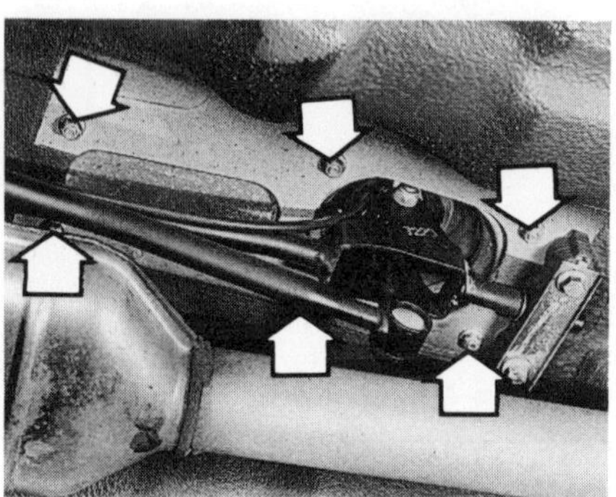

5.9 Gearchange lever housing retaining nut locations (arrowed)

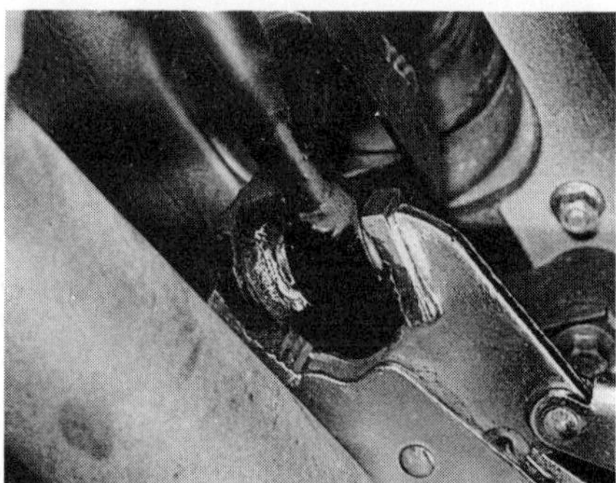

5.13 On refitting ensure all gearchange linkage balljoints are pressed firmly together

11 Carefully check the condition of all linkage joints; if any show signs of stiffness or free play, they must be renewed. Check also the control rod mounting rubber and bush assembly; renew the rubber if it shows any sign of cracks, splits or other deterioration and renew the bush if it is a sloppy fit on the control rod end.

12 The bellcrank assembly must be renewed complete if it is worn or damaged.

Refitting

13 Refitting is the reverse of the removal procedure, noting the following points (photo):

- *(a) Apply a smear of the specified grease to all pivot and bearing surfaces.*
- *(b) Tighten all nuts and bolts securely and ensure that all gearchange linkage balljoints are pressed firmly together.*
- *(c) Where necessary, secure the reverse interlock cable to the control rod with all the relevant cable ties.*
- *(d) If adjustment of the linkage is required, refer to Section 4.*

6 Speedometer drive - removal and refitting

Removal

1 Firmly apply the handbrake then jack up the front of the car and support it on axle stands.

2 From underneath the car, pull out the rubber retaining pin which secures the lower end of the speedometer cable to the transmission housing. Withdraw the cable from the speedometer drive and remove the O-rings from the cable lower end. Discard the O-rings and renew then regardless of their apparent condition.

3 Undo the speedometer drive housing retaining bolt then withdraw the housing and driven gear pinion from the transmission. Separate the pinion and housing and remove the oil seal and O-ring from the pinion housing. Discard the oil seal and O-ring; both should be renewed as a matter of course whenever they are disturbed.

4 Renew the pinion if its teeth are worn or damaged and check the housing for cracks or damage. Note that the speedometer drive gear pinion can be checked visually with the pinion assembly removed by shining a torch into the aperture. If any of the gear teeth are damaged the transmission must be removed from the car and dismantled so that the gear can be renewed; it is pressed onto the differential case.

Refitting

5 On reassembly, fit the new oil seal and O-ring to the housing, then refit the pinion, applying a smear of grease to all components before installation. Insert the assembly into the transmission, rotating the driven pinion until it is felt to engage the teeth of the drive gear pinion, then press the housing into place. **Do not** use excessive force or the drive components may be damaged.

6 When the drive is correctly refitted tighten the retaining bolt securely.

7 Apply a smear of engine oil to the speedometer cable O-rings, then refit the cable to the transmission and secure it in position with the rubber retaining pin. Lower the car to the ground.

7 Oil seals - renewal

Driveshaft oil seal

1 Chock the rear wheels of the car, firmly apply the handbrake then jack up the front of the car and support it on axle stands. Remove the appropriate front roadwheel.

2 Drain the transmission oil as described in Section 2.

3 Slacken and remove the bolt and washer securing the anti-roll bar connecting link to the lower suspension arm, and the two bolts securing the tie bar to the lower suspension arm.

4 Extract the split pins and undo the nuts securing the steering gear track rod end balljoint and the lower suspension arm balljoint to the

7.7 Prise the old seal out of position using a large flat-bladed screwdriver

7.8 Use a suitably sized socket to tap the new seal into position

7.17 Clutch release bearing guide sleeve retaining bolts (arrowed)

swivel hub. Remove the nuts and release the balljoint tapered shanks using a universal balljoint separator.

5 Insert a suitable flat bar in between the inner constant velocity joint and transmission housing then carefully lever the joint out of position, taking great care not to damage the transmission housing.

6 Withdraw the inner constant velocity joint from the transmission and support the driveshaft to avoid damaging the constant velocity joints or gaiters.

7 Carefully prise the oil seal out of the transmission with a large flat-bladed screwdriver (photo).

8 Remove all traces of dirt from the area around the oil seal aperture then apply a smear of grease to the outer lip of the new oil seal. Fit the new seal into its aperture and drive it squarely into position using a suitable tubular drift (such as a socket) which bears only on the hard outer edge of the seal, until it abuts its locating shoulder (photo).

9 Prior to refitting the driveshaft check that the inner constant velocity joint shoulder is smooth and free of burrs and scratches. Small burrs or scratches can be removed using emery cloth, however larger imperfections may require the renewal of the joint. Regardless of its apparent condition, renew the circlip which is fitted to the groove in the inner constant velocity joint splines.

10 Thoroughly clean the driveshaft splines and apply a thin film of grease to the oil seal lips and to the inner constant velocity joint splines and shoulder.

11 Ensure that the circlip is located securely in its groove then locate the joint splines with those of the differential sun gear whilst taking great care not to damage the oil seal. Push the joint fully into the transmission and check that it is securely retained by the circlip by pulling the hub assembly outwards.

12 Insert the lower suspension arm and track rod balljoints into their respective locations in the swivel hub and tighten their retaining nuts to the specified torque (Chapter 10). Secure both nuts with new split pins.

13 Refit the bolts securing the trailing arm and anti-roll bar connecting link to the lower suspension arm and tighten them to the specified torque (Chapter 10).

14 Refit the roadwheel then lower the car to the ground and tighten the wheel nuts to the specified torque (Chapter 10).

15 Refill the transmission with the correct type and quantity of oil as described in Section 2.

Input shaft oil seal

16 Remove the transmission from the car as described in Section 9, then remove the clutch release fork as described in Chapter 6.

17 Undo the three bolts securing the clutch release bearing guide sleeve in position and slide the guide off the input shaft (photo). Discard the bolts; they must be renewed whenever they are disturbed. Carefully lever the oil seal out of the guide using a suitable flat-bladed screwdriver.

18 Before fitting a new seal, check the input shaft's seal rubbing surface for signs of burrs, scratches or other damage which may have caused the seal to fail in the first place. It may be possible to polish away minor faults of this sort using fine abrasive paper, however, more serious defects will require the renewal of the input shaft. Clean any thread locking material from the bellhousing threads using Loctite Chisel and a suitable tap, then degrease thoroughly. Ensure that the input shaft is clean and greased to protect the seal lips on refitting.

19 Dip the new seal in clean oil and fit it to the guide sleeve. Carefully slide the guide sleeve into position then fit the **new** retaining bolts and tighten them to the specified torque wrench setting.

20 Reassemble and lubricate the clutch release mechanism as described in Chapter 6, then wipe off any surplus oil or grease and refit the transmission to the car.

8 Reversing lamp switch – testing, removal and refitting

Testing

1 The reversing lamp circuit is controlled by a plunger-type switch that is screwed into the top of the transmission casing. If a fault develops in the circuit first ensure that the circuit fuse has not blown.

2 To test the switch, disconnect its wires and use a multimeter (set to the resistance function) or a battery and bulb test circuit to check that there is continuity between the switch terminals only when reverse gear is selected. If this is not the case and there are no obvious breaks or other damage to the wires, the switch is faulty and must be renewed.

Removal

3 To remove the switch, disconnect its wiring connector and unscrew it (photo).

Refitting

4 On refitting, apply a smear of sealant to the switch threads and tighten it securely, but do not overtighten it. Re-connect its wiring connector and test the operation of the circuit.

8.3 Disconnecting reversing lamp wiring connector

9.4 Disconnect the clutch cable and free it from the transmission bracket

9.10 Lever out both driveshaft inner CV joints from the transmission

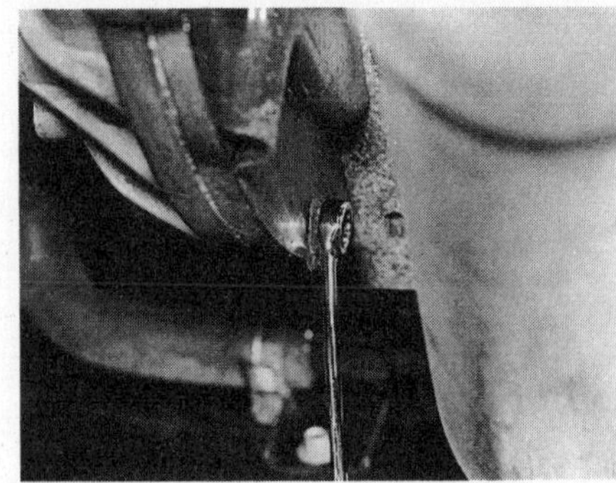

9.13A Undo the flywheel lower cover plate...

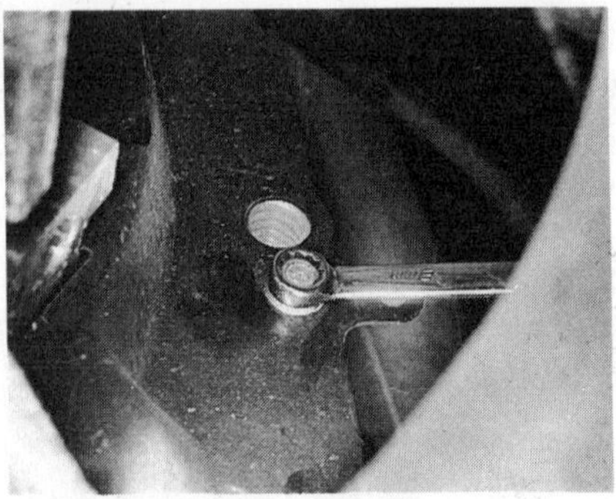

9.13B ...and front flywheel cover plate retaining bolts and remove both covers

9.14 Clutch cable/wiring harness support bracket to transmission bolts (arrowed)

Fig. 7.4 Exploded view of the transmission (Sec 10)

1 Nut
2 Stop plate
3 Synchro-hub
4 Finger
5 Spring
6 Steel ball
7 5th gear synchro-sleeve
8 5th gear selector fork
9 Roll pin
10 Baulk ring
11 Output shaft 5th gear pinion
12 Needle roller bearing
13 Spacer
14 Output shaft ball-bearing
15 Bearing retainer and Torx screws
16 Output shaft 4th gear pinion
17 Circlip – four-speed transmission only
18 Spacer
19 3rd/4th gear synchro-sleeve
20 Segment ring
21 Output shaft 3rd gear pinion
22 Output shaft 2nd gear pinion
23 Baulk ring
24 1st/2nd gear synchro-hub
25 1st/2nd gear synchro-sleeve – with reverse gear
26 Finger
27 Output shaft 1st gear pinion
28 Output shaft roller bearing
29 Output shaft
30 Plastic lubrication insert
31 Bolt
32 Left-hand end cover
33 Rubber gasket
34 Transmission casing
35 Oil seal
36 Oil filler/level plug
37 Sealing washer
38 Bolt
39 Bolt
40 Breather body
41 Breather cap
42 Reversing lamp switch
43 Sealing washer
44 Reverse interlock cable nut
45 1st/2nd gear selector fork
46 5th, 1st/2nd and reverse selector fork shaft
47 3rd/4th gear selector fork
48 3rd/4th selector fork shaft
49 Reverse idler gear shaft
50 Thrust bearing
51 Reverse idler gear pinion
52 Needle roller bearing
53 Reverse gear selector fork
54 Pivot pin
55 Reverse gear locking plunger
56 Spring
57 Locking ring
58 Belleville washer
59 Input shaft 5th gear pinion
60 Bearing retainer and Torx screws
61 Input shaft ball-bearing
62 Input shaft
63 Input shaft ball-bearing
64 Thrustwasher
65 Planetary gear pinion
66 Centre tube
67 Thrustwasher
68 Sun gear pinion
69 Planetary gear shaft
70 Differential side taper roller bearing
71 Differential case and crownwheel assembly
72 Roll pin
73 Retaining ring
74 Speedometer drivegear
75 Speedometer drive pinion
76 Speedometer lower cable retaining rubber dowel
77 O-ring
78 Speedometer drive housing
79 Oil seal
80 Screw
81 Oil seal
82 Roll pin
83 Transmission gear selector lower lever and shaft assembly
84 Bellhousing and intermediate plate assembly
85 Torx screw
86 Bolt
87 Roll pin
88 Combined interlock and detent assembly
89 Plastic cup
90 Bias spring
91 Dowel
92 Oil seal
93 Clutch release bearing guide sleeve
94 Bolt
95 Transmission gear selector upper lever
96 Reverse gear lever assembly
97 Oil drain plug
98 Oil seal

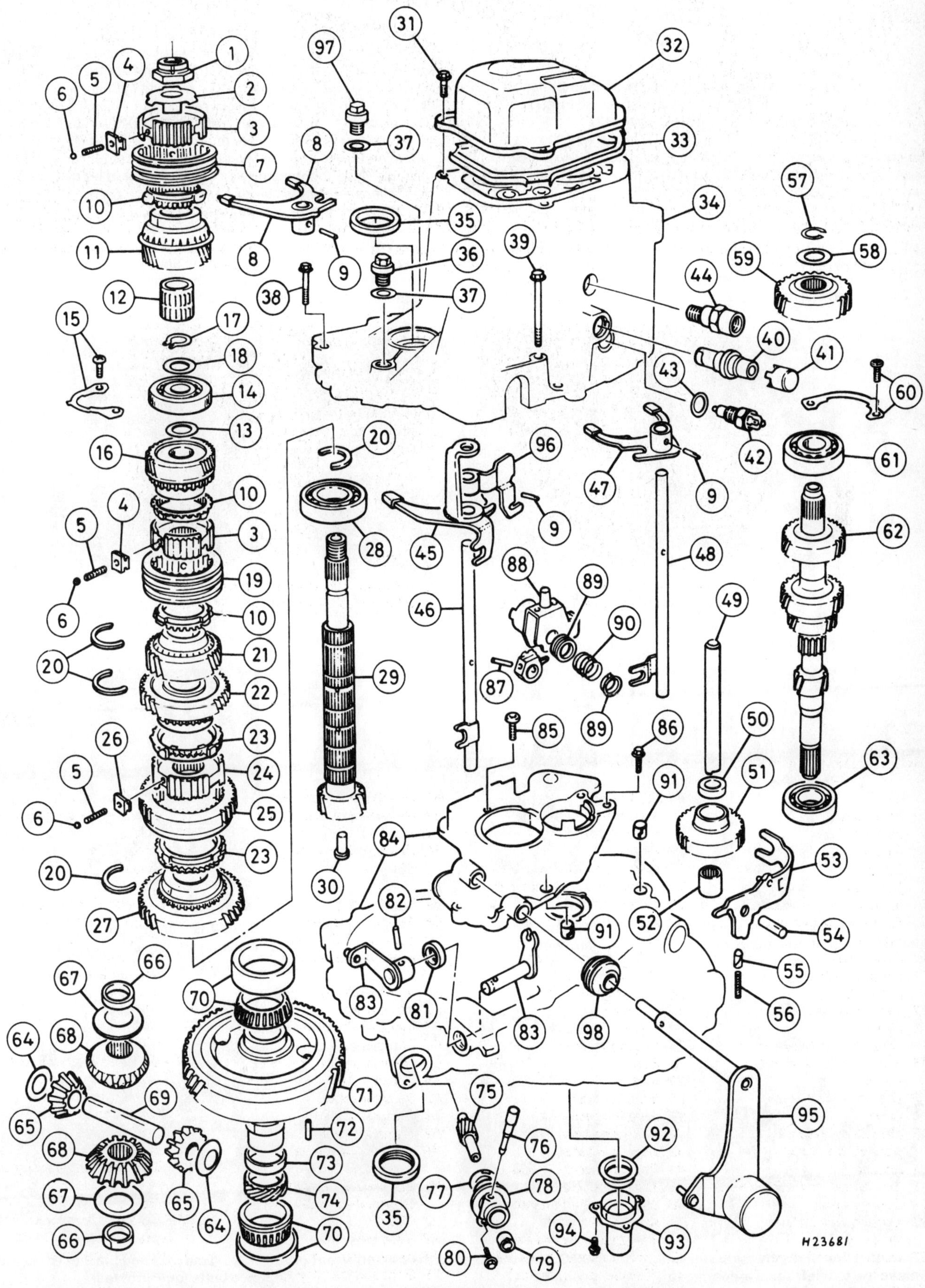
H23681

9 Transmission – removal and refitting

Removal

1 Drain the transmission oil as described in Section 2 then refit the drain and filler plugs and tighten them to the specified torque.
2 Remove the battery as described in Chapter 12.
3 Referring to Section 3, where necessary, unscrew the plastic nut securing the reverse interlock cable to the top of the transmission housing and plug the transmission orifice to prevent the entry of dirt.
4 Trace the clutch cable back from the clutch release lever to the bulkhead and remove the C-clip which retains the outer cable spring in position. Unhook the inner cable from the release lever and free the outer cable from its mounting bracket and position it clear of the transmission (photo).
5 Disconnect the wiring connector from the reversing lamp switch.
6 Firmly apply the handbrake and chock the rear wheels, then jack up the front of the car and support it on axle stands. Remove both front roadwheels.
7 Undo the three bolts securing the front bumper flange to the body then remove the seven front undercover panel retaining bolts and remove the panel from underneath the front of the car.
8 Remove the starter motor as described in Chapter 12.
9 In the absence of the special gearchange linkage balljoint separator (Rover service tool number 18G 1592), use a suitable flat-bladed screwdriver to carefully lever the link rod balljoints off the transmission upper and lower selector levers, taking care not to damage the balljoint gaiters. Move the transmission selector lever fully towards the engine so that it will clear the subframe.
10 Release the driveshaft inner constant velocity joints from the transmission as described in Section 7, paragraph 3 to 7 (photo).
11 Withdraw the rubber retaining pin which secures the speedometer cable in position in the transmission and withdraw the cable. Remove the O-rings from the lower end of the cable and discard them; they must be renewed whenever they are disturbed.

9.15 Remove the rear flywheel cover plate

9.16 Using a support bar to take the weight of the engine (bonnet removed for clarity)

9.18A Unbolt the rear mounting to transmission bolts (arrowed)...

9.18B ...then slacken the connecting link to subframe bracket bolt and pivot the mounting away from the transmission

9.19 Anti-beaming bracket retaining bolt (arrowed)

9.20A Slacken and remove the transmission bracket to mounting bolts...

9.20B ...then lower the transmission and remove the four left-hand mounting to body bolts (arrowed)...

9.20C ...and manoeuvre the mounting out of position

9.20D Transmission bracket is retained by two bolts (one arrowed)

12 Where necessary, slacken and remove the two bolts securing the exhaust front pipe to its mounting bracket.
13 Undo the lower flywheel cover and front flywheel cover retaining bolts and remove both covers from the engine/transmission unit (photos).
14 Unscrew the two bolts securing the clutch cable/wiring harness support bracket to the transmission and remove the bracket (photo).
15 Remove the two rear flywheel cover retaining bolts and remove the cover from the engine/transmission unit (photo).
16 Place a jack with interposed block of wood beneath the engine to take the weight of the engine. Alternatively attach lifting eyes to the engine and fit a hoist or support bar to take the weight of the engine (photo).
17 Place a jack and block of wood beneath the transmission.
18 Undo the two bolts securing the rear engine/transmission mounting assembly bracket to the transmission. Slacken the bolt securing the connecting link to the subframe bracket and pivot the assembly away from the transmission unit (photos).
19 Slacken and remove the bolt securing the anti-beaming bracket in position and remove the bracket (photo).
20 Undo the two bolts securing the transmission bracket to the left-hand engine/transmission mounting then lower the transmission unit. Undo the four engine/transmission mounting to body bolts, and remove the mounting to gain access to the bolts securing the mounting bracket to the transmission. Remove the two bracket retaining bolts and remove the bracket from the transmission unit (photos).
21 On models equipped with air conditioning, remove the bolt securing the air conditioning pipe to the top of the transmission.
22 Remove all the remaining transmission housing to engine bolts then make a final check that all necessary components have been disconnected.
23 Lower the engine and transmission slightly, then release the transmission from the engine. It may initially be tight owing to the locating dowels. Once the transmission is free, lower the jack and remove the unit out from under the car.

Refitting

24 The transmission is refitted by a reversal of the removal procedure bearing in mind the following points:

- *(a) Make sure the dowels are correctly positioned prior to installation.*
- *(b) Apply a little high melting point grease to the splines of the transmission input shaft. Do not apply too much otherwise there is a possibility of the grease contaminating the clutch friction plate.*
- *(c) Renew the driveshaft inner constant velocity joint circlips and install the driveshafts as described in Section 7, paragraph 9 onwards.*
- *(d) Tighten all nuts and bolts to the specified torque.*
- *(e) On completion refill the transmission with the specified type and quantity of oil as described in Section 2.*

10 Transmission overhaul – general information

Overhauling a manual transmission unit is a difficult and involved job for the DIY home mechanic. In addition to dismantling and reassembling many small parts, clearances must be precisely measured and, if necessary, changed by selecting shims and spacers. Internal transmission components are also often difficult to obtain and in many instances, extremely expensive. Because of this, if the transmission develops a fault or becomes noisy, the best course of action is to have the unit overhauled by a specialist repairer or to obtain an exchange reconditioned unit.

Nevertheless, it is not impossible for the more experienced mechanic to overhaul the transmission if the special tools are available and the job is done in a deliberate step-by-step manner so that nothing is overlooked.

The tools necessary for an overhaul include internal and external circlip pliers, bearing pullers, a slide hammer, a set of pin punches, a dial test indicator and possibly a hydraulic press. In addition, a large, sturdy workbench and a vice will be required.

During dismantling of the transmission, make careful notes of how each component is fitted to make reassembly easier and accurate.

Before dismantling the transmission, it will help if you have some idea what area is malfunctioning. Certain problems can be closely related to specific areas in the transmission which can make component examination and replacement easier. Refer to the Fault diagnosis Section at the beginning of this Manual for more information.

Chapter 8 Driveshafts

Contents

Specifications

Type .... Unequal-length solid steel shafts, splined to inner and outer constant velocity joints, dynamic damper on both shafts

Lubrication (overhaul only – see text)

Lubricant type/specification .... Use only special grease supplied in sachets with gaiter kits – joints are otherwise pre-packed with grease and sealed

Torque wrench setting	**Nm**	**lbf ft**
Driveshaft retaining nut	185	137

1 General information

Drive is transmitted from the differential to the front wheels by means of two unequal length, solid steel driveshafts.

Both driveshafts are splined at their outer ends to accept the wheel hubs and are threaded so that each hub can be fastened by a large nut. The inner end of each driveshaft is splined to accept the differential sun gear, and has a groove to accept the circlip which secures the driveshaft to the sun gear.

Constant velocity (CV) joints are fitted to each end of the driveshafts to ensure the smooth and efficient transmission of drive at all the angles possible as the roadwheels move up and down with the suspension, and as they turn from side to side under steering. Both inner and outer constant velocity joints are of the ball-and-cage type.

A dynamic damper is fitted to both the left- and right-hand driveshafts to reduce harmonic vibrations and resonance.

Note: *The only replacement parts listed are the inner constant velocity joint and shaft assemblies, the outer constant velocity joint assemblies and the rubber gaiters; the gaiters are supplied in a kit with the necessary sachets of grease and clips. If any joint is worn or damaged it cannot be reconditioned but must be renewed; in the case of the inner joints, this means that the complete joint/shaft assembly must be renewed.*

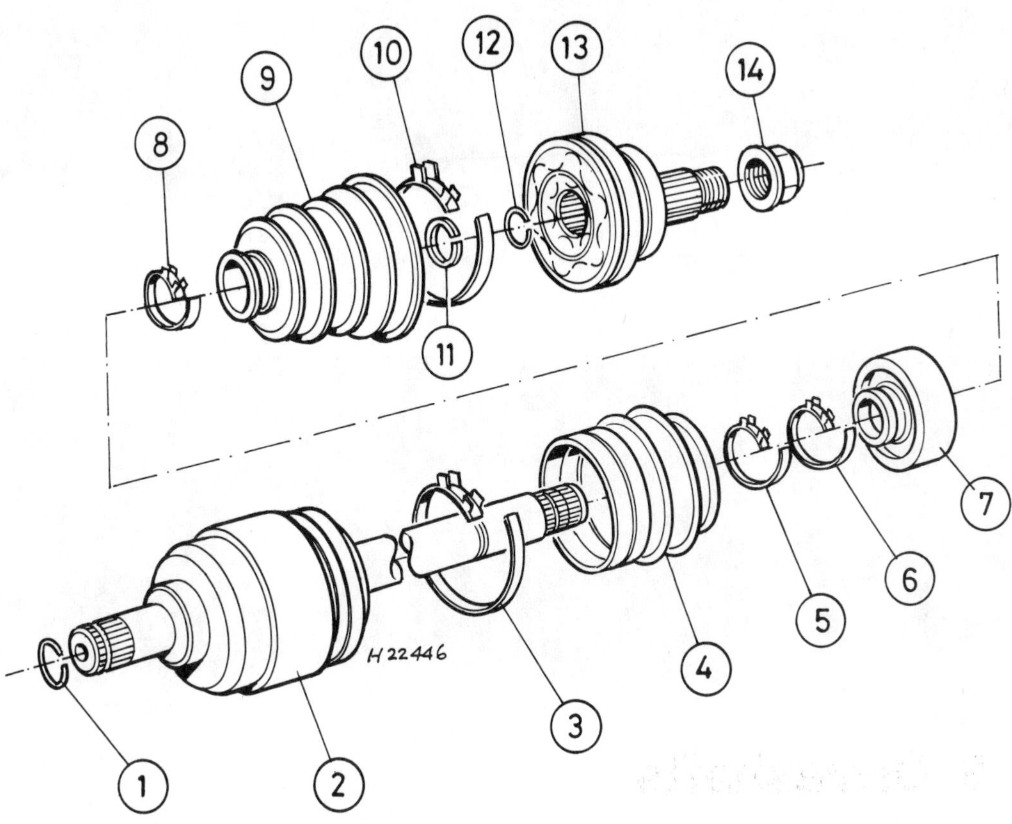

Fig. 8.1 Exploded view of driveshaft assembly (Sec 1)

1 *Circlip*
2 *Inner joint and shaft assembly*
3 *Large gaiter retaining clip*
4 *Gaiter*
5 *Small gaiter retaining clip*
6 *Damper clip*
7 *Dynamic damper*
8 *Small gaiter retaining clip*
9 *Gaiter*
10 *Large gaiter retaining clip*
11 *Stopper ring*
12 *Circlip*
13 *Outer joint assembly*
14 *Driveshaft retaining nut*

2 Driveshafts – removal and refitting

Removal

1 Chock the rear wheels of the car, firmly apply the handbrake then jack up the front of the car and support it on axle stands. Remove the appropriate front roadwheel.

2 Drain the transmission oil as described in Chapter 7.

3 Using a hammer and suitable punch, tap up the staking securing the driveshaft retaining nut to the groove in the constant velocity joint (photo). Note that a new driveshaft retaining nut must be obtained for reassembly.

4 Have an assistant firmly depress the brake pedal to prevent the front hub from rotating, then using a socket and extension bar, slacken and remove the driveshaft retaining nut. Discard the nut.

5 Slacken and remove the bolt and washer securing the anti-roll bar connecting link to the lower suspension arm, and the two bolts securing the tie bar to the lower suspension arm.

6 Extract the split pins and undo the nuts securing the steering gear track rod end balljoint and the lower suspension arm balljoint to the swivel hub. Remove the nuts and release the balljoint tapered shanks using a universal balljoint separator (photo).

7 Carefully pull the swivel hub assembly outwards and withdraw the driveshaft outer constant velocity joint from the hub assembly (photo).

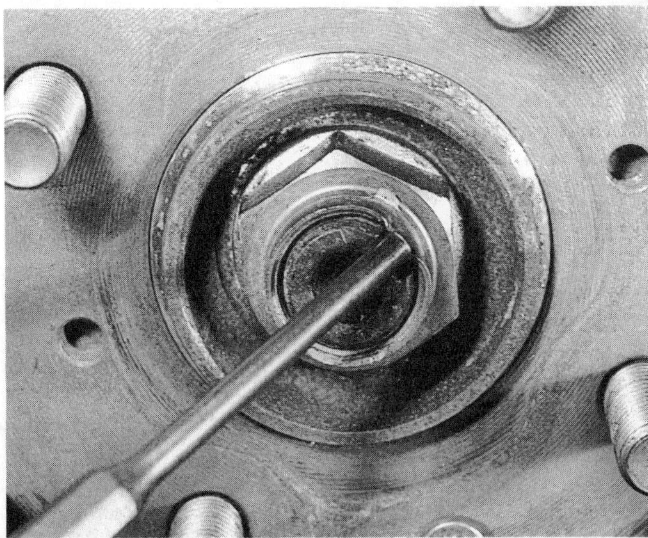

2.3 Use a hammer and suitable punch to tap up the driveshaft nut staking

2.6 Balljoint shanks can be released using a universal balljoint separator

2.7 Pull the swivel hub outwards and disengage the driveshaft outer CV joint

2.8 Carefully lever the driveshaft inner CV joint out of the transmission

2.10A Inspect the outer CV joint oil seal (arrowed) for signs of wear and renew if necessary

2.10B Inner CV joint circlip (arrowed) must be renewed as a matter of course

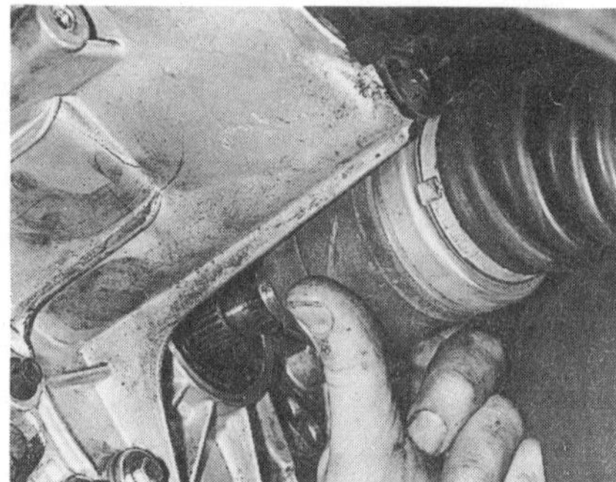
2.12 Refit the driveshaft inner CV joint to the transmission, taking care not to damage the driveshaft oil seal...

2.13 ...and engage the outer CV joint with the swivel hub

2.16A Tighten the driveshaft retaining nut to the specified torque...

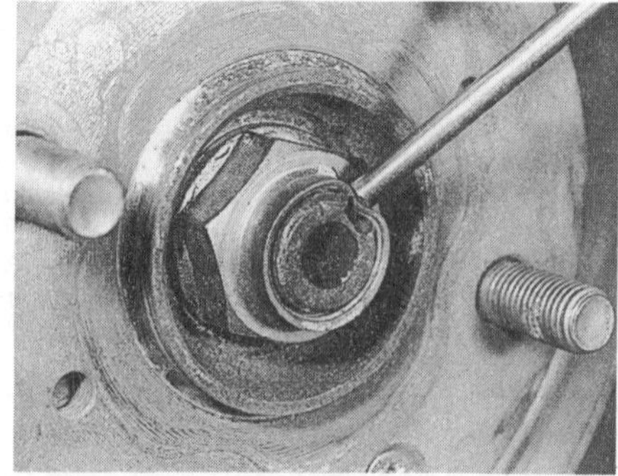
2.16B ...and stake it firmly into the CV joint groove

If necessary the shaft can be tapped out of the hub using a soft-faced mallet.

8 To release the inner constant velocity joint, insert a suitable flat bar in between the joint and transmission housing, then carefully lever the joint out of position, whilst taking great care not to damage the driveshaft oil seal (photo).

9 Support the inner constant velocity joint whilst withdrawing it from the transmission to ensure the oil seal is not damaged and remove the driveshaft from the vehicle.

Refitting

10 Before installing the driveshaft examine the transmission housing driveshaft oil seal for signs of damage or deterioration and, if necessary, renew it referring to Chapter 7 for further information. Similarly inspect the oil seal which is fitted to the outer constant velocity joint for damage or deterioration and renew if necessary. Regardless of its apparent condition, renew the circlip which is fitted to the groove in the inner constant velocity joint splines as a matter of course (photos).

11 Thoroughly clean the driveshaft splines and the apertures in the transmission and hub assembly, and apply a thin film of grease to the oil seal lips and to the driveshaft splines and shoulders. Check that all gaiter clips are securely fastened.

12 Ensure that the circlip fitted to the inner constant velocity joint is located securely in its groove, then locate the joint splines with those of the differential sun gear, taking great care not to damage the oil seal, then push the joint fully into the transmission (photo). Check that the joint is securely retained by the circlip by pulling the shaft outwards.

13 Locate the outer constant velocity joint splines with those of the swivel hub and slide the joint back into position in the hub (photo).

14 Insert the lower suspension arm and track rod balljoints into their respective locations in the swivel hub and tighten the retaining nuts to the specified torque (Chapter 10). Secure both nuts in position using new split pins.

15 Refit the bolts securing the trailing arm and anti-roll bar connecting link to the lower suspension arm and tighten them to the specified torque (Chapter 10).
16 Fit the new driveshaft retaining nut and tighten it to the specified torque setting whilst an assistant firmly depresses the brake pedal. Release the brake, check that the hub rotates freely, then stake the nut firmly into the groove on the constant velocity joint using a suitable punch (photos).
17 Refit the roadwheel then lower the car to the ground and tighten the wheel nuts to the specified torque (Chapter 10).
18 Refill the transmission with the correct type and quantity of oil as described in Chapter 7.

3 Driveshaft rubber gaiters – renewal

Outer joint

1 Remove the driveshaft from the car as described in Section 2.
2 Secure the driveshaft in a vice equipped with soft jaws and release the two rubber gaiter retaining clips by raising the locking tangs with a screwdriver and then raising the end of the clip with pliers. If necessary the gaiter retaining clips can be cut to release them (photo).
3 Slide the rubber gaiter down the shaft to expose the outer constant velocity joint.
4 Using a soft-faced mallet, sharply strike the inner member of the joint to drive it off the end of the shaft (photo). The outer joint is retained on the driveshaft by a circular section circlip and striking the joint in this manner forces the circlip into its groove, so allowing the joint to slide off.
5 Once the joint assembly has been removed, remove the circlip from the groove in the driveshaft splines and discard it. A new circlip must be fitted on reassembly.
6 Withdraw the rubber gaiter from the driveshaft.
7 With the constant velocity joint removed from the driveshaft, thoroughly clean the joint using paraffin, or a suitable solvent, and dry it thoroughly. Carry out a visual inspection of the joint.
8 Move the inner splined driving member from side to side to expose each ball in turn at the top of its track. Examine the balls for cracks, flat spots or signs of surface pitting.
9 Inspect the ball tracks on the inner and outer members. If the tracks have widened, the balls will no longer be a tight fit. At the same time check the ball cage windows for wear or cracking between the windows.
10 If on inspection any of the constant velocity joint components are found to be worn or damaged, it will be necessary to renew the complete joint assembly, since no components are available separately. If the joint is in satisfactory condition, obtain a repair kit consisting of a new gaiter, retaining clips and the correct type and quantity of grease (photo).
11 Tape over the splines on the end of the driveshaft, then fit the small retaining clip onto the gaiter and carefully slide the gaiter onto the shaft.
12 Remove the tape then, ensuring that the stopper ring is securely located in its groove, fit a **new** circlip to the groove in the driveshaft splines (photo). Engage the help of an assistant for the following operations.

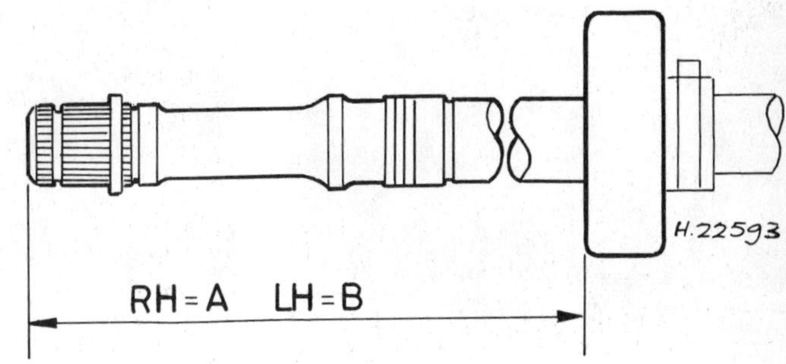

Fig. 8.2 Position the dynamic damper the specified distance from the outer end of the driveshaft (Sec 3)

Right-hand driveshaft (A) – 405 to 411 mm
Left-hand driveshaft (B) – 148 to 154 mm

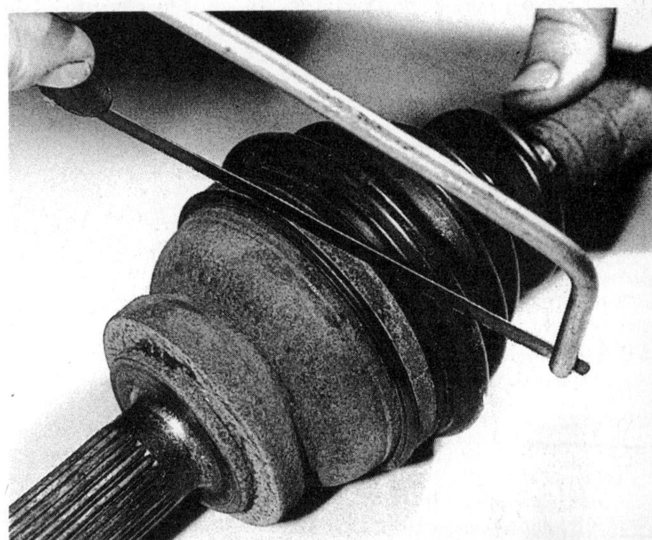

3.2 It may be necessary to cut gaiter clips to release them

13 Position the constant velocity joint over the splines on the driveshaft until it abuts the circlip.
14 Using two small screwdrivers placed either side of the circlip, Compress the clip and at the same time have your assistant firmly strike the end of the joint with a soft faced mallet. This should not require an undue amount of force. If the joint does not spring into place, remove it, reposition the circlip and try again. Do not force the joint, otherwise the circlip will be damaged.
15 Check that the circlip holds the joint securely on the driveshaft end

3.4 Driving outer constant velocity joint off the driveshaft end

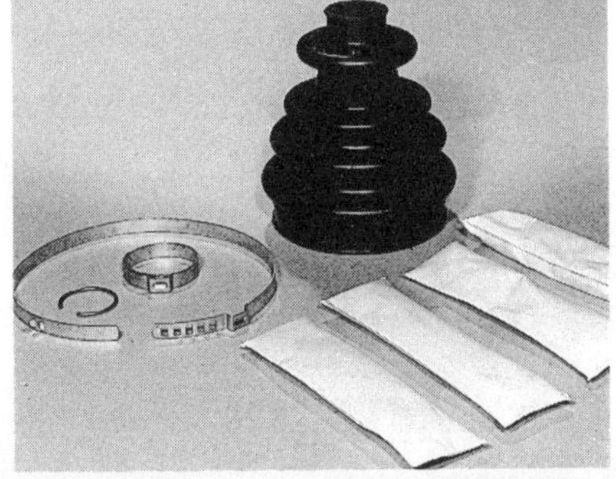

3.10 Components of constant velocity joint gaiter kit

3.12 Ensure stopper ring and new circlip are correctly located before refitting outer constant velocity joint

3.17 Using correct tool to tighten gaiter clip – side cutters can be used if care is exercised

3.22 Cutting inner constant velocity joint clip to release it

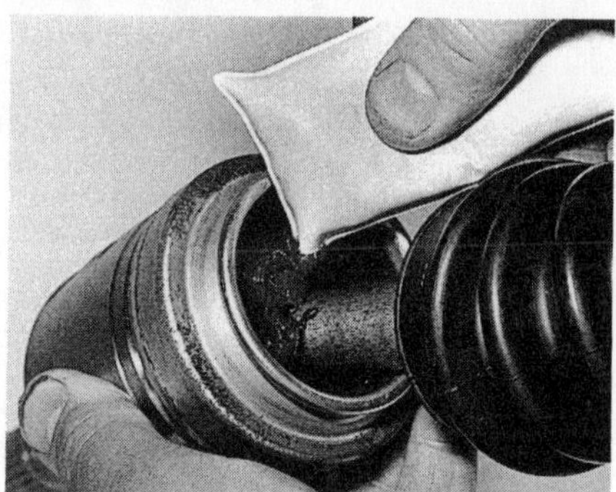

3.24 Pack the inner constant velocity joint with the grease supplied in the gaiter kit

then pack the joint with the grease supplied. Work the grease well into the ball tracks whilst twisting the joint, and fill the rubber gaiter with any excess.

16 Ease the gaiter over the joint and place the large retaining clip in position. Ensure that the gaiter is correctly located in the grooves on both the driveshaft and constant velocity joint.

17 Using pliers, pull the large retaining clip and fold it over until the end locates between the two raised tangs. Hold the clip in this position and bend the tangs over to lock the clip in position. Remove any slack in the gaiter retaining clip by carefully compressing the raised section of the clip. In the absence of the special tool, a pair of side cutters may be used (photo). Secure the small retaining clip using the same procedure.

18 Check that the constant velocity joint moves freely in all directions then refit the driveshaft to the car as described in Section 2.

Inner joint

19 Remove the outer constant velocity joint and gaiter as described above in paragraphs 1 to 5.

20 Tape over the splines on the driveshaft and carefully remove the outer constant velocity joint rubber gaiter.

21 Release the dynamic damper retaining clip and slide the damper off the end of the driveshaft; use liquid soap if necessary to aid damper removal and clean off any rust deposits or similar using emery cloth.

22 Release the inner joint gaiter retaining clips and slide the gaiter off the shaft (photo).

23 Thoroughly clean the joint using paraffin, or a suitable solvent, and dry it thoroughly. Carry out a visual inspection of the joint as described in paragraphs 8 and 9. If on inspection the constant velocity joint components are found to be worn or damaged, it will be necessary to renew the complete joint and shaft assembly, since the joint is not available separately. If the joint is in satisfactory condition, obtain a repair kit consisting of a new gaiter, retaining clips and the correct type and quantity of grease. Although not strictly necessary, it is also recommended that the outer constant velocity joint gaiter is renewed regardless of its apparent condition.

24 On reassembly, pack the joint with the grease supplied in the gaiter kit. Work the grease well into the ball tracks whilst twisting the joint (photo).

25 Clean the shaft, using emery cloth to remove any rust or sharp edges which may damage the gaiter, then slide the inner joint gaiter along the driveshaft.

26 Locate the gaiter in the grooves on the joint and shaft and fit both the large and small retaining clips. Secure the clips in position as described in paragraph 17 and check that the joint moves freely in all directions.

27 Lubricate the shaft and position a new retaining clip on the dynamic damper flange. Slide the dynamic damper onto the shaft so that its clip flange is innermost (faces the inner constant velocity joint). Position the damper as shown in Fig. 8.2 then secure it in position with the retaining clip.

28 Remove any surplus lubricant from the shaft and refit the outer constant velocity joint as described in paragraphs 11 to 18.

4 Driveshaft overhaul – general information

1 If any of the checks described in Chapter 1 reveal wear in any driveshaft joint, first remove the roadwheel trim or centre cap (as appropriate). If the staking is still effective, the driveshaft nut should be correctly tightened; if in doubt use a torque wrench to check that the nut is securely fastened and re-stake it, then refit the centre cap or trim. Repeat this check on the remaining driveshaft nut. Refer to Section 2 for further information.

2 Road test the vehicle and listen for a metallic clicking from the front as the vehicle is driven slowly in a circle on full lock. If a clicking noise is heard this indicates wear in the outer constant velocity joint. This means that the joint must be renewed; reconditioning is not possible.

3 If the outer joint is worn it can be renewed separately (see note, Section 1); the procedure is as described in Section 3, paragraphs 1 to 12.

4 If vibration, consistent with road speed, is felt through the car when accelerating, there is a possibility of wear in the inner constant velocity joints.

5 Remove the driveshafts, then dismantle them as described in Section 3 and check the joints; if any wear or free play is found, the inner joints are worn and the joint and shaft assembly must be renewed (see note, Section 1).

Chapter 9 Braking system

Contents

Specifications

System type

Dual hydraulic circuit split diagonally on models without ABS, and front to rear on models with ABS. Disc front brakes. Drum rear brakes except on models with ABS which have rear disc brakes. Vacuum servo-assistance on all models. Cable-operated handbrake on rear brakes

Front brakes

Type	Disc, with single piston sliding caliper
Disc diameter:	
Models without ABS	238 mm
Models with ABS	262 mm
Disc thickness:	
New:	
Models without ABS	12.80 mm
Models with ABS	21.60 mm
Minimum thickness after machining:	
Models without ABS	10.70 mm
Models with ABS	19.00 mm
Maximum disc run-out	0.02 mm
Brake pad friction material minimum thickness	3.0 mm

Rear brakes

Type:	
Models without ABS	Single leading shoe drum
Models with ABS	Disc, with single piston sliding caliper
Drum brakes:	
Drum diameter:	
New	200 mm
Maximum diameter after machining	204 mm
Maximum drum ovality	0.012 mm
Brake shoe friction material minimum thickness	2.0 mm
Disc brakes:	
Disc diameter	239 mm
Disc thickness:	
New	10 mm
Minimum thickness after machining	8 mm
Maximum disc run-out	0.06 mm
Brake pad friction material minimum thickness	3.0 mm

Torque wrench settings

	Nm	lbf ft
Servo vacuum hose to inlet manifold union bolt	50	37
Brake hose union bolt	38	28
Master cylinder to servo unit nuts	17	12
Master cylinder brake pipe union nuts	24	18
Brake caliper guide pin bolt	32	24
Brake disc retaining screws	12	9
Front brake caliper bracket to hub bolts	81	60
Pressure regulating valve union nuts	14	10
Rear brake drum retaining screws	10	7
Rear wheel cylinder to backplate bolts	10	7
Rear brake caliper bracket to trailing arm bolts	40	30
Handbrake cable to underbody retaining bolts	22	16
ABS modulator mounting nuts	7	5
ABS modulator brake pipe union nuts:		
Upper union nuts	15	11
Lower union nuts	24	18
ABS front wheel sensor retaining bolts	25	19
ABS rear wheel sensor retaining bolts	10	7
ABS wheel sensor wiring bracket bolts	10	7
ABS rear wheel sensor cover and cover strap bolts	10	7
Roadwheel nuts	100	74

1 General information

The braking system is of the servo-assisted, dual circuit hydraulic type. The arrangement of the hydraulic system is such that each circuit operates one front and one rear brake from a tandem master cylinder. Under normal circumstances both circuits operate in unison. However, in the event of hydraulic failure in one circuit, full braking force will still be available at two wheels. On models not equipped with an Anti-lock Braking System (ABS), a pressure regulating valve is also incorporated in the hydraulic circuit to regulate the pressure applied to the rear brakes and reduce the possibility of the rear wheels locking under heavy braking. On models equipped with ABS the pressure regulating valve is fitted is but it is non-operational.

All models are fitted with front disc brakes. Models equipped with ABS are fitted with ventilated discs whereas non-ABS models are fitted with solid discs. The disc brakes are actuated by single piston sliding type calipers which ensures that equal pressure is applied to each disc pad.

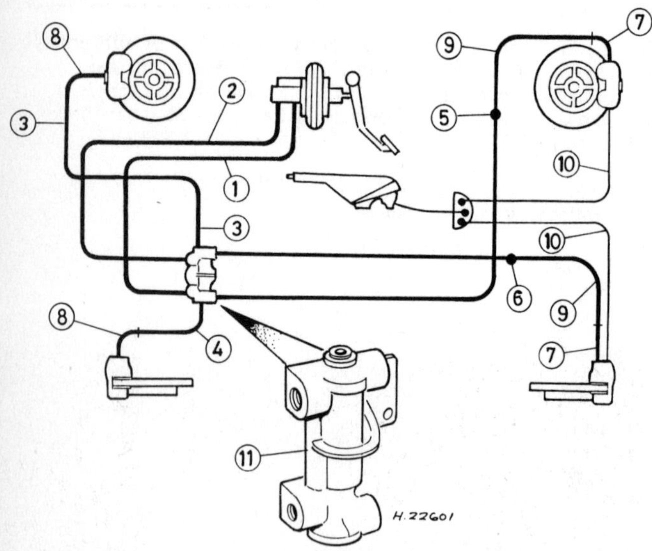

Fig. 9.1 Layout of braking system components – models without ABS (Sec 1)

1 Primary hydraulic circuit
2 Secondary hydraulic circuit
3 Brake pipe – pressure regulating valve to right-hand front hose
4 Brake pipe – pressure regulating valve to left-hand front hose
5 Brake pipe – pressure regulating valve to right-hand rear hose
6 Brake pipe – pressure regulating valve to left-hand rear hose
7 Brake pipe – hose to rear wheel cylinder
8 Brake flexible hose – brake pipe to front brake caliper
9 Brake flexible hose – rear wheel
10 Handbrake cable
11 Pressure regulating valve

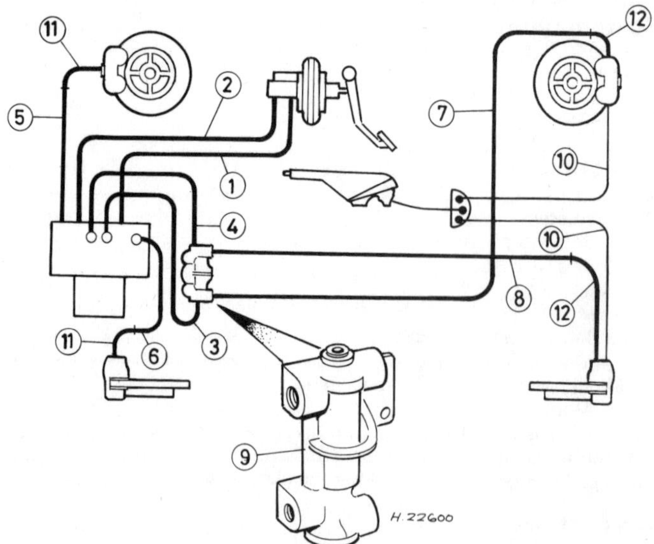

Fig. 9.2 Layout of braking system components – models with ABS (Sec 1)

1 Primary hydraulic circuit
2 Secondary hydraulic circuit
3 Brake pipe – modulator to pressure regulating valve
4 Brake pipe – modulator to pressure regulating valve
5 Brake pipe – modulator to right-hand front hose
6 Brake pipe – modulator to left-hand front hose
7 Brake pipe – modulator to right-hand rear hose
8 Brake pipe – modulator to left-hand rear hose
9 Pressure regulating valve
10 Handbrake cable
11 Brake flexible hose – brake pipe to front brake caliper
12 Brake flexible hose – brake pipe to rear brake caliper

Non-ABS models are fitted with rear drum brakes, incorporating leading and trailing shoes which are actuated by twin piston wheel cylinders. A self-adjust mechanism is incorporated to automatically compensate for brake shoe wear. As the brake shoe linings wear the footbrake operation automatically operates the adjuster mechanism quadrant which effectively lengthens the shoe strut and repositions the brake shoes to remove the lining to drum clearance.

ABS models are equipped with rear disc brakes. The disc brakes are actuated by a single piston sliding caliper which incorporates a mechanical handbrake mechanism. Refer to Section 21 for further information on the ABS operation.

On all models, the handbrake provides an independent mechanical means of rear brake application.

Note: *When servicing any part of the system, work carefully and methodically; also observe scrupulous cleanliness when overhauling any part of the hydraulic system. Always renew components (in axle sets, where applicable) if in doubt about their condition, and use only genuine Rover replacement parts, or at least those of known good quality. Note the warnings given in 'Safety first' and at relevant points in this Chapter concerning the dangers of asbestos dust and hydraulic fluid.*

2 Brake pedal - removal and refitting

Removal

1 Working from inside the car, undo the five screws and remove the right-hand lower facia panel.

2 Extract the R-clip and clevis pin securing the servo unit pushrod to the brake pedal.

3 Using pliers, carefully unhook the brake pedal return spring from the pedal to release all the spring tension.

4 Slacken and remove the nut and washers (as applicable) from the brake pedal pivot bolt then withdraw the pivot bolt and remove the brake pedal and return spring.

5 Examine all brake pedal components for signs of wear, paying particular attention to the pedal bushes, pivot bolt and return spring, renewing as necessary.

Refitting

6 Refitting is a reverse of the removal procedure, but lubricate the bushes, pivot bolt and clevis pin with a multi-purpose grease. On completion check the operation of the pedal and ensure it returns smoothly to the at rest position under the pressure of the return spring.

3 Vacuum servo unit - testing, removal and refitting

Testing

1 To test the operation of the servo unit, depress the footbrake several times to exhaust the vacuum, then start the engine whilst keeping the pedal firmly depressed. As the engine starts there should be a noticeable 'give' in the brake pedal as the vacuum builds up. Allow the engine to run for at least two minutes then switch it off. If the brake pedal is now depressed it should feel normal, but further applications should result in the pedal feeling firmer, with the pedal stroke decreasing with each application.

2 If the servo does not operate as described, inspect the servo unit check valve as described in Section 4.

3 If the servo unit still fails to operate satisfactorily, the fault lies within the unit itself. Repairs to the unit are possible, but special tools are required and the work should be entrusted to a suitably equipped Rover dealer.

Removal

4 Remove the air cleaner assembly as described in Chapter 4.

5 Remove the master cylinder as described in Section 7.

6 Disconnect the vacuum hose connection from the grommet on the servo unit taking great care not to damage or displace the sealing grommet (photo).

Fig. 9.3 Vacuum servo unit and pushrod fixings (Sec 3)

1 *Servo unit mounting nuts*
2 *Pushrod clevis pin*
3 *R-clip*

3.6 Master cylinder mounting nuts 'A' and servo vacuum hose connection 'B'

7 Working from inside the car, undo the five retaining screws and remove the right-hand lower facia panel.
8 Extract the R-clip and clevis pin securing the servo unit pushrod to the brake pedal.
9 Slacken and remove the four nuts securing the servo unit to the engine compartment bulkhead, then remove the unit noting the gasket which is fitted to the rear of the unit.

Refitting

10 Prior to refitting, check the servo unit to vacuum hose sealing grommet for signs of damage or deterioration and renew if necessary.
11 Fit a new gasket to the rear of the servo unit and reposition the unit in the engine compartment.
12 From inside the car ensure the servo unit pushrod is correctly engaged with the brake pedal then refit the servo unit mounting nuts and tighten them securely.
13 Refit the servo unit pushrod to brake pedal clevis pin and secure it in position with the R-clip.
14 Refit the right-hand lower facia panel tightening its retaining screws securely.
15 From inside the engine compartment carefully ease the vacuum hose connection back into position in the servo unit, taking care not to displace the sealing grommet.
16 Refit the air cleaner assembly as described in Chapter 4.
17 Refit the master cylinder as described in Section 7 of this Chapter.
18 On completion, start the engine and check for air leaks at the vacuum hose to servo unit connection and the operation of the braking system.

4 Vacuum servo unit check valve - removal, testing and refitting

Note: *The valve is only available as part of the vacuum hose assembly; do not try to remove it, the servo unit connection, or the inlet manifold union from the hose or air leaks may ensue, necessitating the renewal of the hose assembly.*

Removal

1 Carefully unplug the hose connection from the vacuum servo unit taking care not to damage the sealing grommet.
2 Unscrew the union bolt securing the vacuum hose assembly to the inlet manifold and withdraw the hose assembly from engine compartment. Remove the union bolt from the hose end and discard the sealing washers.

Testing

3 Examine the hose for damage, splits, cracks or general deterioration. Make sure that the check valve inside the hose is working correctly by blowing through the hose from the servo unit connection end. Air should flow in this direction, but not when blown through from the inlet manifold union. Renew the hose and check valve assembly if it is at all suspect.
4 Examine the servo unit sealing grommet for signs of damage or deterioration and renew if necessary.

Refitting

5 Position a new sealing washer on each side of the hose union and refit the hose to inlet manifold union bolt. Ensure that the hose union locating pin is correctly situated between the lugs on the manifold then tighten the union bolt to the specified torque setting (photo).
6 Carefully ease the hose connection into the servo unit sealing grommet taking care not to displace or damage the grommet.
7 On completion, start the engine and check the vacuum hose to servo unit connection for signs of air leaks.

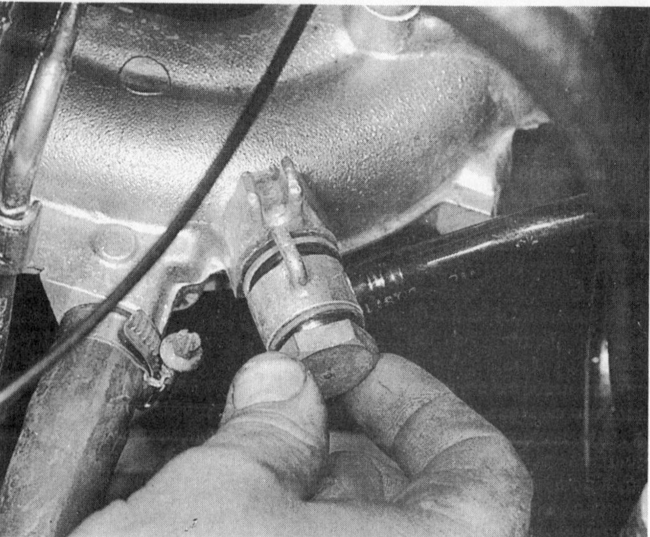

4.5 Ensure hose union locating pin is correctly located between the lugs on the inlet manifold

5 Hydraulic system - bleeding

Note: *Hydraulic fluid is poisonous; wash off immediately and thoroughly in the case of skin contact and seek immediate medical advice if any fluid is swallowed or gets into the eyes. Certain types of hydraulic fluid are inflammable and may ignite when allowed into contact with hot components; when servicing any hydraulic system it is safest to assume that the fluid is inflammable and to take precautions against the risk of fire as though it is petrol that is being handled. Hydraulic fluid is also an effective paint stripper and will attack plastics; if any is spilt, it should be washed off immediately using copious quantities of fresh water. Finally, it is hygroscopic (it absorbs moisture from the air) - old fluid may be contaminated and unfit for further use. When topping-up or renewing the fluid, always use the recommended type and ensure that it comes from a freshly-opened sealed container.*

General

1 The correct operation of any hydraulic system is only possible after removing all air from the components and circuit; this is achieved by bleeding the system.
2 During the bleeding procedure, add only clean, unused hydraulic fluid of the recommended type; never re-use fluid that has already been bled from the system. Ensure that sufficient fluid is available before starting work.
3 If there is any possibility of incorrect fluid being already in the system, the brake components and circuit must be flushed completely with uncontaminated, correct fluid and new seals should be fitted to the various components.
4 If hydraulic fluid has been lost from the system, or air has entered, because of a leak ensure that the fault is cured before proceeding further.
5 Park the car on level ground, switch off the engine and select first or reverse gear, then chock the wheels and release the handbrake.
6 Check that all pipes and hoses are secure, unions tight and bleed screws closed. Clean any dirt from around the bleed screws.
7 Unscrew the master cylinder reservoir cap and top the master cylinder reservoir up to the 'MAX' level line; refit the cap loosely and remember to maintain the fluid level at least above the 'MIN' level line throughout the procedure or there is a risk of further air entering the system.
8 There are a number of one-man, do-it-yourself brake bleeding kits currently available from motor accessory shops. It is recommended that one of these kits is used whenever possible as they greatly simplify the bleeding operation and also reduce the risk of expelled air and fluid being drawn back into the system. If such a kit is not available the basic (two-man) method must be used which is described in detail below.
9 If a kit is to be used, prepare the car as described previously and follow the kit manufacturer's instructions as the procedure may vary slightly according to the type being used; generally they are as outlined below in the relevant sub-section.
10 Whichever method is used, the same sequence must be followed (paras 11 and 12) to ensure the removal of all air from the system.

Bleeding sequence

11 If the system has been only partially disconnected and suitable precautions were taken to minimise fluid loss, it should be necessary only to bleed that part of the system (ie the primary or secondary circuit).

12 If the complete system is to be bled, then it should be done working in the following sequence:

Non-ABS models

(a) Left-hand front brake.
(b) Right-hand rear brake.
(c) Right-hand front brake.
(d) Left-hand rear brake.

ABS models

(a) Left-hand front brake.
(b) Right-hand front brake.
(c) Left-hand rear brake.
(d) Right-hand rear brake.

Bleeding - basic (two-man) method

13 Collect a clean glass jar, a suitable length of plastic or rubber tubing which is a tight fit over the bleed screw and a ring spanner to fit the screw. The help of an assistant will also be required.

14 Remove the dust cap from the first screw in the sequence. Fit the spanner and tube to the screw, place the other end of the tube in the jar and pour in sufficient fluid to cover the end of the tube.

15 Ensure that the master cylinder reservoir fluid level is maintained at least above the 'MIN' level line throughout the procedure.

16 Have the assistant fully depress the brake pedal several times to build up pressure, then maintain it on the final stroke.

17 While pedal pressure is maintained, unscrew the bleed screw (approximately one turn) and allow the compressed fluid and air to flow into the jar. The assistant should maintain pedal pressure, following it down to the floor if necessary and should not release it until instructed to do so. When the flow stops, tighten the bleed screw again, release the pedal slowly and recheck the reservoir fluid level.

18 Repeat the steps given in paragraphs 16 and 17 until the fluid emerging from the bleed screw is free from air bubbles. If the master cylinder has been drained and refilled and air is being bled from the first screw in the sequence, allow approximately five seconds between cycles for the master cylinder passages to refill.

19 When no more air bubbles appear, tighten the bleed screw securely, remove the tube and spanner and refit the dust cap. Do not overtighten the bleed screw.

20 Repeat the procedure on the remaining screws in the sequence until all air is removed from the system and the brake pedal feels firm again.

Bleeding - using a one-way valve kit

21 As their name implies, these kits consist of a length of tubing with a one-way valve fitted to prevent expelled air and fluid being drawn back into the system; some kits include a translucent container which can be positioned so that the air bubbles can be more easily seen flowing from the end of the tube (photo).

22 The kit is connected to the bleed screw, which is then opened. The user returns to the driver's seat and depresses the brake pedal with a smooth, steady stroke and slowly releases it; this is repeated until the expelled fluid is clear of air bubbles.

23 Note that these kits simplify work so much that it is easy to forget the master cylinder reservoir fluid level; ensure that this is maintained at least above the 'MIN' level line at all times.

Bleeding - using a pressure bleeding kit

24 These kits are usually operated by the reservoir of pressurised air contained in the spare tyre, although note that it will probably be necessary to reduce the pressure to a lower limit than normal; refer to the instructions supplied with the kit.

25 By connecting a pressurised, fluid-filled container to the master cylinder reservoir, bleeding can be carried out simply by opening each screw in turn (in the specified sequence) and allowing the fluid to flow out until no more air bubbles can be seen in the expelled fluid.

26 This method has the advantage that the large reservoir of fluid provides an additional safeguard against air being drawn into the system during bleeding.

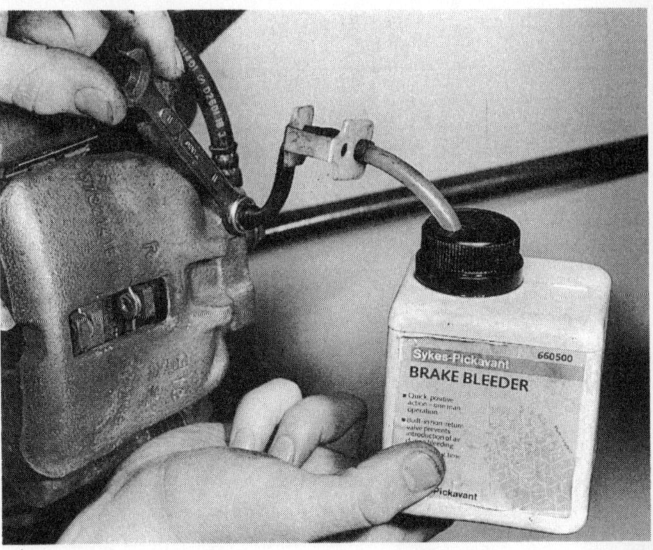

5.21 Bleeding the braking system using a typical one-way valve kit

27 Pressure bleeding is particularly effective when bleeding 'difficult' systems or when bleeding the complete system at the time of routine fluid renewal.

All methods

28 When bleeding is complete and firm pedal feel is restored, wash off any spilt fluid, tighten the bleed screws securely and refit their dust caps.

29 Check the hydraulic fluid level and top up if necessary (Chapter 1).

30 Discard any hydraulic fluid that has been bled from the system; it will not be fit for re-use.

31 Check the feel of the brake pedal. If it feels at all spongy, air must still be present in the system and further bleeding is required. Failure to bleed satisfactorily after a reasonable repetition of the bleeding procedure may be due to worn master cylinder seals.

6 Hydraulic pipes and hoses - renewal

Note: *Before starting work, refer to the note at the beginning of Section 5 concerning the dangers of hydraulic fluid.*

1 If any pipe or hose is to be renewed, minimise fluid loss by removing the master cylinder reservoir cap and then tightening it down onto a piece of polythene (taking care not to damage the sender unit) to obtain an airtight seal. Alternatively flexible hoses can be sealed, if required, using a proprietary brake hose clamp, while metal brake pipe unions can be plugged (if care is taken not to allow dirt into the system) or capped immediately they are disconnected (photo). Place a wad of rag under any union that is to be disconnected to catch any spilt fluid.

2 If a flexible hose is to be disconnected, unscrew the brake pipe union nut before removing the spring clip which secures the hose to its mounting bracket.

3 To unscrew the union nuts it is preferable to obtain a brake pipe spanner of the correct size; these are available from most large motor accessory shops (photo). Failing this a close-fitting open-ended spanner will be required, though if the nuts are tight or corroded their flats may be rounded-off if the spanner slips. In such a case a self-locking wrench is often the only way to unscrew a stubborn union, but it follows that the pipe and the damaged nuts must be renewed on reassembly. Always clean a union and surrounding area before disconnecting it. If disconnecting a component with more than one union make a careful note of the connections before disturbing any of them.

4 If a brake pipe is to be renewed it can be obtained, cut to length and with the union nuts and end flares in place, from Rover dealers. All that is then necessary is to bend it to shape, following the line of the original, before fitting it to the car. Alternatively, most motor accessory shops

6.1 Using a brake hose clamp to minimise the loss of fluid when flexible hoses are disconnected

6.3 Using a brake pipe spanner to unscrew a union nut

can make up brake pipes from kits, but this requires very careful measurement of the original to ensure that the replacement is of the correct length. The safest answer is usually to take the original to the shop as a pattern.

5 On refitting, do not overtighten the union nuts. The specified torque wrench settings, where given, are not high and it is not necessary to exercise brute force to obtain a sound joint. When refitting flexible hoses, always renew any sealing washers used.

6 Ensure that the pipes and hoses are correctly routed with no kinks and that they are secured in the clips or brackets provided. After fitting, remove the polythene from the reservoir and bleed the hydraulic system as described in Section 5. Wash off any spilt fluid and check carefully for fluid leaks.

7 Master cylinder – removal, overhaul and refitting

Note: *Before starting work, refer to the note at the beginning of Section 5 concerning the dangers of hydraulic fluid.*

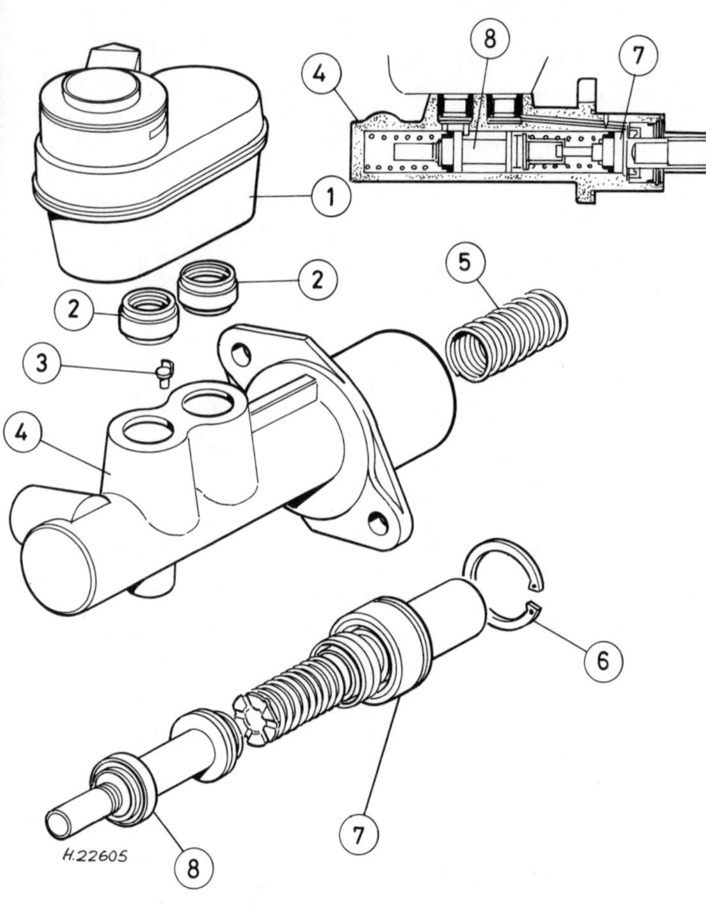

Fig. 9.4 Master cylinder cutaway and exploded view – models without ABS (Sec 7)

1 *Master cylinder reservoir*
2 *Mounting seals*
3 *Secondary piston stop pin*
4 *Master cylinder body*
5 *Spring*
6 *Circlip*
7 *Primary piston*
8 *Secondary piston*

Removal

1 Remove the master cylinder reservoir cap, having disconnected the sender unit wiring connector, and syphon the hydraulic fluid from the reservoir.

Note: *Do not syphon the fluid by mouth, as it is poisonous; use a syringe or an old poultry baster.*

Alternatively, open any convenient bleed screw in the system and gently pump the brake pedal to expel the fluid through a plastic tube connected to the screw (see Section 5).

2 Wipe clean the area around the brake pipe unions on the side of the master cylinder and place absorbent rags beneath the pipe unions to catch any surplus fluid. Unscrew the two union nuts and carefully withdraw the pipes. Plug or tape over the pipe ends and master cylinder orifices to minimise the loss of brake fluid and to prevent the entry of dirt into the system. Wash off any spilt fluid immediately with cold water.

3 Slacken and remove the two nuts and washers securing the master cylinder to the vacuum servo unit then withdraw the unit from the engine compartment. Remove the O-ring from the rear of the master cylinder and discard it.

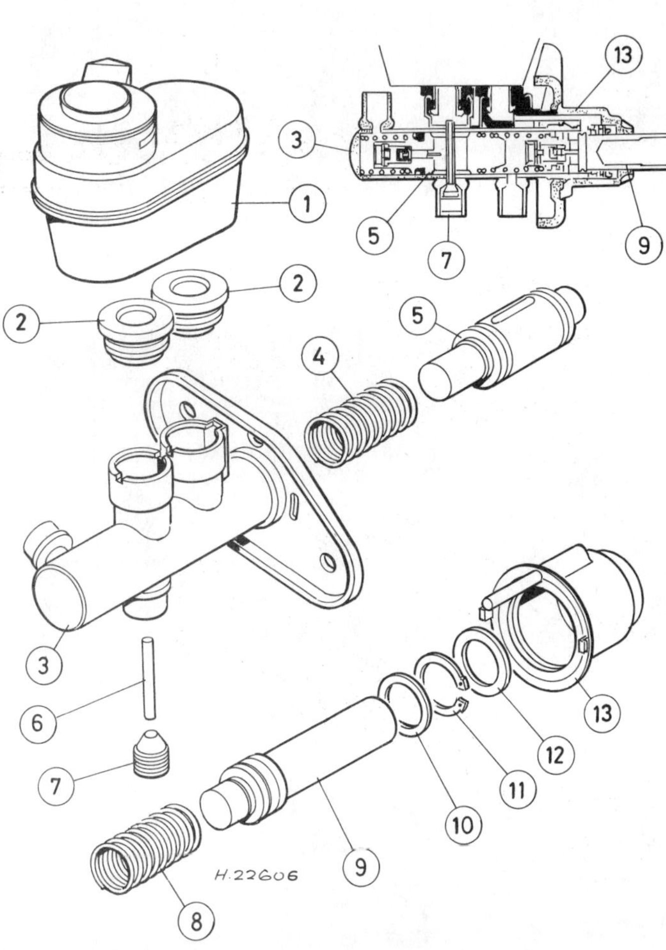

Fig. 9.5 Master cylinder cutaway and exploded view – models with ABS (Sec 7)

1 *Master cylinder reservoir*
2 *Mounting seals*
3 *Master cylinder body*
4 *Spring*
5 *Secondary piston*
6 *Retaining pin*
7 *Grub screw*
8 *Spring*
9 *Primary piston*
10 *Washer*
11 *Circlip*
12 *Flat washer*
13 *Dust cap*

Overhaul

Note: *Before attempting to overhaul the unit, check the price and availability of individual components and compare this with the price of a new or reconditioned unit, as overhaul may not be viable on economic grounds alone.*

4 Remove the master cylinder from the car as described above and clean it thoroughly.

5 Carefully prise the reservoir from the master cylinder body and remove two mounting seals.

6 Prepare a clean working surface and proceed as described under the relevant sub-heading.

Non-ABS models

7 Using a wooden dowel press the primary piston in as far as possible and extract the secondary piston stop pin from the reservoir inlet port, then remove the retaining circlip.

8 Noting the order of removal and the direction of fitting of each component, withdraw the piston assemblies with their springs and seals, tapping the body on to a clean wooden surface to dislodge them. If necessary, clamp the master cylinder body in a vice (fitted with soft jaw covers) and use compressed air of low pressure (applied through the secondary circuit fluid port) to assist the removal of the secondary piston assembly.

9 Thoroughly clean all components using only methylated spirit, isopropyl alcohol or clean hydraulic fluid as a cleaning medium. Never use mineral-based solvents such as petrol or paraffin which will attack the hydraulic system's rubber components. Dry the components immediately using compressed air or a clean, lint-free cloth.

10 Check all components and renew any that are worn or damaged. Check particularly the cylinder bores and pistons; the complete assembly should be renewed if these are scratched, worn or corroded. If there is any doubt about the condition of the assembly or of any of its components, renew it. Check that the body's inlet and bypass ports are clear.

11 If the assembly is fit for further use, obtain a repair kit. Renew all seals and sealing O-rings disturbed on dismantling as a matter of course; these should never be re-used. Renew also any other items included in the repair kit.

12 On reassembly, soak the pistons and the new seals in clean hydraulic fluid. Smear clean fluid into the cylinder bore.

13 Fit the new seals to their pistons using only the fingers to manipulate them into the grooves.

14 Insert the pistons into the bore using a twisting motion to avoid trapping the seal lips. Ensure that all components are refitted in the correct order and the right way round.

15 Press the secondary piston assembly fully up into the bore using a clean wooden dowel, then refit the stop pin.

16 Refit the primary piston assembly, then secure it in position with a new circlip.

17 Press the new mounting seals into the master cylinder body and carefully refit the reservoir ensuring that it is pressed fully into position.

ABS models

18 Carefully prise out the dust cap from the rear of the master cylinder body and remove the flat washer.

19 Using a wooden dowel press the primary piston in as far as possible and extract the circlip and washer. Withdraw the primary piston assembly and spring.

20 Undo the grub screw from the underside of the master cylinder body then use the wooden dowel to press the secondary piston into the body and withdraw the secondary piston retaining pin. Extract the secondary piston assembly and spring. If necessary the piston can be dislodged by tapping the master cylinder body on a wooden block.

21 Examine and overhaul the master cylinder components as described above in paragraphs 9 to 14.

22 Fit the spring to the secondary piston assembly and use a clean wooden dowel to press the assembly fully into the master cylinder bore. Align the slot in the piston with the retaining pin hole then insert the secondary piston retaining pin. Refit the grub screw and tighten it securely.

23 Fit the spring to the primary piston assembly and press the assembly into position using the wooden dowel. Refit the washer and secure the piston assembly in position with the circlip, ensuring that it is correctly located in its groove in the master cylinder bore.

24 Fit the flat washer and refit the dust cap to the rear of the master cylinder body.

25 Align the lugs on the new mounting seals with the slots in the master cylinder body and press them into position. Carefully refit the reservoir ensuring that it is pressed fully into the master cylinder body.

Refitting

26 Remove all traces of dirt from the master cylinder and servo unit mating surfaces and fit a new O-ring to the groove on the master cylinder body.

27 Fit the master cylinder to the servo unit ensuring that the servo unit pushrod enters the master cylinder bore centrally. Refit the master cylinder washers and mounting nuts and tighten them to the specified torque.

28 Wipe clean the brake pipe unions then refit them to the master cylinder ports and tighten them to the specified torque setting.

29 Refill the master cylinder reservoir with new fluid and bleed the hydraulic system as described in Section 5.

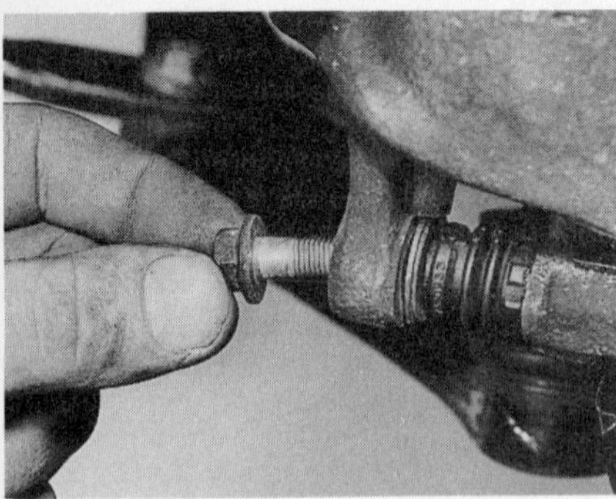
8.2A Remove the lower caliper guide pin bolt...

8.2B ...and pivot the caliper away from the disc

8.3 Remove the circular shim from the caliper piston

8.4 Remove the pads noting the correct position of the pad springs and shims

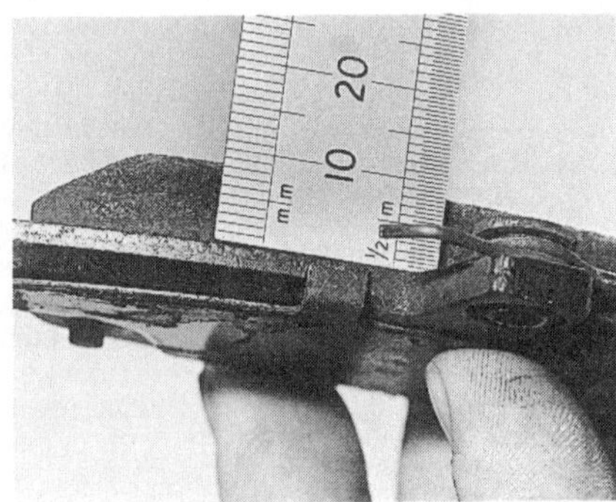

8.5 Measuring thickness of brake pad friction material

8.7 Check condition of guide pins and gaiters before refitting pads

8.8 Fit the pad retainer springs to the caliper bracket...

8.9 ...and install the shims on the pads

8 Front brake pads - renewal

Warning: *Renew both sets of front brake pads at the same time - never renew the pads on only one wheel as uneven braking may result. Note that the dust created by wear of the pads may contain asbestos, which is a health hazard. Never blow it out with compressed air and don't inhale any of it. An approved filtering mask should be worn when working on the brakes. DO NOT use petroleum-based solvents to clean brake parts. Use brake cleaner or methylated spirit only.*

1 Chock the rear wheels, firmly apply the handbrake then jack up the front of the car and support it on axle stands. Remove both front roadwheels.

2 Remove the lower caliper guide pin bolt whilst, if necessary, using a slim open-ended spanner to prevent the guide pin itself from rotating. Pivot the caliper away from the disc to gain access to the brake pads and tie it to the suspension strut using a piece of wire (photos).

3 Remove the circular shim which is fitted to the caliper piston (photo).

4 Remove the brake pads from the caliper mounting bracket whilst noting the correct position of the pad retainer springs and pad shims (photo).

5 First measure the thickness of friction material remaining on each brake pad (photo). If either pad is worn at any point to the specified minimum thickness or less, all four pads must be renewed. Also, the pads should be renewed if any are fouled with oil or grease; there is no satisfactory way of degreasing friction material once contaminated. If any of the brake pads are worn unevenly or fouled with oil or grease, trace and rectify the cause before reassembly. New brake pad kits are available from Rover dealers and include new shims and pad retainer springs.

6 If the brake pads are still serviceable, carefully clean them using a clean, fine wire brush or similar, paying particular attention to the sides and back of the metal backing. Clean out the grooves in the friction

material (where applicable) and pick out any large embedded particles of dirt or debris. Carefully clean the pad retainer springs and the pad locations in the caliper body and mounting bracket.

7 Prior to fitting the pads, check that the guide pins are free to slide easily in the caliper bracket and check that the rubber guide pin gaiters are undamaged (photo). Brush the dust and dirt from the caliper and piston but **do not** inhale it as it is injurious to health. Inspect the dust seal around the piston for damage and the piston for evidence of fluid leaks, corrosion or damage. If attention to any of these components is necessary, refer to Section 9.

8 On refitting, first fit the pad retainer springs to the caliper mounting bracket (photo).

9 Apply a thin smear of high-temperature brake grease (silicone- or PBC/Poly Butyl Cuprysil-based) or anti-seize compound (eg Holts Copaslip) to the sides and back of each pad's metal backing and to those surfaces of the caliper body and mounting bracket which bear on the pads. Fit the shims to the back of both pads and apply a thin smear of lubricant to the back of each shim. Do not allow the lubricant to foul the friction material (photo).

10 Install the brake pads in the caliper mounting bracket ensuring that the friction material is against the disc.

11 If new brake pads have been fitted, the caliper piston must be pushed back into the cylinder to make room for them. Either use a G-clamp or similar tool, or use suitable pieces of wood as levers. Provided that the master cylinder reservoir has not been overfilled with hydraulic fluid there should be no spillage, but keep a careful watch on the fluid level while retracting the piston. If the fluid level rises above the 'MAX' level line at any time the surplus should be syphoned off or ejected via a plastic tube connected to the bleed screw (see Section 7, paragraph 1).

12 Apply a thin smear of the recommended lubricant to the circular shim and fit the shim to the caliper piston. Pivot the caliper body down over the brake pads then refit the bottom guide pin bolt and tighten it to the specified torque wrench setting.

13 Check that the caliper body slides smoothly in the mounting bracket, then depress the brake pedal repeatedly until the pads are pressed into firm contact with the brake disc and normal (non-assisted) pedal pressure is restored.

14 Repeat the above procedure on the remaining front brake caliper.

15 Refit the roadwheels then lower the car to the ground and tighten the roadwheel nuts to the specified torque setting.

16 Check the hydraulic fluid level as described in Chapter 1.

9 Front brake caliper – removal, overhaul and refitting

Note: *Before starting work, refer to the note at the beginning of Section 5 concerning the dangers of hydraulic fluid and to the warning at the beginning of Section 8 concerning the dangers of asbestos dust.*

Removal

1 Chock the rear wheels, firmly apply the handbrake, jack up the front of the car and support on axle stands. Remove the appropriate front roadwheel.

2 Minimise fluid loss either by removing the master cylinder reservoir cap and then tightening it down onto a piece of polythene to obtain an airtight seal (taking care not to damage the sender unit), or by using a brake hose clamp, a G-clamp or a similar tool to clamp the flexible hose.

3 Clean the area around the union, then undo the brake hose union bolt and disconnect the hose from the caliper. Plug the end of the hose and the caliper orifice to prevent dirt entering the hydraulic system. Discard the sealing washers; they must be renewed whenever disturbed.

4 Unscrew the two caliper guide pin bolts whilst, if necessary, using a slim open-ended spanner to prevent the guide pins themselves from rotating.

5 Carefully lift the caliper assembly off the brake pads and remove the circular shim from the caliper piston. Note that the brake pads need not be disturbed and can be left in position in the caliper mounting bracket.

Overhaul

6 With the caliper on the bench, wipe away all traces of dust and dirt, but *avoid inhaling the dust as it is injurious to health.*

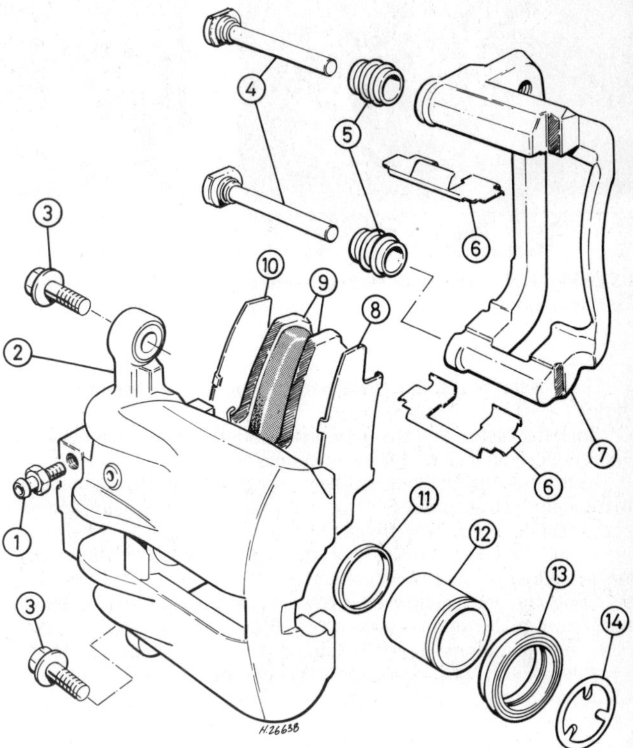

Fig. 9.6 Exploded view of the front brake caliper (Sec 9)

1	*Bleed screw*	8	*Inner pad shim*
2	*Caliper body*	9	*Brake pads*
3	*Guide pin bolt*	10	*Outer pad shim*
4	*Guide pin*	11	*Piston seal*
5	*Gaiter*	12	*Piston*
6	*Pad retainer spring*	13	*Dust seal*
7	*Caliper mounting bracket*	14	*Circular shim*

7 Withdraw the partially ejected piston from the caliper body and remove the dust seal. The piston can be withdrawn by hand, or if necessary pushed out by applying compressed air to the union bolt hole. Only low pressure should be required such as is generated by a foot pump.

8 Using a small screwdriver, extract the piston hydraulic seal whilst taking great care not to damage the caliper bore.

9 Withdraw the guide pins from the caliper mounting bracket and remove the guide pin gaiters.

10 Thoroughly clean all components using only methylated spirit, isopropyl alcohol or clean hydraulic fluid as a cleaning medium. Never use mineral-based solvents such as petrol or paraffin which will attack the hydraulic system's rubber components. Dry the components immediately using compressed air or a clean, lint-free cloth. Use compressed air to blow clear the fluid passages.

11 Check all components and renew any that are worn or damaged. Check particularly the cylinder bore and piston; these should be renewed (note that this means the renewal of the complete body assembly) if they are scratched, worn or corroded in any way. Similarly check the condition of the guide pins and their bores in the mounting bracket; both guide pins should be undamaged and (when cleaned) a reasonably tight sliding fit in the mounting bracket bores. If there is any doubt about the condition of any component, renew it.

12 If the assembly is fit for further use, obtain the appropriate repair kit; the components are available from Rover dealers in various combinations.

13 Renew all rubber seals, dust covers and caps, and the sealing washers disturbed on dismantling as a matter of course; these should never be re-used.

10.3 Using a micrometer to measure brake disc thickness

10.4 Using a dial gauge to check brake disc run-out

10.6 Remove the caliper assembly...

14 On reassembly, ensure that all components are absolutely clean and dry.
15 Soak the piston and the new piston (fluid) seal in clean hydraulic fluid. Smear clean fluid on the cylinder bore surface.
16 Fit the new piston (fluid) seal using only the fingers to manipulate it into the cylinder bore groove. Fit the new dust seal to the piston and refit it to the cylinder bore using a twisting motion, and ensure that the piston enters squarely into the bore. Press the piston fully into the bore, then secure the dust seal to the caliper body.
17 Apply the grease supplied in the repair kit, or a good quality high-temperature brake grease (silicone- or PBC/Poly Butyl Cuprysil-based) or anti-seize compound (eg Holts Copaslip), to the guide pins and fit the new gaiters. Fit the guide pins to the caliper mounting bracket ensuring that the gaiters are correctly located in the grooves on both the guide pin and mounting bracket.

Refitting

18 Refit the circular shim to the piston and carefully slide the caliper into position over the brake pads. Refit the caliper guide pin bolts and tighten them to the specified torque setting.
19 Position a new sealing washer on each side of the hose union and refit the brake hose union bolt. Ensure that the brake hose union is correctly positioned between the lugs on the caliper then tighten the union bolt to the specified torque setting.
20 Remove the brake hose clamp, where fitted, and bleed the hydraulic system as described in Section 5. Note that providing the precautions described were taken to minimise brake fluid loss, it should only be necessary to bleed the relevant front brake.
21 Refit the roadwheel then lower the car to the ground and tighten the roadwheel nuts to the specified torque.

10 Front brake disc – inspection, removal and refitting

Note: *Before starting work, refer to the warning at the beginning of Section 8 concerning the dangers of asbestos dust.*

Inspection

Note: *If either disc requires renewal, both should be renewed at the same time to ensure even and consistent braking.*

1 Chock the rear wheels, firmly apply the handbrake, jack up the front of the car and support on axle stands. Remove the appropriate front roadwheel.
2 Slowly rotate the brake disc so that the full area of both sides can be checked; remove the brake pads, as described in Section 8, if better access is required to the inboard surface. Light scoring is normal in the area swept by the brake pads, but if heavy scoring is found the disc must be renewed. The only alternative to this is to have the disc surface-ground until it is flat again, but this must not reduce the disc to less than the minimum thickness specified.
3 It is normal to find a lip of rust and brake dust around the disc's perimeter; this can be scraped off if required. If, however, a lip has formed due to excessive wear of the brake pad swept area then the disc's thickness must be measured using a micrometer (photo). Take measurements at four places around the disc at the inside and outside of the pad swept area; if the disc has worn at any point to the specified minimum thickness or less, the disc must be renewed.
4 If the disc is thought to be warped it can be checked for run-out (6 mm in from the disc's outer edge) either using a dial gauge mounted on any convenient fixed point, while the disc is slowly rotated, or by using feeler gauges to measure (at several points all around the disc) the clearance between the disc and a fixed point such as the caliper mounting bracket (photo). If the measurements obtained are at the specified maximum or beyond, the disc is excessively warped and must be renewed; however it is worth checking first that the hub bearing is in good condition (Chapters 1 and/or 10). Also try the effect of removing the disc and turning it through 180° to reposition it on the hub; if run-out is still excessive the disc must be renewed.
5 Check the disc for cracks, especially around the stud holes, and any other wear or damage. Renew it if any of these are found.

Removal

6 Unscrew the two bolts securing the caliper mounting bracket to the swivel hub and slide the caliper assembly off the disc (photo). Using a

10.7A ...and remove the disc retaining screws

10.7B If tight, the disc can be drawn off using two 8 mm bolts

11.2 Pressure regulating valve. In the event of failure fluid will seep from plug (arrowed)

piece of wire or string, tie the caliper to the front suspension coil spring to avoid placing any strain on the hydraulic brake hose.

7 Use chalk or paint to mark the relationship of the disc to the hub, then remove the two screws securing the brake disc to the hub and remove the disc. If the disc is a tight fit on the hub it can be drawn off by screwing two bolts into the jacking holes provided (photos).

Refitting

8 Refitting is the reverse of the removal procedure, noting the following points:

- *(a) Ensure that the mating surfaces of the disc and hub are clean and flat.*
- *(b) Align (if applicable) the marks made on removal.*
- *(c) If a new disc has been fitted, use a suitable solvent to wipe any preservative coating from the disc before refitting the caliper.*
- *(d) Tighten the disc retaining screws, caliper bracket bolts and roadwheel nuts to their specified torque wrench settings.*

11 Pressure regulating valve – testing, removal and refitting

Testing

1 A pressure regulating valve is incorporated in the hydraulic braking circuit to regulate the pressure applied to the rear brakes and reduce the risk of the rear wheels locking under heavy braking. The pressure regulating valve is mounted on the right-hand side of the bulkhead in the engine compartment.

2 Specialist equipment is required to check the performance of the valve, therefore if the valve is thought to be faulty the car should be taken to a suitably equipped Rover dealer for testing. However, in the event of an internal failure brake fluid will seep from the plug on the front face of the valve which is situated directly above the lower two hose unions (photo). Repairs are not possible and, if faulty, the valve must be renewed.

Removal

Note: *Before starting work, refer to the note at the beginning of Section 5 concerning the dangers of hydraulic fluid.*

3 Disconnect the sender unit wiring connector and unscrew the master cylinder reservoir filler cap. Place a piece of polythene over the filler neck and securely refit the cap (taking care not to damage the sender unit). This will minimise brake fluid loss during subsequent operations. As an added precaution place absorbent rags beneath the pressure regulating valve brake pipe unions.

4 Wipe clean the area around the brake pipe unions on the pressure regulating valve then make a note of how the pipes are arranged to use as a reference on refitting. Unscrew the union nuts and carefully withdraw the pipes. Plug or tape over the pipe ends and valve orifices to minimise the loss of brake fluid and to prevent the entry of dirt into the system. Wash off any spilt fluid immediately with cold water.

5 Slacken the two bolts which secure the valve to the bulkhead and remove it from the engine compartment.

Refitting

6 Refit the pressure regulating valve to the bulkhead and tighten its mounting bolts securely.

7 Wipe the brake pipe unions clean and refit them to the valve, using the notes made on dismantling to ensure they are correctly positioned. Tighten the union nuts to the specified torque.

8 Remove the polythene from the master cylinder reservoir filler neck and bleed the complete hydraulic system as described in Section 5.

12 Rear brake drum – removal, inspection and refitting

Note: *Before starting work, refer to the warning at the beginning of Section 13 concerning the dangers of asbestos dust.*

Removal

1 Chock the front wheels then jack up the rear of the car and support it on axle stands. Remove the appropriate rear wheel.

2 Use chalk or paint to mark the relationship of the drum to the hub.

3 With the handbrake firmly applied to prevent drum rotation,

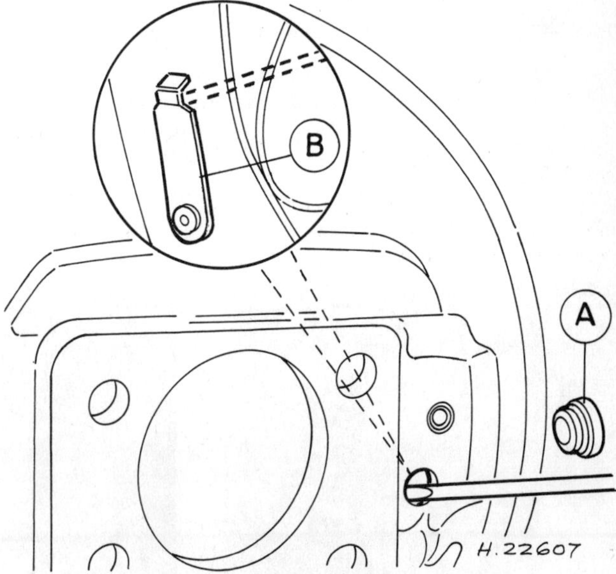

Fig. 9.7 Releasing the handbrake mechanism stop lever (Sec 12)

Remove the rubber grommet (A) and use a small screwdriver to depress the handbrake lever stop (B)

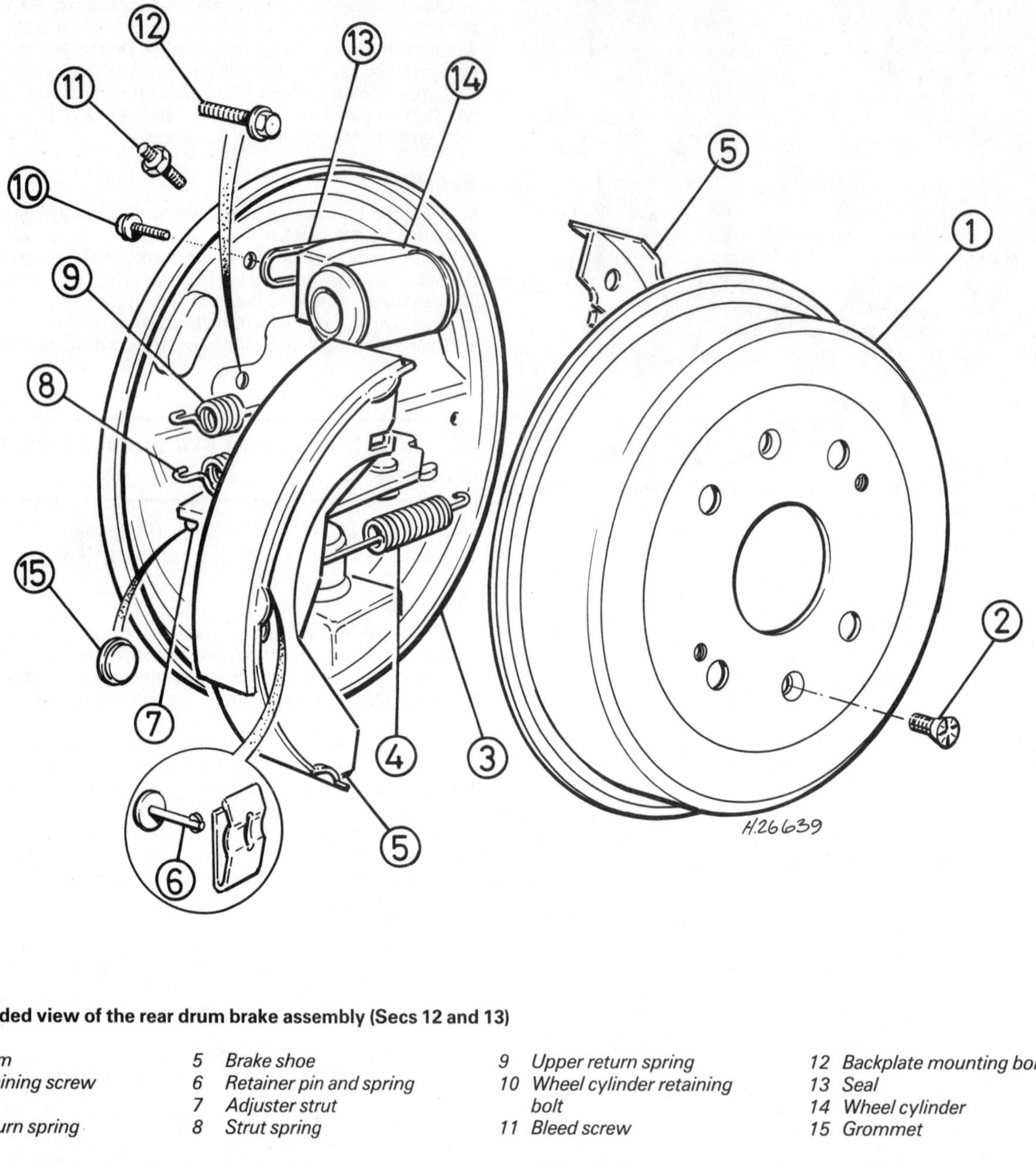

Fig. 9.8 Exploded view of the rear drum brake assembly (Secs 12 and 13)

1 Brake drum
2 Drum retaining screw
3 Backplate
4 Lower return spring
5 Brake shoe
6 Retainer pin and spring
7 Adjuster strut
8 Strut spring
9 Upper return spring
10 Wheel cylinder retaining bolt
11 Bleed screw
12 Backplate mounting bolt
13 Seal
14 Wheel cylinder
15 Grommet

12.3 Removing brake drum retaining screws

12.4A Disengage the handbrake lever stop to increase shoe to drum clearance

12.4B If necessary, the brake drum can be drawn off the hub using two 8 mm bolts

unscrew the drum retaining screws (photo). Fully release the handbrake cable and withdraw the drum.

4 If the drum will not pull away first check that the handbrake is fully released. If the drum will still not come away, remove the grommet from the rear of the backplate and, using a small screwdriver, disengage the handbrake lever stop from behind the lever to increase the shoe to drum clearance (Fig. 9.7). If removal still proves troublesome the brake drum can be drawn off by screwing two bolts into the jacking holes provided (photos).

Inspection

Note: *If either drum requires renewal, both should be renewed at the same time to ensure even and consistent braking.*

5 Working carefully, remove all traces of brake dust from the drum, but *avoid inhaling the dust as it is injurious to health.*

6 Scrub clean the outside of the drum and check it for obvious signs of wear or damage such as cracks around the roadwheel stud holes; renew the drum if necessary.

7 Examine carefully the inside of the drum. Light scoring of the friction surface is normal, but if heavy scoring is found the drum must be renewed. It is usual to find a lip on the drum's inboard edge which consists of a mixture of rust and brake dust; this should be scraped away to leave a smooth surface which can be polished with fine (120 to 150 grade) emery paper. If, however, the lip is due to the friction surface being recessed by excessive wear, then the drum must be renewed.

8 If the drum is thought to be excessively worn, or oval, its internal diameter must be measured at several points using an internal micrometer. Take measurements in pairs, the second at right angles to the first, and compare the two to check for signs of ovality. Provided that it does not enlarge the drum to beyond the specified maximum diameter, it may be possible to have the drum refinished by skimming or grinding; if this is not possible, the drums on both sides must be renewed.

Refitting

9 Refitting is the reverse of the removal procedure, noting the following points:

(a) *On fitting a new brake drum, use a suitable solvent to remove any preservative coating that may have been applied to its interior.*
(b) *Use a clean wire brush to remove all traces of dirt, brake dust and corrosion from the mating surfaces of the drum and the hub flange.*
(c) *Align (if applicable) the marks made on removal.*
(d) *Tighten the drum retaining screws and the roadwheel nuts to their specified torque wrench settings.*

13 Rear brake shoes - renewal

Warning: *Brake shoes must be renewed on both rear wheels at the same time - never renew the shoes on only one wheel as uneven braking may result. Also, the dust created by wear of the shoes may contain asbestos, which is a health hazard. Never blow it out with compressed air and don't inhale any of it. An approved filtering mask should be worn when working on the brakes. DO NOT use petroleum based solvents to clean brake parts. Use brake cleaner or methylated spirit only.*

1 Remove the brake drum as described in Section 12.

2 Working carefully, remove all traces of brake dust from the brake drum, backplate and shoes.

3 Measure the thickness of friction material remaining on each brake shoe at several points; if either shoe is worn at any point to the specified minimum thickness or less, all four shoes must be renewed as a set. Also, the shoes should be renewed if any are fouled with oil or grease; there is no satisfactory way of degreasing friction material once contaminated. Replacement shoes from Rover dealers are only available as an axle set.

4 If any of the brake shoes are worn unevenly or fouled with oil or grease, trace and rectify the cause before reassembly.

5 To remove the brake shoes, first remove the shoe retainer springs and pins, using a pair of pliers to press in each retainer clip until it can be rotated through 90° and released. Ease the shoes out one at a time from the lower pivot point to release the tension of the return spring, then disconnect the lower return spring from both shoes. Ease the upper end of both shoes out from their wheel cylinder locations, taking great care not to damage the wheel cylinder seals, and disconnect the handbrake cable from the trailing shoe. The brake shoe and adjuster strut assembly can then be manoeuvred out of position and away from the backplate (photos). Do not depress the brake pedal until the brakes are reassembled; wrap a strong elastic band around the wheel cylinder pistons to retain them.

6 With the brake shoe assembly on a bench, make a note of the fitted positions of the adjuster strut and springs to use as a guide on reassembly (photo). Carefully ease the adjuster strut from its slot in the trailing shoe and remove the short spring which secures the two components together. Detach the upper return spring and separate the shoes and strut.

7 Examine the adjuster strut assembly for signs of wear or damage paying particular attention to the adjuster quadrant and knurled wheel. If damaged the strut assembly must be renewed. Renew all the brake shoe return springs regardless of their apparent condition.

8 Peel back the rubber protective caps and check the wheel cylinder for fluid leaks or other damage and that both cylinder pistons are free to move easily. Refer to Section 14, if necessary, for information on wheel cylinder overhaul.

9 Prior to installation clean the backplate and apply a thin smear of high-temperature brake grease (silicone- or PBC/Poly Butyl Cuprysil-based) or anti- seize compound (eg Holts Copaslip) to all those surfaces of the backplate which bear on the shoes, particularly the adjuster and the wheel cylinder pistons. Do not allow the lubricant to foul the friction material.

10 Ensure the handbrake lever stop on the trailing shoe is correctly engaged with the lever and is pressed tight against the brake shoe (photo).

11 Fully extend the adjuster strut quadrant and fit the leading brake shoe into the adjuster strut slot, ensuring that the strut spring and knurled wheel are situated on the underside of the strut assembly. Using a screwdriver, move the quadrant away from the knurled wheel and set it in the minimum adjustment position.

13.5A Remove the brake shoe retainer springs...

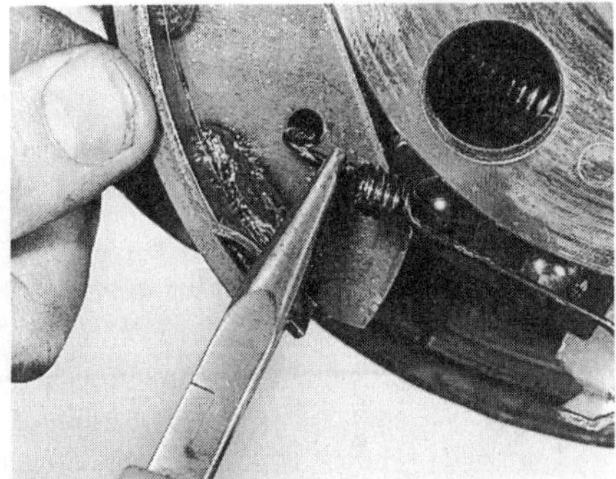
13.5B ...then unhook the lower return spring...

13.5C ...and manoeuvre the shoe and adjuster strut assembly away from the backplate

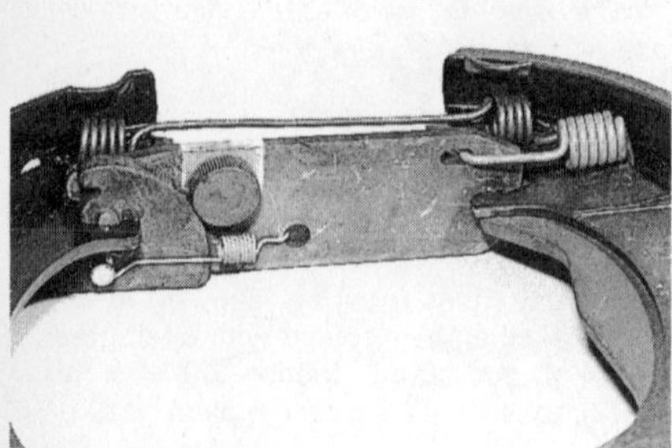

13.6 Correct fitted positions of adjuster strut and springs

13.10 Ensure the handbrake stop lever is correctly located

13.14 Prior to refitting the drum, reset the adjuster strut

12 Fit the upper return spring to its respective location on the leading shoe. Fit the trailing shoe to the upper return spring and carefully ease the shoe into position in the adjuster strut slot. Once in position fit the small spring which secures the trailing shoe to the strut assembly.
13 Remove the elastic band fitted to the wheel cylinder and manoeuvre the shoe and strut assembly into position on the backplate. Locate the upper end of both shoes with the wheel cylinder pistons and fit the handbrake cable to the trailing shoe operating lever. Fit the lower return spring to both shoes and ease the shoes into position on the lower pivot point.
14 Tap the shoes to centralise them with the backplate and refit the shoe retainer pins and springs and secure them in position with the retainer clips. Check that the adjuster quadrant is still in the minimum adjuster position and if necessary reset as follows. Place a block of wood between the trailing shoe and hub, to prevent the shoe moving forwards, then lever the leading shoe away from the hub to release the brake shoe return spring pressure on the adjuster quadrant. With the shoe held in this position reset the quadrant to the minimum adjustment setting (photo). Once the adjuster strut is correctly set, ease the leading shoe back into position then remove the block of wood and check that the shoes are still central.
15 Refit the brake drum as described in Section 12 and repeat the above operation on the remaining rear brake assembly.
16 On completion apply the footbrake repeatedly, to set the shoe to drum clearance, until normal (non-assisted) brake pedal operation returns.
17 Check the handbrake cable operation and, if necessary, adjust as described in Chapter 1.
18 Refit the roadwheels then lower the car to the ground and tighten the roadwheel nuts to the specified torque.
19 Check the hydraulic fluid level as described in Chapter 1.

14 Rear wheel cylinder – removal, overhaul and refitting

Note: *Before starting work, refer to the note at the beginning of Section 5 concerning the dangers of hydraulic fluid and to the warning at the beginning of Section 13 concerning the dangers of asbestos dust.*

Removal

1 Remove the brake shoes as described in Section 13, paragraphs 1 to 5.
2 Minimise fluid loss by removing the master cylinder reservoir cap and then tightening it down onto a piece of polythene to obtain an airtight seal (taking care not to damage the sender unit), or by using a brake hose clamp, a G-clamp or a similar tool to clamp the flexible hose.
3 Wipe away all traces of dirt around the brake pipe union at the rear of the wheel cylinder and unscrew the union nut. Carefully ease the pipe out of the wheel cylinder and plug or tape over its end to prevent dirt entry (photo).
4 Unscrew the two wheel cylinder retaining bolts from the rear of the backplate and remove the cylinder, noting the rubber sealing ring which is fitted between the cylinder and backplate.

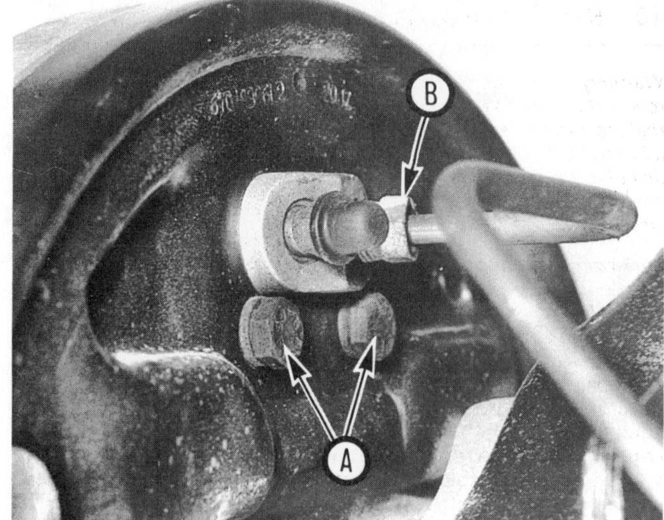

14.3 Wheel cylinder retaining bolts 'A' and brake pipe union nut 'B'

Overhaul

Note: *Before attempting to overhaul the unit, check the price and availability of individual components and the price of a new or reconditioned unit, as overhaul may not be viable on economic grounds alone.*

5 Remove the wheel cylinder from the car and clean it thoroughly.
6 Mount the wheel cylinder in a soft-jawed vice and remove the rubber protective caps. Extract the piston assemblies.
7 Thoroughly clean all components using only methylated spirit, isopropyl alcohol or clean hydraulic fluid as a cleaning medium. Never use mineral-based solvents such as petrol or paraffin which will attack the hydraulic system's rubber components. Dry the components immediately using compressed air or a clean, lint-free cloth.
8 Check all components and renew any that are worn or damaged. Check particularly the cylinder bore and pistons; the complete assembly must be renewed if these are scratched, worn or corroded. If there is any doubt about the condition of the assembly or of any of its components, renew it. Remove the bleed screw and check that the fluid entry port and bleed screw passages are clear.
9 If the assembly is fit for further use, obtain a repair kit. Renew the rubber protective caps, dust caps and seals disturbed on dismantling as a matter of course; these should never be re-used. Renew also any other items included in the repair kit.
10 On reassembly, soak the pistons and the new seals in clean hydraulic fluid. Smear clean fluid on the cylinder bore surface.
11 Fit the new seals to their pistons using only the fingers to manipulate them into the grooves. Ensure that all components are refitted in the correct order and the right way round.
12 Insert the pistons into the bore using a twisting motion to avoid

trapping the seal lips. Apply a smear of rubber lubricant to each piston before fitting the new rubber protective caps.

Refitting

13 Fit a new sealing ring to the rear of the wheel cylinder and place the cylinder in position on the backplate.
14 Refit the wheel cylinder retaining bolts and tighten them to the specified torque.
15 Tighten the brake pipe union nut and, if necessary, remove the clamp from the brake hose.
16 Refit the brake shoes as described in Section 13.
17 Bleed the hydraulic braking system as described in Section 5 noting that if precautions were taken to minimise fluid loss it should only be necessary to bleed the relevant rear brake. On completion check that both the footbrake and handbrake function correctly before taking the car on the road.

15 Rear brake pads – renewal

Warning: *Renew both sets of rear brake pads at the same time – never renew the pads on only one wheel as uneven braking may result. Note that the dust created by wear of the pads may contain asbestos, which is a health hazard. Never blow it out with compressed air and don't inhale any of it. An approved filtering mask should be worn when working on the brakes. DO NOT use petroleum-based solvents to clean brake parts. Use brake cleaner or methylated spirit only.*

1 Chock the front wheels then jack up the rear of the car and support on axle stands. Remove the rear roadwheels.
2 Undo the two bolts securing the caliper shield in position and remove the shield from the rear of the caliper.
3 Remove both the caliper guide pin bolts whilst, if necessary, using a slim open-ended spanner to prevent the guide pins from rotating. Lift the caliper away from the disc noting the upper pad spring which is fitted to the roof of the caliper. Tie the caliper to the suspension strut using a piece of wire to avoid straining the hydraulic hose.
4 Remove the brake pads from the caliper mounting bracket whilst noting the correct fitted positions of the brake pads, pad retainer springs and pad shims.
5 Inspect the pads as described in paragraphs 5 to 7 of Section 8 and, if necessary, renew as a complete axle set.
6 On refitting first fit the pad retainer springs to the caliper mounting bracket.
7 Apply a thin smear of Molykote M77 compound to the sides and back of each pad's metal backing and to those surfaces of the caliper body and mounting bracket which bear on the pads. In the absence of the specified lubricant, a good quality high-temperature brake grease (silicone- or PBC/Poly Butyl Cuprysil-based) or anti-seize compound (eg Holts Copaslip) may be used. Fit the shims to the back of both pads, noting that the smaller shim must be fitted to the piston side pad, and apply a thin smear of lubricant to the back of each shim. Do not allow the lubricant to foul the friction material.
8 Install the brake pads in the caliper mounting bracket ensuring that the friction material is against the disc, and the pad with the smaller shim attached is fitted on the inside.
9 If new pads have been fitted it will be necessary to retract the piston fully into the caliper bore by rotating it in a clockwise direction. This can be achieved using a suitable pair of circlip pliers as a peg spanner or by fabricating a peg spanner for the task. Provided that the master cylinder reservoir has not been overfilled with hydraulic fluid there should be no spillage, but keep a careful watch on the fluid level while retracting the piston. If the fluid level rises above the 'MAX' level line at any time the surplus should be syphoned off or ejected via a plastic tube connected to the bleed screw (see Section 7, paragraph 1).
10 Ensure the upper pad spring is still in position in the caliper then slide the caliper into position in its mounting bracket. When fitting the caliper ensure that the lug on the rear of the piston side pad is located in one of the piston slots. Refit the caliper guide pin bolts and tighten them to the specified torque setting.
11 Depress the footbrake to bring the piston into contact with the pads then check that the lug on the piston side pad is located in one of the piston slots. If necessary, remove the caliper and adjust the piston position as described above. Refit the shield to the rear of the caliper.
12 Repeat the above procedure on the remaining rear brake caliper.
13 Once both calipers have been done, repeatedly depress the brake pedal until normal (non-assisted) pedal operation returns, then repeatedly apply the handbrake to set the handbrake adjustment. Check the operation of the handbrake and, if necessary, adjust the cable as described in Chapter 1.
14 Refit the roadwheels then lower the car to the ground and tighten the roadwheel nuts to the specified torque.
15 Check the hydraulic fluid level as described in Chapter 1.

16 Rear brake caliper – removal, overhaul and refitting

Note: *Before starting work, refer to the note at the beginning of Section 5 concerning the dangers of hydraulic fluid and to the warning at the beginning of Section 15 concerning the dangers of asbestos dust.*

Removal

1 Chock the front wheels, then jack up the rear of the car and support on axle stands. Remove the rear wheel.
2 Undo the two bolts securing the caliper shield in position and remove the shield from the rear of the caliper.
3 Extract the spring clip and clevis pin securing the handbrake cable to the caliper handbrake lever then remove the clip securing the outer cable to its mounting bracket and detach the handbrake cable from the caliper.
4 Minimise fluid loss by removing the master cylinder reservoir cap and then tightening it down onto a piece of polythene to obtain an airtight seal (taking care not to damage the sender unit), or by using a brake hose clamp, a G-clamp or a similar tool to clamp the flexible hose.
5 Clean the area around the hose union, then undo the brake hose union bolt and disconnect the hose from the caliper. Plug the end of the hose and the caliper orifice to prevent dirt entering the hydraulic system. Discard the sealing washers; they must be renewed whenever disturbed.
6 Remove both the caliper guide pin bolts whilst, if necessary, using a slim open-ended spanner to prevent the guide pins from rotating, then lift the caliper away from the disc, noting the upper pad spring which is fitted to the roof of the caliper. Note that the brake pads need not be disturbed and can be left in position in the caliper mounting bracket.

Overhaul

7 With the caliper on the bench, wipe away all traces of dust and dirt, but *avoid inhaling the dust as it is injurious to health.*
8 Using a small screwdriver, carefully prise out the dust seal from the caliper bore.
9 Remove the piston from the caliper bore by rotating it in an anti-clockwise direction. This can be achieved using a suitable pair of circlip pliers as a peg spanner or by fabricating a peg spanner for the task. Once the piston turns freely but does not come out any further the piston can be withdrawn by hand, or if necessary pushed out by applying compressed air to the union bolt hole. Only low pressure should be required such as is generated by a foot pump.
10 With the piston removed, extract the circlip from inside the piston and withdraw the thrustwasher, spring and adjuster nut.
11 Remove the piston (fluid) seal whilst taking great care not to scratch the caliper bore.
12 Extract the circlip from the caliper bore and withdraw the spring cover, spring, spring seat, bearing and adjusting bolt. Then remove the adjusting bolt piston, noting the O-ring fitted to the rear of the piston, and withdraw the small pushrod.
13 Slacken and remove the handbrake lever retaining nut and washer and remove the return spring, lever and dust seal. Withdraw the handbrake mechanism cam from the caliper and remove the cam washer.
14 Withdraw the guide pins from the caliper mounting bracket and remove the guide pin gaiters.
15 Inspect all the caliper components as described in Section 9, paragraphs 10 to 13 and renew as necessary.
16 On reassembly ensure that all components are absolutely clean and dry.

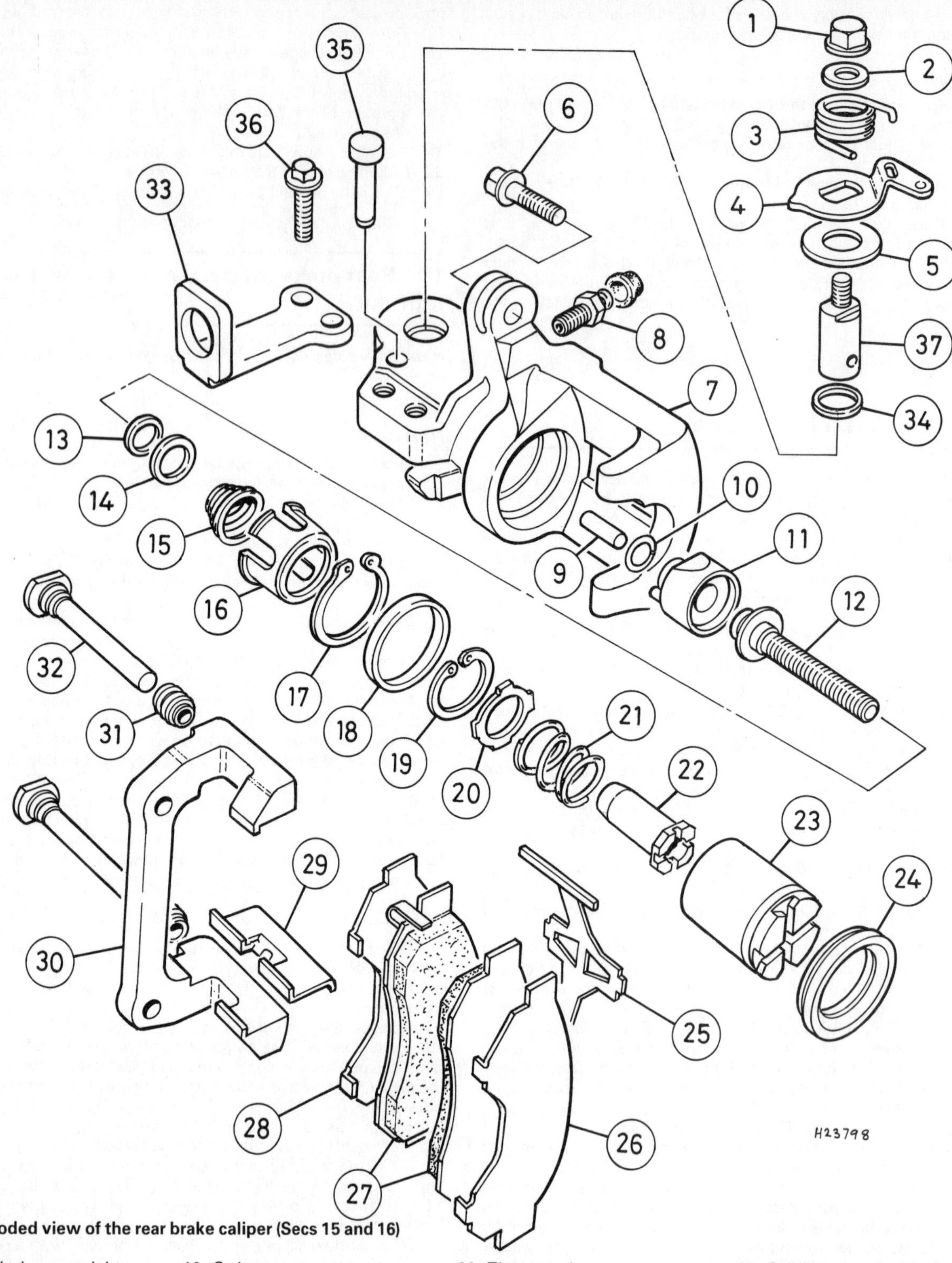

Fig. 9.9 Exploded view of the rear brake caliper (Secs 15 and 16)

1 Handbrake lever retaining nut
2 Washer
3 Return spring
4 Handbrake operating lever
5 Dust seal
6 Guide pin bolt
7 Caliper body
8 Bleed screw
9 Pushrod
10 O-ring
11 Adjusting bolt piston
12 Adjusting bolt
13 Bearing
14 Spring seat
15 Spring
16 Spring cover
17 Circlip
18 Piston seal
19 Circlip
20 Thrustwasher
21 Spring
22 Adjuster nut
23 Piston
24 Dust seal
25 Pad spring
26 Inner pad shim
27 Brake pads
28 Outer pad shim
29 Pad spring
30 Caliper mounting bracket
31 Gaiter
32 Guide pin
33 Handbrake cable mounting bracket
34 Cam washer
35 Pin
36 Bolt
37 Handbrake mechanism cam

17 Apply a good quality high-temperature brake grease (silicone- or PBC/Poly Butyl Cuprysil-based) or anti-seize compound (eg Holts Copaslip) to the handbrake mechanism cam and refit the cam washer and cam to the caliper. Fit the dust seal, lever, return spring and washer and tighten the handbrake lever retaining nut securely.
18 Fit a new O-ring to the adjusting bolt piston then insert the small pushrod into the rear of the piston and install the adjusting bolt piston assembly in the caliper bore. Operate the handbrake lever and check that the piston is free to move smoothly then refit the adjusting bolt, followed by the bearing and spring seat. Fit the spring, so that its tapered end is innermost, then install the spring cover. Secure all the above components in position with the circlip, ensuring that it is correctly seated in the groove in the caliper bore.
19 Locate the adjusting nut with the cutout on the inside of the caliper piston and refit the spring, thrustwasher and circlip. Ensure the circlip is correctly located in its groove.
20 Soak the piston and the new piston (fluid) seal in clean hydraulic fluid. Smear clean fluid on the cylinder bore surface.
21 Fit the new piston (fluid) seal using only the fingers to manipulate it into the cylinder bore groove and refit the piston assembly. Turn the piston in a clockwise direction, using the method employed on dismantling, until it is fully retracted into the caliper bore.
22 Fit the dust seal to the caliper ensuring that it is correctly located in the caliper and also the groove on the piston.
23 Apply the grease supplied in the repair kit, or a good quality high-temperature brake grease (silicone- or PBC/Poly Butyl Cuprysil-based) or anti-seize compound (eg Holts Copaslip), to the guide pins and fit the new gaiters. Fit the guide pins to the caliper mounting bracket ensuring that the gaiters are correctly located in the grooves on both the guide pin and mounting bracket.

Refitting

24 Ensure the upper pad spring is still in position in the caliper then slide the caliper into position in its mounting bracket. When fitting the caliper ensure that the lug on the rear of the piston side pad is located in the centre of the caliper piston at the point where the two piston slots cross. Refit the caliper guide pin bolts and tighten them to the specified torque setting.
25 Position a new sealing washer on each side of the hose union and refit the brake hose union bolt. Ensure that the brake hose union is correctly positioned between the lugs on the caliper then tighten the union bolt to the specified torque setting.
26 Remove the brake hose clamp, where fitted, and bleed the hydraulic system as described in Section 5. Note that providing the precautions described were taken to minimise brake fluid loss, it should only be necessary to bleed the relevant rear brake.
27 Refit the handbrake outer cable to its mounting bracket and secure it in position with the retaining clip. Ensure the return spring is located in the groove in the operating lever then refit the handbrake cable to lever clevis pin and secure it in position with the spring clip.
28 Depress the brake pedal several times until normal (non-assisted) operation returns then check and, if necessary, adjust the handbrake cable as described in Chapter 1.
29 Refit the shield to the rear of the caliper and tighten its retaining bolts securely.
30 Refit the roadwheel then lower the vehicle to the ground and tighten the roadwheel nuts to the specified torque.
31 Check the hydraulic fluid level as described in Chapter 1.

17 Rear brake disc - inspection, removal and refitting

Note: *Before starting work, refer to the warning at the beginning of Section 15 concerning the dangers of asbestos dust.*

Inspection

Note: *If either disc requires renewal, both should be renewed at the same time to ensure even and consistent braking.*

1 Chock the front wheels, then jack up the rear of the car and support on axle stands. Remove the appropriate rear roadwheel.
2 Inspect the disc as described in Section 10, paragraphs 2 to 5.

Removal

3 Undo the two caliper shield retaining bolts and remove the shield from the rear of the caliper.
4 Undo the two bolts securing the caliper mounting bracket to the trailing arm assembly and slide the caliper assembly off the disc. Using a piece of wire or string, tie the caliper to the rear suspension coil spring to avoid placing any strain on the hydraulic brake hose.
5 Use chalk or paint to mark the relationship of the disc to the hub, then remove the two screws securing the brake disc to the hub and remove the disc. If the disc is a tight fit on the hub it can be drawn off by screwing two bolts into the jacking holes provided.

Refitting

6 Refitting is the reverse of the removal procedure, noting the following points:

- (a) *Ensure that the mating surfaces of the disc and hub are clean and flat.*
- (b) *Align (if applicable) the marks made on removal.*
- (c) *If a new disc has been fitted, use a suitable solvent to wipe any preservative coating from the disc before refitting the caliper.*
- (d) *Tighten the disc retaining screws, caliper bracket bolts and roadwheel nuts to their specified torque wrench settings.*

18 Handbrake lever - removal and refitting

Removal

1 With the car parked on level ground, chock the roadwheels so that the car cannot move.
2 From inside the car, prise out the cover from the top of the rear centre console section to gain access to the two retaining screws. Undo the two screws and remove the rear console section.
3 Remove the handbrake lever rubber gaiter and disconnect the wiring connector from the lever warning lamp switch (photo).
4 Slacken and remove the handbrake cable adjusting nut from the rear of the lever and undo the bolts securing the handbrake lever assembly to the floorpan.
5 Lift the handbrake assembly out of position noting the spring which is fitted to the lever adjusting rod.

Refitting

6 Refitting is a reverse of the removal procedure. Prior to refitting the handbrake lever rubber gaiter, adjust the handbrake cable as described in Chapter 1.

18.3 Handbrake lever switch 'A', mounting bolts 'B' and adjusting nut 'C'

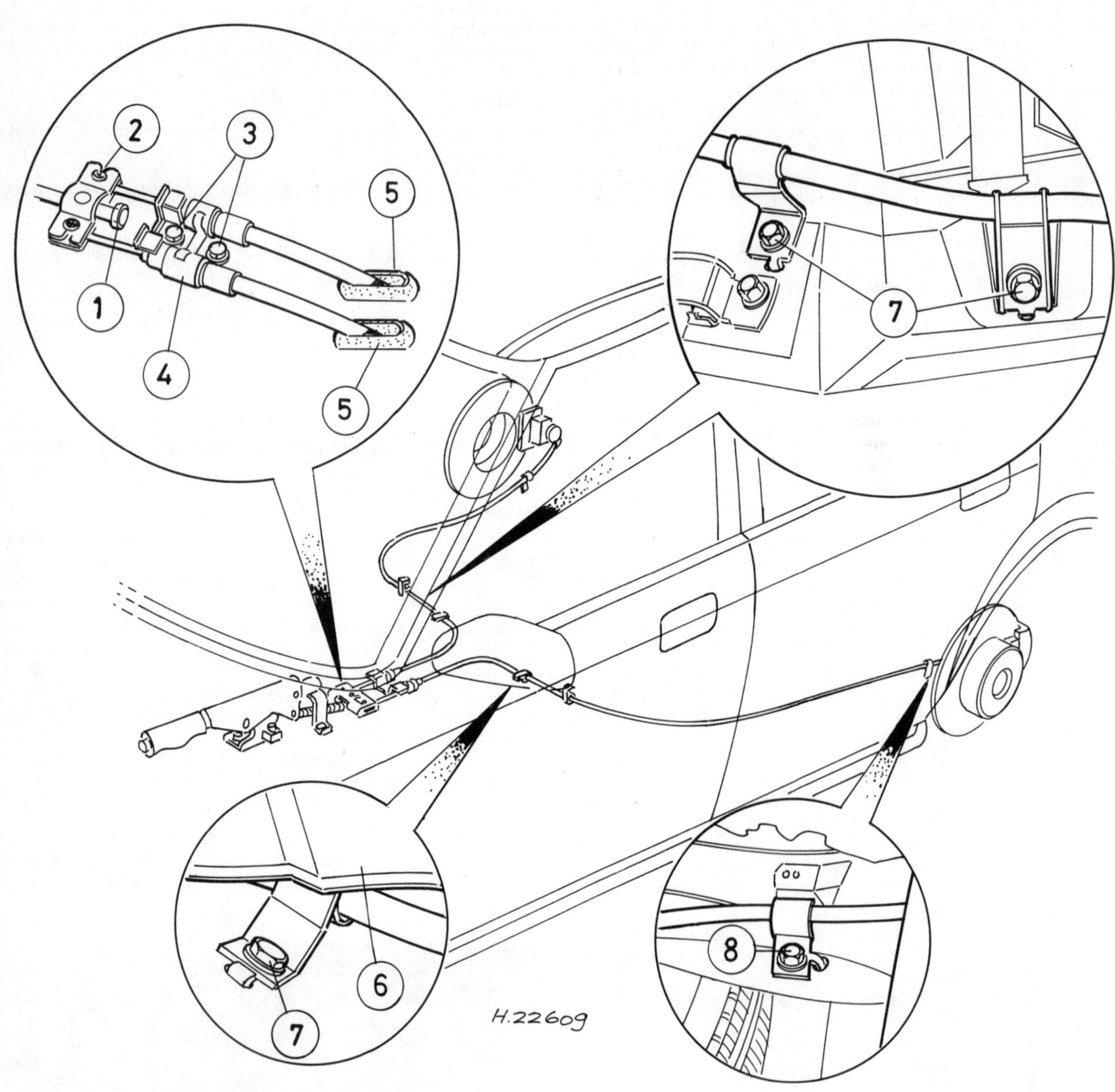

Fig. 9.10 Handbrake mechanism layout (Secs 18 and 19)

1 Handbrake cable adjuster nut
2 Equalizer plate
3 Bolts
4 Cable retaining plate
5 Grommet
6 Exhaust heatshield
7 Bolts – cable to body
8 Bolts – cable to trailing arm

19 Handbrake cables – removal and refitting

Removal

1 Firmly chock the front wheels then jack up the rear of the vehicle and support it on axle stands. The handbrake cable consists of two sections, a right- and left-hand section, which are linked to the lever assembly by an equalizer plate. Each section can be removed individually.

2 From inside the car, prise out the cover from the top of the rear centre console section to gain access to the two retaining screws. Undo

19.4 Handbrake cable adjusting nut 'A', equalizer plate 'B' and outer cable retaining plate bolts 'C'

19.6 Use a 12 mm spanner to compress the outer cable retaining tangs and withdraw the cable from the backplate

the two screws and remove the rear console section.

3 Slacken and remove the handbrake cable adjusting nut from the rear of the lever and disconnect the equalizer plate, noting the spring which is fitted to the lever adjusting rod.

4 Undo the two bolts securing the outer cable retaining plate to the floor pan (photo). Remove the retaining plate then detach the relevant inner cable from the equalizer plate and release the cable grommet from the floorpan.

5 On models equipped with ABS, working from underneath the car, remove the two brake caliper shield retaining bolts and remove the shield from the caliper. Extract the spring clip and clevis pin securing the handbrake cable to the caliper handbrake lever then remove the clip securing the outer cable to its mounting bracket and detach the handbrake cable from the caliper.

6 On non-ABS models remove the relevant rear brake drum as described in Section 12. Remove the trailing shoe retainer spring and pin, using a pair of pliers to press in the retainer clip until it can be rotated through 90° and released. Ease the trailing shoe out of the lower pivot point to release the tension of the return spring, then disconnect the lower return spring from both shoes. Disconnect the handbrake cable from the trailing shoe then use a 12 mm spanner to compress the handbrake cable retaining tangs and withdraw the cable from the rear of the backplate (photo).

7 On all models, release the main silencer from its three rubber mountings and carefully lower the tailpipe section to gain access to the heat shield. Undo the three heat shield retaining bolts and remove the shield from the vehicle underbody.

8 Work along the length of the cable section and remove all the bolts securing the outer cable to the vehicle underbody and trailing arm. Once free withdraw the cable from underneath the vehicle and, if necessary, repeat the procedure for the remaining cable section.

Refitting

9 Refitting is a reversal of the removal sequence noting the following points:

- (a) *Lubricate all exposed linkages and cable pivots with a good quality multi-purpose grease.*
- (b) *Ensure the outer cable grommet is correctly located in the floorpan and that all retaining bolts are tightened to the specified torque.*
- (c) *On non-ABS models relocate the trailing shoe and refit the brake drum as described in Section 12.*
- (d) *On all models, prior to refitting the rear centre console section, adjust the handbrake cable as described in Chapter 1.*

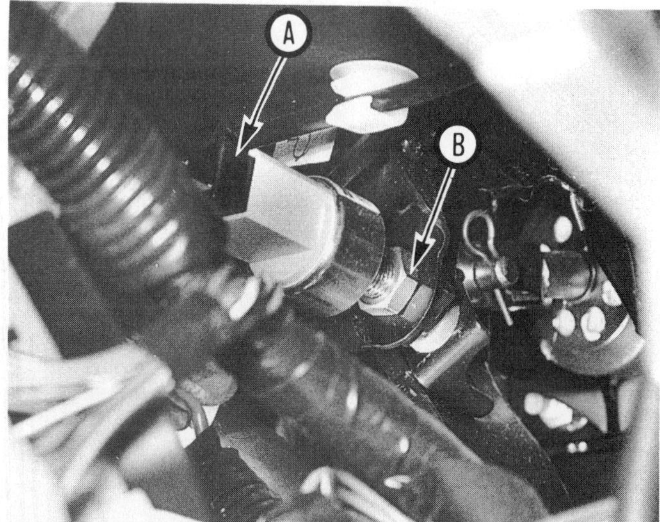

20.2 Stop lamp switch wiring connector 'A' and locknut 'B'

20 Stop lamp switch – removal, refitting and adjustment

Removal

1 Working from inside the car undo the five screws and remove the right-hand lower facia panel.

2 Disconnect the wiring connector from the stop lamp switch (photo).

3 Slacken the stop lamp switch locknut and unscrew the switch from its mounting bracket.

Refitting and adjustment

4 Screw the switch back into position in the mounting bracket.

5 Connect an ohmmeter across the stop lamp switch terminals and screw the switch in until an open circuit is present between the switch terminals. Gently depress the pedal and check that continuity exists between the switch terminals as soon as the pedal is depressed. If necessary, reposition the switch until it operates as specified.

6 Once the stop lamp switch is correctly adjusted, hold the switch stationary and tighten the locknut securely.

7 Connect the wiring connector to the switch and refit the lower facia panel.

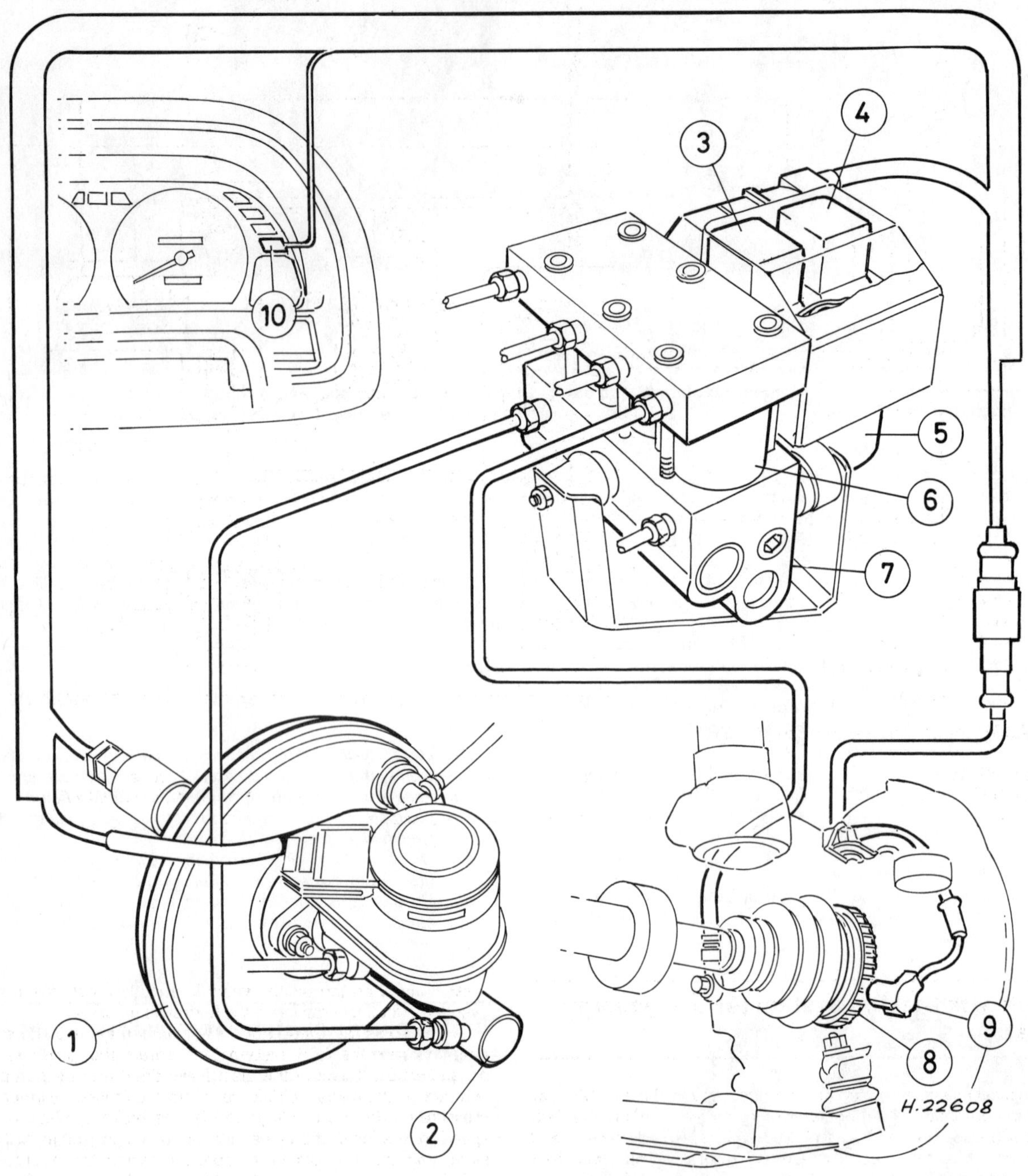

Fig. 9.11 ABS system components (Sec 21)

1 Servo unit
2 Master cylinder
3 Solenoid relay
4 Return pump relay
5 Return pump
6 Solenoid valves
7 Modulator block
8 Reluctor ring
9 Wheel sensor
10 System warning lamp

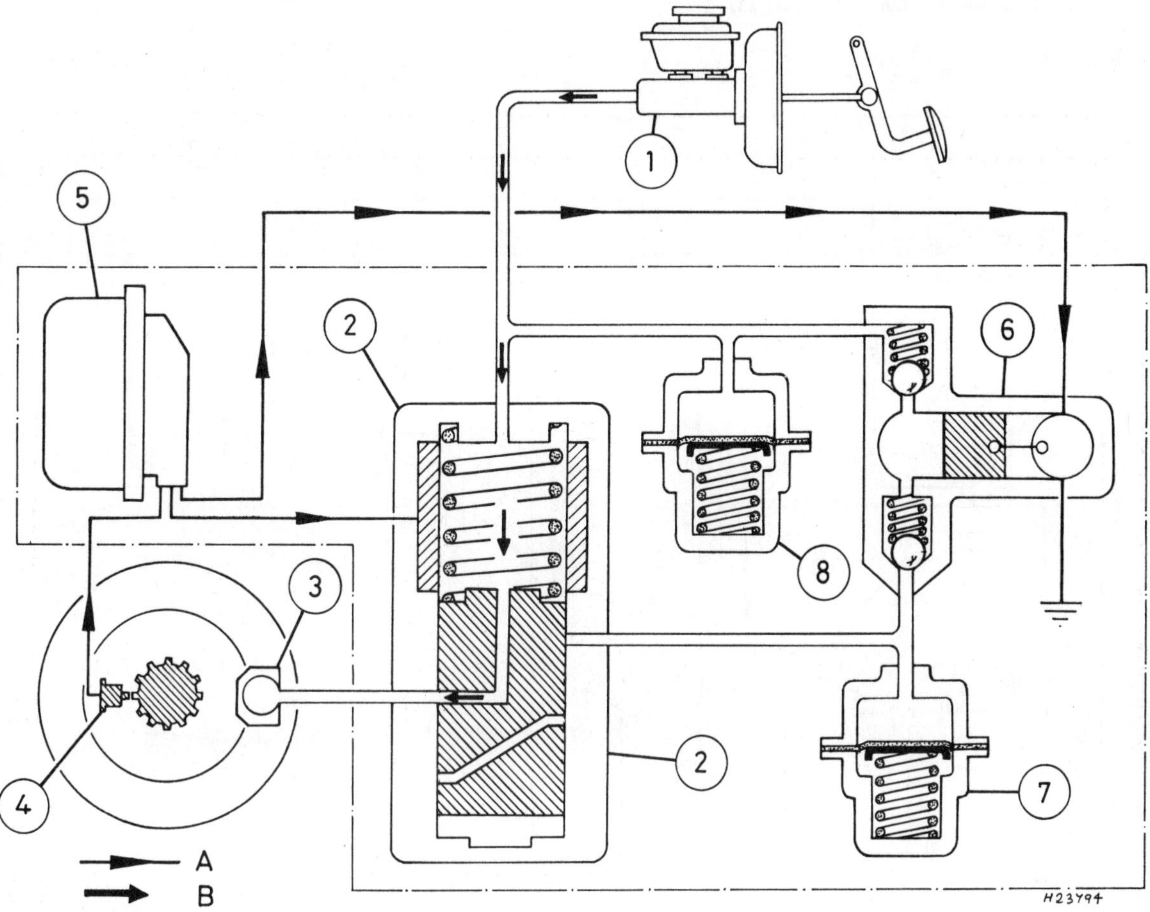

Fig. 9.12 ABS system normal operation (Sec 21)

1 *Master cylinder*
2 *Solenoid valve*
3 *Brake caliper*
4 *Wheel sensor and reluctor ring*
5 *Electronic Control Unit (ECU)*
6 *Return pump*
7 *Accumulator*
8 *Accumulator*
A *Flow of electrical signal*
B *Flow of brake fluid*

21 Anti-lock Braking System (ABS) – general information

ABS is available as an option on all models covered in this Manual. The system comprises of a modulator block which contains the ABS Electronic Control Unit (ECU), the hydraulic solenoid valves and accumulators, and the electrically-driven return pump, and four roadwheel sensors; one fitted to each wheel. The purpose of the system is to prevent wheel(s) locking during heavy braking. This is achieved by automatic release of the brake on the relevant wheel, followed by reapplication of the brake.

The solenoids are controlled by the ECU which itself receives signals from the four wheel sensors (one fitted on each hub), which monitor the speed of rotation of each wheel. By comparing these speed signals from the four wheels, the ECU can determine the speed at which the vehicle is travelling. It can then use this speed to determine when a wheel is decelerating at an abnormal rate compared to the speed of the vehicle and therefore predict when a wheel is about to lock. During normal operation the system functions in the same way as a non-ABS braking system does (Fig. 9.12).

If the ECU senses that a wheel is about to lock the ABS system enters the 'pressure maintain' phase (Fig. 9.13). The ECU operates the relevant solenoid valve in the modulator block which then isolates the brake caliper, on the wheel which is about to lock, from the master cylinder, effectively sealing in the hydraulic pressure.

If the speed of rotation of the wheel continues to decrease at an abnormal rate the ABS system then enters the 'pressure decrease' phase (Fig. 9.14), where the electrically-driven return pump operates and pumps the hydraulic fluid back into the master cylinder, releasing pressure on the brake caliper so that the brake is released. Once the speed of rotation of the wheel returns to an acceptable rate the pump stops and the solenoid valve opens allowing the hydraulic master cylinder pressure to return to the caliper which then reapplies the brake. This cycle can be carried out at up to 10 times a second.

The action of the solenoid valves and return pump creates pulses in the hydraulic circuit. When the ABS system is functioning these pulses can be felt through the brake pedal.

The solenoid valves connected to the front calipers operate independently, but the valve connected to the rear calipers, together with the pressure regulating valve, operates both calipers simultaneously.

The operation of the ABS system is entirely dependent on electrical signals. To prevent the system responding to any inaccurate signals, a built-in safety circuit monitors all signals received by the ECU. If an inaccurate signal or low battery voltage is detected, the ABS system is automatically shut down and the warning lamp on the instrument panel is illuminated to inform the driver that the ABS system is not operational.

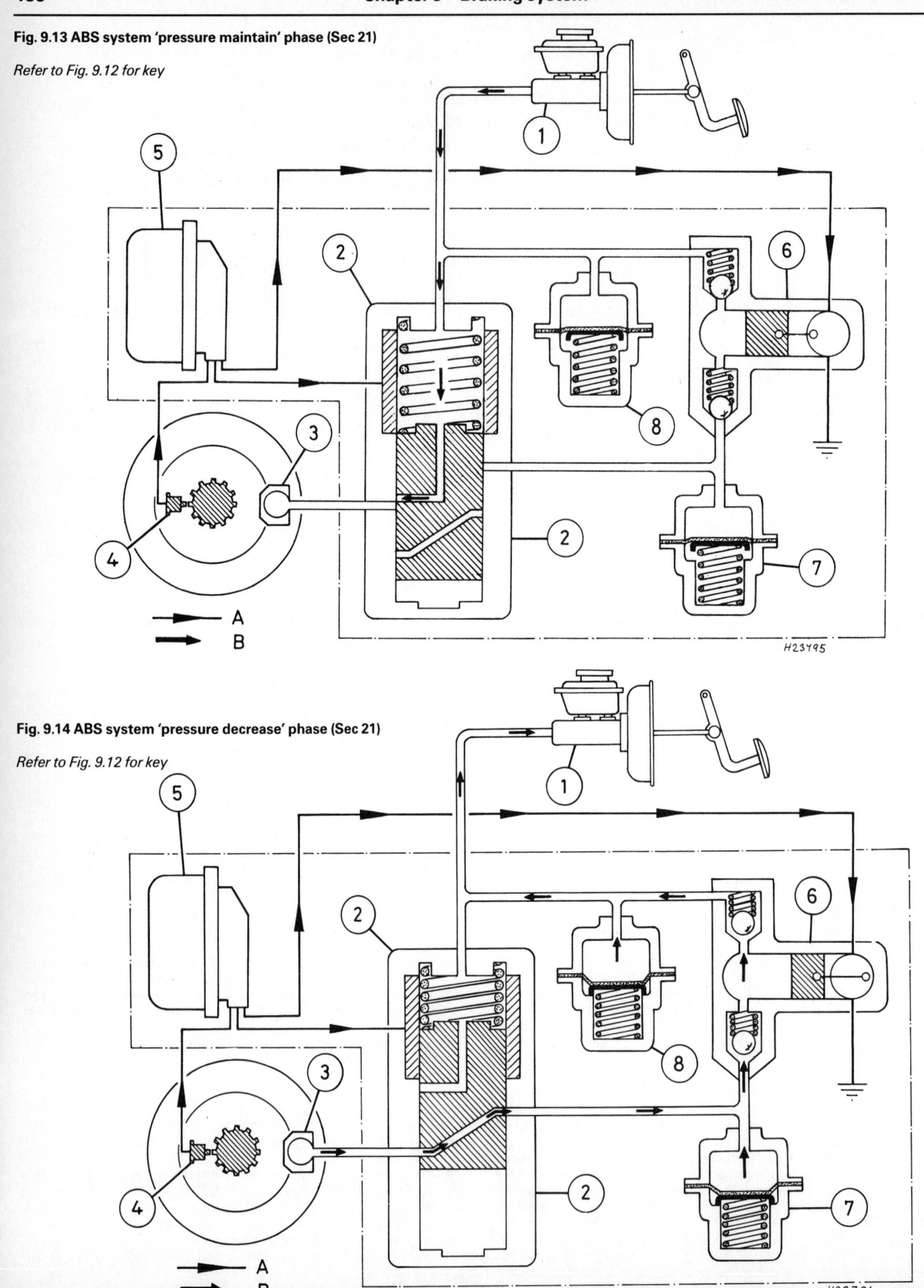

Fig. 9.13 ABS system 'pressure maintain' phase (Sec 21)

Refer to Fig. 9.12 for key

Fig. 9.14 ABS system 'pressure decrease' phase (Sec 21)

Refer to Fig. 9.12 for key

If a fault does develop in the ABS system the car must be taken to a Rover dealer for fault diagnosis and repair.

22 Anti-lock Braking system (ABS) components – removal and refitting

Modulator block

Note: *Before starting work, refer to the note at the beginning of Section 5 concerning the dangers of hydraulic fluid.*

Removal

1 Disconnect the battery negative terminal then undo the screw and remove the modulator relay cover.
2 Disconnect the wiring connectors from the modulator and free the wiring from its retaining clip on the unit.
3 Disconnect the sender unit wiring connector and unscrew the master cylinder reservoir filler cap. Place a piece of polythene over the filler neck and securely refit the cap (taking care not to damage the sender unit). This will minimise brake fluid loss during subsequent operations. As an added precaution place absorbent rags beneath the modulator brake pipe unions.
4 Wipe clean the area around the brake pipe unions then make a note of how the pipes are arranged to use as a reference on refitting. Unscrew the union nuts and carefully withdraw the pipes. Plug or tape over the pipe ends and valve orifices to minimise the loss of brake fluid and to prevent the entry of dirt into the system. Wash off any spilt fluid immediately with cold water.
5 Undo the earth lead retaining nut and slacken the modulator block mounting nuts. Disconnect the earth lead and remove the modulator assembly from the engine compartment.

Note: *Do not attempt to dismantle the modulator block assembly. Overhaul of the unit is a complex job and should be entrusted to a Rover dealer.*

Refitting

6 Refitting is the reverse of the removal procedure noting the following points:

(a) *Tighten the modulator block mounting nuts to the specified torque.*
(b) *Refit the brake pipes to their respective unions and tighten the union nuts to the specified torque.*
(c) *On completion, bleed the braking system as described in Section 5.*

Front wheel sensor

Removal

7 Chock the rear wheels, firmly apply the handbrake, jack up the front of the car and support on axle stands. Remove the appropriate front roadwheel.
8 From inside the engine compartment, disconnect the relevant sensor wiring connector and displace the sensor wiring grommet.
9 From underneath the car, pull the sensor wiring lead through the wing valance then undo the sensor lead bracket retaining bolts and remove the brackets.
10 Slacken and remove the two bolts securing the sensor unit to the wheel hub then remove the sensor and lead assembly.

Refitting

11 Refitting is the reverse of the removal procedure noting the following points:

(a) *Ensure that the sensor and hub sealing faces are clean then refit the sensor and tighten its retaining bolts to the specified torque.*
(b) *Ensure the sensor wiring is correctly routed and all bracket retaining bolts are tightened to the specified torque.*

Rear wheel sensor

Removal

12 Chock the front wheels then jack up the rear of the vehicle and support it on axle stands. Remove the appropriate roadwheel.
13 Trace the wiring back from the sensor to the wiring connector then free the connector from its retaining clips and disconnect it.
14 Undo the sensor lead bracket retaining bolts and remove the brackets.
15 Slacken and remove the bolt securing the strap to the sensor cover then undo the sensor cover retaining bolts and remove the cover.
16 Undo the two bolts securing the sensor to the rear hub assembly and remove it from the car along with the shim which is fitted behind it.

Refitting

17 Refitting is the reverse of the removal procedure noting the following points:

(a) *Ensure the sensor and hub sealing faces are clean then install the sensor and shim and tighten the sensor retaining bolts to the specified torque.*
(b) *Refit the sensor cover, cover strap retaining bolt and sensor lead brackets and tighten all retaining bolts to the specified torque.*
(c) *Reconnect the sensor lead wiring connector and refit the connector to its retaining clip.*

Reluctor rings

Note: *The reluctor rings are not available separately. The front rings being available only as an integral part of the outer constant velocity joint assembly and the rear rings being available only as an integral part of the rear hub.*

General

18 The front reluctor rings are situated on the outer constant velocity joint and the rear reluctor rings are part of the stub axle assembly. Examine the rings for signs of damage such as chipped or missing teeth and renew as necessary (see note above). Refer to Chapter 8 for information on CV joint renewal, and Chapter 10 for details of rear hub renewal.

Relays

General

19 Both the solenoid relay and return pump relay are located in the modulator block assembly. To gain access to them undo the relay cover retaining screw and lift off the cover. Either relay can then be simply pulled out of position. Refer to Chapter 12 for further information on relays.

Chapter 10 Suspension and steering

Contents

Specifications

Front suspension

Type .... Fully independent by MacPherson struts with coil springs and integral shock absorbers. Anti-roll bar mounted onto both lower suspension arms

Rear suspension

Type .... Fully independent double wishbone type, by trailing arms with transverse lateral links, suspension struts with coil springs and integral shock absorbers

Steering

Type	Rack and pinion, power-assisted steering available as an option
Turns lock-to-lock:	
Manual steering	4.0
Power-assisted steering	3.4
Power-assisted steering fluid	Automatic transmission fluid to Dexron II D specification (Duckhams Uni-Matic or D-Matic Automatic Transmission Fluid)

Wheel alignment and steering angles

Note: *All measurements are with car at kerb weight (see 'General dimensions and weights')*

Toe-out in turns	Inside roadwheel 17° 17′, outside roadwheel 16° 21′ ± 2′
Camber angle:	
Front	0° 20′ negative ± 0° 10′
Rear	0° 50′ negative to 0° 50′
Castor angle:	
Front	1° 59′ positive ± 0° 30′
Rear	N/A
Steering axis inclination (SAI) or kingpin inclination (KPI)	12°
Toe setting:	
Front	0° 10′ ± 0° 15′ toe-out
Rear	0° 11′ ± 0° 7.5′ toe-in (each wheel)

Roadwheels

Type:	
214 GSi	Steel (Alloy optional)
All other models	Steel
Size:	
214 S without ABS	4.5 x 13
214 S with ABS, 214, 414 Si and SLi	5 x 14
214 GSi:	
Standard (steel wheels)	5 x 14
Optional (alloy wheels)	5.5 x 14

Tyres

Type	Tubeless, steel-braced radial	
Size:		
214 S without ABS	155 SR 13	
214 S with ABS, 214, 414 Si and SLi	175/65 TR 14	
214 GSi:		
Standard (steel wheels)	175/65 TR 14	
Optional (alloy wheels)	185/60 HR 14	
Pressures (cold) - 155 SR 13 tyres:	**Front**	**Rear**
Normal driving conditions	2.1 bars (30 lbf/in^2)	2.1 bars (30 lbf/in^2)
Loads in excess of four persons	2.1 bars (30 lbf/in^2)	2.3 bars (34 lbf/in^2)
Speeds in excess of 100 mph - all loads	2.2 bars (32 lbf/in^2)	2.2 bars (32 lbf/in^2)
Pressures (cold) - 175/65 TR 14 tyres:	**Front**	**Rear**
All loads - up to 100 mph	2.1 bars (30 lbf/in^2)	2.1 bars (30 lbf/in^2)
All loads - over 100 mph	2.2 bars (32 lbf/in^2)	2.2 bars (32 lbf/in^2)
Pressures (cold) - 185/60 HR 14 tyres:	**Front**	**Rear**
All loads - up to 100 mph	2.1 bars (30 lbf/in^2)	2.1 bars (30 lbf/in^2)
All loads - over 100 mph	2.5 bars (36 lbf/in^2)	2.5 bars (36 lbf/in^2)

Note: *Pressures apply only to original equipment tyres and may vary if any other make or type is fitted; check with the tyre manufacturer or supplier for correct pressures if necessary*

Torque wrench settings

	Nm	lbf ft
Front suspension		
Driveshaft retaining nut	185	137
Front suspension strut:		
Upper mounting nuts	32	24
Swivel hub pinch-bolt	100	74
Brake hose clamp bolt	25	19
Upper mounting plate retaining nut	40	30
Anti-roll bar:		
Mounting clamp bolts	15	11
Connecting link bolts	45	33
Tie bar:		
Lower suspension arm bolts	80	59
Retaining nut	55	41
Lower arm:		
Balljoint retaining nut	60	44
Body pivot bolt	45	33
Rear suspension		
Rear hub nut	185	137
Drum brake backplate to trailing arm bolts	65	48
Disc brake shield to trailing arm bolts	15	11
Brake hose bracket to trailing arm bolts	15	11
Handbrake cable to trailing arm bolts	22	16
Stub axle:		
Retaining nut	170	126
Trailing arm bolts	55	41
Rear suspension strut:		
Upper mounting nuts	32	24
Lower mounting bolt	45	33
Upper mounting plate retaining nut	40	30
Lateral link pivot bolts	45	33
Trailing arm mounting bolts	83	61
Steering		
Steering wheel nut	52	39
Steering column:		
Lower mounting bolt and nut	20	15
Upper mounting bolts	20	15
Upper mounting nuts	13	10
Universal joint pinch-bolts	30	22
Steering gear mounting bolts	42	31
Steering gear mounting nuts	25	19

Torque wrench settings (continued)

	Nm	lbf ft
Power-assisted steering gear:		
Feed pipe union nut	39	29
Return pipe union nut	31	22
Track rod balljoint:		
Retaining nut	44	32
Locknut	55	41
Power steering pump:		
Mounting bolts	48	35
Outlet pipe union nut	55	41
Pulley retaining bolts	9	6
Power steering oil cooler mounting bolts	9	6
Roadwheels		
Roadwheel nuts	100	74

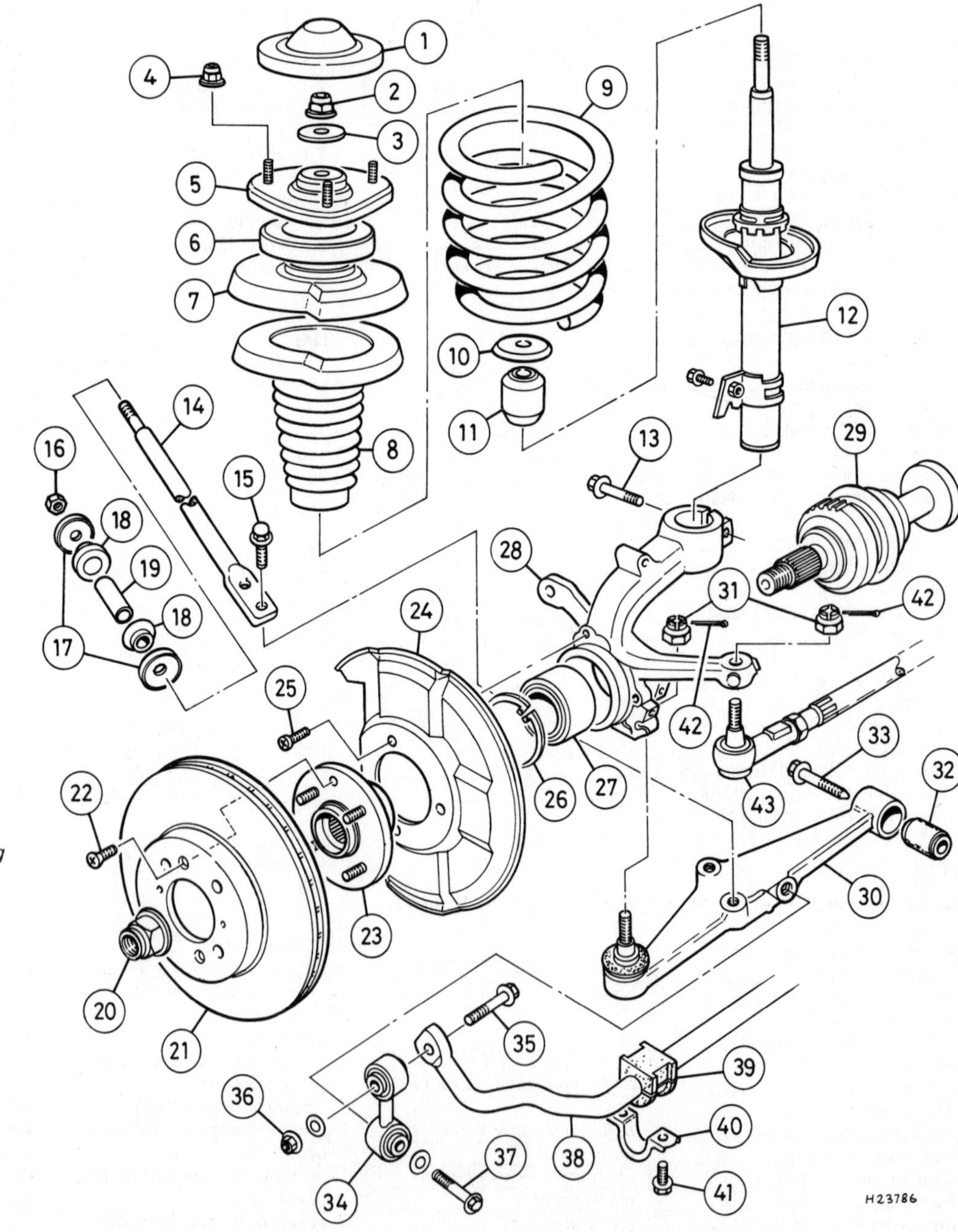

Fig. 10.1 Exploded view of the front suspension components (Sec 1)

1. *Rubber cover*
2. *Self-locking nut*
3. *Washer*
4. *Strut upper mounting nut*
5. *Upper mounting plate*
6. *Bearing*
7. *Upper spring seat*
8. *Dust cover*
9. *Coil spring*
10. *Washer*
11. *Rubber damper stop*
12. *Strut*
13. *Strut lower clamp bolt*
14. *Tie bar*
15. *Bolt – tie bar to lower arm*
16. *Nut – tie bar to subframe*
17. *Flanged washer*
18. *Mounting bush*
19. *Spacer*
20. *Driveshaft retaining nut*
21. *Brake disc*
22. *Disc retaining screw*
23. *Hub*
24. *Disc shield*
25. *Bolt*
26. *Circlip*
27. *Hub bearing*
28. *Swivel hub*
29. *Driveshaft*
30. *Lower suspension arm*
31. *Balljoint retaining nut*
32. *Lower arm pivot bush*
33. *Lower arm pivot bolt*
34. *Anti-roll bar connecting link*
35. *Bolt*
36. *Nut*
37. *Bolt – anti-roll bar connecting link to lower arm*
38. *Anti-roll bar*
39. *Mounting rubber*
40. *Mounting clamp*
41. *Bolt*
42. *Split pin*
43. *Track rod balljoint*

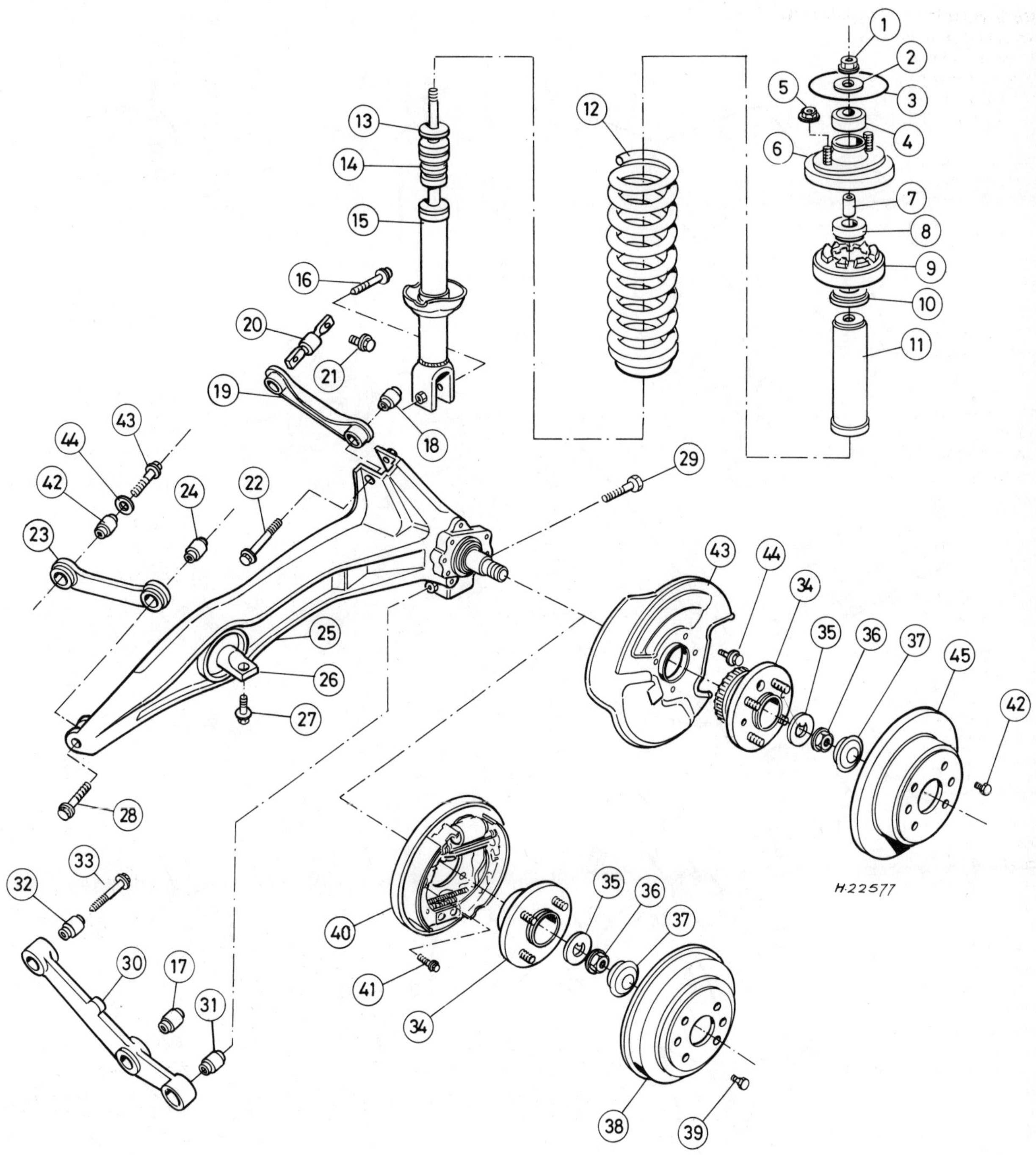

Fig. 10.2 Exploded view of the rear suspension components (Sec 1)

1 *Self-locking nut*
2 *Washer*
3 *Seal*
4 *Mounting rubber*
5 *Strut upper mounting nut*
6 *Upper mounting plate*
7 *Spacer*
8 *Mounting rubber*
9 *Rubber damper*
10 *Dust seal*
11 *Dust cover*
12 *Coil spring*
13 *Stop plate*
14 *Rubber stop*
15 *Strut*
16 *Strut lower mounting bolt*
17 *Strut lower mounting bush*
18 *Rear upper lateral link outer bush*
19 *Rear upper lateral link*
20 *Rear upper lateral link inner bush*
21 *Bolt – rear upper link to body*
22 *Pivot bolt – rear upper link to trailing arm*
23 *Front lateral link*
24 *Front lateral link outer bush*
25 *Trailing arm*
26 *Trailing arm mounting bush*
27 *Bolt – trailing arm to body*
28 *Pivot bolt – front link to trailing arm*
29 *Pivot bolt – rear lower link to trailing arm*
30 *Rear lower lateral link*
31 *Rear lower lateral link outer bush*
32 *Rear lower lateral link inner bush*
33 *Pivot bolt – rear lower link to body*
34 *Rear hub*
35 *Washer*
36 *Rear hub retaining nut*
37 *Hub cap*
38 *Brake drum*
39 *Drum retaining screw*
40 *Backplate assembly*
41 *Backplate mounting bolt*
42 *Disc retaining screw*
43 *Disc shield*
44 *Disc shield mounting bolt*
45 *Brake disc*

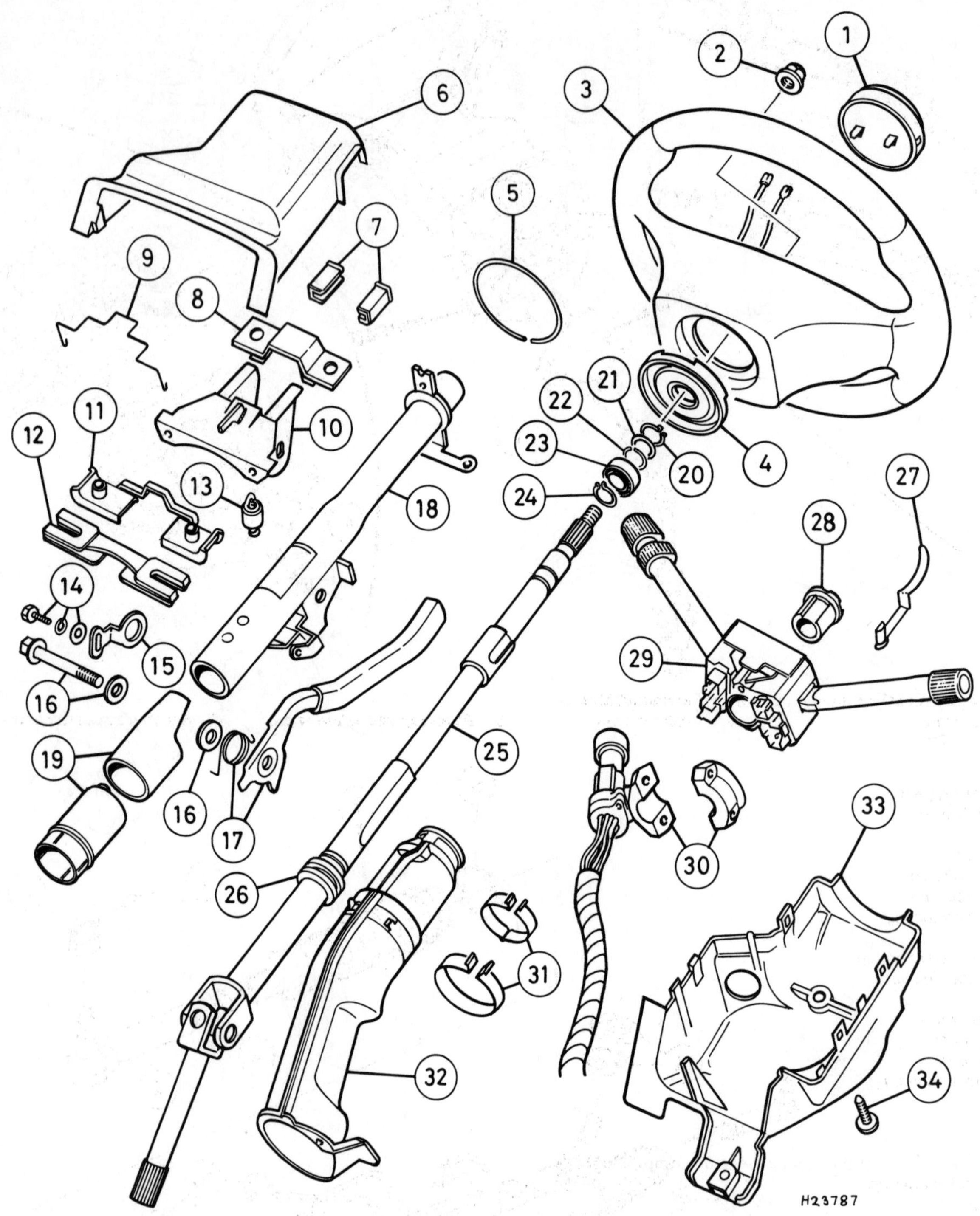

Fig. 10.3 Exploded view of the steering column (Sec 1)

1 Horn button assembly
2 Steering wheel retaining nut
3 Steering wheel
4 Contact ring
5 Snap ring
6 Upper shroud
7 Guide rails
8 Bending plate guide
9 Bending plate spring
10 Bending plate base
11 Upper column holder
12 Bending plate
13 Column hanger spring
14 Tilt adjusting bolt and washers
15 Tilt lock plate
16 Tilt lock bolt and washers
17 Tilt lever and spring
18 Steering column
19 Bush and retainer
20 Circlip
21 Washer
22 Spring washer
23 Bearing
24 Circlip
25 Steering shaft
26 Shaft bush
27 Horn pick-up
28 Indicator cancelling cam
29 Combination switch assembly
30 Ignition switch/steering lock
31 Retaining clips
32 Lower cover
33 Lower shroud
34 Shroud retaining screw

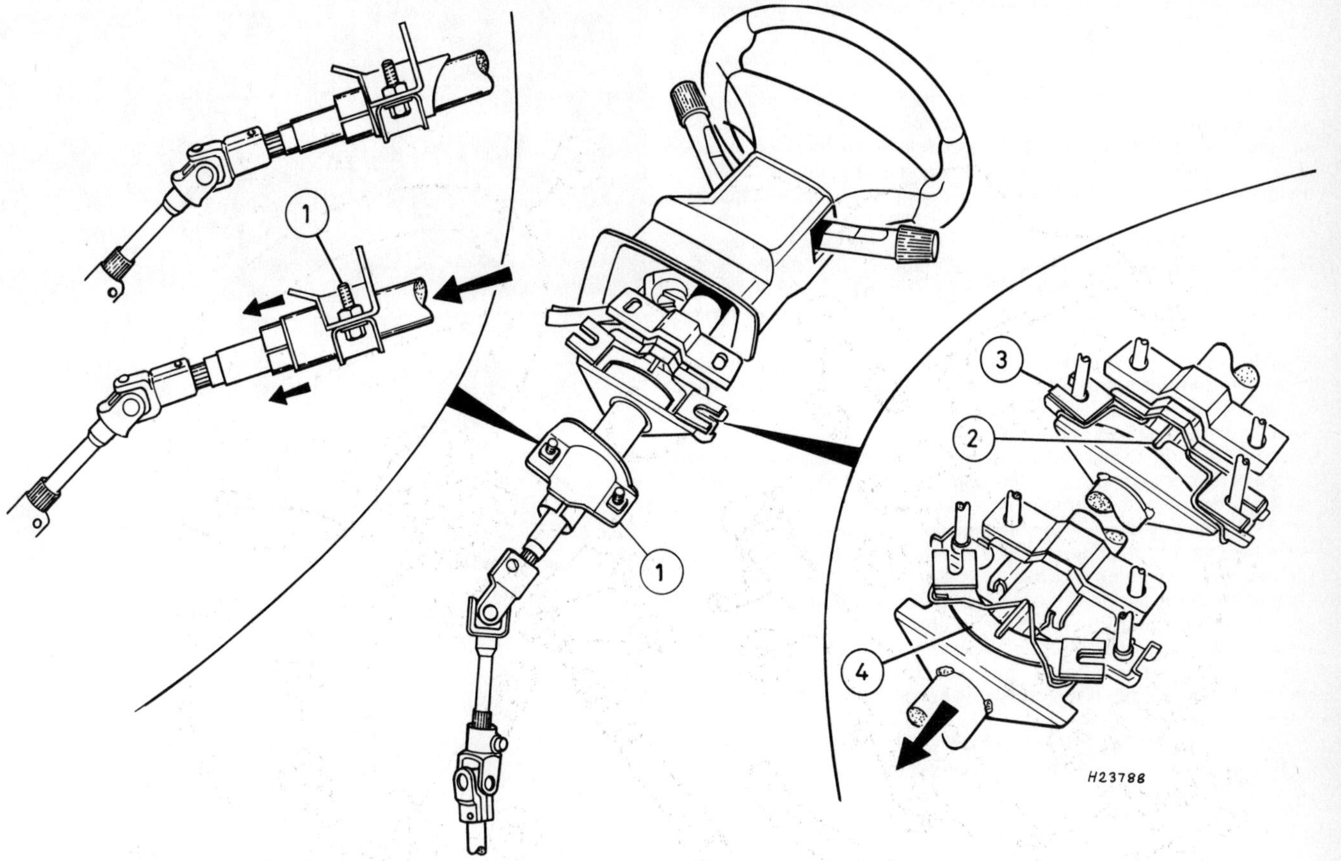

Fig. 10.4 Movement of the steering column under impact (Sec 1)
1 *Lower mounting* 2 *Steering column hook* 3 *Bending plate before impact* 4 *Bending plate after impact*

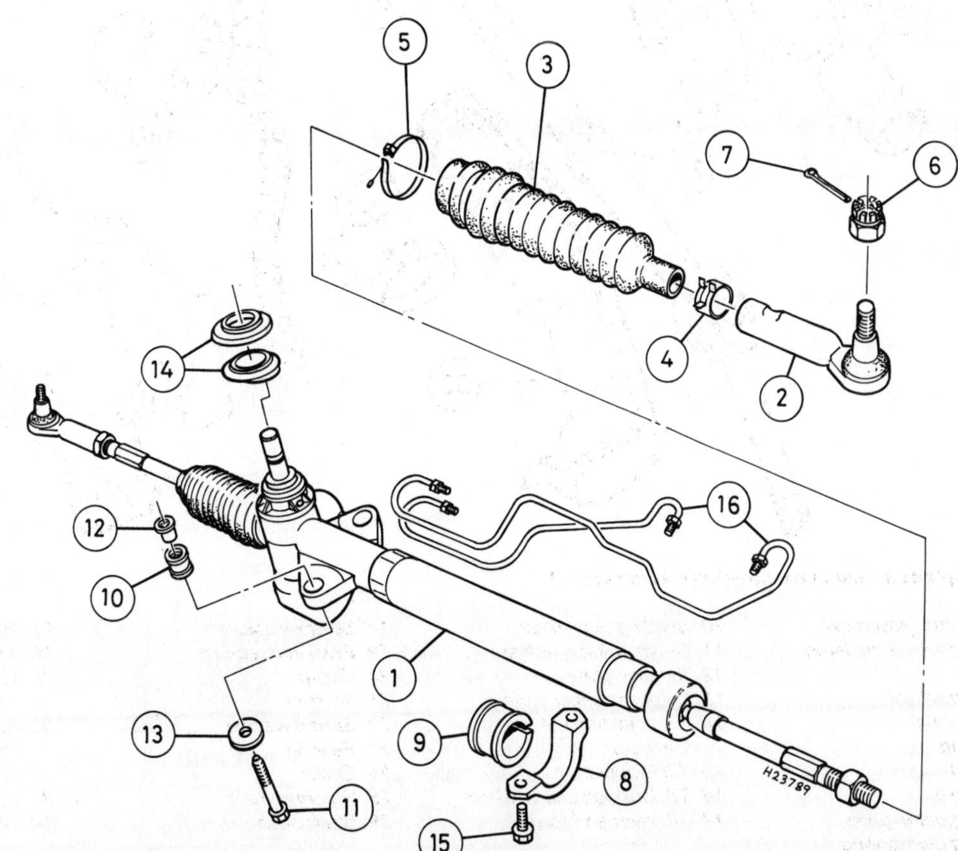

Fig. 10.5 Steering gear components (Sec 1)

1 *Steering rack*
2 *Track rod balljoint*
3 *Steering rack gaiter*
4 *Gaiter outer retaining clip*
5 *Gaiter inner retaining clip*
6 *Balljoint retaining nut*
7 *Split pin*
8 *Mounting clamp*
9 *Mounting bush*
10 *Mounting bush*
11 *Steering rack mounting bolt*
12 *Spacer*
13 *Washer*
14 *Washers*
15 *Steering rack mounting clamp bolt*
16 *Power steering fluid pipes (where fitted)*

1 General information

The independent front suspension is of the MacPherson strut type, incorporating coil springs and integral telescopic shock absorbers. The MacPherson struts are located by transverse lower suspension arms, which utilize rubber inner mounting bushes and incorporate a balljoint at the outer ends, and forward facing longitudinal tie bars. Both lower suspension arms are connected to an anti-roll bar via a small connecting link. The front swivel hubs, which carry the wheel bearings, brake calipers and the hub/disc assemblies, are bolted to the MacPherson struts and connected to the lower arms via the balljoints.

The fully independent rear suspension is of double wishbone type utilising pressed steel trailing arms which have the roadwheel stub axles bolted into their rear ends. These are located longitudinally on the vehicle underbody via a large rubber bush which is situated towards the centre of each arm. Each trailing arm assembly is located transversely by three lateral links, which utilize rubber mounting bushes at both their inner and outer ends. The rear suspension struts incorporate coil springs and integral telescopic shock absorbers and are mounted onto the rear lower lateral link via a rubber mounting bush.

The steering wheel is of the energy-absorbing type to protect the driver in the event of an accident and is attached by a deeply-recessed nut to the steering column which is also collapsible. In the event of an impact, such as in an accident, the lower steering column clamp and the upper column mounting, fitted with energy absorbing bending plates, is designed to allow the column to slide downwards. The downwards movement of the column bends the mounting plates which absorb some of the energy, so lessening the force transmitted to the driver via the steering wheel (Fig. 10.4).

The steering column has a universal joint fitted towards the lower end of its length and its bottom end is clamped to a second universal joint, which is in turn clamped to the steering gear pinion.

The steering gear is mounted onto the engine compartment bulkhead and is connected by two track rods, with balljoints at their outer ends, to the steering arms projecting rearwards from the hub carriers. The track rod ends are threaded to facilitate adjustment.

Power-assisted steering is available as an option on all models. The main components being a rack and pinion steering gear unit, a hydraulic pump which is belt-driven off the crankshaft, and the hydraulic feed and return lines between the pump and steering gear.

2 Front swivel hub assembly – removal and refitting

Removal

1 Chock the rear wheels, firmly apply the handbrake then jack up the front of the vehicle and support it on axle stands. Remove the appropriate front roadwheel.

2 Using a hammer and suitable chisel nosed tool, tap up the staking securing the driveshaft retaining nut to the groove in the outer constant velocity joint.

3 Have an assistant firmly depress the footbrake then using a socket and extension bar, slacken and remove the driveshaft retaining nut. Discard the nut noting that a new driveshaft retaining nut must be obtained for reassembly.

4 If the hub bearings are to be disturbed, remove the brake disc (Chapter 9, Section 10). If not, undo the two bolts securing the caliper mounting bracket to the hub and slide the caliper off the disc. Using a piece of wire, tie the caliper to the suspension strut to avoid placing any strain on the brake hose.

5 On models equipped with ABS remove the front wheel sensor (Chapter 9, Section 22).

6 Slacken and remove the bolt and washer securing the anti-roll bar connecting link to the lower suspension arm and undo the two bolts securing the tie bar to the lower suspension arm.

7 Extract the split pins and undo the nuts securing the steering gear track rod and lower suspension arm balljoints to the swivel hub. Release both the balljoints from the swivel hub using a suitable balljoint separator taking great care not to damage the balljoint gaiters.

8 Slacken the swivel hub to suspension strut clamp bolt then carefully ease the hub off the strut. Once free, pull the hub outwards to free it from the constant velocity joint splines and remove it from the car

2.8 Removing the swivel hub assembly

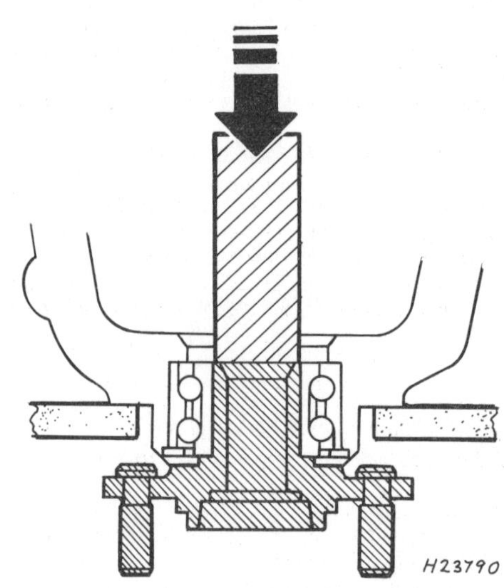

Fig. 10.6 Pressing out hub from the swivel hub (Sec 3)

(photo). Whilst the hub is removed, support the driveshaft by tying it to the suspension strut to avoid damaging the inner constant velocity joint or gaiter.

Refitting

9 Refitting is reversal of the removal procedure noting the following points:

- (a) *Ensure that the lug on the base of the suspension strut correctly engages with the slot in the swivel hub assembly clamp.*
- (b) *Tighten all nuts and bolts to the specified torque.*
- (c) *Where necessary, refit the brake disc and/or ABS wheel sensor as described in the relevant Sections of Chapter 9.*
- (d) *Use new split pins to secure the track rod and lower suspension arm balljoint retaining nuts in position.*
- (e) *When fitting the new driveshaft retaining nut, tighten it to the specified torque then stake it firmly into the groove in the constant velocity joint using a suitable punch.*

3 Front hub bearings – removal and refitting

Note: *The bearing is a sealed, pre-adjusted and pre-lubricated, double-row roller type and is intended to last the car's entire service life without maintenance or attention. Do not attempt to remove the bearing*

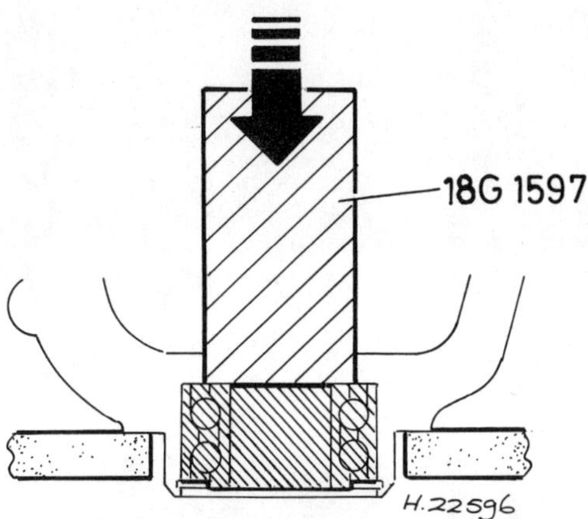

Fig. 10.7 Pressing hub bearing out of swivel hub (Sec 3)

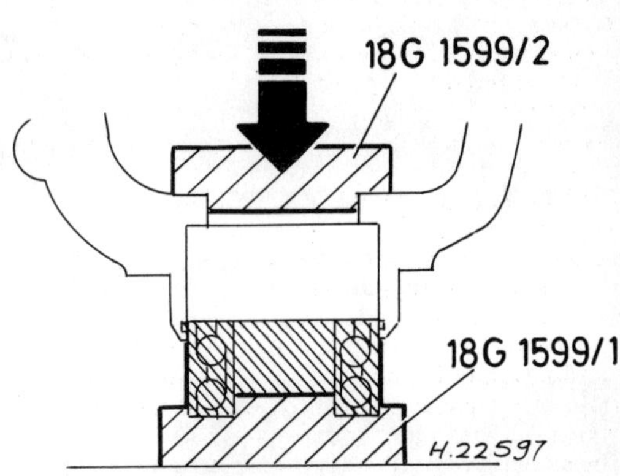

Fig. 10.8 Pressing new hub bearing into swivel hub (Sec 3)

unless absolutely necessary, as it will probably be damaged during the removal operation. Never overtighten the driveshaft nut beyond the specified torque wrench setting in an attempt to 'adjust' the bearing.

Note: *A press will be required to dismantle and rebuild the assembly; if such a tool is not available, a large bench vice and suitable spacers (such as large sockets) will serve as an adequate substitute. The service tool numbers for the special Rover mandrels are given in the accompanying figures. The bearing's inner races are an interference fit on the hub; if the outboard inner race remains on the hub when it is pressed out of the hub carrier, a proprietary knife-edged bearing puller will be required to remove it.*

Removal

1 Remove the swivel hub assembly as described in Section 2, then undo the brake disc shield retaining screws and remove the shield from the hub.

2 Press the hub out of the swivel hub using a tubular spacer (Fig. 10.6). If the bearing's outboard inner race remains on the hub, remove it using a suitable bearing puller (see note above).

3 Extract both circlips from the swivel hub and discard them; they should be renewed whenever they are disturbed.

4 Press the bearing out of the swivel hub using a suitable tubular spacer (Fig. 10.7).

5 Thoroughly clean the hub and swivel hub, removing all traces of dirt and grease and polishing away any burrs or raised edges which might hinder reassembly. Check both for cracks or any other signs of wear or damage and renew them if necessary. As noted above, the bearing and its circlips must be renewed whenever they are disturbed. Note that a replacement bearing kit is available from Rover dealers which consists of the bearing and both circlips.

6 Check the condition of the roadwheel studs in the hub flange. If any are sheared off, stretched or have damaged threads, they can be pressed out of the hub providing that its flange is fully supported; on refitting, support the hub flange and press in the new stud until it seats fully.

Refitting

7 On reassembly, check (if possible) that the new bearing is packed with grease and fit the new circlip to the swivel hub outboard groove. Apply a light film of oil to the bearing inner and outer races and to the matching surfaces in the hub and swivel hub to aid installation of the bearing.

8 Supporting the swivel hub outboard face and, using a suitable tubular spacer which bears only on the bearing's outer race, press in the new bearing until it seats against the circlip (Fig. 10.8). Secure the bearing in position by fitting the second new circlip to the swivel hub's inboard groove.

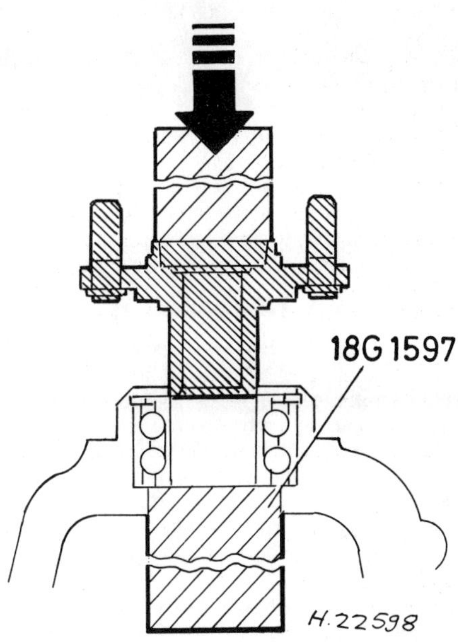

Fig. 10.9 Pressing hub into swivel hub – note support for bearing inner race (Sec 3)

9 Fully supporting the bearing inner race, press the hub into the bearing and swivel hub until the hub shoulder seats against the bearing's inner race (Fig. 10.9). Wipe off any surplus oil or grease.

10 Refit the brake disc shield to the swivel hub and tighten its retaining screws securely.

11 Refit the swivel hub assembly as described in Section 2.

4 Front suspension strut – removal and refitting

Removal

1 Chock the rear wheels, firmly apply the handbrake, then jack up the front of the car and support on axle stands. Remove the appropriate roadwheel.

4.4 Remove the bolt securing the brake hose to the suspension strut

4.6A Remove rubber cover and mark relative positions of strut and body

4.6B Removing a front suspension strut

4.7A Align suspension strut lug with slot in swivel hub (arrowed)

4.7B Tighten suspension strut upper mounting nuts...

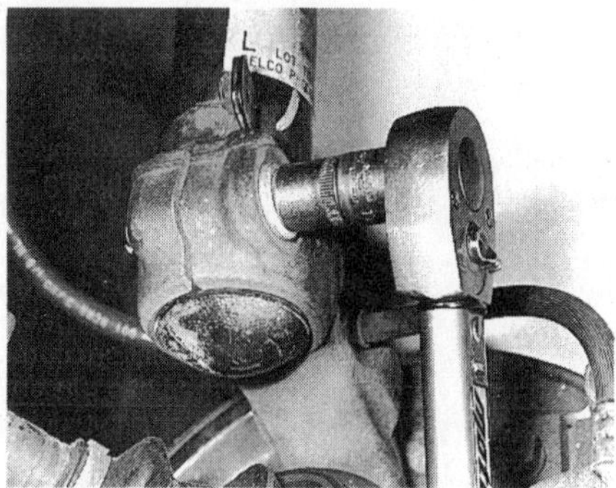
4.7C ...and swivel hub clamp bolt to the specified torque

2 Extract the split pin and undo the nut securing the steering gear track rod balljoint to the swivel hub. Release the balljoint shank using a suitable balljoint separator tool whilst taking care not to damage the balljoint gaiter.
3 Slacken and remove the bolt and washer securing the anti-roll bar connecting link to the lower suspension arm and undo the two bolts securing the tie bar to the lower suspension arm.
4 Undo the bolt securing the brake hose retaining clamp to the strut, then remove the clamp and free the flexible hose (photo).
5 Slacken the swivel hub to suspension strut clamp bolt, then carefully ease the swivel hub assembly off the end of the strut.
6 Working in the engine compartment, remove the rubber suspension strut cover. Use chalk or a dab of paint to mark the relative positions of the suspension strut upper mounting and body. Undo the three strut upper mounting nuts and manoeuvre the strut out from under the wheel arch, noting the seal which is fitted between the upper mounting plate and vehicle body (photos).

Refitting

7 Refitting is a reversal of the removal procedure noting the following points (photos):

(a) *Ensure that the marks made on removal are aligned when installing the strut.*
(b) *Ensure that the lug on the base of the suspension strut correctly engages with the slot in the swivel hub assembly.*
(c) *Tighten all nuts and bolts to the specified torque.*
(d) *Use a new split pin to secure the track rod balljoint retaining nut in position.*

5 Front suspension strut - dismantling, inspection and reassembly

Note: *Before attempting to dismantle the front suspension strut, a suitable tool to hold the coil spring in compression must be obtained. Adjustable coil spring compressors are readily available and are recommended for this operation. Any attempt to dismantle the strut without such a tool is likely to result in damage or personal injury.*

5.2 Compress the coil spring with a suitable pair of spring compressors...

Dismantling

1 With the strut removed from the car as described in Section 4, clean away all external dirt then mount it upright in a vice.
2 Fit the spring compressor and compress the coil spring until all tension is relieved from the upper mounting plate (photo).
3 Slacken the upper mounting retaining nut whilst retaining the strut piston with an Allen key (photo).
4 Remove the nut and washer followed by the mounting plate,

5.3 ...and remove the upper mounting nut whilst retaining the piston with an Allen key

bearing and upper spring seat. Lift off the coil spring and damper piston dust cover and separate the two components. Slide the washer and rubber damper stop off the strut piston.

Inspection

5 With the strut assembly now completely dismantled, examine all the components for wear, damage or deformation and check the bearing for smoothness of operation. Renew any of the components as necessary.

6 Examine the strut for signs of fluid leakage. Check the strut piston for signs of pitting along its entire length and check the strut body for signs of damage. Test the operation of the strut, while holding it in an upright position, by moving the piston through a full stroke and then through short strokes of 50 to 100 mm. In both cases the resistance felt should be smooth and continuous. If the resistance is jerky, or uneven, or if there is any visible sign of wear or damage to the strut, renewal is necessary.

7 If any doubt exists about the condition of the coil spring, carefully remove the spring compressors and check the spring for distortion and signs of cracking. Since no minimum free length is specified by Rover the only way to check the tension of the spring is to compare it to a new component. Renew the spring if it is damaged or distorted or there is any doubt as to its condition.

8 Inspect all other components for signs of damage or deterioration and renew any that are suspect.

Reassembly

9 Reassembly is a reversal of dismantling, making sure that the spring ends are correctly located in the upper and lower seats and that the upper mounting plate retaining nut is tightened to the specified torque.

6 Front suspension anti-roll bar – removal and refitting

Removal

1 Chock the rear wheels, firmly apply the handbrake then jack up the front of the car and support it on axle stands. Remove both front roadwheels.

2 From underneath the car, undo the bolts securing the gearchange control rod rear rubber mounting to the vehicle underbody. Remove the rubber mounting assembly and bolts noting the correct fitted positions of the mounting rubber spacers and mounting plate.

3 Release the exhaust system from its front rubber mountings then undo the three gearchange linkage bellcrank assembly retaining bolts and lower the gearchange linkage assembly down onto the exhaust system.

6.4 Slacken and remove the anti-roll bar to connecting link bolts

6.5 Prior to removal note the position of anti-roll bar mounting bush split (arrowed)

4 Slacken and remove the nuts and washers securing each end of the anti-roll bar to the connecting links and remove the bolts (photo).

5 Mark the location of the clamp bushes on the bar, then undo the mounting clamp retaining bolts and remove the clamps. Make a note of the fitted position of the rubber bush splits to ensure that they are positioned correctly on refitting (photo). Manoeuvre the anti-roll bar out over the gearchange linkage and exhaust system and remove it from the right-hand side of the vehicle.

6 Carefully examine the anti-roll bar components for signs of wear, damage or deterioration, paying particular attention to the mounting rubbers. Inspect the gearchange mechanism control rod mounting rubber and bush for signs of wear or deterioration. Renew worn components as necessary.

Refitting

7 Manoeuvre the anti-roll bar into position from the right-hand side of the vehicle and refit the connecting link bolts. Refit the washers and tighten the nuts finger tight only at this stage.

8 Lubricate the mounting clamp bushes with a solution of soapy water then lever the bar down and slide them into position on the anti-roll bar. Ensure that the splits are on the right side of the bushes then align them with the marks made on dismantling.

9 Refit the anti-roll bar mounting clamps and tighten the retaining bolts to the specified torque setting, then tighten the anti-roll bar to connecting link bolts to the specified torque.

10 Refit the front gearchange mechanism linkage mounting plate assembly retaining bolts and tighten them securely.
11 Apply a smear of grease to the gearchange control rod bush and refit the rear mounting rubber assembly. Tighten the mounting bolts to the specified torque setting (Chapter 7), and check that the gearchange mechanism operates smoothly. Refit the exhaust system to the front mounting rubbers.
12 Refit the roadwheels then lower the car to the ground and tighten the roadwheel nuts to the specified torque.

7 Front suspension anti-roll bar connecting link – removal and refitting

Removal

1 Chock the rear wheels, firmly apply the handbrake, jack up the front of the car and support on axle stands. Remove the appropriate front roadwheel.
2 From underneath the car, slacken and remove the bolt and washer securing the connecting link to the lower suspension arm (photo).
3 Remove the nut and washer securing the connecting link to the anti-roll bar, then withdraw the bolt and remove the connecting link from under the vehicle.
4 Inspect the connecting link rubber mounting bushes for signs of damage and renew them if they are cracked, worn, split or perished. The bushes are a press fit in the connecting link and can be pressed out and in using a vice and two suitable sized tubular drifts, such as sockets (one which bears on the hard outer edge of the bush and another which bears against the edge of the connecting link).

Refitting

5 Refitting is the reverse of the removal sequence, tightening both the connecting link bolts to the specified torque setting.

7.2 Anti-roll bar connecting link

8 Front suspension tie bar – removal and refitting

Removal

1 Chock the rear wheels, firmly apply the handbrake, jack up the front of the car and support on axle stands. Remove the appropriate front roadwheel.
2 From underneath the front of the vehicle, slacken and remove the

8.3 Tie bar retaining nut is accessed from front of subframe

8.4 Tie bar to lower suspension arm bolts

8.5 Renew tie bar mounting bushes if damaged (arrowed)

8.6 Fit flange washer, spacer and mounting bush onto tie bar...

8.7 ...then refit the tie bar to the subframe and install second mounting bush and flange washer

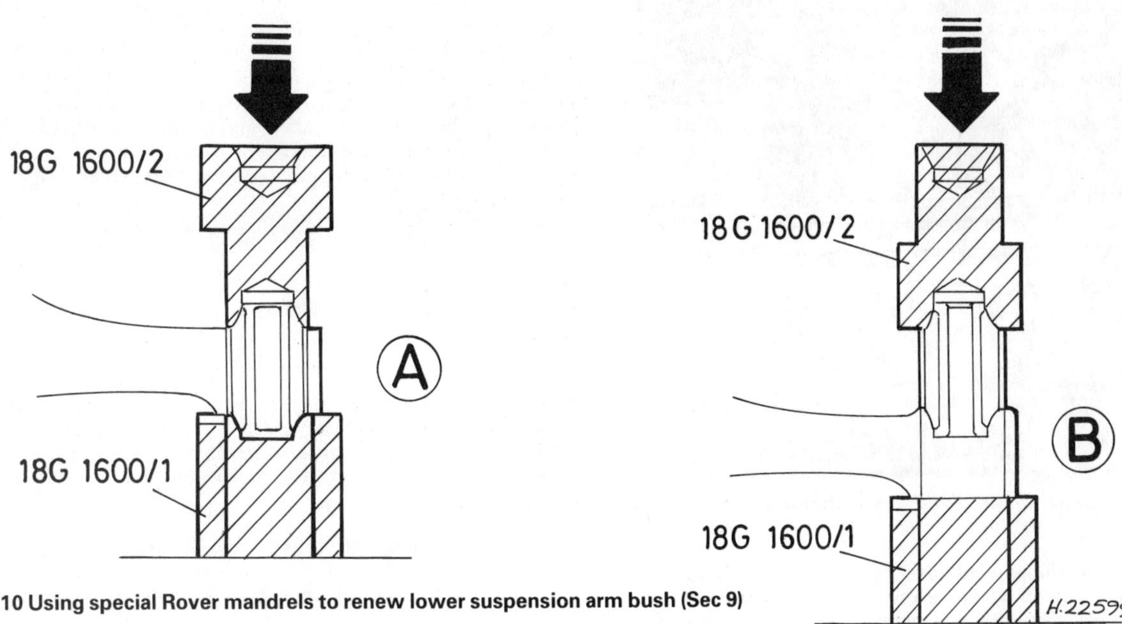

Fig. 10.10 Using special Rover mandrels to renew lower suspension arm bush (Sec 9)

A Removing old bush *B Fitting new bush*

three bolts securing the bumper flange to the body. Remove the seven bolts securing the front undercover panel to the body and remove the panel.

3 Undo the nut securing the front of the tie bar to the front subframe then remove the flanged washer and mounting bush, noting which direction the flange is facing (photo).

4 Undo the two bolts securing the tie bar to the lower suspension arm, then remove the rod from the car, and slide the spacer, mounting bush and flanged washer off the tie bar (photo).

5 Examine all the components for signs of wear or damage, paying particular attention to the mounting bushes and tie bar threads, and renew components as necessary (photo).

Refitting

6 Slide the flange washer, mounting bush and spacer onto the tie bar threads. Ensure that the flange of the washer is facing away from the mounting bush and that the rounded surface of the bush is facing the washer (photo).

7 Refit the tie bar to the front subframe and fit the second mounting bush and flanged washer. Ensure the flat surface of the mounting bush is facing the subframe and that the flange of the washer is facing away from the mounting bush then refit the tie bar nut, tightening it finger tight only at this stage (photo).

8 Refit the tie bar to lower suspension arm bolts and tighten them to the specified torque, then tighten the tie bar retaining nut to the specified torque setting.

9 Refit the front undercover panel and tighten all the panel and bumper flange bolts securely.

10 Refit the roadwheel then lower the car to the ground and tighten the roadwheel nuts to the specified torque.

9 Front suspension lower arm – removal, overhaul and refitting

Removal

1 Chock the rear wheels, firmly apply the handbrake, jack up the front of the car and support on axle stands. Remove the appropriate front roadwheel.

2 Slacken and remove the bolt and washer securing the anti-roll bar connecting link to the lower suspension arm and undo the two bolts securing the tie bar to the lower suspension arm.

9.4A Release the balljoint from the swivel hub assembly...

3 Extract the split pin and undo the nut securing the lower arm balljoint to the swivel hub. Release the balljoint shank using a suitable balljoint separator tool whilst taking care not to damage the balljoint gaiter.

4 Undo the lower suspension arm to body pivot bolt and withdraw the lower arm from the vehicle (photos).

Overhaul

Note: *The lower arm balljoint is an integral part of the lower arm assembly and is not available separately. If renewal of the balljoint is necessary the complete lower arm assembly must be renewed.*

5 Thoroughly clean the lower arm and the area around the arm mountings, removing all traces of dirt and underseal if necessary, then check carefully for cracks, distortion or any other signs of wear or damage. Check that the lower arm balljoint moves freely without any sign of roughness and that the balljoint gaiter shows no sign of deterioration and is free from cracks and splits. Examine the shank of the pivot bolt for signs of wear or scoring. Renew worn components as necessary.

9.4B ...then remove pivot bolt (arrowed) and withdraw lower suspension arm

6 Check the lower arm inner pivot bush; if it is worn, cracked, split or perished it must be renewed. The renewal of the bush is best left to a Rover dealer as a press, a special bush removal/refitting mandrel and a support are required (Rover Service Tool Numbers 18G 1600/2 and 18G 1600/1 respectively). While the old bush can be extracted using a strong bench vice and suitable sockets it is unlikely that new bushes can be installed successfully without the shaped mandrel (Fig. 10.10).

Refitting

7 Offer up the lower arm and fit the arm to body pivot bolt. Tighten the bolt by hand only at this stage.
8 Insert the lower arm balljoint shank into the swivel hub and tighten its retaining bolt to the specified torque. Secure the balljoint nut in position with a new split pin.
9 Refit the tie bar and anti-roll bar connecting link to lower arm bolts and tighten them to the specified torque.
10 Refit the roadwheel then lower the car to the ground and tighten the roadwheel nuts to the specified torque.
11 With the car standing on its wheels, rock the suspension to settle the lower arm bush in position then tighten the lower arm to body pivot bolt to the specified torque setting.
12 Check and, if necessary, adjust the front wheel alignment as described in Section 26.

10 Rear hub and bearings - removal and refitting

Note: *The bearing is a sealed, pre-adjusted and pre-lubricated, double-row tapered-roller type and is intended to last the car's entire service life without maintenance or attention. Never overtighten the hub nut beyond the specified torque wrench setting in an attempt to 'adjust' the bearings*

Note: *The bearing is an integral part of the hub and cannot be purchased separately. If renewal of the bearing is necessary the complete hub assembly must be renewed as a unit. The only component which is available separately are roadwheel studs.*

Removal

1 Chock the front wheels, then jack up the rear of the vehicle and support it on axle stands. Remove the appropriate rear roadwheel.
2 Prise out the cap from the centre of the hub assembly and, using a hammer and suitable chisel nosed tool, tap up the staking securing the hub retaining nut to the groove in the stub axle (photo).
3 Have an assistant firmly depress the footbrake then using a socket and extension bar, slacken but do not remove the hub retaining nut.

10.2 Prise off centre cap to gain access to rear hub nut

10.9A Refit the hub...

10.9B ...and washer, ensuring its tooth engages with the stub axle groove

10.11A Tighten the hub retaining nut to the specified torque...

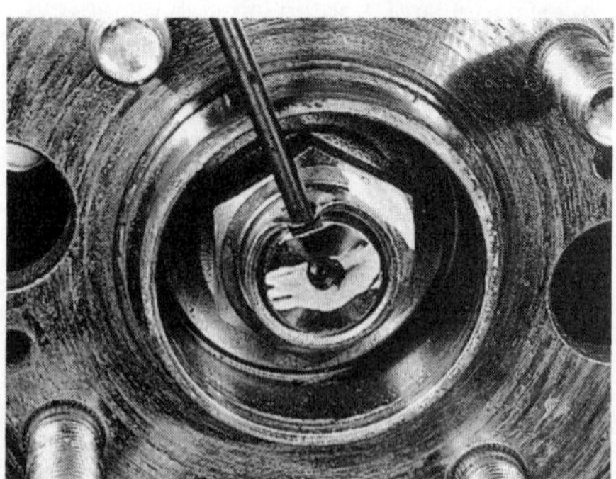

10.11B ...then stake it firmly into the stub axle groove

11.2A On models fitted with rear drum brakes, use a 12 mm spanner to compress the handbrake cable retaining tangs

11.2B Backplate retaining bolts (arrowed) - rear drum brake models

11.4 Stub axle retaining nut 'A'. Torx bolts are accessed via four holes (arrowed)

4 Remove the brake drum or disc (as applicable) as described in the relevant Section of Chapter 9.
5 Once the brake drum/disc has been removed, remove the hub nut and toothed washer and pull the hub assembly off the stub axle. If necessary the hub can be drawn off the stub axle using a three-legged puller. Discard the nut noting that a new hub retaining nut must be obtained for reassembly.
6 Check that there is no sign of free play in the hub bearing and that the bearing inner race rotates smoothly and easily without any sign of roughness. If there is any sign of wear or damage to the hub assembly or bearing the complete hub assembly must be renewed as a unit.
7 Check the condition of the roadwheel studs in the hub flange. If any are sheared off, stretched or have damaged threads, they can be pressed out of the hub providing that its flange is fully supported. On refitting, support the hub flange and press in the new stud until it seats fully.

Refitting

8 Prior to refitting the hub inspect the stub axle for signs of wear or scoring and, if necessary, renew as described in Section 11.
9 Apply a thin smear of grease to the hub bearing seal and refit the hub assembly. Refit the toothed washer, ensuring that its tooth locates with the groove in the stub axle, and install the new hub nut (photos). Tighten the hub nut by hand only.
10 Refit the brake drum or disc (as applicable) as described in the relevant Section of Chapter 9, but do not refit the roadwheel.
11 Have an assistant firmly apply the footbrake then tighten the hub retaining nut to the specified torque. Release the brake and check that the hub rotates smoothly then stake the hub retaining nut fully into the stub axle groove (photos). Refit the hub centre cap.
12 Refit the roadwheel then lower the car to the ground and tighten the roadwheel nuts to the specified torque.
13 Check and, if necessary, adjust the rear wheel alignment as described in Section 26.

11 Rear stub axle - removal and refitting

Removal

1 Remove the rear hub assembly as described in Section 10.
2 On models fitted with rear drum brakes remove the lower brake shoe return spring, then disconnect the handbrake cable from the trailing shoe, referring to Chapter 9, Section 13 for further information. Undo the bolts securing the handbrake cable and brake hose brackets to the trailing arm then use a 12 mm ring spanner to compress the handbrake cable retaining clip and withdraw the cable from the backplate. Remove the four bolts securing the backplate to the trailing arm and carefully ease the backplate assembly outwards and off the end of the stub axle (photos). Position the backplate assembly out of the way of the stub axle and tie it to the rear suspension unit coil spring using a piece of wire.
3 On models fitted with rear disc brakes, undo the four disc shield retaining bolts and remove the shield from the trailing arm.
4 On all models, using a socket and extension bar, undo the large stub axle retaining nut from the rear of the trailing arm assembly (photo).
5 Slacken and remove the four Torx bolts securing the stub axle mounting plate to the trailing arm assembly, then withdraw the stub axle and remove it from the vehicle.
6 Examine the stub axle spindle and mounting plate for signs of wear or damage such as scoring or cracking. If damaged, the stub axle must be renewed.

Refitting

7 Refitting is a reverse of the removal procedure noting the following points:

(a) *Tighten all the nuts and bolts to the specified torque settings.*
(b) *Refit the hub as described in Section 10.*

12 Rear suspension strut - removal and refitting

Removal

1 Chock the front wheels, then jack up the rear of the vehicle and support it on axle stands. Remove the appropriate rear roadwheel.
2 Slacken and remove both the pivot bolts securing the rear lower lateral link to the body and trailing arm. On models equipped with ABS undo the bolts securing the wheel sensor wiring lead bracket to the lower arm and release the wiring. On all models undo the lower suspension strut mounting bolt and remove the rear lower lateral link.
3 From inside the luggage compartment, prise off the trim cap to gain access to rear suspension strut upper mounting nuts on 214 models, while on 414 models remove the relevant luggage compartment side trim panel to gain access (photo).

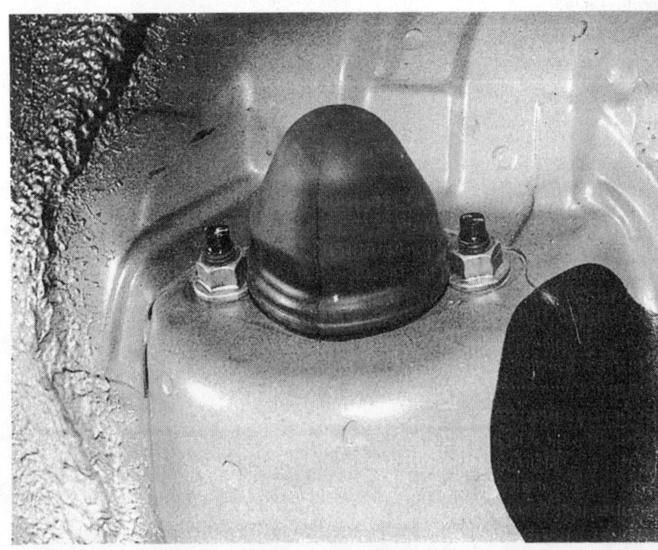

12.3 On 414 models remove the luggage compartment side trim to gain access to strut upper mounting nuts

4 Remove the rubber cover and use chalk or a dab of paint to mark the relative positions of the suspension strut upper mounting and body. Undo the two suspension strut upper mounting nuts and manoeuvre the strut out from under the wheel arch, noting the seal which is fitted between the upper mounting plate and vehicle body (photo).

Refitting

5 Prior to refitting, examine the rear lower lateral link mounting bushes as described in Section 14, and renew any which are worn or damaged.

6 Ensure the rubber seal is in position on the upper mounting plate then refit the suspension strut, aligning the marks made on removal (where necessary), and refit the upper mounting nuts. Tighten the nuts to the specified torque setting and refit the rubber cover and trim cap/panel.

7 Offer up the lower lateral link and refit the lower suspension strut mounting bolt followed by both the lower lateral link pivot bolts. Tighten the bolts only loosely at this stage. On models equipped with ABS refit the wheel sensor wiring bracket retaining bolts and tighten them securely.

8 Refit the roadwheel then lower the car to the ground and tighten the roadwheel nuts to the specified torque.

9 With the car standing on its wheels, rock the car to settle the disturbed components in position then tighten the lower lateral link pivot bolts and the lower suspension strut mounting bolt to the specified torque.

13 Rear suspension strut – dismantling, inspection and reassembly

Note: *Before attempting to dismantle the rear suspension strut, a suitable tool to hold the coil spring in compression must be obtained. Adjustable coil spring compressors are readily available and are recommended for this operation. Any attempt to dismantle the strut without such a tool is likely to result in damage or personal injury.*

Dismantling

1 With the strut removed from the car as described in Section 12, clean away all external dirt then mount it upright in a vice.

2 Fit the spring compressor and compress the coil spring until all tension is relieved from the upper mounting plate.

3 Slacken the upper mounting retaining nut whilst retaining the strut piston with an Allen key.

4 Remove the nut and washer followed by the mounting plate assembly, noting the correct fitted positions of the mounting rubbers and spacer, and upper spring rubber damper. Remove the coil spring then lift the dust seal and cover off the damper and slide the damper stop plate and rubber stop off the strut piston.

Inspection

5 Examine all the rear suspension strut components using the information given for the front suspension strut in Section 5.

Reassembly

6 Reassembly is a reversal of the removal procedure ensuring that the spring ends are correctly located in the upper and lower seats and that the upper mounting plate retaining nut is tightened to the specified torque setting.

12.4 Removing rear suspension strut

14 Rear suspension lateral links – removal, inspection and refitting

Removal

1 Chock the front wheels, then jack up the rear of the car and support it on axle stands. Remove the appropriate rear roadwheel.

Front lateral link

2 Mark the position of the lateral link body pivot bolt in relation to the body. This mark can then be used as a guide on refitting.

3 Slacken and remove both the pivot bolts securing the front lateral link to the body and trailing arm and remove the link from the vehicle (photo).

Rear upper lateral link

4 Slacken and remove the pivot bolt securing the rear upper lateral link to the trailing arm assembly (photo).

5 Undo the two bolts securing the inner mounting to the vehicle body and remove the link assembly from the car.

Rear lower lateral link

6 Slacken and remove both the pivot bolts securing the lower rear lateral link to the body and trailing arm. On models equipped with ABS, undo the bolts securing the wheel sensor wiring lead bracket to the lower arm and release the wiring. On all models undo the lower suspension mounting bolt and remove the rear lower lateral link (photo).

14.3 Front lateral link to body mounting bolt (arrowed) is slotted to permit rear wheel alignment

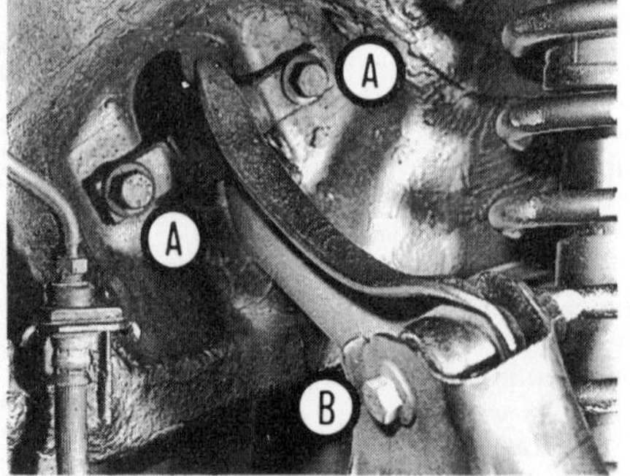

14.4 Rear upper lateral link to body bolts 'A' and trailing arm pivot bolt 'B'

14.6 Removing rear lower lateral link

14.7 Examine lateral link bushes for signs of wear and renew if necessary

15.3 Remove retaining clip and free the brake hose from the trailing arm

Inspection

7 Examine the lateral link for signs of cracking and check the mounting bushes for signs of wear or deterioration and renew as necessary. The bushes are a press fit in the link and can be pressed out and in using a vice and two suitable sized tubular drifts, such as sockets (one which bears on the hard outer edge of the bush and another which bears against the edge of the lateral link) (photo).

Note: *When renewing the inner bush on the rear upper lateral link, mark the position of the bush mounting plate in relation to the lateral link before removing the worn bush. Fit the new bush so that the mounting plate is in the same position in relation to the lateral link. This avoids placing any undue strain on the rubber bush when the link is refitted to the vehicle.*

8 Examine the pivot bolt shanks for signs of wear or damage such as scoring, and renew as necessary.

Refitting

9 Refitting is the reverse of removal noting the following points:

- *(a) Refit the pivot bolts and tighten them only loosely.*
- *(b) When refitting the front lateral link align the inner pivot bolt using the marks made on dismantling.*
- *(c) With the car standing on its wheels, rock the suspension to settle all the disturbed components in position then tighten all the disturbed pivot bolts to the specified torque.*
- *(d) Check and, if necessary, adjust the rear wheel alignment as described in Section 26.*

15 Rear suspension trailing arm - removal and refitting

Removal

1 Chock the front wheels then jack up the rear of the vehicle and support it on axle stands. Remove the appropriate rear roadwheel, then follow the procedure under the relevant sub heading.

Non-ABS models

2 Remove the rear hub assembly as described in Section 10.

3 Undo the bolts and remove the clips securing the handbrake cable and brake hose brackets to the trailing arm (photo). Remove the four bolts securing the backplate to the trailing arm and carefully ease the

15.8 Trailing arm mounting bolts (arrowed)

backplate assembly outwards and off the end of the stub axle. Position the backplate out of the way of the stub axle and tie it to the rear suspension unit coil spring using a piece of wire.

ABS models

4 Remove the two brake caliper shield retaining screws and remove the shield from the caliper.

5 Slacken and remove the bolts securing the handbrake cable and brake hose retaining clamps to the trailing arm. Undo the two bolts securing the caliper mounting bracket to the trailing arm and slide the caliper off the disc. Tie the caliper to the rear suspension strut coil spring to avoid placing any strain on the hydraulic hose or handbrake cable.

6 Remove the ABS rear wheel sensor (Chapter 9, Section 22).

All models

7 Slacken and remove the three pivot bolts securing the front lateral link, rear lower lateral link and rear upper lateral link to the trailing arm.

8 Remove the two bolts securing the trailing arm mounting bracket to the vehicle body, then manoeuvre the trailing arm assembly out of position and away from the vehicle (photo).

9 Inspect the trailing arm for signs of damage such as cracks, paying particular to the areas around the mounting bolt holes, and examine the

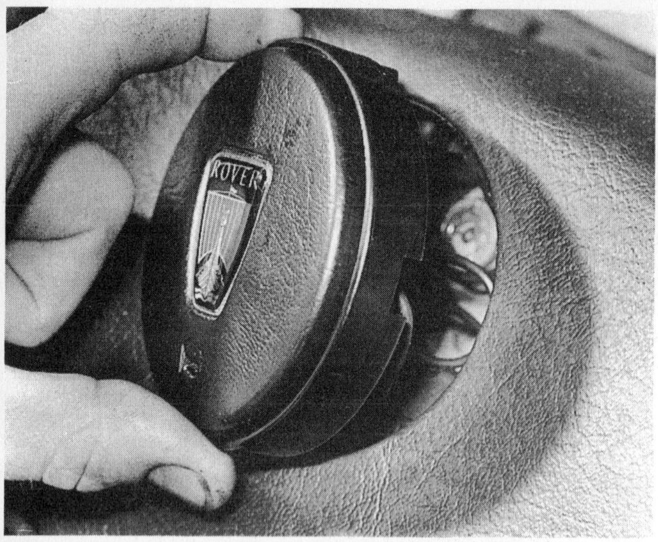

16.2A Remove the horn button from the steering wheel...

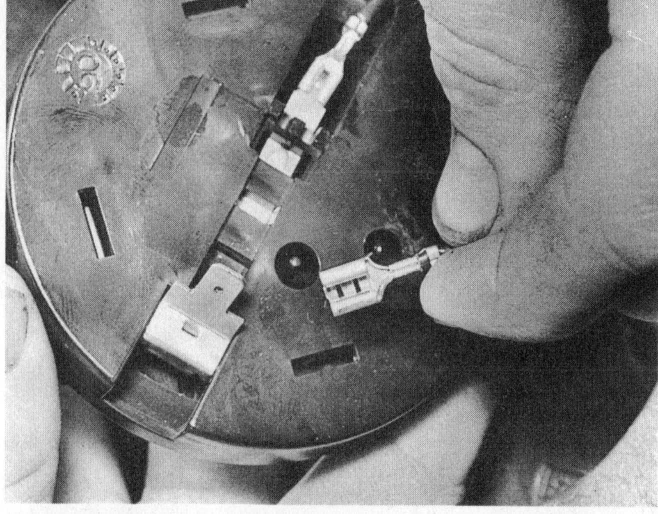

16.2B ...and disconnect the wiring from the button terminals

mounting bush for signs of damage and deterioration. If either the arm or bush show signs of wear or damage the trailing arm and bush assembly must be renewed as a unit since neither component is available separately.

Refitting

10 Refitting is the reverse of removal noting the following points:

- *(a) Manoeuvre the trailing arm into position and tighten its mounting bolts to the specified torque.*
- *(b) Refit all the pivot bolts and tighten them only loosely.*
- *(c) On non-ABS models tighten the backplate retaining bolts to the specified torque and refit the hub as described in Section 10.*
- *(d) On ABS models tighten the brake caliper mounting bracket bolts to the specified torque and refit the wheel sensor as described in Chapter 9.*
- *(e) With the car standing on its wheels, rock the suspension to settle all the suspension components in position then tighten all the disturbed pivot bolts to their specified torque setting.*
- *(f) Check and, if necessary, adjust the rear wheel alignment as described in Section 26.*

16.5A On refitting ensure steering wheel cut-outs are correctly engaged with indicator cancelling cam tabs (arrowed)...

16 Steering wheel – removal and refitting

Removal

1 Set the front wheels in the straight-ahead position. The steering wheel spokes should be horizontal.

2 Carefully prise out the horn button assembly from the centre of the steering wheel, then disconnect the wires from the horn terminals and remove the horn button assembly (photos).

3 Using a socket, unscrew and remove the steering wheel retaining nut.

4 Mark the steering wheel and steering column shaft in relation to each other then lift the steering wheel off the column splines. If it is tight, tap it up near the centre, using the palm of your hand, or twist it from side to side whilst pulling upwards to release it from the shaft splines.

Refitting

5 On refitting, check that the steering column splines are clean. Refit the wheel, entering the cut-outs on its lower surface with the direction indicator cancelling cam tabs and aligning the marks made on dismantling; this should leave the wheel positioned as described in paragraph 1 above (photos).

6 Tighten the steering wheel nut to the specified torque wrench setting, then reconnect the horn wiring to the horn terminals and press the horn into position in the centre of the wheel.

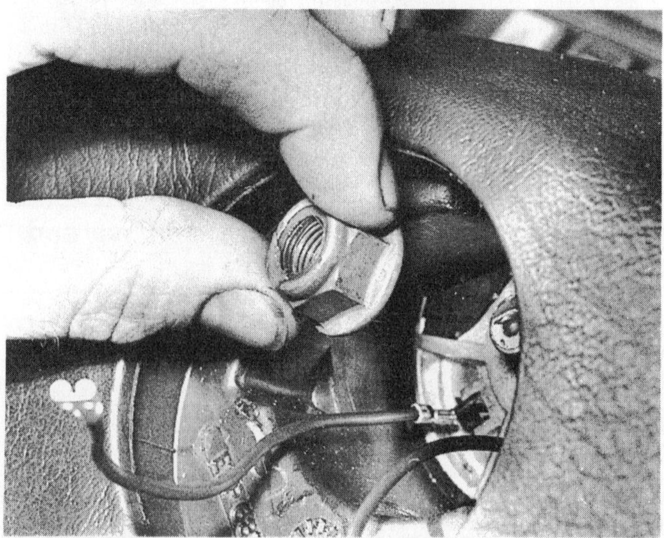

16.5B ...then refit the retaining nut

17.3A Prise off the snap ring...

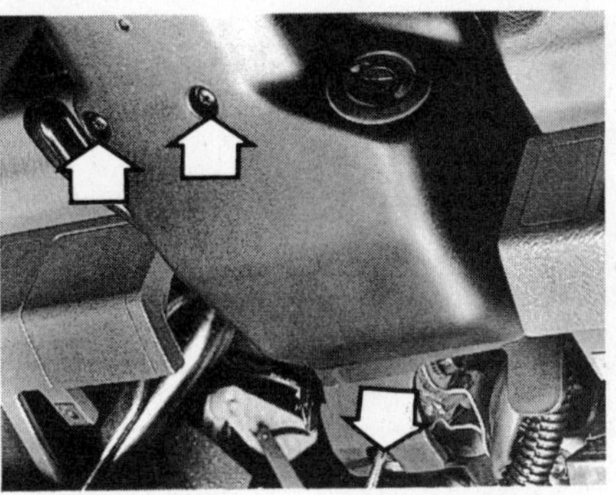

17.3B ...undo the lower shroud retaining screws (arrowed)...

17.3C ...and remove both lower and upper shrouds

17.5 Combination switch assembly is retained by two screws (remaining screw location arrowed)

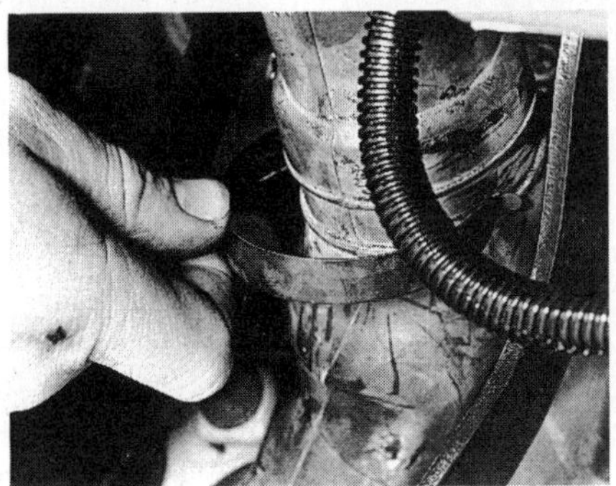

17.7A Remove the retaining clips...

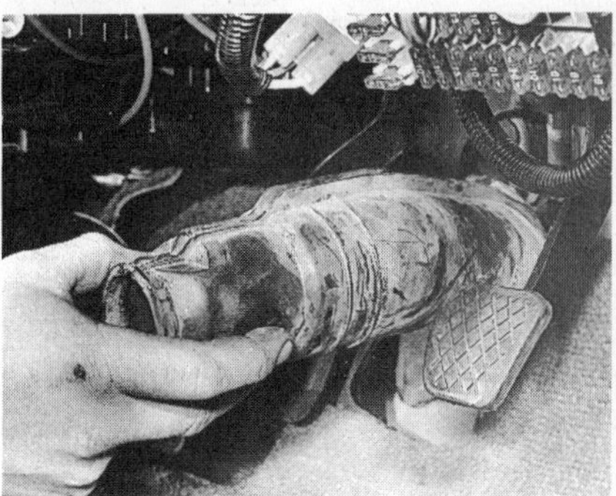

17.7B ...and withdraw the lower steering column cover

17.9 Steering column lower mounting clamp components

17.14 Ensure that the indicator cancelling cam is correctly engaged with the combination switch assembly

17 Steering column – removal and refitting

Removal

1 Insert the key to ensure the steering column is unlocked, then release the column tilt lever and position the steering wheel at the lowest possible position. Remove the steering wheel as described in Section 16.

2 Disconnect the battery negative terminal then undo the five right-hand lower facia panel retaining screws and remove the panel from the facia.

3 Prise the large snap ring which secures the two halves of the steering column shroud together from the top of the shrouds and remove the ignition key. Undo the three screws securing the lower shroud to the steering column and remove both the upper and lower steering column shrouds (photos).

4 Lift the indicator cancelling cam off the steering column and disconnect the wiring connectors from the rear of the steering column combination switch assembly.

5 Undo the two combination switch retaining screws and slide the assembly off the end of the steering column (photo).

6 Trace the ignition switch wiring back to its wiring connectors and disconnect them from the main wiring loom.

7 Pull back the driver's footwell carpet and remove the two studs securing the lower column cover to the floor. Remove the two retaining clips from the upper end of the cover and withdraw the cover (photos).

8 Using a hammer and punch, white paint or similar, mark the exact relationship between the steering column shaft and shaft to steering gear universal joint, then slacken and remove the pinch-bolt securing the joint to the column shaft.

9 Undo the nut and bolt securing the lower steering column mounting clamp in position and remove the clamp (photo). Slacken and remove the two nuts and bolts securing the upper mounting assembly to the

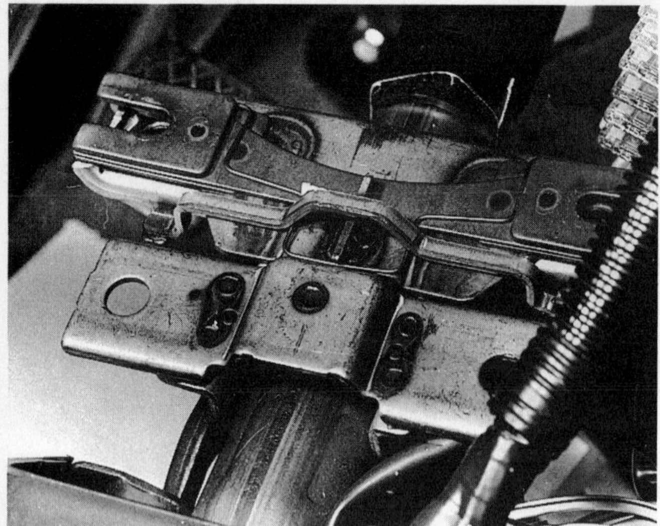

18.5 Fitted positions of upper mounting assembly components

vehicle then disengage the column from its mounting studs and universal joint then remove it from the vehicle.

Refitting

10 Before refitting the steering column, closely examine the upper mounting assembly for damage or misalignment as described in Section 18.

11 Align the marks made on dismantling and engage the steering column shaft splines with those of the universal joint.

12 Locate the upper mounting bracket assembly over its mounting studs and refit the upper mounting nuts and bolts. Refit the lower mounting clamp and tighten its retaining nut and bolt to the specified torque setting, then tighten the upper mounting nuts and bolts to their specified torque settings.

13 Refit the universal joint to steering column pinch-bolt and tighten it to the specified torque. Refit the lower cover over the steering column and secure it in position with the retaining clips and studs.

14 Refit the combination switch to the column and tighten its screws securely. Refit the indicator cancelling cam to the steering column, ensuring that it is correctly located with the switch assembly, and reconnect the combination and ignition switch wiring connectors (photo). Ensure that the wiring is correctly routed and secured by any relevant clips.

15 Offer up the two halves of the steering column shroud and refit the three retaining screws to the lower shroud. Ensure the shroud halves are clipped firmly together, then refit the snap ring to its groove.

16 Refit the lower facia panel, tightening its retaining screws securely, then refit the steering wheel as described in Section 16.

18 Steering column – overhaul

1 With the steering column removed from the car as described in Section 17, fit the ignition key and check that the steering lock is off. Remove the circlip from the upper end of the column shaft, and lift off the washer and spring washer.

2 Carefully withdraw the steering shaft from the lower end of the steering column; note the inner circlip fitted to the shaft upper end.

3 Inspect the steering shaft for straightness and for signs of impact and damage to the collapsible portion. Check for signs of wear, such as scoring, on the shaft bush and check the steering shaft universal joint for signs of damage or roughness in the joint bearings. If any damage or wear is found on the steering shaft, shaft bush or universal joint, the shaft must be renewed as an assembly.

4 Inspect the steering column for signs of damage and renew if necessary. Closely examine the column upper mounting and tilt assembly for signs of damage or distortion, paying particular attention to the upper mounting bending plate and its spring retainer. The bending plate is designed to distort in the event of an impact hitting the steering wheel and must be renewed, along with its spring retainer, if it is not completely straight. Renew other components as necessary.

5 If renewal of any of the upper mounting or steering column tilt assembly components is necessary, make a note of the correct fitted positions of all components before dismantling the assembly. Use this as a guide when reassembling all the components to ensure they are correctly fitted. Ensure that the ends of the bending plate spring retainer are correctly located in the holes in the mounting bracket and the retainer is hooked over the claw situated in the centre of the bracket (photo).

6 Apply a smear of grease to the steering shaft and column bearing surfaces and to the shaft bush. If a new steering shaft is being installed, transfer the inner circlip from the old shaft onto the second groove in the upper end of the new shaft.

7 Insert the steering shaft into position in the steering column and refit the spring washer and flat washer to the upper end of the steering shaft, securing them in position with the circlip. Ensure that the circlip is correctly located in its groove and check that the shaft rotates freely in the column. Remove the ignition key and check that the steering lock functions correctly.

8 Before installing the column assembly, check the steering shaft to steering gear universal joint for signs of wear or damage and smoothness of operation. If there is any sign of roughness in the joint bearing it must be renewed before refitting the steering column as described in Section 18.

19 Steering lock/ignition switch – removal and refitting

Removal

1 Remove the steering column from the car as described in Section 17.

2 Securely clamp the column assembly in a vice equipped with soft jaws taking great care not to overtighten the vice and distort the steering column.

3 Centre-punch the two steering lock shear bolts then drill off the heads of the bolts. Note that new shear bolts must be obtained for refitting.

4 Withdraw the steering lock/ignition switch, then unscrew the remains of the shear bolts using a self-locking wrench or similar on the exposed ends.

Refitting

5 On refitting, carefully align the assembly on the steering column, lightly tighten the bolts and check that the steering lock works smoothly.

6 Tighten the shear bolts evenly until their heads shear off.

7 Refit the steering column as described in Section 17.

20 Steering gear rubber gaiters – renewal

1 Remove the track rod balljoint as described in Section 25, and unscrew the locknut from the track rod end.

2 Using a pair of pliers, release the outer steering gear gaiter retaining clip and slide it off the track rod end. Remove the inner gaiter retaining clip by cutting it, then slide the gaiter off the end of the track rod.

3 Thoroughly clean the track rod and the steering gear housing, using fine abrasive paper to polish off any corrosion, burrs or sharp edges which might damage the new gaiter's sealing lips on installation. Repair kits which consist of new gaiters and retaining clips are available from Rover dealers.

4 Fit the new rubber gaiter ensuring that it is correctly seated in the grooves in the steering gear housing and track rod.

5 Check that the gaiter is not twisted or dented then secure it in position using new retaining clips.

6 Refit the locknut and balljoint onto the track rod end as described in Section 25.

21.3 Steering column universal joint pinch-bolts (arrowed)

21.7 Gearchange linkage bellcrank mounting bolt locations (arrowed)

21.9 Power steering pipes and steering gear right-hand mounting bolts (arrowed)

21 Steering gear – removal, overhaul and refitting

Removal

1 Chock the rear wheels, firmly apply the handbrake, jack up the front of the car and support on axle stands. Remove the appropriate front roadwheel.

2 Working from inside the car, peel back the driver's footwell carpet and remove the studs securing the lower steering column cover to the floor. Remove the two retaining clips from the upper end of the cover and withdraw the cover.

3 Mark the relative positions of the steering gear pinion and joint to use as a guide on refitting then slacken and remove the two universal joint pinch-bolts (photo). Slide the universal joint up the steering column shaft splines until it is free from the steering gear pinion.

4 Extract the split pins and undo the nuts securing the steering gear track rod balljoints to the swivel hubs. Release the balljoint shanks using a suitable balljoint separator tool whilst taking care not to damage the balljoint gaiters.

5 From underneath the car, slacken and remove the bolt securing the rear engine/transmission mounting connecting link to the subframe bracket, then remove the three subframe bracket retaining bolts and remove the bracket, releasing it from the exhaust mounting rubber. Undo the two bolts securing the connecting link and bracket assembly to the transmission housing and remove the assembly from the vehicle.

6 Undo the three front exhaust pipe to manifold retaining nuts and, where necessary, the two bolts securing the front pipe mounting bracket to the vehicle. Release the intermediate exhaust section from its mountings and lower the front of the exhaust system.

7 In the absence of the special gearchange linkage balljoint separator (Rover service tool Number 18G 1592), use a suitable flat-bladed screwdriver carefully lever the lower gearchange rod balljoint off the gearchange linkage bellcrank assembly. Remove the three bolts securing the assembly to the subframe (photo).

8 Using a suitable stout bar, lever down the rear of the engine/transmission unit and insert a block of wood between the transmission and subframe to hold it in position. This is necessary to gain the required clearance to remove the steering gear.

9 On models equipped with power-assisted steering, remove the bolt securing the feed and return pipe mounting bracket to the subframe. Mark the pipe union bolts to ensure they are correctly positioned on reassembly, then unscrew the pipe to steering gear union nuts (photo). Be prepared for fluid spillage and position a suitable container beneath the pipes whilst unscrewing the union nuts. This fluid must be disposed of and new fluid of the specified type used when refilling (Chapter 1). Plug the pipe ends and steering gear orifices to prevent excessive fluid leakage and the entry of dirt into the hydraulic system.

10 On all models, fully extend the left-hand track rod then undo the two left-hand steering gear mounting bolts and remove the mounting bracket. Undo the two right-hand mounting bolts, noting the mounting bushes and spacers, and free the steering gear pinion from its cutout.

11 Initially move the steering gear to the left, to free the right-hand track rod from the subframe, then manoeuvre the assembly out from the right-hand side of the vehicle. Remove the washers from the steering gear pinion.

Overhaul

12 Examine the steering gear assembly for signs of wear or damage and check that the rack moves freely throughout the full length of its travel with no signs of roughness or excessive free play between the steering gear pinion and rack. The steering gear is available only as a complete assembly with no individual components, with the exception of the track rod balljoints and rubber gaiters, being available separately. Therefore, if worn, the complete assembly must be renewed. Track rod balljoint and rubber gaiter renewal are covered in Sections 25 and 20 respectively of this Chapter.

13 Inspect the steering gear mounting bushes for signs of damage or deterioration and renew as necessary.

Refitting

14 Refit the washers to the pinion and, with the left-hand track rod fully extended, manoeuvre the steering gear into position from the right-hand side of the vehicle. Once both the track rods are located in the subframe cutouts, refit the mounting clamp and bolts, ensuring that the mounting bushes and spacers are correctly positioned, and tighten the mounting bolts to the specified torque.

15 Centralise the steering gear rack so that both track rods are protruding by an equal distance.

16 On models equipped with power-assisted steering, wipe clean the feed and return pipe unions then refit them to their respective positions on the steering gear and tighten the union nuts to the specified torque. Refit the bolt securing the pipe retaining bracket to the subframe and tighten securely.

17 The remainder of the refitting procedure is direct reversal of removal, noting the following points:

(a) Tighten all nuts and bolts to the specified torque settings.
(b) Secure the track rod balljoint retaining nuts in position with new split pins.
(c) When refitting the universal joint to the steering gear pinion splines, ensure that the front wheels are pointing in the straight-ahead direction then, if necessary, align the marks made on dismantling and check that the steering wheel spokes are horizontal.
(d) On completion check and, if necessary, adjust the front wheel alignment as described in Section 26.
(e) On models equipped with power-assisted steering bleed the hydraulic system as described in Section 24.

22 Power steering pump – removal and refitting

Removal

1 Slacken, but do not remove, the three power steering pump pulley retaining bolts, then remove the power steering pump drivebelt as described in Chapter 1.

2 Position a suitable container beneath the power steering pump to catch any spilt fluid, then slacken the inlet hose retaining clip and disconnect the hose from the top of the steering pump. Undo the bolt securing the outlet pipe retaining bracket to the pump, then unscrew the

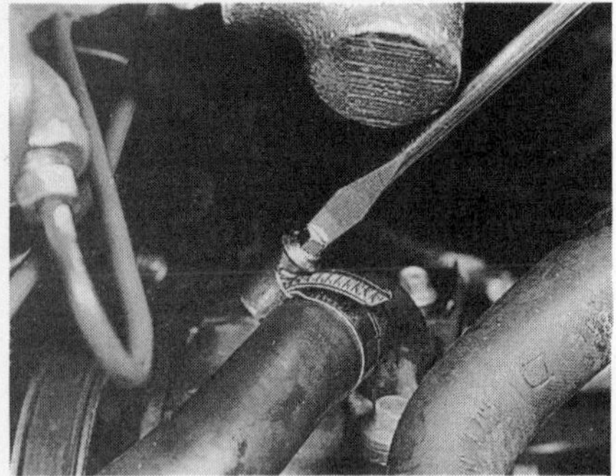

22.2A Slacken the retaining clamp and disconnect the inlet hose from the pump

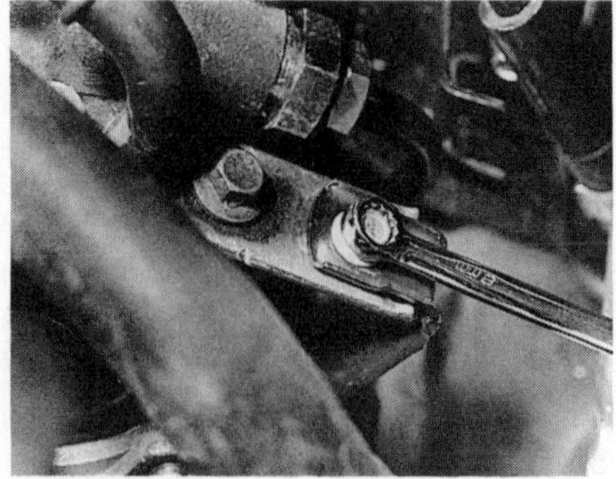

22.2B Remove the outlet pipe bracket retaining bolt...

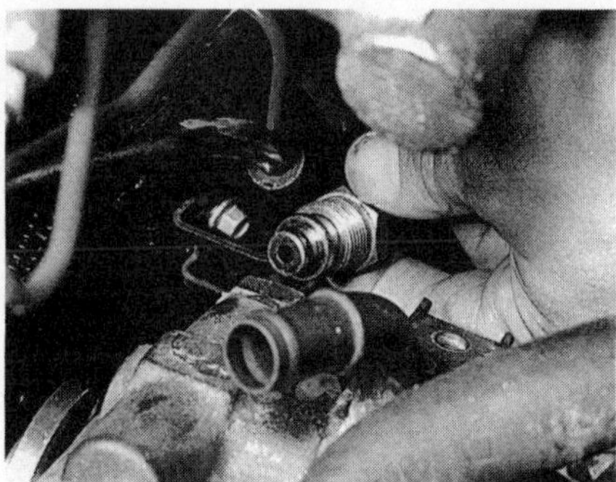

22.2C ...and unscrew the outlet pipe union nut from the pump

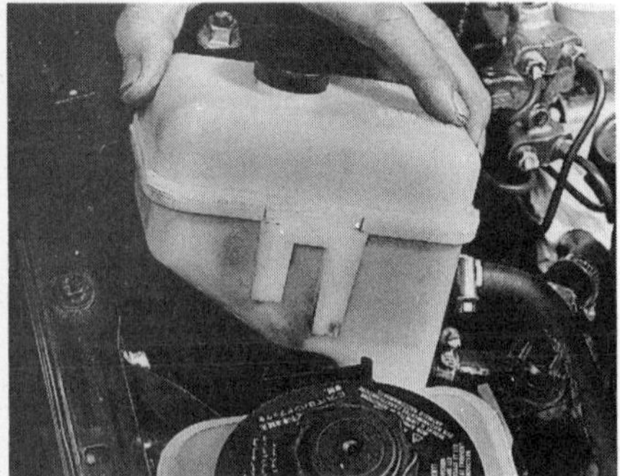

22.3 Remove the power steering fluid reservoir from the retaining clamp and position it clear of the pump

22.4A Remove the pulley retaining bolts (arrowed)...

22.4B ...and withdraw pulley. Note FRONT mark on pulley face (arrowed)

22.5A Unscrew the power steering pump mounting bolts (three arrowed)...

22.5B ...and remove the pump

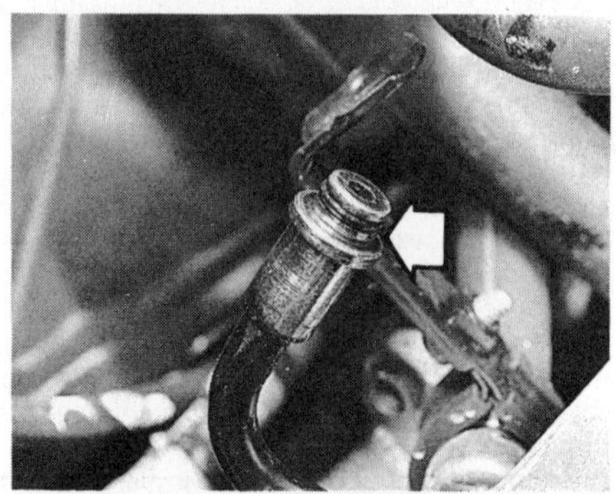

22.7 Always renew outlet pipe O-ring (arrowed) whenever disturbed

23.3 Slacken clamps and disconnect hoses from power steering oil cooler

23.4A Power steering oil cooler upper mounting bolts (arrowed)

23.4B Oil cooler lower mounting bolt can be accessed via bumper grille

outlet pipe union nut and disconnect the pipe from the pump, noting the O-ring which is fitted to the union (photos). Plug the hose ends and pump unions to prevent excessive fluid loss and the possible entry of dirt into the system.
3 Remove the reservoir from its mounting bracket and position it clear of the pump assembly (photo).
4 Unscrew the pump pulley retaining bolts and remove the pulley. Check that the front face of the pulley is marked FRONT, if not mark it using a dab of white paint. The mark can then be used to ensure that the pulley is correctly refitted (photos).
5 Undo the five bolts (three on the right-hand side of the pump, and two on the left-hand side) securing the power steering pump to the mounting bracket and remove the pump from the engine (photos).
6 The power steering pump is a sealed unit and cannot be repaired. If faulty the pump assembly must be renewed.

Refitting

7 Refitting is a reverse of the removal procedure noting the following points (photo):

- (a) *Tighten the pump mounting bolts to the specified torque.*
- (b) *Fit a new O-ring to the pump outlet pipe union and tighten the union nut to the specified torque.*
- (c) *Ensure the pulley is correctly installed and lightly tighten its mounting bolts.*
- (d) *Refit and adjust the drivebelt as described in Chapter 1, and tighten the pulley mounting bolts to the specified torque.*
- (e) *On completion bleed the hydraulic system as described in Section 24.*

23 Power steering oil cooler - removal and refitting

Removal

1 Remove the right-hand headlamp assembly as described in Chapter 12.
2 Remove the bonnet lock as described in Chapter 11.
3 Position a suitable container beneath the power steering oil cooler hose connections to catch any spilt fluid, then slacken the hose retaining clips and disconnect both hoses (photo). Plug the hose and oil cooler ends to prevent excessive fluid loss and the possible entry of dirt into the system.
4 Undo the three oil cooler mounting bracket retaining bolts, then manoeuvre the oil cooler assembly out from between the front bumper and body (photos).

Refitting

5 Refitting is the reverse of the removal procedure. On completion bleed the hydraulic system as described in Section 24.

24 Power steering system - bleeding

Note: *Avoid holding the steering at full lock for long periods of time. Failure to do so could lead to overheating, and possible damage, of the power steering pump and steering gear.*
1 Remove the cap from the power steering fluid reservoir and fill the reservoir with the specified fluid.
2 Disconnect the distributor wiring at the connector, to prevent the engine from starting, then turn the engine over for approximately 5 seconds to prime the power steering pump.
3 Reconnect the distributor wiring, then check the reservoir fluid level is between the MAX and MIN level markings on the side of the reservoir, topping up if necessary.
4 Start the engine and allow it to idle for approximately 30 seconds with the front wheels pointing in the straight-ahead position. After 30 seconds turn the steering onto full lock in one direction, hold it there for a few seconds, then turn it onto full lock in the opposite direction and hold it there for a few seconds. Return the front wheels to the straight-ahead position. Repeat this procedure until air bubbles cease to appear in the fluid reservoir.
5 If, when turning the steering, an abnormal noise is heard from the fluid lines, it indicates that there is still air in the system. Check this by turning the wheels to the straight-ahead position and switching off the engine. If the fluid level in the reservoir rises, then air is present in the system and further bleeding is necessary.
6 Once all traces of air have been removed from the power steering hydraulic system turn the engine off and allow the system to cool. Once cool, check that fluid level is up to the MAX mark on the power steering fluid reservoir, topping up if necessary.

25 Track rod balljoint - removal and refitting

Removal

1 Apply the handbrake, then jack up the front of the vehicle and support it on axle stands. Remove the appropriate front roadwheel.
2 If the balljoint is to be re-used, use a straight-edge and a scriber, or similar, to mark its relationship to the track rod.
3 Holding the balljoint, unscrew its locknut by one quarter of a turn.
4 Extract the split pin and undo the nut securing the steering gear track rod balljoint to the swivel hub. Release the balljoint shank using a suitable balljoint separator tool whilst taking care not to damage the balljoint gaiter (photo).
5 Counting the **exact** number of turns necessary to do so, unscrew the balljoint from the track rod. If the locknut is to be removed, mark its

25.4 Using a universal balljoint separator to free track rod balljoint from swivel hub

25.9 Secure the balljoint retaining nut in position with a new split pin

position on the track rod and count the number of turns required to remove it so that it can be returned exactly to its original position on reassembly.

6 Carefully clean the balljoint and the threads. Renew the balljoint if its movement is sloppy or if it is too stiff, if it is excessively worn or if it is damaged in any way; carefully check the stud taper and threads. No grease leakage should be visible.

Refitting

7 If necessary, screw the locknut onto the track rod by the number of turns noted on removal. This should align the locknut with the mark made on dismantling.

8 Screw the balljoint onto the track rod by the number of turns noted on removal. This should bring the balljoint to within a quarter of a turn from the locknut, with the alignment marks that were made (if applicable) on removal lined up.

9 Refit the balljoint shank to the swivel hub and tighten its retaining nut to the specified torque setting. Use a new split pin to secure the retaining nut in position (photo).

10 Refit the roadwheel then lower the car to the ground and tighten the roadwheel nuts to the specified torque setting.

11 Check and, if necessary, adjust the front wheel alignment as described in Section 26.

26 Wheel alignment and steering angles - general information

Wheel alignment and steering angles - general

1 A car's steering and suspension geometry is defined in five basic settings - all angles are expressed in degrees and the steering axis is defined as an imaginary line drawn through the centres of the front suspension upper and lower balljoints, extended where necessary to contact the ground.

2 **Camber** is the angle between each roadwheel and a vertical line drawn through its centre and tyre contact patch when viewed from the front or rear of the car. Positive camber is when the roadwheels are tilted outwards from the vertical at the top; negative camber is when they are tilted inwards.

3 Camber is not adjustable is given for reference only; while it can be checked using a camber checking gauge, if the figure obtained is significantly different from that specified the car must be taken for careful checking by a professional, as the fault can only be caused by wear or damage to the body or suspension components.

4 **Castor** is the angle between the steering axis and a vertical line drawn through each roadwheel's centre and tyre contact patch when viewed from the side of the car. Positive castor is when the steering axis is tilted so that it contacts the ground ahead of the vertical; negative castor is when it contacts the ground behind the vertical.

5 Castor is not adjustable and is given for reference only; while it can be checked using a castor checking gauge, if the figure obtained is significantly different from that specified the car must be taken for careful checking by a professional, as the fault can only be caused by wear or damage to the body or suspension components.

6 **Steering axis inclination/SAI** - also known as **kingpin inclination/KPI** - is the angle between the steering axis and a vertical line drawn through each roadwheel's centre and tyre contact patch when viewed from the front or rear of the car.

7 SAI/KPI is not adjustable and is given for reference only.

8 **Toe** is the difference, viewed from above, between lines drawn through the roadwheel centres and the car's centre-line. 'Toe-in' is when the roadwheels point inwards, towards each other at the front, while 'toe-out' is when they splay outwards from each other at the front.

9 At the front, the toe setting is adjusted by screwing the track rods in or out of their balljoints to alter the effective length of the track rod assemblies.

10 At the rear, the toe setting is adjusted by slackening the front lateral link to body pivot bolt and repositioning the bolt in its mounting slot thereby altering the position of the trailing arm assembly.

11 **Toe-out on turns** - also known as turning angles or Ackermann angles - is the difference, viewed from above, between the angles of rotation of the inside and outside front roadwheels when they have been turned through a given angle.

12 Toe-out on turns is set in production and is not adjustable as such, but can be upset by altering the length of the track rods unequally. It is essential, therefore, to ensure that the track rod lengths are exactly the same and that they are turned by the same amount whenever the toe setting is altered.

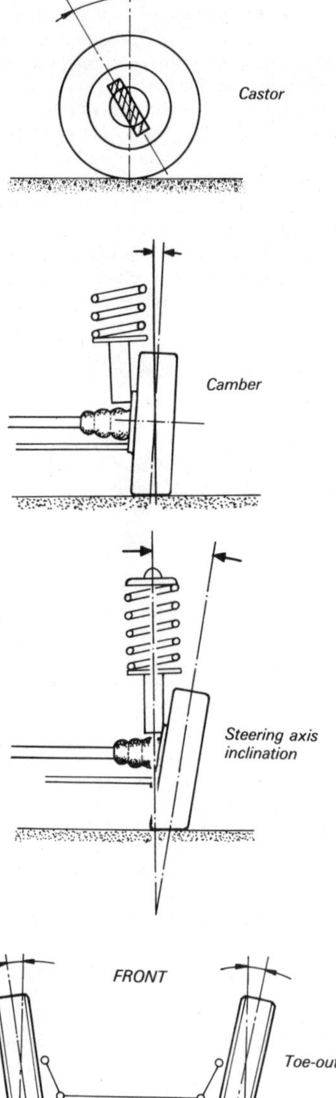

Fig. 10.11 Wheel alignment and steering angles (Sec 26)

Checking - general

13 Due to the special measuring equipment necessary to check the wheel alignment and the skill required to use it properly, the checking and adjustment of these settings is best left to a Rover dealer or similar expert; note that most tyre-fitting shops now possess sophisticated checking equipment.

14 For **accurate** checking, the car **must** be at the kerb weight specified in *'General dimensions and weights'*.

15 Before starting work, always check first that the tyre sizes and types are as specified, then check the pressures and tread wear, the roadwheel run-out, the condition of the hub bearings, the steering wheel free play and the condition of the front suspension components (Chapter 1). Correct any faults found.

16 Park the car on level ground, check that the front roadwheels are in the straight-ahead position, then rock the rear and front ends to settle the suspension, release the handbrake and roll the car backwards 1 metre, then forwards again to relieve any stresses in the steering and suspension components.

Toe-out on turns - checking and adjusting

17 As far as the home mechanic is concerned, this can be checked only using a pair of scuff plates.

18 Prepare the car as described in paragraphs 14 to 16 above. Roll the car backwards, check that the front roadwheels are in the straight-ahead position, then roll it forwards on to the scuff plates until each front roadwheel is seated squarely on the centre of each plate.

19 Turn the steering wheel first one way until the outside roadwheel is at the specified angle; record the angle of the inside roadwheel. Next, turn the steering wheel back through the straight-ahead position and repeat the check on that side.

20 If, in either check, the inside roadwheel is not at the angle specified, check that both track rod assemblies are exactly the same length by counting the exposed threads inboard of the locknuts. If the lengths are different this can be corrected by screwing the track rods in or out of the balljoints, but this will affect the toe setting (see below) and the steering wheel position.

21 If the angles are incorrect but the track rods are the same length and the steering mechanism components are known from the preliminary checks to be unworn, then there is damage to, or distortion of, part of the steering mechanism, the front suspension or the body itself. This will require careful checking, preferably by an expert such as a Rover dealer, as soon as possible.

Toe setting - checking and adjusting

22 As far as the home mechanic is concerned, the toe setting can be checked only using a pair of scuff plates, in which the roadwheels are rolled across a moveable plate which records any deviation (or scuff) of the tyre relative to the straight-ahead position as it moves across the plate. While such gauges are available in relatively inexpensive form from accessory outlets, only an individual owner can decide whether the expense is justified, in view of the small amount of use such equipment would normally receive.

Front wheel toe setting

23 Prepare the car as described in paragraphs 14 to 16 above.

24 Roll the car backwards, check that the roadwheels are in the straight-ahead position, then roll it across the scuff plates so that each front roadwheel passes squarely over the centre of its respective plate. Note the angle recorded by the scuff plates.

25 To ensure accuracy, repeat the check three times and take the average of the three readings.

26 If the roadwheels are running parallel, there will of course be no angle recorded; if a deviation value is shown on the scuff plates, compare the reading obtained for each wheel with that specified. If the value recorded is outside the set tolerance, the toe setting is incorrect and must be adjusted.

27 If adjustment is required, apply the handbrake then jack up the front of the car and support it securely on axle stands. First clean the track rod threads; if they are corroded, apply penetrating fluid before starting adjustment. Release the rubber gaiter outboard clips, peel back the gaiters and apply a smear of grease so that both are free and will not be twisted or strained as their respective track rods are rotated.

28 Use a straight-edge and a scriber or similar to mark the relationship of each track rod to its balljoint then, holding each balljoint in turn, unscrew its locknut fully (photo).

29 Alter the length of both track rods (by exactly the same amount) by screwing them into or out of the balljoints one-quarter of a turn at a time and rechecking the toe setting until it is correct; shortening the track rods (screwing them into their balljoints) will reduce toe-in/increase toe-out. If the track rods are not provided with squared sections that permit the use of a spanner, they must be rotated using a self-locking wrench.

30 To ensure that the track rod lengths remain equal, always rotate them in the same direction (viewed from the centre of the car).

31 When the setting is correct, hold the balljoints and tighten the locknuts securely. Check that the balljoints are seated correctly in their sockets and count the exposed threads to check the length of both track rods. If they are not the same then the adjustment has not been made equally and problems will be encountered with tyre scrubbing in turns; also, the steering wheel spokes will no longer be horizontal when the wheels are in the straight-ahead position.

32 If the track rod lengths are the same, check that the toe setting has been correctly adjusted by lowering the car to the ground and preparing it (paragraph 16 above), then re-checking the toe setting (paragraphs 24 to 26); re-adjust if necessary. If the setting is correct tighten the track rod balljoint locknuts to the specified torque. Ensure that the rubber gaiters are seated correctly and are not twisted or strained, then refit the clips to secure their outboard ends.

26.28 Adjusting front wheel alignment

Rear wheel toe setting

33 The procedure for checking the rear toe setting is the same as described for the front in paragraphs 23 to 26, except that the rear wheels rather than the front wheels are rolled across the scuff plates.

34 If adjustment is necessary, chock the rear wheels then jack up the rear of the car and support it on axle stands.

35 Mark the relative position of the front lateral link to body pivot bolt to use as a reference. Slacken the bolt then, using a suitable piece of wood, lever the front of the trailing arm assembly to either move the lateral link pivot bolt inwards (to increase toe-in) or outwards (to decrease toe-in) (photo). As an approximate guide the distance the pivot bolt should be moved is equal to the distance that the wheel is out of alignment. Note also that both bolts should be positioned at approximately the same place in their respective slot as the opposite lateral link pivot bolt. Once both right- and left-hand front lateral link pivot bolts are positioned correctly tighten them to the specified torque setting.

36 Check that the toe setting has been correctly adjusted by lowering the car to the ground and preparing it (paragraph 16 above), then rechecking the toe setting (paragraphs 24 to 26). Repeat the adjustment procedure, if necessary, until the correct toe setting is obtained for each wheel.

26.35 Rear wheel alignment is adjusted by repositioning front lateral link to body pivot bolt in its slot

Chapter 11 Bodywork and fittings

Contents

Specifications

Torque wrench setting	**Nm**	**lbf ft**
Front bumper mounting bolts	10	7
Rear bumper:		
Mounting nuts	22	16
Mounting bolt	10	7
Bonnet hinge mounting bolts	10	7
Bonnet lock mounting bolts	10	7
Bonnet release lever mounting bolts	10	7
Wheel arch liner screws	10	7
Door glass regulator and top slide bolts	6	4
Door glass to regulator bolts	6	4
Door glass channel nut and bolt	6	4
Door hinge bolts	24	18
Boot lid hinge bolts	10	7
Boot lid lock retaining bolts	10	7
Boot lid lock cylinder retaining bolt	10	7
Tailgate hinge nuts and bolts	10	7
Front seat slide mounting bolts	45	33
Rear seat hinge bolts - 214 models	25	19
Rear seat back bolts - 414 models	10	7
Seat belt fastenings:		
Mounting bolts - front and rear	32	24
Front belt upper mounting nut	25	19
Inertia reel upper mounting bolt	9	6
Inertia reel lower mounting bolt	32	24
Rear side belt guide retaining bolts	32	24
Facia mounting bolts	9	6

1 General information

The bodyshell is made of pressed-steel sections in three- and five-door Hatchback and four-door Saloon versions. Most components are welded together but some use is made of structural adhesives; the front wings are bolted on.

The bonnet, door, tailgate and some other vulnerable panels are made of zinc-coated metal; once assembled, the entire body is given an eight-stage pretreatment process including a high-pressure wash before painting. The first coat of primer is applied by cathodic electro-deposition, followed by four coats of paint and two of lacquer; an anti-stone chip coating (finished in matt black, where exposed) is applied to the outer faces of the sills and the corresponding surfaces of the front and rear wings. A PVC coating is applied to the underbody, followed by a coating of protective wax; all chassis members, box-sections and sills are injected with liquid cavity wax.

Several of the body cavities are then filled with 'expand-in-place' foam. This process features a two-part liquid silicon foam and hardener mix which is injected into the cavities after the body has been painted and wax treated. The foam improves the noise insulation of the vehicle and is also flame retardant. On top of this the foam is also hydrophobic (repels water).

Extensive use is made of plastic materials, mainly on the interior but also in exterior components such as the wheel arch liners. The plastic front wheel arch liners are fitted to improve the body's resistance to corrosion.

2 Maintenance – bodywork and underframe

The general condition of a vehicle's bodywork is the one thing that significantly affects its value. Maintenance is easy but needs to be regular. Neglect, particularly after minor damage, can lead quickly to further deterioration and costly repair bills. It is important also to keep watch on those parts of the vehicle not immediately visible, for instance the underside, inside all the wheel arches and the lower part of the engine compartment.

The basic maintenance routine for the bodywork is washing – preferably with a lot of water, from a hose. This will remove all the loose solids which may have stuck to the vehicle. It is important to flush these off in such a way as to prevent grit from scratching the finish. The wheel arches and underframe need washing in the same way to remove any accumulated mud which will retain moisture and tend to encourage rust. Paradoxically enough, the best time to clean the underframe and wheel arches is in wet weather when the mud is thoroughly wet and soft. In very wet weather the underframe is usually cleaned of large accumulations automatically and this is a good time for inspection.

Periodically, except on vehicles with a wax-based underbody protective coating, it is a good idea to have the whole of the underframe of the vehicle steam cleaned, engine compartment included, so that a thorough inspection can be carried out to see what minor repairs and renovations are necessary. Steam cleaning is available at many garages and is necessary for the removal of the accumulation of oily grime which sometimes is allowed to become thick in certain areas. If steam cleaning facilities are not available, there are one or two excellent grease solvents available such as Holts Engine Degreasant, which can be brush applied. The dirt can then be simply hosed off. Note that these methods should not be used on vehicles with wax-based underbody protective coating or the coating will be removed. Such vehicles should be inspected annually, preferably just prior to winter, when the underbody should be washed down and any damage to the wax coating repaired using Holts Undershield. Ideally, a completely fresh coat should be applied. It would also be worth considering the use of such wax-based protection for injection into door panels, sills, box sections, etc, as an additional safeguard against rust damage where such protection is not provided by the vehicle manufacturer.

After washing paintwork, wipe off with a chamois leather to give an unspotted clear finish. A coat of clear protective wax polish like the many excellent Turtle Wax polishes, will give added protection against chemical pollutants in the air. If the paintwork sheen has dulled or oxidised, use a cleaner/polisher combination such as Turtle Wax Hard Shell to restore the brilliance of the shine. This requires a little effort, but such dulling is usually caused because regular washing has been neglected. Care needs to be taken with metallic paintwork, as special non-abrasive cleaner/polisher is required to avoid damage to the finish. Always check that the door and ventilator opening drain holes and pipes are completely clear so that water can be drained out. Brightwork should be treated in the same way as paintwork. Windscreens and windows can be kept clear of the smeary film which often appears by the use of proprietary glass cleaner like Holts Mixra. Never use any form of wax or other body or chromium polish on glass.

3 Maintenance – upholstery and carpets

Mats and carpets should be brushed or vacuum cleaned regularly to keep them free of grit. If they are badly stained remove them from the vehicle for scrubbing or sponging and make quite sure they are dry before refitting. Seats and interior trim panels can be kept clean by wiping with a damp cloth and Turtle Wax Carisma. If they do become stained (which can be more apparent on light coloured upholstery) use a little liquid detergent and a soft nail brush to scour the grime out of the grain of the material. Do not forget to keep the headlining clean in the same way as the upholstery. When using liquid cleaners inside the vehicle do not over-wet the surfaces being cleaned. Excessive damp could get into the seams and padded interior causing stains, offensive odours or even rot. If the inside of the vehicle gets wet accidentally it is worthwhile taking some trouble to dry it out properly, particularly where carpets are involved. *Do not leave oil or electric heaters inside the vehicle for this purpose.*

4 Minor body damage – repair

Note: *For more detailed information about bodywork repair, Haynes Publishing produce a book by Lindsay Porter called The Car Bodywork Repair Manual. This incorporates information on such aspects as rust treatment, painting and glass-fibre repairs, as well as details on more ambitious repairs involving welding and panel beating.*

The colour bodywork repair photographic sequences between pages 32 and 33 illustrate the operations detailed in the following sub-sections.

Repairs of minor scratches in bodywork

If the scratch is very superficial, and does not penetrate to the metal of the bodywork, repair is very simple. Lightly rub the area of the scratch with a paintwork renovator like Turtle Wax Color Back, or a very fine cutting paste like Holts Body+Plus Rubbing Compound, to remove loose paint from the scratch and to clear the surrounding bodywork of wax polish. Rinse the area with clean water.

Apply touch-up paint to the scratch using a fine paint brush; continue to apply fine layers of paint until the surface of the paint in the scratch is level with the surrounding paintwork. Allow the new paint at least two weeks to harden, then blend it into the surrounding paintwork by rubbing the scratch area with a paintwork renovator or a very fine cutting paste such as Holts Body+Plus Rubbing Compound or Turtle Wax Color Back. Finally apply wax polish from one of the Turtle wax range of wax polishes.

Where the scratch has penetrated right through to the metal of the bodywork, causing the metal to rust, a different repair technique is required. Remove any loose rust from the bottom of the scratch with a penknife, then apply rust inhibiting paint such as Turtle Wax Rust Master, to prevent the formation of rust in the future. Using a rubber or nylon applicator fill the scratch with bodystopper paste like Holts Body+Plus Knifing Putty. If required, this paste can be mixed with cellulose thinners such as Holts Body+Plus Cellulose Thinners, to provide a very thin paste which is ideal for filling narrow scratches. Before the stopper-paste in the scratch hardens, wrap a piece of smooth cotton rag around the top of a finger. Dip the finger in cellulose thinners and quickly sweep it across the surface of the stopper-paste in the scratch; this will ensure that the surface of the stopper-paste is slightly hollowed. The scratch can now be painted over as described earlier in this Section.

Repairs of dents in bodywork

When deep denting of the vehicle's bodywork has taken place, the first task is to pull the dent out, until the affected bodywork almost attains its original shape. There is little point in trying to restore the original shape completely, as the metal in the damaged area will have stretched on impact and cannot be reshaped fully to its original contour. It is better to bring the level of the dent up to a point which is about 3 mm below the level of the surrounding bodywork. In cases where the dent is very shallow anyway, it is not worth trying to pull it out at all. If the underside of the dent is accessible, it can be hammered out gently from behind, using a mallet with a wooden or plastic head. Whilst doing this, hold a suitable block of wood firmly against the outside of the panel to absorb the impact from the hammer blows and thus prevent a large area of the bodywork from being 'belled-out'.

Should the dent be in a section of the bodywork which has a double skin or some other factor making it inaccessible from behind, a different technique is called for. Drill several small holes through the metal inside the area – particularly in the deeper section. Then screw long self-tapping screws into the holes just sufficiently for them to gain a good purchase in the metal. Now the dent can be pulled out by pulling on the protruding heads of the screws with a pair of pliers.

The next stage of the repair is the removal of the paint from the damaged area, and from an inch or so of the surrounding 'sound' bodywork. This is accomplished most easily by using a wire brush or abrasive pad on a power drill, although it can be done just as effectively by hand using sheets of abrasive paper. To complete the preparation for filling, score the surface of the bare metal with a screwdriver or the tang of a file, or alternatively, drill small holes in the affected area. This will provide a really good 'key' for the filler paste.

To complete the repair see the Section on filling and respraying.

Repairs of rust holes or gashes in bodywork

Remove all paint from the affected area and from an inch or so of the surrounding 'sound' bodywork, using an abrasive pad or a wire brush on a power drill. If these are not available a few sheets of abrasive paper will do the job most effectively. With the paint removed you will be able to judge the severity of the corrosion and therefore decide whether to renew the whole panel (if this is possible) or to repair the affected area. New body panels are not as expensive as most people think and it is often quicker and more satisfactory to fit a new panel than to attempt to repair large areas of corrosion.

Remove all fittings from the affected area except those which will act as a guide to the original shape of the damaged bodywork (eg headlamp shells, etc.). Then, using tin snips or a hacksaw blade, remove all loose metal and any other metal badly affected by corrosion. Hammer the edges of the hole inwards in order to create a slight depression for the filler paste.

Wire brush the affected area to remove the powdery rust from the surface of the remaining metal. Paint the affected area with rust inhibiting paint such as Turtle Wax Rust Master; if the back of the rusted area is accessible treat this also.

Before filling can take place it will be necessary to block the hole in some way. This can be achieved by the use of aluminium or plastic mesh, or aluminium tape.

Aluminium or plastic mesh or glass fibre matting is probably the best material to use for a large hole. Cut a piece to the approximate size and shape of the hole to be filled, then position it in the hole so that its edges are below the level of the surrounding bodywork. It can be retained in position by several blobs of filler paste around its periphery.

Aluminium tape should be used for small or very narrow holes. Pull a piece off the roll and trim it to the approximate size and shape required, then pull off the backing paper (if used) and stick the tape over the hole; it can be overlapped if the thickness of one piece is insufficient. Burnish down the edges of the tape with the handle of a screwdriver or similar, to ensure that the tape is securely attached to the metal underneath.

Bodywork repairs – filling and respraying

Before using this Section, see the Sections on dent, deep scratch, rust holes and gash repairs.

Many types of bodyfiller are available, but generally speaking those proprietary kits which contain a tin of filler paste and a tube of resin hardener are best for this type of repair like Holts Body + Plus or Holts No Mix which can be used directly from the tube. A wide, flexible plastic or nylon applicator will be found invaluable for imparting a smooth and well contoured finish to the surface of the filler.

Mix up a little filler on a clean piece of card or board – measure the hardener carefully (follow the maker's instructions on the pack) otherwise the filler will set too rapidly or too slowly. Alternatively, Holts No Mix can be used straight from the tube without mixing, but daylight is required to cure it. Using the applicator apply the filler paste to the prepared area; draw the applicator across the surface of the filler to achieve the correct contour and to level the surface. As soon as a contour that approximates to the correct one is achieved, stop working the paste – if you carry on too long the paste will become sticky and begin to 'pick-up' on the applicator. Continue to add thin layers of filler paste at twenty minute intervals until the level of the filler is just proud of the surrounding bodywork.

Once the filler has hardened, excess can be removed using a metal plane or file. From then on, progressively finer grades of abrasive paper should be used, starting with a 40 grade production paper and finishing with a 400 grade wet-and-dry paper. Always wrap the abrasive paper around a flat rubber, cork, or wooden block – otherwise the surface of the filler will not be completely flat. During the smoothing of the filler surface the wet-and-dry paper should be periodically rinsed in water. This will ensure that a very smooth finish is imparted to the filler at the final stage.

At this stage the 'dent' should be surrounded by a ring of bare metal, which in turn should be encircled by the finely 'feathered' edge of the good paintwork. Rinse the repair area with clean water, until all of the dust produced by the rubbing-down operation has gone.

Spray the whole area with a light coat of primer, either Holts Body + Plus Grey or Red Oxide Primer – this will show up any imperfections in the surface of the filler. Repair these imperfections with fresh filler paste or bodystopper, and once more smooth the surface with abrasive paper. If bodystopper is used, it can be mixed with cellulose thinners to form a really thin paste which is ideal for filling small holes. Repeat this spray and repair procedure until you are satisfied that the surface of the filler, and the feathered edge of the paintwork are perfect. Clean the repair area with clean water and allow to dry fully.

The repair area is now ready for final spraying. Paint spraying must be carried out in a warm, dry, windless and dust free atmosphere. This condition can be created artificially if you have access to a large indoor working area, but if you are forced to work in the open, you will have to pick your day very carefully. If you are working indoors, dousing the floor in the work area with water will help to settle the dust which would otherwise be in the atmosphere. If the repair area is confined to one body panel, mask off the surrounding panels; this will help to minimise the effects of a slight mis-match in paint colours. Bodywork fittings (eg chrome strips, door handles, etc.) will also need to be masked off. Use genuine masking tape and several thicknesses of newspaper for the masking operations.

Before commencing to spray, agitate the aerosol can thoroughly, then spray a test area (an old tin, or similar) until the technique is mastered. Cover the repair area with a thick coat of primer; the thickness should be built up using several thin layers of paint rather than one thick one. Using 400 grade wet-and-dry paper, rub down the surface of the primer until it is really smooth. While doing this, the work area should be thoroughly doused with water, and the wet-and-dry paper periodically rinsed in water. Allow to dry before spraying on more paint.

Spray on the top coat using Holts Dupli-color Autospray, again building up the thickness by using several thin layers of paint. Start spraying in the centre of the repair area and then, using a circular motion, work outwards until the whole repair area and about 2 inches of the surrounding original paintwork is covered. Remove all masking material 10 to 15 minutes after spraying on the final coat of paint.

Allow the new paint at least two weeks to harden, then, using a paintwork renovator or a very fine cutting paste such as Turtle Wax Color Back or Holts Body + Plus Rubbing Compound, blend the edges of the paint into the existing paintwork. Finally, apply wax polish.

Plastic components

With the use of more and more plastic body components by the vehicle manufacturers (eg bumpers, spoilers, and in some cases major body panels), rectification of more serious damage to such items has become a matter of either entrusting repair work to a specialist in this field, or renewing complete components. Repair of such damage by the DIY owner is not really feasible owing to the cost of the equipment and materials required for effecting such repairs. The basic technique involves making a groove along the line of the crack in the plastic using a rotary burr in a power drill. The damaged part is then welded back together by using a hot air gun to heat up and fuse a plastic filler rod into the groove. Any excess plastic is then removed and the area rubbed down to a smooth finish. It is important that a filler rod of the correct plastic is used, as body components can be made of a variety of different types (eg polycarbonate, ABS, polypropylene).

Damage of a less serious nature (abrasions, minor cracks, etc.) can be repaired by the DIY owner using a two-part epoxy filler repair material such as Holts Body + Plus or Holts No Mix which can be used directly from the tube. Once mixed in equal proportions (or applied directly from the tube in the case of Holts No Mix), this is used in similar fashion to the bodywork filler used on metal panels. The filler is usually cured in twenty to thirty minutes, ready for sanding and painting.

If the owner is renewing a complete component himself, or if he has repaired it with epoxy filler, he will be left with the problem of finding a suitable paint for finishing which is compatible with the type of plastic used. At one time the use of a universal paint was not possible owing to the complex range of plastics encountered in body component applications. Standard paints, generally speaking, will not bond to plastic or rubber satisfactorily, but Holts Professional Spraymatch paints to match any plastic or rubber finish can be obtained from dealers. However, it is now possible to obtain a plastic body parts finishing kit which consists of a pre-primer treatment, a primer and coloured top coat. Full instructions are normally supplied with a kit, but basically the method of use is to first apply the pre-primer to the component concerned and allow it to dry for up to 30 minutes. Then the primer is applied and left to dry for about an hour before finally applying the special coloured top coat. The result is a correctly coloured component where the paint will flex with the plastic or rubber, a property that standard paint does not normally possess.

5 Major body damage – repair

Where serious damage has occurred, or large areas need renewal due to neglect, it means that complete new panels will need welding in, and this is best left to professionals. If the damage is due to impact, it will also be necessary to check completely the alignment of the bodyshell, and this can only be carried out accurately by a Rover dealer using special jigs. If the body is left misaligned, it is primarily dangerous as the car will not handle properly, and secondly, uneven stresses will be imposed on the steering, suspension and possibly transmission, causing abnormal wear, or complete failure, particularly to such items as the tyres.

6 Front bumper – removal and refitting

Removal

1 Firmly apply the handbrake then jack up the front of the vehicle and support it on axle stands.
2 Remove the headlamps as described in Chapter 12.
3 Remove the four screws securing the bumper to the right-hand wheel arch liner, then undo the three screws securing the top of the liner to the body and prise out the screw retaining plugs. Free the right-hand wheel arch liner from the front bumper and repeat the complete procedure for the left-hand wheel arch.
4 Undo the three bolts securing the bumper to the front undercover panel followed by the four bolts securing the bumper mounting plates to the body mounting brackets (photo).
5 Release both the left- and right-hand bumper slides from their retaining studs and pull the bumper away from the vehicle in a forwards direction.
6 If necessary, the bumper mounting plates, trim strip and number plate can be removed from the bumper and the bumper mountings can be unbolted from the vehicle. Renew the components as necessary and/or transfer them to the new bumper.

Refitting

7 Refitting is a reverse of the removal sequence ensuring that the bumper mounting bolts are tighten to the specified torque.

6.4 Front bumper mounting plate to bracket bolts

7 Rear bumper – removal and refitting

Removal

1 Chock the front wheels then jack up the rear of the vehicle and support it on axle stands.

214 models

2 From underneath the vehicle, undo the four screws securing the undercover panel to the left-hand side of the bumper and remove the panel.
3 Remove the screw securing the left-hand wheel arch liner to the body, and the screw securing the right-hand wheel arch liner to the bumper.
4 Undo the bolt, situated next to the towing hook, securing the underside of the bumper to the vehicle.
5 Open the tailgate and from inside the luggage compartment, prise out the two circular grommets to gain access to the bumper mounting nuts, then undo both nuts and remove the flat washers.
6 Release both the left- and right-hand bumper slides from their mountings and pull the bumper away from the vehicle in a rearwards direction, noting the sealing washer and two flat washers which are fitted to each of the bumper mounting studs.

7.8 Remove rubber grommet to gain access to bumper mounting nut

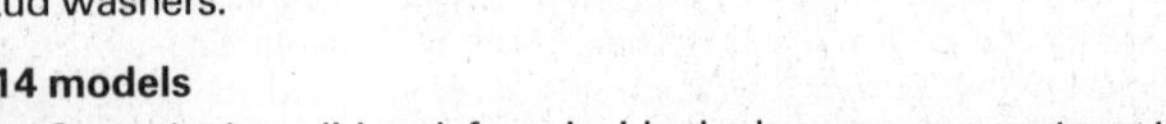

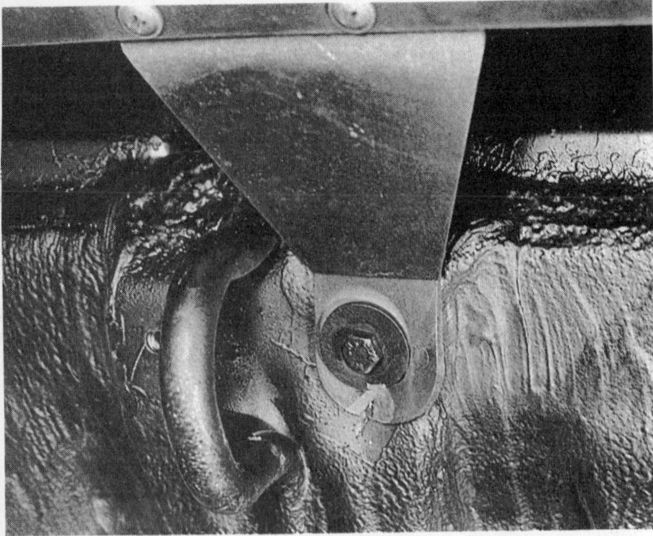

7.9 Rear bumper centre mounting bracket to body bolt – 414 models

7 If a new bumper is being fitted, transfer the trim strip and mounting stud washers.

414 models

8 Open the boot lid and, from inside the luggage compartment, prise out the two circular grommets to gain access to the bumper mounting nuts, then undo both nuts and remove the flat washers (photo).
9 From underneath the car, slacken and remove the two nuts and washers securing the bumper mounting brackets to the body and undo the bolt securing the bumper centre mounting bracket to the body (photo).
10 Remove the screw securing the left-hand wheel arch liner to the wheel arch.
11 Release both the left- and right-hand bumper slides from their mountings and pull the bumper away from the vehicle in a rearwards direction, noting the sealing washers which are fitted to each of the bumper mounting studs.
12 If necessary, the bumper mounting brackets and trim strip can be removed from the bumper and either renewed or transferred to a new bumper.

Refitting

13 Refitting is a reverse of the removal sequence ensuring that the bumper mounting nuts and bolts are tightened to their specified torque settings.

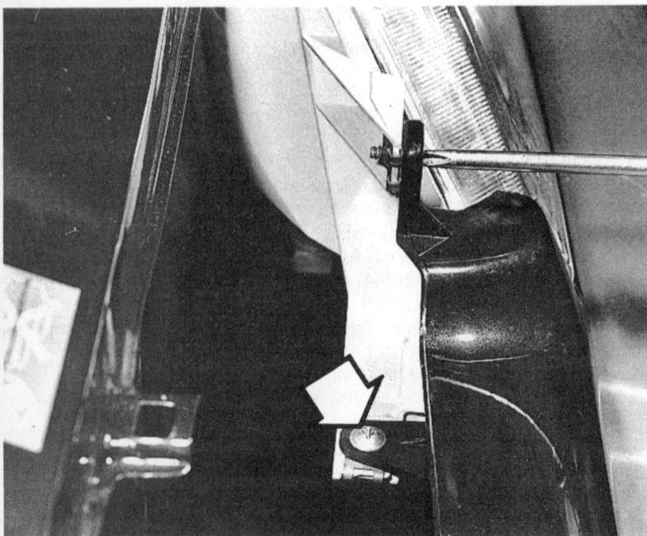

8.1 Radiator grille left-hand retaining screws

8 Radiator grille – removal and refitting

Removal

1 Open the bonnet, then remove the four screws securing the radiator grille to the headlamp assemblies and remove the grille from the car (photo).

Refitting

2 Fit the grille into position between the headlamps and tighten its retaining screws securely.

9 Bonnet – removal, refitting and adjustment

Removal

1 Open the bonnet and get an assistant to support it then, using a pencil or felt tip pen, mark the outline position of each bonnet hinge relative to the bonnet to use as a guide on refitting.
2 Disconnect the windscreen washer supply pipe from the T-piece, then undo the bonnet retaining bolts and, with the help of an assistant, carefully lift the bonnet clear, noting any shims which may be fitted between the bonnet and hinge (photos). Store the bonnet out of the way in a safe place.

Refitting and adjustment

3 Offer up the bonnet, position the shims (where fitted) between the bonnet and hinges, and loosely fit the retaining bolts (photo). Align the

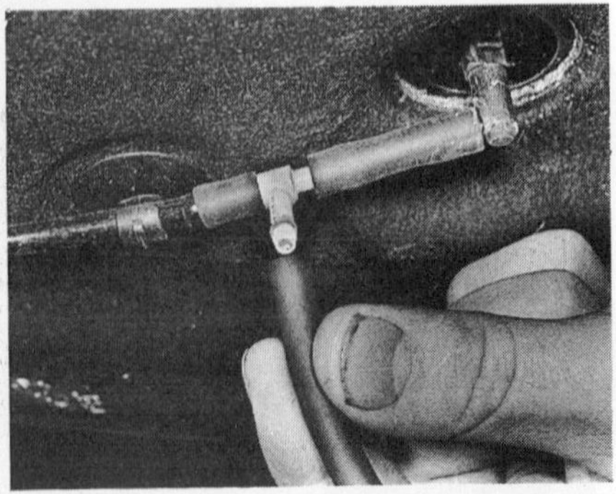

9.2A Disconnect the washer supply pipe...

9.2B ...and remove the bonnet with the aid of an assistant

9.3 Bonnet retaining bolts

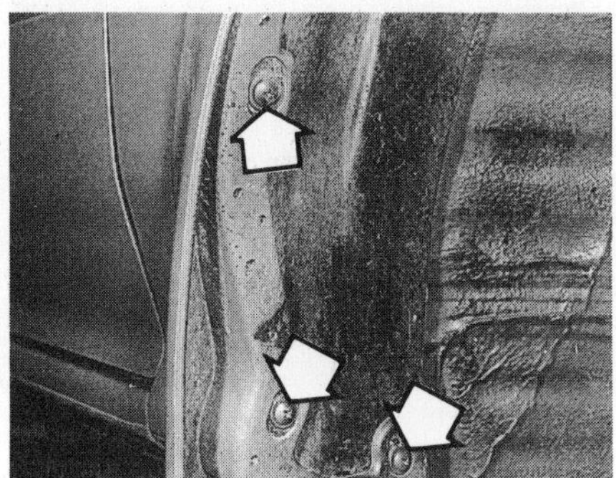
10.2 Mudflap retaining screws (arrowed)

10.3 Remove the right-hand wheel arch liner...

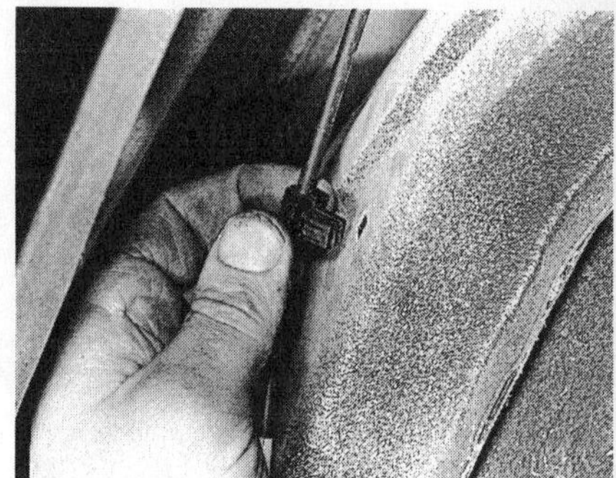
10.4 ...and release the cable retaining clips from the wheel arch

hinges with the marks made on removal (where applicable) then tighten the retaining bolts securely and reconnect the windscreen washer supply pipe.

4 Close the bonnet and check for alignment with the adjacent panels. If necessary, slacken the hinge bolts and realign the bonnet to suit. Once the bonnet is correctly aligned tighten the hinge bolts to the specified torque.

5 Check that the bonnet height is correct with that of the front wings and, if necessary, adjust by altering the height of the bonnet rubber stops.

6 Once the bonnet is correctly aligned, check that the bonnet fastens and releases in a satisfactory manner. If adjustment is necessary, remove the plastic lock cover then slacken the bonnet lock retaining bolts and adjust the position of the lock to suit. Once the lock is operating correctly tighten its retaining bolts to the specified torque and refit the lock cover.

10 Bonnet release cable - removal and refitting

Removal

1 With the bonnet open, carefully prise off the plastic lock cover, then disconnect the inner cable from the lock operating mechanism and release the outer cable from the lock bracket.

2 Undo the three screws securing the right-hand mudflap to the wheel arch and remove the mudflap (photo).

3 Remove the four screws securing the right-hand wheel arch liner to the front bumper, then undo the six screws securing the liner to the wheel arch and prise out the screw retaining plugs. Manoeuvre the wheel arch liner out from under the wheel arch (photo).

4 Release the cable from its retaining clips in the engine compartment and under the right-hand wing. Pull the cable through from under the right wheel arch (photo).

5 From inside the car, undo the two bolts securing the bonnet release lever to the vehicle then release the cable sealing grommet from under the facia panel. Pull the cable through from inside the car and remove it from the vehicle.

Refitting

6 Feed the cable through from inside the car until the bonnet release lever is in position. Tighten the lever mounting bolts to the specified torque and refit the sealing grommet.

7 From under the right-hand wheel arch feed the cable through into the engine compartment then fit the cable to the two retaining clips situated under the wheel arch.

8 Ensure the cable is correctly routed around the engine compartment and retained by all the necessary retaining clips then connect the cable to the bonnet lock.

9 Refit the right-hand wheel arch liner and press the six screw retaining plugs back into position. Refit the retaining screws and the liner to bumper screws and tighten all wheel arch liner screws to the specified torque. Refit the mudflap.

10 Check that the bonnet fastens and releases in a satisfactory manner. If adjustment is necessary, slacken the bonnet lock retaining bolts and adjust the position of the lock to suit. Once the lock is operating correctly tighten its retaining bolts to the specified torque and refit the lock cover.

11 Bonnet lock - removal, refitting and adjustment

Removal

1 Remove the radiator grille as described in Section 8.

2 Carefully prise off the plastic cover from the lock then mark the outline of the bonnet lock on the body to use as a guide on refitting (photo).

3 Slacken and remove the three bonnet lock retaining bolts then

11.2 Remove the plastic bonnet lock cover...

11.3A ...and undo three retaining bolts (remaining two arrowed)...

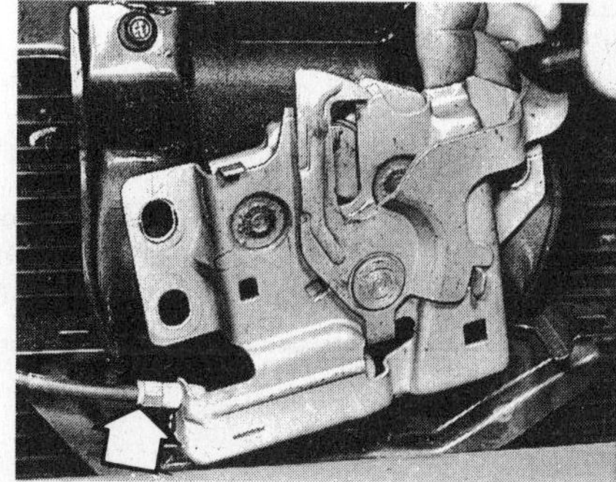
11.3B ...then remove the lock and disconnect the release cable (arrowed)

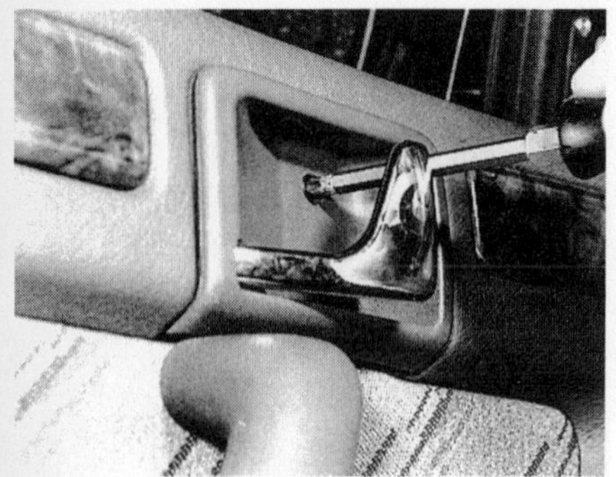
12.2A Undo the retaining screw...

12.2B ...and remove inner door handle escutcheon

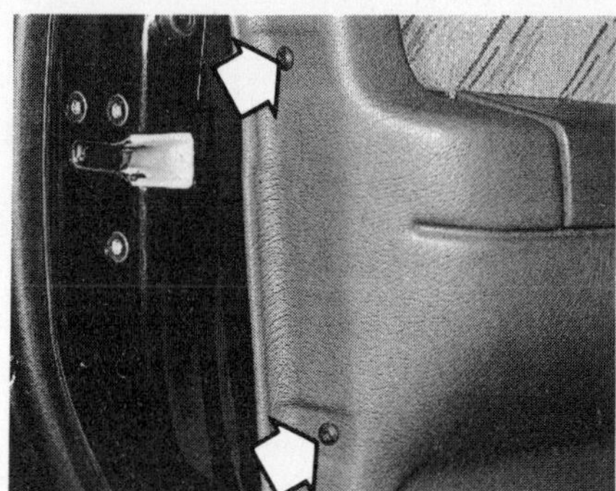
12.4A Front door trim panel retaining screws

12.4B Removing front armrest retaining screw

12.5 On models equipped with electric windows disconnect wiring connectors as trim panel is removed

12.6 Fit horseshoe clip (arrowed) to manual regulator handle before refitting the handle to the regulator

withdraw the lock and disconnect the inner cable from the lock operating mechanism. Release the outer cable from the lock bracket and remove the lock from the car (photos).

Refitting and adjustment

4 Refit the release cable to the lock operating mechanism then align the lock with the marks made on removal and tighten the lock retaining bolts to the specified torque.

5 Check that the bonnet fastens and releases in a satisfactory manner. If adjustment is necessary, slacken the bonnet lock retaining bolts and adjust the position of the lock to suit. Once the lock is operating correctly tighten its retaining bolts to the specified torque and refit the lock cover and radiator grille.

12 Door inner trim panel – removal and refitting

Removal

1 Open the door and carefully prise out and remove either the mirror inner trim panel (front door) or window inner trim panel (rear door).

2 Undo the door inner handle escutcheon retaining screw and remove the escutcheon (photos).

3 On models equipped with manual windows, remove the window regulator handle horseshoe clip by hooking it out with a screwdriver or bent piece of wire, then pull the handle off the spindle and remove the regulator escutcheon.

4 Remove the screws securing the inner trim panel and armrest to the door noting that on certain models the armrest mounting screws may be hidden behind trim caps (photos).

5 Release the door trim panel studs by carefully levering between the panel and door with a suitable flat-bladed screwdriver. When all the studs are released lift the panel upwards and away from the door. Note that on models with electric windows it will be necessary to disconnect the switch wiring connector(s) as the panel is removed (photo).

Refitting

6 Refitting the trim panel is the reverse of removal, noting the following points (photo):

(a) *Check the trim panel retaining studs for breakage and renew them as necessary.*

(b) *When refitting the window regulator handle (where fitted), fit the clip to the handle first then push the handle onto the regulator spindle.*

13 Door window glass and regulator – removal and refitting

Removal

Front door window glass and regulator

1 Remove the front door inner trim panel as described in Section 12.

2 Undo the four screws securing the speaker to the door then withdraw the speaker and disconnect its wiring connectors.

3 Undo the two armrest support bracket retaining screws and remove the bracket from the door (photo).

4 On models equipped with electric windows, temporarily connect the window switch wiring connector(s) and position the glass so that access can be gained to both the glass retaining bolts via the cutaway in the door panel. If work is being carried out on the right-hand door, unplug the wiring connectors from the window control unit then undo the control unit mounting screws and remove the unit from the door panel (photo). Release any relevant wiring retaining clips from the door.

5 On models equipped with central locking disconnect the wiring connectors from the door lock motor unit and release the wiring retaining clips from the door panel. If work is being carried out on the left-hand door, unplug the wiring connectors from the central locking control unit then undo the control unit mounting screws and remove the unit from the door panel (photo).

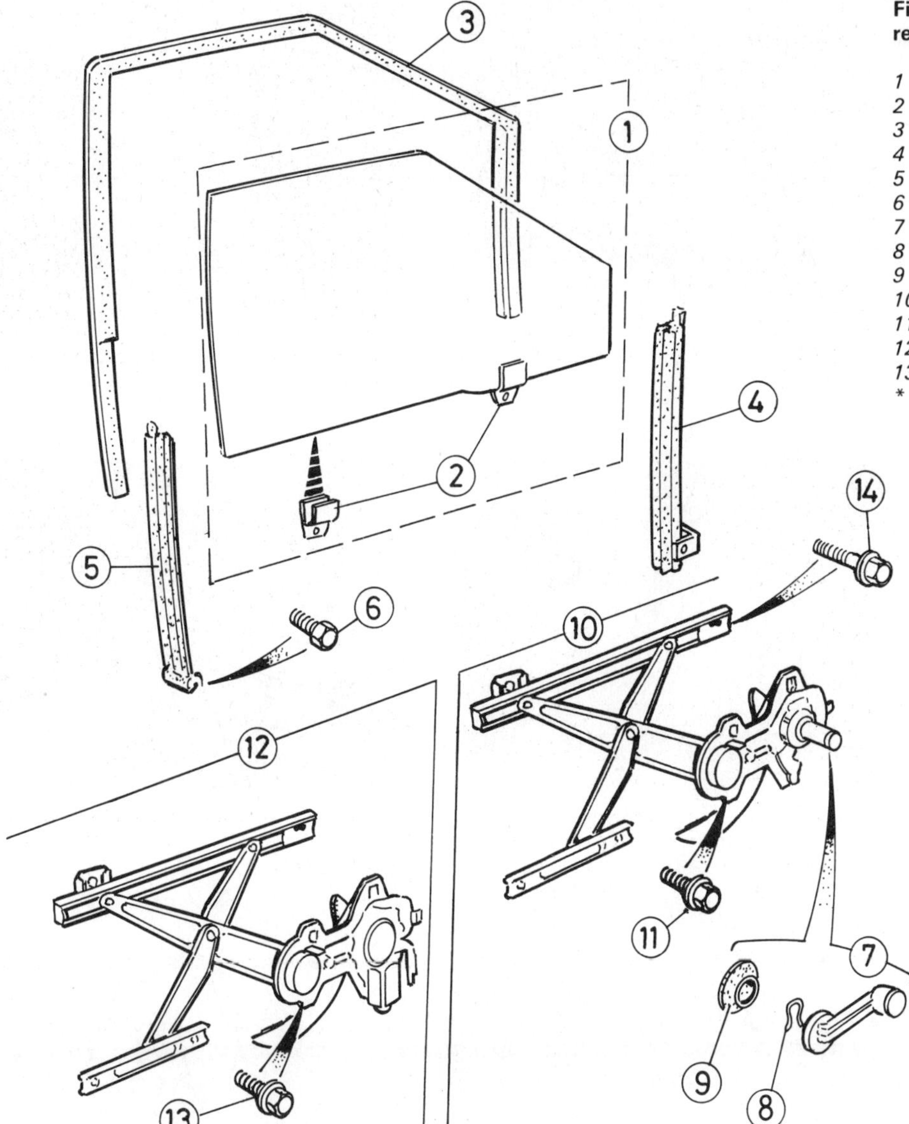

Fig. 11.1 Front door window glass and regulator components (Sec 13)

1 *Window glass*
2 *Window glass mounting brackets*
3 *Sealing strip*
4 *Window glass front channel*
5 *Window glass rear channel*
6 *Bolt*
7 *Regulator handle **
8 *Regulator handle retaining clip **
9 *Regulator escutcheon **
10 *Manual window regulator assembly **
11 *Bolt **
12 *Electric window regulator assembly **
13 *Bolt **
* *Not fitted to all models*

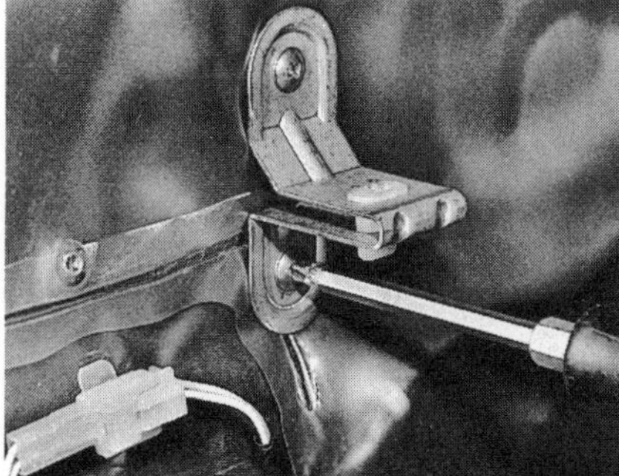

13.3 Armrest support bracket is retained by two screws

13.4 On models equipped with electric windows the control unit must be removed when working on the right-hand door

13.5 On models equipped with central locking the control unit must be removed when working on the left-hand door

6 On models equipped with manual windows temporarily refit the regulator handle and position the glass so that its retaining bolts can be accessed through the cutaway in the door.

7 On all models carefully peel back the polythene watershield to gain access to the regulator components (photo).

8 Slacken and remove the bolt securing the front glass channel to the door then carefully disengage the channel from the window glass.

9 Undo the two bolts securing the window glass to the regulator then lift up the glass and manoeuvre it out of the door (photo).

10 Slacken and remove the six regulator assembly retaining bolts and manoeuvre the assembly out through the door panel cutaway.

Rear door window glass and regulator

11 Remove the rear door inner trim panel as described in Section 12.

Fig. 11.2 Rear door window glass and regulator components (Sec 13)

1 Window glass
2 Window glass mounting brackets
3 Sealing strip
4 Window glass front channel
5 Window glass rear channel
6 Bolt
7 Nut
8 Spacer
*9 Regulator handle **
*10 Regulator handle retaining clip **
*11 Regulator escutcheon **
*12 Manual window regulator assembly **
*13 Bolt **
*14 Electric window regulator assembly **
*15 Electric window regulator **
*16 Electric window motor **
*17 Bolt **
** Not fitted to all models*

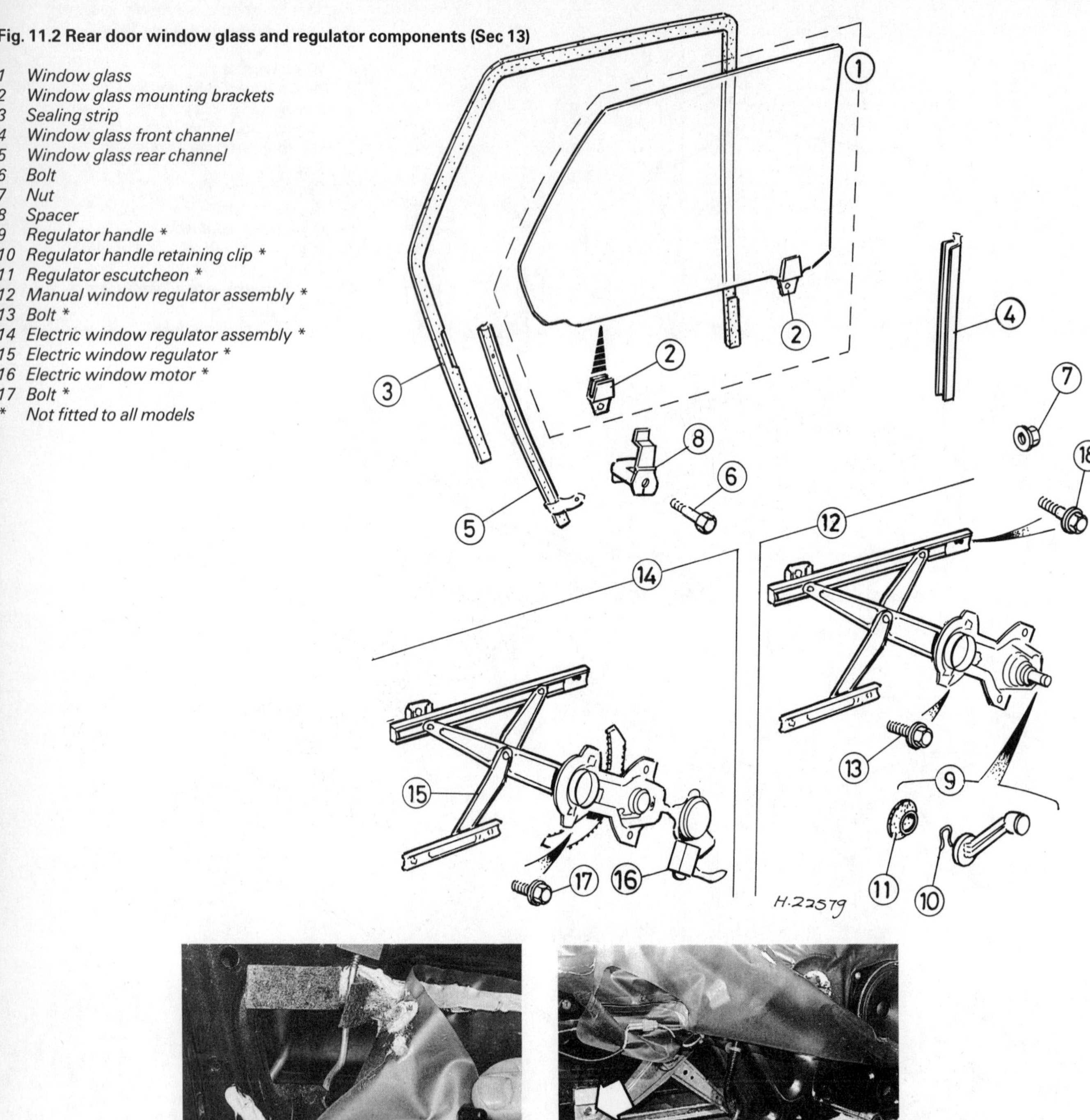

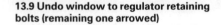

13.7 Carefully peel back polythene watershield to gain access to regulator components

13.9 Undo window to regulator retaining bolts (remaining one arrowed)

12 Where necessary, disconnect the wiring from the central locking motor and free any relevant wiring clips from the door panel.

13 Temporarily refit the regulator handle or reconnect the switch wiring connector (as applicable) and position the window glass so the retaining bolts can be accessed through the cutaway in the door panel.

14 Undo the two arm rest support bracket retaining screws then remove the bracket from the door and carefully peel back the polythene watershield.

15 Undo the window outer rear trim panel retaining screw and remove the panel from the door.

16 Remove the screw securing the outer window sealing strip to the rear of the door then carefully prise the strip out of the door panel and remove it from the car.

17 Slacken and remove the bolt securing the lower end of the rear window glass channel to the door panel and recover the spacer, through which the bolt passes, from inside the door panel. Undo the nut securing the channel to the door then release the rear channel from the window glass and rubber sealing strip and remove it from the door.

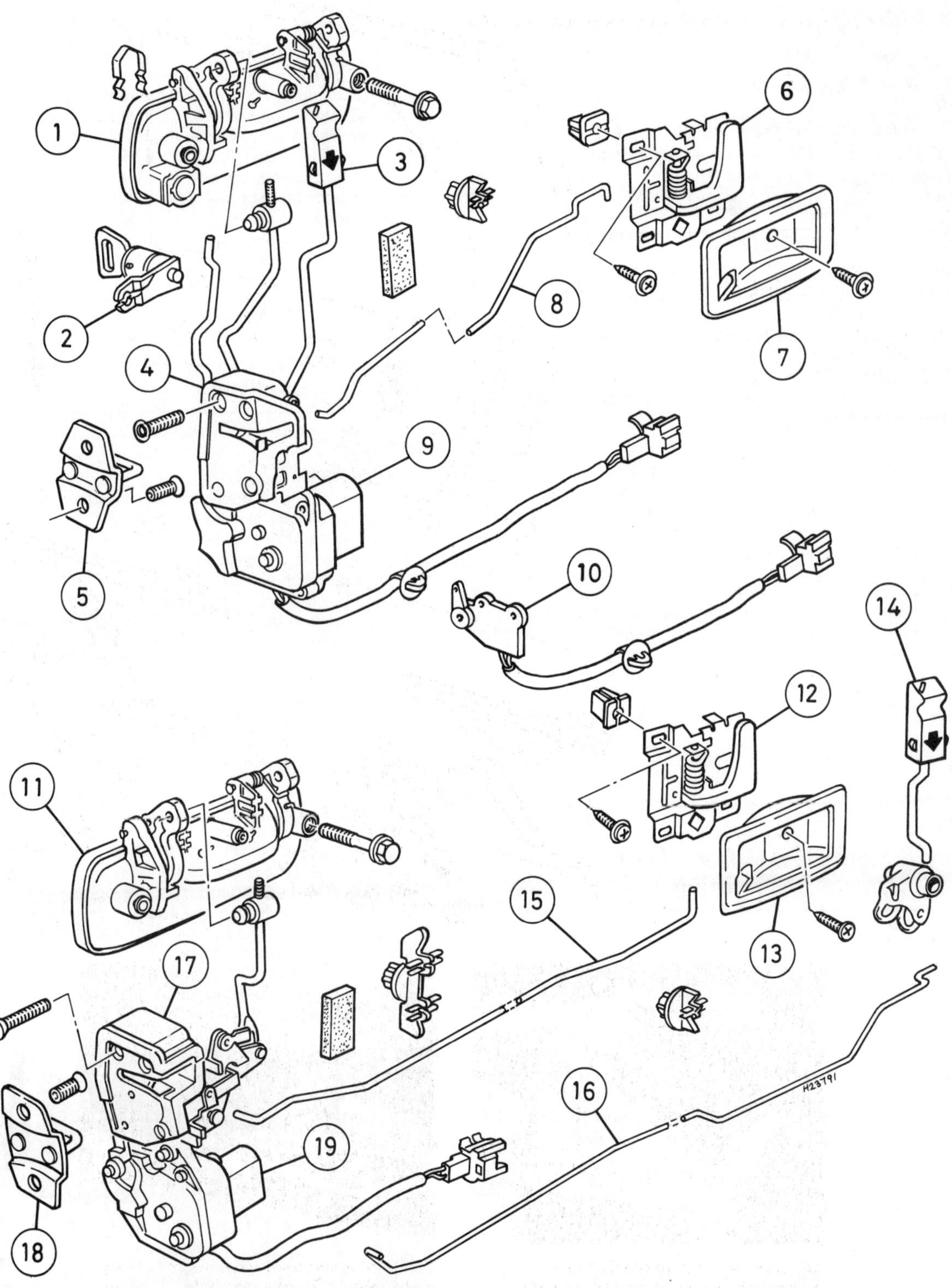

Fig. 11.3 Door lock and handle components (Sec 15)

Front door – items 1 to 10
1 Exterior handle
2 Door lock cylinder
3 Interior lock button
4 Lock assembly
5 Lock striker
6 Interior handle
7 Interior handle escutcheon
8 Link rod – interior handle to lock
*9 Central locking motor – passenger door **
*10 Central locking switch – driver's door **

Rear door – items 11 to 19
11 Exterior handle
12 Interior handle
13 Interior handle escutcheon
14 Interior lock button
15 Link rod – interior handle to lock
16 Link rod – interior lock button to lock
17 Lock assembly
18 Lock striker
*19 Central locking motor **
** Not fitted to all models*

18 Undo the two bolts securing the window glass to the regulator then lift up the glass and manoeuvre it out of the door.
19 Slacken and remove the six regulator assembly retaining bolts and manoeuvre the assembly out through the door panel cutaway.

Refitting

Front door window glass and regulator

20 Refit the regulator to the door panel and lightly tighten its retaining bolts. Operate the regulator mechanism, either using the handle or by connecting the switch, to align the top slide then tighten the retaining bolts to the specified torque.
21 Install the window glass and tighten the glass to regulator bolts to the specified torque.
22 Refit the front glass channel, ensuring that it is correctly located in position, then tighten its retaining bolt lightly. Operate the regulator mechanism a few times to align the channel with the window glass, checking that the window travels up and down smoothly, then tighten the channel bolt to the specified torque.
23 Refit the polythene watershield to the door ensuring that it is securely stuck down around the edges. The remainder of refitting is a reversal of the removal procedure.

Rear door window glass and regulator

24 Refit the regulator and glass as described in paragraphs 20 and 21.
25 Relocate the rear window glass channel with the rubber sealing strip and window glass then refit its retaining nut. Position the spacer inside the door panel then refit the channel lower bolt, ensuring it passes through the spacer and tighten both the channel retaining nut and bolt lightly. Operate the regulator mechanism a few times to align the channel with the window glass, checking that the window travels up and down smoothly, then tighten the channel retaining nut and bolt to the specified torque setting.
26 Refit the polythene watershield to the door ensuring that it is securely stuck down around the edges. The remainder of refitting is a reversal of the removal procedure.

14 Quarterlight glass (3-Door Hatchback models) - removal and refitting

Removal

1 Remove the rear window parcel shelf, then fold the rear seat cushion fully forwards and remove the rear seat back as described in Section 26. Remove the rubber seal from the rear seat back retaining catch.
2 Remove the four screws securing the rear seat side trim panel to the luggage compartment carpet and carefully peel the front door sealing strip away from the door pillar so that the front edge of the trim panel is freed. The panel can then be released by carefully prising it away from the body, using a large flat-bladed screwdriver to release the retaining clips, and removed from the car.
3 Remove the single retaining screw securing the rear quarterlight trim panel in position then carefully prise the panel away from the body and remove it from the car.
4 Remove the upper seat belt mounting cover then undo the retaining nut and remove the seat belt from its mounting point.
5 Undo the upper door pillar trim panel retaining screw and peel the door sealing strip away from the front edge of the panel. Release all the panel retaining clips and remove it from the car.
6 Mark the position of the quarterlight rear catch on the body then remove the three hinge retaining screws.
7 Support the window glass then undo the front hinge retaining screws and remove the glass from the car.
8 Examine the window seal for signs of damage or deterioration and renew if necessary. To renew the seal, first undo the two nuts securing the outer door pillar trim panel in position and remove the panel. The old seal can then be removed and the new seal installed. Once the seal is correctly positioned refit the outer trim panel and tighten its retaining screws securely.

Refitting

9 Refitting is a reverse of the removal sequence noting the following points:

(a) *Align the rear window catch with the marks made on dismantling and lightly tighten the retaining screws.*
(b) *Close the window and check that it is correctly aligned with the surrounding bodywork. Adjust, if necessary, by repositioning the hinge then tighten all the hinge retaining screws securely.*
(c) *Where possible, renew any broken trim panel retaining clips.*
(d) *Tighten the seat belt upper mounting nut to the specified torque.*
(e) *On completion ensure all trim panels are securely retained and the door sealing strip is correctly located on the pillar.*

15 Door lock, lock cylinder and handles - removal and refitting

Removal

Front door lock

1 Remove the front door window glass as described in Section 13, then remove the lock cylinder as described in paragraph 15.
2 Position the window sealing strip clear of the lock assembly and, where necessary, release the wiring retaining clips from the door panel.
3 Remove the three screws securing the interior handle to the door panel and free the operating rod from the retaining clips.
4 Undo the two bolts securing the exterior handle to the door then remove the three door lock retaining screws (photo).
5 Partially withdraw the lock and handle assembly then disconnect the interior and exterior handle connecting rods from the lock and remove both handles from the door. Disconnect the inner lock button operating rod from the lock and remove the button.
6 Disconnect the wiring connector from the central locking motor (where fitted) and manoeuvre the lock assembly out of the door.

Rear door lock

7 Remove the rear door window glass as described in Section 13.
8 Remove the screw securing the inner lock button pivot to the door panel then release the button operating rod from its retaining clips. Disconnect the operating rod from the lock assembly and remove the inner button assembly from the door.
9 Free the interior handle operating rod from its retaining clips and disconnect the rod from the lock.
10 Undo the two bolts securing the exterior handle to the door then remove the three door lock retaining screws.
11 Partially withdraw the lock assembly then disconnect the exterior

15.4 Door lock retaining screws (Torx type)

15.15 Front door lock cylinder operating rod 'A' and circlip 'B'

15.17 Interior handle retaining screws (arrowed)

15.19 Exterior handle retaining bolts (arrowed)

handle operating rod and remove the exterior handle and lock assembly from the door.

Front door lock cylinder

12 Ensure the window glass is fully up then remove the door inner trim panel as described in Section 12.

13 Where necessary, disconnect the wiring connectors from the central locking (left-hand door) or electric window (right-hand door) control unit then undo the unit retaining screws and remove it from the door panel. Disconnect the wiring from the central locking motor and release any relevant retaining clips from the door panel.

14 Undo the two armrest support bracket retaining screws then remove the bracket and carefully peel back the polythene watershield to gain access to the lock components.

15 Disconnect the operating rod from the lock cylinder retaining clip then remove the circlip and withdraw the cylinder from the door (photo).

Interior handle

16 Remove the inner trim panel as described in Section 12.

17 Undo the screws securing the interior handle to the door then disconnect the handle from its operating rod and remove it from the car (photo).

Exterior handle

18 Remove the inner trim panel as described in Section 12 and carefully peel back the polythene watershield to gain access to the exterior handle retaining bolts.

19 Disconnect the operating rod from the handle then undo the two retaining bolts and remove the handle from the door (photo).

Refitting

20 Refitting is the reverse of the removal sequence noting the following points:

- *(a) Ensure that all operating rods are securely held in position by the retaining clips.*
- *(b) Apply grease to all lock and operating rod pivot points.*
- *(c) Before installing the inner trim panel, thoroughly check the operation of all the door lock handles and, where necessary, the central locking system and ensure that the polythene watershield is securely stuck to the door.*

16 Door – removal, refitting and adjustment

Removal

1 Open the door and peel back the wiring gaiter or displace the wiring grommet from the front edge of the door panel. Carefully withdraw the wiring from the door until the wiring connector(s) emerge. Disconnect the block connector(s) and tape the door side of the connectors to the door frame to prevent them falling back into the door panel.

16.5 Remove wheel arch liner to gain access to front door hinge retaining bolts (arrowed)

Note: *If there is insufficient slack in the wiring to be able to withdraw the wiring connectors from the door panel, it will be necessary to remove the inner trim panel as described in Section 12, and peel back the polythene watershield to gain access to them.*

2 Using a pencil or felt tip pen, mark the outline position of each door hinge relative to the door to use as a guide on refitting.

3 Remove the retaining clip and extract the pin securing the door check link to the door pillar.

4 Have an assistant support the door and undo the nuts which secure the upper and lower hinges to the door then remove the door from the car.

5 If necessary, the hinges can then be unbolted and removed from the door pillar having first marked the relative position of the hinge on the pillar. To gain access to the front door hinge bolts it will first be necessary to remove the wheel arch liner as described in paragraphs 2 and 3 of Section 10 (photo).

Refitting and adjustment

6 The door is refitted by a reverse of the removal procedure. Align the hinges with the marks made on removal and tighten the bolts to the specified torque.

7 On completion, shut the door and check that the door is correctly aligned with all surrounding bodywork with an equal clearance all around. If necessary, adjustment can be made by slackening the hinge bolts and moving the door. Once the door is positioned correctly tighten the hinge bolts to the specified torque.

8 Once the door is correctly aligned check that the door closes easily,

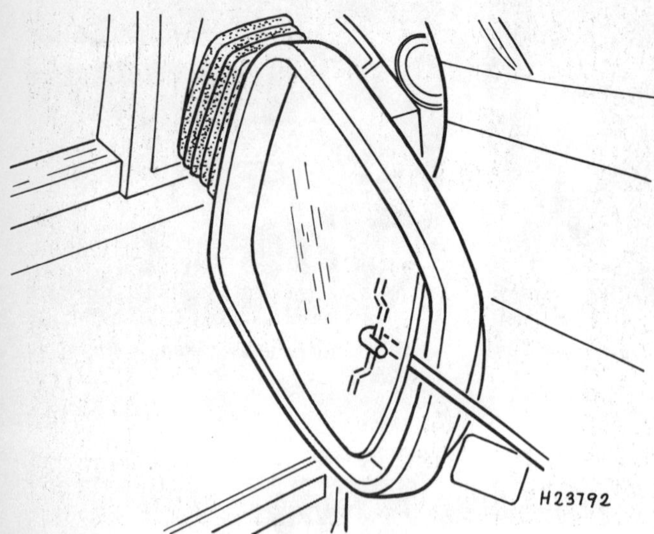

Fig. 11.4 Removing mirror glass – models equipped with electric mirrors (Sec 17)

is flush with the adjacent panels and does not rattle when closed. If not slacken the door striker retaining screws and reposition the striker. Once the door operation is satisfactory tighten the striker retaining screws securely.

17 Exterior mirror – removal and refitting

Removal

Mirror glass

1 On models equipped with manual mirrors, heat the mirror glass with a hairdryer to soften the adhesive used to stick the glass to its mounting plate. Once warm the mirror glass can be levered out of position.

2 On models equipped with electric mirrors position the mirror so that access can be gained to the rear of the outer edge of the glass. Using a piece of welding rod or other suitable wire, bend the end of the rod into a hook. Locate the hook with the spring clip on the rear of the mirror glass and pull the clip outwards to release the mirror (Fig. 11.4). Disconnect the wiring connectors from the mirror heated element and remove the glass from the car (photo).

Mirror assembly

3 Carefully prise the mirror inner trim panel from the door (photo).

4 Disconnect the mirror wiring connector (where necessary) then slacken and remove the three screws and mounting plate securing the mirror to the door and remove the mirror assembly (photos).

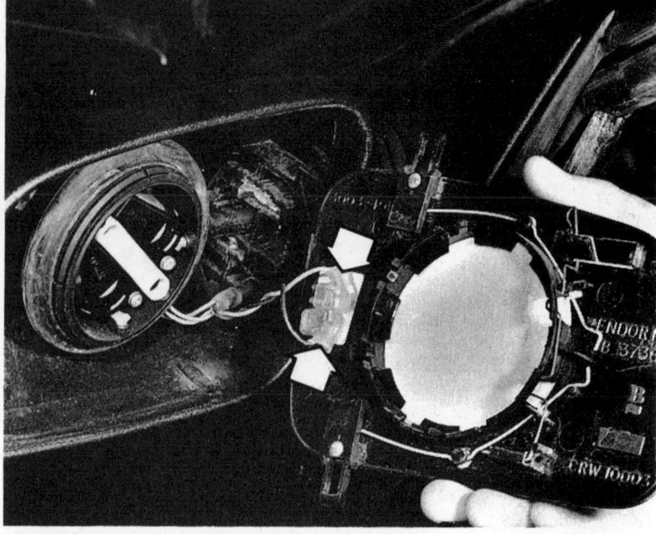

17.2 Disconnect wiring connectors (arrowed) and remove mirror glass – electrically operated mirrors

Refitting

Mirror glass

5 On models equipped with manual mirrors first ensure that all traces of old adhesive are removed from the mounting plate. Remove the backing from the new mirror and press the glass firmly into place and adjust to the required position.

6 On models equipped with electric mirrors connect the wiring connectors to the heated element terminals then align the mirror spring clip with the motor mounting point. Press the mirror glass firmly onto the motor and check that it is securely retained by the spring clip then adjust the mirror to the required position.

Mirror assembly

7 Refitting is a reverse of the removal procedure.

18 Boot lid – removal, refitting and adjustment

Removal

1 Open the boot lid then disconnect the release outer cable from the lock bracket and release the inner cable from the lock operating mechanism.

2 Disconnect the wiring connectors from the boot lid lock warning lamp switch.

3 Remove the access cover from the left-hand side of the boot lid and free the release cable from all its retaining clips and ties on the boot lid and hinge. Tie a piece of string to the end of the cable then withdraw the

17.3 Remove the mirror inner trim panel...

17.4A ...disconnect the wiring connector then undo mirror retaining screws (remaining two arrowed)...

17.4B ...and remove mirror assembly from the door

cable from the boot lid. Untie the string from the cable end and leave it in position in the boot lid. The string can then be used on refitting to draw the cable through into position.

4 Remove the right-hand access cover from the boot lid and repeat the operation in paragraph 3 for the warning lamp wiring, again leaving the string in position in the boot lid.

5 Using a felt tip pen or pencil, mark the outline of each hinge on the boot lid.

6 With the aid of an assistant, undo the four hinge retaining bolts and lift the boot lid away from the car.

Refitting and adjustment

7 Offer up the boot lid, aligning the hinges with the marks made on dismantling, and tighten the hinge bolts securely. Tie the left-hand piece of string to the boot release cable and use the string to draw the cable through the boot lid, then repeat the procedure using the right-hand piece of string to draw the warning lamp switch wiring through the lid and untie both pieces of string.

Note: *If a new boot lid is being installed it will be necessary to centralise the boot lid on its hinges and feed the release cable and wiring through the boot lid.*

8 Connect the release inner cable to the lock operating mechanism and refit the outer cable to its respective position on the lock. Secure the release cable to the boot lid hinge using the necessary retaining clips.

9 Connect the warning connectors to the boot lock warning lamp switch and secure the wiring to the right-hand hinge using all the necessary retaining clips.

10 Refit both the left- and right-hand access covers to the boot lid.

11 Close the boot lid and check that it is correctly aligned with all surrounding bodywork with an equal clearance all around. If necessary, adjustment can be made by slackening the hinge bolts and repositioning the boot lid. Once correctly positioned, tighten the hinge bolts to the specified torque.

12 Once the boot lid is correctly aligned ensure that it closes without slamming and is securely retained. If not, slacken the boot lid striker retaining bolts and reposition the striker. Once the boot lid operation is satisfactory tighten the striker retaining bolts securely.

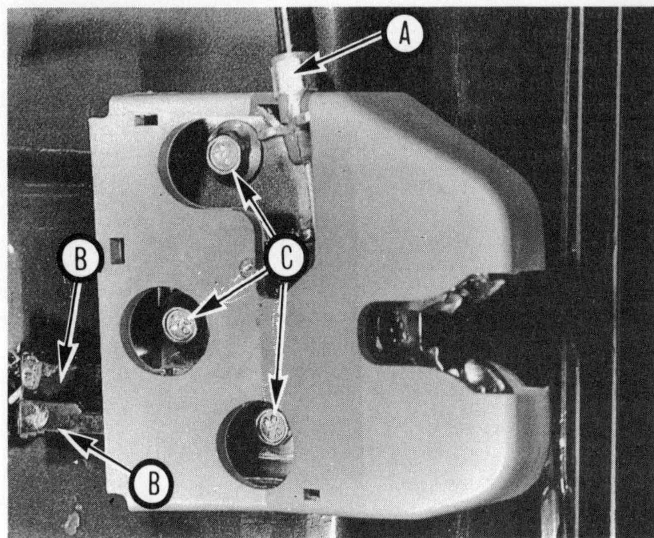

19.2 Boot lid lock release cable 'A', warning lamp wiring connectors 'B' and retaining bolts 'C'

19.7 Boot lid lock cylinder retaining bolt and operating rod

19 Boot lid lock and lock cylinder – removal and refitting

Removal

Boot lid lock

1 Open the boot lid then disconnect the release outer cable from the lock bracket and release the inner cable from the lock operating mechanism.

2 Disconnect the wiring connectors from the boot lid lock warning lamp switch (photo).

3 Carefully prise off the boot lid lock cover then undo the three bolts securing the lock to the boot lid.

4 Partially withdraw the lock then disconnect the lock cylinder operating rod from the rear of the assembly and remove the lock from the vehicle.

5 If necessary, remove the right-hand access cover from the boot lid, then disconnect the operating rod from the lock cylinder and remove it from the car.

Boot lid lock cylinder

6 Open the boot lid and remove the right-hand access cover.

7 Detach the operating rod from the lock cylinder and remove the bolt securing the cylinder to the boot lid (photo).

8 Manoeuvre the lock cylinder out of the boot lid. Remove the lock cylinder gasket and discard it. A new gasket should be used on refitting.

Refitting

Boot lid lock

9 Refitting is a reversal of the removal sequence. Tighten the lock retaining bolts to the specified torque. On completion check that the boot lid closes without slamming and is securely retained when shut. If not, slacken the boot lid striker retaining bolts and reposition the striker. Once the boot lid operation is satisfactory tighten the striker retaining bolts securely.

Boot lid lock cylinder

10 Refitting is a reverse of the removal procedure ensuring that a new gasket is fitted to the cylinder and its retaining bolt is tightened to the specified torque.

20 Boot lid/tailgate and fuel filler flap release cables – removal and refitting

Removal

1 Remove the driver's seat and rear seats as described in Section 26.

2 Undo the right-hand front sill finisher and carpet retainer screws and remove the sill finisher and carpet retainer from the car (photo).

3 Remove the boot lid/tailgate and fuel filler release lever handles, then lift the flap situated on the top of the release lever cover to gain access to the retaining screw. Undo the screw and lift off the release lever cover (photos).

4 On four- and five-door models, open the right-hand rear door and

20.2 Remove right-hand sill finisher

undo the two screws securing the sill finisher to the floor then, remove the sill finisher and carpet retainer. Carefully prise out the lower trim panels from the centre and rear door pillars.

5 On three-door models, remove the four screws securing the right-hand lower rear seat side trim panel to the luggage compartment carpet and carefully peel the front door sealing strip away from the door pillar so that the front edge of the trim panel is freed. The panel can then be released by carefully prising it away from the body, using a large flat-bladed screwdriver to release its retaining clips, and removed from the car.

6 On all models, remove the cap from the driver's seat belt lower anchorage bolt then undo the bolt and free the belt from the floor. Release the trim clips securing the carpet to the floor and peel back the carpet to gain access to the release cables.

7 Open the boot lid/tailgate, prise out the screw caps (where necessary) and undo the screws securing the luggage compartment rear inner trim panel in position. Remove the panel from the car. Release any relevant retaining clips and remove the luggage compartment carpet.

8 Closely examine the luggage compartment left-hand side trim panel and remove any relevant retaining screws. Carefully prise the panel away from the body and remove it from the luggage compartment (photo).

Boot lid/tailgate release cable

9 On 414 models release the outer cable from the boot lid lock bracket and release the inner cable from the lock/striker operating mechanism. Remove the left-hand access cover from the boot lid and the release cable from all its retaining clips and ties on the boot lid and hinge. Tie a piece of string to the end of the cable then withdraw the cable from the boot lid. Untie the string from the cable end and leave it in position in the boot lid. The string can then be used on refitting to draw the cable through into position.

10 On 214 models, undo the tailgate striker retaining screws then withdraw the striker and detach the release cable.

11 On all models, release the cable from all the retaining clips in the luggage compartment then, from inside, pull the cable through into the car. Work back along the length of the cable and free it from any relevant retaining clips. Disconnect the outer cable from the release lever mounting bracket then detach the inner cable from the lever and withdraw the cable from the car (photo).

Fuel filler release cable

12 Detach the fuel filler release cable from the left-hand side of the luggage compartment (photo). The cable can then be removed as described in paragraph 11.

20.3A Remove the release lever handles...

20.3B ...then undo lever cover retaining screw...

20.3C ...and remove the cover

20.8 Removing the left-hand luggage compartment trim panel - 414 models

20.11 Detach the relevant cable from the release lever assembly and withdraw it from the car

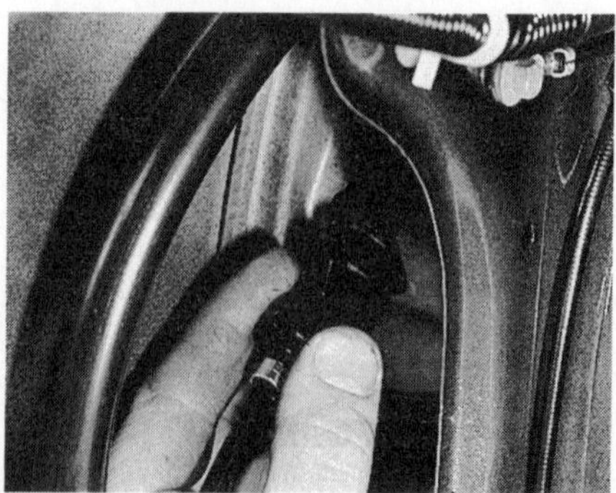

20.12 Disconnecting fuel filler release cable - 414 models

Refitting

13 Refitting is a reversal of the removal procedure noting the following points:

- (a) *Ensure the cable is correctly routed and retained by any relevant clips and check the release lever operates satisfactorily before proceeding further.*
- (b) *Where possible, renew any broken trim panel retaining clips.*
- (c) *Ensure all carpets and trim panels are properly located and securely retained by all necessary clips and screws.*
- (d) *Tighten the lower seat belt anchorage bolt to the specified torque setting.*

21 Tailgate – removal, refitting and adjustment

Removal

1 Open the tailgate and undo the two screws securing the tailgate inner trim panel to the tailgate and carefully prise out the screw retaining plugs.
2 Using a large flat-bladed screwdriver, work around the outside of the trim panel and carefully prise it away from the tailgate to free all the retaining clips. Once all the retaining clips have been freed remove the trim panel.
3 Disconnect the two wiring block connectors, situated on the right-hand side of the tailgate, which connect the tailgate electrical components to the main wiring loom. Tie a piece of string around the wiring side of the block connector, then displace the grommet from the upper right-hand corner of the tailgate and withdraw the wiring. Once free, untie the string from the end of the wiring and leave it in place in the tailgate. The string can then be used to draw the wiring back through into position on refitting.
4 Disconnect the washer hose from the tailgate grommet.
5 Using a felt tip pen or pencil, mark the relative positions of the hinges on the tailgate.
6 Have an assistant support the tailgate then raise the spring clips and pull the support struts off their balljoint mountings on the tailgate. Undo the four hinge retaining bolts and remove the tailgate from the vehicle, noting any shims which may be fitted between the hinge and tailgate.

Refitting and adjustment

7 Offer up the tailgate, positioning any shims necessary between the hinge and tailgate, and refit the hinge bolts. Press the support struts firmly onto the balljoint mountings and clip the spring clips back into position. Align the hinges with the marks made on removal, or centralise the hinges, and tighten the retaining bolts to the specified torque.
8 Tie the string around the end of the tailgate wiring and draw the wiring back into position. Untie the string, then reconnect the wiring connectors and relocate the grommet in the tailgate.
9 Renew any broken retaining clips, then refit the inner trim panel to the tailgate. Ensure the panel is securely clipped in position then refit the screw retaining plug and tighten the screws securely. Reconnect the washer hose to the tailgate grommet.
10 On completion shut the tailgate and check that it is correctly aligned with the surrounding bodywork. If adjustment is necessary, slacken the hinge bolts and reposition the tailgate as necessary. Once alignment is correct tighten the hinge bolts to the specified torque. If the correct alignment is not possible by repositioning the tailgate it will be necessary to alter the hinge to body position. To do this, peel away the tailgate sealing strip from the top edge of the body and carefully prise the top of the right- and left-hand tailgate pillar trim panels until the headlining can be peeled back sufficiently to gain access to the hinge retaining nuts. Slacken the hinge nuts and reposition the tailgate noting that, as a guide, Rover state there should be a gap of approximately 7 mm along the top edge of the tailgate. Once correctly positioned, tighten the retaining nuts to the specified torque then relocate the headlining, trim panels and tailgate sealing strip.
11 Adjust the height of the tailgate by screwing the rubber stop in or out, as necessary, then check that the tailgate closes easily and does not rattle when closed. If adjustment is necessary slacken the tailgate striker retaining screws and reposition the striker as necessary. Once the tailgate operation is satisfactory tighten the striker retaining bolts securely.

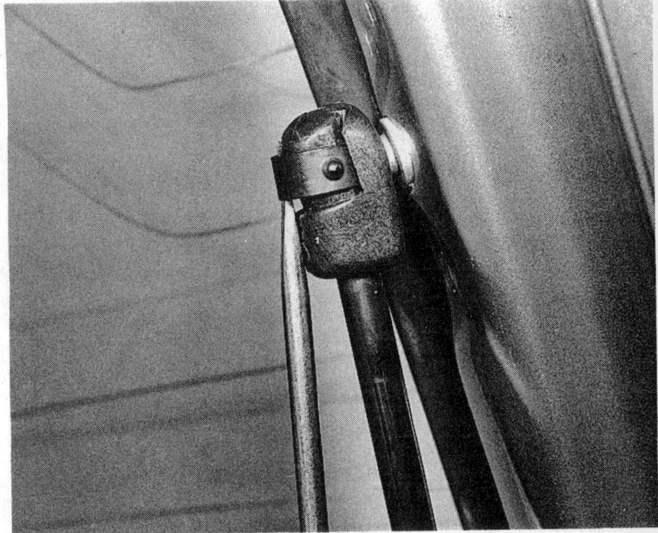

22.2 Raising tailgate support strut spring clip to release mounting

22 Tailgate support strut – removal and refitting

Removal

1 Support the tailgate in the open position using a stout piece of wood, or with the help of an assistant.
2 Raise the spring clip and pull the support strut off its balljoint mounting on the tailgate (photo). Repeat the procedure for the strut to body mounting and remove the strut from the car.

Refitting

3 Refitting is the reverse sequence of removal ensuring that the strut is pressed firmly onto each of its balljoints and the spring clips are correctly positioned.

23 Tailgate lock and lock cylinder – removal and refitting

Removal

Tailgate lock

1 Open the tailgate and undo the two screws securing the tailgate inner trim panel to the tailgate and carefully prise out the screw retaining plugs (photo).
2 Using a large flat-bladed screwdriver, work around the outside of the trim panel and carefully prise it away from the tailgate to free all the retaining clips. Once all the clips have been freed, remove the trim panel.
3 Disconnect the operating rod from the lock and then remove the plastic cover from outside of the lock (photo). Using a felt tip pen or pencil, mark the relative position of the lock assembly on the tailgate.
4 Undo all the tailgate lock retaining bolts and remove the lock assembly from the car.

Tailgate lock cylinder

5 Open the tailgate and remove the right-hand access panel from the tailgate trim.
6 Disconnect the operating rod from the lock cylinder, then undo the retaining bolt and remove the cylinder from the tailgate.

Refitting

Tailgate lock

7 Refitting is a reverse of the removal sequence. Align the lock with the marks made on dismantling. On completion check that the tailgate closes easily and does not rattle when closed. If adjustment is necessary

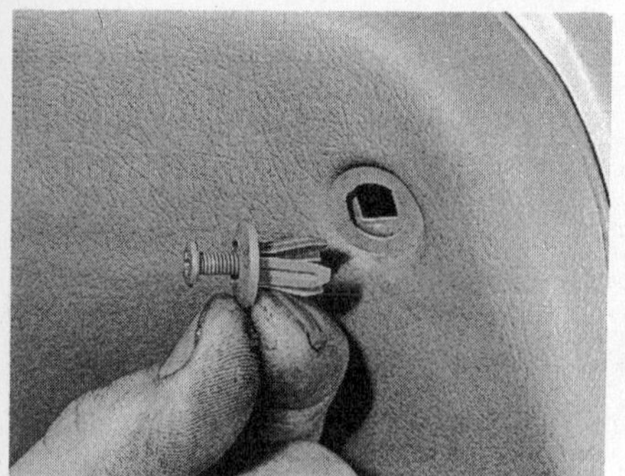
23.1 Tailgate inner trim panel retaining screw and plug

23.3 Remove plastic cover to gain access to tailgate lock retaining bolts (arrowed)

23.7 Tailgate striker retaining screws (Torx type)

slacken the tailgate striker retaining screws and reposition the striker as necessary (photo). Once the tailgate operation is satisfactory tighten the striker retaining bolts securely.

Tailgate lock cylinder

8 Refitting is a reverse of the removal procedure.

24 Windscreen, fixed rear quarterlight and tailgate/rear window glass - general information

These areas of glass are secured by the tight fit of the weatherstrip in the body aperture; although they are not fixed by the direct-bonding method used on many modern vehicles, the removal and refitting of these areas of fixed glass is still difficult, messy and time-consuming for the inexperienced. It is also difficult, unless one has plenty of practice, to obtain a secure, waterproof fit. Furthermore, the task carries a high risk of breakage; this applies especially to the laminated glass windscreen. In view of this, owners are strongly advised to have this sort of work carried out by one of the many specialist windscreen fitters.

25 Body exterior trim panels - general information

The exterior body and door trim strips are held in position with a special adhesive tape. Removal requires the trim to be heated, to soften the adhesive, and possibly cut away from the door surface. Due to the high risk of damage to the vehicle's paintwork during this operation it is recommended that the work should be entrusted to a Rover dealer.

26 Seats - removal and refitting

Removal

Front seats

1 Slide the seat fully backwards, then slacken and remove the two torx bolts securing the front of the seat slides to the floor (photo).
2 Slide the seat fully forwards then undo the two torx bolts securing the rear of the seat slides to the floor and remove the seat from the car.

Rear seat cushion - 214 models

3 Carefully prise off the hinge covers from the front of the seat cushion, then undo the two torx bolts securing the hinges to the floor. The cushion can then be lifted out of position and removed from the car (photo).

Rear seat cushion - 414 models

4 Remove the bolt securing the rear of the cushion to the seat back then lift the rear of the seat cushion (photo).
5 Disengage the cushion retaining clips from the front of the seat cushion and remove it from the car.

Rear seat back - 214 models

6 Remove the rear window parcel shelf then fold the seat backs fully forwards.
7 Peel back the carpet to gain access to the centre hinge, then remove

26.1 Front seat slides are secured to the floor by Torx bolts

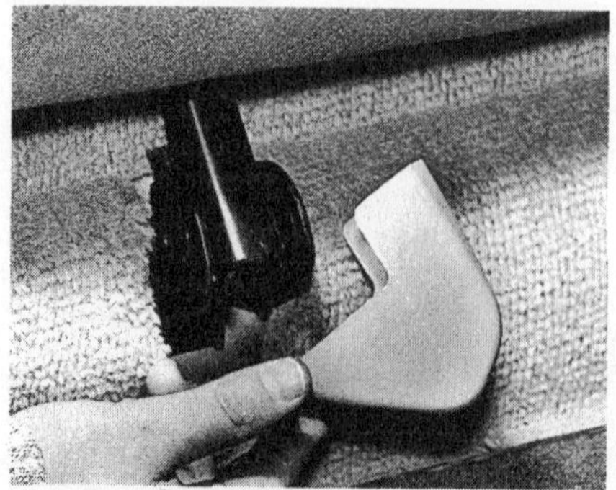
26.3 On 214 models remove seat cushion hinge covers to gain access to retaining bolts

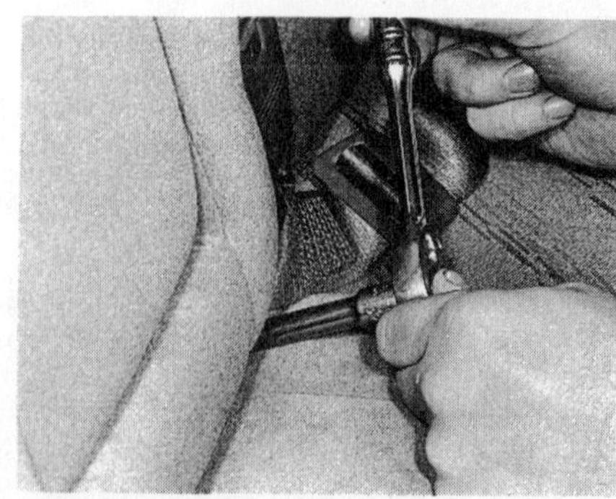
26.4 Removing rear seat cushion retaining bolt - 414 models

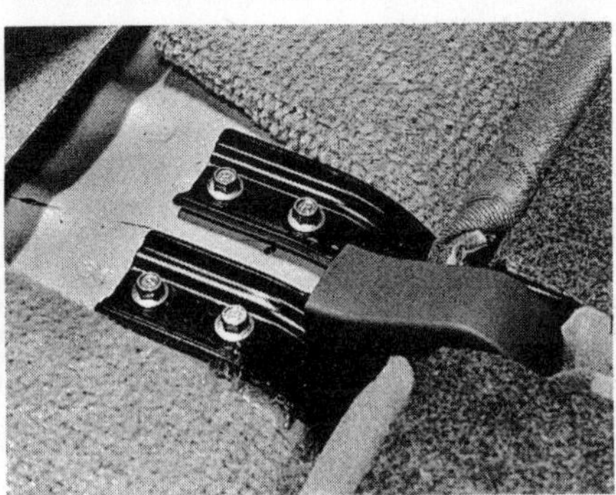
26.7 Rear seat back centre hinge retaining bolts - 214 models

26.10 Rear seat back retaining bolt - 414 models

the hinge cover and undo the bolts securing the hinge to the floor (photo).
8 Disengage the rear seat back pivot pins from the body and remove the assembly from the car.

Rear seat back - 414 models

9 Remove the rear seat cushion as described in paragraphs 4 and 5.
10 Remove the three bolts securing the bottom of the seat back to the body then pull the seat back forwards to release it from its retaining clips, and remove it from the car (photo).

Refitting

11 Refitting is the reverse of removal tightening the seat or hinge mounting bolts (as applicable) to the specified torque setting.

27 Interior trim - general information

Interior trim panels

1 The interior trim panels are secured using either screws or various types of trim fasteners, usually studs or clips.
2 Check that there are no other panels overlapping the one to be removed; usually there is a sequence that has to be followed that will become obvious on close inspection.
3 Remove all obvious fasteners, such as screws. If the panel will not come free, it is held by hidden clips or fasteners. These are usually situated around the edge of the panel and can be prised up to release them; note, however that they can break quite easily so replacements should be available. The best way of releasing such clips in the absence of the correct type of tool, is to use a large flat-bladed screwdriver. Note in many cases that the adjacent sealing strip must be prised back to release a panel.
4 When removing a panel, **never** use excessive force or the panel may be damaged; always check carefully that all fasteners have been removed or released before attempting to withdraw a panel.
5 Refitting is the reverse of the removal procedure; secure the fasteners by pressing them firmly into place and ensure that all disturbed components are correctly secured to prevent rattles. If adhesives were found at any point on removal, use white spirit to remove all traces of old adhesive, then wash off all traces of spirit using soapy water; use a suitable trim adhesive (a Rover dealer should be able to recommend a proprietary product) on reassembly.

Carpets

6 The passenger compartment floor carpet is in one piece and is secured at its edges by screws or clips, usually the same fasteners used to secure the various adjoining trim panels.
7 Carpet removal and refitting is reasonably straightforward but very time-consuming due to the fact that all adjoining trim panels must be removed first, as must components such as the seats, the centre console and seat belt lower anchorages.

Headlining

8 The headlining is clipped to the roof and can be withdrawn once all fittings such as the grab handles, sun visors, sunroof (if fitted), windscreen and rear quarterlights and related trim panels have been removed and the door, tailgate and sunroof aperture sealing strips have been prised clear.
9 Note that headlining removal requires considerable skill and experience if it is to be carried out without damage and is therefore best entrusted to an expert.

28 Seat belts - removal and refitting

Removal

Front seat belt - four- and five-door models

1 Carefully prise the lower door pillar trim panel out of position and remove it from the car.
2 Remove the cover from the upper belt mounting, undo the seat belt retaining nut and detach the belt (photo).

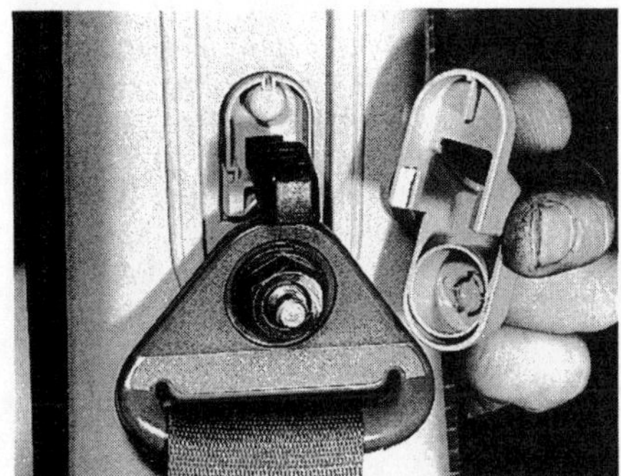
28.2 Remove the cover to reveal the front seat belt upper mounting nut

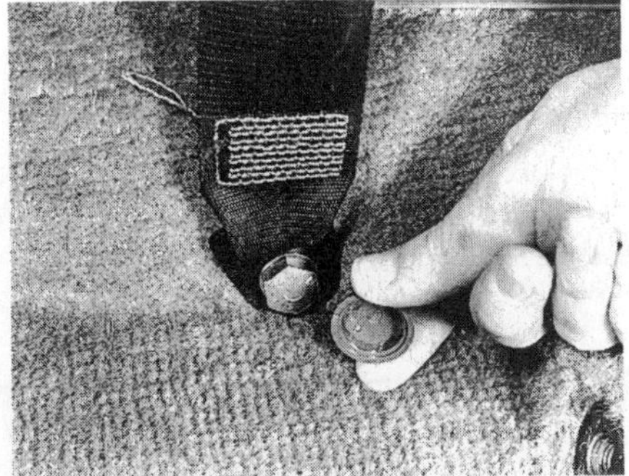
28.3 Prise off the trim cap and remove front seat belt lower mounting bolt

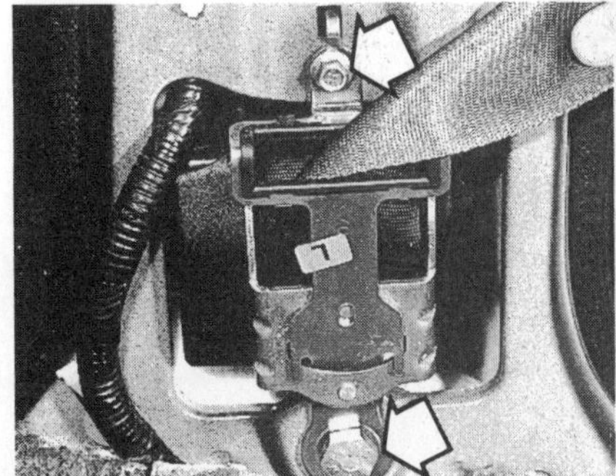
28.4 Front seat belt inertia reel retaining bolts (arrowed)

28.14 Remove cover to gain access to rear seat belt lower retaining bolt

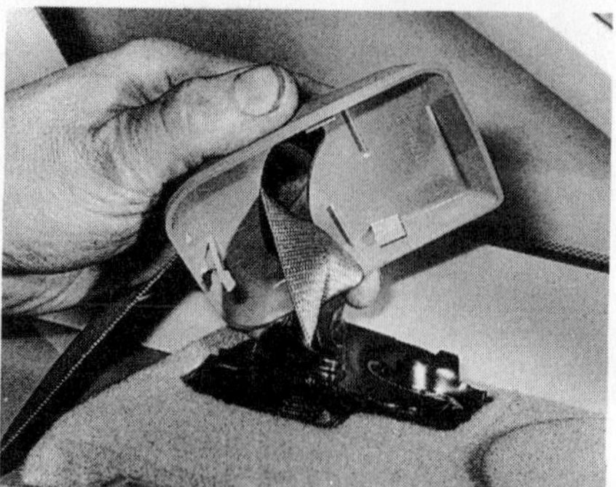

28.15A Prise off the cover...

28.15B ...and remove the seat belt guide retaining bolts

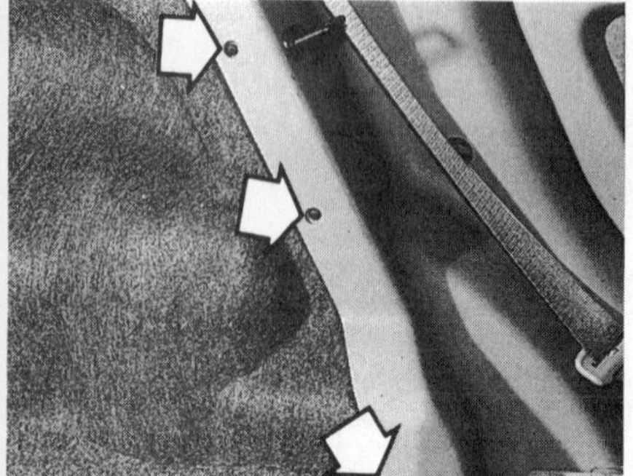

28.16A Remove rear door pillar trim panel retaining screws...

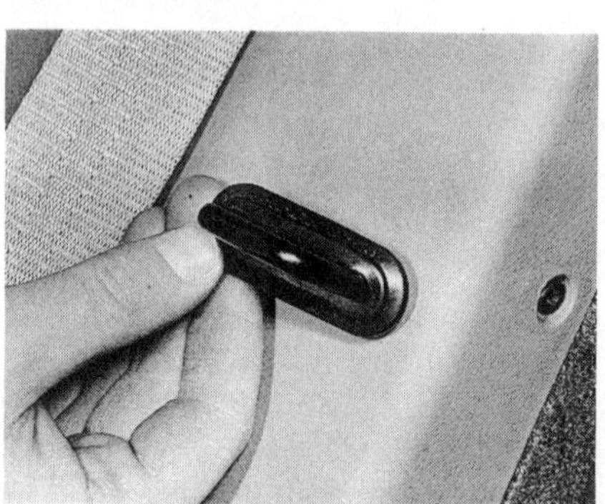

28.16B ...and remove the seat catch rubber seal

28.20 Rear seat side belt lower mounting bolt...

3 Remove the cap from the lower seat belt mounting bolt then undo the bolt and detach the belt from the floor (photo).

4 Undo the two bolts securing the inertia reel to the door pillar and remove the reel and belt assembly from the car (photo).

Front seat belt – three-door models

5 Remove the rear window parcel shelf then fold the rear seat cushion fully forwards and remove the rear seat back as described in Section 26. Remove the rubber seal from the rear seat back mounting catch.

6 Prise out the lower seat belt mounting point cover then slacken and remove the lower mounting bolt and detach the belt from the body.

7 Remove the four screws securing the lower rear seat side trim panel to the luggage compartment carpet and carefully peel the front door sealing strip away from the door pillar so that the front edge of the trim panel is freed. The panel can then be released by carefully prising it away from the body, using a large flat-bladed screwdriver to release its retaining clips, and removed from the car.

8 Prise off the cover from the upper seat belt mounting then undo the nut securing the belt to the inertia reel and detach the belt.

9 Prise off the covers from the seat belt lower mounting bar bolts then undo both bolts. Disengage the mounting bar from the belt and remove it from the car.

10 Release the seat belt from its door pillar guide, then slacken and remove the two inertia reel retaining bolts and remove the belt and inertia reel from the car.

Front seat belt stalk – all models

11 Remove the seat from the car as described in Section 26. undo the seat belt stalk to seat mounting bolt and remove the stalk.

Rear seat side belt – five-door models

12 Remove the rear window parcel shelf and fold the rear seats fully forwards.

13 Carefully examine the luggage compartment side trim panel and remove all its retaining screws. If the right-hand panel is being removed, prise out the luggage compartment lamp from the trim panel, disconnect the lamp wiring and remove it from the car. Release the trim panel and remove it from the luggage compartment.

14 Remove the cover from the lower seat belt mounting point then undo the mounting bolt and detach the belt from the body (photo).

15 Prise off the cover from the seat belt upper guide point and undo the two seat belt guide retaining bolts (photos).

16 Undo the six screws securing the rear door pillar trim panel in position and remove the rubber seal from the rear seat back mounting catch. Remove the trim panel to gain access to the inertia reel (photos).

17 Undo the two bolts securing the inertia reel to the body and remove the belt and reel assembly from the car.

Rear seat side belt – four-door models

18 Remove the rear seat cushion and back as described in Section 26.

19 Carefully examine the luggage compartment side trim panel and

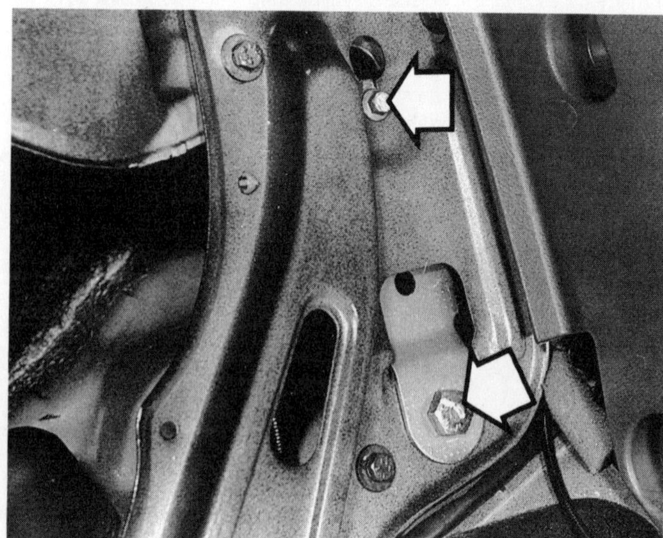

28.22 ...and inertia reel retaining bolts (arrowed) – four-door models

remove all its retaining screws. Release the trim panel and remove it from the luggage compartment.
20 Remove the lower seat belt mounting bolt and detach the belt from the body (photo).
21 Prise off the cover from the seat belt upper guide point and undo the two seat belt guide retaining bolts.
22 Undo the two bolts securing the inertia reel to the body and remove the belt and reel assembly from the car (photo).

Rear seat side belt – three-door models

23 Remove the rear window parcel shelf then fold the rear seat fully forwards and remove the rear seat back as described in Section 26. Remove the rubber seal from the seat back mounting catch.
24 Carry out the operations described in paragraphs 13 to 15.
25 Carefully peel the front door sealing strip away from the door pillar so that the front edge of the rear seat side trim panel is freed. Release the panel by carefully prising it away from the body, using a large flat-bladed screwdriver and remove it from the car to gain access to the inertia reel.
26 Undo the two bolts securing the inertia reel to the body and remove the seat bolt and inertia reel assembly from the car.

Rear seat centre belt and buckles

27 On 214 models, fold the rear seat cushion fully forwards, and on 414 models remove the rear seat cushion as described in Section 26.
28 The centre belt and/or buckle assembly can then be removed by freeing the buckle(s) from the rear seat back and removing the mounting bolt(s).

Refitting

29 Refitting is the reversal of removal noting the following points:
- (a) *Tighten all the seat belt, seat belt guide, seat belt stalk and inertia reel mounting nuts and bolts (as applicable) to the specified torque setting.*
- (b) *Where possible, renew any broken trim panel retaining clips.*
- (c) *On completion ensure all trim panels are securely held by their retaining clips and, if disturbed, the door sealing strips are correctly located.*

29 Sunroof – general information

A sunroof is available as an option on all models; both an electrically operated sunroof and a manual sunroof being available.

Due to the complexity of the sunroof mechanism considerable expertise is needed to repair or replace sunroof components successfully. Removal of the sunroof first requires the headlining to be removed which is a complex and tedious operation and not a task to be undertaken lightly (See Section 27). Any problems with the sunroof should therefore be referred to a Rover dealer.

On models equipped with an electrically operated sunroof, if the sunroof motor fails to operate, first check the relevant fuse. If the fault cannot be traced and rectified the sunroof can be opened and closed manually using a suitable torx wrench or Allen key. Use a coin to unscrew the circular access cover in the panel in the headlining, situated between the sun visors and insert the wrench into the drive spindle. Rotate the key to move the sunroof to the required position. A suitable wrench was supplied with the vehicle and should be in the luggage compartment where it is stowed next to the wheel trim remover.

30 Centre console – removal and refitting

Removal

1 Prise out the cover, situated just in front of the handbrake lever, from the rear centre console section to gain access to the two retaining bolts (photo).
2 Undo the two bolts, then slide the rear console section backwards to free it from the retaining bracket and front console section, then remove it from the car (photos).
3 Unscrew the gearchange lever knob, then prise off the reverse gear

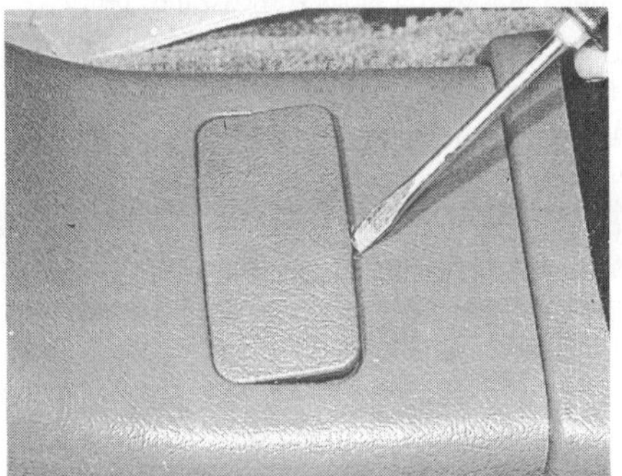

30.1 Prise out the cover...

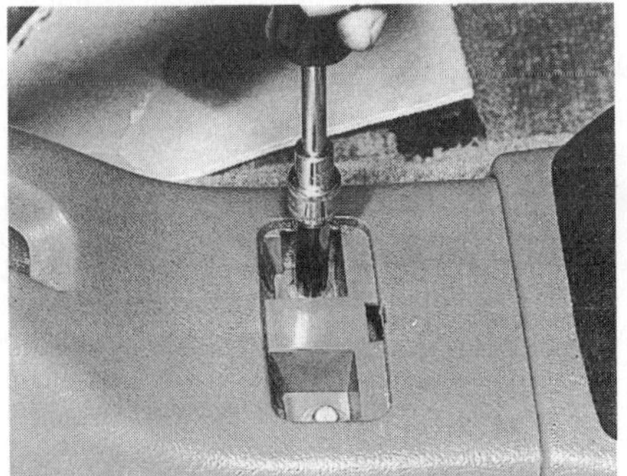

30.2A ...then undo the retaining bolts...

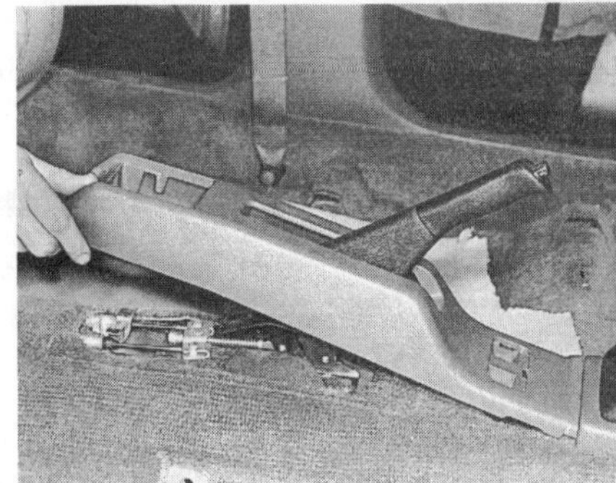

30.2B ...and remove the centre console rear section – front seats removed for clarity

30.3 Prise off the reverse gear selector slide retaining clip...

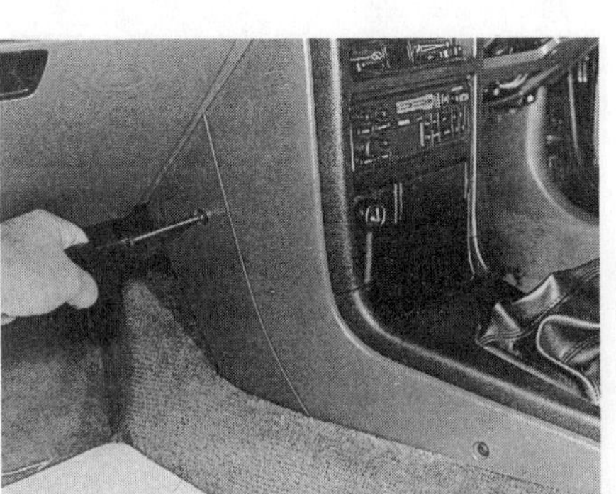

30.4A ...then remove the front console section retaining screws...

30.4B ...and remove the console section from the car

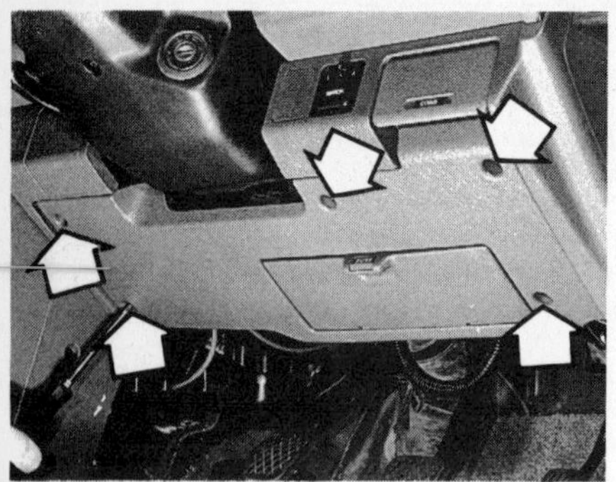

31.5 Right-hand lower facia panel retaining screws (arrowed)

31.7A Heater control panel retaining screws 'A' and lower central facia panel retaining screws 'B'

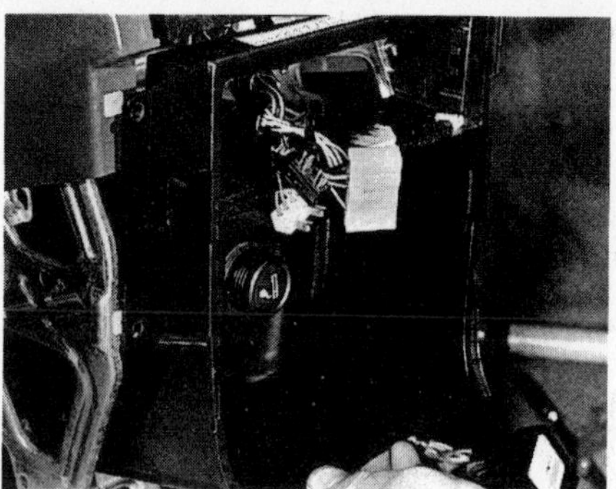

31.7B Withdraw the central facia panel...

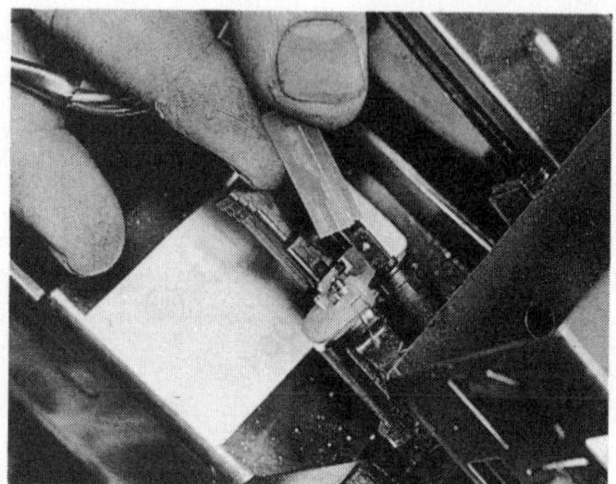

31.7C ...disconnect the wiring connectors...

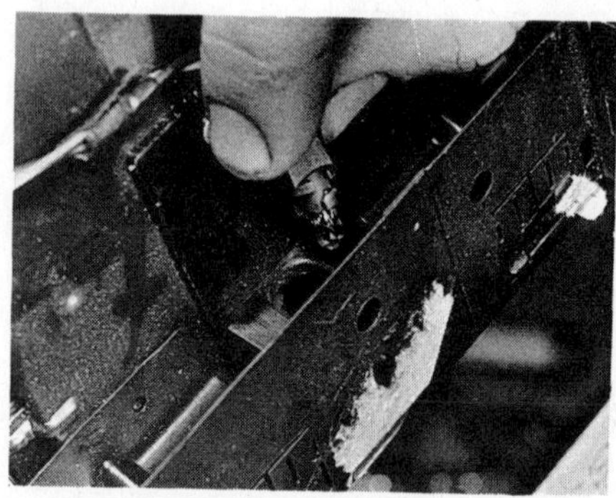

31.7D ...and remove the ashtray illumination bulb

selector slide retaining clip and disengage the slide from the gearchange lever (photo).

4 Remove the four front console section retaining screws and remove it from the car (photos).

Refitting

5 Refitting is a reversal of the removal procedure.

31 Facia – removal and refitting

Removal

1 Disconnect the battery negative terminal and from within the engine compartment, unscrew the union nuts and separate the two halves of the speedometer cable.

2 Remove the centre console as described in Section 30.

3 Slide the front seats rearwards and remove the radio/cassette player as described in Chapter 12.

4 Working on the passenger side of the facia, remove the mat from the facia tray, then carefully prise out the clock mounting trim panel. Disconnect the wiring connector from the rear of the clock and remove the trim panel.

5 Undo the five right-hand lower facia panel retaining screws and remove the panel (photo).

6 Remove the nuts and bolts securing the steering column assembly to the body and remove the lower mounting clamp. Carefully lower the column assembly away from the facia, releasing the wiring from any necessary retaining clips, and rest it on the driver's seat taking great care to ensure that no strain is placed on any of the column wiring.

7 Slacken and remove the four screws securing the heater control panel to the facia, then undo the four screws securing the lower central panel to the facia. Partially withdraw the lower central facia panel then disconnect the wiring and remove the cigar lighter and ashtray illumination bulbs. Remove the lower central panel from the car (photos).

8 With the panel removed, disconnect the two block connectors from the relay module and release the wiring retaining clip from the facia

31.9 Slacken the two facia mounting bolts and remove relay module mounting bracket (arrowed)

31.11A Remove door demister duct...

31.11B ...then slacken and remove the facia right-hand upper...

31.11C ...and lower mounting bolts

31.12A Facia centre mounting bolt is accessed via clock aperture

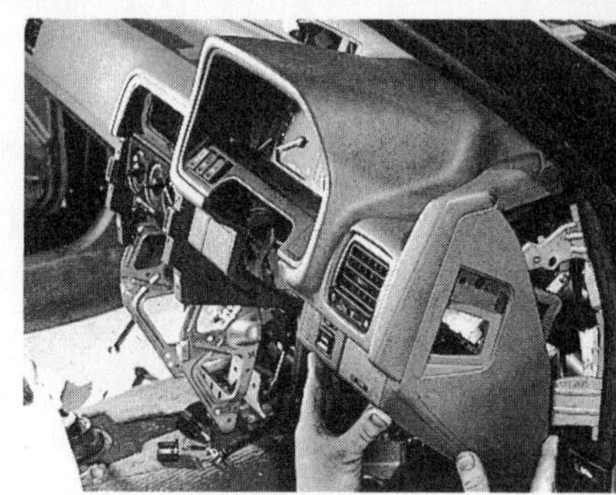
31.12B Removing facia assembly

mounting bracket. Use a screwdriver to release the retaining clip and remove the relay module.

9 Slacken the two bolts securing the facia to the mounting bracket on the transmission tunnel and remove the bolts along with the relay module mounting bracket (photo).

10 Open the glovebox and remove the door demister duct from the left-hand end of the facia. Slacken and remove the two left-hand facia mounting bolts then close the glovebox.

11 Remove the door demister duct from the right-hand end of the facia and undo the two right-hand facia mounting bolts (photos).

12 Slacken and remove the centre facia mounting bolt which is accessed through the clock aperture. Partially withdraw the facia until access can be gained to the wiring block connectors situated behind the right-hand end of the facia and the speedometer cable (photos). Reach behind the facia then press in the speedometer cable retaining clip and disconnect the cable from the instrument panel. Disconnect the facia/instrument panel wiring block connectors and carefully manoeuvre the facia assembly out of the vehicle.

Refitting

13 Offer up the facia and reconnect the four wiring connectors. Refit the speedometer cable to the instrument panel ensuring it is clipped securely in position.

14 Manoeuvre the panel into position, ensuring that the heater control panel is correctly positioned, then refit the facia mounting bolts and tighten them to the specified torque.

15 The remainder of the refitting procedure is a reversal of removal, noting the following points:

(a) *Tighten the steering column mounting nuts and bolts to the specified torque (Chapter 10), noting that the lower clamp nut and bolt should be tightened first.*

(b) *On completion, reconnect the battery and check that all electrical components and switches function correctly.*

Chapter 12 Electrical system

Contents

Specifications

System type .... 12 volt, negative earth

Battery

Type	Maintenance-free (sealed for life) lead-acid	
Battery code (Lucas):		
Standard equipment	063	
For cold climates	063S	
Battery performance:	**Cold cranking**	**Reserve capacity**
063	360 amps	60 amps
063S	405 amps	70 amps

Alternator

Type	Lucas/Magneti Marelli A127-65
Output – @ 14 volts and 6000 rpm	65 amps
Regulated voltage	14 volts maximum
Brush minimum protrusion	5 mm approx (see text)
Voltage regulator	Lucas 21TR

Starter motor

Type	Lucas M79
Rating	0.8 kW
Brush minimum length	3.5 mm approx (see text)

Fuses

Fuse	Rating (amps)	Circuit(s) protected
1	10	Clock, instruments, direction indicators and dim-dip unit
2	10	Starter signal
3	15	Central locking
4	10	Cigar lighter
5	10	Dim-dip resistor
6	30	Sunroof
7	10	Right-hand sidelamps, tail lamp and number plate lamps
8	10	Left-hand sidelamps, tail lamp and interior lamps
9	10	Fog lamps
10	10	Left-hand headlamp dipped beam
11	10	Right-hand headlamp dipped beam
12	15	Radio/cassette memory, clock and interior lamps
13	15	Front windscreen washers and wipers
14	10	Engine management system
15	15	Cooling fan, tailgate washer and wiper
16	15	Reversing lamps, stop lamps and electric windows
17	10	Cigar lighter, Multi-function unit and radio/cassette player
18	10	Electric door mirrors
19	15	Headlamp dim-dip
20	15	Fuel pump
21	15	Right-hand headlamp main beam
22	15	Left-hand headlamp main beam
23	25	Heated rear window and heated door mirrors
24	20	Heater blower motor
25	15	ABS system
26	15	Left-hand rear electric window
27	15	Right-hand rear electric window
28	15	Left-hand front electric window
29	15	Right-hand front electric window

Fusible links

Link	Rating (amps)	Circuit(s) protected
1	40	ABS pump
2	40	Lighting and cigar lighter
3	40	Ignition switch
4	40	Electric window relay, sunroof, central locking and heated rear window
5	40	Ignition switch
6	60	Main relay, fuel pump relay and lambda sensor relay

Relays and control units

Component	Location
Starter relay	Engine compartment fusebox, centre relay of the right-hand three
Intake manifold heater relay	Engine compartment fusebox, rear relay of the right-hand three
Main relay	Engine compartment fusebox, front relay of the right-hand three
Fuel pump relay	Engine compartment fusebox, front relay of the left-hand two
Cooling fan relay	Engine compartment fusebox, rear relay of the left-hand two
Direction indicator relay	Behind right-hand lower facia panel (square relay)
Heated rear window relay	Behind right-hand lower facia panel (circular relay)
Cigar lighter relay, Fog lamp relay, Horn relay and Main beam relay	Part of relay module, mounted on the transmission tunnel behind lower central facia panel
Electric window relay	Behind the lower central facia panel
Electric window control unit	Behind right-hand front door inner trim panel
Central locking control unit	Behind left-hand front door inner trim panel
Air conditioning relay	Mounted on left-hand side of engine compartment bulkhead
Dim-dip relay	Behind right-hand lower facia panel
Windscreen wiper relay	Behind right-hand lower facia panel
Sunroof relay	Behind right-hand lower facia panel
Lambda sensor relay - catalytic converter models only	Engine compartment fusebox, next to fusible links
Tailgate wiper relay	Behind right-hand luggage compartment trim

Bulbs

	Fitting	Wattage
Headlamps:		
Dip/main beam bulb	H4	60/55
Individual main beam bulb	H1	55
Front sidelamps	Capless	5
Direction indicator lamps	Bayonet	21
Direction indicator side repeater lamps	Capless	5
Interior lamp	Festoon	5

Bulbs (continued)	Fitting	Wattage
Instrument panel warning and illumination	Integral with holder (with exception of rear illumination panel bulb which is capless)	14V, 1.4 or 3W
Glovebox lamp	Festoon	5
Luggage compartment lamp	Bayonet	10
Reversing lamps	Bayonet	21
Tail lamps	Capless	5
Stop lamps	Bayonet	21
Rear foglamps	Bayonet	21
Number plate lamps	Capless	5

Torque wrench settings	Nm	lbf ft
Alternator:		
Pulley retaining nut	25	19
Mounting/pivot/adjusting arm bolts	25	19
Starter motor to transmission bolts	45	33
Starter motor support bracket fasteners:		
Bracket front half to motor nuts	25	19
Bracket front half to rear half bolt	45	33
Bracket rear half to transmission bolts	25	19
Wiper arm spindle nut	14	10
Wiper motor mounting bolts	9	6
Windscreen wiper linkage spindle assembly bolts	9	6

1 General information and precautions

Warning: *Before carrying out any work on the electrical system, read through the precautions given in Safety First! at the beginning of this Manual.*

The electrical system is of 12 volt negative earth type, and consists of a battery, alternator, starter motor and related electrical accessories, components and wiring.

The battery, charged by the alternator which is belt-driven from the crankshaft pulley, provides a steady amount of current for the ignition, starting, lighting and other electrical circuits.

The starter motor is of the pre-engaged type incorporating an integral solenoid. On starting, the solenoid moves the drive pinion into engagement with the flywheel ring gear before the starter motor is energised. Once the engine has started, a one-way clutch prevents the motor armature being driven by the engine until the pinion disengages from the flywheel.

It is necessary to take extra care when working on the electrical system to avoid damage to semi-conductor devices (diodes and transistors), and to avoid the risk of personal injury. In addition to the precautions given in *Safety first!* at the beginning of this Manual, observe the following when working on the system:

Always remove rings, watches, etc., before working on the electrical system. Even with the battery disconnected, capacitive discharge could occur if a component's live terminal is earthed through a metal object. This could cause a shock or nasty burn.

Do not reverse the battery connections. Components such as the alternator, fuel injection/ignition system ECU, or any other having semi-conductor circuitry could be irreparably damaged.

If the engine is being started using jump leads and a slave battery, connect the batteries *positive to positive* and *negative to negative* (see *'Booster battery (jump) starting')*. This also applies when connecting a battery charger.

Never disconnect the battery terminals, the alternator, any electrical wiring or any test instruments when the engine is running.

Do not allow the engine to turn the alternator when the alternator is not connected.

Never 'test' for alternator output by 'flashing' the output lead to earth.

Never use an ohmmeter of the type incorporating a hand-cranked generator for circuit or continuity testing.

Always ensure that the battery negative lead is disconnected when working on the electrical system.

Before using electric-arc welding equipment on the car, disconnect the battery, alternator and components such as the fuel injection/ignition system ECU to protect them.

2 Electrical fault finding – general information

1 A typical electrical circuit consists of an electrical component, any switches, relays, motors, fuses, fusible links or circuit breakers related to that component and the wiring and connectors that link the component to both the battery and the chassis. To help you pinpoint an electrical circuit problem, wiring diagrams are included at the end of this Manual.

2 Before tackling any troublesome electrical circuit, first study the appropriate wiring diagrams to get a complete understanding of what components are included in that individual circuit. Trouble spots, for instance, can be narrowed down by noting if other components related to the circuit are operating properly. If several components or circuits fail at one time, then the problem is probably in a fuse or earth connection, because several circuits are often routed through the same fuse and earth connections.

3 Electrical problems usually stem from simple causes, such as loose or corroded connections, a blown fuse, a melted fusible link or a faulty relay. Visually inspect the condition of all fuses, wires and connections in a problem circuit before testing the components. Use the diagrams to note which terminal connections will need to be checked in order to pinpoint the trouble spot.

4 The basic tools needed for electrical fault finding include a circuit tester or voltmeter (a 12-volt bulb with a set of test leads can also be used), a continuity tester, a battery and set of test leads, and a jumper wire, preferably with a circuit breaker incorporated, which can be used to bypass electrical components. Before attempting to locate a problem with test instruments, use the wiring diagram to decide where to make the connections.

Voltage checks

5 Voltage checks should be performed if a circuit is not functioning properly. Connect one lead of a circuit tester to either the negative battery terminal or a known good earth. Connect the other lead to a connector in the circuit being tested, preferably nearest to the battery or fuse. If the bulb of the tester lights, voltage is present, which means that the part of the circuit between the connector and the battery is problem free. Continue checking the rest of the circuit in the same fashion. When you reach a point at which no voltage is present, the problem lies between that point and the last test point with voltage. Most problems can be traced to a loose connection.

Note: *Bear in mind that some circuits are only live when the ignition switch is switched to a particular position.*

Finding a short circuit

6 One method of finding a short circuit is to remove the fuse and

Fig. 12.1 Location of electrical system earth points (Sec 2)

1 *Behind left-hand headlamp – E1*
2 *Behind right-hand headlamp – E2*
3 *Base of right-hand front door pillar – E3*
4 *Beneath right-hand rear lamp cluster – E4*
5 *Beneath left-hand rear lamp cluster – E5*
6 *Centre of tailgate/boot lid – E6*
7 *Bonnet lock platform – E7*

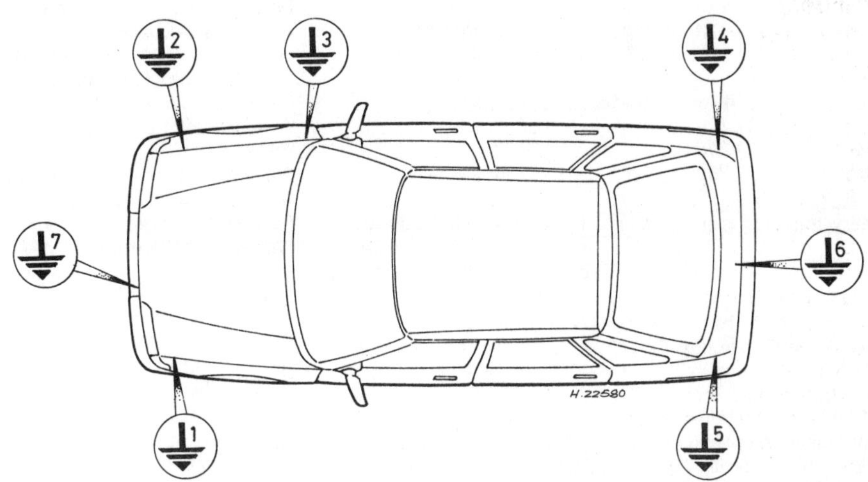

connect a test light or voltmeter to the fuse terminals with all the relevant electrical components switched off. There should be no voltage present in the circuit. Move the wiring from side to side while watching the test light. If the bulb lights up, there is a short to earth somewhere in that area, probably where the insulation has rubbed through. The same test can be performed on each component in the circuit, even a switch.

Earth check

7 Perform an earth test to check whether a component is properly earthed. Disconnect the battery and connect one lead of a self-powered test light, known as a continuity tester, to a known good earth point. Connect the other lead to the wire or earth connection being tested. If the bulb lights up, the earth is good; if not, the earth is faulty.

8 If an earth connection is thought to be faulty, dismantle the connection and clean back to bare metal both the bodyshell and the wire terminal or the component's earth connection mating surface. Be careful to remove all traces of dirt and corrosion, then use a knife to trim away any paint, so that a clean metal to metal joint is made. On reassembly, tighten the joint fasteners securely; if a wire terminal is being refitted, use serrated washers between the terminal and the bodyshell to ensure a clean and secure connection. When the connection is remade, prevent the onset of corrosion in the future by applying a coat of petroleum jelly or silicone-based grease or by spraying on (at regular intervals) a proprietary ignition sealer such as Holts Damp Start or a water dispersant lubricant such as Holts Wet Start.

9 The car's wiring harness has seven multiple-earth connections, each one being identified in the wiring diagrams by a reference number (E1 to E7). Each of these earth connections serves several circuits; their locations are as follows:

E1 Behind the left-hand headlamp.
E2 Behind the right-hand headlamp.
E3 Base of the right-hand front door pillar.
E4 Beneath the right-hand rear lamp cluster.
E5 Beneath the left-hand rear lamp cluster.
E6 Centre of the tailgate/boot lid.
E7 Bonnet lock platform.

Continuity check

10 A continuity check is necessary to determine if there are any breaks in a circuit. With the circuit off (ie no power in the circuit), a self-powered continuity tester can be used to check the circuit. Connect the test leads to both ends of the circuit (or to the positive end and a good earth), and if the test light comes on, the circuit is passing current properly. If the light does not come on, there is a break somewhere in the circuit. The same procedure can be used to test a switch, by connecting the continuity tester to the switch terminals. With the switch turned on, the test light should come on.

Finding an open circuit

11 When checking for possible open circuits, it is often difficult to locate them by sight because oxidation or terminal misalignment are hidden by the connectors. Merely moving a connector on a sensor or in the wiring harness may correct the open circuit condition. Remember this when an open circuit is indicated when fault finding in a circuit. Intermittent problems may also be caused by oxidized or loose connections.

General

12 Electrical fault finding is simple if you keep in mind that all electrical circuits are basically electricity flowing from the battery, through the wires, switches, relays, fuses and fusible links to each electrical component (light bulb, motor, etc.) and to earth, from which it is passed back to the battery. Any electrical problem is an interruption in the flow of electricity from the battery.

3 Battery – testing and charging

1 In normal use, the battery should not require charging from an external source unless very heavy use is made of electrical equipment over a series of journeys that are too short to allow the charging system to keep pace with demand. Otherwise, a need for regular recharging points to a fault either in the battery or in the charging system.

2 If, however, the car is laid up for long periods (in excess of thirty days at a time) the battery will lose approximately 1% of its charge per week. This figure is for a disconnected battery; if the battery is left connected, circuits such as the clock (where fitted) will drain it at a faster rate. To prevent this happening, always disconnect the battery negative lead whenever the car is to be laid up for a long period. To keep the battery fully charged it should be given regular 'refresher' charges every six weeks or so. This is particularly important on 'maintenance-free' batteries, which will suffer permanent reduction of charge capacity if allowed to become fully discharged.

3 If a discharged battery is suspected the simplest test for most owners is as follows. Leave the battery disconnected for at least two hours, then measure the (open circuit, or no-load) voltage using a sensitive voltmeter connected across the battery terminals. Compare the reading obtained with the following:

Voltmeter reading	Charge condition
10.50 volts	*Fully discharged – battery scrap*
12.30 volts	*50% charged*
12.48 volts	*75% charged*
12.66 volts or more	*Fully charged*

4 If frequent topping-up is required, and the battery case is not fractured, the battery is being over-charged; the voltage regulator will have to be checked.

5 If the car covers a very small annual mileage, it is worthwhile checking the specific gravity of the electrolyte every three months to determine the state of charge of the battery. Use a hydrometer to make the check, and compare the results with the following table:

	Normal climates	Tropics
Discharged	*1.120*	*1.080*
Half charged	*1.200*	*1.160*
Fully charged	*1.280*	*1.230*

6 If the battery condition is suspect, first check the specific gravity of electrolyte in each cell. A variation of 0.040 or more between any cells indicates loss of electrolyte or deterioration of the internal plates.
7 A further test can be made only by a battery specialist using a battery heavy discharge meter. Alternatively, connect a voltmeter across the battery terminals and operate the starter motor with the ignition coil HT lead disconnected from the distributor and earthed, and with the headlamps, heated rear window and heater blower switched on. If the voltmeter reading remains above approximately 9.5 volts, the battery condition is satisfactory. If the voltmeter reading drops below 9.5 volts and the battery has already been charged, it is proven faulty.
8 In winter when heavy demand is placed on the battery (starting from cold and using more electrical equipment), it is a good idea occasionally to have the battery fully charged from an external source. The battery's bench charge rate depends on its code (see a Rover dealer or Lucas agent for details); for most owners the best method will be to use a trickle-charger overnight, charging at a rate of 1.5 amps. Rapid 'boost' charges which are claimed to restore the power of the battery in 1 to 2 hours are **not** recommended, as they can cause serious damage to the battery plates through overheating and may cause a sealed battery to explode.
9 Ideally, the battery should be removed from the car before charging and moved to a well-ventilated area. As a minimum precaution, both battery terminal leads must be disconnected (negative lead first) before connecting the charger leads.

Warning: *The battery will be emitting significant quantities of (highly-inflammable) hydrogen gas during charging and for approximately 15 minutes afterwards; do not allow sparks or naked flames near the battery or it may explode.*

10 Continue to charge the battery until all cells are gassing vigorously and no further rise in specific gravity or increase in no-load voltage is noted over a four-hour period. When charging is complete, turn the charger off before disconnecting the leads from the battery.

4 Battery - removal and refitting

Removal

1 First check that all electrical components are switched off to avoid a spark occurring as the negative lead is disconnected. If the radio/cassette unit has a security code, de-activate the code temporarily and re-activate it when the battery is re-connected; refer to the instructions and code supplied with the unit.
2 Slacken the terminal clamp nut then lift the clamp and negative (-) lead from the terminal. This is the terminal to disconnect before working on any electrical component on the car. If the terminal is tight, carefully ease it off by moving it from side to side.
3 Raise the plastic cover from the positive (+) terminal clamp and slacken the clamp nut, then lift the clamp and lead from the terminal.
4 Unscrew the clamp bolt and remove the clamp from the battery tray (photo).
5 Lift the battery from the tray keeping it upright and taking care not to allow it to contact your clothing.
6 If the battery tray is to be removed, first release any relevant wiring harness clips from the tray. Unscrew the six bolts securing the battery tray in position and remove the tray. If necessary, undo the two bolts securing the battery tray mounting bracket to the body and remove the bracket (photos).
7 Clean the battery terminal posts, clamps, tray and battery casing. If the bodywork is rusted as a result of battery acid spilling onto it, clean it thoroughly and re-paint with reference to Chapter 11.
8 Whenever the battery is removed, check it for cracks and leakage.

Refitting

9 Refitting is the reverse of the removal procedure. Ensure that the terminal posts and leads are cleaned before re-connection. Smear petroleum jelly on the terminals after reconnecting the leads. Always connect the positive terminal clamp first and the negative terminal clamp last.

5 Charging system - testing

1 If the ignition warning lamp fails to light when the ignition is switched on, first check the alternator wiring connections for security. If satisfactory, check that the warning lamp bulb has not blown and is secure in its holder. If the lamp still fails to light check the continuity of the warning lamp feed wire from the alternator to the bulbholder. If all is satisfactory, the alternator is at fault and should be renewed or taken to an auto-electrician for testing and repair.
2 If the ignition warning lamp lights when the engine is running, stop the engine and check that the drivebelt is correctly tensioned (see Chapter 1) and that the alternator connections are secure. If all is so far satisfactory, check the alternator brushes and commutator as described in Section 7. If the fault persists, the alternator should be renewed or taken to an auto-electrician for testing and repair.
3 If the alternator output is suspect even though the warning lamp functions correctly, the regulated voltage may be checked as follows.
4 Connect a voltmeter across the battery terminals and start the engine.
5 Increase engine speed until the voltmeter reading remains steady; this should be approximately 12 to 13 volts and no more than 14 volts.
6 Switch on as many electrical accessories (eg the headlamps, heated rear window and heater blower) as possible and check that the alternator maintains the regulated voltage at around 13 to 14 volts.
7 If the regulated voltage is not as stated, the fault may be due to worn brushes, weak brush springs, a faulty voltage regulator, a faulty diode, a

4.4 Battery clamp bolt

4.6A Battery tray retaining bolts (arrowed)

4.6B Battery tray mounting bracket retaining bolts (viewed from underneath)

6.8A On models without air conditioning remove the cover from the rear of the alternator...

6.8B ...and disconnect the wiring connector

6.9A Slacken the upper pivot mounting bolts...

6.9B ...and the lower adjusting arm bolt 'A' then rotate the adjuster bolt 'B' to slacken drivebelt tension

severed phase winding or a worn or damaged commutator. The brushes and commutator may be checked, but if the fault persists the alternator should be renewed or taken to an auto-electrician for testing and repair.

6 Alternator - removal and refitting

Removal

1 Disconnect the battery negative lead.

2 Firmly apply the handbrake then jack up the front of the car and remove the right-hand front roadwheel.

3 From underneath the front of the vehicle, slacken and remove the three bolts securing the bumper flange to the body. Remove the seven bolts securing the front undercover panel to the body and remove the panel.

Models equipped with air conditioning

4 Undo the two bolts and washers securing the heat shield to the rear of the alternator then remove the nut securing the heat shield to the engine and lift the shield out of the engine compartment.

5 Disconnect the wiring connector from the rear of the alternator.

6 Slacken the adjuster pulley retaining nut then turn the pulley adjusting bolt until sufficient drivebelt free play is obtained to be able to disengage the drivebelt from the alternator pulley.

7 Slacken and remove the three bolts securing the alternator to its mounting bracket then manoeuvre the alternator out of the engine compartment.

Models without air conditioning

8 Unscrew the three nuts and washers securing the rear cover to alternator and remove the cover. Release the wire retaining clip and disconnect the alternator wiring connector (photos).

9 Slacken the lower alternator to adjusting arm bolt and the two upper alternator pivot bolts then slacken the drivebelt adjusting bolt until sufficient free play is obtained to disengage the drivebelt from the alternator pulley (photos).

10 Remove the alternator adjusting arm and upper pivot bolts and manoeuvre the alternator out of the engine compartment.

Refitting

11 If a new alternator is being installed it will be necessary to remove the pulley and cooling fan from the old unit. To do this slacken the pulley retaining nut whilst preventing it from rotating by either using a suitable

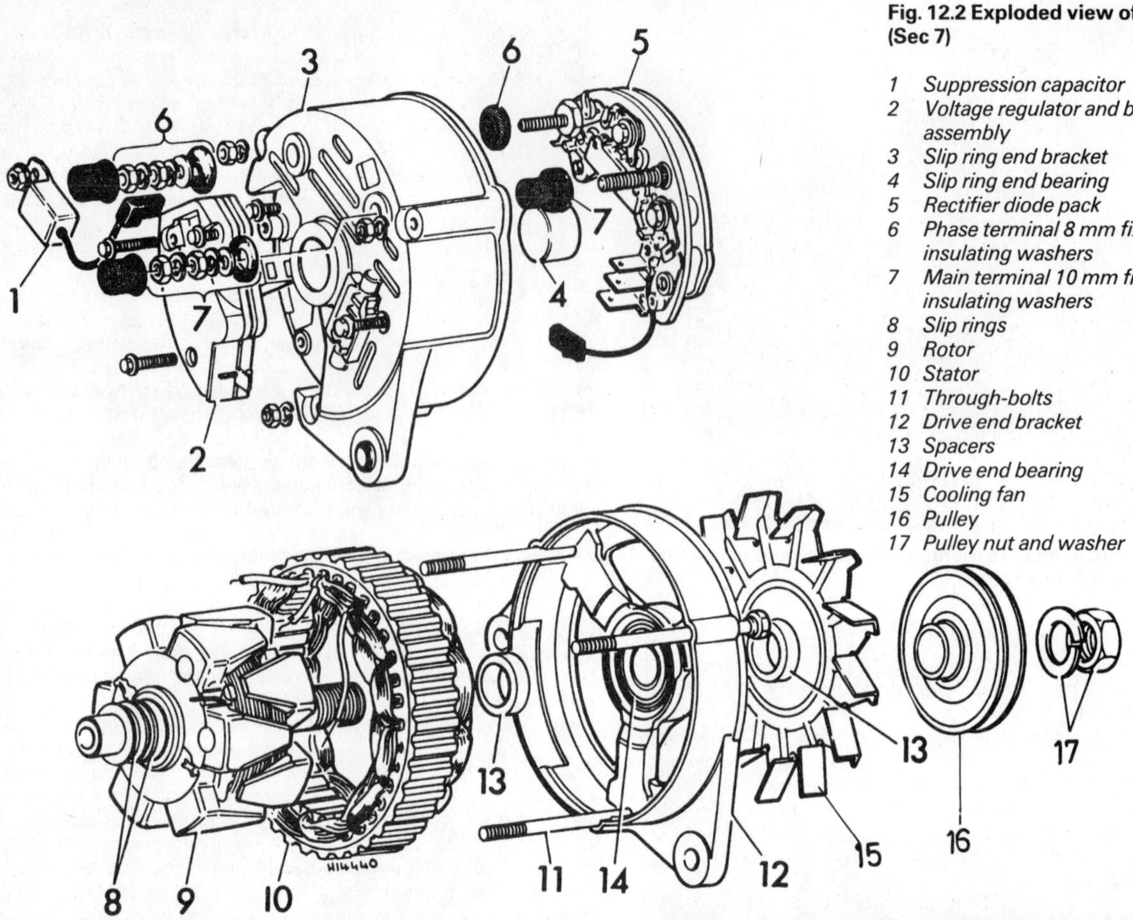

Fig. 12.2 Exploded view of the alternator (Sec 7)

1 *Suppression capacitor*
2 *Voltage regulator and brush holder assembly*
3 *Slip ring end bracket*
4 *Slip ring end bearing*
5 *Rectifier diode pack*
6 *Phase terminal 8 mm fixings and insulating washers*
7 *Main terminal 10 mm fixings and insulating washers*
8 *Slip rings*
9 *Rotor*
10 *Stator*
11 *Through-bolts*
12 *Drive end bracket*
13 *Spacers*
14 *Drive end bearing*
15 *Cooling fan*
16 *Pulley*
17 *Pulley nut and washer*

Allen key to retain the alternator shaft or by clamping the pulley firmly in a vice equipped with soft jaws. Remove the pulley, cooling fan and fan washer from the old alternator and, ensuring that the pulley and shaft mating surfaces are clean, install them on the new unit. Tighten the pulley retaining nut to the specified torque whilst using the method employed on removal to retain the pulley.

Models equipped with air conditioning

12 Manoeuvre the alternator into position then refit its mounting bolts and tighten them to the specified torque.

13 Locate the drivebelt on the alternator pulley then adjust the drivebelt tension as described in Chapter 1.

14 Reconnect the wiring connector to the rear of the alternator then refit the heat shield, tightening its retaining nut and bolts securely, and reconnect the battery.

Models without air conditioning

15 Manoeuvre the alternator into position then refit the adjusting arm and pivot bolts and tighten them lightly.

16 Locate the drivebelt on the alternator pulley and adjust the drivebelt tension as described in Chapter 1.

17 Reconnect the wiring connector to the rear of the alternator then refit the rear cover, tightening its retaining nuts securely, and reconnect the battery.

7 Alternator brush holder and voltage regulator assembly - renewal

Note: *The vast majority of actual alternator faults are due to the voltage regulator or to the brushes. If the renewal of either of these assemblies does not cure the fault, the advice of an expert should be sought as to the best approach; for most owners the best course of action will be to renew the alternator as a complete unit. In many cases overhaul will not be viable on economic grounds alone.*

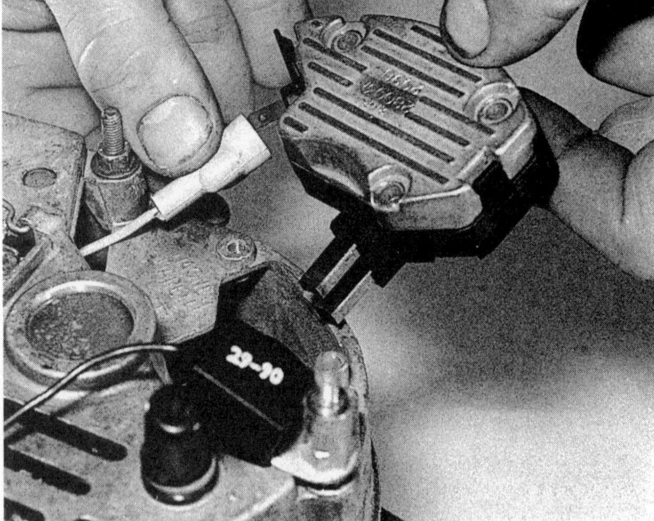

7.2 Remove the voltage regulator/brush holder from the alternator and disconnect the wiring lead

1 While it is physically possible to remove the voltage regulator and brush holder assembly with the alternator in place on the car, owners are advised to remove the alternator, as described in Section 6, so that it can be serviced in clean working conditions.

2 Unscrew the screws securing the voltage regulator and brush holder assembly to the alternator. Lift off the regulator/brush holder, disconnect the electrical lead and remove the regulator/brush holder from the alternator (photo).

3 In most cases the brushes will have wear limit marks in the form of a

7.3 When alternator brushes are worn to ends of wear limit marks (where given), they must be renewed

groove etched along one face of each brush; when these marks are erased by wear, the brushes are worn out (photo). If no marks are provided, measure the protrusion of each brush from the brush holder end to the tip of the brush. No dimension is given by Rover but as a rough guide 5 mm should be regarded as a minimum. If either brush is worn to or below this amount, renew the voltage regulator and brush holder assembly. If the brushes are still serviceable, clean them with a solvent-moistened cloth. Check that the brush spring pressure is equal for both brushes and holds the brushes securely against the slip rings. If in doubt about the condition of the brushes and springs compare them with new components.

4 Clean the slip rings with a solvent-moistened cloth, then check for signs of scoring, burning or severe pitting. If worn or damaged, the slip rings should be attended to by an auto-electrician.

5 Refitting is the reverse of the removal procedure.

8 Starting system - testing

Note: *Refer to the warnings given in Safety first! and in Section 1 of this Chapter before starting work.*

1 If the starter motor fails to operate when the switch is operated, the following may be the cause.

- *(a) The battery is faulty.*
- *(b) The electrical connections between the ignition switch, solenoid, battery and starter motor are somewhere failing to pass the necessary current from the battery through the starter to earth.*
- *(c) The solenoid is faulty.*
- *(d) The starter relay is faulty.*
- *(e) The starter motor is mechanically or electrically defective.*

2 To check the battery, switch on the headlamps. If they dim after a few seconds the battery is discharged; recharge or renew the battery. If the lamps glow brightly operate the ignition switch and see what happens to the lamps. If they dim then you know that power is reaching the starter motor; therefore the starter motor must be removed and renewed or overhauled to cure the fault. If the lamps stay bright (and no clicking sound can be heard from the solenoid) there is a fault in the circuit or solenoid; see below. If the starter turns slowly when switched on, but the battery is in good condition, then either the starter must be faulty or there is considerable resistance in the circuit.

3 If the circuit is suspected, disconnect the battery terminals (including the earth connection to the body), the starter/solenoid wiring and the engine/transmission earth lead, thoroughly clean their connections and refit them, then use a meter or test lamp to check that full battery voltage is available at the solenoid terminal of the battery positive lead and that the earth is sound. Smear petroleum jelly around the battery terminals to prevent corrosion. Corroded connections are the most frequent cause of electrical system malfunctions.

4 If the battery and all connections are in good condition, check the circuit first by disconnecting the wire from the solenoid blade terminal. Connect a meter or test lamp between the wire end and the terminal and check that the wire is live when the ignition switch is operated. If it is, then the circuit is sound; if not, proceed to paragraph 7.

5 The solenoid contacts can be checked by putting a voltmeter or test lamp across the main cable connection on the starter side of the solenoid and earth. When the switch is operated, there should be a reading or lighted bulb. If there is no reading or lighted bulb, the solenoid is faulty and should be renewed.

6 If the circuit and solenoid are proved sound, the fault must be in the starter motor; remove it and check the brushes as described in Section 10. If the fault does not lie in the brushes, the motor windings must be faulty; in this event the motor must be renewed, unless an auto-electrical specialist can be found who will overhaul the unit at a cost significantly less than that of a new or exchange starter motor.

7 If the circuit is thought to be faulty, first check the starter relay which is situated in the engine compartment fusebox. A simple test is to temporarily replace it with one of the other relays from the fusebox, such as the cooling fan relay, which is known to be in a good condition. If this resolves the fault the starter relay is faulty and must be renewed. If not, check the ignition switch and wiring using the equipment and procedures outlined in Section 2 of this Chapter, referring to the wiring diagrams for full details.

9 Starter motor - removal and refitting

Removal

1 Disconnect the battery negative lead.

2 Firmly apply the handbrake then jack up the front of the car and support it on axle stands.

3 From underneath the front of the vehicle, slacken and remove the three bolts securing the bumper flange to the body. Remove the seven bolts securing the front undercover panel to the body and remove the panel.

9.4 Starter solenoid main terminal nut 'A' and spade connector 'B'

9.5 Starter motor support bracket to transmission bolts

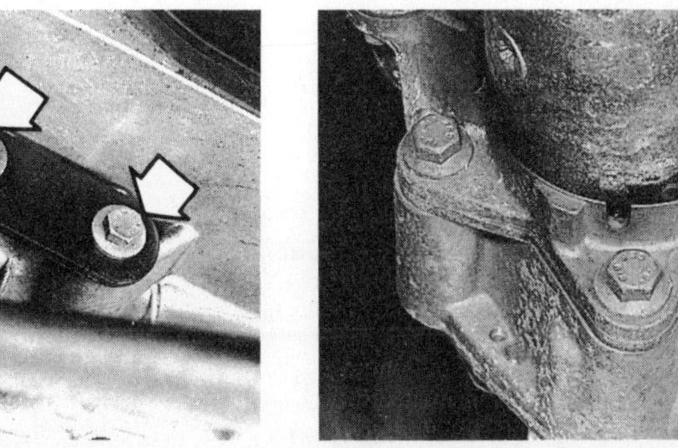

9.6A Starter motor lower mounting bolts (viewed from underneath)

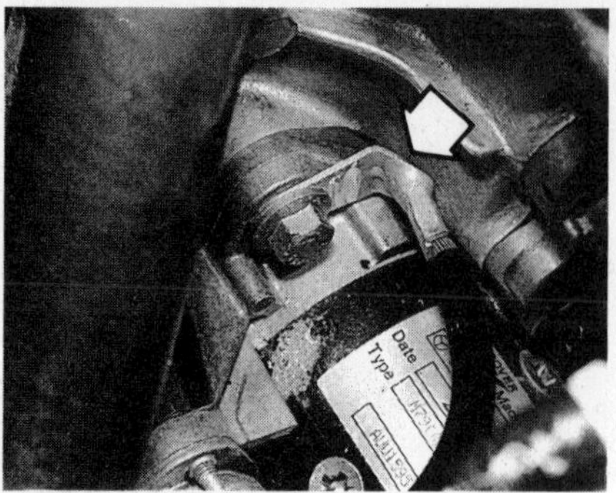

9.6B Starter motor upper mounting bolt and earth strap (arrowed) (viewed from above)

9.6C Removing the starter motor

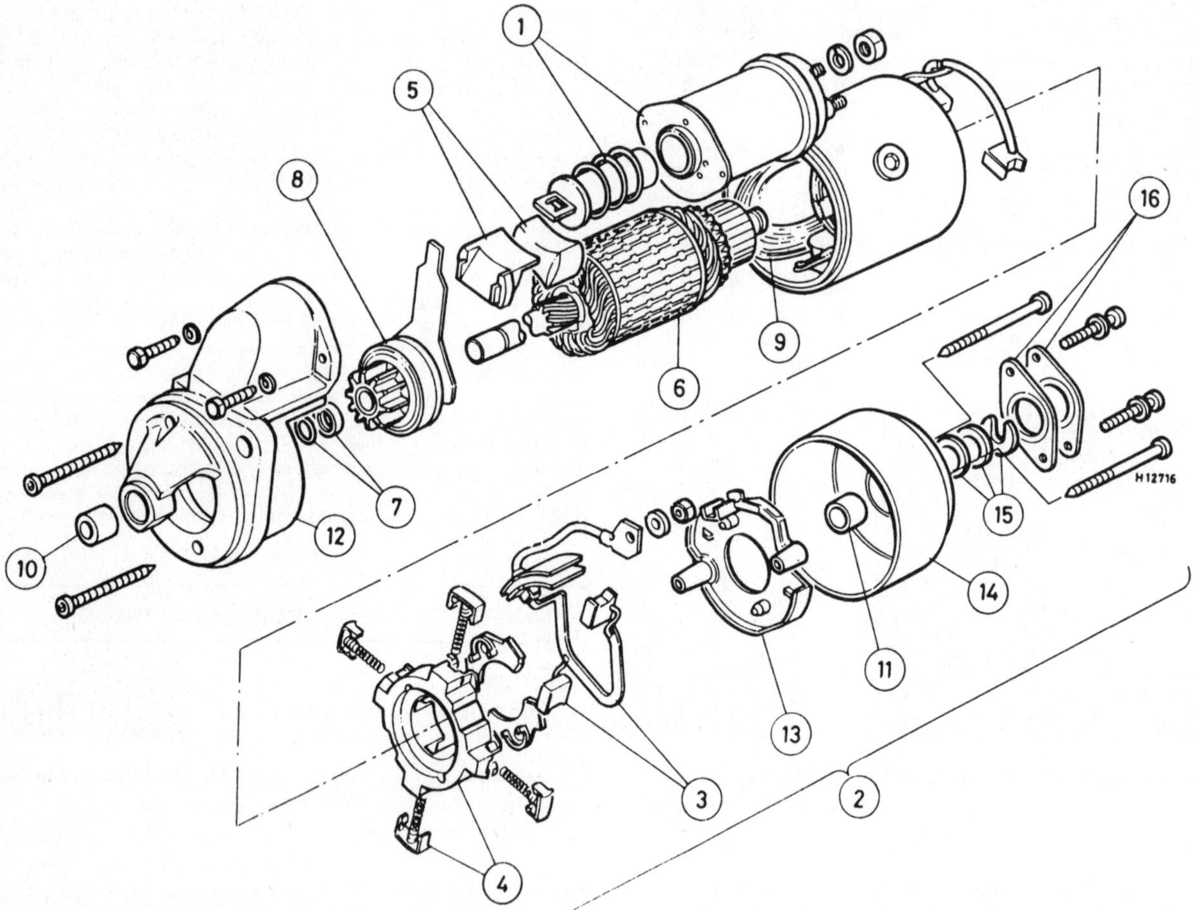

Fig. 12.3 Exploded view of the starter motor (Sec 10)

1 Solenoid and plunger
2 Commutator end cover assembly
3 Positive brush assembly
4 Negative brushes and brush holder
5 Solenoid engaging lever pivot and grommet
6 Armature
7 Jump ring and thrust collar
8 Drive pinion assembly
9 Field coils and yoke
10 Drive end bush
11 Commutator end bush
12 Motor drive end bracket
13 Insulating plate
14 Motor end cover
15 C-clip and thrustwashers
16 Cover and gasket

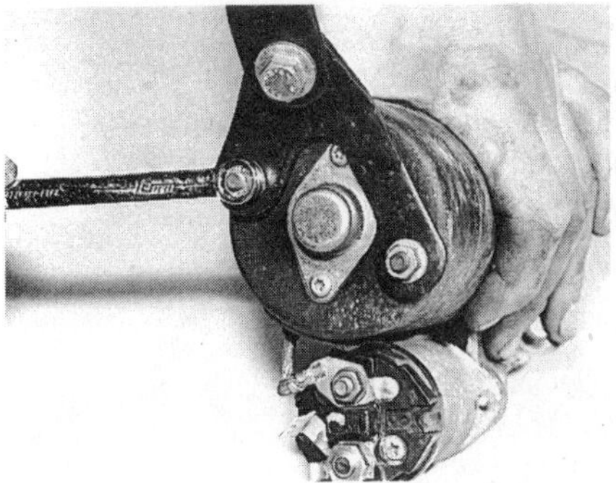

10.2 Undo the retaining nuts and remove the support bracket from the starter motor

10.3 Remove cover to gain access to armature C-clip

10.4A Note alignment marks between yoke and grommet...

10.4B ...then remove the through bolts...

10.4C ...and withdraw the end cover

10.6A Remove plastic insulating plate...

10.6B ...then remove brush spring caps and springs...

10.6C ...and remove the positive brush assembly from the motor

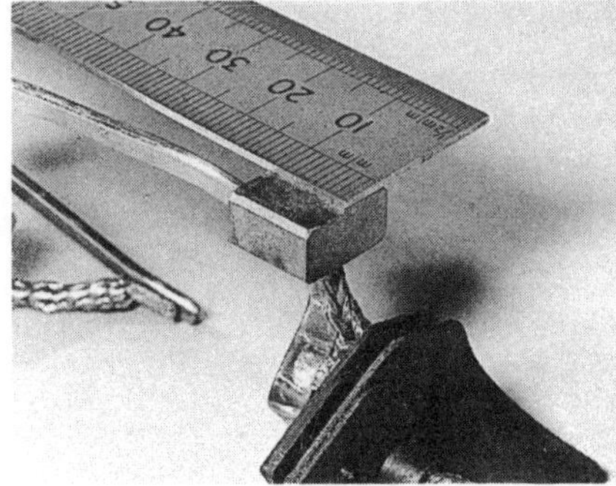

10.7 Measuring the length of starter motor brushes

4 Undo the nut and disconnect the battery cable from the main solenoid terminal. Carefully disconnect the spade connector from the solenoid (photo).

5 Unscrew the two bolts securing the starter motor support bracket to the transmission (photo).

6 Slacken and remove the three starter motor mounting bolts, noting the earth strap which is fitted to the upper bolt, and manoeuvre the starter motor out from underneath the car (photos).

Refitting

7 Refitting is a reverse of the removal sequence, tightening all nuts and bolts to their specified torque settings.

10 Starter motor - brush and solenoid renewal

1 Remove the starter motor as described in Section 9.

Brushes

2 Undo the two nuts securing the support bracket to the rear of the starter motor and remove the bracket (photo).

3 Undo the two screws and remove the small cover and gasket from the centre of the starter motor end cover (photo). Prise out the C-clip and withdraw any thrustwashers fitted to the armature end.

4 Noting the alignment marks between the end cover or grommet and the yoke, unscrew the two through bolts and withdraw the end cover (photos).

5 Carefully prise off the negative (field coil) brushes retaining caps from the brush holder assembly then remove the springs and slide the brushes out of the holder.

6 Remove the nut and spring washer securing the positive brush lead to the solenoid terminal and slide the brush holder assembly off the end of the commutator. Withdraw the plastic insulating plate then remove the positive brush retaining caps and springs and remove the positive brushes from the holder (photos).

7 In most cases the brushes will have wear limit marks in the form of a

10.14 Unscrew the nut and disconnect the starter motor lead from the solenoid terminal

10.15 Remove solenoid retaining bolts (one arrowed)...

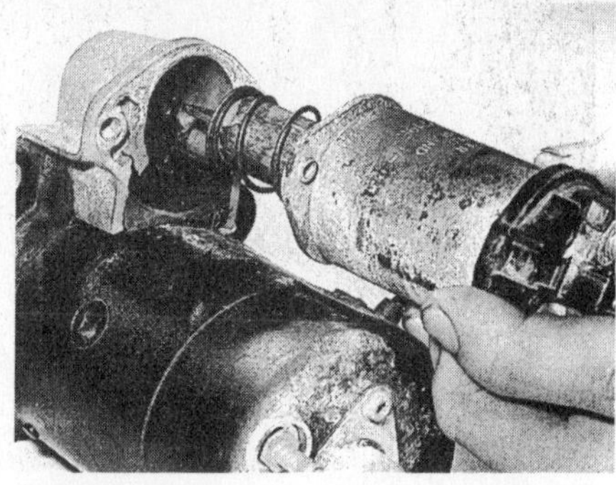

10.16 ...then release solenoid plunger from its lever and remove assembly from the motor

groove etched along one face of each brush; when the brushes are worn down to these marks, they are worn out and must be renewed. If no marks are provided, measure the length of each brush (photo). No dimension is given by Rover but as a rough guide 3.5 mm should be regarded as a minimum. If any brush is worn below this amount, renew the brushes as a set. If the brushes are still serviceable, clean them with a solvent-moistened cloth. Check that the brush spring pressure is equal for all brushes and holds the brushes securely against the commutator. If in doubt about the condition of the brushes and springs compare them with new components.

8 Clean the commutator with a solvent-moistened cloth, then check for signs of scoring, burning, excessive wear or severe pitting. If worn or damaged, the commutator should be attended to by an auto-electrician.

9 On refitting, slot the positive brushes into position in the brush holder then refit the insulating plate, ensuring that the small threaded brackets are correctly positioned on the brush holder and locate with the pins on the insulating plate.

10 Fit the brush holder assembly to the commutator and slot the negative (field coil) brushes into position in the brush holder. With all the brushes in position, fit the brush springs and secure them in position with the retaining caps. Check that the brushes are free to move in their holders against spring pressure.

11 Refit the starter motor end cover, engaging it with the grommet, and align the marks noted on removal. Tighten the cover through bolts securely.

12 Refit any necessary thrustwashers to the end of the armature and secure them in position with the C-clip. Refit the gasket and small cover to the end cover and tighten its retaining screws securely. Connect the positive brush lead to the solenoid terminal and tighten the nut securely.

13 Refit the support bracket to the motor and tighten its retaining nuts to the specified torque.

Solenoid

14 Slacken and remove the nut and spring washer securing the starter motor (positive brush) lead to the solenoid and disconnect the lead from the solenoid terminal (photo).

15 Unscrew the two bolts and spring washers securing the solenoid to the starter motor drive end bracket (photo).

16 Release the solenoid plunger from the starter engaging lever, then withdraw the solenoid, noting the spring which is fitted to the plunger (photo).

17 Refitting is the reverse of the removal procedure. Ensure that the solenoid, its plunger and the motor/solenoid mating surfaces are clean and lubricate the plunger/starter engaging lever surfaces with a smear of grease (Rover recommend Shell Alvania).

11 Fuses, fusible links and relays – general information

Fuses

1 Most of the fuses are located behind the panel in the right-hand lower facia panel, with a few odd fuses being located in the fusebox on the left-hand side of the engine compartment.

2 Access to the fuses is gained by removing the fusebox lid/cover. Symbols on the reverse of the lid/cover indicate the circuits protected by the fuses and five spare fuses are supplied together with plastic tweezers to remove and fit them (photo). Further details on fuse ratings and circuits protected are given in the Specifications Section of this Chapter.

3 To remove a fuse, first switch off the circuit concerned (or the ignition), then fit the tweezers and pull the fuse out of its terminals. Slide the fuse sideways from the tweezers. The wire within the fuse is clearly visible; if the fuse is blown the wire will be broken or melted.

4 Always renew a fuse with one of an identical rating; never use a fuse with a different rating from the original or substitute anything else. Never renew a fuse more than once without tracing the source of the trouble. The fuse rating is stamped on top of the fuse; note that the fuses are also colour-coded for easy recognition.

5 If a new fuse blows immediately, find the cause before renewing it again; a short to earth as a result of faulty insulation is most likely. Where a fuse protects more than one circuit, try to isolate the defect by switching on each circuit in turn (if possible) until the fuse blows again.

6 If any of the spare fuses are used, always replace them immediately so that a spare of each rating is available.

11.2 Fuses can be removed using plastic tweezers supplied (arrowed)

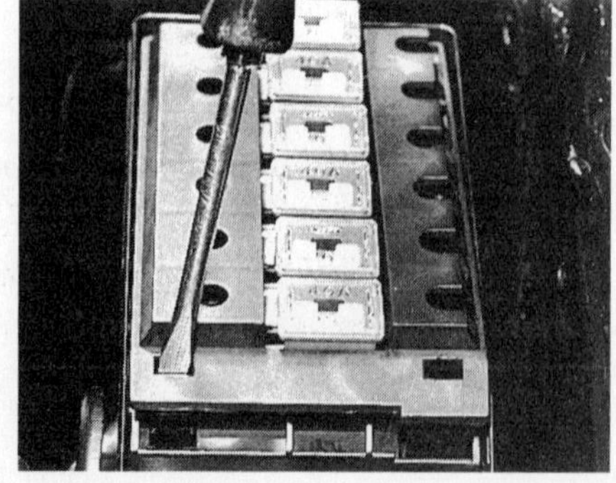

11.9A Unclip the plastic cover...

11.9B ...then undo the retaining screws and remove fusible link

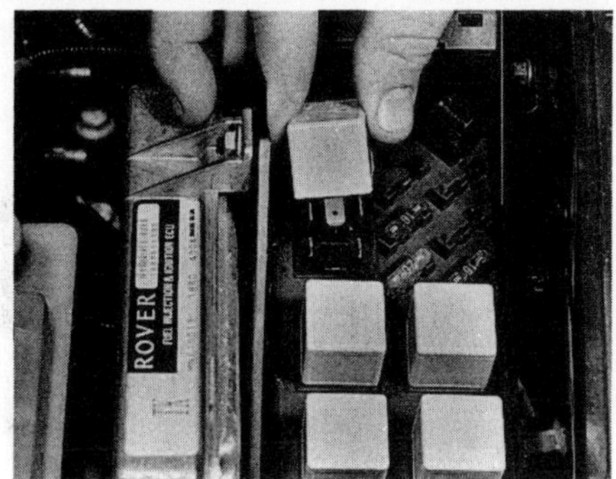

11.13 Engine compartment fusebox relays. Relays are a push fit

11.14A Use a screwdriver to release the relay module retaining clip...

11.14B ...then slide the module out of position and disconnect its wiring connectors

Fusible links

7 The fusible links are located in the rear of the fusebox situated on the left-hand side of the engine compartment. Unclip the lid to gain access to them.
8 Details of link ratings and circuits protected are given in the Specifications Section of this Chapter; the links are numbered on the rear of the fusebox lid.
9 To remove a fusible link, first ensure that the circuit concerned is switched off then prise off the small black plastic cover. Slacken the two link retaining screws then lift the fusible link out of the fusebox (photos). The wire within the fusible link is clearly visible; if the fuse is blown it will be broken or melted.

Note: *A blown fusible link indicates a serious wiring or system fault which must be diagnosed before the link is renewed.*

10 Always renew a fusible link with one of an identical rating; never use a link with a different rating from the original or substitute anything else. On refitting tighten the link retaining screws securely and refit the link cover.

Relays

11 The Specifications Section of this Chapter gives full information on the location and function of the various relays fitted; refer to the relevant wiring diagram for details of wiring connections.
12 If a circuit or system controlled by a relay develops a fault and the relay is suspect, operate the system; if the relay is functioning it should be possible to hear it click as it is energized. If this is the case the fault lies with the components or wiring of the system. If the relay is not being energized, then either the relay is not receiving a main supply or a switching voltage or the relay itself is faulty. Testing is by the substitution of a known good unit but be careful; while some relays are identical in appearance and in operation, others look similar but perform different functions.
13 To renew a relay, ensure that the ignition switch is off, then simply pull direct from the socket and press in the new relay (photo).
14 Certain relays are contained in the relay module which is situated behind the lower central facia panel. To remove this, first remove the lower central panel from the facia as described in Section 31 of Chapter 11. Disconnect its two wiring block connectors then release its retaining clip and slide to the left to withdraw it from the mounting bracket (photos). The complete module must be renewed, even if only one of the relays is faulty.

12 Switches – removal and refitting

Note: *Disconnect the battery negative lead before removing any switch, and reconnect the lead after refitting the switch.*

Ignition switch

1 Refer to Chapter 10, Section 19, for details of switch removal and refitting. A Rover dealer will be able to tell you whether the switch can be obtained separately from the steering lock.

Steering column combination switch

2 Remove the steering wheel and steering column shrouds, then disconnect the switch wiring as described in Chapter 10, Section 17, paragraphs 1 to 4.
3 Each individual switch can be removed by unscrewing its two retaining screws and sliding the switch out of the housing (photos).
4 To remove the complete assembly, slacken and remove the two retaining screws and slide the assembly off the steering column.
5 Refitting is the reverse of the removal procedure, referring to Chapter 10, Section 17 for further information.

Instrument panel and facia switches

6 Check that the switch is in the 'off' position, then taking great care not to scratch or damage the switch or its surround, prise it out using a suitable flat-bladed screwdriver. Withdraw the switch until the connector plug appears then disconnect the wiring connector and

12.3A Individual combination switches can be removed by slackening their retaining screws...

12.3B ...and sliding the switch out of the main assembly

12.6A Carefully prise facia switches out of position...

12.6B ...and disconnect their wiring connectors

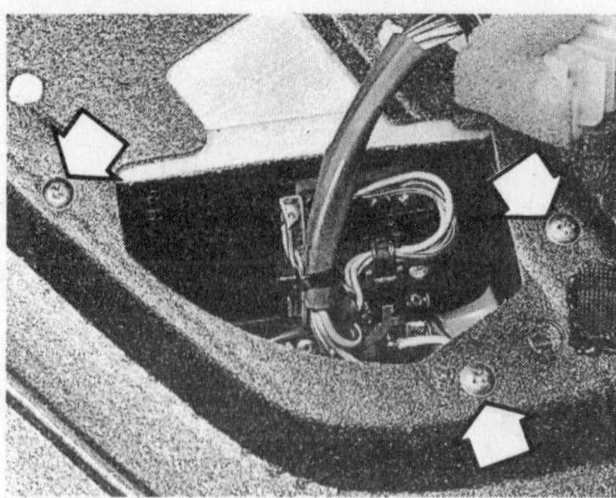

12.9 Driver's side electric window switch retaining screws (arrowed)

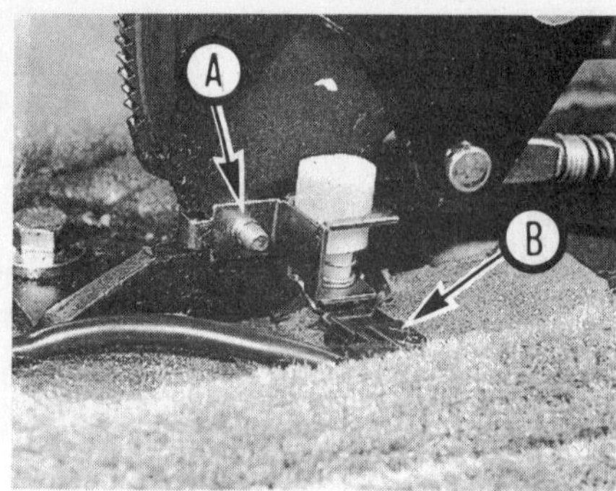

12.15 Handbrake warning lamp switch retaining screw 'A' and wiring connector 'B'

remove the switch (photos). Tie a piece of string to the wiring connector to prevent it from falling behind the facia panel.

7 On refitting, connect the wiring connector to the switch and press the switch into position until the retaining clips click into place.

Electric window switches

8 Remove the door inner trim panel as described in Chapter 11.

9 Undo the retaining screws and remove the switch from the trim panel (photo).

10 On refitting tighten the switch screws securely and refit the door inner trim panel as described in Chapter 11.

Courtesy lamp switches

11 With the door open, undo the two screws securing the switch to the body. Pull out the switch and tie a piece of string to the wiring to prevent it dropping into the body.

12 Disconnect the switch and remove it from the vehicle.

13 Refitting is a reverse of removal.

Handbrake warning lamp switch

14 From inside the car, carefully prise out the cover from the top of the centre console rear section to gain access to the two retaining screws. Undo the two screws and remove the rear centre console section.

15 Disconnect the wiring connector from the switch then slacken and remove the retaining screw and remove the switch from the handbrake lever quadrant (photo).

16 Refitting is a reverse of the removal procedure.

13 Bulbs (exterior lamps) - renewal

General

1 Whenever a bulb is renewed, note the following points.

(a) *Disconnect the battery negative lead before starting work.*

(b) *Remember that if the lamp has just been in use the bulb may be extremely hot.*

(c) *Always check the bulb contacts and holder, ensuring that there is clean metal-to-metal contact between the bulb and its live(s) and earth. Clean off any corrosion or dirt before fitting a new bulb.*

(d) *Wherever bayonet-type bulbs are fitted (see Specifications) ensure that the live contact(s) bear firmly against the bulb contact.*

(e) *Always ensure that the new bulb is of the correct rating and that it is completely clean before fitting; this applies particularly to headlamp bulbs (see below).*

Headlamp

2 Working in the engine compartment, twist off the relevant circular plastic cover and remove it from the rear of the headlamp unit (photo).

3 Unplug the wiring connector, then press together the ears of the bulb retaining clip and release it from the rear of the lamp (photo).

4 Withdraw the bulb.

5 When handling the new bulb, use a tissue or clean cloth to avoid touching the glass with the fingers; moisture and grease from the skin can cause blackening and rapid failure of this type of bulb. If the glass is accidentally touched, wipe it clean using methylated spirit.

6 Refitting is the reverse of the removal procedure; ensure that the new bulbs locating tabs are correctly located in the lamp cutouts.

Front sidelamp

7 Working in the engine compartment, twist off the large circular plastic cover and remove it from the rear of the headlamp unit.

8 Pull the bulbholder from the headlamp reflector.

9 Pull the capless (push fit) bulb out of its socket.

10 Refitting is the reverse of the removal procedure.

Front direction indicator

11 Working in the engine compartment, undo the indicator lamp upper retaining screw and withdraw the lamp (photo).

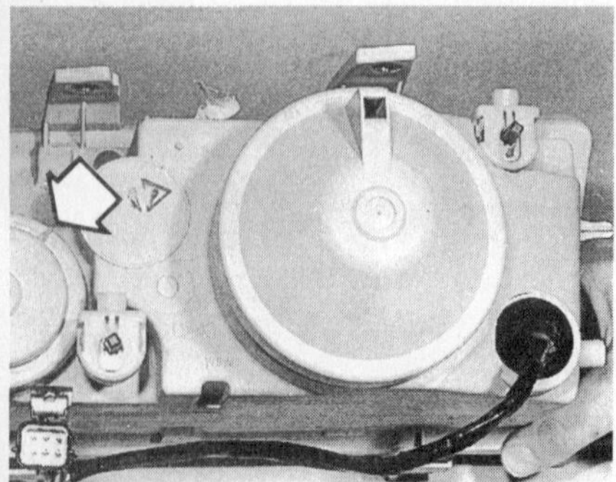

13.2 Remove the large circular cover to access dip/main beam bulb and side lamp bulbs and smaller cover (arrowed) to access individual main beam bulb

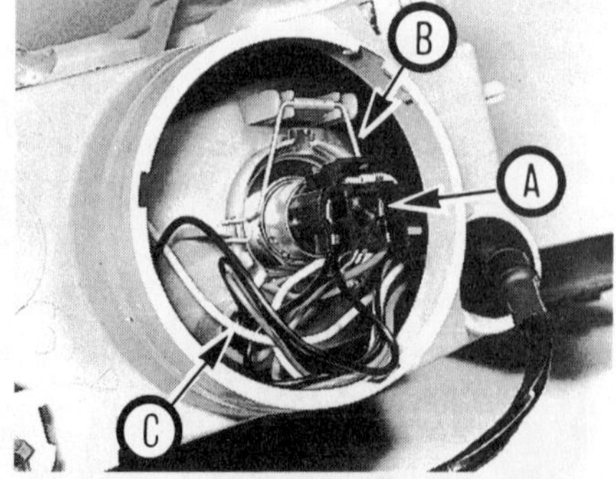

13.3 Headlamp dip/main beam bulb wiring connector 'A', retaining clip 'B' and sidelamp bulbholder 'C' - headlamp removed for clarity

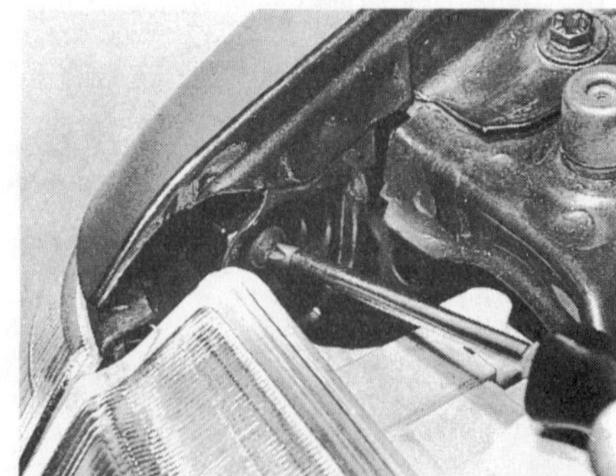

13.11 Remove the retaining screw...

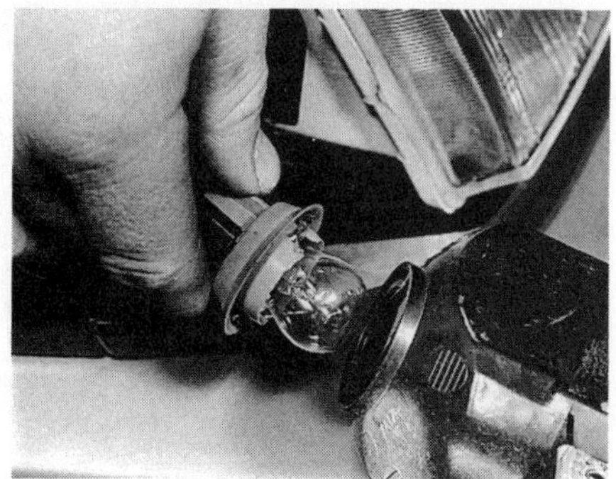
13.12 ...then withdraw the indicator lamp and twist the bulbholder free

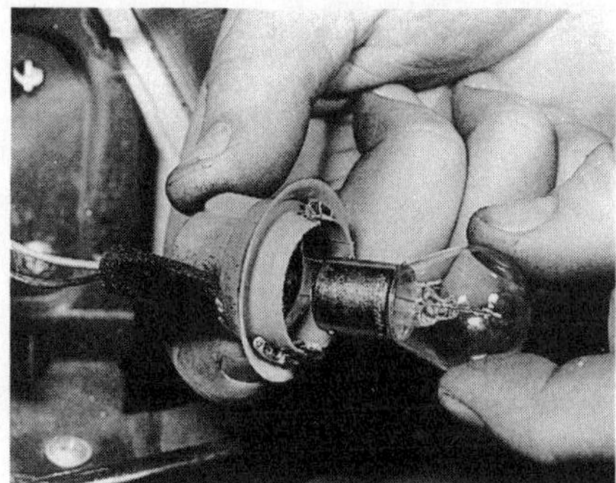
13.13 Indicator bulbs are of the bayonet type

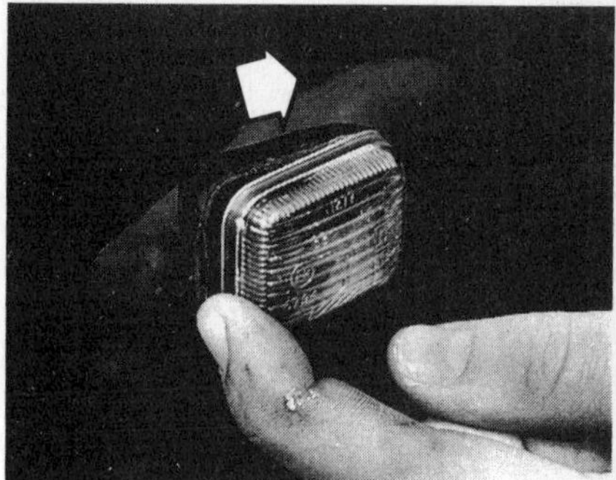
13.15 Push indicator side repeater lamp to the right...

13.16 ...then withdraw the lamp and pull out the bulbholder

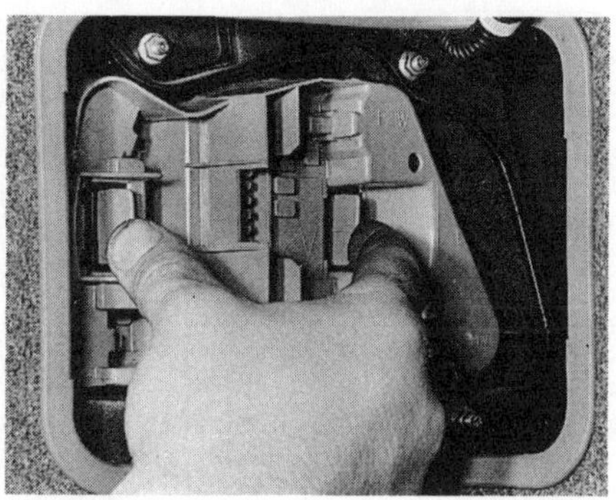
13.19 Depress the catches and withdraw the rear lamp bulb panel

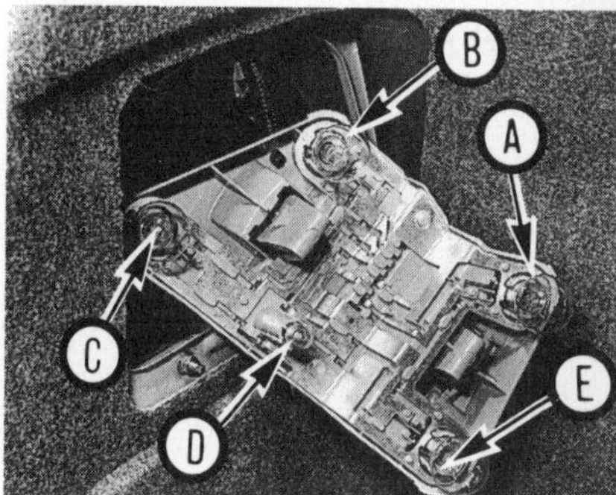

13.20A Rear lamp cluster bulbs: direction indicator 'A', reversing lamp 'B', fog lamp'C', tail lamp 'D' and stop lamp 'E'

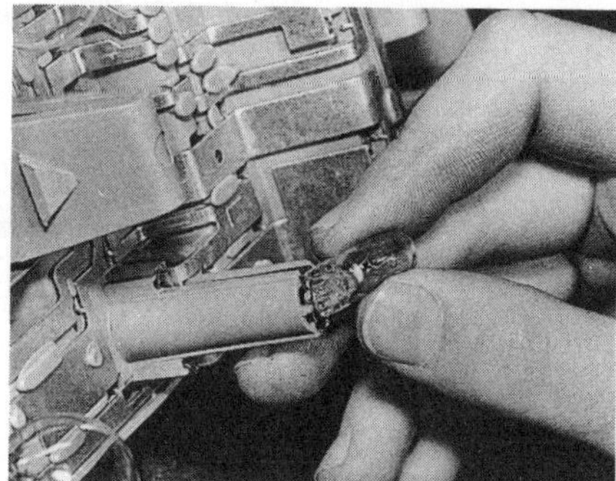
13.20B Rear cluster tail lamp bulb is of capless type...

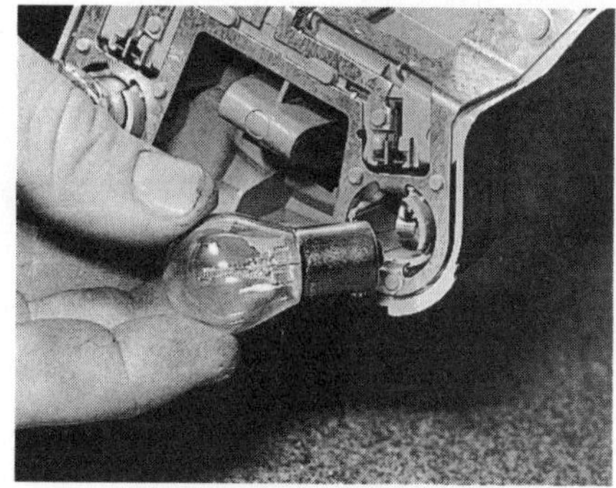
13.20C ...whereas all other bulbs have a bayonet type fitting

12 Twist the bulbholder in an anti-clockwise direction to free it from the lamp and remove it from the lamp unit (photo).
13 The bulb is a bayonet fit in the holder and can be removed by pressing it and twisting in an anti-clockwise direction (photo).
14 Refitting is a reverse of the removal procedure.

Front direction indicator side repeater

15 Push the lamp unit towards the right to free its retaining clips then withdraw it from the wing (photo).
16 Pull the bulbholder out of the lamp unit then pull the capless (push fit) bulb out of its holder (photo).
17 Refitting is a reverse of the removal procedure.

Rear lamp cluster

18 From inside the luggage compartment, remove the relevant rear cover from the lamp.
19 Depress the catches and withdraw the bulb panel from the lens unit (photo).
20 The relevant bulb can then be removed from the panel, noting that the tail lamp bulb is of the capless (push fit) type whereas all other bulbs have a bayonet fitting (photos).
21 Refitting is the reverse of the removal sequence noting that the rubber seal must be renewed if damaged.

Number plate lamps

22 Undo the two mounting screws and remove the number plate lamp lens and seal.
23 Withdraw the lamp and remove the clip from the top of the lamp body to gain access to the bulb.
24 The bulb is of the capless (push fit) type and can be pulled out of the lamp unit.
25 Refitting is a reverse of the removal procedure.

14.9 Luggage compartment lamp bulb is of the bayonet type

14.13A Instrument panel illumination bulbholder is a twist fit in the panel...

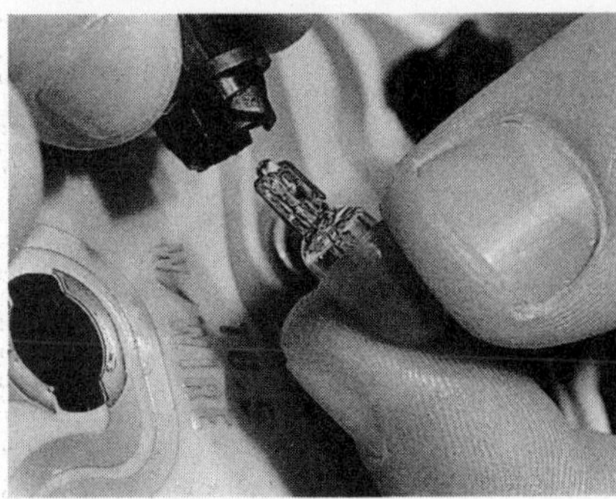
14.13B ...the bulb being of the capless type

14 Bulbs (interior lamps) - renewal

General

1 Refer to Section 13, paragraph 1.

Courtesy lamps

2 Carefully prise the lens off the lamp unit then remove the festoon bulb from its end contacts.
3 Fit the new bulb using a reversal of the removal procedure, but check the tension of the spring contacts and if necessary bend them so that they firmly contact the bulb end caps.

Glovebox lamp

4 Open up the glovebox and undo the two switch/lamp assembly retaining screws. Disconnect the wiring connector and remove the switch/lamp unit from the glovebox.
5 Depress the lens retaining lug and remove the lens assembly from the unit.
6 Release the festoon bulb from its contacts and remove it from the lens.
7 Fit the new bulb using a reversal of the removal procedure, but check the tension of the spring contacts and if necessary bend them so that they firmly contact the bulb end caps.

Luggage compartment lamp

8 Carefully prise the lamp out of the trim panel using a suitable flat-bladed screwdriver.
9 The bulb is a bayonet fit and can be removed by pressing it in and twisting anti-clockwise (photo).
10 Refitting is a reverse of the removal procedure.

Instrument panel illumination and warning lamps

11 Remove the instrument panel as described in Section 17.
12 Twist the relevant bulbholder (see Fig. 12.4) anti-clockwise and withdraw it from the rear of the panel.
13 All bulbs, with the exception of the main panel illumination bulb, are integral with their holders. The main panel illumination bulb is of the capless type and is a push fit in its holder (photos). Be very careful to ensure that the new bulbs are of the same rating as those removed; this is especially important in the case of the ignition/battery charging warning lamp.
14 Refitting is the reverse of the removal procedure.

Facia illumination bulbs

15 To renew the various facia illumination bulbs it will first be necessary to remove the relevant facia panel to gain access to the bulb. Refer to Section 31 of Chapter 11 for information on facia panel removal and refitting.

Switch illumination bulbs

16 All of the facia panel switches are fitted with illuminating bulbs; some are also fitted with a bulb to show when the circuit concerned is operating. These bulbs are an integral part of the switch assembly and cannot be obtained separately. Bulb replacement will therefore require the renewal of the complete switch assembly.

15 Exterior lamp units - removal and refitting

Note: *Disconnect the battery negative lead before removing any lamp unit, and reconnect the lead after refitting the lamp.*

Headlamp

1 Open up the bonnet, then undo the four screws securing the radiator grille to the headlamps and remove the grille from the car.
2 Remove the screw securing the indicator lamp assembly to the wing and position the lamp unit clear of the headlamp assembly.
3 Undo the two headlamp retaining screws which were situated

15.3A Slacken and remove the headlamp retaining screws (remaining one arrowed)...

15.3B ...and the two headlamp retaining bolts

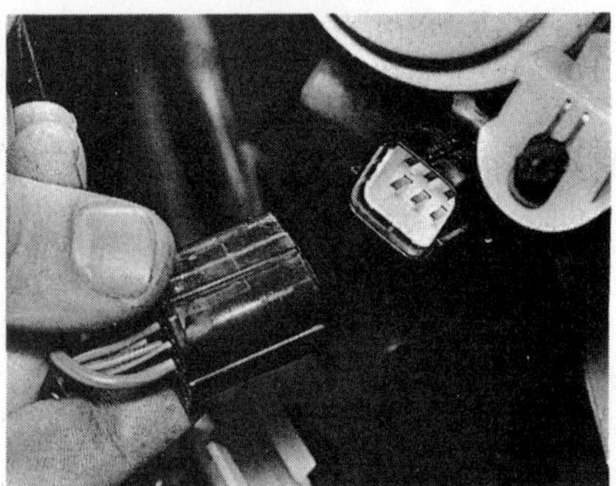
15.4 Disconnect the wiring connector

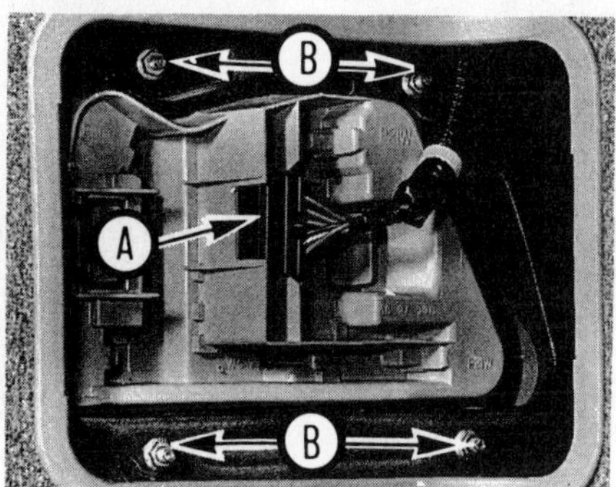

15.14 Disconnect the wiring connector 'A' and remove the rear lamp unit retaining nuts 'B'

15.15 Withdraw the rear lamp unit noting the rubber seal

17.2A Carefully prise left-hand switch assembly out of the instrument panel shroud...

17.2B ...then withdraw the assembly and disconnect wiring connectors

17.4 On models without an electric sunroof remove cover from right-hand side of instrument panel shroud

behind the indicator lamp and undo the two upper headlamp retaining bolts (photos).

4 Disconnect the headlamp wiring connector (photo).

5 Gently pull the headlamp upwards to release it from its lower retainer then remove the headlamp and lower finisher trim panel assembly from the car.

6 If necessary, the lower finisher can be removed from the headlamp by removing the retaining screw and releasing the two retaining clips.

7 Refitting is a reversal of the removal procedure. On completion adjust the headlamp aim as described in Chapter 1.

Front direction indicator

8 Open up the bonnet and remove the indicator lamp upper retaining screw.

9 Withdraw the lamp unit from the wing, then twist the bulbholder in an anti-clockwise direction to free it from the lamp and remove the lamp unit from the car.

10 Refitting is the reverse of the removal procedure.

Front direction indicator side repeater

11 Push the lamp unit towards the right to free its retaining clips then withdraw it from the wing.

12 Pull the bulbholder out and remove the lamp from the car.

13 Refitting is a reverse of the removal procedure.

Rear lamp cluster

14 Working from within the luggage compartment, remove the relevant rear lamp cover and disconnect the lamp wiring connector (photo).

15 Undo the four nuts securing the lamp unit to the body and remove the unit from the car noting the rubber seal which is fitted between the lamp unit and body (photo).

16 Refitting is a reversal of the removal procedure noting that the rubber seal must be renewed if damaged.

Number plate lamps

17 Undo the two mounting screws and remove the number plate lamp lens and seal.

18 Withdraw the lamp unit until the wiring connector appears then disconnect the connector and remove the unit from the car.

19 Refitting is the reverse of the removal procedure noting that the rubber seal must be renewed if damaged.

16 Dim-dip headlamp system - general information

1 The system comprises the dim-dip unit mounted behind the right-hand lower facia panel and a resistor situated behind the left-hand headlamp assembly.

2 The dim-dip unit is supplied with current from the sidelamp circuit and energised by a feed from the ignition switch. When energised, the unit allows battery voltage to pass through the resistor to the headlamp dipped-beam circuits; this lights the headlamps with approximately one-sixth of their normal power so that the car cannot be driven using sidelamps alone.

17 Instrument panel - removal and refitting

Removal

1 Working in the engine compartment, disconnect the battery negative lead, then unscrew the union nut which secures the upper and lower sections of the speedometer cable together.

2 Position the steering column in its lowest possible height setting then, using a suitable flat-bladed screwdriver, carefully prise out the switch assembly from the left-hand side of the instrument panel shroud. Disconnect the switch wiring connector and remove the switch assembly (photos).

3 On models equipped with an electric sunroof repeat the above operation for the sunroof switch.

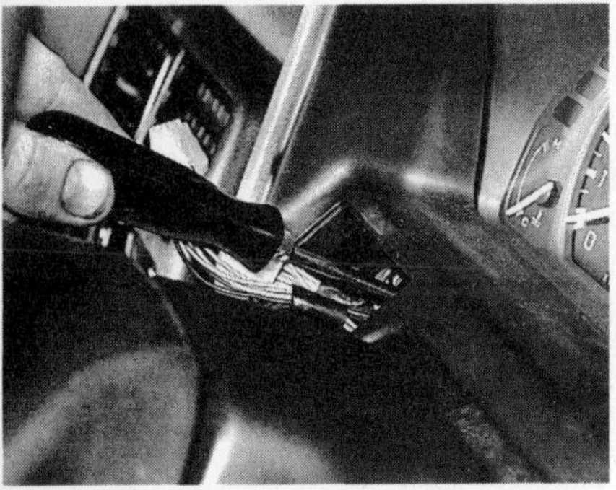

17.5A Instrument panel shroud lower retaining screws are accessed through switch apertures

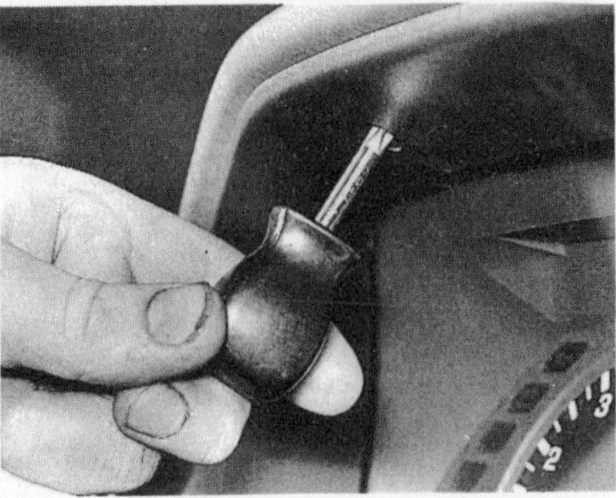

17.5B Remove upper retaining screws...

17.5C ...then withdraw the instrument panel shroud

17.6A Remove instrument panel upper (arrowed) and lower retaining screws...

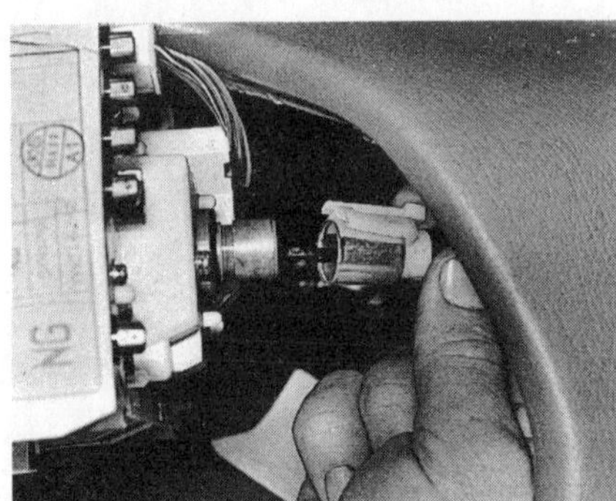

17.6B ...then disconnect the speedometer cable...

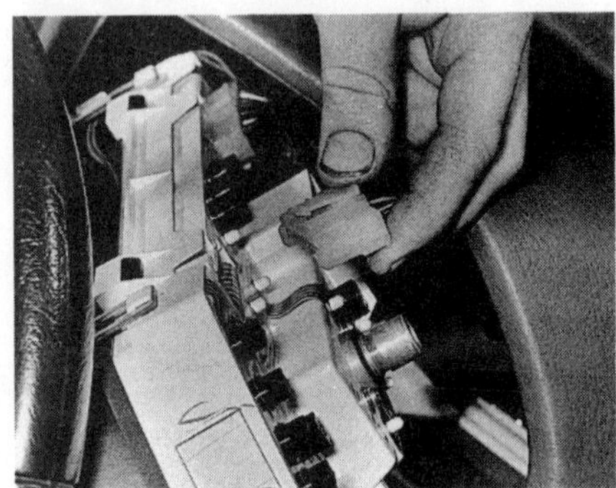

17.6C ...and wiring connectors...

4 On models without an electric sunroof carefully prise out the cover from the right-hand lower corner of the instrument shroud (photo).

5 Remove the four instrument panel shroud retaining screws and remove the shroud from the facia (photos).

6 Undo the four screws securing the instrument panel to the facia and carefully withdraw the panel until access can be gained to the rear of the panel. Release the speedometer cable retaining clip then disconnect the cable and three wiring block connectors from the panel (photos).

7 Remove the instrument panel from the facia (photo).

17.7 ...and withdraw the instrument panel from the facia

Refitting

8 Refitting is a reverse of the removal procedure. On completion check the operation of all the panel warning lamps and instrument shroud switches to ensure that they are functioning correctly.

18 Instrument panel components – removal and refitting

General

1 Remove the instrument panel as described in Section 17 then proceed as described under the relevant sub heading.

Instrument illumination panel

Removal

2 Remove the screws securing the right- and left-hand upper mounting brackets to the panel assembly and remove both brackets (photos).

3 Release the rear illumination panel bulbholder by twisting it in an anti-clockwise direction then remove the illumination panel from the top of the instruments (photo).

Refitting

4 Refitting is a reversal of the removal procedure.

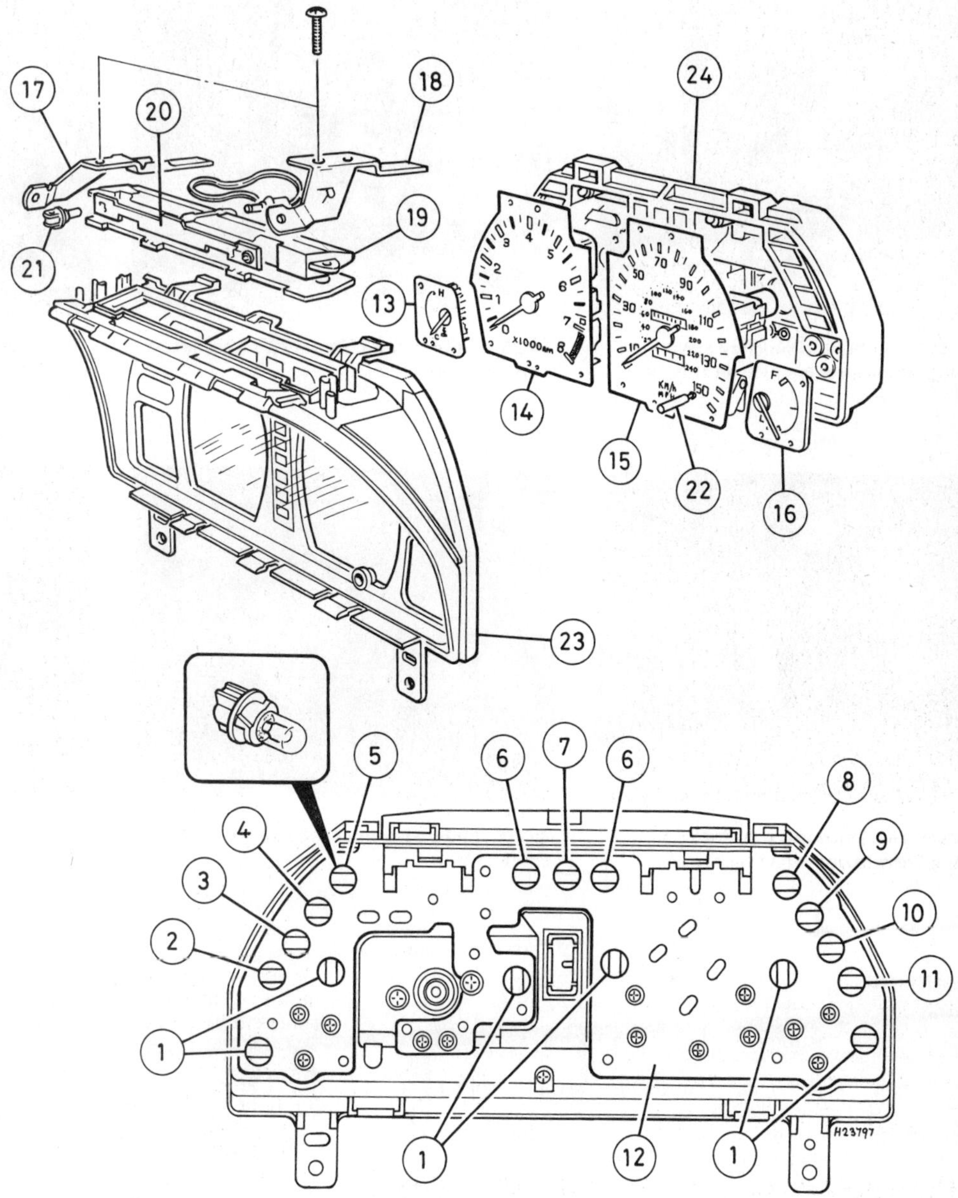

Fig. 12.4 Exploded view of the instrument panel (Sec 18)

1 Panel rear illumination bulbs
2 ABS warning lamp bulb (where fitted)
3 Boot open warning lamp bulb
4 Hazard warning lamp bulb
5 Brake fail/handbrake warning lamp bulb
6 Direction indicator warning lamp bulb
7 Main beam warning lamp bulb
8 Oil pressure warning lamp bulb
9 Ignition/charging lamp warning bulb
10 Choke warning lamp bulb – carburettor models
11 Caravan/trailer indicator warning lamp bulb
12 Printed circuit
13 Coolant temperature gauge
14 Tachometer
15 Speedometer
16 Fuel gauge
17 Left-hand support bracket
18 Right-hand support bracket
19 Illumination panel cover
20 Illumination panel printed circuit
21 Panel front illumination bulb
22 Tripmeter reset knob
23 Instrument panel cover
24 Instrument panel case

H23797

18.2A Unscrew retaining screws...

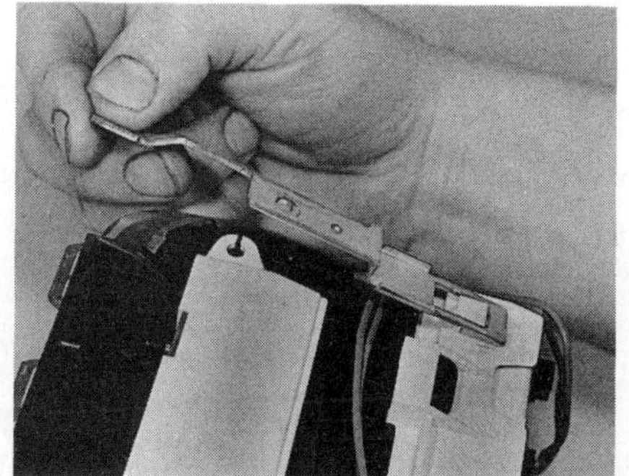

18.2B ...and remove upper mounting brackets from the instrument panel

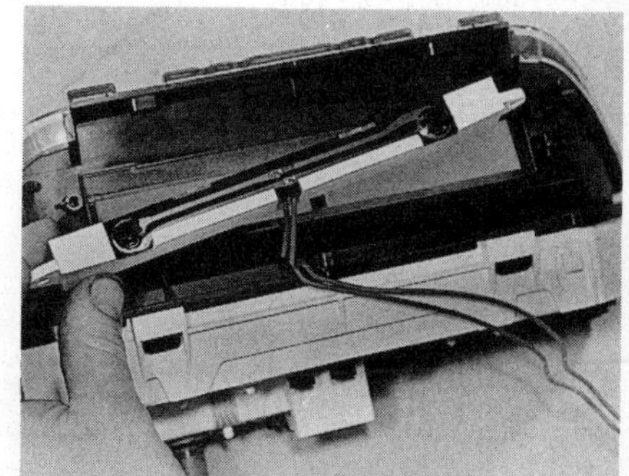

18.3 Removing instrument illumination panel

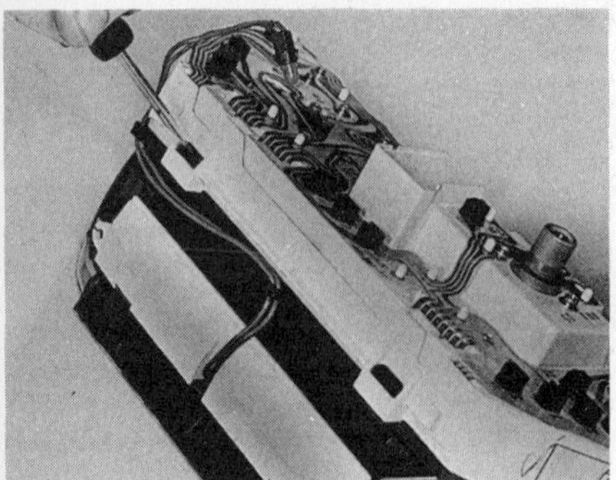
18.6 Release the retaining clips and separate instrument panel case and cover

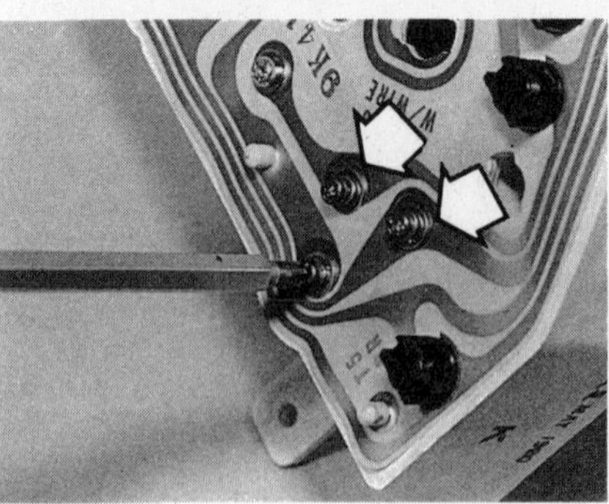
18.7A Remove retaining screws (remaining two arrowed)...

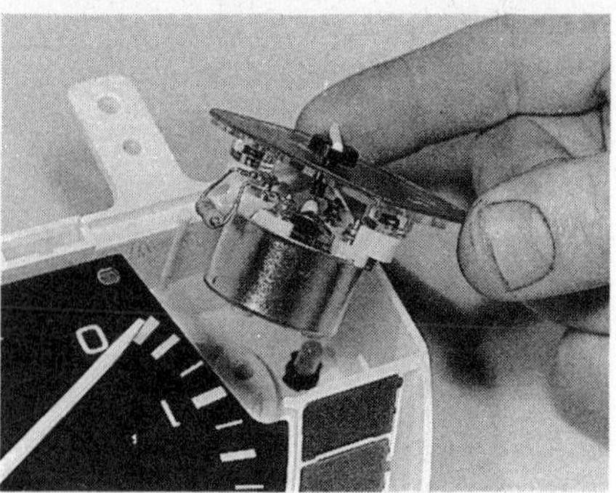
18.7B ...and remove relevant instrument from the panel case – temperature gauge shown

20.2A Carefully prise out the clock mounting trim strip...

20.2B ...and disconnect the clock wiring connector

20.3 Clock is retained by two screws

Instruments

Removal

5 Remove the instrument illumination panel as described in paragraphs 2 and 3.
6 Release the instrument panel cover retaining clips and lift the cover off the instrument panel case (photo).
7 The individual instruments can then be removed separately by unscrewing the retaining screws (photos). When removing the speedometer note the foam washer which is fitted around the base of the instrument stalk.

Refitting

8 Refitting is a reversal of the removal procedure.

Printed circuit

Removal

9 Remove the speedometer, tachometer, fuel gauge and temperature gauge from the meter case as described in paragraphs 5 to 7.
10 Remove all the bulbholders from the rear of the case by twisting them in an anti-clockwise direction, then release the printed circuit from its retaining pins and remove it from the case.

Refitting

11 Refitting is a reverse of the removal sequence.

19 Cigar lighter – removal and refitting

Removal

1 Disconnect the battery negative lead.
2 Remove the lighter element, then carefully prise out the metal surround, followed by the plastic body. Note the wiring connections before disconnecting them and tie a piece of string around the connector to prevent it from falling back inside the facia.

Refitting

3 Refitting is the reverse of the removal procedure.

20 Clock – removal and refitting

Removal

1 Disconnect the battery negative lead.
2 Using a suitable flat-bladed instrument, carefully prise out the clock mounting trim strip from the facia. Withdraw the trim and disconnect the wiring connector from the rear of the clock. Tie a piece of string around the connector to prevent it from falling back inside the facia (photos).
3 Undo the two clock retaining screws and remove the clock from the trim strip (photo).

Refitting

4 Refitting is a reversal of the removal procedure.

21 Horn – removal and refitting

Removal

1 Disconnect the battery negative terminal.
2 Remove the front bumper as described in Chapter 11.

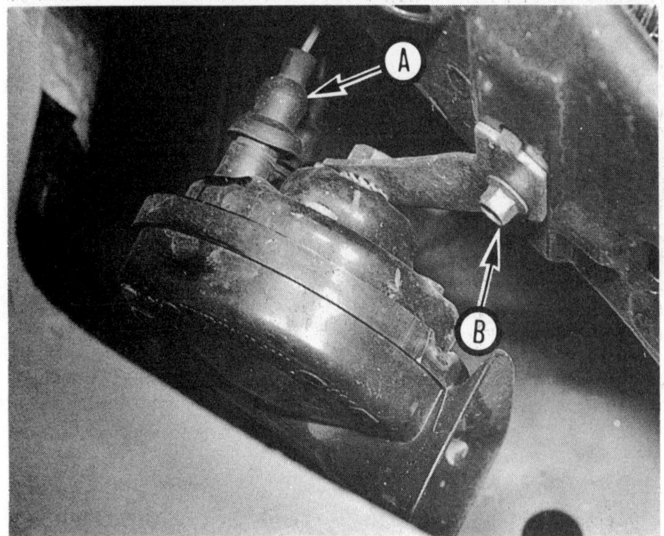

21.3 Horn wiring connectors 'A' and retaining bolt 'B'

3 Disconnect the horn wiring connectors and unbolt the horn(s) from the body (photo).

Refitting

4 Refitting is a reversal of the removal procedure.

22 Speedometer drive cable – removal and refitting

General

1 The drive cable is in two parts; the lower cable runs from the transmission to a point just below the fuel filter, while the upper cable runs from that point to the rear of the instrument panel.

Upper cable

Removal

2 Remove the instrument panel as described in Section 17 and make a note of the correct routing of the speedometer cable.
3 Working in the engine compartment, release the cable sealing grommet from the engine compartment bulkhead and withdraw the cable section from the bulkhead.

Refitting

4 If a new cable is being installed transfer the grommet from the old cable to the new cable.
5 Have an assistant feed the cable in through the engine compartment bulkhead whilst checking from inside the car that the cable is following the correct route behind the demister duct then over the pedal mounting bracket and through the steering column support bracket.
6 Once the cable is correctly routed, refit the sealing grommet to the bulkhead then draw the cable through until the coloured tape on the outer cable abuts the sealing grommet.
7 Refit the instrument panel as described in Section 17 then reconnect the speedometer cable sections and tighten the union nut securely.

Lower cable

Removal

8 Apply the handbrake then jack up the front of the car and support it on axle stands to improve access to the lower end of the cable.
9 Pull out the rubber retaining pin which secures the lower end of the cable in position then withdraw the cable from the transmission.
10 Slacken the union nut securing the upper and lower cable sections together then disconnect the two cable sections (photo).

22.10 Slacken the union nut and disconnect the two speedometer cable sections

22.11 Lower cable O-rings (arrowed) must be renewed whenever they are disturbed

11 Release the lower cable from any relevant retaining clips or ties and remove it from the car. Remove the O-rings from the lower end of the cable and discard them; these should be renewed as a matter of course whenever they are disturbed (photo).

Refitting

12 Lubricate the cable lower end fitting O-rings with engine oil and insert the end fitting into the transmission. Refit the rubber retaining pin to secure the cable in position.
13 Ensure the cable section is correctly routed and is retained by any necessary clamps or ties.
14 Connect the upper cable to the lower cable and tighten the union nut securely. Lower the car to the ground.

23 Multi-function unit (MFU) – general information, removal and refitting

General information

1 The multi-function unit (MFU) is mounted onto the rear of the

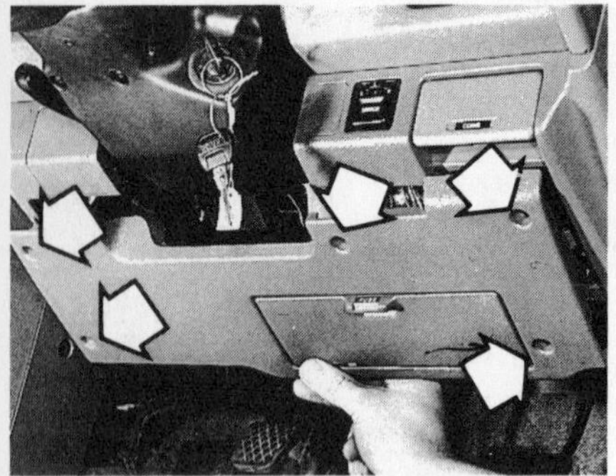
23.6 Remove retaining screws (locations arrowed) and withdraw the right-hand lower facia panel

23.7A Release the left-hand fuse panel...

23.7B ...and disconnect wiring connectors from the front of the fusebox

23.8 Fusebox retaining nut locations (arrowed)

23.9A Release the Multi-Function Unit (MFU) from the rear of the fusebox...

23.9B ...and disconnect the wiring connector

fusebox which is located behind the right-hand lower facia panel. The unit controls the following functions:

- (a) *Front and rear wiper system delay intervals.*
- (b) *Heated rear window timer.*
- (c) *Courtesy lamp delay.*
- (d) *Lamps-on warning bleeper.*

2 The MFU also has a self diagnostic mode where it checks out all the relevant circuits it controls.

3 To start the diagnostic sequence, press the heated rear window switch and turn on the ignition switch on simultaneously. Release the heated rear window switch as soon as the ignition switch is turned on, the MFU should then bleep to indicate it has entered its diagnostic mode, then press the heated rear window switch for a second time. Subsequent operations of the interior lamp switches, wiper switches and headlamp switch will result in a bleep from the MFU as it receives a signal. If the unit does not bleep a fault is indicated in the relevant circuit. A third press on the heated rear window switch will enter the MFU into the second stage of its diagnostic sequence. The MFU will now operate each of its functions in turn starting with the heated rear window, followed by the front and rear wipers and finally the courtesy lamp will operate for approximately two seconds if there are no faults. When all the checks are complete turn the ignition switch off to take the MFU out of its diagnostic sequence.

4 If a fault appears in one of the circuits controlled by the MFU, check the relevant relay (where fitted) and wiring using the equipment and procedures outlined in Sections 2 and 11 of this Chapter, referring to the wiring diagrams for full details. If this fails to locate the fault, it is likely that the MFU is at fault. The MFU is a sealed unit and must be renewed even if only one of its control functions is faulty.

Removal

5 Disconnect the battery negative terminal.

6 Undo the five retaining screws and remove the right-hand lower facia panel (photo).

7 Release the left-hand fuse panel from the side of the main fusebox and disconnect the two wiring block connectors from the front of the fusebox (photos).

8 Remove the two fusebox retaining nuts then partially withdraw the fusebox until the upper wiring block connector(s) can be disconnected (photo).

9 Carefully turn the fusebox assembly around and disconnect the block connector from the MFU. Release the MFU from the rear of the fusebox and remove it from the car (photos).

Refitting

10 Refitting is a reversal of the removal procedure ensuring that all the wiring connectors are correctly refitted. On completion reconnect the battery terminal and check that all electrical circuits function correctly.

24 Windscreen wiper motor and linkage – removal and refitting

Removal

1 Operate the wiper motor then switch it off so that the wiper blades return to the rest position.

2 Stick a piece of masking tape along the edge of each wiper blade to use as an alignment aid on refitting, then open up the bonnet.

3 Slacken and remove the wiper arm spindle nuts and pull the arms off their spindles (photos). If necessary, the arms can be levered off their spindles using a large flat-bladed screwdriver.

4 Carefully prise out the seven trim caps from the ventilation grille to gain access to the grille retaining screws. Slacken and remove all the retaining screws then release the eight retaining clips situated along the front edge of the grille and remove the grille from the car.

5 Using a large flat bladed screwdriver, carefully lever the wiper

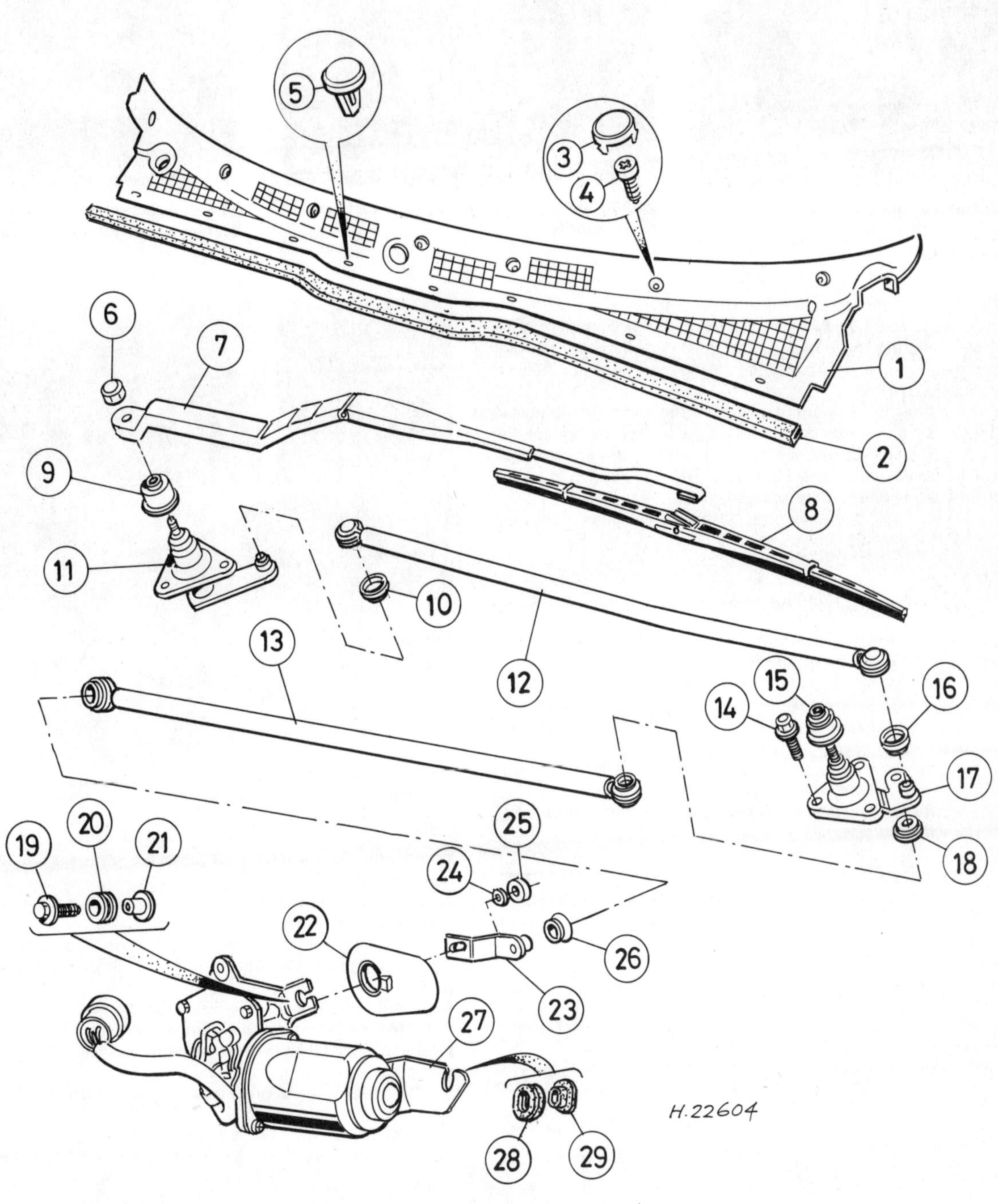

Fig. 12.5 Exploded view of the windscreen wiper motor and linkage (Sec 24)

1 *Ventilation grille*
2 *Sealing strip*
3 *Trim cap*
4 *Screw*
5 *Retaining clip*
6 *Wiper arm spindle nut*
7 *Wiper arm*
8 *Wiper blade*
9 *Spindle cap*
10 *Dust seal*
11 *Right-hand spindle assembly*
12 *Connecting rod*
13 *Operating rod*
14 *Bolt*
15 *Spindle cap*
16 *Dust seal*
17 *Left-hand spindle assembly*
18 *Dust seal*
19 *Wiper motor mounting bolt*
20 *Mounting rubber*
21 *Spacer*
22 *Water shield*
23 *Wiper motor crank arm*
24 *Spring washer*
25 *Nut*
26 *Dust seal*
27 *Wiper motor*
28 *Mounting rubber*
29 *Spacer*

24.3A Slacken the spindle nuts...

24.3B ...and remove the wiper arms from their spindles

24.6 Windscreen wiper motor mounting bolt locations (lower bolt hidden)

linkage arm off the wiper motor crank arm balljoint.

6 Disconnect the wiring connector from the wiper motor and remove the four bolts securing the motor to the bulkhead, then remove the motor from the engine compartment taking care not to lose its mounting rubbers (photo).

7 Remove the three bolts securing the right-hand wiper arm spindle in position then, using a large flat-bladed screwdriver, disconnect the linkage rod from the spindle balljoint and remove the spindle assembly.

8 Disconnect the two linkage rods from the left-hand wiper arm spindle assembly balljoints and remove the rods.

9 Undo the three left-hand wiper arm spindle retaining bolts and remove the spindle assembly.

Refitting

10 Refitting is a reversal of the removal procedure, noting the following points:

- (a) *Examine the wiper motor mounting rubbers for signs of damage or deterioration and renew if necessary.*
- (b) *Tighten the wiper arm spindle assembly and wiper motor mounting bolts to the specified torque and ensure all linkage balljoints are pressed firmly together.*
- (c) *Ensure the wiper arm spindles are clean then align the wiper blades with the tape fitted on removal and press the arms firmly onto the spindles. Tighten the wiper arm spindle nuts to the specified torque.*

25 Tailgate wiper motor - removal and refitting

Removal

1 Operate the wiper motor then switch it off so that the wiper blade returns to the rest position.

2 Stick a piece of masking tape along the edge of the wiper blade to use as an alignment aid on refitting.

3 Prise off the wiper arm spindle nut cover then slacken and remove the wiper arm spindle nut and pull the arm off its spindle (photo). If necessary, the arm can be levered off using a large flat-bladed screwdriver.

25.3 Remove cover to reveal tailgate wiper arm spindle nut

4 Undo the spindle retaining nut then remove the toothed washer and rubber seal (photos).

5 Open up the tailgate and undo the two screws securing the tailgate inner trim panel to the tailgate and carefully prise out the screw retaining plugs.

6 Using a large flat-bladed screwdriver, work around the outside of the trim panel and carefully prise it away from the tailgate to free all its retaining clips. Once all the retaining clips have been freed remove the trim panel.

7 Disconnect the wiring connector and undo the three bolts securing

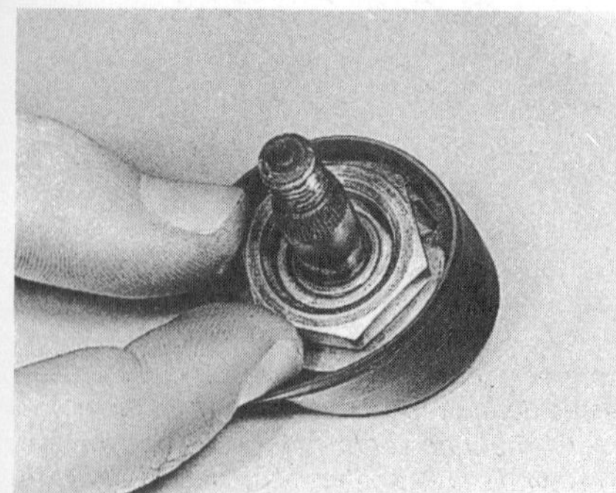
25.4A Unscrew the wiper spindle retaining nut...

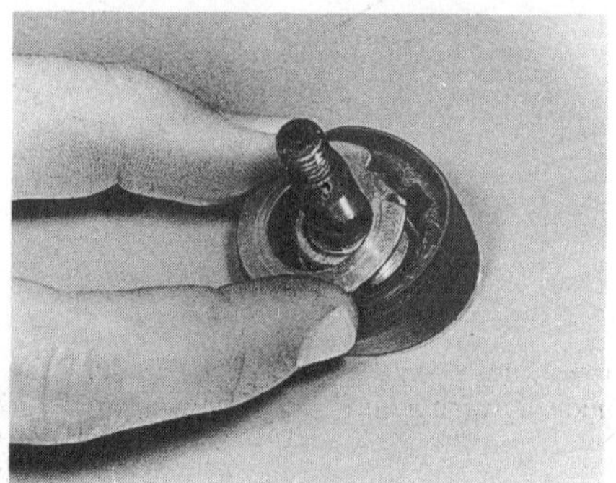
25.4B ...and withdraw the toothed washer and rubber seal

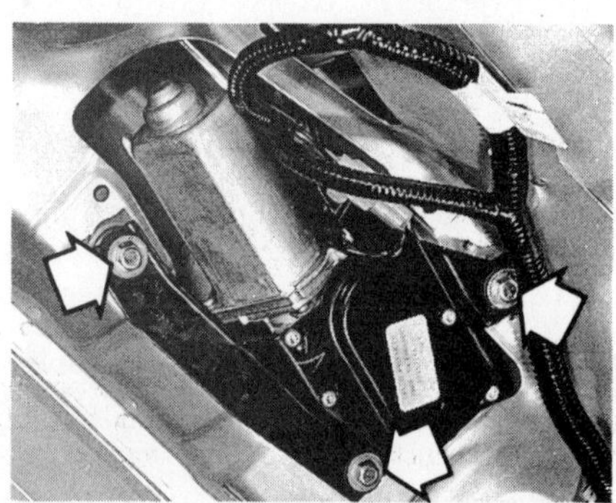
25.7 Tailgate wiper motor mounting bolts (arrowed)

Fig. 12.6 Windscreen/tailgate washers system components (Sec 26)

1 *Windscreen washer tube T-piece connector*
2 *Windscreen washer tube*
3 *Reservoir cap*
4 *Reservoir mounting nut*
5 *Reservoir mounting bolt*
6 *Washer pump retaining clip*
7 *Reservoir mounting bolt*
8 *Wiring connector*
9 *Windscreen washer pump*
10 *Seal*
11 *Washer reservoir*
12 *Wiring connector**
13 *Tailgate washer pump**
14 *Seal**
15 *Tailgate washer tube**
16 *Non-return valve**
* *Fitted to 214 models only*

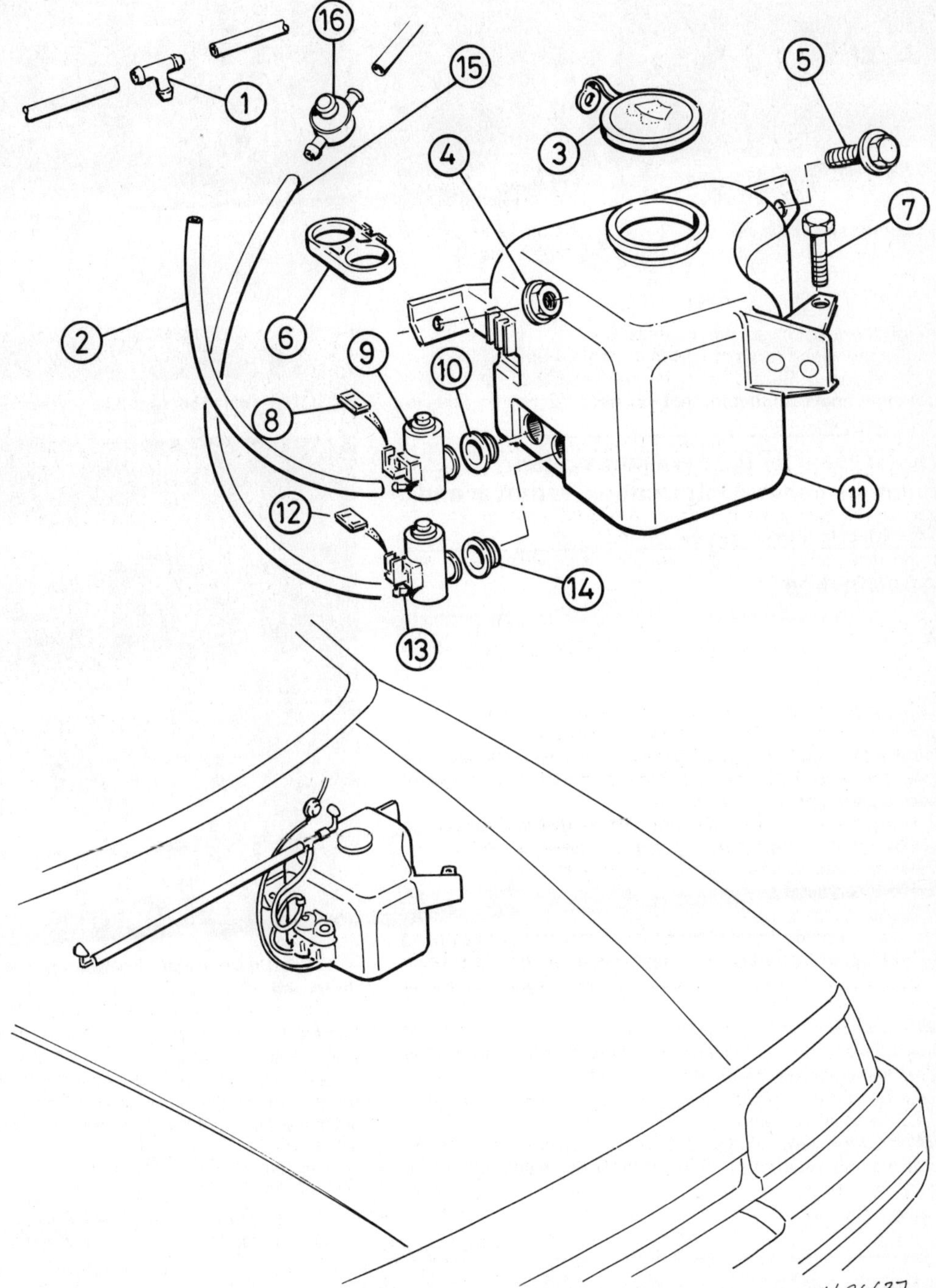

the wiper motor to the tailgate (photo). Remove the motor from the tailgate noting the three motor mounting rubbers and the washer and rubber seal which are fitted to the wiper spindle.

Refitting

8 Refitting is a reverse of the removal procedure, noting the following points:

(a) *Examine the wiper motor mounting rubbers and spindle seals for signs of damage and deterioration and renew if necessary.*
(b) *Tighten the wiper motor mounting bolts to the specified torque.*
(c) *Ensure the wiper arm spindle is clean then align the wiper blade with the tape fitted on removal and press the arm firmly onto the spindle. Tighten the wiper arm spindle nut to the specified torque and refit the nut cover.*

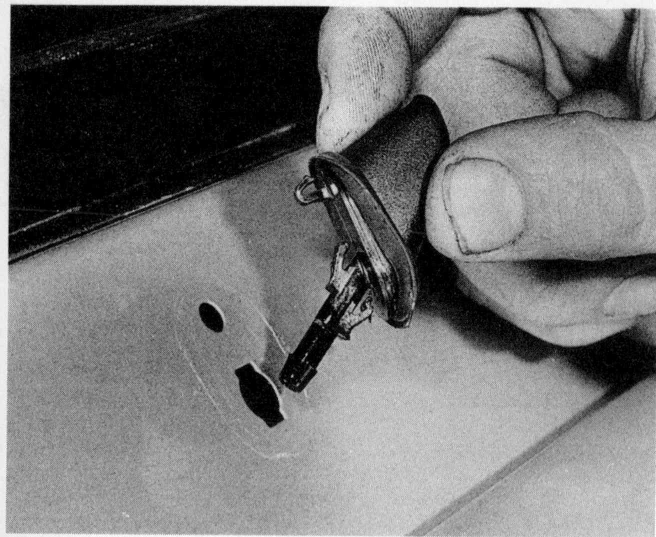

26.5 Removing tailgate washer jet - 214 models

27.3A Use DIN tools to release retaining clips...

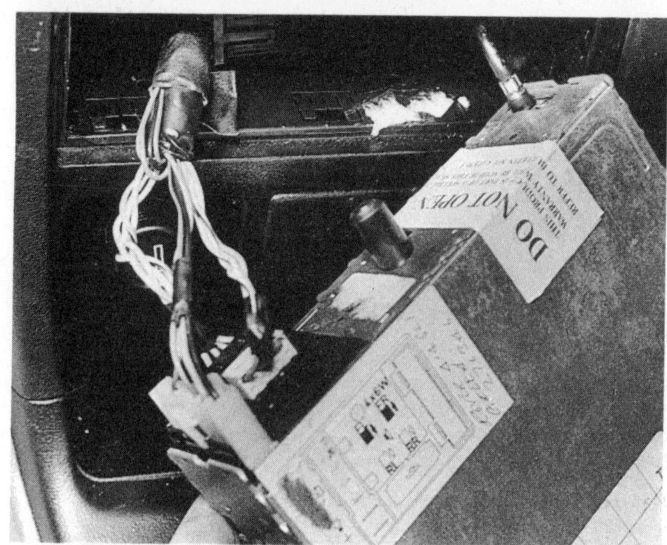

27.3B ...then withdraw the radio/cassette unit and disconnect the aerial and wiring connectors

26 Windscreen/tailgate washer system components - general information, removal and refitting

General Information

1 The windscreen washer reservoir is situated in the rear left-hand corner of the engine compartment with the washer system pump being mounted on the side of the reservoir. On 214 models the reservoir is also used to supply the tailgate washer system via a second pump.

Removal

2 To remove the washer reservoir and pump(s), unscrew the mounting nut and bolts and lift the reservoir from the left-hand corner of the engine compartment.
3 Disconnect the wiring connector(s) from the pump(s) then disconnect the plastic tubing from the reservoir and remove the assembly from the car.
4 Empty the reservoir of any remaining fluid then undo the retaining screws and separate the pump(s) and reservoir.
5 If necessary the windscreen washer nozzles can carefully be prised out of the ventilation grille and disconnected from the tubing. On 214 models, prise the washer jet out and remove it from the tailgate (photo).
6 If trouble is experienced at any time with the flow to the tailgate washer, check that the non-return valve is not blocked; it is fitted in the tube next to the reservoir and should allow fluid to pass only outwards to the jet.

Refitting

7 Refitting is a reversal of removal. Ensure that the washer tubes are not trapped when refitting the reservoir and note that the connectors for the pumps are colour-coded to aid correct reconnection on reassembly.

27 Radio/cassette player - removal and refitting

Note: *The following removal and refitting procedure is for the range of radio/cassette units which Rover fit as standard equipment. Removal and refitting procedures of non-standard units may differ slightly.*

Removal

1 Referring to the instructions supplied with the radio/cassette unit, temporarily de-activate the security code.
2 Disconnect the battery negative lead.
3 To remove the unit, two standard DIN extraction tools are required. These are two U-shaped rods which are inserted into the four small holes in the front of the unit to release the unit retaining clips. The tools may possibly be obtained from a Rover dealer or any audio accessory outlet, or can be made out of 3 mm (0.12 in) wire rod such as welding rod. Using the tools, push back the clamps on the left and right-hand sides, withdraw the unit and disconnect the wiring plugs and aerial (photos).

Refitting

4 Refitting is the reverse of the removal procedure. On completion connect the battery negative terminal and reactivate the security code.

28 Speakers - removal and refitting

Removal

Front speaker

1 Remove the front door inner trim panel as described in Chapter 11, Section 12.
2 Undo the three speaker retaining screws then withdraw the speaker, disconnect the speaker wiring connectors and remove the speaker from the door (photos).

Rear speaker - 214 models

3 Prise off the trim cap from the rear seat belt upper mounting point,

28.2A Slacken the three retaining screws...

28.2B ...then withdraw the speaker from the door and disconnect the wiring connectors

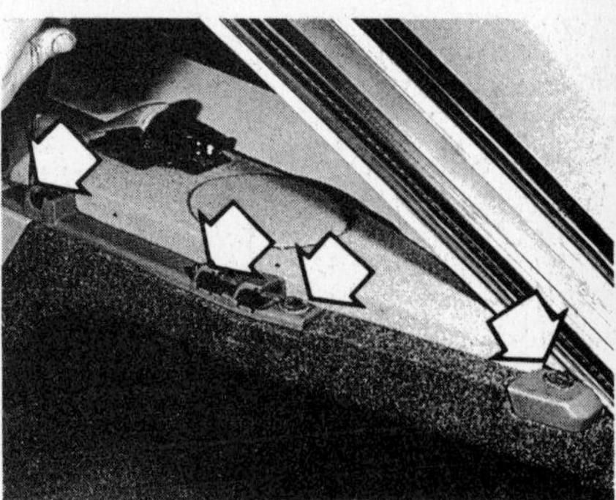

28.4 Rear speaker grille panel retaining screw locations (arrows) - 214 models

28.5 On 214 models rear speakers are retained by four screws

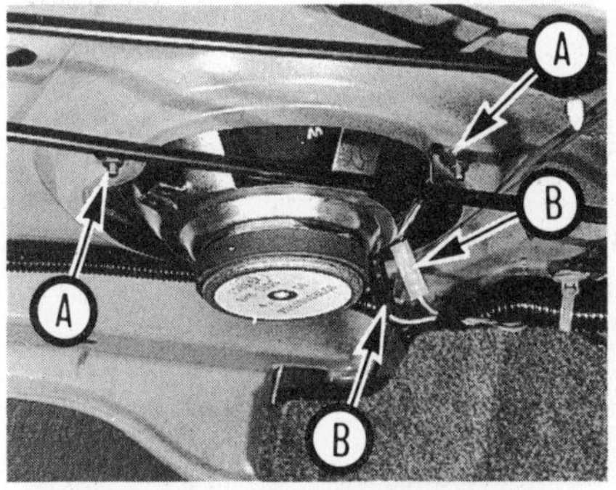

28.6 Rear speaker retaining nuts 'A' and wiring connectors 'B' - 414 models

then slacken and remove the two seat belt guide retaining bolts.
4 Open up the tailgate, then remove the four screws securing the speaker grille panel and position the panel clear of the speaker (photo).
5 Undo the four speaker retaining screws then lift out the speaker, disconnect the wiring connectors and remove the speaker from the car (photo).

Rear speaker - 414 models

6 Working from inside the luggage compartment, disconnect the speaker wiring connections and undo the three nuts securing the speaker to the parcel shelf (photo).
7 The speaker can then be lifted away from the parcel shelf from inside the car.

Refitting

8 Refitting is a reverse of the removal procedure.

29 Radio aerial - removal and refitting

Removal

1 Remove the radio/cassette player as described in Section 27.
2 Undo the five screws securing the right-hand lower facia panel and remove the panel to gain access to the relay mounting bracket. Remove the relay mounting bracket retaining bolt.
3 Trace the aerial lead back along its length and free it from any retaining clips or ties. Tie a long piece of string around the aerial end plug.
4 Undo the two screws securing the aerial to the roof and remove the aerial and sealing rubber. Carefully withdraw the aerial lead until the plug comes out of the aerial aperture then untie the string and leave it in position in the car.

Refitting

5 Securely tie the string around the aerial lead plug and fit the rubber seal to the aerial.
6 From inside the car, gently pull the string through the radio aperture whilst feeding the aerial lead in through the roof. When the aerial lead plug emerges on the inside of the car untie the string.
7 Ensure the rubber seal is correctly located on the base of the aerial then tighten the aerial retaining screws securely.
8 Refit the aerial lead to the necessary retaining clips and ties then refit the relay mounting bracket and right-hand lower facia panel, tighten all retaining screws and bolts securely.
9 Refit the radio/cassette unit as described in Section 27.

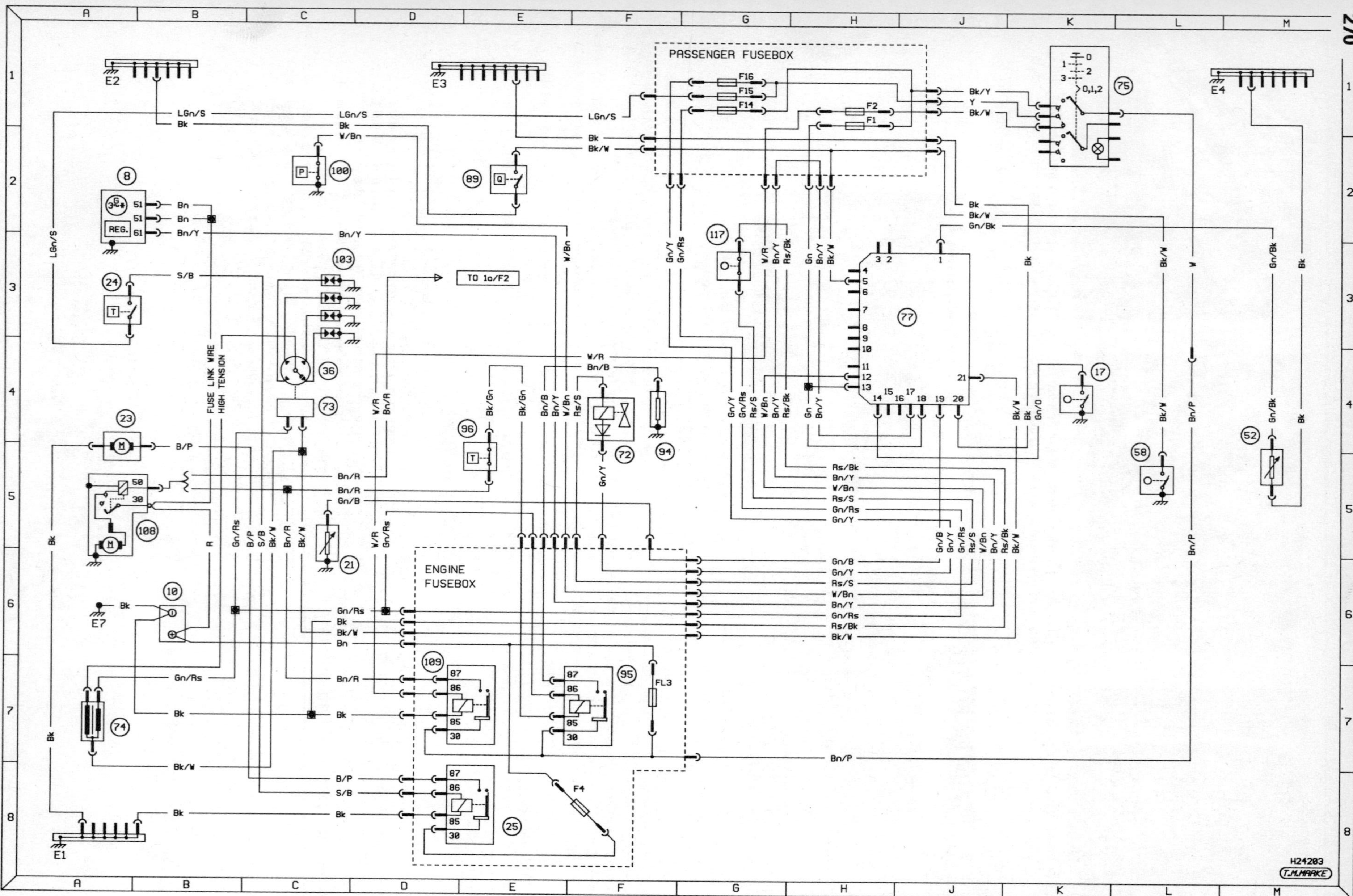

Diagram 1: Starting, charging, ignition (carburettor models), cooling fan, warning lamps and gauges. All models

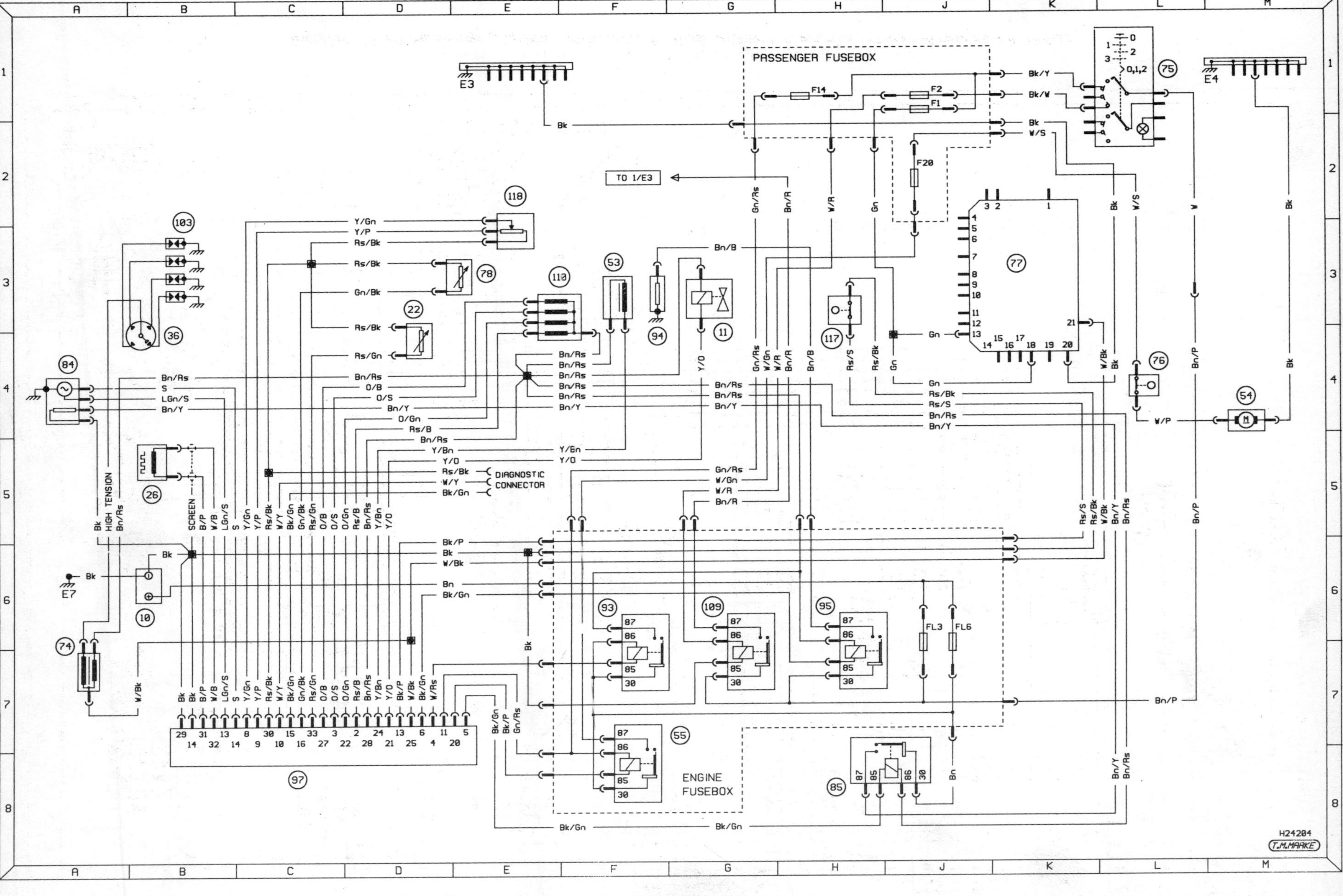

Diagram 1a: Modular engine management – single point injection

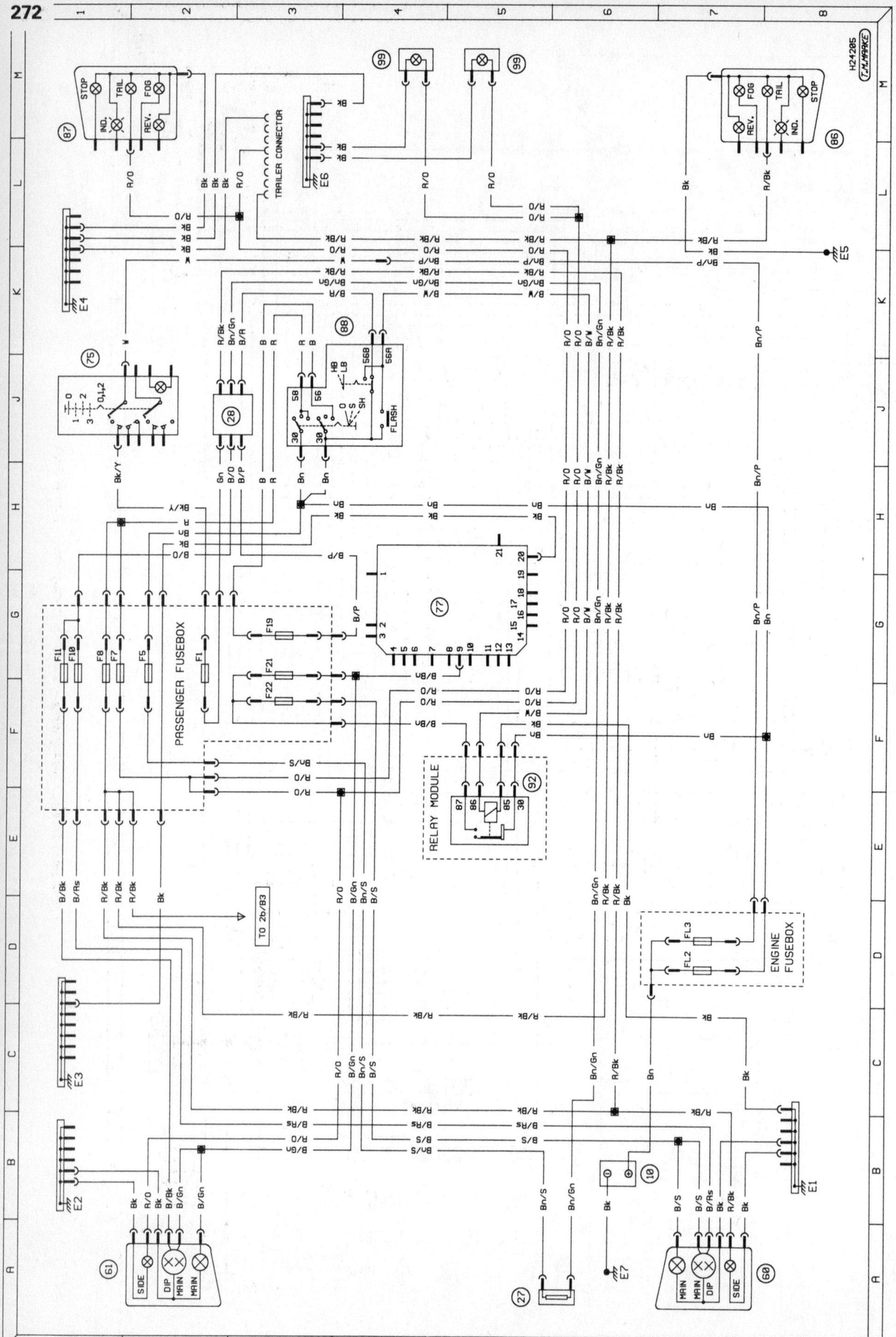

Diagram 2: Exterior lighting – sidelamps and headlamps. All models

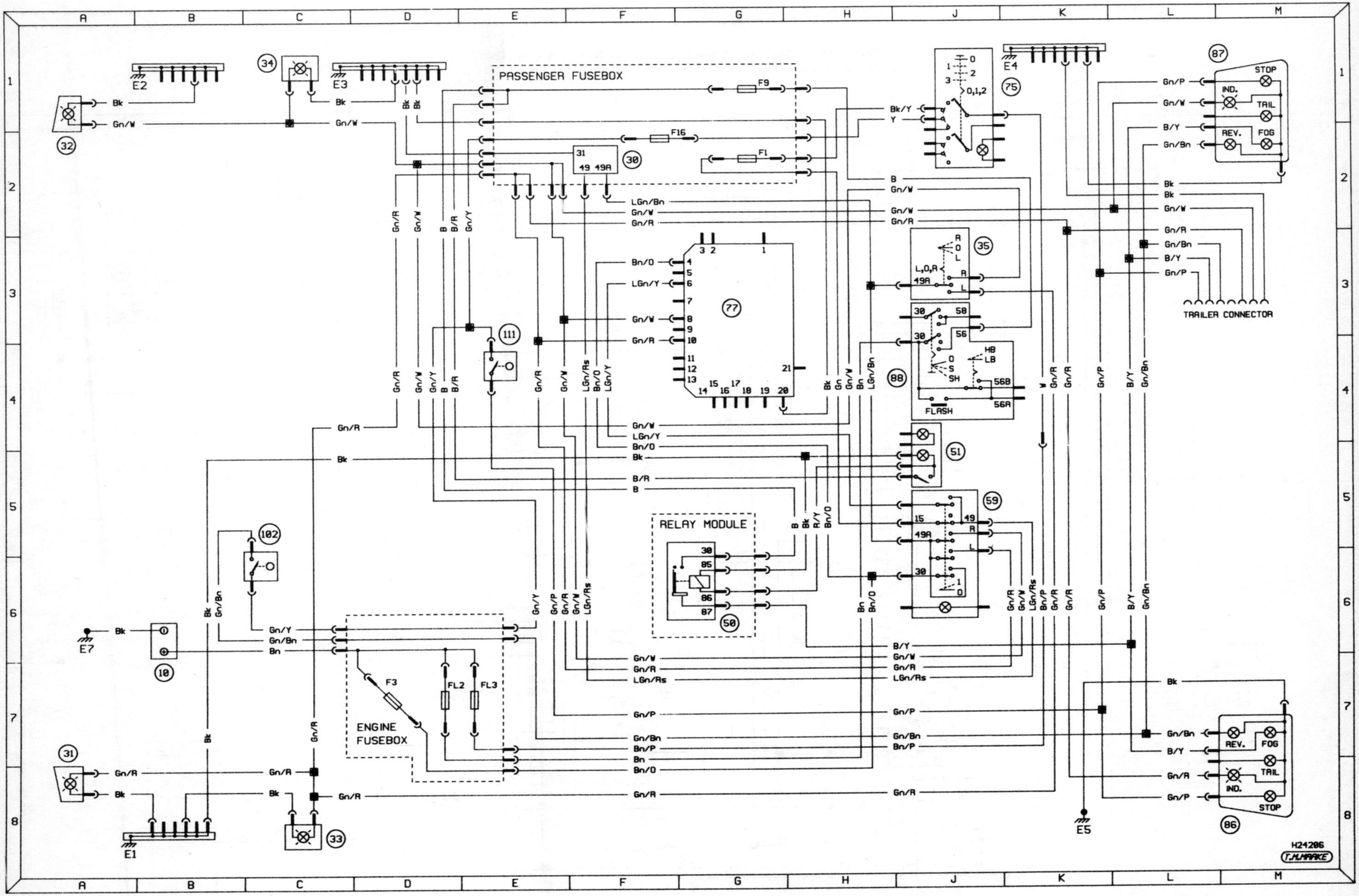

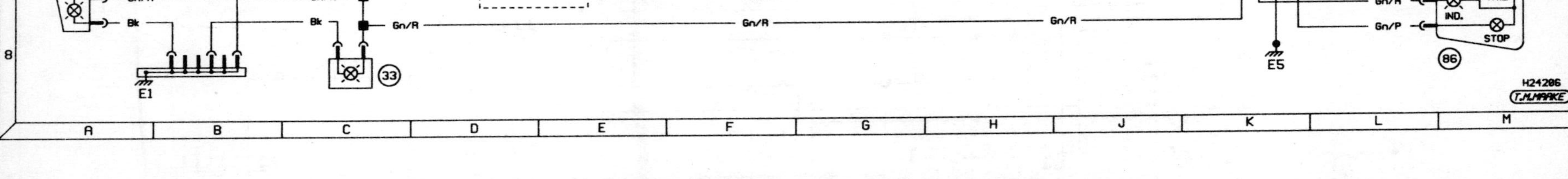

Diagram 2a: Exterior lighting – signal/warning lamps. All models

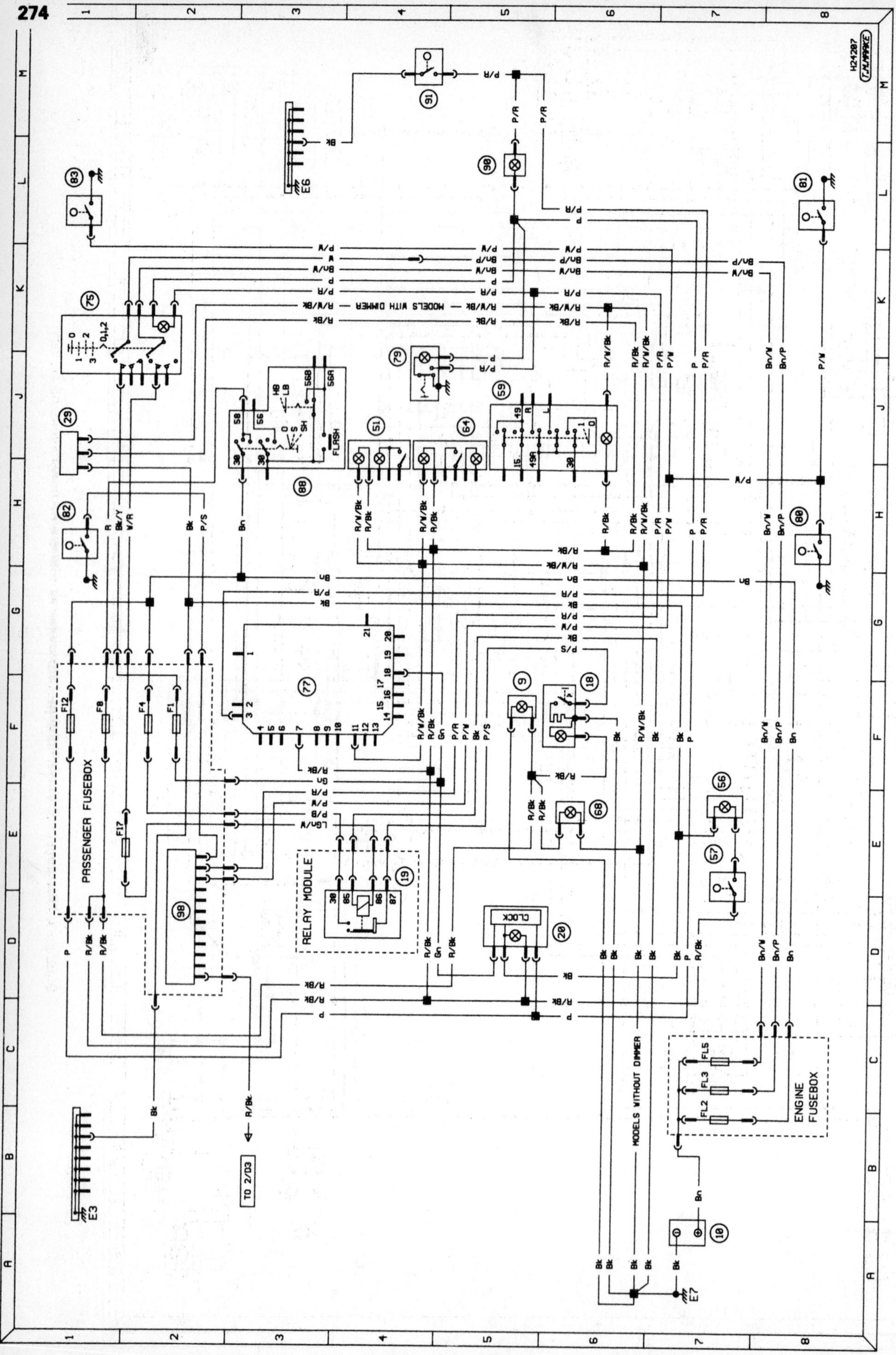
PASSENGER FUSEBOX
F12
F8
F4
F1
F17
RELAY MODULE
CLOCK
ENGINE FUSEBOX
FL5
FL3
FL2
MODELS WITH DIMMER
MODELS WITHOUT DIMMER
FLASH
TO 2/D3
E3
E6
E7
H24287
T.M.MARKE

Diagram 2b: Interior lighting and associated circuits. All models

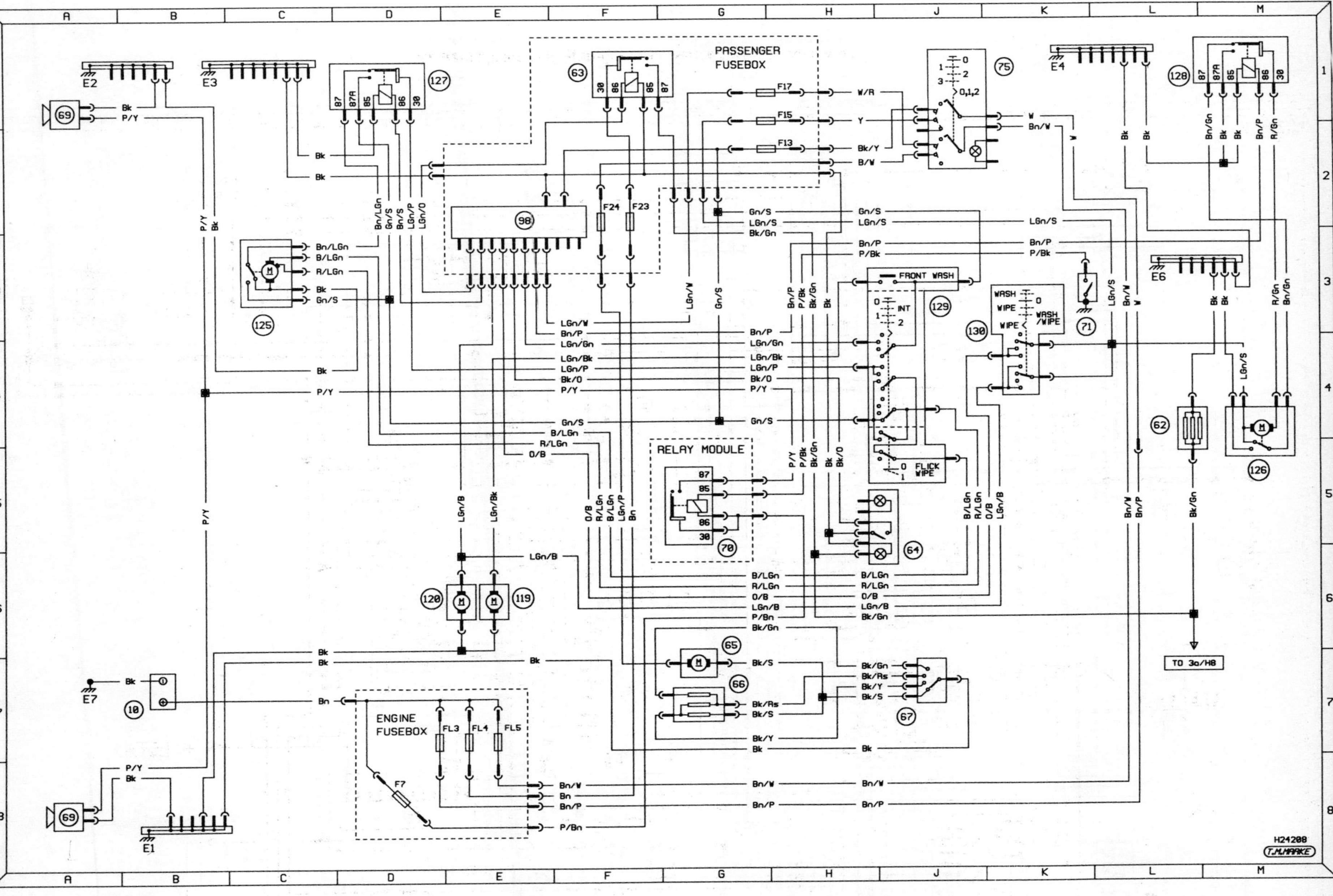

Diagram 3: Ancillary circuits – wash/wipe, heater blower and heated rear window. All models

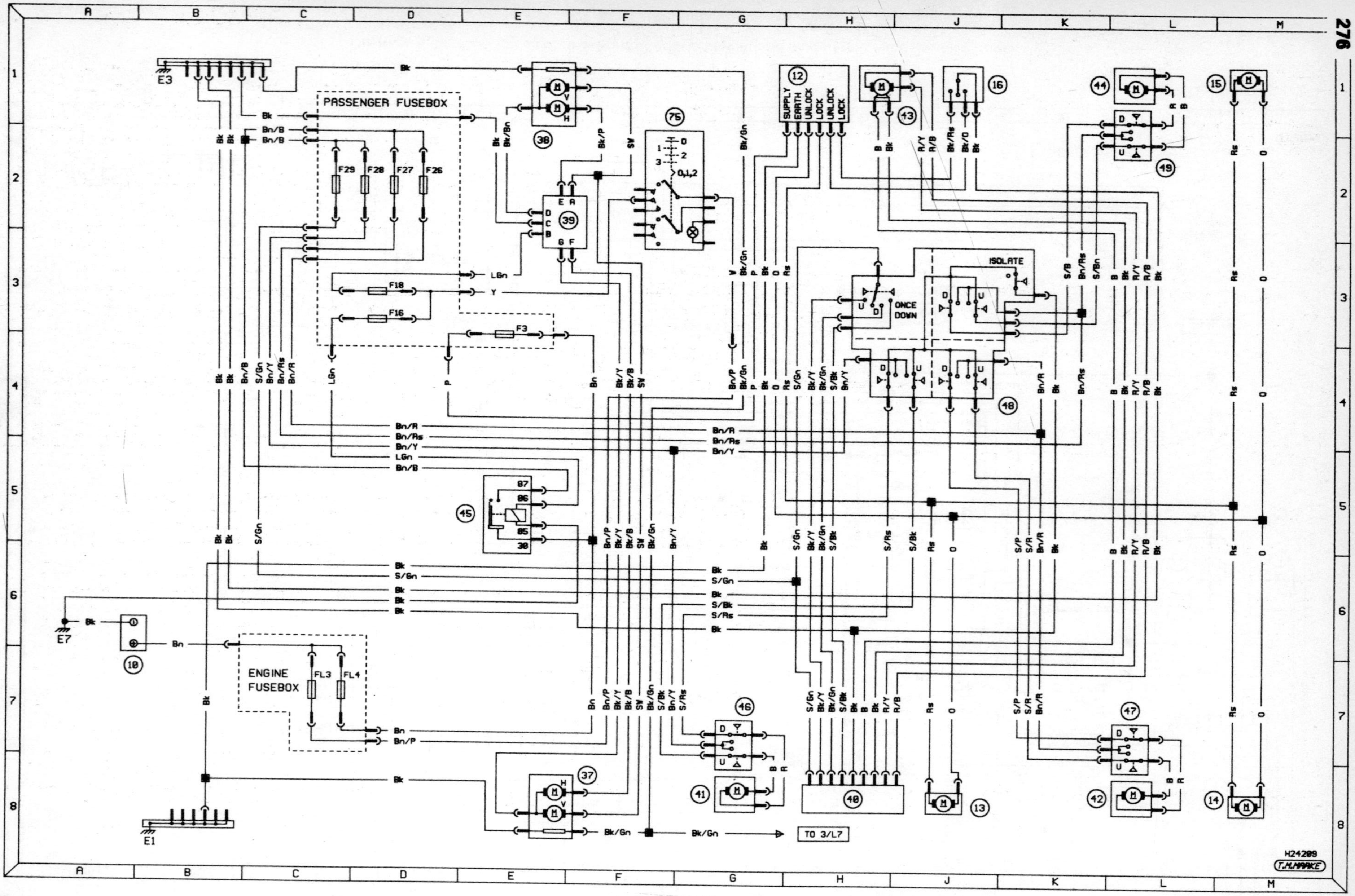

Diagram 3a: Ancillary circuits – electric windows, mirrors and central locking

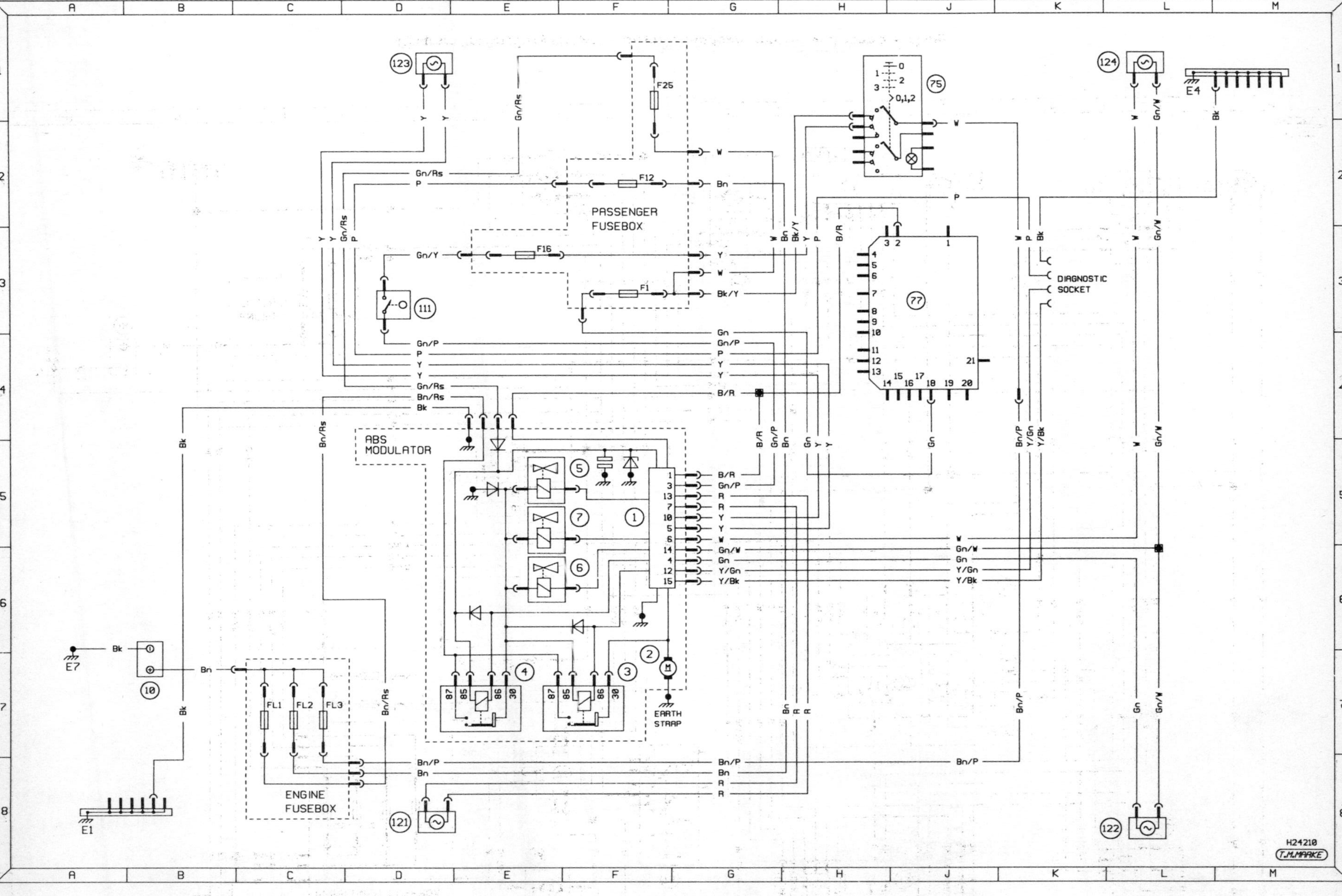

Diagram 4: Anti-lock braking system

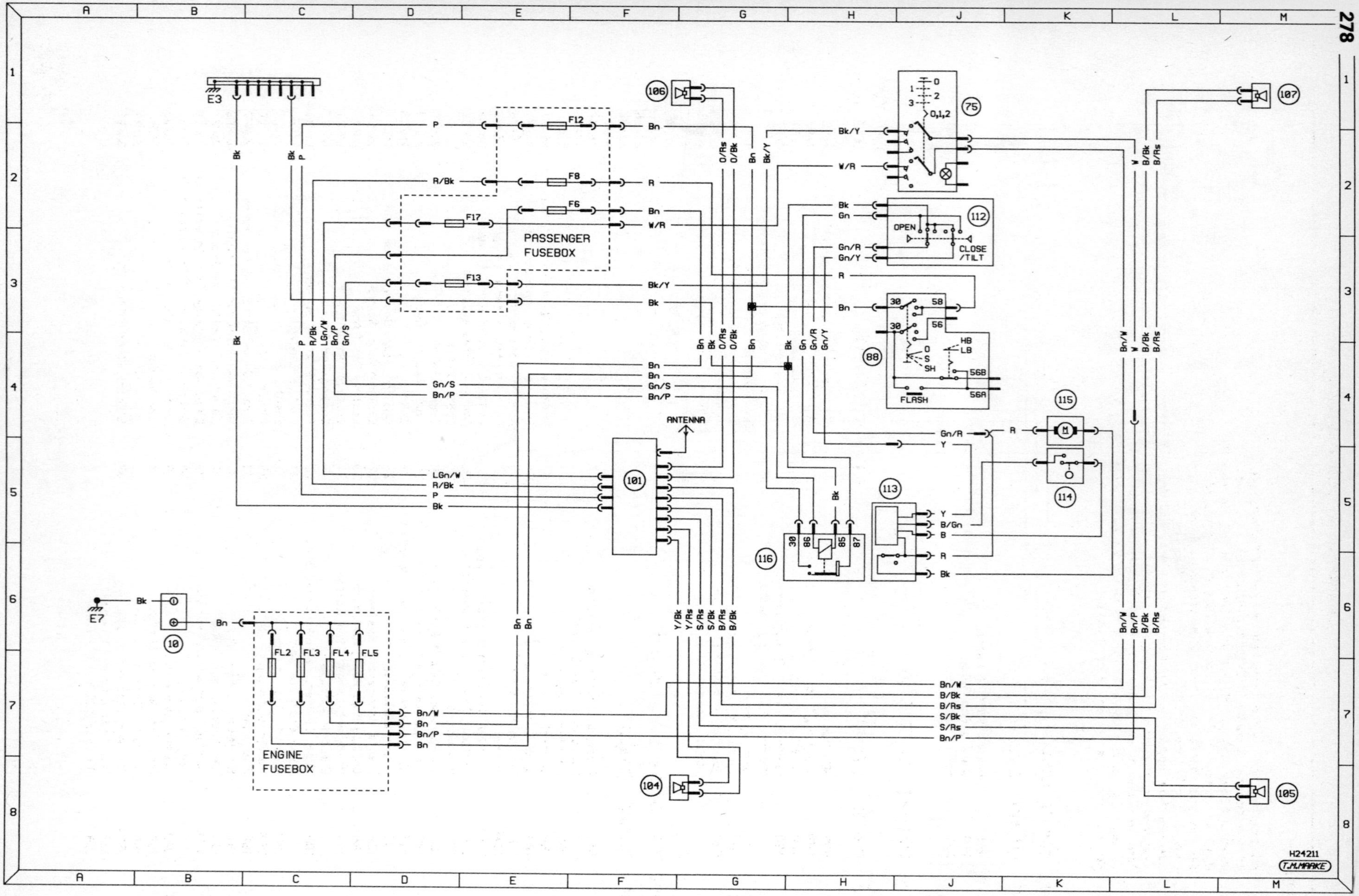

PASSENGER FUSEBOX

ENGINE FUSEBOX

ANTENNA

OPEN

CLOSE /TILT

FLASH

H24211

T.M.MARKE

Diagram 5: In-car entertainment and electric sunroof

NOTES:

1. All diagrams are divided into numbered circuits depending on function e.g. Diagram 2: Exterior lighting.
2. Items are arranged in relation to a plan view of the vehicle.
3. Items may appear on more than one diagram so are found using a grid reference e.g. 2/A1 denotes an item on diagram 2 grid location A1.
4. Complex items appear on the diagrams as blocks and are expanded on the internal connections page.
5. Feed wire colour varies dependant on the circuit supplied but all earth wires are coloured black or have a black tracer.
6. Not all items are fitted to all models.

ENGINE COMPARTMENT FUSEBOX

FUSE	RATING	CIRCUIT
3	10A	Hazard Warning Lamps
4	25A	Cooling Fan Relay
7	15A	Horn

ENGINE COMPARTMENT FUSEBOX

FUSE -LINK	RATING	CIRCUIT
FL1	40A	ABS Pump
FL2	40A	Lighting, Cigar Lighter
FL3	40A	Ignition Switch
FL4	40A	Electric Window Relay, Sunroof, Central Door Locking, Heated Rear Window
FL5	40A	Ignition Switch
FL6	60A	Main Relay, Fuel Pump Relay, Lambda Sensor Relay

PASSENGER COMPARTMENT FUSEBOX

FUSE	RATING	CIRCUIT
1	10A	Clock, Instruments, Direction Indicators, Dim/Dip Unit
2	10A	Starter Signal
3	15A	Central Locking
4	10A	Cigar Lighter
5	10A	Dim/Dip Resistor
6	30A	Sunroof
7	10A	RH Side, Tail, Number Plate Lamps
8	10A	LH Side, Tail, Interior Illumination
9	10A	Fog Lamps
10	10A	LH Headlamp Dipped Beam
11	10A	RH Headlamp Dipped Beam
12	15A	Clock, Interior Lamps, Radio Memory
13	15A	Front Wash/Wipe
14	10A	Engine Management System
15	15A	Cooling Fan, Rear Wash/Wipe
16	15A	Reversing Lamps, Stop Lamps, Electric Windows
17	10A	Cigar Lighter, Multi-Function Unit, Radio Cassette Unit
18	10A	Electric Door Mirrors
19	15A	Headlamp Dim/Dip
20	15A	Fuel Pump
21	15A	RH Headlamp Main Beam
22	15A	LH Headlamp Main Beam
23	25A	Heated Rear Window, Heated Door Mirrors
24	20A	Heater Blower Motor
25	15A	Anti-lock Braking System
26	15A	LH Rear Electric Window
27	15A	RH Rear Electric Window
28	15A	LH Front Electric Window
29	15A	RH Front Electric Window

ITEM	DESCRIPTION	DIAGRAM/ GRID REF.
1	ABS Electronic Control Unit	4/F5
2	ABS Pump	4/F7
3	ABS Pump Relay	4/F7
4	ABS Solenoid Relay	4/E7
5	ABS Solenoid Valve LH Front	4/F5
6	ABS Solenoid Valve Rear	4/F6
7	ABS Solenoid Valve RH Front	4/F5
8	Alternator	1/A2
9	Ashtray Illumination	2b/F5
10	Battery	1/B6, 1a/B6, 2/B6, 2a/B6, 2b/A7, 3/B7, 3a/B7, 4/B7, 5/B6
11	Canister Purge Solenoid (Cat. Only)	1a/G3
12	Central Locking Control Unit	3a/H1
13	Central Locking Motor LH Front	3a/J8
14	Central Locking Motor LH Rear	3a/M8
15	Central Locking Motor RH Rear	3a/M1
16	Central Locking Switch	3a/J1
17	Choke Switch	1/K4
18	Cigar Lighter	2b/F6
19	Cigar Lighter Relay	2b/E4
20	Clock	2b/D5
21	Coolant Temp. Gauge Sender Unit	1/C1
22	Coolant Temp. Sensor	1a/D4
23	Cooling Fan Motor	1/A4
24	Cooling Fan Switch	1/A3
25	Cooling Fan Relay	1/E8
26	Crank. Position Sensor	1a/B5
27	Dim/Dip Resistor	2/A5
28	Dim/Dip Unit	2/J2
29	Dimmer Unit	2b/J1
30	Direction Indicator Flasher Relay	2a/F2
31	Direction Indicator LH Front	2a/A8
32	Direction Indicator RH Front	2a/A1
33	Direction Indicator Side Repeater LH	2a/C8
34	Direction Indicator Side Repeater RH	2a/C1
35	Direction Indicator Switch	2a/J3
36	Distributor	1/C4, 1a/B3
37	Electric Door Mirror LH	3a/E8

H24200

ITEM	DESCRIPTION	DIAGRAM/ GRID REF.
38	Electric Door Mirror RH	3a/E1
39	Electric Door Mirror Switch	3a/F2
40	Electric Window Control Unit	3a/H8
41	Electric Window Motor LH Front	3a/G8
42	Electric Window Motor LH Rear	3a/L8
43	Electric Window Motor RH Front	3a/H1
44	Electric Window Motor RH Rear	3a/L1
45	Electric Window Relay	3a/E5
46	Electric Window Switch LH Front	3a/G7
47	Electric Window Switch LH Rear	3a/L7
48	Electric Window Switch RH Front	3a/J4
49	Electric Window Switch RH Rear	3a/L2
50	Foglamp Relay	2a/G6
51	Foglamp Switch	2a/J5, 2b/J4
52	Fuel Gauge Sender Unit	1/M4
53	Fuel Injector	1a/F3
54	Fuel Pump	1a/M4
55	Fuel Pump Relay	1a/F8
56	Glove Box Lamp	2b/E7
57	Glove Box Lamp Switch	2b/E7
58	Handbrake Warning Switch	1/L5
59	Hazard Warning Lamp Switch	2a/J5, 2b/J5
60	Headlamp Unit LH	2/A7
61	Headlamp Unit RH	2/A2
62	Heated Rear Window	3/L4
63	Heated Rear Window Relay	3/F1
64	Heated Rear Window Switch	2b/J5, 3/J5
65	Heater Blower Motor	3/G7
66	Heater Blower Resistor Pack	3/G7
67	Heater Blower Switch	3/J7
68	Heater Blower Switch Illumination	2b/E6
69	Horn	3/A1, 3/A8
70	Horn Relay	3/G5
71	Horn Switch	3/K3
72	Idle Solenoid	1/F4
73	Ignition Amplifier Module	1/C4
74	Ignition Coil	1/A7, 1a/A7
75	Ignition Switch	1/K1, 1a/L1, 2/J1, 2a/J1, 2b/K1, 3/J1, 3a/F2, 4/J1, 5/J1
76	Inertia Switch	1a/L4
77	Instrument Cluster	1/J3, 1a/K3, 2/G4, 2a/G3, 2b/G3, 4/J3
78	Intake Air Temp. Sensor	1a/E3
79	Interior Lamp	2b/J4
80	Interior Lamp Door Switch LH Front	2b/H8
81	Interior Lamp Door Switch LH Rear	2b/L8
82	Interior Lamp Door Switch RH Front	2b/H1
83	Interior Lamp Door Switch RH Rear	2b/L1
84	Lambda Sensor (Cat. Only)	1a/A4
85	Lambda Sensor Relay (Cat. Only)	1a/H8
86	Lamp Cluster LH Rear	2/M8, 2a/M8
87	Lamp Cluster RH Rear	2/M1, 2a/M1
88	Light Switch	2/J3, 2a/J4, 2b/J3, 5/J4
89	Low Brake Fluid Sender Unit	1/E2
90	Luggage Comp. Lamp	2b/L5
91	Luggage Comp. Lamp Switch	2b/M4
92	Main Beam Relay	2/E5
93	Main Relay	1a/F6
94	Manifold Heater	1/F4, 1a/F3
95	Manifold Heater Relay	1/F7, 1a/H6
96	Manifold Temp. Switch	1/E4
97	MEMS Unit	1a/C7
98	Multi-Function Unit	2b/D2, 3/E2
99	Number Plate Lamp	2/M4, 2/M5
100	Oil Pressure Switch	1/C2
101	Radio/Cassette Unit	5/F5
102	Reversing Lamp Switch	2a/C5
103	Spark Plugs	1/C3, 1a/B3
104	Speaker LH Front	5/F8
105	Speaker LH Rear	5/M8
106	Speaker RH Front	5/F1
107	Speaker RH Rear	5/M1
108	Starter Motor	1/A5
109	Starter Relay	1/D7, 1a/G6
110	Stepper Motor	1a/E3
111	Stop-Lamp Switch	2a/E4, 4/D3
112	Sunroof Control Switch	5/J2
113	Sunroof Control Unit	5/H5
114	Sunroof Microswitch	5/K5
115	Sunroof Motor	5/K4
116	Sunroof Relay	5/H6
117	Throttle Pedal Switch	1/G3, 1a/H3
118	Throttle Potentiometer	1a/E2
119	Washer Pump Front	3/E6
120	Washer Pump Rear	3/E6
121	Wheel Sensor LH Front	4/D8
122	Wheel Sensor LH Rear	4/L8
123	Wheel Sensor RH Front	4/D1
124	Wheel Sensor RH Rear	4/L1
125	Wiper Motor Front	3/C3
126	Wiper Motor Rear	3/M4
127	Wiper Relay Front	3/D1
128	Wiper Relay Rear	3/M1
129	Wiper Switch Front	3/J3
130	Wiper Switch Rear	3/K3

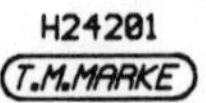

Key to wiring diagrams (continued)

INTERNAL CONNECTION DETAILS

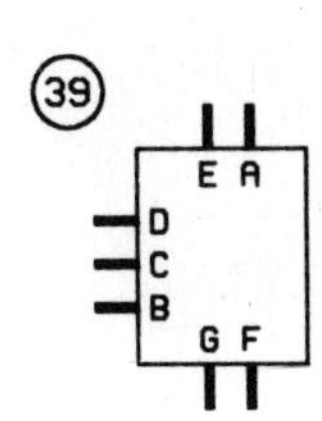

INTERNAL CONNECTIONS FOR ITEM 39

LH	B	C	A	F	G
UP					
DOWN					
LEFT					
RIGHT					

RH	B	C	A	F	G
UP					
DOWN					
LEFT					
RIGHT					

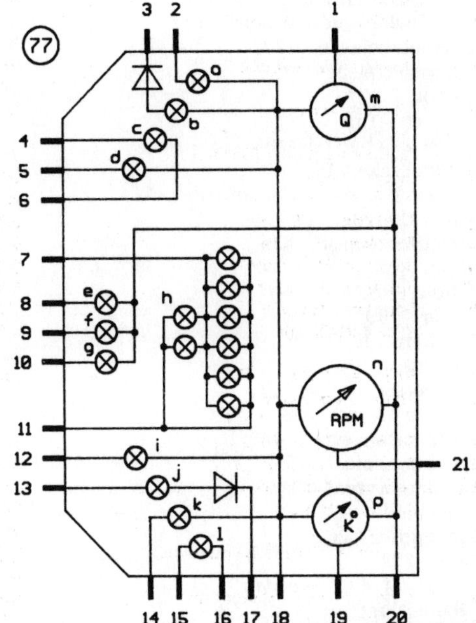

KEY TO INSTRUMENT CLUSTER (ITEM 77)

a = ABS Warning Lamp
b = Tailgate Open Warning Lamp
c = Hazard Warning Lamp
d = Handbrake/Low Brake Fluid Warning Lamp
e = RH Direction Indicator Lamp
f = Main Beam Warning Lamp
g = LH Direction Indicator Lamp
h = Instrument Illumination
i = Oil Pressure Warning Lamp
j = Ignition Warning Lamp
k = Choke Warning Lamp
l = Trailer Warning Lamp
m = Fuel Gauge
n = Tachometer
p = Coolant Temperature Gauge

WIRE COLOURS

B	Blue	R	Red
Bk	Black	Rs	Pink
Bn	Brown	S	Grey
LGn	Light Green	V	Violet
Gn	Green	W	White
O	Orange	Y	Yellow
P	Purple		

KEY TO SYMBOLS

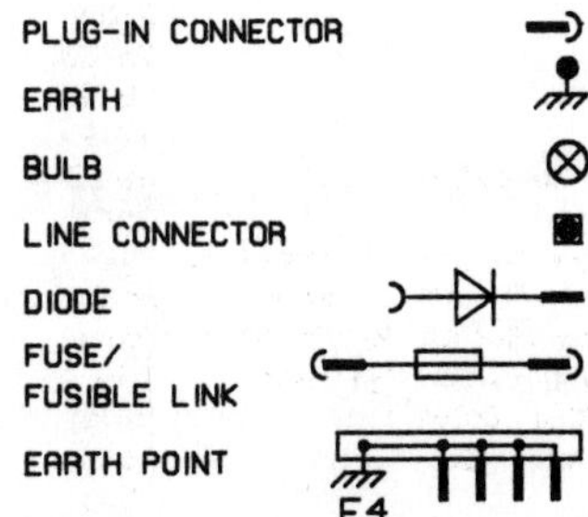

Internal connection details, wire colours and key to symbols

Index

E

F

G

H

I

J

L

M

N

O

P